PLEA ROLLS OF THE EXCHEQUER OF THE JEWS

preserved in

THE NATIONAL ARCHIVES

(formerly the Public Record Office)

Volume VI

EDWARD I, 1279–81

Edited by

PAUL BRAND, F.B.A.

THE JEWISH HISTORICAL SOCIETY OF ENGLAND

33 SEYMOUR PLACE, LONDON W1H 5AP

2005

Published in 2005 by
THE JEWISH HISTORICAL SOCIETY OF ENGLAND
33 SEYMOUR PLACE, LONDON W1H 5AP

ISBN 0-902528-40-8

Printed in Great Britain by 4edge Limited, Hockley, Essex

CONTENTS

PREFACE

During the preparation of this volume I have accumulated numerous debts to friends and colleagues. I have first to thank the Jewish Historical Society of England for inviting me to work on the volume and also for giving me the opportunity to present the lectures which form the basis for its introduction. I would also like to give particular thanks to successive officers of the Society, particularly the late Dr Richard Barnett, Malcolm Brown, Edgar Samuel and Dr Jeremy Schonfield, for their patience and their encouragement for my work on the volume and support for its publication. I also have to thank my erstwhile colleagues in the old Public Record Office, Dr Daphne Gifford and Frederick Mabbs, for suggesting my name to the Society and encouraging me to work on this volume. Thanks are also due to Jennifer Morrissey and Janette Swaine for typing or word-processing parts of this volume; such errors as may be found are either my errors in transcription or in parts that I word-processed for myself. I am also grateful for encouragement received at a significant stage in my work from my old friend, Professor Bob Stacey, and for the continuing patience and support of my wife Vanessa. The work on this volume was completed in the congenial as well as stimulating surroundings of All Souls College, Oxford, which has done me the honour of supporting my scholarly work by electing me to a Senior Research Fellowship. I trust this volume will help to justify the confidence of my colleagues in the value of my research.

PAUL BRAND

INTRODUCTION
THE EXCHEQUER OF THE JEWS, 1265–1290

The Exchequer of the Jews was that part of the machinery of royal government whose special concern was with matters relating to the Jewish community. It came into existence towards the end of the twelfth century and functioned for around a century until the Jewish community was expelled from England in 1290. There have been a number of excellent general scholarly studies of the Exchequer of the Jews or of specific aspects of history.[1] The most recent of these is now almost half a century old and none has concentrated in detail on the history of the institution during the last quarter of a century of its existence, which is by far the best documented period of its whole history.[2] What follows is a study that concentrates primarily on that period but also looks at the wider history where that is relevant.

It is divided into five sections:

- I discusses the evidence as to the actual physical location of the Exchequer of the Jews during this period, and about the times when it was in session and open for business.
- II deals with the main administrative functions of the Exchequer of the Jews and the jurisdiction which it exercised as a court. In passing, it also discusses those functions which might have been expected to fall within the province of the Exchequer of the Jews, but which were in fact performed by other parts of the royal administration.
- III examines the functions and responsibilities of the various officials associated with the Exchequer of the Jews; how, and by whom they were appointed; their background and previous experience and the immediate context of their appointment; what they were paid; other functions they discharged while in office; the reasons for their removal; and the subsequent careers of such officials elsewhere.
- IV investigates the ways in which the Exchequer of the Jews was subject to external scrutiny and supervision by the Exchequer and by other parts of the royal administration.
- V looks at the various records created and preserved by the Exchequer of the Jews which constitute our main source of information about it.

The study begins with the re-establishment of the Exchequer of the Jews in Michaelmas term 1265 after the defeat of the Montfortians at the

[1] The most notable works are: Thomas Madox, *The History and Antiquities of the Exchequer* (London, 1711), chapter VII; Charles Gross, 'The Exchequer of the Jews of England in the Middle Ages' in *Papers Read at the Anglo-Jewish Historical Exhibition* (London, 1888) at pp. 170-230; J.M. Rigg, introductions to *Select Pleas, Starrs etc., of the Jewish Exchequer, 1220-1284* (Selden Society, 15: 1901) and *Calendar of the Plea Rolls of the Exchequer of the Jews, vol. I* (Jewish Historical Society: 1905); Sir Hilary Jenkinson, introduction to *Calendar of the Plea Rolls of the Exchequer of the Jews, vol. III* (Jewish Historical Society: 1929); H.G. Richardson, *The English Jewry under Angevin Kings* (London, 1960), particularly chapters VI and VII; C.A.F. Meekings, 'Justices of the Jews, 1218-68: a Provisional List' in *Bulletin of the Institute of Historical Research,* 28 (1955), at pp. 173-188.

[2] All references to unpublished manuscripts in this study, unless otherwise specified, are to documents in the The National Archives (formerly the Public Record Office), London. The published Calendars of the Plea Rolls of the Exchequer of the Jews are abbreviated hereafter as *EJ* and Rigg's volume of *Select Pleas, Starrs etc. of the Jewish Exchequer, 1220-1284* jointly published by the Selden Society and the Jewish Historical Society will be referred to as *Select Pleas.*

battle of Evesham.[3] It ends with the dissolution of the Exchequer of the Jews, probably after it had held a last session in Michaelmas term 1290,[4] at the time of the Expulsion.

[3] Robert of Fulham and John le Moyne were only formally appointed as Justices of the Jews on 5 December 1265, but had been acting as such since at least 14 November: *see* Appendix I. William of Middleton had also been appointed the keeper of rolls and writs of the Exchequer of the Jews by mid-November: below, p. 38. Between the battle of Lewes (May 1264) and the battle of Evesham (August 1265), the Exchequer of the Jews, like the rest of the machinery of government, was under the ultimate control of Simon de Montfort, earl of Leicester. The appointment in January 1265 of Hamon Hauteyn as one of two Justices of the Jews was probably intended to conciliate the earl of Gloucester (*see* further on this below at p. 28) and in May 1265 two new Justices of the Jews were appointed on the nomination of the Lord Edward, though one of these was probably removed from office before he acted: C.A.F. Meekings, 'Justices of the Jews, 1218-68: a Provisional List', *B.I.H.R.*, xxviii (1955), p. 182.

[4] A royal writ addressed to the Barons of the Exchequer, dated 7 November 1290, ordered them to consult with the former Justices of the Jews (*'justiciarii nuper ad custodiam Judeorum assignati'*) on a particular matter relating to a Jewish debt: E 159/64, m. 7d. The last Justices of the Jews, William of Carleton and Peter of Leicester, were paid not only the half-yearly instalments of their fees which fell due at Michaelmas 1289 and Easter 1290 (C 62/66, m.2: in the *liberate* writs, dated 24 July 1290, they are simply described as Justices of the Jews), but also a final instalment in respect of Michaelmas 1290 (C 62/67, m. 3: in these *liberate* writs, dated 4 June 1291, they are described as being the former Justices of the Jews). Although the payment was in respect of the half-year preceding the date when the instalments became due, it seems unlikely that they would have been paid all of the instalment due at Michaelmas 1290 unless still in office on that day.

I *Location and Sessions*

(i) *Location*

The Exchequer of the Jews was one of those courts and departments of government which were in semi-permanent residence in the royal palace of Westminster, like the Exchequer proper, the main body with responsibility for financial administration, and the court known as the Common Bench or Court of Common Pleas, ultimately an offshoot of the Exchequer, but by now independent of it, and of increasing importance as the leading court for the hearing of civil litigation.The precise location of the Exchequer of the Jews at Westminster is revealed by an order given in 1235 for the enlargement of the premises housing it so as to include a solar, cellar and chimney. This places the Exchequer of the Jews in a chamber on the west side of Westminster hall, on the opposite side to the river Thames.[1] By 1260, the Exchequer of the Jews also possessed its own 'wardrobe', separate from, but close to, the main room or rooms of the court.[2] This is probably to be identified with the 'treasury' of the Exchequer of the Jews which is mentioned in later references. Evidence from 1265 suggests that the Exchequer of the Jews may have held its sessions elsewhere during the period when the Lord Edward controlled it (1262-5);[3] and in 1267, when the earl of Gloucester marched on London and the Exchequer moved to St. Paul's, the Exchequer of the Jews appears to have moved, albeit only temporarily, to Ludgate.[4]

The Exchequer of the Jews is known to have left Westminster on two later occasions as well.[5] On both occasions the move was to Shrewsbury, and the Exchequer of the Jews was accompanied by the other two Westminster-based institutions, the Exchequer and the Common Bench. The first move was associated with a royal expedition against the Welsh prince, Llewellyn ap Gruffydd, which was summoned to Worcester for mid-Summer 1277. For the benefit of litigants summoned to the King's service, the three Westminster-based institutions and the court of King's Bench were ordered to transfer themselves to Shrewsbury for Michaelmas term 1277.[6] The Exchequer of the Jews held its sessions that term in the castle at Shrewsbury,[7] but had probably made the return journey to Westminster in time for the following Hilary term.[8] The second move was also associated with military activity against the Welsh, and was ordered by the King on 10 April 1282. The Exchequer of the Jews, like the Exchequer, was ordered to be at Shrewsbury for mid-Summer's day,[9] and probably held its sessions at Shrewsbury from Michaelmas term 1282 to Trinity term 1283 (inclusive).[10]

The subsequent fate of the buildings at Westminster which had been used to house the Exchequer of the Jews is not clear. The later Star Chamber was on the east, not the west, side of Westminster Hall. This renders improbable any connection between the Chamber and the Exchequer of the Jews.[11] In 1294, an assize was

[1] *Close Rolls, 1234-7*, p. 100. The enlargement was to be made at the expense of the Jews of England.

[2] E 159/33, m. 10.

[3] *Close Rolls, 1264-8*, pp. 19, 52.

[4] *EJ*, i, pp. 151, 154. For the removal of the Exchequer to St. Paul's *see* E 159/41, m. 6d. These same events led to the court not sitting in Easter term 1267: E 9/7, m. 1.

[5] That the Exchequer of the Jews was still located in premises outside Westminster hall proper in 1274 is indicated by *EJ*, ii, pp. 176-7.

[6] The ordinance of the King and council ordering the transfer, which is referred to as the *statutum regis* in E 13/5, m. 19, survives in manuscript in three different versions: C 49/66, no. 8; C 49/69, no. 17; E 175/1, no. 14. It is printed from one of these by G.O. Sayles in *Select Cases in the Court of King's Bench*, vol. II, (Selden Soc. 57: 1938), pp. cxxvii - cxxxviii.

[7] C. Roth, *A History of the Jews in England* (3rd edition, Oxford, 1964), p. 111, n. 3 is in error in stating that sessions were held in the abbey at Shrewsbury. The ordinance appears to assign the Exchequer of the Jews to the abbey, but its sessions were in fact held in the castle, as is shown by C 62/54, m. 4.

[8] Curiously, the plea-roll for Michaelmas term 1277 (E 9/25) unlike the corresponding roll of the Bench (CP 40/21, m. 1) does not make it clear that the proceedings which it records are being held at Shrewsbury. One plea-roll entry appears to envisage that the Exchequer of the Jews would still be at Shrewsbury in Hilary term (*EJ*, iii, p. 289), though it is known that the Common Bench had by then returned to Westminster (CP 40/23, m. 1).

[9] *Cal. Close Rolls, 1279-88*, p. 150. The Common Bench was ordered to be at Shrewsbury at the beginning of June.

[10] The Plea Rolls of the Exchequer of the Jews from Michaelmas term 1282 to Trinity term 1283 (E 9/40A, 40B, 41, 42, 43) all record the fact that sessions are being held at Shrewsbury. The single surviving membrane from a plea-roll of Michaelmas term 1283 (E 9/67) does not make it clear where sessions are being held, but it is known that the Common Bench returned to Westminster for that term (CP 40/51, m.1) and that the Exchequer was ordered to do so (E 159/56, m. 2d). The timing is curious, for parliament was held at Shrewsbury at Michaelmas 1283, and it might have been expected that practical convenience would dictate that the Westminster-based institutions stay on at Shrewsbury for that term. For an allowance made to the sheriffs of London of eight shillings for the cost of the carriage of the rolls, charters and memoranda of the Exchequer of the Jews from London to Shrewsbury in 11 Edward I *see* C 62/60, m. 3.

[11] R.A. Brown, H.M. Colvin and A.J. Taylor, *The History of the King's Works*, vol. I. (London, 1963), pp. 545-6; the suggestion is made by Roth (*op. cit.*, pp. 110-11).

adjourned before assize justices at Westminster *in Judaismo*. The assize was probably heard in what had been the buildings of the Exchequer of the Jews and shows that they were then still identified with the institution which had once housed them.[12] Given their location it seems possible that the buildings were those subsequently used for the storage of records of the Common Bench and known as 'Paradise' and 'Hell.'[13]

(ii) *Chronology of sessions*

The Exchequer of the Jews, in common with the Exchequer and the Common Bench and the King's Bench, was open for the transaction both of legal and (so it would seem) administrative business only for part of the year.[14] This was during four main terms, named after four festivals of the Christian church which preceded each of them (Hilary, Easter, Trinity, Michaelmas). The legal business of the Exchequer of the Jews, as of the other institutions, was recorded as taking place on particular 'days' within these terms. These days occur, normally, at intervals of about one week, and it is clear from other evidence that what is recorded as taking place on a particular 'day' might, in reality, have occurred at any time within the succeeding week (and sometimes even later than that). The exact duration of the four terms varied somewhat from year to year. This was probably in response to the exigencies of business as well as to the demands of the Christian calendar. The terms observed by the Exchequer of the Jews were not the same as those of the Common Bench or of the Exchequer, but were closely related to those of both institutions. At the maximum, it was open for business for rather under half the year.

Hilary term opened for the Exchequer of the Jews on the octave of the feast of St. Hilary (20 January) and normally continued until at least the week beginning 3 February (three weeks after the feast of St. Hilary, or the morrow of the feast of the Purification of the Virgin).[15] In some, but perhaps not all, years it continued until the quindene of the feast of the Purification (the week beginning 17 February).[16] In at least six years during this period, proceedings are also recorded for a return-day of the morrow of Ash Wednesday (a movable feast).[17] The term of the Exchequer of Pleas opened one week earlier (on the morrow of the feast of St. Hilary) and normally continued until the week beginning with the morrow of Ash Wednesday. The Common Bench opened on the same day as the Exchequer of the Jews but is not normally recorded as having done any business later than the quindene of the feast of the Purification of the Virgin.

Easter term opened for the Exchequer of the Jews on the quindene of Easter (the Monday after the second Sunday after Easter) and continued until either the week beginning three weeks later (the fifth week after Easter)[18] or to the week commencing on the Friday of that same week (the morrow of the feast day of the Ascension).[19] The Exchequer of Pleas also regularly commenced proceedings for this term one week earlier (on the morrow of the close of Easter), but concluded proceedings on the morrow of the Ascension. The Common Bench opened on the same day as the Exchequer of the Jews, and also closed with the morrow of Ascension return-day.

Trinity term was always complicated by the fact that some of its return-days were calculated with reference to Trinity Sunday, a movable feast whose date changes with that of Easter Sunday, while others were calculated by reference to fixed feast-days. The term began for the Exchequer of the Jews at the octave of Trinity (the Monday after the first Sunday after Trinity Sunday) and proceedings might then be recorded for two and three weeks after Trinity.[20] Proceedings are also normally recorded for the morrow of the feast of St. John the Baptist (the week beginning 25 June) and for return-days a week, a fortnight and three weeks after that festival. The term sometimes continued until a return-day beginning on the morrow of the feast of St. Margaret (21 July)[21] or even until a return-day beginning on the morrow of the feast of St. James (26 July).[22] The Exchequer of Pleas again opened one week earlier (on the morrow of Trinity Sunday) and closed at around the end of July, like the Exchequer of the Jews. The Common Bench opened on the same day as the Exchequer of the Jews, but seems normally to have closed after the return-day a fortnight after the feast of St. John the Baptist.

12 CP 40/104, m. 143.

13 Brown et al., *op. cit.*, pp. 542-3.

14 But for evidence indicating that the justices of the Jews transacted certain kinds of business out of term and away from Westminster see Paul Brand, 'Jews and the Law in England, 1275-90' in *Eng. Hist. Rev.*, 115 (2000), 1138-58 at 1144-7.

15 Years when this is the last return-day for which proceedings are recorded are 1282 (E 9/39, m. 5) and 1283 (E 9/41, m. 2).

16 Hilary terms which continued until this return-day include those in 1268 (E 9/9, m. 6), 1275 (E 9/18, m. 4) and 1276 (E 9/49, m. 2).

17 In 1268 (E 9/9, m. 6) (week beginning 23 February); 1273 (E 9/13, m. 4) (week beginning 23 February); 1275 (E 9/18, m. 7) (week beginning 28 February); 1278 (E 9/26, m. 5) (week beginning 3 March); 1279 (E 9/30, m. 3d) (week beginning 16 February); 1280 (E 9/34, m. 9) (week beginning 7 March).

18 Five weeks after Easter is the last return-day mentioned in the roll for 1277 (E 9/23, m. 6). In 1279, the last return-day mentioned is a Month after Easter (E 9/31, m. 3).

19 Proceedings are recorded for this return-day in 1275 (E 9/19, m. 4) and 1278 (E 9/27, m. 7).

20 No proceedings are recorded for the latter return-day in 1272 (E 9/12), 1273 (E 9/14), 1275 (E 9/20), 1278 (E 9/28) or 1281 (E 9/38).

21 In 1266 (E 9/6, m. 1: as a return-day of a Month after the feast of St. John the Baptist); 1275 (E 9/20, mm. 14, 20, 20d); 1280 (E 9/36, mm. 1, 5d).

22 In 1272 (E 9/12, m. 4) 1273 (E9/14, m. 13) and 1278 (E 9/63, mm. 1, 12, 12d). In 1272 and 1273 proceedings are also recorded for the morrow of St. Margaret (E 9/12, mm. 2, 4; E 9/14, m. 13).

Michaelmas term for the Exchequer of the Jews commenced at the octave of the feast of St. Michael (6 October). In the earlier part of the 1270s it continued in several years until as late as a return-day for the morrow of the feast of St. Nicholas (7 December);[23] but it is uncertain, from the unsatisfactory nature of the surviving evidence, whether this was also true of the later period. The Exchequer of Pleas followed the general pattern of other terms by opening one week earlier (on the morrow of Michaelmas) and regularly remained open until a return-day on the morrow of the feast of St. Nicholas. The Common Bench opened on the same day as the Exchequer of the Jews, but ended with a return-day at the quindene of the feast of St. Martin (25 November).

[23] In 1273 (E 9/15, mm. 6d, 7), 1274 (E 9/17, mm. 6, 13), 1275 (E 9/21, m. 8) and 1276 (E 9/68, m. 1d).

II *The administrative functions and jurisdictional powers of the Exchequer of the Jews*

The plea rolls of the Exchequer of the Jews are the main record of its activities. The name given to this series of rolls suggests that the Jewish Exchequer functioned simply as a law court, for the same name is given to the rolls which record the exclusively legal business of the main common law courts and to the rolls which record litigation in the Exchequer of Pleas. The name is, however, a misleading guide to their content. What the rolls in fact record is the mixture of purely legal business and largely administrative activities that was heard and performed by the Exchequer of the Jews. The account which follows is an attempt to analyse the main administrative functions performed by the Jewish Exchequer and the main constituent elements in the court's jurisdiction. The discussion is illustrated mainly, but not exclusively, by examples drawn from the period under consideration, the last quarter-century of the existence of the Exchequer of the Jews.

(i) *Administrative functions*

(a) *Chirograph chests.* From 1194 onwards there had existed a network of local chirograph chests (*archae*) in all the main centres of Jewish settlement in England.[1] Initially, there were no more than six or seven but by 1220 there were seventeen and later still more, though sometimes only for limited periods of time.[2] By 1269 it could be asserted (and the assertion is repeated more forcefully in the statute of Jewry of 1275) that Jews ought not to reside outside the towns that had such chests.[3] Each chirograph chest was administered by two Christian chirographers and two Jewish chirographers plus one or two clerks.[4] The clerks were responsible for writing the chirographs or bonds recording acknowledgments of debt to Jewish creditors in the presence of both the debtor and the creditor,[5] and an undated form of oath apparently belonging to the early 1270s requires them to have personal knowledge of the debtor and to be satisfied that he held lands in his own right that he could oblige to the creditor or to act only on the testimony of two respectable witnesses and the debtor's own affirmation on oath, and also to write their own names in the bond and to sign them with a quasi-notarial sign.[6] Prior to 1233, chirographs were bipartite in form, with the part sealed by the debtor going to the creditor and a second unsealed but otherwise identical copy going to the chirograph chest. Thereafter chirographs became tripartite with the debtor getting a third unsealed copy.[7] In 1239 a further change was made which ensured that it was the sealed part that went into the chest and the unsealed 'foot' that now went to the creditor.[8] The chirographers were in charge of the chirograph chest itself. Under the original scheme, there were to be three keys to each chest. One was to be shared by the two Christian chirographers, a second by the two Jewish chirographers, and a third was to be in the custody of a third clerk appointed centrally and responsible for keeping a roll of transcripts of bonds, and each of these locks was to be sealed. The centrally appointed clerk is not found in later practice and by 1239 each of the individual chirographers had his own key.[9] It

[1] *Chronica Rogeri de Hovedene*, ed. W. Stubbs (Rolls Series: 1868-71), iii, 266-7.

[2] Joe Hillaby, 'A magnate among the marchers: Hamo of Hereford, his family and clients, 1218-53', *Jewish Historical Studies 31* (1988-90), 23-82 at 23-4.

[3] *Close Rolls, 1268-72*, p. 116; *Stat. Realm*, i, p. 221a. *Cf.* H.G. Richardson, *The English Jewry under Angevin Kings* (London, 1960), pp. 14-22.

[4] The original scheme of 1194 had envisaged the employment of two clerks for each chest. Later evidence, though not conclusive, suggests that there was only a single clerk except at London and York (for the latter *see EJ*, ii, p. 181 and *EJ*, i, p. 303). In 1275, an order was given for two clerks to be chosen at Devizes, but only one was chosen: *EJ*, iii, pp. 42-3. The original scheme also envisaged that at at each chest there would also be a clerk appointed by William de St Mere Eglise and William de Chimilli (apparently the justices of the Jews) who would keep a transcript of all the bonds. It is not clear whether these clerks were ever appointed and, if so, how quickly they disappeared.

[5] For the requirement of the presence of both parties see the legislation of 1239: *Liber de Antiquis Legibus*, pp. 237-8; BL MS. Additional 62534, ff. 257v-258r.

[6] BL MS. Additional 62534, f. 265r.

[7] Richardson, *English Jewry under Angevin Kings*, p. 294.

[8] Prior to 1239 it was the (unsealed) foot of the chirograph that was deposited in the chest, but thereafter the chest contained the part sealed by the debtor and the creditor got the unsealed 'foot': *Liber de Antiquis Legibus*, pp. 237-8; BL MS. Additional 62534, ff. 257v-258r.

[9] *Liber de Antiquis Legibus*, pp. 237-8; BL MS. Additional 62534, ff. 257v-258r.

was probably the need to assemble all of the chirographers before the chest could be opened that explains the grace period of ten days allowed for placing the official part in the chest.[10] The chirographers were collectively responsible for the safe custody of chirographs in their chest and the eventual withdrawal of the chirograph from the chest when the debt was paid in full or when instructed to do so by the Exchequer of the Jews. The original arrangements of 1194 had, as had been seen, envisaged the appointment of a special clerk to keep a transcript of all bonds and that he would also compile one of three rolls recording payments on the bonds, with the Christian chirographers keeping a second and the Jewish chirographers a third. Later evidence makes no mention of separate rolls recording payments but does suggest that it was the chirographers who kept a roll recording the names of debtors and creditors, the total owed, the year and day of payment and the names of the witnesses.[11]

The Exchequer of the Jews appears to have exercised an almost exclusive control over the *appointment and dismissal* of both chirographers and clerks, although the actual choice of a new chirographer or clerk might sometimes be left to a local jury.[12] Each newly appointed official had to take an oath of good conduct.[13] This might be taken either locally or at the Exchequer of the Jews. The names of the sureties for the new official's good conduct, usually two in number, if found locally, had to be returned to the Exchequer of the Jews, to be entered as of record on the plea-rolls.[14] Prior to 1275, there appears to have been a fairly rapid turn-over of such officials. After 1275, when usury was prohibited by the statute of Jewry, the chests became of less importance and the turn-over much slower. Only one change of chirographer and clerk is recorded on the rolls between Michaelmas 1275 and Hilary 1277;[15] none at all between Easter 1279 and Trinity 1281.

From time to time, local chirograph chests were closed and their contents enrolled. This was normally accompanied by an *appuramentum* (a 'cleansing') of the bonds they contained, to distinguish between those which had become void on full payment or satisfaction of the debt, those where only part of the debt had been satisfied, and the 'clear' bonds, where the whole of the debt was still owed.[16] Such an operation was normally undertaken in preparation for the imposition of a tallage, to allow an assessment to be based on the sums still owed to individual creditors, and the tallage would normally lead to some of the 'clearer' bonds passing into the King's hands. During this period, orders for the general closing and subsequent re-opening of the chirograph chests came not from the Exchequer of the Jews, but from the royal chancery, and it was the same body which issued individual commissions for the enrolling and 'cleansing' of the contents of the local chests. The justices of the Jews were generally among those commissioned for this purpose, but only on an individual basis, and not *ex officio*.[17]

(b) *Tallage assessment and collection.* A tallage of the Jews of England, and the closely related fines paid in lieu of such tallage, or for respite from tallage for a limited period, were forms of extraordinary taxation which, like other types of tallage (those levied by the Crown from inhabitants of the royal desmesne, or by lords from their villeins), appear to have required no consent from those liable to pay them, though they were probably discussed and approved in advance by the King's council. Although the amount of information we possess about some of the Jewish tallages and fines of this period is small, it is enough to allow the confident assertion that

[10] This is mentioned in the legislation of 1239 with the severe punishment awaiting the chirographer who retained the chirograph beyond that period: *Liber de Antiquis Legibus*, pp. 237-8; BL MS. Additional 62534, ff. 257v-258r. It is also mentioned in the undated chirographer's oath (probably of c. 1270) found in BL MS. Additional 62534, f. 256r.

[11] This is mentioned in the oath of the Christian chirographers of c. 1270 recorded in BL MS. Additional 62534, f. 256r.

[12] For the direct appointment of new chirographers *see EJ*, i, p. 153; *EJ*, ii, pp. 43, 49, 108, 114, 183, 240. For the election of new chirographers *see Select Pleas*, p. 11; *EJ*, i, pp. 69, 82, 135, 152; *EJ*, ii, pp. 14, 107, 149, 238, 270, 273; *EJ*, iii, pp. 42-3. For the direct appointment of new clerks *see EJ*, i, pp. 71, 150; *EJ*, ii, pp. 114, 146, 181. For the election of new clerks *see EJ*, i, p. 135; *EJ*, ii, p. 62; *EJ*, iii, pp. 42-3.

[13] The form of the oaths taken c. 1270 by both clerks and Christian chirographers is recorded in BL MS. Additional 62534 at f. 256r.

[14] *Select Pleas*, p. 11; *EJ*, i, pp. 69, 82, 135, 152; *EJ*, ii, pp. 14, 114, 149, 238, 270, 273.

[15] *EJ*, iii, pp. 42-3.

[16] For a commission to make an *appuramentum* with detailed instructions *see Cal. Pat. Rolls, 1272-81*, p. 158 (cf. *ibid*, p.184). A writ issued under the attestation of Hamon Hauteyn for the transfer of certain bonds from the Hereford chest after its *appuramentum* in 1273 mentions that both the scrutiny of the chest (the enrolment of its contents) and the subsequent *appuramentum* had been authorized by the King's council: E 143/1/3, no. 4.

[17] There were scrutinies of the chests at London and Colchester (and perhaps elsewhere) in 1269 made by John of Weston, Walter de la Croce and William of Middleton: *Close Rolls, 1268-72*, pp. 50, 54; E 159/47, m. 3d; E 159/45, m. 8A. There was a scrutiny of the chest at Norwich by William of Middleton in 1272/3, and of the chest at Canterbury by Ellis of Hertford: *Cal. Pat. Rolls, 1266-72*, p. 708; E 159/47, m. 4. In February 1273 four commissioners (including the two Justices of the Jews) were ordered to make a scrutiny of between four and six chests each: *Cal. Pat. Rolls, 1272-81*, p. 6. A total of twenty-two commissioners, working in groups of two, were ordered to make scrutinies of between one and four chests each in November 1275: *Cal. Pat. Rolls, 1272-81*, pp. 126-7. For the resulting records *see* C 47/9/48 (Colchester), C 47/9/49 (York), E 101/249/31 (Exeter) and E 9/22, m. 18 (Hereford). Three commissions were issued during 1276 for work on the scrutiny of the London chest: *Cal. Pat. Rolls, 1272-81*, pp. 148, 158, 184. Further scrutinies appear to have been made in 1277 (*Cal. Close Rolls, 1272-9*, p. 432, cf. *ibid.*, p. 215), 1281 (*Cal. Pat. Rolls, 1272-81*, pp. 458, 459) and 1286 (*Cal. Pat. Rolls, 1281-92*, p. 227; E 159/59, mm. 23d, 27d).

neither the original assessment of tallage nor the apportionment of fines (the assessment of particular sums as due from individuals) nor even the subsequent collection of tallages or fines from the individuals concerned, was ever in this period the *ex officio* concern of the Exchequer of the Jews or its officials. On each occasion when tallages or fines were levied, specific individuals were commissioned for these tasks, and the Exchequer of the Jews was, at most, called in after the process of collection had begun, with the remit of enforcing payment of the arrears.[18]

c) *Chevage collection.* A much lighter, if more regular, form of taxation paid by the Jews of England was chevage *(capitagium),* an annual poll tax of three pence per person payable by all Jews, both male and female, aged twelve or over. The payment is first mentioned in the 1275 statute of Jewry,[19] though it is possible that it predates that statute.[20] The actual collection of the tax was entrusted to commissioners specially appointed by chancery writ,[21] and the proceeds went (from at least 1278 onwards) to the *Domus Conversorum.*[22] The whole arrangement was, however, under the supervision of the Exchequer of the Jews, before whom the collectors were required to present their accounts.[23]

(d) *Residence controls.* In 1265 it appears to have been a well-established feature of royal control over the Jewish community in England that no Jew could change his place of residence without securing official permission to do so. It was the Exchequer of the Jews to which (at least during the period up to 1276) any application for permission to move had to be made.[24] A small sum was paid for such permission, and the local sheriffs concerned were notified of the granting of permission by a writ from the Exchequer of the Jews.[25] Unlicensed residence in a town could (and did) lead to the issuing of orders by the Exchequer of the Jews for the seizure of the body, goods and chattels of the Jew or Jews concerned, and might lead to the forfeiture of the latter.[26] It was also the Exchequer of the Jews which, in 1275, was made responsible for supervising the transfer of Jews resident in towns allocated in dower to the Queen Mother to other near-by towns remaining in the King's possession.[27] After 1276, the evidence for this side of the activities of the Exchequer of the Jews seems largely to disappear,[28] though it is known that in 1277 action was taken by the Exchequer of the Jews to enforce that part of the statute of Jewry which prohibited the residence of the Jews in towns which did not possess chirograph chests,[29] and that in 1284 it was instructed to take action of a similar kind once more.[30]

(e) *Inquisitions post mortem.* By 1265, it had long been established that at the death of a Jew, the king was entitled by way of relief to a sum equal to one third of the value of his movable goods, his outstanding debts, and of the value (but for one year only) of any houses or other immovable property in his possession.[31] By 1268 at latest, there existed a writ of standard form sent by the Exchequer of the Jews to the appropriate local sheriff(s) ordering a full inquiry to be held as to the goods and chattels (especially gold, silver and other valuables), bonds in chirograph chests and immovable property which a deceased Jew had held on the day he fell sick of the illness of which he died, or (in the case of sudden, violent death) on the day of his death, a kind of Jewish analogue to the inquisition *post mortem* into the lands held by a deceased Christian tenant-in-chief at the time of his death.[32] It was on the basis of these inventories and their valuations that the widow or sons of the deceased were allowed to satisfy the King for his third share, normally by granting him 'clear' debts to the

[18] For full details of the arrangements made for the tallages and related payments of this period *see* Appendix V.

[19] *Stat. Realm,* i, p. 221a.

[20] In 1240 Jeremy of Caxton and William of Hardel were commissioned to make a scrutiny of the chests in eight English counties, and to make inquiries as to various *capitula.* The local sheriff was ordered to let them know the names, and produce the bodies, of all Jews aged over twelve (the age at which chevage was later payable): *Close Rolls 1237-42,* pp. 238-9. Some system of regular checking-up on all adult Jews (with perhaps a payment made on each occasion) is implied by the regulation of 1239 requiring each Jew to stay for a year at his place of residence at Michaelmas: *Liber de Antiquis Legibus,* p. 237.

[21] *Cal. Pat. Rolls, 1272-81,* p. 240; *EJ,* vi, no. 492; *Cal. Pat. Rolls, 1281-92,* p. 398.

[22] *EJ,* vi, no. 492; *Cal. Pat. Rolls, 1272-81,* p. 372.

[23] *EJ,* vi, no. 492 (6 Edward I). But the account of the keeper of the *Domus Conversorum* for 8-13 Edward I appears to have been rendered in the main Exchequer: E 101/249/24. This has been edited by Michael Adler in the Appendix of documents attached to his article on the 'History of the "Domus Conversorum"' in *Trans. Jew. Hist. Soc.* 4 (1899-1901), pp. 16-75 at pp. 59-63.

[24] But for temporary residence permits issued by Chancery in 1275 *see Cal. Close Rolls, 1272-9,* pp. 259, 260.

[25] *EJ,* i, pp. 134, 150; *EJ,* ii, pp. 13, 48, 50, 51, 52, 103, 104, 145, 151, 163, 173, 242, 243, 278; *EJ,* iii, pp. 109, 127.

[26] *Select Pleas,* pp. 61, 82; *EJ,* iii, pp. 59-60. But for orders from the Chancery for the removal of Jews from particular towns *see Cal. Close Rolls, 1272-9,* pp. 50, 130; *Cal. Close Rolls, 1279-88,* p. 241; and for the issuing by Chancery of an order for a proclamation to be made that Jews were not to live outside towns in the counties of Oxfordshire and Berkshire *see Close Rolls, 1268-72,* p. 116.

[27] *Cal. Pat. Rolls, 1272-81,* p.76; *Select Pleas,* p. 85.

[28] For evidence of temporary residence permits being issued by Chancery in 1277 see *Cal. Close Rolls, 1279-88,* pp. 370, 376, 382, 385.

[29] *EJ,* iii, pp. 317, 319.

[30] *Cal. Close Rolls, 1279-88,* p. 256.

[31] The King's third is mentioned as early as 1220 (*EJ,* i, p. 37) but is probably older. That the King's entitlement was only to a third of the annual value, not of the full value, of immovable property is shown by *EJ,* vi, nos. 351, 475. See also below, p. 13 and n. 107.

[32] The earliest example seems to be *EJ,* i, pp. 201-2.

appropriate value.[33] A similar inquisition was held when a Jew converted to Christianity.[34] In such a case, prior to 1280, all his possessions were forfeit;[35] thereafter the convert was allowed to keep half and the *Domus Conversorum* was given the other half.[36]

(f) *Licences for the purchase and sale of property.* Under the terms of the statute of Jewry of 1275, it became necessary for any Jew wishing to dispose of real property (messuages, rents etc.) which he held, whether to fellow-Jews or to Christians, to obtain a royal licence to do so.[37] Such licences were issued not by the Exchequer of the Jews, but by Chancery. However, both the letters patent licensing the transaction and the charter recording the transaction were, it seems, normally recorded on the Plea Rolls of the Exchequer of the Jews.[38] Even prior to 1275, it was not uncommon for vendors and purchasers to obtain royal confirmation or ratification of such transactions. These also were obtained from Chancery, and not from the Exchequer of the Jews.[39]

The only known bar in 1265 to the acquisition of urban property by Jews was one imposed in or before 1248 on Jews acquiring property in London from Christian vendors.[40] This was not an absolute prohibition, but merely required the Jewish purchaser to obtain a royal licence for his purchase.[41] From 1271 onwards, however, Jews were prohibited from acquiring any title, whether for life or in fee, to real property in future. This was a prohibition to which there appear to have been no licenced exceptions.[42]

(g) *Licences for the sales of debts to Christians.* Another type of transaction which came, during the course of this period, to require a licence was the sale of any debt by a Jewish creditor to a Christian. The requirement of a licence was introduced by the statute of Jewry of 1269 and the licences regularly recited its terms.[43] Again, the licences themselves were issued by Chancery, not by the Exchequer of the Jews, though it seems to have been normal practice for the latter to enrol the terms of such licences, as well as the starr recording the terms of the sale.[44] It seems not to have been uncommon, though not as yet strictly necessary,[45] for the parties to similar sales to obtain a royal confirmation of the transaction prior to the statute.[46] Such confirmations were also then given for sales by Jews to Christians of rent-charges, a practice forbidden by legislation in 1269.[47] When debts were sold prior to 1269, they were sold with the interest accumulated up to the date of sale, a practice also specifically forbidden in 1269.[48]

(ii) *Jurisdiction*

(a) *Litigation about title to real property.* The Exchequer of the Jews exercised a jurisdiction over cases concerning title to real property (primarily houses and rents in towns) in which either of the litigants concerned was Jewish.[49] The writs and forms of action used in such litigation appear to have closely resembled those in use for similar litigation in other royal courts. This includes writs of right,[50] writs of entry both within the degrees[51] and in the *post*,[52] writs of cosinage,[53] and writs of dower.[54] The 1271 statute of Jewry required the original writs necessary for the initiation of such litigation to be issued by the Exchequer of the Jews itself rather than by Chancery, which issued all writs initiating similar litigation in other royal courts.[55] This may also reflect the

[33] This was not yet the general practice in the 1250s when the treasurer and the justices of the Jews advised such a course since 'Jews do not keep their terms for fines made': C 145/21, no. 4.

[34] For examples *see EJ*, vi, nos. 653, 691.

[35] For evidence of this rule *see Close Rolls, 1253-4*, p. 24; *EJ*, i, pp. 132, 194.

[36] *Cal. Pat. Rolls, 1272-81*, pp. 370-1. By special favour, individual converts were occasionally allowed to keep all their possessions. For examples see *Cal. Close Rolls, 1279-88*, pp. 25, 28.

[37] *Stat. Realm*, i, p. 221a.

[38] For example, *see Cal. Pat. Rolls 1272-81*, p. 332 and *EJ*, vi, no. 294.

[39] For examples *see Cal. Pat. Rolls, 1258-66*, pp. 544, 565; *Cal. Pat. Rolls, 1266-72*, pp. 82, 255, 572, 606, 621, 664-5. For confirmations in the form of licences *see Cal. Pat. Rolls, 1272-81*, pp. 42, 43, 88. For one licence given by the Exchequer of the Jews in 1274 *see EJ*, ii, pp. 173, 191.

[40] *Close Rolls, 1247-51*, p. 65.

[41] *See ibid.* for an early licence; and *cf. Cal. Pat. Rolls, 1266-72*, p. 646 for a confirmation which is tantamount to a licence.

[42] *Liber de Antiquis Legibus*, pp. 235-6.

[43] *Cal. Pat. Rolls, 1266-72*, p. 376. The first licence under the statute was issued in July 1269: *Cal. Pat. Rolls, 1266-72*, pp. 359-60.

[44] e.g. *EJ*, ii, p. 276 (and *Cal. Pat. Rolls, 1272-81*, p. 83); *EJ*, iii, p.115 (and *Cal. Pat. Rolls, 1272-81*, p. 115); *EJ*, vi, nos. 875-6, 918 (and *Cal. Pat. Rolls, 1272-81*, p. 425).

[45] For examples of unconfirmed sales *see EJ*, i, pp. 136-8, 154-5, 157, 209, 211, 212.

[46] For examples *see Cal. Pat. Rolls, 1258-66*, pp. 614, 628; *Cal. Pat. Rolls 1266-72*, pp. 29, 67, 177 (and *cf. Select Pleas*, p. 177), 184, 185 (and *cf. EJ*, i, p.195 and *Select Pleas*, p. 46), 235, 261.

[47] For examples *see Cal. Pat. Rolls, 1266-72*, pp. 37, 38, 69, 117 (and *cf. EJ*, i, p. 117), 122, 123 (and *cf. EJ*, i, p. 197), 164, 166, 170, 172 (and *cf. EJ*, i, p.195), 177 (and *cf. Select Pleas*, pp. 43-5), 179 (and *cf. EJ*, i, pp. 193, 206), 180 (and *cf. EJ*, i, pp. 193, 206, 207), 182 (and *cf. EJ*, i, pp. 207-8), 184, 185 (and *cf. EJ*, i, p.195 and *Select Pleas*, p. 46), 186 (and *cf. EJ*, i, p. 210), 307, 309.

[48] Above, n. 43.

[49] For litigation where the plaintiff or demandant was Jewish *see EJ*, i, pp.118-19, 192; *EJ*, ii, pp. 35, 93-4; *EJ*, iii, p. 242. For litigation where the defendant or tenant was Jewish *see EJ*, i, pp. 2, 7, 16, 36, 129, 147; *EJ*, ii, pp. 124, 197, 210, 215-6. For litigation where both parties were Jewish *see EJ*, iii, p.258.

[50] E.g. *EJ*, i, p.147.

[51] E.g. *EJ*, ii, p. 35; *EJ*, iii, p. 242.

[52] E.g. *EJ*, iii, p. 242.

[53] E.g. *Select Pleas*, p. 36.

[54] E.g. *Select Pleas*, p. 52; *EJ*, i, p. 192.

[55] *Liber de Antiquis Legibus*, pp. 235-6.

earlier practice. It is not clear whether or not the Exchequer of the Jews had enjoyed an *exclusive* jurisdiction in all real property litigation involving Jews prior to 1271.[56] There is some evidence to suggest that it may not have done. In 1244 we learn only in passing of litigation about real property (a messuage in Canterbury) involving a Jewish tenant which had been removed into the Exchequer of the Jews from the court of the prior of Canterbury, but we cannot be certain whether this removal was in order to secure the benefit of a formal record of the demandant's quitclaim in the Exchequer of the Jews or whether the grounds for the removal were that the case was outside the jurisdiction of the prior's court.[57] The *Liber de Antiquis Legibus* suggests that the citizens of London in 1250 recovered their jurisdiction over actions concerning title to real property in the City involving Jews.[58] This jurisdiction had been lost again by 1279, but perhaps only as a direct result of the legislation of 1271.[59] A case concerning title to land in Marlborough involving a Jewish tenant that was removed into the Exchequer of the Jews from the town court in 1270 suggests that, if the Exchequer of the Jews did then claim a jurisdictional monopoly over such cases, this fact was unknown either to the royal Chancery (which must have issued the royal writ initiating the litigation) or to the town court in question.[60] Prior to 1275, and the introduction of a system of licensing all property transactions involving Jews, the Exchequer of the Jews also, on occasion, appears to have been willing to entertain purely collusive actions to secure the transfer of real property rights,[61] and at least one such action is known to have led to the drawing-up of a final concord.[62]

In addition the Exchequer of the Jews exercised what appears to have been an exclusive jurisdiction[63] in all cases in which the King sought to recover real property which had once been in the possession of a Jewish tenant and which had escheated to him when the Jew was converted to Christianity[64] or been convicted of a felony.[65] It was one of the peculiarities of real property law as it applied to the acquisition and tenure of property by Jews that, from whomsoever the property was acquired and to whomsoever services were done for it, the property once in Jewish hands was considered to be held in chief of the King. Any conviction of a Jew for felony or forfeiture on conversion therefore led to the property escheating to the King.[66] The closest analogy here is that supplied by the acquisition of land by a villein, whose acquisitions of property were, in law, liable to confiscation by his lord, to being treated as having been made by the lord, but in such a case the lord would hold the land of the lord of whom the villein was to have held it, not hold it free of that lord's claims, as here.

(b) *Litigation about movable property.* The Exchequer of the Jews also exercised jurisdiction in cases where a plaintiff was seeking the return by the defendant of movable property which belonged to him, if either of the litigants was Jewish. Almost all of the cases where the plaintiff was Jewish arose out of arrangements made by Jews to confide movables for temporary safe custody to neighbours in times of civil disturbances,[67] whereas the cases in which the defendant was Jewish normally concerned arrangements for the deposit of movables as the security

56 It was clearly intended to do so after the statute of 1271: *ibid.* But for litigation involving a Jewish tenant heard elsewhere after the statute *see* e.g. JUST 1/1219B, m. 10d (1273).

57 *EJ*, i, p. 97. For litigation by the assize of nuisance against a Jewish defendant in the 1236 Hampshire eyre *see* JUST 1/775, m. 9d; and for a final concord made in the 1248 Surrey eyre quitclaiming half a messuage in Southwark to a Jewish tenant *see* CP 25(1)/226/13, no. 51.

58 *Liber de Antiquis Legibus*, p. 16.

59 *Cal. Close Rolls 1272-9*, p. 547 and *cf. Cal. Close Rolls, 1279-88*, p. 8. Among the grievances of the citizens of London in 1281 was the fact that when Jews were impleaded by writ of right for London tenements in the Husting court, they secured writs attested by the Justices of the Jews to forbid the mayor and sheriffs to hear the pleas concerned: G.O. Sayles, 'The Sources of Two Revisions of the Statute of Gloucester, 1278', *Eng. Hist. Rev.*, 52 (1937), 467-74 at 474. For an earlier royal prohibition under the great seal to the mayor and sheriffs of London stopping them hearing land litigation brought against Aaron son of Vives by a Christian demandant *see* Corporation of London Records Office, Hustings Pleas of Land Roll 3, m. 5 and schedule (the writ sent). But for land litigation in the Hustings involving Jewish litigants in 1280 and 1285 *see* Ibid, Roll 8, m.1 and Roll 14, m. 5. Land transfers in London involving Jewish grantors or grantees continued down to 1290 to be registered on occasion on the Hustings Rolls of Deeds and Wills: *see* Corporation of London Records Office, Hustings Deeds and Wills Roll 4, nos. 10 (1268), 127 (1272); Roll 12, no. 54 (1281); Roll 13, nos. 49, 58, 108 (1282) and Roll 19, no. 14 (1290).

60 *EJ*, i, pp. 224-5 and see preceding note.

61 E.g. *EJ*, i, pp. 143, 167.

62 *A Cartulary of the Hospital of St. John the Baptist*, vol. II, ed. H.E. Salter (Oxford Historical Society 68: 1915), pp. 41-2 (no. 525): made in Easter term 1263, and apparently part of a bipartite (and not as might have been expected, a tripartite) document. In 1272 an inventory of the treasury of the Exchequer of the Jews' records among its contents *due fines levate in curia de Judaismo in quadam bursa*: E 101/249/15.

63 But for such a case being summoned to King's Bench in 1253 *see Close Rolls, 1251-3*, p. 451.

64 E.g. *EJ*, ii, pp. 288, 295; *EJ*, iii, pp. 22, 34-5, 177; *Select Pleas*, pp. 99-100 (a single case).

65 E.g. *EJ*, i, p. 167; *EJ*, ii, pp. 210, 257.

66 It was this point that was being made, albeit rather unclearly, in the Close Roll entry of 1249 (*Close Rolls, 1247-51*, p. 346) which Roth takes as reaffirming a royal prerogative of confiscating a Jew's property at his death (*op. cit.*, p. 101 and n.1). For the background to this particular forfeiture *see Cal. Inq. Misc.*, i, nos. 428, 522 and, more generally, V.D. Lipman, *The Jews of Medieval Norwich* (Jewish Historical Society of England, 1967), pp. 59-62.

67 For cases arising out of arrangements made in times of disturbance *see Select Pleas*, pp. 31-3; *EJ*, i, pp. 131, 132-3; *Select Pleas*, pp. 37-8; *EJ*, i, pp. 142, 143-4, 145, 169. For goods entrusted to a neighbour when Jews were expelled from a village by royal order *see EJ*, vi, nos. 563-4, and for goods allegedly pledged to Christians *see Select Pleas*, pp.17-18, and pp. 63-4.

for a loan of money.[68] The jurisdiction over such cases was not an exclusive one for certain local courts are also known to have heard such cases as well.[69] The forfeiture of a Jew's movable goods to the Crown, for whatever cause, also led to actions brought by the King in the Exchequer of the Jews to recover such of their goods as were in the possession of third parties.[70]

(c) *Trespass jurisdiction.* The Exchequer of the Jews possessed and exercised a jurisdiction over cases of trespass where either of the parties was Jewish or if the trespass was closely connected with a Jewish debt, even where neither of the parties was Jewish. The types of trespass mentioned on the Plea Rolls include physical assault,[71] imprisonment aggravated by the seizure of goods and chattels,[72] breaking into houses and seizure of their contents,[73] ejection from a house,[74] ejection of a creditor or his assign from land in their possession for the payment of a debt, or the seizure of the movable goods on such land,[75] ejection of a debtor from his house by a creditor taking possession of the debtor's lands or the commission of waste by such a creditor,[76] defamation,[77] deception (all the cases relate to chirographs),[78] and various types of wrongdoing and neglect of duty connected with the system of chirograph chests.[79]

(d) *Jurisdiction over felonies.* The Exchequer of the Jews exercised a crown pleas jurisdiction over appeals of felony (private prosecutions of serious crime) where either of the parties was Jewish,[80] and also over cases where Jews were indicted of felony.[81] It appears also to have exercised an *ex officio* jurisdiction to inquire into the deaths of any Jew who appeared to have been murdered.[82] Crown pleas, in the later thirteenth century, were normally tried and determined either at the increasingly infrequent sessions of the general eyre or (but only in the case of prisoners already in custody) at sessions of the justices of gaol delivery. It would appear that crown pleas cases involving Jews did not enjoy an automatic exemption from the normal criminal justice system,[83] and that, in order to ensure that such a case was heard in the Exchequer of the Jews, it was necessary to apply specially either to the Exchequer of the Jews,[84] or to Chancery,[85] for a writ authorising the release of the imprisoned Jew on bail to appear in the Exchequer of the Jews.

(e) *Privilege jurisdiction.* A further area of jurisdiction was over civil actions (not involving title to land) brought

68 For examples, see *EJ*, i, pp. 22, 139-40; *EJ*, vi, nos. 105, 423, 429, 447, 1129.

69 The constable of the Tower of London is known to have exercised a jurisdiction in cases concerning the pledging of chattels, if the chattels were worth less than forty shillings: *Close Rolls, 1259-61*, p. 385. *Cf. EJ*, ii, p. 211. A similar jurisdiction may have been exercised by other local constables and sheriffs. For evidence that some kind of jurisdiction was exercised by the constable of Exeter in cases involving Jews in 1220 *see EJ*, i, p.18; and by the constable of Winchester in cases involving Jews in 1270 *see Cal. Pat. Rolls, 1266-72*, p. 417. For the wider significance in other types of local court of a forty shillings limitation *see* J.S. Beckerman, 'The Forty-Shilling Jurisdictional Limit in Medieval English Personal Actions,' *Legal History Studies, 1972i*, pp. 110-17. The chancellor of the university of Oxford also exercised a jurisdiction over certain types of litigation involving Jews and students of the university: *Close Rolls, 1259-61*, pp. 360-1; *Cal. Close Rolls, 1272-9*, pp. 232-3; *Cal. Pat. Rolls 1281-92*, p. 236.

70 *EJ*, vi, nos. 674, 684, 692-3, 739, 940-3, 945-7, 1002, 1004, 1005, 1012, 1029-32, 1045, 1050, 1103, 1112-15, 1178-9, 1186, 1230.

71 For such cases being brought by Jews *see EJ*, i, p. 242; *EJ*, ii, pp. 87, 94-5, 130 and (where the king was involved, because the Jew had come to the town by royal order) *EJ*, iii, p. 5 (and *cf.*, pp. 8-9, 40-1). For such cases being brought by a Christian *see EJ*, vi, no. 107. For physical assault and robbery *see: EJ*, ii, pp. 130-1 (and *cf. ibid.*, pp. 138-9, 195-6, 200, 206, 216-17, 219-20, 227, 232, 286, 302).

72 *EJ*, i, pp. 224-5.

73 *EJ*, ii, pp. 142-3, 241; *EJ* ii, pp. 223-4. For a break in followed by the removal of the tiles on the roof of the house *see EJ*, ii, p. 263.

74 *EJ*, ii, pp. 95-96 (and *cf. ibid.*, p.119). For hindrance to the building of a house *see EJ*, ii, p. 129.

75 E.g. *EJ*, i, pp. 158-9; *EJ*, iii, p.160.

76 E.g. *EJ*, i, pp.160-1; *EJ*, i, p.178; *EJ*, ii, p. 26; *EJ*, ii, pp. 31-2; *EJ*, vi, no. 254.

77 *EJ*, i, p. 305; *EJ*, ii, p. 33; *EJ*, ii, p. 224.

78 *Select Pleas*, pp. 41-42; *ibid.*, pp. 54-6; *EJ*, i, p. 285; *EJ*, i, pp. 286-7; *EJ*, i, p. 292; *EJ*, ii, p. 206; *EJ*, iii, pp. 24, 82, 180, 181; *EJ*, ii, pp. 139, 140; *Select Pleas*, pp. 83-4; *EJ*, ii, pp. 200, 213-14, 218, 258; *EJ*, ii, pp. 136, 138-9, 191, 196, 198; *EJ*, ii, pp. 227, 229-30, 258, 298, *EJ*, iii, pp. 83, 148, *Select Pleas*, pp. 86, 91.

79 *EJ*, i, pp. 27-8, 43-4; *EJ*, i, p. 97; *EJ*, i, pp. 106-7; *EJ*, i, pp. 127-8; *EJ*, i, p.132; *EJ*, i, pp. 160, 182-3 and *Select Pleas*, pp. 51-2; *EJ*, i, pp. 162-3; *Select Pleas*, pp. 38-9; *EJ*, ii, pp.1-2, 94.

80 For appeals by Christians against Jews *see Select Pleas*, pp. 4-5; *EJ*, i, pp. 296-7; *EJ*, ii, p. 56; *EJ*, ii, p. 110; *EJ*, iii, pp.157-8, 162-3; *EJ*, iii, pp. 185-6, 189; *EJ*, iii, p. 288; *EJ*, vi, nos. 503, 632. For an appeal removed to the Exchequer of the Jews because the vouchee of the appellee was Jewish see *Select Pleas etc.*, p.78. For appeals by Jews against Christians see *EJ*, i, p. 46 (and *cf. ibid.*, p. 31); *EJ*, i, pp. 130-1. For appeals by Jews against Jews see *EJ*, i, p. 39; *EJ*, i, pp. 33, 42-3, 45, 50-1; *EJ*, i, pp. 69, 76; *Select Pleas etc.*, pp. 11-12. For an appeal by a Christian against a Christian, heard in the Exchequer of the Jews because it involved a Jewish debt, see *EJ*, i, pp. 250-1.

81 *EJ*, i, p. 107; *EJ*, i, p. 280; *EJ*, ii, p. 149.

82 *EJ*, i, p. 31 (*cf. ibid.*, p. 46); *EJ*, ii, pp. 44-5, 186, 249. For an indictment of Christians for the death of a Jew removed into the Exchequer of the Jews for trial *see EJ*, iii, pp. 248, 292-3.

83 For Jews being indicted at the eyre and then outlawed *see Close Rolls 1261-4*, p. 208; *Cal. Pat. Rolls, 1281-92*, p. 221. For Jews being tried before special oyer and terminer commissions, *see* e.g. *Cal. Close Rolls, 1266-72*, p. 400; *Cal. Pat. Rolls, 1272-81*, pp. 244-5, 227, 290; *Cal. Pat. Rolls 1281-92*, pp. 98, 397. For Jews being tried at gaol delivery sessions *see* e.g. *Cal. Pat. Rolls, 1266-72*, p. 278; *Cal. Pat. Rolls, 1281-92*, p. 258, 259, 282, 402.

84 E.g. *EJ*, i, p. 69; *EJ*, i, p. 134; *EJ*, ii, p. 12; *EJ*, ii, pp. 63, 103; *EJ*, ii, pp. 64, 101.

85 E.g. *Cal. Close Rolls, 1272-79*, p. 271; *Cal. Close Rolls, 1279-88*, p.158.

by any of the justices of the Jews,[86] or by the clerks,[87] or serjeants of the Exchequer of the Jews.[88] A curious feature of this privilege jurisdiction was that former clerks continued to avail of it for several years after severing their links with the court. William of Middleton, who had ceased to be keeper of rolls and writs in 1276, was, for example, still bringing litigation in the Exchequer of the Jews seven years later.[89] The Exchequer was the only other royal court in this period whose officials were able to make use of a similar privilege jurisdiction, and in its case the jurisdiction seems to have been even more extensive and more valuable since it also protected them against being sued in any other court.[90]

(f) *Acknowledgments of debt.* A further privilege enjoyed by the officials of the Exchequer of the Jews, and one enjoyed presumably without payment of a fee, was that they could have acknowledgments of indebtedness made by their debtors recorded on the plea-rolls of the court.[91] This was a facility also enjoyed, though probably only in return for a payment, by certain Jewish creditors.[92] Similar facilities were also enjoyed by the officials of other royal courts. The main advantage secured was probably in the ease and speed of levying the sum acknowledged as owed once it became due.

(g) *Debt.* The greatest part, by far, of the business of the Exchequer of the Jews during the last quarter of a century of its existence was connected with the practice of Jews lending money to Christians on the security of their lands, and the subsequent efforts of the creditors or their assigns to secure repayment of the moneys loaned plus (where appropriate) interest.[93] At first sight, it appears surprising that the plea rolls of the Exchequer of the Jews contain so few entries relating to the attempts of Jewish creditors to secure repayment of loans from their original debtors. Far more common are entries relating to attempts to secure repayment from those to whom the lands of such debtors had subsequently passed, or relating to the attempts of those to whom the debts had passed (particularly the King) to secure repayment. When a debt recorded in a chirograph became due, the original creditor does indeed seem to have had to obtain a writ from the Exchequer of the Jews to the local sheriff to instruct the debtor to repay the debt and, if he failed to do so, to place the creditor in possession of chattels of the debtor to the value of the sum owed. Only if these did not suffice to pay the debt was the sheriff instructed to place the creditor in possession of the debtor's lands as well, to hold until he had received what was owed out of the profits of the land.[94] Such a writ would, however, be issued without the debtor being summoned to appear at the Jewish Exchequer and probably merely on production of the creditor's part of the chirograph and the writ was not, it seems, returnable into the Exchequer of the Jews either. Both the issuing of the writ and the action undertaken under it would normally go unrecorded there. The statute of Jewry of 1275 brought about significant changes in these procedures. Under its provisions, a creditor was only to be allowed to take possession of at most one half of the debtor's chattels, and only to be given seisin of one half of the debtor's tenements (excluding his house), and both were to be valued by a jury before delivery.[95] The creditor now had to sue out two writs: one to have the chattels and lands belonging to the debtor valued and the valuation returned to the Exchequer of the Jews; a second to put the creditor in possession of half of the movables and half the lands and maintain him in possession till the debt was repaid. This order was now sometimes enrolled with a summary of the valuation.[96]

Only slightly more common are entries on the plea-rolls relating to the attempts of creditors to sue third parties for a share of a debt owed to the creditor by a living debtor. A case of 1276 explains why. Third parties were normally only liable for such a share if the debtor was insolvent and they had acquired lands from him after he had contracted the debt.[97] Much more common are entries relating to the attempts of creditors to sue third parties for a share of a debt owed to the creditor by a

[86] The earliest example of such a case seems to be in 1267: *EJ*, i, p.141, (*cf. ibid.*, p. 144) (John le Moyne).

[87] The earliest example of such a case seems also to be in 1267: *EJ*, i, p.143 (William of Middleton).

[88] The earliest example of such a case seems to be in 1268: *EJ*, i, p. 170 (Roger of Kinton).

[89] E 9/43, m.1.

[90] There is no evidence that a similarly extensive privilege was ever enjoyed by the officials of the Exchequer of the Jews.

[91] The earliest example of a debt being recorded on the plea-rolls in this way seems to be in 1267: *EJ*, i, p.144.

[92] Debts to Jews were also sometimes recorded on the rolls of the court of Common Pleas: e.g. CP 40/13, m. 77; CP 40/15, m. 95d, and in Chancery e.g. *Cal. Close Rolls, 1272-9*, pp. 326, 343-4, 345, 357; *Cal. Close Rolls, 1279-88*, pp. 60, 124, 238; *Cal. Close Rolls, 1288-96*, p. 117.

[93] After the enactment of the statute of Jewry of 1275 it became illegal for Jews to make new loans of money at interest, and interest ceased to accumulate on loans already made and not repaid: *Stat. Realm*, i, pp. 221-221a. There are comparatively few cases where a Christian creditor can be found suing a Jewish debtor, but for an example *see EJ*, iii, p. 31.

[94] The rule that the sheriff or local bailiff needed a royal warrant to place a creditor in seisin of the debtor's lands is apparent in the earliest rolls: *EJ*, i, pp. 41, 48. For evidence of its observance in the post-1265 period *see* e.g. *EJ*, i, p.185; *EJ*, ii, pp. 255-6. The form of the writ which required primarily distraint on chattels, and seizure of lands only if the chattels did not suffice for the debt, can be deduced from *EJ*, ii, pp. 255-6, and from the post-1275 version of the same writ (for which see next footnote).

[95] *Stat. Realm*, i, 221-221a.

[96] For examples see *EJ*, vi, nos. 327, 328, 751, 752.

[97] *EJ*, iii, pp.159-60 and *cf. EJ*, i, p.73. It was, however, possible, it seems, for the King, as a matter of grace, to allow individual Jewish creditors to levy their debts by taking possession of such lands, as well as those retained by the debtor, even where the debtor was not insolvent: *see Cal. Pat. Rolls, 1258-66*, pp. 521, 547, 581, 585, 617, 646; *Close Rolls, 1264-8*, p.166; *Cal. Pat. Rolls, 1266-72*, pp. 13, 21, 24, 51, 95.

debtor who has since died. Here, the general principle followed seems to have been that not only the heir but all those in possession of lands which the debtor had possessed when contracting the debt or afterwards were liable for a share of the debt proportionate to their share of the debtor's lands.[98] In these circumstances it was normally necessary for the creditor to secure the appearance of the tenants at the Exchequer of the Jews and to obtain a judgment against them there.[99] Such tenants might answer that the debt claimed had been paid in whole or in part,[100] or that there were other tenants in addition to those whom the creditor was suing who were liable for a share of the debt.[101] They might, alternatively, claim that the debtor had not possessed such an interest in the land they held at the time he had contracted the debt or subsequently that it or they could be held liable for his debts,[102] or that their title to the land was not derived from him.[103] Alienees would frequently vouch the heir of the debtor to acquit them of their share of the debt by virtue of charters from the debtor, and succeed in transferring liability for that share to his heir.

Debts were commonly granted or sold by Jewish creditors to both Christians and Jews, and from the mid-1260s, if not before, such grants were commonly, perhaps invariably, and possibly necessarily, recorded in starrs, enrolled in the starr section of the Exchequer of the Jews plea-rolls.[104] Such an assign seems, originally at least, to have been regarded as no more than the 'representative' of the original creditor. Writs against the debtor had to be sued out in the name of the creditor, though at the cost of the assign, and it was necessary for the creditor to promise *not* to pardon the debt to the debtor after the sale had taken place.[105] The remedies and procedures available to such assigns seem to have been identical with those available to the original creditor, and to have gone unrecorded, or been recorded on the plea rolls, in much the same way.[106]

Debts also passed on a considerable scale into the hands of the King. This occurred for a variety of reasons: by the grant of the widow or children of a deceased creditor in settlement of the King's claim to one third of the value of the chattels and debts of deceased Jews,[107] by grant of the creditor himself in settlement of tallage owed to the King, by the working of the law, either because the creditor had converted to Christianity,[108] or because he or she had been condemned to death for felony,[109] or had become a fugitive when accused of felony.[110] Much of the time, and effort, of the Exchequer of the Jews went towards levying these sums for the King. It was not, however, the only institution used for this purpose, as both the ordinary Exchequer,[111] and special commissioners[112] were also employed to do this. The writs sent to local sheriffs ordering or authorising them to levy Jewish debts (including the sums which had become due to the King through amercements and fines imposed in the course of proceedings in the Exchequer of the Jews) were not normally transcribed in full on the Plea Rolls,[113] though those rolls do record intermittently the despatching of summonses to particular sheriffs.[114] Nor did the action taken by the sheriffs in response to these writs necessarily lead to an entry on the rolls. If all that happened was that the sheriff levied part or all of the sum owed, then this was not recorded, though the sheriff would be required to account for the sum raised (by producing the money, or a tally recording its payment to an authorised receiver of moneys, generally the Receipt of the Exchequer) when, periodically, he was summoned to render his account at the Exchequer of the Jews.[115] Only if there was some kind of complication or difficulty, as there frequently was, particularly when old debts were being levied from the tenants of the lands possessed by a debtor when entering into the debt, was an entry necessary. In certain circumstances, it was also possible for others to utilize the rather swifter and more efficient procedures at the King's disposal for the levying of his debts. This might happen if the King granted to some

[98] *Cf. EJ*, i, p. 215.

[99] This rule was restated in the statute of Jewry of 1275 (*Stat. Realm*, i, p. 221). It is alluded to in 1268, though in a way that suggests that it was then possible, as of grace, for the King to waive it: *EJ*, i, p.197. For evidence of a Jewish creditor being put into possession of lands held by a third party for a debt owed by a deceased creditor under a writ issued by the Exchequer of the Jews, but apparently without any appearance there by the third party *see* the record of an assize of novel disseisin heard in the 1268 Wiltshire eyre, which quotes most of the writ, on JUST 1/998A, m. 2.

[100] E.g. *EJ*, vi, no. 413.

[101] E.g. *EJ*, vi, no. 102.

[102] E.g. *EJ*, vi, no. 197; *EJ*, i, pp. 6, 26.

[103] E.g. *EJ*, i, pp.100-1.

[104] The earliest I have noted is in Trinity term 1266: *EJ*, i, pp. 136-7.

[105] E.g. *EJ*, i, p. 138; *EJ*, iii, p. 307; *EJ*, vi, no. 875.

[106] As already noted (above, p. 9) Christian assigns, as from 1269, ceased to be able to claim the interest on debts assigned to them, and had to seek royal permission for the assignment to be made.

[107] The King was already entitled to his third at the time of the earliest plea-rolls: above, n. 31.

[108] But see above, p. 9.

[109] E.g. *EJ*, vi, nos. 949, 1180.

[110] E.g. *EJ*, vi, no. 985.

[111] In 1260, the Exchequer of the Jews was even ordered to transfer all debts over twenty marks to the great Exchequer for them to be levied through it: *Close Rolls, 1259-61*, p. 38. Entries on the Memoranda Rolls in the 1270s and 1280s appear to indicate that Jewish debts continued to be levied through the great Exchequer during this period.

[112] See e.g. *Cal. Pat. Rolls, 1272-81*, p. 364.

[113] But for examples *see EJ*, i, pp. 205-6.

[114] E.g. *EJ*, ii, pp. 162, 184; *EJ*, iii, p.190 (estreats of pleas); *EJ*, vi, no. 703.

[115] For the summoning of sheriffs to render account for Jewish debts in the Exchequer of the Jews *see EJ*, i, pp. 135, 150, 151, 154, 250, 256; *EJ*, ii, pp. 64-5, 107, 163, 174, 272; *EJ*, iii, pp. 49, 51, 92, 93, 203-4, 294, 317.

third party debts which had been in his possession,[116] or if a creditor agreed that the King should have a certain proportion of the money levied in return for his "assistance."[117]

There was also another side to the functions of the Exchequer of the Jews in relation to debts: where it was the debtor, rather than the creditor, who took the initiative. It was possible, in this period, for individual debtors to secure from the King a pardon of their debts. Such pardons might be issued not just for debts which had passed into the King's hands,[118] but also for debts still in the hands of creditors.[119] Such pardons were issued by Chancery and the only role of the Exchequer of the Jews was to ensure that the 'official' copies of the relevant bonds were withdrawn from the treasury of the Exchequer of the Jews or from the local chirograph chest and handed over to the beneficiary. An alternative form of pardon, and one less favourable to the debtor, released him from all liability to pay the creditor interest on the money borrowed,[120] or allowed him to repay the creditor what he had actually borrowed rather than the sum he was recorded as owing in the chirograph which recorded the debt.[121] Again, such pardons were issued by Chancery and the role of the Exchequer of the Jews was normally limited to ensuring the withdrawal of the relevant bond once the sum owed was paid.[122] It is not clear whether, when the king pardoned a debt owed to a Jewish creditor, he was obliged to compensate the creditor by allowances against debts owed to the Crown, or by the grant of debts in the King's hands. Certainly, such compensation was sometimes awarded (though only ever for the principal, not for interest);[123] and there is clear evidence of the King acknowledging an obligation to compensate under such circumstances. It may well have been much more common than the surviving evidence would suggest,[124] and possibly even have been the normal practice.

Lesser acts of royal grace obtainable by debtors included (prior to the enactment of the statute of Jewry) the temporary suspension for a limited period of the accumulation of interest on a loan,[125] and the temporary prohibition of any measures to enforce repayment of a debt.[126] Again, it was Chancery that was responsible for the issuing of the requisite royal orders with the Exchequer of the Jews playing at most a subsidiary role in securing their execution. As we have already seen, prior to 1275 and the enactment of the statute of Jewry, a creditor was entitled to secure possession of a debtor's chattels and, if necessary, of all of his lands in order to ensure prompt repayment of his loan.[127] Another way in which the king could show grace or favour to a debtor was by ordering that he be allowed to pay off his debt in fixed (and easy) instalments. Again this was a favor granted not just to debtors who had come to owe their debt to the Crown, but also to those who still owed their debt to a Jewish creditor. Sometimes, all that was ordered was the attermination of a debt: that it should be paid off at the rate of so much money a year.[128] More common was an order for the justices of the Jews to have the debtor's lands valued, as a preliminary to (and basis for) the assignment to the debtor of 'reasonable terms' for the repayment of his debt.[129] Something also obtainable only

116 E.g. *EJ*, vi, no. 455.

117 E.g. *EJ*, ii, p. 20 (one-third), 45 (one half), 52-3 (one quarter); *EJ*, vi, no. 117 (one quarter).

118 For pardons of specific debts which had come into the King's hands *see* e.g. *Close Rolls 1264-8*, pp. 403, 404; *Cal. Pat. Rolls, 1266-72*, pp. 430, 441; *Close Rolls, 1268-72*, pp. 175-6; *Cal. Close Rolls, 1272-9*, pp. 458, 472-3; *Cal. Close Rolls, 1279-88*, pp. 258, 259, 329-330. For pardons covering all the Jewish debts of a particular debtor in the king's hands *see Cal. Pat. Rolls, 1272-81*, pp. 334, 335-6; *Cal. Close Rolls, 1279-88*, p. 387.

119 For pardons of specific debts to specific creditors *see* e.g. *Close Rolls, 1264-8*, pp.78, 214-5, 309-10, 343, 350-1, 431; *Close Rolls, 1268-72*, p. 187; *Cal. Pat. Rolls, 1281-92*, pp. 228, 234. For pardons of all debts to specific debtors *see Close Rolls, 1264-8*, pp. 201-2, 203; *Close Rolls, 1268-72*, p.153; *Cal. Pat Rolls, 1266-72*, pp. 502, 503. For pardons of all debts to all Jewish creditors *see Cal. Pat. Rolls, 1258-66*, pp. 648, 661 and *Close Rolls, 1264-8*, pp. 199, 200.

120 E.g. *Close Rolls, 1264-8*, pp. 266, 333-4 (but see also *ibid.* pp. 351, 403); *Close Rolls, 1268-72*, pp. 56, 202, 583-4 (but see n. 122); *Cal. Close Rolls, 1272-9*, p. 177.

121 E.g. *Close Rolls, 1268-72*, pp. 222, 479 (and *cf. ibid.*, p. 346).

122 Both the Justice of the Jews and the Barons of the Exchequer co-operated in the proceedings required to establish the original sum or sums borrowed by the abbey of Stratford of master Elias son of master Moses in 1275-6. For related material see *Close Rolls, 1268-72*, pp. 583-4; *Cal. Close Rolls, 1272-9*, pp. 8, 140, 172-3, 271, 320; E 159/49, m. 7d; E 13/3, mm. 9d, 17; *EJ*, iii, pp. 223-4, 285-6 and iv, p.128.

123 The clearest statement of this obligation is in *Close Rolls, 1264-8*, p. 431. For a pardon which (as calendered) says nothing of compensation but for which compensation was clearly ordered, see *Cal. Close Rolls 1272-9*, pp. 187, 306.

124 *See Cal. Close Rolls, 1272-9*, p. 306 (*EJ*, iv, 306), which refers to a previous, unrecorded order to make such an allowance. There is no mention of allowance, it would seem, in the pardon proper: *Cal. Close Rolls, 1272-9*, p. 187. See also *EJ*, iii, p. 64, referring to an apparently unrecorded order for an allowance to be made to Manser son of Aaron. For the pardon *see EJ*, ii, p. 306.

125 E.g. *Close Rolls, 1264-8*, pp. 160, 180, 265-6, 305, 306; *Close Rolls, 1268-72*, pp. 370, 486.

126 In the case of these prohibitions, it is not always easy to know whether or not the debt in question is one which has already come to the King's hands. For examples *see Close Rolls, 1264-8*, pp. 339, 466; *Cal. Close Rolls, 1272-9*, pp. 8, 30, 65, 96, 137, 150, 154-5, 157, 194, 222, 465.

127 Above, p. 12.

128 For examples of the attermination of debts in the King's hands *see Cal. Close Rolls, 1272-9*, pp. 105, 152, 362-3; *Cal. Close Rolls, 1279-88*, pp. 5, 166, 275. For examples of the attermination of debts owed to Jewish creditors *see Close Rolls, 1264-8*, pp. 194, 274, 351; *Close Rolls, 1268-72*, pp. 219, 314; *Cal. Pat. Rolls, 1266-72*, p. 505; *Cal. Close Rolls, 1272-9*, pp. 184-5.

129 For examples of such orders issued between 1265 and 1272 *see Close Rolls, 1264-8*, pp.78, 145, 152-3, 202, 265, 278, 279, 294, 423-4, 444-5. There was then a halt to the issuing of

from Chancery and not from the Exchequer of the Jews (though it was the latter which enforced its observance) was a grant to the alienee of land once held by a debtor that the land he now held should not be liable for a share of the debtor's debts, and that the creditor should be allowed to take measures to enforce payment only against other lands which belonged or had belonged to the debtor concerned.[130] This was, of course, of value principally where the debtor or his heirs were unable to fulfil the obligation they would normally have assumed on the alienation of the land concerned of acquitting the alienee of all claims for Jewish debts.

These were all matters of greater or lesser royal grace and favour. More a matter of law, right and justice were two main forms of actual litigation initiated in the Exchequer of the Jews by debtors or persons alleged to be debtors: the action of *unlawful distraint* and the action of *account*. The action of *unlawful distraint* was a type of trespass action, in which a plaintiff sued a defendant for having had him distrained for a debt, which he claimed not to owe. The defendant might, in reply, deny that he had ever taken such action, or had it taken.[131] More commonly, he would avow the action taken, and the parties take issue as to whether the debt had already been levied,[132] or whether the bond on which action had been taken was or was not genuine.[133] Much more common, however, is the action of *account*. This action, as brought in the Exchequer of the Jews, was only, at most, a very distant relation of the form of action of the same name found in other royal courts. There the action functioned as a way of compelling the managers (bailiffs) of landed estates to render an account of the period they had managed such estates and pay over any balance that had then accrued, or of compelling the employees or partners in commercial ventures to perform a similar obligation. In the Exchequer of the Jews, the action of account was an action brought by a debtor against his creditor, whose primary purpose (in form at least) was to make the creditor[134] state in court how much the debtor owed him in all, and to produce the chirographs by virtue of which this claim was made.[135] Commonly, perhaps almost invariably, when a plaintiff initiated this action, his opponent was currently taking steps to enforce the payment of his debt and it would seem that by merely initiating it the debtor was entitled to suspension, for up to a year, of whatever measures the creditor was employing for this purpose.[136] Some plaintiffs may, indeed, have brought the action merely in the hope of securing some respite.[137] Others, however, had more legitimate purposes. For some, it was a necessary preliminary to the attermination of their debts. When money was owed to several creditors, it was necessary that the precise total owed to each be ascertained before the process of attermination could be completed.[138] For others, it was a means of ensuring that a debt owed by a previous tenant of the land was levied not from them but from a warrantor,[139] or not levied at all.[140] For yet others it was a way of ensuring that a creditor did not exact more than was owed to him, after receiving various payments and the proceeds of earlier distraints,[141] observed the terms of a starr of acquittance which had been burnt by accident,[142] only demanded (and received) a lesser sum than that contained in the chirograph when the parties had agreed to this in a collateral agreement,[143] or observed the terms of a related agreement.[144] In some cases, the action was a way of challenging the validity of the chirograph itself.[145] In others, it seems merely to have been a way of securing an acknowledgement from a creditor that his debt had now been paid in full.[146]

Related to the action of account, in the sense that it was often a preliminary to such an action and indeed always envisaged the possibility of such an action or actions then taking place, was the process in use by 1244,[147] and of which there are earlier forerunners,[148]

such orders until Edward I's return from the Crusade, when some kind of general guidelines were agreed as to the issuing of such orders. They were in the future only made available to those who without such an attermination would be unable to support themselves and their families (on which *see Cal. Close Rolls, 1272-9*, p. 103). For examples of such orders *see Cal. Close Rolls, 1272-9*, pp. 97, 100, 101, 102, 104, 105, 106, 137, 149, 176, 180-1. For orders for extent and attermination issued after the statute of 1275 *see Cal. Close Rolls, 1272-9*, pp. 321, 335, 357, 409; *Cal. Close Rolls, 1279-88*, p. 466. For variants still more favourable to debtors *see Close Rolls, 1264-8*, pp. 479-80; *Cal. Close Rolls, 1272-9*, pp. 214-15, 359, 395.

[130] For examples *see Cal. Pat. Rolls, 1266-72*, pp. 34, 210 (during a lease), 255 (a debt owed by a Jew), 398, 401, 449, 522-3, 577; *Cal. Close Rolls, 1272-9*, p. 181; *Cal. Pat. Rolls, 1272-81*, p. 249.

[131] E.g. *EJ*, i, pp. 283-4; *EJ*, ii, pp. 134-5, 253-4; *EJ*, iii, pp. 169-70.

[132] E.g. *EJ*, i, p. 185.

[133] e.g. *EJ*, i, pp.185, 229-30; *EJ*, ii, pp. 210-11.

[134] If the original creditor had alienated the debt, then both he and the alienee would have to put in an appearance in court to answer: e.g. *EJ*, i, pp. 161, 162, 179. However, a tenant who was in possession of the debtor's lands only at the will of a creditor was not a proper party to such a suit: *EJ*, vi, no. 779.

[135] The writs initiating such litigation seem normally to have been issued by the Exchequer of the Jews itself: *see* e.g., *Select Pleas*, p.42; *EJ*, ii, p. 12. They might, however, be issued by Chancery: see *EJ*, iii, pp. 9-10.

[136] *EJ*, i, pp. 223, 273; *Select Pleas*, p. 42.

[137] E.g. *EJ*, i, p.174; *EJ*, ii, p. 231.

[138] E.g. *EJ*, i, pp. 177, 182 (and *Close Rolls, 1264-8*, p. 279); *EJ*, ii, pp. 221, 224, 260, 261, 292; *EJ*, iii, pp. 36, 55 (and *Cal. Close Rolls, 1272-9*, pp. 97, 103).

[139] E.g. *EJ*, i, p. 284; *EJ*, vi, no. 578.

[140] *EJ*, ii, pp. 124-6.

[141] E.g. *EJ*, i, pp. 188, 188-90, 286; *EJ*, ii, pp.121-2; *EJ*, iii, pp. 6-7, 256-7; *EJ*, vi, no. 403.

[142] *EJ*, ii, p.79.

[143] E.g. *EJ*, i, pp. 146-7, 159-60, 161, 168, 300-1; *EJ*, ii, pp. 284-5, 295; *EJ*, iii, pp. 9-10.

[144] E.g. *EJ*, i, pp.188-90.

[145] E.g. *EJ*, i, p.162; *Select Pleas*, p. 41; *EJ*, ii, pp. 288-9; *EJ*, iii, pp. 167-8.

[146] E.g. *EJ*, i, p. 279; *EJ*, ii, pp. 31, 32, 227.

[147] *Pipe Roll 10 Richard I*, p. 210; *Select Pleas*, pp. 9, 12-13.

[148] *Close Rolls, 1234-7*, pp. 87, 462.

under which a local sheriff or constable was ordered to ensure that proclamation was made in the synagogue on two or three sabbaths, requiring any Jew with claims against a particular individual to appear at the Exchequer of the Jews on a future (specified) date to account with him.[149] The precise purpose of this procedure is not clear. In some cases, it may have been a preliminary to a sale of part of the individual's lands, showing a potential purchaser the extent of the indebtedness attaching to the lands. In others, it may reflect ignorance of what Jewish debts had been contracted by an ancestor.

[149] E.g. *EJ*, i, pp.75-6, 106, 193, 194, 197, 198, 199, etc.

In the case of a debtor whose debt had passed to the King, the actions of unjust distraint and account were not available but the evidence suggests that such debtors were in practice able to challenge the amounts demanded from them both by appearing in the Exchequer of the Jews and objecting there to such demands,[150] and by purchasing royal writs to the Exchequer of the Jews outlining their case, and ordering an investigation of it.[151]

[150] E.g. *EJ*, vi, nos. 306, 949.
[151] E.g. *EJ*, vi, nos. 142, 190, 307, 702.

III *The Personnel of the Exchequer of the Jews*

The Justices of the Jews

The most important of the office-holders associated with the Exchequer of the Jews in this, as in earlier periods, were the officials who are generally referred to in contemporary documents as the 'Justices assigned to the custody of the Jews' (*Justiciarii ad custodiam Judeorum assignati*).[1] I will nonetheless hereafter follow the more convenient modern practice of calling them the 'Justices of the Jews'.

(a) *Functions and responsibilities*

The Justices of the Jews were in overall charge of all business done in and by the Exchequer of the Jews, not just of the jurisdiction which it exercised as a court, but also of its various administrative functions. Royal orders relating to both aspects of its work were addressed to them as the officials in charge of the institution as a whole, and the plea-rolls made for the individual Justices record items of business relating to both sides of the work of the institution. They were not, then, purely judicial officials, unlike, say, their contemporaries appointed as justices of the common law courts. They are more closely reminiscent in their combination of judicial and administrative functions of the justiciars of twelfth and early thirteenth century England or of late twelfth to fourteenth century Ireland than of their fellow-justices. It should, however, be remembered that the one Latin word *justiciarius* was used both for justiciars and for the justices of the common law courts, though we now choose to translate it by two different English words.

The overall control exercised over the Exchequer of the Jews by the Justices was reflected also in their general responsibility for all that was done there. The procedures followed by the Exchequer when reviewing judgments made in the Exchequer of the Jews on writs of error seem to indicate that it was the Justices who were held responsible for judgments given there, though not, in practice, to the extent of imposing penalties on them for giving erroneous judgments.[2] It seems probable, however, that they were, at least in theory, also exposed to the possibility of being accused and tried for judicial misconduct, the fate which befell so many of the justices of Edward I in 1290, and which led to the levying of large fines from those who were convicted.[3] On the administrative side, they were certainly held responsible for all money received in the Exchequer of the Jews on behalf of the king,[4] as well as for what was done with the Jewish bonds belonging to the king which had been entrusted to their custody.[5]

In practice, much of the routine business of the Exchequer of the Jews, as of other royal courts and departments, was probably informally delegated by the Justices to their subordinates, with the justices merely reading through the relevant entry on the plea-roll,[6] or checking the relevant judicial writ before allowing it to be sent out. It was certainly possible for routine business to be done in the Exchequer of the Jews in the absence of all of its Justices. We only know that neither of the Justices of the Jews was present in the Exchequer of the Jews at the beginning of Michaelmas term 1273 because some more difficult business then arose which had to be postponed pending their arrival.[7] The inference is that routine business could be transacted without them and that the

[1] Other phrases were sometimes used to refer to them in this period but all seem to be variants on the same basic formula - omitting *assignati* for example, or emphasizing that the justices were royal justices (*justiciarii regis*; *justiciarii nostri*). Their older alternative title, that of custodians or wardens (*custodes*) of the Jews, had fallen entirely into disuse by this time.

[2] See below, pp. 47-8.

[3] *State Trials of the Reign of Edward the First, 1289-1293*, ed. T.F. Tout and Hilda Johnstone (Camden Soc., 3rd. series, vol. 9:1906)), *passim*. However, none of the Justices of the Jews disgraced in this period seems to have been convicted of *judicial* misconduct, in the strict sense of that term.

[4] See below, pp. 46-7.

[5] See below, p. 47.

[6] Hence perhaps Hamon Hauteyn's refusal to deliver up his plea-rolls in 1286 '... *eo quod ipsos rotulos nondum examinaverat et quod non ausus fuit eosdem rotulos advocare, presertim cum clerici sui multa potuerunt irrotulare que ipse non potuit advocare*': *Select Cases in the Court of King's Bench, vol. I*, ed. G.O. Sayles (Selden Soc., vol. 55: 1936), p. clv. A similar answer was also given by his colleague Ludham: *Ibid.*, p. clvi. This may simply reflect a caution as to the possible gap between what had been done in their presence and what had been enrolled, but may perhaps also reflect the much greater need for caution about matters done in their absence.

[7] *EJ*, ii, pp. 76, 147.

record of such business would not normally indicate that they had not been present for it.

(b) *Numbers and relative status*

The normal complement of Justices of the Jews during this period, the number normally serving together in the Exchequer of the Jews at any one time, seems to have been no more than two. There may have been three for a brief period in 1266 (Fulham, Orlestone and Esporun) though this is not certain, since it is not clear when Esporun left office, nor when Orlestone took office.[8] There were certainly three (Fulham, Orlestone and Watford) for the whole of 1267 and part of 1268 and again from mid-1271 to early 1272, when they were Fulham, Watford and Pasket.[9] Master Henry de Bray was paid as a Justice from 1282 to 1287 and was described as a Justice of the Jews in a document of December 1288. For much of this period, however, he also held the demanding position of escheator of England south of Trent, which may have left little time for acting as a Justice of the Jews, and when Hauteyn and Ludham were called to account for their period as justices in 1286, no mention was made of master Henry sharing responsibility with them for any part of their period of office.[10] It is not clear, therefore, whether master Henry should really be accounted a full Justice, and whether, therefore, it can be said that there were three Justices of the Jews between 1282 and 1286 and perhaps for part of 1287 and 1288. Nor is it clear whether Bray is to be regarded as having been a companion to William of Carleton during the period before Peter of Leicester's appointment in 1286-7. If not, this appears to be the only period when the Exchequer of the Jews was reduced to a single justice.

A complement of two or, at most, three justices means that the Exchequer of the Jews had a smaller judicial staff than any of the other royal courts of the period. The court of King's Bench in this period generally had three, and sometimes four, justices;[11] the Common Bench four, and sometimes five, justices;[12] while the Exchequer, from the mid-1270s, always had at least three Barons in addition to the Treasurer and the Chancellor of the Exchequer.[13] Two or at most three is also a smaller complement than had been customary in the Exchequer of the Jews itself prior to 1265, when there had normally been three or even four justices.[14] This reduction may reflect a decline in the amount of business done by the Exchequer of the Jews. But the reduction is also perhaps to be explained simply by the creation in 1265 of the new post of Keeper of the Rolls and Writs of the Exchequer of the Jews, a post whose holder may have performed many of the functions of a Justice, though without the same status or the same remuneration.[15]

As between those who were given the title of Justice of the Jews, there was, as will be seen, no differentiation in respect of the salaries they received.[16] Nor is there any reason to believe that the formal appointment of Justices allocated to them a particular place or seniority as Justices.[17] It nonetheless seems clear that for most, if not all, of our period, one of the Justices was treated as senior or superior to his colleague or colleagues. When, in 1267, a seal was needed to seal a box being sent to the Exeter chirograph chest and the official seal of the Exchequer of the Jews was not available because it had been lost during the baronial wars, it was Robert of Fulham's own seal that was used, and surviving judicial writs of 1269 and 1271 bear his name as witness.[18] Hamon Hauteyn seems to have been regarded as the senior Justice for most, if not all, of his period of office. In 1275, an order was made that his name should be given as witness in all writs issued by the Exchequer of the Jews; and it was presumably because he was the senior Justice that in 1277 responsibility for custody of his plea-roll was shared between his own chief clerk and the keeper of rolls and writs.[19] There is also some evidence that William of Carleton was regarded as the senior Justice during the final years of the Jewish Exchequer. It was he who witnessed a judicial writ issued on 22 July 1287 which survives in an almost contemporary copy and another judicial writ issued on 20 July 1288 which survives in a late fourteenth century copy.[20]

[8] For full details see Appendix I.

[9] For full details see Appendix I.

[10] For full details of Master Henry de Bray's period as a justice of the Jews see Appendix I; for Hauteyn and Ludham being called to account for their period as Justices of the Jews see below, pp. 35-8

[11] *Select Cases.... King's Bench, vol. I*, p. lxiii. But between 1265 and 1272, there seem to have been only two permanent justices at the most in the court: C.A.F. Meekings, *List of Various Common Law Records* (P.R.O. Lists and Indexes, Supplementary Series, no. 1 (New York, 1970)), pp. 45-6.

[12] *Select Cases.... King's Bench, vol. I*, pp. cxxxv-cxxxvii. Between 1265 and 1272, however, there were only two or three: *Bracton's Note Book*, ed. F.W. Maitland, vol. I (London, 1887), pp. 144-5.

[13] These figures are derived from the unpublished Memoranda and Liberate Rolls.

[14] Meekings, *Justices of the Jews, 1218-1268*.

[15] See further below, pp. 38-41.

[16] See below, pp. 29-30.

[17] As will be seen, however (below, p.19), few of the formal instruments of appointment were enrolled, so their exact terms cannot now be known.

[18] Below, p. 49 and note 4; C 145/15, no. 13, m. 1 and C 145/17, no. 3, m. 3 (but for a writ of 1272 which is attested by Watford see C 145/17, no. 3, m. 1). For a transcript of another writ of 5 July 1271 attested by Fulham see JUST 1/365, m. 70d.

[19] *Cal. Close Rolls, 1272-9*, p.167 (and for writs of 2 August 1273 and 15 May 1278 attested by him see E 143/1/3, no. 4); below, p. 37. Note also the existence of an entry on the plea-roll for Michaelmas term 1278 where the initial writ summoning the case was authorized by Ludham alone, and the entry was apparently cancelled because Hauteyn did not agree with his colleague's action: *EJ*, v, no. 859.

[20] JUST 1/541A, m. 24 (By this date Peter of Leicester was

(c) *Appointment: the formalities*

Some thirteen men in all are known to have acted at some time during this period as Justices of the Jews.[21] The Chancery rolls contain, however, a copy of only one set of *letters patent of appointment,* those issued for the appointment on the same day of John le Moyne and Robert of Fulham.[22] It is just possible that some of the Justices were appointed by word of mouth,[23] but much more probable that in all cases letters patent were issued, but that it was generally not thought necessary to enrol them.[24] *Letters close of association* were appropriate when a newly appointed Justice was to join colleagues who had been appointed some time before. Only one set of letters close of this kind was enrolled during this period for a Justice of the Jews. Again, it seems probable that they were issued on other occasions, but not enrolled.[25] The close connexion between the main Exchequer and the Jewish Exchequer is illustrated by another type of letters close sometimes, and perhaps always, issued on the appointment of a new Justice. These were addressed to the Treasurer and Barons of the Exchequer, and ordered them to deliver to the new Justice his own key to the treasury of the Exchequer of the Jews. Such letters close are known to have been issued on the appointment of Thomas Esporun in 1266, because a copy of them was enrolled on one of the Exchequer memoranda rolls.[26] They were also issued in 1273 on the appointment of Hamon Hauteyn and Robert of Ludham. On this occasion the Treasurer and Barons were also instructed to deliver the records of the Exchequer of the Jews to them.[27] Before taking office, the newly appointed Justices probably also took an *oath of faithful service* to the king. Such an oath is occasionally mentioned in connexion with the appointment of Justices of the Jews prior to 1265,[28] and is known to have been taken by other justices during this period.[29] Although direct evidence of this seems to be lacking, it is a reasonable inference that the Justices of the Jews continued to take it as well.

(d) *Appointment: the background and prior experience of the justices, and the immediate context of their appointment*

In accordance with what had by 1265 become long established practice, all thirteen of the Justices appointed during this period were Christians. There had been no Jewish Justice of the Jews since the late twelfth century, and such an appointment had in the meanwhile become unthinkable. In the much more recent past, the *presbiter Judeorum* had been ascribed the status of a Justice, though not appointed as such. There is, however, no evidence that such a status was attributed to him in this period.[30]

already serving as his colleague); BL MS. Harley 3697, f. 84v. For a reference to a plea brought by Cok Hagin against the abbot of Langley heard before William of Carlton and his colleagues, the Justices of the Jews, see Bodleian Library MS. Bodley 242, f. 74v.

21 For full details of their periods of office, see below, Appendix I.

22 C 66/84, m. 40 (= *Cal. Pat. Rolls 1258-66*, p. 517): *De justiciariis assignatis ad custodiam Judeorum.* Rex omnibus etc. salutem. Sciatis quod assignavimus dilectos et fideles nostros Johannem le Moyne et Robertum de Fulleham Justiciarios nostros ad custodiam Judeorum nostrorum quamdiu nobis placuerit. In cujus etc. Teste ut supra.

23 Sayles suggests that in the thirteenth century, the justices of the court of King's Bench may have been appointed in this way: *Select Cases in the Court of King's Bench, vol. IV,* ed. G.O. Sayles (Selden Soc., vol. 74: 1955), pp. xi-xii.

24 The only earlier patent of appointment I have noted is *Patent Rolls, 1216-25*, p. 154.

25 *Close Rolls, 1264-8*, p. 286 (on behalf of Master William of Watford). For earlier examples see *Close Rolls, 1231-1234*, p. 569; *Close Rolls, 1234-1237*, p. 237; *Close Rolls, 1237-1242*, p. 17; *Close Rolls, 1247-1251*, pp. 234, 330. Such letters were presumably also issued on the appointment of Esporun, Orlestone and Pasket as justices, and perhaps for the appointments of Bray and Leicester.

26 E 159/40, m. 8 (Hilary communia). *Magistro Thome de Wymundeham Thesaurario de tercia clave Judaismi liberata Thome Espurun.* Rex mandat eisdem quod liberent predicto Thome, quem rex assignavit justiciarium suum ad custodiam Judeorum una cum aliis Justiciariis ad hoc assignatis, terciam clavem arche thesauri sui de debitis et rotulis Judeorum ad ea facienda et exequenda que ad officium illud pertinent.

27 These letters close survive in two variants, one on the Close Roll, the other on the Memoranda Roll (i) C 54/90, m.10 (= *Cal. Close Rolls, 1272-9*, p. 6): *De justiciariis Judeorum.* Quia Rex constituit Hamonem Hautayn et Robertum de Ludham Justiciarios suos ad custodiam Judeorum suorum, mandatum est thesaurario et baronibus de scaccario quod eisdem Hamoni et Roberto claves arche Judaismi una cum rotulis, brevibus et omnibus aliis Judaismum illud contingentibus liberent, prout aliis Justiciariis ibidem prius fieri consuevit. Datum per manum W. de Merton' cancellarii apud Westm' .xxvij. die Januarii' (ii) E 159/47, m. 4 (Hilary communia): *Baronibus pro Hamone Hautein et Roberto de Ludham.* Cum Rex constituerit dictum Hamonem Hauten et Robertum de Ludham Justiciarios suos ad custodiam Judeorum, mandavit baronibus quod eisdem Hamoni et Roberto claves arche Judaismi una cum rotulis, brevibus et omnibus aliis officium illud contingentibus liberent, prout aliis Justiciariis regis ibidem prius fieri consuevit. Datum per manum W. de Merton cancellarii regis apud Westm' .xviij. die Januarii etc. Breve est in forulo marescalli'. The Justices were presumably given custody of the rolls and writs because William of Middleton had not yet been re-appointed as Keeper of the Rolls and Writs. However, when he was re-appointed, it was the Treasurer and Barons of the Exchequer rather than the Justices of the Jews who were ordered to deliver the rolls and writs to him, so the earlier transfer may not have taken place: below, p. 39. For earlier letters close of a similar kind *see Close Rolls, 1242-7*, p.416 and *Close Rolls, 1256-59*, p. 392.

28 E.g. in 1237 (*Close Rolls, 1234-7*, p. 237), in 1250 (*Close Rolls 1247-51*, p. 330), and in 1256 (*Close Rolls, 1254-6*, p. 269).

29 For the oath taken by the justices in eyre see C 54/95, m. 1d (Close Roll, 6 Edward I). For the oath of the justices as modified in 1290 *see* E 368/61, m. 10.

30 See further, below, p. 44.

Despite the hostility of the Church to ordained clerks serving as justices in lay courts,[31] clerical justices, in the broadest sense, were in a small majority in the court. Of the thirteen Justices of this period five (master William of Watford, master Henry de Bray, Robert of Ludham, William of Carleton and Peter of Leicester) were ordained clerics and are known to have held ecclesiastical benefices;[32] and a further two (Thomas Esporun and Robert of Fulham) are both described, on more than one occasion, as being king's clerks,[33] a term generally held to imply ordination as well as service to the king. Neither, however, seems to have been in possession of a benefice (an almost invariable accompaniment to ordination, especially in the case of an ordained clerk in the service of the king) and Robert of Fulham, at least, was enough of a layman to have had a wife,[34] and to have been succeeded by an apparently legitimate son and heir.[35] The Exchequer of the Jews was not, however, distinctive in its large-scale recruitement of clerics as Justices. During this same period eleven of the twenty-two justices appointed to the Common Bench were clerics,[36] and six of the eleven justices appointed to the court of King's Bench.[37]

(i) *Clerical justices*

Two of the clerical justices, William of Watford and Henry de Bray, are both commonly accorded in the records the title of master (*magister*). In both cases, the title probably denotes possession of a university degree,[38] though we know nothing further of the university careers of either man. University graduates are also to be found serving as justices in other royal courts in this period, though only in small numbers. Master Roger of Seaton was a justice of the Common Bench (1268-71, 1273), chief justice of an eyre circuit (1271-2) and chief justice of the Common Bench (1274-8). Master Richard of Staines was an eyre justice (1268-9), a justice of King's Bench (1269-74), a justice of the Common Bench (1274-6) and finally chancellor of the Exchequer (1276-7). Master Ralph of Farningham was a justice of the Common Bench from 1275 to 1278 and Master Robert of Thorp a justice of the Common Bench from 1290 to 1291.

Little more is known about *master William of Watford.* He probably came from the Watford in Hertfordshire,[39] and is first encountered in the records in 1256, when he

[31] R.V. Turner, 'Clerical Judges in English Secular Courts: the Ideal versus the Reality,' *Medievalia et Humanistica*, iii (1972), pp. 75-98.

[32] *Master William of Watford* was presented to the church of Chesham, co. Bucks in 1258-9 by the abbot of Woburn: *Rotuli ... Ricardi Gravesend*, p. 236. His benefices were sequestered by the bishop of Bath and Wells in 1273: E 13/2, m. 1d. *Master Henry de Bray* was presented to the church of Cledey, in the diocese of St. David's, in 1275 by the king: *Cal. Pat. Rolls, 1272-81*, p.75; presented to the church of 'Landaddok', in the diocese of Llandaff, in 1276 by the king: *Ibid.*, p. 160 (and resigned in 1280: *Ibid.*, p. 417); presented to the church of 'Llantheliou', in the diocese of Llandaff, in 1277 by the king: *Ibid.*, p. 234; presented to the church of Woodford Halse, co. Northants, in or before 1282 by the abbot of Rocester, and given custody of it and admitted to the same church on ordination as subdeacon in 1284: *Reg. Oliver Sutton*, ii, pp. 36-7. The same church was vacated by him on his institution to the church of Lutterworth, co. Leics: *Ibid.*, p. 72. He was also allegedly parson of Stretton Sugwas, co. Herefs., at some date prior to 1294: CP 40/103, m. 136d. In 1292 the bishops of Lincoln and Coventry and Lichfield were ordered to sequestrate his benefices for his debts to the king but the latter returned that he possessed none in his diocese: E 159/66, m. 63. He was also a recipient of a clerical protection in 1297: CP 40/116, m. 135d; *Cal. Pat. Rolls, 1292-1301*, p. 236. *Robert of Ludham* was the recipient of a clerical protection as parson of the churches of Scole and Knapton, co. Norfolk, in 1294: *Cal. Pat. Rolls, 1292-1301*, p. 117. He sold his tithes of sheaves and hay of the church of Quainton to a burgess of Reading in 1280: E 9/27, m. 9. *William of Carleton* was the recipient of a clerical protection as parson of the church of North Creake, co. Norfolk, in 1294: *Cal. Pat. Rolls, 1292-1301*, p.121. He was still parson of the church in 1309, when a mortmain licence was given for a grant to him and his successors as parsons of the church: *Cal. Pat. Rolls, 1307-13*, p. 159. William built the chancel of North Creake church which still survives: N. Pevsner, *The Buildings of England: North-West and South Norfolk* (London, 1962), pp. 270-1. He was granted custody of the church of Beddington, co. Surrey, in 1294 *(Reg...Pontissara*, vol. I, p. 64), and was litigating as parson of the same church in 1300: CP 40/131, m. 217. At some date between 1297 and 1311 he was parson of the church of North Cave, co. Yorks: *Reg...Henry Woodlock, vol. II*, pp. 1016-7. *Peter of Leicester* was litigating as parson of Preston Bagot, co. Warwicks, in 1279: CP 40/31, m. 11d; was said to have recently resigned from the church of Budbrooke, co. Warwicks in 1303: CP 40/146, m. 162. He was parson of the church of Cleeve, co. Gloucs, by 1287: JUST 1/541B, m. 11d. He held the prebend of Bishopshull in Lichfield cathedral at the time of his death: *Le Neve's Fasti*, new edn., vol. x, p. 20.

[33] Thomas Esporun: *Cal. Pat. Rolls, 1247-58*, pp. 117, 505; *Cal. Liberate Rolls, 1251-60*, p.145; *Close Rolls, 1259-61*, pp. 45, 298; *Cal. Liberate Rolls, 1267-72*, nos. 1028, 1169. Robert of Fulham: *Cal. Liberate Rolls, 1251-60*, p. 440; *Close Rolls, 1256-9*, pp. 87, 90; *Close Rolls, 1259-61*, p. 298.

[34] *Essex Feet of Fines*, vol I, p.185. Robert's widow, Joan, was being sued for a debt in the Exchequer of Pleas in 1276: E 13/4, m. 5.

[35] For a reference in 1286 to Edmund, the son and heir of Robert of Fulham, the former Justice of the Jews, see E 159/59, m. 26d.

[36] Roger of Missenden; master Roger of Seaton; Martin of Littlebury; Stephen Heym; Robert Fulks; Ralph de Hengham; master Richard of Staines; master Ralph of Farningham; Roger of Leicester; William of Brunton; Ellis of Beckingham. One of the lay justices, Thomas Weyland, had once been a subdeacon.

[37] Master Richard of Staines; Martin of Littlebury; William of Saham; Ralph de Hengham; Walter of Wimborne; Ellis of Sutton.

[38] *cf.* A.B. Emden, *A Biographical Register of the University of Oxford to 1500*, vol. I (Oxford, 1957), pp. xv-xvi.

[39] In favour of a Hertfordshire origin are (i) his association with John of Gaddesden, who also came from Hertfordshire, when first encountered in the records (see below); (ii) the fact that in 1270 he was suing Henry of Buckland for trespass in his lay tenement at Buckland and 'Bradenach' in that county: *Select Cases in the Exchequer of Pleas*, ed. H. Jenkinson and B.E.R. Fermoy (Selden Society vol. 48: 1932), pp. 56-7; (iii) the fact that after his outlawry it was thought he might be living in Essex or Hertfordshire (or in Surrey or Sussex): *EJ*, iii, p. 16.

was one of the members of an embassy led by John of Gaddesden and the bishop of Ely to Alphonso X, king of Castile.[40] Early in the following year, he himself led a smaller embassy on a return visit to Castile,[41] and at Christmas that year, and at Whitsun 1258, received robes from the King as one of his clerks.[42] Thereafter, he may have retired to his living at Chesham;[43] but it seems more probable that he was making a career as a canon lawyer or in ecclesiastical or private lay administration. He is only mentioned once during this period in the royal records, when appointed by the King in 1261 to act as his proctor in making an appeal concerning the election of the prior of St. Swithin's Winchester,[44] and it has not proved possible so far to find any evidence as to what he was doing during this period.[45] His appointment as a Justice in 1267 cannot therefore be explained by reference to any recent record of royal service, nor even by reference to a recent period of administrative experience in the service of some other master, and remains an enigma.

Rather more is known about the background and prior experience of the other university graduate. *Master Henry de Bray* was the son of William de Bray and came from Hinton in Woodford Halse in Northamptonshire.[46] The John, Richard, and Thomas de Bray who stood surety for him in 1290 were probably close relatives and quite possibly brothers.[47] In the late 1260s and early 1270s, Master Henry was the business agent of John de Verdun, a landowner of baronial rank in the West Midlands and in Ireland.[48] The two seem to have parted company on bad terms. Master Henry alleged in 1277 that Verdun had disseised him of land at Cottesbach in Leicestershire and imprisoned him in his castle at Alton until he had quitclaimed this land. Verdun's son and heir (Theobald) claimed that master Henry had been found to owe his father two hundred pounds when he rendered an account to him, had been imprisoned because of that debt, and had granted the land to John in settlement of it.[49] Despite this contretemps, Master Henry's next move was upwards, into the service of the king. In 1273 he was commissioned to levy arrears of clerical taxation (a triennial tenth granted by the pope to the late king) in five dioceses of England and Wales (Lincoln, Coventry and Lichfield, Worcester, St. David's, Hereford) and he was described in the commission as being a king's clerk.[50] Later that same year, he was appointed bailiff of various honours and castles in South and West Wales which had come into the king's hands on the death of George de Cantilupe. These were the honour and castle of Abergavenny in Monmouthshire, the honour and

[40] *Cal. Pat. Rolls, 1247-58*, p.487. For the background to this embassy see F.M. Powicke, *King Henry III and the Lord Edward* (Oxford, 1947), pp. 232-6. He may also be the William of Watford to be found acting as an attorney for John of Gaddesden in litigation in the Common Bench in Trinity and Michaelmas terms 1253: KB 26/149, m. 4d; KB 26/148, m. 4d.

[41] *Close Rolls, 1256-9*, pp. 98, 117; *Cal. Liberate Rolls, 1251-60*, p. 353.

[42] *Close Rolls, 1256-9*, pp. 178, 219-20.

[43] Above, n. 32.

[44] *Cal. Pat. Rolls, 1258-66*, p. 150. There had been a long dispute between the monks of St. Swithin's and the bishop of Winchester about the claim by the monks of the right to elect their own prior: *VCH Hants*, ii, p. 109.

[45] It is, however, known from litigation heard in the 1271 Kent eyre that he took a ten year lease of a messuage and a carucate of land of Sutton-at-Hone in Kent at Michaelmas 1264, but ceased paying the rent a year later: JUST 1/365, m. 71d. For other litigation in the same eyre apparently relating to the same holding see JUST 1/365, m. 35d.

[46] Two quitclaims and one grant made to him in 1289 all specifically style him the son of William de Bray of Hinton: KB 27/116, m. 26; KB 27/118, m. 45; KB 27/120, m. 4. In 1301 he claimed to possess one third of the manor of Hinton by purchase from John de Bray: CP 40/136, m. 60; and in the same year he arranged for an annuity of five pounds a year to be paid to himself there: CP 40/158, m. 78d.

[47] *Cal. Close Rolls, 1288-96*, p. 96. This John de Bray may be the same as the man from whom master Henry claimed in 1301 to have acquired one third of the manor of Hinton. He is almost certainly the John de Bray to whom master Henry de Bray granted lands in Clipstone, Sibbertoft, Kelmarsh and Oxenden in Northamptonshire, which he had been granted shortly before his death by Silvester de Swinford, and which Silvester's brother, John, sought to recover by mort d'ancestor in 1290-1 (and which Margery widow of William de Swinford sought to recover as her dower in 1292): CP 40/81, m. 32; CP 40/91, m. 235d; CP 40/95, m. 96; CP 40/95, m. 198. When Silvester's widow, Emma, made a quitclaim of these lands to master Henry de Bray and John de Bray in 1288 she described John as her brother, but not master Henry: *Cal. Close Rolls, 1288-96*, p. 32. Richard de Bray may be the same man as the Richard de Bray who also acted as an attorney for John de Verdun while he went away on crusade in 1270: below, n. 48. He may also perhaps be the Richard de Bray who succeeded master Henry de Bray as rector of Woodford Halse in 1289: *Reg. Oliver Sutton*, ii, pp. 36-7. Thomas de Bray is perhaps to be identified with the Thomas de Bray given an estate in remainder in fee tail with his wife Sarah in the manor of Grandborough, Warwickshire, after a fee tail in possession for Thomas de 'Farendon' and his wife Emma and a life estate in remainder for master Henry: *Warwicks Fines, vol. II*, p. 20, no. 1063. By 1363-4 one William de Bray, the son of Henry, the son of Thomas and Sarah, was claiming to be entitled to the manor: *William Salt Society*, vol. 13, p. 34.

[48] In Michaelmas term he and other bailiffs of John de Verdun were being sued in an action of *contra formam feoffamenti* for distraining Roger Bydulf to perform suit to John's court of Alton in Staffordshire contrary to the provisions of chapter 9 of the statute of Marlborough: KB 26/194, m. 36. The case had still not come to trial in Easter term 1271: KB 26/202, m. 5. In July 1270, Henry and Richard de Bray were named as John's attorneys while he was on crusade with the Lord Edward in the Holy Land: *Cal. Pat. Rolls, 1266-72*, p. 443. In Trinity term 1271 it was as John de Verdun's steward that he promised in the Exchequer that John's debts to the King would be paid: E 159/45, m. 16. John de Verdun appointed him his attorney in a plea in the 1272 Staffordshire eyre: JUST 1/802, m. 39.

[49] CP 40/19, m. 6. Eleanor de Verdun was the current tenant of the land and vouched John to warranty. Master Henry denied that there had been any arrears on his account.

[50] *Cal. Pat. Rolls, 1272-81*, p. 11; C 62/52, m. 7 (allowed twenty-four pounds expenses for this in 1276).

castle of Penrose in the same county and the castle of Kilgerran in Pembrokeshire.[51] He retained control of the most important of these, the honour and castle of Abergavenny, until 1281, when he was allowed to reach an arrangement with William de Valence to transfer custody of them to him.[52] The custody of Kilgerran had been transferred to Valence by the king in 1275.[53] What happened to Penrose is unclear. During his term of office, Master Henry became embroiled in a number of disputes with the men of the honour of Abergavenny,[54] but this does not seem to have influenced the decision to transfer its custody to Valence. He was also entrusted during this period with various other administrative and judicial responsibilities in South and West Wales.[55]

In October 1281 Master Henry was commissioned, together with two other Justices of the Jews (and originally also John of Cobham, a Baron of the Exchequer, though his name was omitted from a revised commission shortly afterwards) to search the chirograph chests for all charters, starrs and other muniments relating to Jewish debts which had passed into the ownership of the King. The deeds were to be transcribed on to three separate rolls: one for the Exchequer, another for the Exchequer of the Jews, a third for Master Henry to take to the king.[56] The following month, it was ordered that Master Henry be paid ten pounds for the purchase of parchment and ink for this purpose, and to pay the clerks making the transcripts.[57] These transcripts were then to be used to prepare estreats to each sheriff to collect the money owed, and the money thus collected was to be recorded and kept separately.[58] It was perhaps shortly after this that Master Henry became himself a Justice,[59] but it is not clear that this meant that he now took a full share in all the other work of the Exchequer of the Jews as well. He may simply have continued to bear responsibility only for levying money due to the king but with the added status of a Justice of the Jews.[60] In any case, his appointment as escheator of England south of the Trent in February 1283 probably prevented him thenceforward playing much part in the running of the institution.[61]

The other five non-graduate 'clerks' who became Justices of the Jews in this period all shared a common background. This was of prior service in the main Exchequer, four as part of its clerical staff, the fifth as a Baron. *Thomas Esporun* was the only one of the five to have also had prior experience as a Justice of the Jews.[62] Thomas had been appointed to the clerical post of deputy-chamberlain of the Exchequer by one of the hereditary chamberlains, Margery de Rivers, countess of Devon, in 1245,[63] an appointment renewed by the King after her death in 1252.[64] In a bureaucratic reorganization of 1255, he lost that part of the deputy chamberlainship which was exercised in the great Exchequer of Receipt.[65] In 1251, he had been entrusted with a message from Henry III to the Treasurer and Barons of the Exchequer concerning the purchasing of gold with the

[51] *Cal. Fine Rolls, 1272-1307*, pp. 12-13.

[52] *Cal. Pat. Rolls, 1272-81*, p. 426; *Cal. Close Rolls, 1279-88*, p. 116. Master Henry was able to sell the custody because in 1279 he had become 'custodian' rather than 'bailiff' of the honour and castle, paying a set farm for them of four hundred marks a year: *Cal. Pat. Rolls, 1272-81*, p. 305.

[53] *Cal. Fine Rolls, 1272-1307*, p. 45.

[54] These had begun as early as 1278 when a commission of oyer and terminer was issued to enquire into trespasses and wrongs allegedly committed by Master Henry and his servants to the men of Abergavenny, and their counter-charges of similar wrongs committed by those men: *Cal. Pat. Rolls, 1272-81*, p. 294. For subsequent related commissions see *Ibid.*, p. 339, *Cal. Close Rolls, 1279-88*, p. 84, and *The Welsh Assize Roll, 1277-1284*, ed. J.C. Davies (Board of Celtic Studies, Univ. of Wales, History and Law Series, no. 7: 1940), pp. 178-81.

[55] *Cal. Pat. Rolls, 1272-81*, pp. 56, 119, 126, 166, 182.

[56] *Cal. Pat. Rolls, 1272-81*, pp. 458, 459. This commission appears to be a follow-up to the commissions of November 1279 which had authorised various commissioners to go to the chirograph chests and to take out all chirographs, bonds, tallies, charters, feoffments, starrs, and other deeds belonging to condemned, fugitive or converted Jews and deliver them to the Treasurer and Barons of the Exchequer: *Cal. Close Rolls, 1279-88*, p. 41. John of Cobham and Adam of Winchester had then been commissioned to levy the debts to the King's use: *Cal. Pat. Rolls, 1272-81*, p. 364; E 358/53, m. 5d.

[57] C 62/58, m. 5. In January 1282, the sheriff of Northamptonshire was ordered to pay master Henry de Bray another £15 towards his expenses in this matter: *Cal. Close Rolls, 1279-88*, p. 146.

[58] E 159/55, m. 4 (Easter communia, 1282): *Baronibus pro rege.* Rex mandavit eisdem quia modis omnibus scire vult per quos, qualiter et quo modo negocium de extractis Judaismi, quod nuper de diversis debitis expediri precepit, fiat et expediatur, quod totam pecuniam provenientem de eodem Judaismo per extractas predictas, maxime factas per magistrum Henricum de Bray, in quadam cista in thesauraria per se poni faciant salvo custodiendum usque adventum Regis apud Westm'; proffrum autem singulorum vicecomitum de extractis illis, quantum videlicet quilibet per se proferat et solvat et qua de causa, et ad quam summam proffrum hujusmodi attingat, et de quo tempore, in quodam rotulo per se conscribi et irrotulari faciant, proviso eciam quod pecunia predicta sic per se posita salvo custodiatur, nec aliquid inde quoquo modo amoveatur donec aliud inde dederit in mandatis.

[59] See below Appendix I.

[60] But the survival of portions of three rolls for Michaelmas term 1282 (below, Appendix III) suggests that he may have played a somewhat wider role.

[61] *Cal. Pat. Rolls, 1281-92*, p. 58.

[62] The only other Justice appointed in this period also to have held office as a Justice prior to this period is Hamon Hauteyn: below, p. 28.

[63] E 368/16, m. 8d. In July 1251, the treasurer and barons were ordered to ensure that she paid him wages (*stipendia*) for the time that he had been in residence at the Exchequer as her deputy, in accordance with what had been paid to his predecessors in that office: *Close Rolls, 1247-51*, p. 473. His connexion with Margery went back to 1235 when he was appointed her attorney for litigation in the Middlesex eyre: JUST 1/536, m. 3.

[64] *Close Rolls, 1251-3*, p. 162 (but note that this refers only to the deputy chamberlainship of the Exchequer of Receipt).

[65] *Close Rolls, 1254-6*, p. 30.

King's income from Jewish sources,[66] but his first real connection with Jewish affairs came only in the following year, when he was one of those commissioned (together with Edward of Westminster, a Baron of the Exchequer, and William le Bretun, a Justice of the Jews) to enquire into the 'concealments of the Jewry' in the city of London and elsewhere.[67] In October 1255, he was instructed to go to Wallingford to monitor on the King's behalf the payment of debts and of tallage by the Jews of England to Richard of Cornwall.[68] Shortly after this, he is described for the first time as being a Justice of the Jews,[69] and he remained a Justice until some time between February and June 1259.[70] Esporun seems then to have returned, at least for a while, to service as a clerk in the Exchequer and received robes as such at Whitsun and Christmas 1260.[71] He may then have gone into retirement, since the evidence connecting him with the Exchequer ceases.[72] His reappointment as a Justice of the Jews in 1266 was perhaps only an emergency measure, the temporary calling of an experienced justice out of retirement to fill a gap in the ranks of the Justices.

Robert of Fulham's surname appears to be the only evidence of any link between Robert and the Middlesex village of Fulham.[73] He can only be traced as a landowner, on a small scale, in the south of Essex. He held property at Vange,[74] Mountnessing[75] and 'Ginge Joybert' and 'Ginge Laundry' (both now in Buttsbury)[76] and jointly with his wife (and perhaps in her right) at Runwell.[77] In 1247, he had been appointed to the clerical position of deputy constable of the Exchequer by the hereditary constable, the earl of Hereford, who was himself a major Essex landowner.[78] Robert retained this post until Michaelmas 1264, when he was promoted to the position of King's Remembrancer of the Exchequer.[79] Just one year later he was appointed a Justice of the Jews at a time when the Exchequer of the Jews was being reconstituted after the king's victory at the battle of Evesham.[80] It is possibly relevant that he had by then acquired some experience of levying Jewish debts owed to the king. In August 1261 he had been commissioned to levy such debts in ten Midland counties. He was also commissioned at the same time to levy non-Jewish royal debts in the same counties.[81] It is probably not relevant that it was Robert who had been singled out in 1258 to compose and write "... certain charters in English and French, made by ordinance of the king's council .... sent through all counties of England ..."[82] Competence, even in writing, in both languages and also in Latin was probably quite common,[83] and Fulham was probably chosen for the job as a trustworthy clerk rather than for any special linguistic abilities which might be of particular use to a justice of the Jews.[84]

The earliest mention of *Robert of Ludham* as an Exchequer clerk is in Michaelmas term 1259,[85] but it seems probable that he had already by then served in the Exchequer as a clerk for some considerable period, since only three years later he was of sufficient seniority to be entrusted with the temporary custody of four East

[66] *Close Rolls, 1247-51*, p. 473.

[67] *Close Rolls, 1251-3*, p. 226.

[68] *Cal. Pat. Rolls, 1247-58*, p. 444. On the temporary grant of the Jews of England (or rather, of the income arising from them) to Richard of Cornwall by his brother Henry III in 1255-6 see *Cal. Pat. Rolls, 1247-58*, pp. 400-1, 439-40; *Close Rolls, 1256-9*, p. 14.

[69] He was perhaps already a Justice of the Jews when an order was given on 7 November 1255 that he be paid twenty marks a year while on the King's service in the Exchequer of the Jews: *Cal. Liberate Rolls, 1251-60*, p. 251. He had previously (in August 1252) been granted an annual fee of ten pounds a year while on the King's service at the Exchequer: *Ibid*, pp. 64-5. The first specific reference to him as a Justice of the Jews is, however, on 6 July 1256: *Close Rolls, 1254-6*, p. 426.

[70] He was still a Justice of the Jews on 9 February 1259: *Chartulary of the Priory of Boxgrove*, ed. L. Fleming (Sussex Record Soc. 59: 1960), p. 44. He had ceased to be one by 6 June 1259: *Close Rolls, 1256-9*, p. 392.

[71] *Close Rolls, 1259-61*, pp. 45, 298.

[72] But note that in 1263 he was one of the witnesses to a deed granting Adam de Stratton the office of weigher at the Exchequer: *Cal. Charter Rolls*, ii, p.50. In July 1264, in the aftermath of the battle of Lewes, he was granted a protection till the feast of All Saints following: *Cal. Pat. Rolls, 1258-66*, p. 334.

[73] But note that in 1232-3 a Robert of Fulham occurs among the witnesses to a charter of the abbey of Colchester granting property in London in the parish of St. Dunstan in the East to Ledulf *Teutonicus*. Other witnesses to the charter include Walter and Edward of Fulham: *Cartularium Monasterii Sancti Johannis Baptiste*, ed. S.A. Moore (Roxburghe Club, 2 vols., London 1897), ii, 588-90. This suggests that he may have come from a London family originally from Fulham.

[74] *Close Rolls, 1254-6*, p. 404; *Close Rolls, 1264-8*, p. 544; CP 40/18, m. 7d.

[75] *Essex Feet of Fines*, vol. I, p. 243.

[76] *Essex Feet of Fines*, vol. I, p. 172, JUST 1/236A, m. 6.

[77] *Essex Feet of Fines*, vol. I, p. 185.

[78] E 159/24, m. 2.

[79] D. Crook, 'The Early Remembrancers of the Exchequer', *Bulletin of the Institute of Historical Research*, 53 (1980), p. 11-23 at p. 22. The appointment may not have been intended to be permanent, since John Peverel was appointed to act as deputy-constable only for as long as Fulham was unable to act. But note also the terms under which the earl of Hereford presented Nicholas of Blaby to the same post in Hilary term 1269. He was appointed under Fulham, and to act only when he was absent from the post: E 159/42, m. 6.

[80] Below, Appendix I.

[81] *Cal. Pat. Rolls, 1258-66*, p. 187; *cf. Close Rolls, 1259-61*, p. 436: *Close Rolls, 1261-4*, p. 10. For his efforts in 1257 to levy moneys owed to the King in Lincolnshire and transport the money raised to Chester see *Close Rolls, 1256-9*, pp. 87, 90; *Cal. Pat. Rolls, 1247-58*, p. 578.

[82] *Cal. Liberate Rolls, 1251-60*, p. 440. *Cf.* M.T. Clanchy, *From Memory to Written Record* (2nd. Edition, London, 1993), pp. 221-3.

[83] Cf. Clanchy, *op. cit.*, especially chapters 6 and 7.

[84] It was also his position as a senior Exchequer clerk which led to his appointment as temporary custodian of the liberty of Bury St. Edmund's in March 1262 and of the abbey of Peterborough in March 1263: *Cal. Pat. Rolls, 1258-66*, p. 204; *Close Rolls, 1261-4*, pp. 216-17.

[85] E 159/33, m. 1d.

Anglian towns (Norwich, Ipswich, Dunwich and Yarmouth), apparently in order to ensure that money owed to the king was levied from their citizens.[86] Again, no definite evidence seems to exist to link Robert with either the Loudham in Norfolk or the Ludham in Suffolk from which his surname derived, though his property acquisitions both before and after he became a justice of the Jews suggest that he came from, or had close links with, the Suffolk-Norfolk border. In or before 1251 he had acquired an annual pension of eighteen shillings receivable from the north Suffolk religious house of Herringfleet (alias St. Olave's).[87] In 1257 he acquired a small area of land at Thorpe Parva (in Billingford) in the south of Norfolk,[88] and more extensive property at Gunton, Corton, Yarmouth (Northtown) and Pakefield, in north Suffolk and south Norfolk.[89] During the 1270s, he made two acquisitions of the reversions of land at Herringfleet after the death of their current tenants;[90] and by 1281 he had a manor there, and may have been engaged in building work on a manor house.[91] In 1283 he acquired the life tenancy of extensive lands at Weybread, 'Istede' and 'Otinton' in Suffolk[92] and less extensive lands at Lound in the same county.[93] By 1285 he had also acquired the Suffolk manor of Cookley.[94] In Norfolk, in 1278 he acquired the reversion of some marshland at 'Wheatacreburgh' (?Burgh St. Peter) after the death of two brothers then holding this land.[95] He also acquired property outside East Anglia. By 1260 he had acquired property at Chalfont St. Giles in Buckinghamshire[96] and in 1261 he acquired a messuage at Southwark, perhaps to use as residence during Exchequer terms, from one Nicholas Taylor of Yarmouth and his wife Alice.[97] By 1280 he had also acquired a life interest in the manor and advowson of Pampisford in Cambridgeshire.[98] It may also be our Robert of Ludham who was in the position in 1282 of being able to settle land at Send in Surrey on Thomas son of Robert of Papworth and his wife Alice.[99] Robert of Ludham probably remained an Exchequer clerk until shortly before his appointment as a Justice of the Jews, though in Michaelmas term 1271 he was already suing in the Exchequer as a former clerk of that institution in connection with an assault on his servants.[100] The immediate context of his appointment early in 1273 appears to have been the wish to appoint a new (but experienced) team of justices at the beginning of the new reign to run the Exchequer of the Jews.

Peter of Leicester belonged to a later generation of Exchequer clerks. He probably came from the city of Leicester, since in 1300 he was in the position to grant a messuage there to the collegiate church of St. Mary's Leicester.[101] He had a brother named Thomas who was acting as his agent at Bishop's Cleeve in Gloucestershire in 1287,[102] and who is almost certainly the Thomas of Leicester who made a final concord with Peter in 1291 concerning land at Claverdon and two other villages in Warwickshire, which settled the lands on Thomas and his issue by his wife Alice, with remainder over to any other issue of Thomas and reversion to Peter and his heirs.[103] It was Thomas's daughter, Juliana of Leicester, who was born about 1280, who succeeded Peter in his lands after his death.[104] His first appearance in the records is in 1275, when he was appointed the attorney of Osbert of Bereford (Barford), the sheriff of Warwickshire and Leicestershire, when Osbert was to render his account at the Exchequer.[105] This may mark Peter's first contact with the Exchequer, or he may have been appointed as being a clerk already in service at the Exchequer who was known to the sheriff through his local contacts. Peter had certainly entered the Exchequer bureaucracy by 1278 when he was appointed a deputy chamberlain in the Exchequer of Receipt by one of the hereditary chamberlains, the earl of Warwick.[106] Peter

86 *Cal. Pat. Rolls, 1258-66*, p. 204. He was still acting in this capacity in August 1262: *Ibid.*, p. 235. At Michaelmas 1262, orders were given for him to be paid (or allowed) ten marks as expenses for his work, and a further ten marks for his expenses in levying royal debts in the counties of Norfolk and Suffolk: E 159/37, m. 9.

87 In 1259 at the instance of the Barons of the Exchequer and in view of the house's poverty, he remitted eight years' arrears of the annuity and agreed not to claim the annuity during the period of office of the current prior: E 159/33, m. 1d.

88 CP 25 (1)/158/85, no. 1276.

89 CP 25 (1)/214/25, no. 37.

90 CP 25(1)/215/33, no. 3; CP 25(1)/215/34, no.4.

91 CP 40/92, m. 64d: a Common Bench plea in Hilary term 1292 in which William Fegge of Great Yarmouth sought a debt of five marks eleven shillings and four pence, by virtue of an alleged agreement made between them at Great Yarmouth on St. Barnabas day, 9 Edward I (11 June 1281) under which he was to receive this payment for carrying stone to the manor. Robert waged his law that he did not owe the money. Some such agreement must, nonetheless, have lain behind the litigation.

92 CP 25(1)/215/35, no. 29.

93 CP 25(1)/215/35, no. 34. In 1285 he also acquired the advowson of Lound: CP 25(1)/215/37, no. 16.

94 In June 1285, he was granted free warren in all his demesne lands at Cookley: *Cal. Ch. Rolls*, ii, p. 289, and see CP 25 (1)/216/42, no. 6; CP 40/153, m. 266.

95 CP 25(1)/159/108, no. 131.

96 E 159/34, m. 6d. For later evidence of his interests here see CP 40/42, m. 131 and CP 40/103, m. 68d.

97 CP 25(1)/226/17, no. 16.

98 *Cal. Inq. Post Mortem*, ii, no. 381 and *see* CP 25(1)/25/39, 9 Edward I, no. 6.

99 E 159/46, m. 1d.

100 E 159/46, m. 1d.

101 *Cal. Pat. Rolls, 1292-1301*, p. 524. The preliminary inquisition *ad quod damnum* (C 143/31, no. 15) shows that he also held three crofts in the town.

102 JUST 1/541B, m. 11d.

103 CP 25(1)/245/34, no.18: calendared in *Warwickshire Feet of Fines, vol. II*, p. 24, no. 1087.

104 *Cal. Inquisitions Post Mortem*, iv, no. 216; CP 40/161, m. 129d. Juliana was by then the wife of Walter 'de Beruthorp'.

105 E 159/50, m. 15.

106 E 159/52, m. 3d. The appointment was made when the chamberlainship was restored to the earl after a temporary seizure caused by the malpractices of the previous deputy cham-

seems to have retained this post up to the time of his appointment as a Justice of the Jews in 1287,[107] apparently on secondment from the Exchequer in order to provide a second full-time justice in the aftermath of the upheaval caused by the dismissal and disgrace of Hauteyn and Ludham.

The remaining clerical justice of the Jews, *William of Carleton* probably derived his surname from East Carleton in Norfolk about five miles east of Wymondham.[108] He may be the man of that name whose misconduct while bailiff of different Norfolk hundreds and under-constable of Norwich is mentioned in the 1274-5 Hundred Rolls enquiry.[109] He is almost certainly the William of Carleton who acted as the attorney of a number of Norfolk litigants in the Common Bench between 1275 and 1277 and who stood surety for a litigant in the same court in 1282. By 1283, Carleton had probably entered the service of Robert of Tattershall, a major baronial landowner, whose main estates were in Norfolk and Lincolnshire, since he was one of two attorneys appointed by him to act for him during his absence abroad in that year.[110] A continuing connection with Robert and his family is perhaps indicated by William's purchase of the wardship of Robert's lands from the Crown after his death some twenty years later, long after he had passed into the king's service.[111] William was first appointed a Baron of the Exchequer in or before Michaelmas term 1285,[112] and his appointment at that level of seniority probably indicates many years of experience prior to that in the service of the Tattershalls and possibly others. William of Carleton seems to have remained a Baron for about a year[113] before being appointed as a Justice of the Jews to replace the disgraced Hauteyn and Ludham.[114]

berlain, William of Bradcote. Peter had been one of William's mainpernors to answer the charges made against him: *Cal. Close Rolls, 1272-1279*, p. 459.

107 Below, Appendix I.

108 After his death his executors included master Henry of Kenningham, whose name suggests he came from the next village to East Carleton: *Reg ... Henry Woodlock*, ii, 1016-7. In 1299 he had assisted in the resettlement of lands in five villages close to East Carleton: CP 25 (1)/161/118, no. 788 (he was pardoned the proffer for permission to make this concord: CP 40/129, m. 99d).

109 *Rot. Hund.*, i, 473, 474, 476-480, 5121-513, 530, 532, 537. It may also be the same William who is named as one of the executors of William of Middleton, late bishop of Norwich, in 1289: CP 40/78, m. 2d.

110 *Cal. Pat. Rolls, 1281-92*, p.109.

111 *Cal. Pat. Rolls, 1301-7*, pp. 161-2; *Cal. Close Rolls, 1302–7*, p. 516. And note that in 1286 he possessed a life interest in Robert of Tattershall's Suffolk manor of Shelley: JUST 1/48, m. 16.

112 E 13/12, m. 8d. He is also mentioned as a baron in Hilary term 1286 (E 159/59, m. 6).

113 During the first period of service as a baron of the Exchequer, Carleton also acted with master Henry de Bray as keeper of the vacant abbey of Ramsey: *Cal. Pat. Rolls, 1281-92*, p. 250.

114 Below, Appendix I.

(ii) *lay justices*

Six non-clerical Justices of the Jews were appointed during this period and for all except the final years of the Exchequer of the Jews the general policy seems to have been followed of always ensuring that there was at least one lay Justice serving in the court. All the lay Justices were drawn from the gentry of southern England and all but one can be shown to have had some prior administrative experience in either seignorial or royal service. The exception is *William of Orlestone,* who was appointed a Justice in 1266,[115] and who was only thirty-six at the time of his appointment.[116] William belonged to the minor Kent gentry, having inherited lands worth thirty pounds a year from his father the year before his appointment.[117] The main family manor, Orlestone, near Romney Marsh, was held in chief of the king by knight service for two knight's fees of the escheated honour of Haughley.[118] William had at least two brothers. These were John, whose widow held lands at Rucking in Kent of William's inheritance at the time of William's death;[119] and master Robert, who in 1279 renounced his claim to a half share of those of the family lands at Orlestone and Rucking which were held in gavelkind in return for a life pension of two marks a year.[120] When William died in 1283, he was succeeded by his son and heir John, by then aged 30.[121] John was also heir to William's wife, Joan of Popeshall (from Popeshall near Dover), who was dead by 1293.[122]

Two Justices had a prior record of service only in seignorial administration. One was *Ralph of St. Osyth's* who acted as a Justice of the Jews for a brief period only in 1272.[123] A case brought in the court *coram rege* in Michaelmas term 1260 indicates that at that time Ralph was a bailiff of Hugh de Vere, earl of Oxford, at Castle Hedingham in Essex, and may have been his steward. He also appears at the 1262 Essex Eyre, again as the earl's bailiff, but in connection with the earl's court at Earls Colne in Essex.[124] Ralph came from St. Osyth's on the Essex coast, holding lands there to the value of thirty pounds a year plus other lands to the value of fifteen pounds a year at 'Adderle' (probably Ardleigh) in the

115 Below, Appendix I.

116 *Cal. Inq. Post Mortem*, i, no. 879: his age is given here as 35.

117 C 132/45, no. 12, calendared in *Cal. Inq. Post Mortem*, i, no. 879; *Rotuli de Oblatis et Finibus*, ii, p. 420.

118 *Cal. Inq. Post Mortem*, i, no. 879.

119 C 133/39, no. 3, calendared in *Cal. Inq. Post Mortem*, ii, no. 527.

120 CP 25(1)/98/59, no. 91.

121 *Cal. Inq. Post Mortem*, ii, no. 527.

122 JUST 1/375, m. 41.

123 Below, Appendix I.

124 KB 26/168, m. 17d; JUST 1/236B, m. CR 2d. He also acted as his attorney in the 1257 Suffolk eyre: JUST 1/820, m. 11. He appears as second witness to an undated agreement between Ely priory and Hugh de Vere, earl of Oxford, relating to land at Shudy Camps in Cambridgeshire: BL MS. Egerton 3047, ff. 163v-164r.

same county. These lands were held by knight service of the earl of Oxford.[125] From Common Bench litigation of 1279 we learn that his heiresses were the two daughters of a son John, who had predeceased him, but that a younger son Philip claimed that his father had granted him these lands prior to his death.[126]

The second was *William Pasket*. He is first mentioned in a case in the 1248 Berkshire eyre.[127] In 1254 he acted on behalf of the King in land pleas in the Common Bench and King's Bench and authorised a royal writ to the constable of Windsor for a man's release.[128] Richard of Cornwall was, at the relevant time, one of the two regents acting during the absence of Henry III in France, and it is probable that Pasket was in fact acting for Richard in both matters. He had certainly entered Richard's service by 1258,[129] and is mentioned as his bailiff in 1268,[130] and as his steward in 1269.[131] William had been appointed a Justice by May 1271.[132] He must have owed his appointment to Richard of Cornwall, in whose service he had been. Richard's nephew, the lord Edward, who had played an increasingly important role in the government of England since the battle of Evesham, had just gone off on crusade. Richard was also, it seems, able at around the same time to secure the appointment of Stephen Heym as a Justice of the Common Bench.[133] Stephen Heym's previous career also marks him out as an obvious protégé of Richard of Cornwall.[134] Pasket's appointment was not, however, apparently connected with Henry III's grant of the Jewry of England to Richard for one year from Michaelmas 1271. The grant was made only some time after his appointment and specifically reserved to the king the pleas, perquisites and escheats of the Jewry.[135] William may have come from Buckinghamshire. He can be shown to have held land in the south of the county at Langley, Wraysbury and Iver,[136] but in 1262 was claiming lands as his uncle's heir at Haddenham in the west of the county, too.[137] He seems also to have acquired lands in the neighbouring counties of Northamptonshire (at Towcester[138] and Snorscumbe (in Everdon));[139] in Bedfordshire (at Wrestingworth, in exchange for the land at Snorscumbe),[140] and in Hertfordshire (in and around Clothall).[141]

Two of the Justices had experience both in local administration and in private service. *John le Moyne* was another minor tenant-in-chief. His main estate, the manor of Great Shelford in Cambridgeshire, was held by the serjeanty of supervising the making or repair of the king's crown, and was worth just over sixteen pounds a year at the time of his death.[142] It may have been this John le Moyne who had been appointed in 1238 as an assessor and collector of the tax of a thirtieth in Huntingdonshire.[143] It was certainly the future Justice who accompanied Henry III on his expedition to Gascony in May 1253,[144] and who returned to Gascony with the lord Edward two years later.[145] In the period

[125] CP 40/30, m. 28d. For other lands acquired or held by Ralph at Ardleigh of John de Boville see E 326/97 and 99 (both of them undated). In 1248 he had acquired the reversion of lands and rent at Maplestead and Castle or Sible Hedingham: *Essex Feet of Fines*, i, p. 164. In 1260, as Ralph son of Walter of St. Osyth's, he had granted or settled lands in a number of villages close to St. Osyth's on Lawrence the son of Lawrence of Frowyk and his wife: *Ibid*, p. 240.

[126] CP 40/30, m. 28d: the litigation was brought by the executors of Hawise de Vere, countess of Oxford, against Philip of St. Osyth's, claiming that the wardship of Ralph's grand-daughters belonged to the countess.

[127] *The Roll and Writ File of the Berkshire Eyre of 1248*, ed. M.T. Clanchy (Selden Soc. 90: 1972-3), no. 230.

[128] KB 26/154, m.1; KB 26/152, m. 14d; *Close Rolls, 1253-4*, p. 88.

[129] *Rot. Hund.*, vol. I, p. 18. In Michaelmas term 1259 William was suing in the court *coram rege*, ostensibly on the king's behalf, against the prioress of Studley, claiming that the advowson of the church of Beckley should have escheated to the king on the loss of Normandy. The bishop of Lincoln subsequently claimed that the prioress had granted him the advowson. He was then induced to surrender it to Richard of Cornwall by the king: KB 26/161, mm. 21, 9d. Pasket had again presumably been acting for Richard.

[130] *Cal. Charter Rolls*, ii, p. 99. In 1268 he also acted as Richard's attorney in a plea in the Common Bench: KB 26/195, m. 38d.

[131] KB 26/191, m. 6d; and see JUST 1/1210, m. 11d (where he is essoined as Richard's attorney). In 1270 he was appointed as attorney for a Common Bench plea by Richard's son, Henry: KB 26/200A, m. 40.

[132] Below, Appendix I.

[133] *Cal. Liberate Rolls, 1267-72*, no. 1476.

[134] *The Earliest English Law Reports. Vol. I.*, ed. Paul Brand (Selden Soc. 111: 1996), p. cxxvii.

[135] *Cal. Pat. Rolls, 1266-72*, pp. 545-6. The grant in fact amounted to giving Richard the right to levy the last two thousand marks of a tallage of six thousand marks. Henry III prevented Richard from levying the whole sum, though he subsequently promised to pay it in full to his executors: *Ibid.*, p. 671; *Cal. Pat. Rolls, 1272-81*, p. 4.

[136] E 132/2/15 (a roll of deeds, mainly of William Pasket, transcribed apparently for Cecilia, one of his two daughters and coheiresses), m. 3d (quitclaim by Cecilia to her sister Parnel and brother in law, William of Chillingham, of all the right belonging to her by inheritance from William Pasket in the lands and tenements in the villages of Langley and Wraysbury held by William of Fulham and his wife (? the widow of William Pasket)), m. 4d (acquisition by William Pasket of lands at Iver).

[137] JUST 1/58, m. 2; CP 25(1)/16/37, no. 9.

[138] E 132/2/15, m. 4d.

[139] CP 25(1)/174/42, no. 708. See also the related deeds in E 132/2/15, m. 4d.

[140] CP 25(1)/283/14, no. 349.

[141] E 132/2/15, mm. 1-4, 1d-3d. The Alina, daughter of Richard of Gatesbury, and niece of Simon, lord of Clothall, given land at Clothall jointly with William Pasket (m. 1), was perhaps William's future wife. William's acquisitions of land here may be explicable by reference to this marriage.

[142] *Close Rolls, 1242-7*, p. 182; *Close Rolls, 1259-61*, pp. 376-377; *Book of Fees*, ii, pp. 902, 917, 1552.

[143] *Cal. Liberate Rolls, 1226-40*, p. 310.

[144] *Cal. Pat. Rolls, 1247-58*, pp. 215, 231, 245.

[145] *Close Rolls, 1254-6*, p. 187; *Cal. Pat. Rolls, 1247-58*, p. 409.

between these two trips to Gascony, John had served as sheriff of his home county of Cambridgeshire and of its linked neighbour Huntingdonshire. He seems to have been appointed while still in Gascony.[146] John was appointed sheriff of the two counties again in the immediate aftermath of the battle of Evesham, but held the shrievalty for only a matter of months, relinquishing it shortly before becoming a Justice.[147] During the ten year period between his two periods of service as sheriff, John is also to be found in the service of one of the relatives of Henry III's queen, Peter of Savoy. Peter was a major Cambridgeshire landlord as lord of the honour of Richmond.[148] He was going overseas as Peter's messenger at the time of the Oxford parliament of 1258.[149] In 1261 he was in the service of another alien lord, Ingram de Fiennes.[150] Whether these two (and the lord Edward) were the only lords he served during this period, and the precise nature of his service to them, are both unknown.

Hamon Hauteyn was the longest serving non-clerical Justice of our period and the only one to have served (albeit only briefly) a previous term as a Justice. A final concord made in 1244 between William le Breton and Hamon's father, Robert, arranged that William should hold land to the use of (that is, as a trustee for) Hamon and his wife Margery for the following four years.[151] It seems reasonable to deduce from this that Margery was a relative of William. If William is the man of that name who was a Justice of the Jews,[152] and such an identification is only possible, not certain, Hamon would seem to be the only Justice in this period to have been related, if only by marriage, to a previous Justice. Hamon had succeeded his father in the family lands by late in 1247.[153] These lands placed him securely in the ranks of the gentry. The main family holdings were the Norfolk manors of Hellesdon (near Norwich) and Oxnead, which had been in the family's possession since the time of Domesday Book. They were then held by Godwin Halteyn. From his name, Godwin would appear to have been of Anglo-Saxon origin but he seems to have been an Anglo-Saxon who did well out of the Norman Conquest, since in the time of the Confessor the manors had been held by other men to whom he does not appear to have been related.[154] When Domesday Book was compiled, both manors were held in chief of the king. By 1185 the Hauteyn family had come to hold both manors as mesne tenants owing knight service to the de Bohuns, subsequently earls of Hereford.[155] By the time of Hamon's own death, the two manors were probably worth in excess of thirty-five pounds a year.[156] Hamon also held two manors in Lincolnshire, at Scredington and at Shillingthorpe in the parish of Braceborough. Both seem to have come into the family's possession through the marriage (between 1169 and 1185) of Theobald Hauteyn to Agnes, the daughter of Robert de Grelley,[157] and both were also held by knight service.[158] The manor of

146 *Cal. Pat. Rolls, 1247-58*, p. 223; *List of Sheriffs for England and Wales* (P.R.O. Lists and Indexes, ix), p. 12 and see *Close Rolls, 1253-4*, pp. 36, 317.

147 *Cal. Pat. Rolls, 1258-66*, p. 445; *List of Sheriffs*, p. 12. His removal was paid for by the bishop of Ely, perhaps because he had dispute with the bishop over Great Shelford: E 159/40, m. 8; *Close Rolls, 1264-8*, p. 356; KB 26/195, m. 14d. For his appointment see Appendix I.

148 For the lands held of the honour in Cambridgeshire see *Cal. Inq. Post Mortem*, ii, no. 381, pp. 319-321; for the demesne manors of the honour in the county: *Cal. Charter Rolls*, i, p. 259.

149 *Close Rolls, 1256-9*, p. 235.

150 *Close Rolls, 1259-61*, p. 456.

151 *Lincoln Fines*, i, pp. 360-1.

152 On William le Breton and his career see C.A.F. Meekings, *Crown Pleas of the Wiltshire Eyre, 1249* (Wiltshire Archaelogical and Natural History Society, Records Branch, 16: 1960), pp. 129-30.

153 Robert's widow was suing in the Cambridgeshire eyre of the autumn of 1247 for her dower share of the many lands alienated by her husband during their marriage that had formed part of the Norfolk and Lincolnshire manors of the family: JUST 1/81, mm. 14d, 15, 15d. Robert had probably died earlier that year.

154 *Domesday Book*, ii, pp. 271a-271b.

155 *Rotuli de Dominabus*, p. 55. The 1166 return of Humphrey de Bohun mentions one Walter *de Hayntone* as holding two knights' fees of him: *Red Book of the Exchequer*, i, p. 242. Round was probably right to emend this to Walter Hauteyn (*Rotuli de Dominabus*, p. xlvi). The Hauteyn family later owed the service of two knights and one hundred shillings to the earls of Hereford not just for these two manors but also for two other Norfolk manors at Barnham Broom and Herringby and for one hundred acres of Skeyton in the same county: CP 40/115, m. 70d. In 1302 the manor of Hellesdon by itself was said to owe the earl of Hereford the service of half a knight; and the manor of Oxnead and the lands at Skeyton and Tottingham were said to owe the earl a quarter of a knight's fee: *Feudal Aids*, iii, pp. 390, 419.

156 Two-thirds of the manor of Oxnead was leased by the king to Hamon's son and heir William from 1291 onwards for seventeen pounds a year, indicating a total valuation for the manor as a whole of in excess of twenty-five pounds a year: E 372/143, m. 12. The remaining third was held by Hamon's widow in dower. For the context of this and other similar leases see below, p. 38 and n. 309. There was no similar lease of two-thirds of the manor of Hellesdon, because Hamon's widow had successfully claimed to hold the whole manor in frankmarriage: below, p. 38 and n. 308. It can, however, be deduced from the 1244 final concord (above, n. 151) that the manor was then worth at least twenty pounds a year. In 1265, Oxnead had been valued at a little under twenty pounds a year, Hellesdon at only around eleven pounds a year: C 145/29, nos. 19, 20 (=*Cal. Inq. Misc.*, i, nos. 828, 829). Hamon's brother Bartholomew also held lands at Hellesdon in 1265 worth thirty-three shillings and four pence: C 145/29 no. 20 (=*Cal. Inq. Misc.*, i, no. 829). In 1185, however, Oxnead had been valued at ten pounds a year, and Hellesdon at eighteen pounds: *Rotuli de Dominabus*, p. 55.

157 *Registrum Antiquissimum*, vii, ed. K. Major (Lincon Record Soc. 46: 1953), pp. 131-2; *Lincoln Fines*, i, p. 115.

158 In 1242/3, Hamon's father Robert was said to hold one knight's fee at Scredington of William Dyve, together with half a knight's fee of Parnel de Vallibus and one twenty-eighth of a knight's fee of Walter of Threckingham: *Book of Fees*, ii, p. 1033 (and see pp. 1003, 1027). In 1256 Hamon made a final concord with Thomas Amys and his wife Christine concerning one and a half knight's fees at Scredington, under whose terms they were to

Scredington was worth only around eleven pounds a year at the time of his death,[159] and Hamon had by then granted the other manor of Shillingthorpe in fee tail to his daughter Alice and her first husband, Walter of Stirchley.[160] Hamon had also held lands at Ravenserodd in Yorkshire,[161] and lands at Bourne in Cambridgeshire, worth about ten pounds a year, which he alienated to a Bartholomew Hauteyn, who was probably his brother.[162]

Hamon Hauteyn's first known involvement in local government was at the very beginning of the 'period of baronial reform' when, in August 1258, he was appointed as one of the four knights who were to enquire into the misdeeds of sheriffs and others in his home county of Norfolk.[163] Like Fulk Peyforer, he went on from this to become sheriff of the county himself in the following October and retained the shrievalty until early January 1260.[164] At Michaelmas 1259 he was appointed sheriff of Lincolnshire, retaining this shrievalty for over two years.[165] Hamon seems to have fought on the baronial side at the battle of Lewes in 1264, possibly as part of the household of the earl of Gloucester.[166] He was then appointed a Justice of the Jews for the first time,[167] and it is tempting, in view of his later known links with the earl, to see his appointment as being owed to the earl's influence or to the desire of the earl of Leicester to retain his support.[168] The inquisitions held in the aftermath of the battle of Evesham indicate that both Hamon and his brother Bartholomew were known Montfortians. Unlike the earl of Gloucester, they do not seem to have transferred their loyalty back to the King before the battle.[169] During 1266, Hamon was twice given safe-conducts to come to negotiate at court but received no general pardon.[170] In June 1267, he was a participant in the earl of Gloucester's march on London in support of the 'Disinherited' and was given a safe-conduct as one of the earl's messengers.[171] Shortly afterwards, he was pardoned for his role in these events and received his pardon as one of the earl's bachelors, one of his household knights.[172] In October 1268 he received a further pardon, this time for his part in the battle of Lewes, again as a member of the earl's household.[173] In 1267/8, he is also to be found attesting to at least one deed as the earl's steward.[174] It is not known how long he remained in the earl's service or whether his reappointment as a Justice early in 1273 owed anything to the earl's influence.[175] The only further reference to him in the records of the intervening period is to his appointment as a gaol delivery justice at Great Yarmouth in September 1272.[176] Hamon Hauteyn brought one other relevant experience to his appointment as a Justice. His father, Robert, had contracted debts to various Jewish creditors on the security of his lands,[177] and part of the money was still outstanding at his death. By the time of his reappointment as a justice in 1273 (if not before) Hamon had gained personal experience of the workings of the Exchequer of the Jews as a tenant of the lands of a deceased debtor.[178]

Fulk Peyforer is the only member of the group to have

hold half the demesne land there in return for the service of one knight's fee: *Lincoln Fines*, ii, pp. 112-13. In 1303 one Robert Hauteyn was said to be the tenant of three quarters of a knight's fee and one eighth of a knight's fee at Scredington: *Feudal Aids*, iii, p. 129. In 1212 Robert Hauteyn was said to owe Gilbert de Gaunt the service of one twelfth of a knight's fees for Shillingthorpe (*Book of Fees*, i, p. 182), but in 1242/3 he was said to owe Gilbert one-fifth of a knight's fee for his land here (*Ibid.*, ii, pp. 1051, 1067).

159 In 1270, Hamon was returned as holding sixteen bovates here in demesne worth eight marks a year (*EJ*, i, p. 261), but this may well be an under-valuation. After Hamon's death, two-thirds of the manor were leased to his son William for seven pounds and ten shillings a year by the king, indicating an annual value of eleven pounds and five shillings for the manor as a whole: E 401/119. In 1303, William sold the manor to the Exchequer clerk, Walter of Norwich, for one hundred pounds: CP 25(1)/134/70, no. 20.

160 In 1214 the Hauteyn family holding here was described as comprising six bovates: *Lincoln Fines*, i, p. 115. In 1244 it was a holding of one carucate here that was to be settled on Hamon, Margery and Hamon's heirs: *Ibid.*, pp. 360-361. Margery unsuccessfully claimed the manor after Hamon's death but it was retained by Alice and her second husband, William of Shedworth: CP 40/79, m. 65; CP 40/81, m. 49; CP 40/83, m. 85.

161 For litigation brought by Hamon to recover these lands see KB 26/162, m. 7. By 1287 they were held of him by sub-tenants: *Cal. Inq. Mortem*, iv, no. 468 (pp. 354, 356).

162 CP 40/106, mm. 246, 246d. Between 1291 and 1299, two-thirds of these lands were leased by the king to Hamon's son, William, for five pounds a year: E 372/143, m. 46d. His daughter Alice and her second husband also unsuccessfully sought these lands after Hamon's death: *Cal. Inq. Post Mortem*, ii, no. 797; *Cal. Close Rolls, 1288-96*, p. 176.

163 *Cal. Pat. Rolls, 1247-58*, p. 648.

164 *Ibid.*, pp. 654, 655.

165 *List of Sheriffs*, p. 78. He had been instructed to relinquish to it in July 1261: *Cal. Pat. Rolls, 1258-66*, p. 163.

166 *Cal. Pat. Rolls, 1266-72*, p. 268.

167 *Close Rolls, 1264-8*, p. 11, 19, 32, 52; Meekings, *art. cit.*, p. 182.

168 M. Altschul, *A Baronial Family in Medieval England: the Clares, 1217-1314* (Baltimore, 1965), pp. 107-8.

169 *Cal. Inq. Misc.*, i, nos. 828-9. It may, however, be significant that only Bartholomew's lands were granted away by the king after Evesham (*Rotuli Selecti*, p. 255), and that it was the earl of Gloucester's bailiff who took the rent owed to Hamon at Hellesdon at Michaelmas 1265.

170 *Cal Pat. Rolls, 1258-66*, pp. 529, 563.

171 *Cal. Pat. Rolls, 1266-72*, p. 143.

172 *Ibid.*, p. 147.

173 *Ibid.*, p. 268.

174 *Oseney Cartulary*, vol. V, ed. H.E. Salter (Oxford Hist. Soc. 98: 1935), pp. 252-3.

175 Below, Appendix I.

176 C 66/90, m. 4d.

177 Lipman, *Jews of Medieval Norwich*, pp. 187, 215, 227; *EJ*, i, pp. 57, 61; *Close Rolls, 1231-4*, pp. 498, 508.

178 *EJ*, i, p. 261. The experience was also one shared by Fulk Peyforer: *EJ*, ii, pp. 58, 180. For a Jewish debt of William Pasket quitclaimed after his death see *EJ*, iii, p. 81.

had experience only of local administration in the king's service. Fulk belonged to an older generation of the Kent gentry than Orlestone. By the time he was appointed a Justice of the Jews in 1272,[179] he was already in his mid-fifties.[180] He, too, was a minor tenant-in-chief, holding the manor of West Peckham by the serjeanty of looking after a sparrow-hawk for the king from Michaelmas to the feast of the Purification of the Virgin each year,[181] but he had lost possession of this manor by the time of his death,[182] part of it having passed to the earl of Gloucester through the earl's acquisition of Jewish debts.[183] He retained other lands, however,[184] and at the time of his death (in 1277) they were worth just under fifty pounds a year.[185] From 1260 onwards he was also a tenant-in-chief in right of his wife, holding the serjeanty of the custody of the palace of Westminster and the Fleet prison.[186] Fulk possessed considerable experience of local administration. In 1256 he had acted as a gaol delivery justice at Rochester,[187] and in August 1258, in the immediate aftermath of the parliament of Oxford, he was one of the four knights appointed to enquire into the misdeeds of sheriffs and others in Kent.[188] In late October of the same year, he was himself appointed sheriff of the county,[189] and retained that position until December 1259.[190] In 1260 he was commissioned to tallage the royal demesne and towns in Kent and four other south-eastern counties (Surrey, Sussex, Essex and Hertfordshire),[191] and in 1263 was acting as a sub-escheator in Kent.[192] A second term of office as sheriff (from mid-June 1264 to August 1265)[193] coincided with the period of Montfortian rule. He seems not to have been penalized for this after the royalist victory at the battle of Evesham and in December 1265, was even commissioned to extend the lands of the king's Montfortian enemies in four south Midland counties.[194] Fulk served a third term as sheriff of Kent from late 1267 to October 1268.[195] It is possible that Fulk owed both his escape from the measures taken against those who co-operated with the Montfortian regime and his eventual appointment as a Justice of the Jews to the influence of the earl of Gloucester. He certainly held land of the earl,[196] though there seems to be no other evidence to link them, and the earl's acquisition of part of Fulk's lands by the early 1270s hardly looks like the act of a good lord.[197]

(e) *payment*

When authority was given in September 1266 for John le Moyne to be paid for half a year's service in the Exchequer of the Jews, the sum authorised was twenty five marks.[198] This presumably indicates that he had been promised an annual salary of fifty marks, a salary at the level first authorised for Justices of the Jews in 1260.[199] His colleagues were not so lucky. Such payments as can be traced of the other Justices appointed between 1265 and the death of Henry III indicate that they were all paid at the rate of only forty marks a year,[200]

179 Below, Appendix I.

180 This deduction as to his age rests on the evidence of *Kent Feet of Fines*, p. 127, which shows him as a party to a final concord in 1236. It seems probable that the final concord would have been invalid had he not then reached the age of twenty-one.

181 *Book of Fees*, ii, p. 1379.

182 *Cal. Inq. Post Mortem*, ii, no. 230.

183 *Rot. Hundredorum*, i, p. 205b.

184 These lands included (1) half a knight's fee at *East Barming*, held of the earl of Gloucester in 1242-3: *Book of Fees*, ii, pp. 662, 671. At his death, this manor was said to be held by a rent of twenty shillings and suit of court only: *Cal. Inq. Post Mortem*, ii, no. 230; (2) unspecified land to the value of £15, held in gavelkind of the abbot of St. Augustine's Canterbury: *Cal. Inq. Post Mortem*, ii, no. 230; (3) half a carucate at *Boughton Malherbe*, held as one eighth of a knight's fee, and acquired by him in 1255 (*Kent Feet of Fines*, pp. 270-1), perhaps to be identified with the land at *Colbridge* in Boughton Malherbe, held by him of Hamo de Gatton at the time of his death: *Cal. Inq. Post Mortem*, ii, no. 230; (4) *Boyworth marsh*, held of the heirs of Reginald of Cornhill by the service of one sore sparrowhawk: *Ibid*, and (5) *Elmley marsh [in Sheppey]* said to be held of the heirs of Thomas Abelyn for twelve marks a year, and forty shillings a year to the prior of Tonbridge: *Ibid.*

185 C 133/17, no. 13.

186 *Cal. Inq. Post Mortem*, ii, no. 230. Margery's heir, Ralph of Leaveland, brought an action against Fulk's executors for damage and deterioration to the Fleet prison while it was in Fulk's custody: E 13/8, m. 6d.

187 *Cal. Pat. Rolls, 1247-58*, p. 471. As yet there was no requirement that gaol delivery justices possess any experience or qualifications as professional lawyers.

188 *Ibid.*, p. 646. On these commissions (one of which was issued in respect of each county) see R.F. Treharne, *The Baronial Plan of Reform* (Manchester, 1932), pp. 108-11.

189 *Cal. Pat. Rolls, 1247-58*, p. 655.

190 *Cal. Pat. Rolls, 1258-66*, p. 64.

191 *Ibid.*, p. 76.

192 *Ibid.*, p. 291; *Cal. Liberate Rolls, 1260-7*, p. 126.

193 *Cal. Pat. Rolls, 1258-66*, p. 325; *Close Rolls, 1264-8*, p. 289.

194 *Cal. Pat. Rolls, 1258-66*, p. 651.

195 *Cal. Pat. Rolls, 1266-72*, pp. 173, 269; *List of Sheriffs*, p. 67.

196 Above, n. 184.

197 Above, n. 183.

198 *Cal. Liberate Rolls, 1260-7*, p. 236.

199 *Ibid.*, p. 10.

200 A standing order was given for the payment of this sum to Fulham and Esporun in February 1266 (*Cal. Liberate Rolls, 1260-7*, pp. 200-1) and in May 1271 the Exchequer was ordered to allow the bailiffs of Lincoln the one hundred shillings they had paid to Fulham towards his annual fee of forty marks (*Cal. Liberate Rolls, 1267-72*, no. 1510). William of Orlestone was paid twenty marks in respect of Easter 1266, Easter 1267 and Easter 1268, indicating an annual salary of forty marks: *Cal. Liberate Rolls, 1260-7*, pp. 242, 295; *Cal. Liberate Rolls, 1267-72*, no. 319 (and see no. 104). Master William of Watford was paid the twenty marks of an annual fee of forty marks due at Easter 1268: *Cal. Liberate Rolls, 1267-72*, no. 288.

the same salary as that which had been paid to John de Wyvill between 1246 and 1255.[201]

The Justices of the Jews, in common with other royal justices, received no regular salaries during the early years of Edward I's reign, not just during the king's absence from the country but also for some years after his return, though they did receive some irregular payments during this period.[202] In 1278, however, they and the other royal justices were put back on regular annual salaries, and once more at the rate of forty marks. Payments at this rate can be traced for Hamon Hauteyn and Robert of Ludham,[203] master Henry de Bray,[204] William of Carleton[205] and Peter of Leicester.[206] Such a salary gave them parity with the puisne (junior) justices of the Common Bench, King's Bench and the General Eyre, and also with the Barons of the Exchequer, the Chancellor of the Exchequer, and the Treasurer's Remembrancer.

(f) *Additional administrative and judicial functions*

The Exchequer of the Jews was in session at Westminster (or Shrewsbury) for, at most, half the year.[207] Its justices were, however, active also during vacations, partly in activities closely connected with their functions as justices of the Jews, partly on unconnected judicial and administrative activities. Most closely connected with their official functions was their work in receiving presentments from individual communities and from their Christian neighbours locally in the towns where Jews were resident in answer to a set of fifteen 'articles of the Jewry'. We have only indirect evidence of these sessions through related entries on the Plea Rolls of the Exchequer of Jews and then only from the late 1270s, but it seems possible that they had long been one of the vacation tasks of the Justices of the Jews and that they also continued during the 1280s.[208] They seem to have conducted these enquiries *ex officio*, for there is no evidence of them being specially commissioned to hold them. Other activities connected with the Jewish community, however, such as the scrutiny of Jewish chirograph chests, the levying of Jewish tallage, the determining of civil and criminal cases involving individual Jews and relating to forfeited Jewish chattels, did require specific commissions and so can be more easily traced. In February 1273 Hauteyn and Ludham were commissioned to make scrutinies of the Jewish chirograph chests in certain towns,[209] and similar commissions were subsequently issued (in November 1275) to Ludham to act with a colleague in making a scrutiny of the chests in four other towns,[210] to Hauteyn and a colleague (in January 1276) to make a scrutiny of the chests in two towns,[211] to Ludham and a colleague to make a scrutiny and purification of the London chests (in December 1276),[212] and to Hauteyn,

[201] Meekings, *art. cit.*, p. 180. But note that such payments as can be traced to his predecessors and to one of his successors, Ralph de Hotot, were at the still lower rate of twenty pounds a year: *Ibid.*

[202] In August 1273 Hauteyn and Ludham each received twenty five marks for their expenses in office and for their expenses in scrutinising the Jewish *arche:* C 62/49, m. 2. In November 1273 Hauteyn alone received a further twenty marks for his expenses while in office as a Justice of the Jews: C 62/49, m. 1, and in December 1273 Ludham received a similar payment: C 62/50, m. 8. In November 1276, orders were given that both be paid ten pounds by the Lucchese merchants in aid of their expenses as Justices of the Jews: *Cal. Pat. Rolls, 1272-1281*, p. 168.

[203] *Cal. Pat. Rolls, 1272-1281*, p. 304 (3 March 1279: twenty marks in respect of (Michaelmas) 6 Edward I); C 62/55, m. 1 (15 November 1279: like sum for Michaelmas 7 Edward I); C 62/56, m. 2 (10 November 1280: like sum for Michaelmas 8 Edward I): C 62/57, m. 4 (12 October 1281: like sum for Michaelmas 9 Edward I); C 62/60, m. 4 (30 May 1284: like sum for Easter 12 Edward I); C 62/61, m. 8 (28 December 1284: like sum for Michaelmas 12 Edward I); C 62/61, m. 7 (26 April 1285: like sum for Easter 13 Edward I); C 62/61, m. 2 (12 October 1285: like sum for Michaelmas 13 Edward I); C 62/62, m. 2 (3 May 1286: like sum for Easter 14 Edward I).

[204] C 62/61, m. 8 (28 December 1284: twenty marks for Michaelmas 12 Edward I); E 159/64, m. 16 (28 April 1287: allowance of forty marks a year for 12-15 Edward I). But note that in 1284 the sheriff of Northamptonshire was allowed £15 paid to Master Henry as a Justice of the Jews for his expenses in that office in 10 Edward I: E159/57, m. 9.

[205] C 62/63, m. 3 (8 December 1286: twenty marks for Michaelmas 14 Edward I); C 62/63, m. 2 (8 May 1287: like sum for Easter 15 Edward I): C 62/64, m. 4 (25 November 1287: like sum for Michaelmas 15 Edward I): C 62/64, m. 3 (25 May 1288: like sum for Easter 16 Edward I); C 62/65, m. 3 (4 July 1289: twenty marks each for Michaelmas 16 Edward I and Easter 17 Edward I), C 62/66, m. 2 (24 July 1290: twenty marks each for Michaelmas 17 Edward I and Easter 18 Edward I); C 62/67, m. 3 (4 June 1291: twenty marks for Michaelmas 18 Edward I).

[206] C 62/64, m. 4 (7 December 1287: twenty marks for Michaelmas 15 Edward I); C 62/64, m. 3 (25 May 1288: like sum for Easter 16 Edward I); C 62/65, m. 3 (4 July 1289: twenty marks each for Michaelmas 16 Edward I and Easter 17 Edward I); C 62/66, m. 2 (24 July 1290: twenty marks each for Michaelmas 17 Edward I and Easter 18 Edward I); C 62/67, m. 3 (4 June 1291: twenty marks for Michaelmas 18 Edward I).

[207] Above, section I, at p. 4.

[208] Brand, 'Jews and the Law in England', 1144-7.

[209] *Cal. Pat. Rolls, 1272-81*, p. 6: the towns assigned to Hauteyn were Northampton, Nottingham, York, Lincoln and Stamford; the towns assigned to Ludham were Bedford, Cambridge, Colchester and Sudbury. The other two commissioners were the former Justice of the Jews, Thomas Esporun, and the future Keeper of Rolls and Writs of the Exchequer of the Jews, Adam of Winchester.

[210] *Ibid.*, p. 127 (Winchester, Wilton, Oxford and Devizes). The colleague was William Gerberd. Ludham was given one hundred shillings for his expenses in doing this: *Cal. Close Rolls, 1272-9*, p. 288. Several other pairs of commissioners were appointed at the same time to make scrutinies of the Jewish chests in an number of other towns: *Cal. Pat. Rolls, 1272-81*, pp. 127-8.

[211] *Cal. Close Rolls, 1272-9*, p. 263 (Lincoln and Stamford). Hauteyn was authorised to choose his own colleague.

[212] *Cal. Pat. Rolls, 1272-81*, p. 184; the colleague was Ralph of Broughton. In February 1277, the sheriff of Norfolk was allowed the payment of ten marks to Ludham in expenses for this purpose: C 62/53, m. 6.

Ludham and Bray to make a general scrutiny of chests and to transcribe the deeds they contained, to facilitate the levying of Jewish debts which had passed into the king's hands (in October 1281).[213] Hauteyn and Ludham were also commissioned, in May 1275, to act with William of Middleton (keeper of rolls and writs in the Exchequer of the Jews) to levy the arrears of the Jewish tallage of 1273-4, though responsibility for this was subsequently transferred to others;[214] and William of Carleton was commissioned with two others in 1287 to assess a Jewish tallage.[215] Hauteyn was commissioned in July 1281, together with Walter of Kent, the keeper of the queen's gold, to enquire into Jewish debts belonging to the king in the counties of Lincolnshire, Nottinghamshire, Yorkshire, Leicestershire, and Northamptonshire.[216] They were also commissioned for criminal business involving Jews. In October 1277, Hauteyn was commissioned (with William de Brayboef) to enquire into a serious assault on Abraham son of Benedict at Winchester, and the taking of his goods;[217] and in February 1278 (with Bartholomew de Briaunzon) to enquire into allegations of coin-clipping made against Isaac of Berkhamsted.[218] In February 1283, Hauteyn was commissioned, more generally, to enquire into allegations of Jews dealing in sheets made from coin-clipping and in sheets of silvered tin with foreign merchants, [219] though he was later replaced on this commission by others.[220] These allegations seem to be connected with others as to the alleged robbery of merchants of the count of Holland, which Hauteyn and the earl of Cornwall were commissioned to hear,[221] though again they were later replaced by others, eventually including William of Carleton.[222] William of Carleton was also associated (in October 1286) with the trial of Isaac son of Isaac Polet at the Tower of London on a charge of murder.[223] Other commissions on Jewish matters to individual justices of the Jews include one issued in December 1276 to Hamon Hauteyn (and John of Cobham) to determine a plea initiated in the Exchequer of the Jews and subsequently evoked to the Exchequer concerning the alleged forgery of a deed in the name of Roger de Leyburn;[224] one issued to Hauteyn and others (in November 1279) for the sale of houses forfeited by Jews in Lincoln, Stamford and Warwick;[225] one issued to Hauteyn and Walter of Kent (in January 1280) concerning the goods of the late Jacob of Oxford, whom Edward I had granted to the queen consort Eleanor;[226] and a commission issued in January 1288 to William of Carleton to enquire into concealed Jewish goods.[227]

Other tasks assigned to them, however, were quite unconnected with Jewish matters. Hamon Hauteyn regularly acted as one of the gaol delivery justices for the London gaol of Newgate from at least 1276 to the time of his downfall,[228] and was sometimes commissioned for gaol deliveries at the Tower of London.[229] He was also commissioned to hear and determine appeals in London,[230] Middlesex,[231] and Suffolk,[232] and trespass cases in East Anglia and the Home Counties,[233] and to review cases which had been heard in the city courts of London.[234] He was even appointed in 1275 as one of the commissioners to assess a tax of one fifteenth in London and Middlesex.[235] Robert of Ludham acted as an assize justice in East Anglia (the counties of Norfolk, Suffolk, Cambridgeshire, and Huntingdonshire) between 1279 and 1284;[236] and was also commissioned to hear and determine trespass cases mainly in East Anglia.[237] William of Carleton, while a Justice of the Jews, was

213 *Cal. Pat. Rolls, 1272-81*, pp. 458, 459. See also above, p. 22.

214 Below, Appendix V.

215 Below, Appendix V.

216 *Cal. Pat. Rolls, 1272-81*, p. 473.

217 *Cal. Pat. Rolls, 1272-81*, p. 244.

218 *Ibid.*, p. 287.

219 *Cal. Pat. Rolls, 1281-92*, p. 56.

220 *Ibid.*, pp. 128-34.

221 *Ibid.*, p. 98.

222 *Ibid.*, p. 291.

223 JUST 3/36/1, m. 33.

224 *Cal. Pat. Rolls, 1272-81*, p. 236. For the earlier proceedings in the Exchequer of the Jews see *EJ*, ii, pp. 227, 229 (=*Select Pleas*, p. 84), 229-30, 258 (=*Select Pleas*, p. 86), 298; *EJ*, iii, pp. 39 (=*Select Pleas*, p. 91), 83, 148; and in the Exchequer: E 368/50, m. 1d. See also *Cal. Close Rolls, 1272-9*, p. 144; *Cal. Pat. Rolls, 1272-81*, pp. 334, 335; E 159/51, m. 21.

225 *Cal. Pat. Rolls, 1272-81*, p. 337.

226 *Ibid*, p. 407.

227 *Cal. Pat. Rolls, 1281-92*, p. 291.

228 The proceedings at these sessions are recorded on JUST 3/35B, and show that sessions were held within the Exchequer of the Jews term as well as outside it. The modern roll consists of a number of annual rolls sewn together. These rolls were probably delivered into the Exchequer by Hamon's son and heir, William, in response to a royal mandate to him to do so issued in November 1293: *Cal. Close Rolls, 1288-96*, p. 335. In July 1285, Hauteyn was given ten pounds towards his expenses as a gaol delivery justice at Newgate: C 62/61, m.3.

229 e.g. *Cal. Pat. Rolls, 1272-81*, p. 474; *Cal. Pat. Rolls, 1281-92*, pp. 257, 258.

230 *Cal. Pat. Rolls, 1272-81*, p. 347; *Cal. Pat. Rolls, 1281-92*, p. 205.

231 *Cal. Pat. Rolls, 1272-81*, p. 32.

232 *Ibid.*, p. 116.

233 e.g. *Cal. Pat. Rolls, 1272-81*, pp. 66, 111, 179, 468; *Cal. Pat. Rolls, 1281-92*, pp. 81, 91, 100, 103, 144, 211.

234 e.g. *Cal. Pat. Rolls, 1272-81*, pp. 339, 348, 407, 414, 467, 472.

235 *Cal. Close Rolls, 1272-9*, p. 251. He was given ten pounds for his expenses in executing this commission: C 62/52, m. 6.

236 JUST 1/1244 is a roll of assizes heard before Roger Loveday between 1279 and 1282. For many of these his associate was Robert of Ludham. Most of the assizes were heard outside the term time of the Exchequer of the Jews, but some were not. In May 1281 Ludham was paid ten pounds for his expenses as an assize justice (C 62/57, m. 9), in July 1281 another twenty marks (*Cal. Close Rolls, 1279-1288*, p. 95), in June 1282 a further twenty marks (C 62/58, m. 2), in July 1282 ten pounds (*Ibid.*) and in September 1284 twenty pounds in respect of 11 Edward I (C 62/60, m. 2).

237 *Cal. Pat. Rolls, 1272-81*, pp. 115, 179, 285, 286, 407, 409, 470; *Cal. Pat. Rolls, 1281-92*, pp. 42, 49, 73, 81, 98.

commissioned (with William of Middleton) to settle disputes between the merchants of England and Holland at Yarmouth[238] and to audit the accounts of the bailiffs of Dunwich;[239] Peter of Leicester, to act as a custodian of the vacant bishopric of Norwich.[240]

(g) *Removal from office and subsequent fate*

Almost a third of the Justices of this period (four out of thirteen) held office for less than a year. It was probably death that removed Ralph of St. Osyth's from office, since in April 1273 it was his son Philip who was responsible for handing over his father's records to the current Justices.[241] No such easy explanation is available for the removal of his colleague Fulk Peyforer, who lived on for another five years after his removal, playing a part only in local affairs as he had done prior to his original unexplained appointment.[242] The appointment of the remaining two Justices may always have been intended to be temporary. Certainly, in both cases, it is clear from subsequent commissions to them that they had not done anything to cause a loss of confidence in their integrity or abilities. On leaving the Exchequer of the Jews John le Moyne was first appointed a custodian of the vacant see of Norwich (and acted as such from February to June 1266) and was then commissioned to assist in the enforcement of a new customs duty in the north of England.[243] In November 1267 he became sheriff of Northamptonshire[244] and in December 1268 was also appointed escheator of England south of the Trent.[245] The date of his relinquishment of these two offices (August 1270)[246] suggests that he may have been planning to go on a Crusade with the lord Edward, but he seems not to have gone, and in 1272-3 was making alternative plans for a pilgrimage to Santiago.[247] He died in 1275.[248] Thomas Esporun may have been called out of retirement to serve as a Justice. If so, this was not the last call to be made on his services. In 1270 he was commissioned to levy money owed to the king in three south-eastern counties (Kent, Surrey, and Sussex); and the commission describes him as still being a king's clerk.[249] In 1273 he was commissioned to make scrutinies of the Jewish chirograph chests in four towns (Winchester, Oxford, Marlborough, Wilton);[250] but this seems to be the last mention of him.

A further two Justices held office for about two years. William Pasket may have been removed from office by death. Certainly, it was his heiresses who were bringing litigation in the Exchequer of the Jews in Trinity term 1273 against Hagin son of master Moses and others;[251] but the Exchequer seems to have believed that he was still alive at Michaelmas term 1272, some time after he had ceased to be a justice.[252] It is more probable, then, that his removal is to be connected with the disgrace of master William of Watford, though he was not directly implicated in master William's misconduct. William of Orlestone survived another fifteen years after his removal, and during this period was commissioned to perform various functions, mainly in connection with his own home county of Kent.[253] There are no clues as to the reasons for his removal. It remains as unexplained as his original appointment.

The remaining seven Justices all held office for somewhat longer periods. William of Carleton and Peter of Leicester both remained Justices until the Exchequer of the Jews itself was abolished, and then went on to successful careers elsewhere in the royal service, back in the Exchequer. William's first assignment was to assist in making the property arrangements for the marriage of Edward I's daughter, Margaret, to the son of the duke of Brabant,[254] but soon after his return from Brabant, he was reappointed a Baron of the Exchequer,[255] and in 1303 became Chief Baron.[256] He was reappointed at the

[238] *Ibid.*, p. 276.

[239] *Ibid.*, p. 320.

[240] *Ibid*, pp. 301, 312.

[241] Below, p. 50, and n. 7.

[242] In 1273 he was commissioned to enquire as to who was responsible for the guarding of felons in churches in Canterbury (*Cal. Pat. Rolls, 1272-81*, pp. 6, 32) but by 1274 he was said to be sick to the point of death (*EJ*, ii, p. 80). He had recovered by the following year when he was commissioned to collect a tax of one twentieth in Kent and as one of the custodians of the heavily indebted Kent abbey of Faversham: *Cal. Close Rolls, 1272-9*, p. 83; *Cal. Pat. Rolls, 1272-81*, p. 102. In 1277 he was commissioned for a special gaol delivery at Maidstone: *Ibid.*, p. 240. He was dead by mid-November 1277: *Cal. Inq. Post Mortem*, ii, no. 230.

[243] *Cal. Pat. Rolls, 1266-72*, p. 3.

[244] *List of Sheriffs*, p. 92.

[245] *List of Escheators for England* (List and Index Society, 72: 1971), p. 1.

[246] *Ibid.*; *List of Sheriffs*, p. 92.

[247] *Cal. Pat. Rolls, 1266-72*, pp. 327, 343; *Cal. Close Rolls, 1272-9*, p. 50.

[248] His death took place between June and October 1275: *Cal. Close Rolls, 1272-9*, p. 240; *Cal. Fine Rolls, 1272-1307*, p. 53.

[249] *Cal. Liberate Rolls, 1267-72*, nos. 1028, 1169.

[250] *Cal. Pat. Rolls, 1272-81*, p. 6.

[251] *EJ*, ii, p. 27.

[252] E 159/47, m. 2d.

[253] In 1275, he was paid expenses for crossing the Channel to await Erard de Valery and Gaston de Béarn, and then escorting them into England: C 62/51, m. 3. Their point of entry was almost certainly in Kent. From January 1276 till 20 October 1283 he was bailiff of the port of Dover and responsible for passages in and out of the port: *Cal. Pat. Rolls, 1272-81*, p. 128; *Cal. Pat. Rolls, 1281-92*, p. 86; E 159/57, m. 1. In May 1282 he was also appointed keeper of the city of Canterbury: *Cal. Pat. Rolls, 1281-92*, p. 19; E 159/57, m. 3d. In 1278 he acted as a gaol delivery justice at Maidstone (*Cal. Close Rolls, 1279-88*, p. 456) and was appointed in 1281 to hear and determine an appeal: *Cal. Pat. Rolls, 1272-81*, pp. 474-5. He died on 11 November 1283 at daybreak: *Cal. Inq. Post Mortem*, ii, no. 527.

[254] *Cal. Pat. Rolls, 1281-92*, pp. 384, 387, 431. He returned to Brabant on related business in 1297: *Cal. Pat. Rolls, 1292-1301*, p. 226; *Cal. Close Rolls, 1296-1302*, p. 17.

[255] E 159/64, m. 8.

[256] T.F. Tout, *The Place of the Reign of Edward II in English History* (Manchester, 1914), pp. 240-1.

beginning of Edward II's reign,[257] but was allowed to go into partial retirement in October 1308,[258] and was dead by July 1311.[259] Peter of Leicester headed the panel of justices hearing allegations of misconduct against the judges and other officials of Edward I during 1292.[260] In January 1293 he too was appointed a Baron of the Exchequer.[261] He retained that position until 1303,[262] and died early in 1304.[263] Robert of Fulham's removal from office in 1272, after seven years of service, is probably (like that of William Pasket) to be connected with Watford's disgrace, though he, too, was not directly implicated in Watford's misconduct.[264] He died not long afterwards. He was still alive in late April 1273,[265] but was dead by the end of Michaelmas term 1274.[266]

The careers of the remaining four Justices all ended with their disgrace. It should not, however, be concluded from this that the Justices of the Jews were especially badly behaved. During the 'State Trials' which began in 1289 all but one of the justices of the Common Bench, all the justices of King's Bench and all but one of the surviving Eyre justices who had sat as justices of the eyres held between 1286 and 1289 were similarly disgraced for various forms of misconduct.[267] Master Henry de Bray's disgrace can be dismissed quite briefly. It seems to have been for non-official misbehaviour or for misconduct in his other capacity of escheator of England south of the Trent; not for any misconduct as a Justice of the Jews. He had almost certainly ceased to be in any sense a Justice of the Jews before that disgrace occurred.[268] Master William of Watford's disgrace occurred in 1272, after he had served for five years, and was indirectly caused by the finding of a forged bond for ninety pounds among the bonds of the recently deceased Poitevin son of Benedict le Joefne when they were delivered into the Exchequer.[269] The Exchequer had been entrusted with responsibility for levying the large sum of one hundred and twenty pounds which Poitevin had owed to the King,[270] and it had instructed the Exchequer of the Jews to send it all the bonds that had belonged to the deceased for this purpose.[271] At the end of Hilary term 1272,[272] William Pasket and the two Christian chirographers of the London chirograph chest brought to the Exchequer a box containing seventeen bonds of the deceased still 'with wax' (apparently, with the debtor's seal still attached) and one without. This was a bond for ninety pounds allegedly made on 10 December 1228 (13 Henry III) and thus dating from before the time when the parts of chirographs deposited in chests were those sealed by the debtor.[273] Closer examination revealed that the parchment on which it was written was new, but had been rubbed and crumpled to give it an appearance of

[257] *Cal. Pat. Rolls, 1307-13*, p. 7.

[258] *Ibid.*, p. 139.

[259] His will was proved in the London Hustings in July 1311: *Cal... Wills, Hustings*, vol. I, p. 221.

[260] *State Trials*, pp. 8-9, 20; JUST 1/541B, mm. 1-3, 38-45.

[261] E 159/66, m. 17.

[262] For payments authorised to him as a baron between 1293 and 1303 see C 62/68, mm. 5, 2, 1; C 62/69, mm. 3, 2; C 62/70, m. 2; C 62/75, m. 3; C 62/77, m. 1; C 62/78, m. 2; C 62/79, m. 2.

[263] On 6 February 1304, he was one of those commissioned to assess a tallage: *Cal. Pat. Rolls, 1301-7*, p. 201. The writ of *diem clausit extremum* on his death was issued on 30 March 1304: *Cal. Inq. Post Mortem*, iv, no. 216. His will was not, however, proved in London until March 1305: *Cal... Wills, Hustings*, vol. I, p. 168.

[264] See below.

[265] When he, Orlestone and Watford were adjourned in the Exchequer at the quindene of Easter for rendering their account as Justices of the Jews till three weeks after Michaelmas: E 159/37, m. 4d.

[266] E 159/49, m. 15; E 13/3, m. 6.

[267] Paul A. Brand, 'Edward I and the Judges: the 'State Trials' of 1289-93' in *Thirteenth Century England: I*, ed. P.R. Coss and S.D. Lloyd (Woodbridge, 1986), pp. 31-40; Paul Brand, 'Ethical Standards for Royal Justices in England, c. 1175-1307', *The University of Chicago Law School Round Table* 8 (2001), 250-74.

[268] Below, Appendix I.

[269] All details of the case unless otherwise stated, are derived from the record of Watford's trial in the Exchequer as enrolled on a separate undated membrane included in the Trinity *communia* section of the King's Remembrancer's Memoranda Roll: E 159/46, m. 9. A transcript of this entry will be found in Appendix II (i).

[270] It is not clear why it was the Exchequer and not the Exchequer of the Jews that was given this responsibility. Nor does the enrolment explain why Poitevin owed such a large sum to the king. Perhaps it was for tallage.

[271] The Exchequer had originally instructed the Jewish Exchequer only to send bonds of the deceased to the value of the sum owed to the king, but those sent were found inadequate for the purpose, and so the Exchequer had issued further instructions for sending all the bonds, so that it could make its own choice.

[272] The enrolment says only that the delivery was made on 'a certain Thursday'. It does, however, tell us that the original order for the delivery of bonds to the value of the debt owed to the king was made in Hilary term 1272; and that on the Friday preceding that Thursday the Jewish Exchequer was supposed to be ending its sessions and its senior justice, Robert of Fulham, had already gone home. Since the enrolment itself records proceedings during Trinity term 1272, this points to the end of Hilary term or the end of Easter term, when the Exchequer was in session but not the Exchequer of the Jews, as the time when the delivery was made. The end of Easter term is probably to be excluded on the evidence of an adjournment of a plea between Guy de Rocheford and unnamed *perfidi judei* concerning a false charter and other matters to the morrow of the Ascension recorded on the Memoranda Roll: E 159/46, m. 6d. If, as seems certain, the plea arose out of Guy's challenge to the bond produced on this Thursday, that challenge must have taken place prior to the end of Easter term. Other evidence is provided by a royal mandate to the Exchequer, enrolled with the *communia* of Easter term, instructing them not to take proceedings against master Elias son of master Moses or his wife in connection with a bond in the names of Poitevin le Jovene and John de Rocheford, since neither of them made any claim to any part of the debt: E 159/46, m. 7. This also indicates that by Easter term the bond had already been challenged.

[273] Above, p. 6.

age. It was challenged as a forgery by the grandson and heir of the alleged debtor, Guy de Rocheford. An official enquiry was held in the Exchequer in Trinity term 1272 in an attempt to discover who had been responsible for the presence of this forged bond among the bonds delivered into the Exchequer. It took sworn evidence from all those suspected of being implicated.[274] This established that when Poitevin's bonds had been taken out of the treasury of the Exchequer of the Jews six days before their delivery to the Exchequer, they had not included this bond.[275] It also established that they had been placed in a separate box at Watford's own instigation and that he had then taken the box home with him; that he had subsequently instructed his clerk to draw up a writ ordering the chirographers of the chest to accept delivery of the box; and that he had then sent for one of the Jewish chirographers to take delivery of it. Watford provided an ingenious explanation as to why he had made these arrangements for the bonds to pass from the Exchequer of the Jews to the Exchequer by way of the London chirograph chest. He also attempted to direct suspicion at the Jewish chirographer concerned (Aaron Crespin) and at his servant and perhaps also, indirectly, at his own colleague, William Pasket. He asserted that all the time the box had been in his custody it had been secured by two lengths of strap, joined at the front by an impression of Pasket's seal, and at the rear by an impression of his own seal. When the box had been delivered into the Exchequer (and, according to the Christian chirographers, also when it was delivered into their custody) it had been secured by a single length of strap, whose ends were joined by an impression of Pasket's seal only. The implication seems to be that it had been opened while the chest had been in the custody of Aaron Crespin, and that it was later closed and resealed with the knowledge and assistance of William Pasket. Aaron denied the allegation made against him, claiming that when had had (unwillingly) taken delivery of the box, it was then already secured by only a single length of strap, joined only by Pasket's seal, and pointed the finger of suspicion back at Watford himself. He claimed that he had seen the two sons-in-law of the late Poitevin, the only persons who stood to gain from the insertion of the forged bond,[276] at Watford's house when he had called to take delivery of the box. If we are to believe Aaron's story, the box must always have been secured only by the single strap, joined by Pasket's seal; and the forged bond had been inserted into it *before* it was thus secured.

The treasurer and barons took advice from other legal experts - Martin of Littlebury (the senior justice of the Common Bench), John of Cockfield (a King's Bench justice) and Lawrence del Brok (then either the king's serjeant or also a King's Bench justice) - before giving judgment. No one was held directly responsible for inserting the forged bond in the box but master William of Watford was held culpable for breach of an important rule that formed part of the custom of the Exchequer of the Jews in having delivered the box to a Jewish chirographer and not to the Christian chirographers. It was held also that he had behaved incorrectly in various other ways: in having taken the box home, and having had his clerk draw up a writ to the chirographers in the absence of (and thus without the consent of) his colleagues. He was remanded to gaol till further orders were received from the King.[277]

During the same term, a further allegation was made against Watford by Peter le Marchaunt of Mapledurham in Hampshire.[278] Peter claimed that Watford had also placed another unsealed and forged bond, this time one for sixty-four pounds, in the treasury of the Jewish Exchequer at the instigation of Benedict of Winchester. The alleged creditor was Elyas son of Chera; the alleged debtor, Peter's father, Robert. Peter also claimed that it had been Watford alone who had taken the forged bond out of the treasury and delivered it to Benedict on the authority of a royal writ issued in Benedict's favour.[279] Benedict had then taken the bond to the Winchester chirograph chest and secured execution on the debt, thereby gaining possession of Peter's chattels and Peter's lands at Mapledurham from 12 March to 7 June 1272. Watford claimed that the bond was genuine but did not specifically deny having placed it in the treasury; he also claimed that the withdrawal had been made by all the justices and not himself alone. Peter sought judgment against him, asserting that his defence had tacitly admitted the first charge, but the Exchequer adjourned the case to the following Michaelmas term, and released

[274] These were two of the three Justices of the Jews (Pasket and Watford), the two Christian chirographers of the London chirograph chest (John le Ferrun and John le Fort), one of its Jewish chirographers (Aaron Crespin), his servant Samuel, and Poitevin le Jeofne's two sons-in-law, Poitevin le Fort and Isaac of Northampton. If evidence was taken from others as well, it is not mentioned in the enrolment.

[275] All that the enrolment states is that at this stage there were only seventeen bonds, but the clear implication is that the seventeen were the seventeen genuine bonds.

[276] The enrolment makes it plain that the two sons-in-law had already made fine with the king to secure the assets of the deceased in the names of their wives, who were Poitevin's heiresses.

[277] There seems to be no evidence of any further action being taken against the two sons-in-law, though the forged bond can only have been inserted in the box in order to benefit them and presumably at their instigation. Proceedings may have been started against them prior to the conviction of Watford (above, n. 272), but there is no subsequent trace of them.

[278] This case is also recorded on the same separate membrane among the *communia* for Trinity term on the King's Remembrancer's Memoranda Roll: E 159/46, m. 9d. It is transcribed in Appendix II (ii). Unless otherwise stated, my account is based on the facts stated in this enrolment.

[279] There is no suggestion that this writ was not genuine. It was perhaps the royal writ issued in late December 1271 which directed that he be assigned sixty pounds of the king's debts in the treasury of the Exchequer of the Jews, as recompense for the gift, loans and 'courtesies' of Benedict to the King and the lord Edward: *Close Rolls, 1268-1272*, pp. 451-2.

Watford on bail.[280] In that term, the case was re-pleaded and issue joined between them. Both parties agreed that the case should be decided by the evidence or verdict of Watford's former colleagues and the clerks and serjeants of the Exchequer of the Jews. Watford was once more released on bail,[281] but this time did not appear to answer his bail. The measures subsequently taken against him in an attempt to secure his appearance culminated in his outlawry.[282] Peter also brought proceedings in the Exchequer of the Jews against Benedict of Winchester for having instigated Watford's misdeeds. Benedict successfully pleaded that, as an alleged accessory, he was not liable to answer the charge until Watford was convicted of the principal offence.[283] The allegedly forged bond was delivered into the custody of the Exchequer while the case against Watford was pending.[284] Eventually, probably in Michaelmas term 1275, and possibly in return for Peter dropping any further proceedings against him, Benedict agreed to the defacement of the bond (and the remission of the debt).[285] The major difficulty is in seeing why Benedict should have wanted a forged bond inserted in the treasury and delivered to him, when he was entitled to receive a genuine bond or bonds. Perhaps the plan was (or was thought to be) that he receive both genuine *and* forged bonds.

In the same term (Trinity term 1272) yet another allegation was made against Watford, but this time by a Jew, Jacob of Oxford. He claimed that Watford had wrongly extracted from a chirograph chest a bond for fifty marks belonging to Jacob and delivered it to Jacob's debtor, Margery, the widow of Abel of St. Martin.[286] No defence is recorded to this charge, and the allegation seems not to have been followed up.[287]

The chain of events which eventually led to the disgrace of Hauteyn and Ludham began in Trinity term 1286, when they were called into the Exchequer to render their accounts as Justices of the Jews.[288] Although the Justices of the Jews were not among the officials who regularly rendered accounts at the Exchequer, there is no evidence that they contested their liability to do so. The records do not explain why they were being called upon to account at this particular juncture, nor do they make clear whether the presence in the Exchequer on the relevant day (28 June) of the two senior justices of the Common Bench and King's Bench (Weyland and Hengham) in addition to the treasurer, an Exchequer Baron (John of Cobham) and the Treasurer's Remembrancer (Nicholas de Castello) had been arranged in advance because difficulties had been anticipated, or was merely hurriedly arranged on the day once difficulties had arisen. After the two justices had taken what seems to have been the customary oath required of those rendering accounts at the Exchequer, promising to charge themselves with all moneys they had received on behalf of the king other than moneys in payment of their salaries, they were asked to account. Both men denied having received *any* monies for which they were accountable. When asked to produce relevant official records, they denied having any receipt roll,[289] and asked for time to check their plea-rolls before they handed them in. The latter might not have been thought an unrea-

[280] This mainprise is recorded on E 159/46, m. 10. His previous recorded mainprises (to 14 July, and to 28 July, 1272) to answer plaints against him, and to stand to right, may also have covered appearances to answer in the other case against him: E 159/46, mm. 8, 8d. The order on 10 July 1272 to the treasurer and barons for his release on mainprise to appear on 25 July before the King to answer the King and others, does not seem to have been effective in its apparent object, that of securing the permanent supersession of Exchequer proceedings against him: *Close Rolls, 1264-8*, p. 492.

[281] The mainprise in Trinity term had been to the quindene of Michaelmas 1272, and the further pleadings probably took place then or soon afterwards. The King's Remembrancer's Memoranda Roll for 1272-3 records a further mainprise of master William to hear judgment in the Exchequer at the feast of St. Katherine the Virgin (25 November 1272): E 159/47, m. 2d.

[282] He had absconded prior to Henry III's death. The sheriff of Essex was then instructed to distrain him, and when he returned that Watford had no lay tenement, the bishop of Bath and Wells was instructed to distrain him for the quindene of Martinmas (1273). The bishop sequestered his benefices but returned that he could not be found. The sheriff of Somerset was then instructed to arrest him, and eventually to exact him: E 159/46, m. 9d; E 13/2, mm. 1d, 5d; E 159/48, m. 4. By Michaelmas term 1275, Master William had been outlawed. Peter appears then once more to have been attempting to bring proceedings against him in the Exchequer of the Jews: *EJ*, ii, p. 16.

[283] *EJ*, i, pp. 286-7. Benedict was also mainprised to appear in the Exchequer on 28 July 1272 to answer Peter and any others who wished to implead him: E 159/46, m. 8d.

[284] E 159/47, m. 4.

[285] E 159/50, m. 3d.

[286] E 159/46, m. 14d.

[287] For an incident which occurred during Hamon Hauteyn's scrutiny of the chirograph chest at York in 1277, in which a box was found containing a writ attested by Watford, which was sealed with a suspect seal, see *EJ*, iii, p. 309. Abraham Levy was tried on suspicion of involvement, but cleared. No verdict was passed on Master William of Watford's part in the matter.

[288] Unless otherwise specified, the following account is drawn from the record of proceedings against Hauteyn and Ludham enrolled on the Lord Treasurer's Remembrancer's Memoranda Roll, which has been printed by Sayles in *Select Cases ... King's Bench, vol. I* at pp. clv-clix. There is no corresponding entry on the Memoranda Roll of the King's Remembrancer.

[289] There were of course receipt rolls which recorded money levied by the Exchequer of the Jews during their period of office and paid into the Exchequer of Receipt. These were records of the latter institution, and not under the control of the Justices of the Jews, and it was not these that the Exchequer was after. What it wanted was the records which recorded the monies paid directly to the Justices. There is no evidence that in this period these were recorded on separate receipt rolls, but such payments were sometimes recorded on the plea-rolls of the justices (below, p. 47, and n. 10). The relevant entries seem, in fact, however, to have been dismissed by those who investigated the affairs of the Jewish Exchequer during the summer of 1286, for Hauteyn and Ludham seem not to have been made to account for the sums they had received.

sonable request, if made only in respect of the most recent rolls, but Hauteyn and Ludham were apparently making it in respect of the whole (or at least a major part) of the rolls made during their thirteen years of office. This led on to questions about the custody of the plea-rolls, their answers indicating that a majority of them were being kept at the homes of the Justices and not (as the Exchequer clearly considered ought to have been the case) in the treasury of the Jewish Exchequer. In the light of these unsatisfactory answers, the Justices were now suspended, though not dismissed, from office and arrangements made for an independent investigation over the summer into the affairs of the Exchequer of the Jews.[290] Further proceedings took place in the following Michaelmas term in the presence of the earl of Cornwall, who was acting as regent during the King's absence abroad.[291] The investigation of Hauteyn's plea-rolls had uncovered a payment of thirty marks made to him for his assistance by two Jews from Bedford, Joce Batecok and Jacob of Bedford, when they and Benne of Bedford were being tried for robbery before him at the Tower of London in 1283.[292] Hauteyn was asked to explain why he had not charged himself in his account with this money,[293] and was unable to provide a convincing explanation for not have done so.[294] The investigation had also, moreover, uncovered something which implicated Ludham as well as Hauteyn. In November 1276, Edward I had authorised the justices to provide master Elias son of master Moses with compensation from the debts belonging to the king in the treasury for the debts owed master Elias by the abbot of Stratford which the king had recently pardoned.[295] Master Elias, otherwise rabbi Elijah Menahem, was a scholar and physician and one of the most distinguished Jews of his generation;[296] the writ authorising the assignment of royal debts to him in return for the debts owed him by the abbot of Stratford was one of the last stages in a complicated story which went back to the end of the reign of Henry III.[297] An investigation by the Justices in Hilary term 1277 as to the extent of the abbot's indebtedness had concluded that this amounted to

290 It is during this period between his suspension from office and his final downfall that Hauteyn is to be found attesting a judicial writ returnable into the court of King's Bench, and another related judicial writ, both concerning a dispute over the church of Clandon in Surrey. Transcripts of both writs are to be found in Cambridge Univ. Library MS. Additional 3584 at ff. 245v-247r. See also G.D.G. Hall in *Early Registers of Writs*, ed. E. de Haas and G.D.G. Hall (Selden Soc. 87: 1970), p. xcvi.

291 These proceedings are all stated to have taken place on 16 October 1286.

292 For the record of this case see *Select Pleas*, pp. 125-7. Hauteyn heard the case by virtue of a special commission to do so, not as a justice of the Jews: *Cal. Pat. Rolls, 1281-92*, p. 98 (and *cf. ibid.*, p. 56).

293 He was accused of having received the money in terms which placed as unfavourable a gloss on his actions as was possible. The enrolment also records him as having been charged with receiving not thirty, but forty, marks. This may be a scribal error, but may also be an attempt to trap him into further damaging admissions.

294 Hauteyn claimed that he believed that it had been intended to arrange that the money should go to the Queen, but could provide no warrant for making such a payment and no evidence that he had paid the money to her. It was at this point in the proceedings that Hauteyn was induced to waive a writ obtained from the king at Paris in July, instructing the Exchequer not to proceed to judgment against him if he had committed a serious offence without first consulting the king. It is not clear why he did so. Perhaps he was advised that if he did not, his treatment might prove still harsher.

295 References to this writ will be found not only on the plea-rolls of both Justices (*EJ*, iii, pp. 285-6; *EJ*, iv, no. 458) but also in an enrolled version of a writ to the Treasurer and Barons of the Exchequer issued shortly afterwards: *Cal. Pat. Rolls, 1272-9*, p. 320.

296 Roth, *op. cit.*, pp. 113-14, 121, 127; idem, *The Intellectual Activities of Medieval English Jewry* (British Academy Supplemental Papers, no. VIII), pp. 36-7; idem, 'Elijah of London: the most illustrious English Jew of the Middle Ages', *Trans. Jewish Historical Soc.*, 15 (1939-45), pp. 29-61.

297 In November 1272 the abbey of Stratford was pardoned all usuries and penalties on the debts owned to Master Elias in respect of land purchased of William Bucuinte at Mountnessing in Essex, provided the principal was paid: *Close Rolls, 1268-72*, pp. 583-4. In January or February 1273, a further order was given that the abbey should not be distrained to pay any Jewish debts until Edward I returned to England: *EJ*, ii, p. 14 (28 January); *Cal. Close Rolls, 1272-9*, p. 8 (10 February). In December 1274, the abbey was, more generally, pardoned the penalties and usuries on all Jewish debts it owed, at the instance of the Queen mother: *Cal. Close Rolls, 1272-9*, p. 140. In Hilary term 1275, the Barons of the Exchequer were ordered to discover, as best they could, the principal owed by the abbey (E 159/49, m. 7d and for an adjournment in the Exchequer of Pleas in this case from the morrow of Ash Wednesday to the quindene of Easter, *see* E 13/3, m. 9d) and in May of the same year they (and the Justices of the Jews) were given further instruction on the matter, directing their attention to the money already paid, and to the fixing of terms for what still remained unpaid (*Cal. Close Rolls, 1272-9*, pp. 172-3). During Trinity term 1275 the matter was investigated by the Exchequer. The Christian jurors said that the bond for three hundred marks (two hundred pounds) had been entered into by the abbot's predecessor to satisfy an earlier bond of William Bucuinte to Master Elias' wife, Fluria, for sixty pounds; and that one hundred and twenty five marks had been paid towards satisfaction of the debt. They also said that another bond of one hundred and fifty pounds had been entered into to satisfy an earlier debt of fifty-seven and a half marks. The Jewish jurors, however, said that the bond for three hundred marks was not just in satisfaction of the original debt of sixty pounds, but also for the provisions of warranty and defence against all other Jewish creditors, and that the original loan behind the bond for one hundred and fifty pounds had been one hundred and ten pounds. The barons did not feel able to resolve the difficulties raised by these inconsistencies or by the plea advanced by Master Elias that, by virtue of the privileges granted by the charters of the king's predecessors, he should not be obliged to plead against the debtors who had entered into bonds to him, but was entitled to secure repayment of the sums mentioned in their bonds. They therefore sent the case to the king's council for their decision: E 13/3, m. 17. The council seems not to have taken a decision on the matter, but instead arranged a compromise. The Justices of the Jews were told by royal writ in February 1276 that Master Elias had pardoned the

£250.[298] The relevant entry on Hauteyn's plea-roll, however, allegedly showed that master Elias had been assigned royal bonds in excess of that sum; and that he had only been made answerable for part of the difference.[299] More serious still was the fact that the entry contained several erasures and interlineations.[300] It was clearly suspected that the original entry had been deliberately altered on one or more occasions, erasing the debts originally assigned to master Elias once they had been paid and putting other debts which belonged to the King in their place.[301] Adam of Winchester, the Keeper of Rolls and Writs of the Exchequer of the Jews, gave evidence that the plea roll in question and other plea rolls had been taken to the London home of master Elias by the justices and by Hauteyn's then chief clerk (John of Bayfield) and that alterations had been made in it there at the request of master Elias, but he could give no firm information as to the original contents of the entry.[302] Without such information, it could not be proved that the debts erased had not simply been restored to the King. The Exchequer, therefore, sent for the plea-rolls of the other justice, Ludham. The relevant entry on his roll agreed exactly with that on Hauteyn's roll (in its final version); but it was noticed at once that the membrane on which it was written was of different parchment to the rest of the roll, the entries on it written in a different ink, and that the membrane contained much more than the other membranes of the same roll. Under questioning, Ludham's (chief) clerk admitted that the membrane had only just been written and had been substituted for the original membrane in order that the entries on rolls of the two justices should exactly correspond, but was unable to say where the original membrane now was. The membrane was never recovered. Hauteyn and Ludham both eventually confessed their parts in the alteration of Hauteyn's roll, and Ludham also admitted that he had indeed ordered his clerk to write the new membrane.[303] It proved impossible, however, to demonstrate that the actions of the justices had defrauded the King of any of his debts.

The two justices were not particularly harshly treated. Both were allowed to make fine with the king in £1,000 for all offences against him committed while in office.[304]

abbey not only the penalties and usuries of their debts, but also all of the principal other than twenty five marks: *Cal. Close Rolls, 1272-9*, p. 271; and in Trinity term 1276 a starr of Master Elias in those terms was enrolled in the Exchequer of Jews: *EJ*, iii, pp. 223-4. In return, the king seems to have agreed that he would himself compensate master Elias for the debts owed by the abbey. The writ of November 1276 was the fulfilment of his side of the bargain.

298 The Justices found 'by record' that the abbot had owed the sum of three hundred and fifty pounds but had paid one hundred pounds of this. An agreement about this matter may also have been part of the agreement reached before the king's council early in 1276: above, n. 297. In effect, the decision conceded the claim of master Elias that it was wrong to go behind the abbot's bonds. The total of two hundred and forty pounds mentioned in the 1286 record is clearly an error. The other figures in the record are also inconsistent.

299 The enrolment records that the debts assigned to master Elias came to a total of two hundred and ninety pounds, but that this was only thirty pounds more than the sum to which he was entitled. It is also conceded that he had been charged by the Justices with repayment of a surplus of ten pounds. The conclusion then reached is that master Elias had wrongfully benefited to the extent of twenty pounds from the debts assigned at the expense of the king. To make the arithmetic work, two hundred and ninety pounds must be read as either two hundred and eighty or two hundred and seventy pounds: two hundred and eighty if the two plea-rolls are correct in stating the abbot's net indebtedness as two hundred and fifty pounds; the smaller sum if this enrolment is correct in stating the indebtedness as two hundred and forty pounds, (see above, n. 298). A greater problem still is posed by the survival of the relevant enrolment in two versions on two different rolls (above, n. 295) made for the two justices. This indicates that only a single debt of three hundred and sixty pounds was assigned to master Elias; that he was not charged with repayment of any part of it to the king; but that he was required to pay all the surplus to Aaron son of Vives. It also indicates, however, that the Justices had agreed that if the debt assigned had not been levied by the quindene of Easter following, master Elias might opt to levy the debt from other bonds that had been set aside for this purpose. It can be deduced from later entries that master Elias had exercised his option: see *EJ*, vi, nos. 63, 1000. The explanation seems to be that the clerk responsible for the 1286 enrolment has either deliberately (as a result of himself not understanding what had happened) or accidentally (in the process of condensing his material) confused this first enrolment made in Hilary term 1277 and a subsequent enrolment recording master Elias' exercise of his option. This excessive assignment of bonds to master Elias mentioned in the 1286 enrolment as being recorded on Hauteyn's roll is that recorded in this subsequent enrolment, which seems to have been on a roll that does not survive.

300 Again, there is no evidence of such erasures and interlineations in the two enrolments made in Hilary 1277, and the reference must be to the subsequent enrolment.

301 This would mean that at all times the enrolment would provide a warrant for the royal debt then being levied to the use of master Elias, but that he would have received payment much in excess of what was owed him at the expense of the King.

302 It is one of the curious features of these proceedings that, although Adam admitted that he had shared custody of Hauteyn's roll with Hauteyn's own chief clerk, there is no hint of any blame having been attached to him from the alteration of the roll. Nor does any suspicion appear to have attached itself to him, not even when Hauteyn claimed that he had been present in person when the entry was changed.

303 Ludham's confession was made on his sick-bed in his house at London, where he was thought to be in danger of dying. Two Barons of the Exchequer, William of Middleton, the former Keeper of Rolls and Writs of the Exchequer of the Jews, and William of Carleton, the future Justice of the Jews, received it.

304 The enrolment of Hauteyn's fine notes specifically that the fine did not exempt him from being accountable to the King and Queen for all moneys received on their behalf, nor from answering any private complainants. He was also mainperned to appear before the King as and when required. Ludham's original fine was one thousand marks but this was increased to one thousand pounds on 7 December, when he had recovered sufficiently to come to the Exchequer. He was also made to find mainpernors for a further appearance at the Exchequer at the quindene of Easter following.

Some of the justices convicted during the 'State Trials' were treated even more leniently. Nicholas of Stapleton's fine was only 300 marks, those of Roger of Leicester and Walter of Hopton 500 marks. But others were treated much more harshly. William of Saham's fine was 3,000 marks; Solomon of Rochester's £4,000; William of Brunton's 6,000 marks and Ralph de Hengham's 10,000 marks.[305] Hauteyn died while on an overseas journey some three years later.[306] He had, as yet, paid off none of his fine, and so his lands were seized into the king's hands.[307] His son and heir, William, was allowed to recover possession of the lands in 1291,[308] but only as a lessee of the crown, paying off his father's debt by way of an annual rent of £37 a year on the lands.[309] Ludham's debt was attermined at one hundred marks a year in 1290,[310] but he seems to have had difficulty in keeping up regular payments at this rate,[311] and when he died in 1296, almost half of the fine was still to be paid.[312]

(ii) *The Keepers of Rolls and Writs of the Exchequer of the Jews*

The only other official of the Exchequer of the Jews to be paid by the Crown during this period was the *Keeper of Rolls and Writs*. The post appears to have been created only at the beginning of our period, for the first known reference to a holder of this office is in mid-November 1265.[313] The similarly titled clerks in the Common Bench and in the Eyre circuits are known to have compiled their own plea rolls and the 'Rex' roll produced by the Keeper of Writs and Rolls of the Common Bench was, prior to 1253, the authoritative record of proceedings in the court, though reduced thereafter to the status of a subsidiary, duplicate roll along with the rolls of the puisne justices of the court.[314] No such plea-roll was ever compiled by or for the keeper of rolls and writs of the Exchequer of the Jews. It is not even certain that he played any part in the writing of the roll made for the senior justice of the court, though he is known to have shared responsibility for the custody of that roll with the senior justice's own chief clerk.[315] He also had sole responsibility for the custody of all writs sent to or returned into the court with everything attached to them,

305 Brand, 'Ethical Standards for Royal Justices', pp. 265-73.

306 His widow was suing for dower in Trinity term 1289: CP 40/79, m. 65. We know that he died on an overseas journey from an incidental reference to this: *Cal. Close Rolls, 1288-96*, p. 176. The purpose of that journey is unknown.

307 *Cal. Close Rolls, 1288-96*, p. 89. He owed a total of £1,140.12.9d., representing the fine for trespass and two other debts: E 372/143, m. 11.

308 But note that Hamon Hauteyn's widow held one third of the manors of Oxnead and Scredington and of the lands at Bourne in dower: *Cal. Close Rolls, 1288-96*, p. 89; CP 40/83, m. 35. As her dower lands they were not liable for any share of the debt. She was also not liable for any share of the debt in respect of the manor of Hellesdon which she held as tenant for life under the settlement envisaged by the fine of 1244 (above, p. 27): E 159/65, mm. 44d, 45. In 1291 she joined with Hamon's heir, the remainderman under settlement, to convey the manor of Hellesdon to Walter of Barnham and his wife Maud: CP 25(1)/160/116, no. 594. She later made a further quitclaim of the same manor in return for a joint life estate with Alice Aungevin in lands at Barnham Broom and elsewhere: CP 40/192, m. 16. Late in 1291, Margery was summoned to the Exchequer to answer for having consented to the fine without seeking the king's licence, but was allowed to make a fine of twenty shillings for her offence: E 159/65, m. 46. Nor did the manor of Shillingthorpe, which Hauteyn had granted away prior to making the fine, have to bear any share of liability for the debt.

309 E 401/119; E 372/138, m. 34d; E 372/143, mm. 12, 46d. For the regular payments made by William Hauteyn between 1291 and 1301 see E 401/119 (15 October 1291), 124 (18 October 1292), 126 (1 May 1293), 128 (26 October 1293), 129 (12 May 1294), 132 (28 October 1294), 134 (5 May 1295), 138 (26 October 1295), 139 (16 July 1296), 140 (7 December 1296), 141 (5 July 1297), 144 (10 February 1299), 145 (Summer 1299). The next payments exclude any payment in respect of Bourne: E 401/147 (19 February 1300), 149 (27 June 1301).

310 The concession had been made by the king's council. We hear of it only when he had already fallen into arrears. In Trinity term 1290, he was allowed to 'recover' his terms, that is, resume payment at the agreed rate, instead of being distrained to pay the whole sum at once, provided he paid fifty marks later the same term: E 159/63, m. 13d. The payment is recorded as having been made on 10 July 1290 (though this too was two days late): E 401/113. There seems to be no record of earlier payments.

311 Regular payment was made between July 1290 and May 1292: E 401/113 (10 July 1290 - fifty marks); /116 (24 October 1290 - fifty marks); /117 (22 May 1291 - fifty marks; 20 June 1291 - fifty-seven shillings); /119 (31 October 1291 - thirty pounds, nine shillings and eight pence, making fifty marks in all when added to the June payment); /121 (10 May 1292 - fifty marks). But there is then a hiatus in the record of payments until October 1294, when regular (but lesser) payments resumed: E 401/132 (21 October 1294 - thirty marks); /134 (23 April 1295 - ten marks); /138 (24 October and 8 November 1295 - forty-nine marks); /139 (13 April 1296 - ten marks only). The payments made in 1295 and 1296 appear to reflect the transfer of responsibility for forty of the hundred marks owed to the grantees of Ludham's life interest in the manor of Pampisford: E 159/66, m. 40.

312 The last recorded payment by him was on 13 April 1296 (above, n. 311). On 10 October 1296 his executors paid a further eighty pounds: E 401/140. cf. also E 372/144, m. 44. Measures were taken in 1308 to collect the remainder of the fine from the tenants of his lands. The uncollected portion was then said to amount to £449 and a half a mark: E 13/30, m. 48.

313 *Cal. Lib. Rolls, 1260-7*, pp. 185-6. But see also below, n. 320.

314 Paul Brand, *The Making of the Common Law* (London, 1992), p. 386, note 124.

315 Above, n. 302. This responsibility probably existed only so long as the plea-rolls concerned remained outside the treasury of the Exchequer of the Jews. When William of Middleton left office in 1276, a memorandum carefully distinguished between those rolls (of the period 52 Henry III - 2 Edward I) which he had handed into the treasury, and those rolls (of 3 Edward I) which he handed over to his successor: *EJ*, iii, pp. 214-15. Once in the treasury, their custody was the responsibility solely of those who possessed keys to it, the Justices.

like his counterparts in the Common Bench and in the Eyre.[316] The keeper of rolls and writs in the Common Bench is known to have performed a semi-judicial function in the expedition of the court's routine procedural business, perhaps because of its obvious and close association with his custodial responsibilities;[317] his counterpart in the Exchequer of the Jews may well have performed a similar function.[318] He was certainly considered sufficiently responsible to be given on occasion the task of taking jury verdicts locally on cases pleaded to issue in the court.[319]

Appointments to this post were made directly by the king.[320] Such appointments (and re-appointments of persons who had previously served in the past) took place on seven occasions in this period. The chancery rolls contain only one copy of *letters patent of appointment,* those issued on the appointment of Thomas Bacon in April 1266;[321] and one copy of the *letters close* issued to William of Middleton, in August 1271, requiring him to resume the office.[322] Letters close were probably also always issued to the justices of the Jews, authorising and requiring them to admit the Keeper of Rolls and Writs to his office, but again only a single example of such an order was enrolled, the one issued on the reappointment of William of Middleton in 1271.[323] When the new appointee took over from a previous holder of the office who was still in post, a mandate also went to the office-holder being superseded to deliver to his successor the records in his custody, and such mandates were enrolled both in 1271 when master John Tripacy was superseded by William of Middleton,[324] and in 1276 when William of Middleton was superseded by Adam of Winchester.[325] No examples survive of mandates to the Justices of the Jews to deliver the records in their custody to a new keeper, though when Thomas Bacon was dismissed in Octber 1266 he was ordered to deliver the records then in his custody to the Justices.[326] Such an order must then have been issued in favour of William of Middleton. One other type of formal document does, however, survive, that issued on William of Middleton's reappointment as Keeper of Rolls and Writs at the beginning of the reign of Edward I after his own previous appointment had been terminated by the death of Henry III. The lapsing of his appointment seems to have meant that the custody of the records of his office returned in theory (and perhaps also in practice) to the Treasurer and Barons of the Exchequer. On his reappointment it was they who were instructed to deliver them to him.[327]

The post of Keeper of Rolls and Writs was held by just four men. Two can be dismissed quite briefly. *Thomas Bacon* was appointed early in April 1266 and superseded late in October of the same year.[328] Little is known about him except that in 1272-3 he was suing a number of his debtors under the privilege jurisdiction of the Exchequer of the Jews as a former clerk,[329] and that in 1279-80 he was acting as the attorney of William of Leybourne in seeking money owed to William on Jewish debts acquired by him in the Exchequer of the Jews.[330] *Master John Tripacy* of Thornborough in Buckinghamshire relinquished the office in August 1271.[331] When he was appointed to it is uncertain, though it must have been after April 1268.[332] Master John's father, Richard Tripacy, had also been a tenant of land at Thornborough, and John had at least one, and possibly two, brothers who

[316] The 1276 memorandum (above, n. 315) also refers to the transfer of custody of these various other documents: see also below. Again, responsibility for their custody probably ceased once they had been handed in to the treasury of the Jewish Exchequer.

[317] Brand, *Making of the Common Law*, pp. 176-7.

[318] It was perhaps because he was present that routine business could be transacted in the absence of both Justices at the octave of Michaelmas 1273: above, pp. 17-18.

[319] For examples see *EJ*, ii, p. 60; *EJ*, vi, no. 1129.

[320] It should, however, be noted that when William of Middleton was re-appointed to the post in 1271, the letters close directing him to return to the duties of the office spoke of his having previously held the office *per nos et Edwardum primogenitum nostrum* (*Close Rolls, 1268-72*, p. 368). It is not clear whether this means that when he was appointed in 1265 or re-appointed in 1266, the appointment was made jointly by the King and his son or by the King at the request of his son; or whether it means that he had been appointed as Keeper of Rolls and Writs by Edward during the period he had controlled the Exchequer of the Jews (above, p. 3) and the appointment had later been confirmed or extended by the King.

[321] C 66/84, m. 21 (= *Cal. Pat. Rolls, 1258-66*, p. 577): '*De rotulis et brevibus Judaismi commissis.* Rex omnibus etc. salutem. Sciatis quod commissimus dilecto clerico nostro Thome Bakun rotulos et brevia nostra Judaismi nostri custodienda quamdiu nobis placuerit, ita quod percipiat per annum ad scaccarium nostrum decem libras, videlicet centum solidos ad scaccarium nostrum sancti Michaelis et centum solidos ad scaccarium nostrum Pasche, ad se sustentandum in officio predicto quamdiu steterit in eodem'.

[322] *Close Rolls, 1268-72*, p. 368.

[323] *Ibid.*

[324] *Ibid.*

[325] C 66/95, m. 19 (= *Cal. Pat. Rolls, 1272-81*, p. 148): '*De rotulis et brevibus Judaismi liberandis.* Mandatum est Willelmo de Middelton' quod rotulos et brevia Judaismi regis liberet Ade de Wynton' custodienda quamdiu regi placuerit. Et hoc nullatenus omittat. In cujus etc. Teste ut supra'.

[326] *Close Rolls, 1264-8*, p. 216.

[327] C 54/90, m. 9 (= *Cal. Close Rolls, 1272-9*, p. 7): '*De rotulis Judaismi commissis.* Cum rex commiserit Willelmo de Middelton' rotulos et brevia Judaismi sui que sunt in custodia thesaurarii et baronum de Scaccario custodienda quamdiu Regi placuerit, mandatum est eisdem thesaurario et baronibus quod eidem Willelmo rotulos et brevia predicta liberetis, sicut predictum est. Datum ut supra'.

[328] Above, notes 321, 326.

[329] *EJ*, i, pp. 287, 307; *EJ*, ii, p. 82. All the debtors came from Kent.

[330] *EJ*, vi, nos. 13, 17-18, 324.

[331] Above, n. 322.

[332] His predecessor, William of Middleton, was paid as keeper of rolls and writs in April 1268: below, n. 372.

also took university degrees.[333] In 1266 master John was given a life exemption from service as a juror or local royal official against his own wishes.[334] He is nonetheless, to be found acting as the bailiff of the Buckinghamshire hundred of Aylesbury in 1272.[335] Nothing else of significance is known about him.

William of Middleton appears to have been the first keeper of rolls and writs, and to have been appointed by mid-November 1265.[336] He held the post until June 1276, with what were probably only brief intermissions caused by the appointments of Bacon,[337] and then of Tripacy[338] and by the death of Henry III. He seems to have come from the Middleton which is close to King's Lynn in Norfolk.[339] The absence of references to him in official records prior to his appointment may be because his previous experience had been gained in the service of the lord Edward.[340] Certainly, when he was re-appointed in 1271, the letters close directing him to return to the duties of the office, refer to the fact that he had previously held the office through appointment by the king and the lord Edward;[341] and he regularly acted on Edward's behalf in the Exchequer of the Jews in connection with the levying of moneys owed to Edward as a result of Edward's period in control of the Jewry.[342] Both in this period and subsequently he can be shown to have had close links with the man who was Edward's confidential clerk before becoming his chancellor, Robert Burnell, acting as his attorney and witnessing his deeds.[343] Middleton's relinquishment of the post was due to his promotion to Keeper of Rolls and Writs in the Common Bench.[344] He held this latter post for just over two years.[345] He then acted as keeper of the vacant see of Canterbury for almost half a year.[346] In 1285 he was appointed a Baron of the Exchequer and remained one until 1290;[347] in 1285 he was also appointed as one of the assize justices for the counties of Essex and Hertfordshire - his colleagues on this circuit being the chief justice of the Common Bench, Thomas Weyland, and a fellow baron, John of Cobham.[348] He did not die until shortly before Easter 1300.[349]

His successor, *Adam of Winchester,* had also been in the service of Edward I before he ascended the throne. He is described as a clerk of the lord Edward in March 1264,[350] and again in Michaelmas 1272,[351] and it was probably as a trusted clerk in the service of Edward that he was given the various tasks assigned to him between 1265 and his appointment as Keeper of Rolls and Writs in 1276. These included his appointment in May 1265 on Edward's nomination as a Justice of the Jews, though it is probable that he never acted as such.[352] They also include a commission, in February 1266, to make enquiries about the seizure of the lands and goods of Simon de Montfort and others of the king's enemies;[353] the collection of the profits of justice of the city of Bristol to pay a fine the city owed for trespass between Michaelmas 1266 and Midsummer 1270;[354] supervision on Edward's behalf of the work of the collectors of new customs duties in 1272-3;[355] the scrutiny of Jewish chirograph chests, in 1273;[356] a commission to make

333 *Luffield Priory Charters,* vol. II, ed. G.R. Elvey (Northants Record Soc., 26: 1975), pp. lix-lx.

334 *Cal. Pat. Rolls, 1266-72,* p. 1.

335 JUST 1/60, m.5.

336 On 14 November 1265 a standing order was given for payment of his salary: above, n. 313, and see also n. 372.

337 Above, n. 321.

338 Above, n. 332.

339 *EJ,* i, pp. 144-5. In 1290 his title to property at Middleton and in the neighbouring villages (or towns) of Runton, Hardwick, King's Lynn, North and West Lynn, North and South Clenchwarton, Tilney and West Winch was confirmed by final concord: CP 25(1)/160/116, no. 568.

340 Our William of Middleton needs to be distinguished from two contemporaries of the same name: (1) a fellow cleric who was archdeacon of Canterbury (1275-1278) and bishop of Norwich (1278-1288), often known as *master* William of Middleton; (2) a layman, who was the son and heir of the Richard of Middleton, who had been Henry III's chancellor from 1269 to 1272.

341 Above, n. 320.

342 *EJ,* i, pp. 135, 174, 257; E 159/42, m. 28; *Cal. Pat. Rolls, 1258-66,* p. 554 (where Gilbert is clearly an error for William); *Cal. Pat. Rolls, 1272-81,* p. 87.

343 *Cal. Pat. Rolls, 1266-72,* p. 283, 284, 450; *Cal. Pat. Rolls, 1272-81,* pp. 156, 254; *Close Rolls, 1268-72,* pp. 399, 404; *Cal. Close Rolls, 1272-9,* pp. 120, 249, 255, 321, 430, 491; *Cal. Close Rolls, 1279-88,* pp. 57, 114, 120, 195, 423, 478; *Cal. Close Rolls, 1288-96,* pp. 116, 121; CP 25(1)/159/105, no. 56; CP 25(1)/159/110, no. 192.

344 *Cal. Pat. Rolls, 1272-81,* p. 146.

345 Until 10 August 1278: *Ibid.,* p. 276.

346 *Ibid.,* pp. 278, 316.

347 C 62/62 mm. 2, 3, 4; /63, m. 3; /64, mm. 3, 4; /65, m. 3; /67, m. 5.

348 *Cal. Close Rolls, 1279-88,* p. 365.

349 In Easter term 1300 there was litigation in the Common Bench about the advowson of the church of Runton in Norfolk. Its last incumbent, now dead, was one William of Middleton, presented to the church in the reign of Henry III by Maud, the ancestor of Simon Bigod of Felbrigg: CP 40/133, m. 155d. This looks like our William. The identification is made certain by another case in the same term about the advowson of the Suffolk church of Worlington. Its last incumbent, now dead, was also said to have been a William of Middleton presented in the reign of Henry III by Clemencia de Scales: CP 40/133, m. 78d. In Easter term 1280 our William had sued in the Jewish Exchequer under its privilege jurisdiction for money owed for corn belonging to his church of Worlington: *EJ,* vi, no. 416.

350 *Cal. Charter Rolls,* ii, pp. 246-7. There is no evidence, however, of him holding a benefice, and it is known that he was married. Property at Barton Stacey in Hampshire was leased to him and his wife in 1278: *EJ,* v, no. 374.

351 E 159/47, m. 1d.

352 *Close Rolls, 1264-8,* pp. 52, 62.

353 *Cal. Pat. Rolls, 1258-66,* p. 655.

354 *Cal. Close Rolls,1272-9,* p. 392; C 62/49, m. 1.

355 *Cal. Pat. Rolls, 1266-72,* p. 717; *Cal. Pat. Rolls, 1272-81,* p. 4.

356 *Cal. Pat. Rolls, 1272-81,* p. 6 (Bristol, Exeter, Gloucester, Worcester, Hereford, and Warwick). He was given five marks for this work: C 62/49, m. 4.

purchases in connection with Edward's coronation, in 1274;[357] a commission to act as an assessor of the lay fifteenth in the county of Kent in 1275;[358] and temporary custody of his own home town of Winchester, of which he was also a citizen.[359] He retained the post of Keeper of Rolls and Writs until the time of the dissolution of the Exchequer of the Jews.[360] He died not long afterwards.[361]

Middleton and Winchester were both also commissioned to perform a number of tasks that did not form part of their official functions. Middleton, as has already been seen, acted as Edward's attorney in the Exchequer of the Jews.[362] He was also appointed by John le Moyne in 1268 to render account on his behalf at the Exchequer for the time John had been a Justice of the Jews.[363] Middleton was employed on several occasions to make scrutinies of particular Jewish chirograph chests;[364] and on one occasion (between 1274 and 1276) was among those commissioned to levy arrears of a Jewish tallage.[365] He was also employed to audit the accounts of the tax (of one twentieth) granted towards the expenses of Edward in going on crusade and to levy arrears of that tax;[366] and on general oyer and terminer commissions.[367] Winchester was rather less active. In 1276 he was commissioned to hear an account;[368] in 1277 assigned a role in levying Jewish tallage;[369] in 1280 commissioned to levy money due to the king on forfeited Jewish bonds.[370] His last such commission, however, seems to have been in 1281 when he was commissioned to enquire into the concealment of forfeited Jewish goods in Oxfordshire and Berkshire.[371]

The salary attached to the office was ten pounds a year.[372] A similar salary was paid to the Keeper of Rolls and Writs in the Eyre during the 1280s; the Keeper of Rolls and Writs in the Common Bench in this period only received the more modest salary of ten marks a year.[373]

(iii) *The other clerks of the Exchequer of the Jews*

There were also a number of other clerks at work in the Exchequer of the Jews who were neither appointed by the Crown nor paid by it. We normally learn of their existence only from passing references to them on the plea-rolls, most commonly through their use of the court's

357 *Cal. Close Rolls, 1272-9*, pp. 69, 118.

358 *Cal. Close Rolls, 1272-9*, p. 251. He was later given twenty pounds for this work: C 62/52, m. 9.

359 *Cal. Pat. Roll, 1272-81*, p. 60; *Cal. Fine Rolls, 1272-1307*, p. 45. He retained it only till 3 September 1275: *Ibid.*, p. 51. For indirect evidence of his property interests in Winchester see *Cal. Pat. Rolls, 1266-72*, p. 390; *Cal. Pat. Rolls, 1272-81*, p. 360; *EJ*, vi, no. 29.

360 For payments made to him see below, n. 372.

361 In April 1292 the king asked the Exchequer to inform him as to the debts which Adam had owed him at the time of his death: E 159/65, m. 21d.

362 Above, p. 40 and n. 342.

363 E 159/43, m. 18.

364 *Cal. Pat. Rolls, 1266-72*, pp. 382, 708; *Cal. Pat. Rolls, 1272-81*, p. 126; *Cal. Close Rolls, 1272-9*, pp. 220, 289.

365 Below, Appendix V.

366 *Cal. Pat. Rolls, 1266-72*, pp. 548, 591, 682, 683, 710, 714; *Cal. Pat. Rolls, 1272-81*, pp. 61, 154, 163; *Cal. Close Rolls, 1272-9*, pp. 220, 289; E 159/48, m. 2d.

367 *Cal. Pat. Rolls, 1266-72*, pp. 688, 705; *Cal. Pat. Rolls, 1272-81*, pp. 5, 9.

368 *Cal. Close Rolls, 1272-9*, p. 317.

369 He was given a key to the tallage chest: E 368/50, m. 2.

370 *Cal. Pat. Rolls, 1272-81*, p. 364. He was given ten pounds for his work: C 62/56, m. 8.

371 *Cal. Pat. Rolls, 1272-81*, p. 470.

372 (i) A standing order for payment of this sum to *William of Middleton* was given on 14 November 1265 and renewed on 22 November 1266: *Cal. Liberate Rolls, 1260-7*, pp. 185-6, 249. On 3 November 1271 it was ordered instead that he be allowed this amount each year when he rendered accounts: *Cal. Liberate Rolls, 1267-72*, no. 1702. On 20 April 1268 he was paid his salary for 52 Henry III by the sheriff of Cambridgeshire and Huntingdonshire: C 62/52, m. 1; C 47/35/6, no. 1. The salary due for 1 Edward I was paid by Nicholas of Hereford: C 62/50, m. 2. On 13 July 1275 orders were given for payment of the salary for 2 and 3 Edward I: C 62/51, m. 5; (ii) when *Thomas Bacon* was appointed, it was at this salary: *Cal. Pat. Rolls, 1258-66*, p. 577; (iii) for *Adam of Winchester,* a whole series of payments and allowances can be traced: one of ten pounds made by the sheriffs of London prior to 6 May 1277 when they were given an allowance for this: C 62/53, m. 5; one of seven pounds made by the citizens of Winchester prior to 22 November 1277 when they were given an allowance for this: C 62/54, m.4; an allowance made in Trinity term 1278 against the money he owed for silver plate he had received in the course of the coin-clipping enquiries: *EJ*, v, no. 665; an allowance made on 6 July 1279 against debts he owed at the Exchequer of the Jews of ten shillings in respect of Christmas 1277 (for robes) and fifty shillings for Easter 1278: *CCR 1272-9*, p. 533; one of five pounds for the period from St John's day to Christmas day 1278 made by John of London, escheator, prior to 12 January 1279 when he received an allowance for this: C 62/55, m. 7; one of £7 10s for the period from Christmas 1278 to Michaelmas 1279 made by the same John prior to 24 July 1279 when he received an allowance for this: C 62/55, m. 5; one of £2 10s for the period Michaelmas to Christmas 1279 made by the same John before 15 November 1279 when he received an allowance for this: C 62/55, m.1; two payments of £5 and £2 10s made by Thomas de Normanville, the king's steward, in respect of Easter 1280 and in part payment for Michaelmas 1280 made by Thomas prior to 10 November 1280 when received an allowance for this: C 62/56, m. 2; two payments of £10 and £5 made by the sheriff of Hampshire in respect of the period from Christmas 1280 to Christmas 1281 and from Christmas 1281 to St John the Baptist 1282 made prior to 24 April 1282 when he received an allowance for this: C 62/58, m. 3; two payments of £10 each made by the sheriff of Wiltshire in respect of 11 and 12 Edward and made prior to 7 January 1285 when he received an allowance for this: C 62/61, m.7; a payment of £5 made by the exchequer in respect of Easter 1286 on 3 May 1286: C 62/62, m. 2; two payments of £5 each made by the exchequer in respect of Michaelmas 1286 and Easter 1287 on 24 June 1287: C 62/63, m. 2; two payments of £5 and £10 made in respect of Michaelmas 1288 and Easter and Michaelmas 1289 on 19 October 1289: C 62/65, m. 2.

373 *Select Cases ... King's Bench, vol. I*, pp. cxlviii - cxlix.

privilege jurisdiction. Certain of these clerks are specifically referred to on the rolls as the clerks 'of' particular justices. This presumably means that it was those justices who had engaged them in their service and may mean that it was those justices who also paid them, though they may have been remunerated solely through fees payable by those who had business with the court.

Most is known about one of Hamon Hauteyn's clerks, *John of Bayfield.* He was responsible, as early as 1273, for the writing of Hauteyn's plea-roll;[374] and in or after 1277 he was an active participant with his master and others in the alteration of an entry on one of his rolls.[375] He seems to have come from the village of Bayfield in the north of Norfolk. In 1278 he settled land there and in three neighbouring villages (Saxlingham, Glandford, and Letheringsett) on himself for life, with remainder over in fee simple to a son named Thomas.[376] The settlement was almost certainly intended to ensure that his illegitimate son would, in effect, inherit his father's lands. Further details about his family emerge from a settlement made in 1282 recorded in a final concord,[377] and from an assize of novel disseisin brought in the 1286 Norfolk eyre.[378] The settlement was made when John acquired lands in four mid-Norfolk villages (Brandon, Coston, Barnham Broom, and 'Dereford'). Under it he himself took a fee tail interest, with successive remainders over to Agnes of Bayfield (clearly the Agnes daughter of John of Bayfield who is mentioned in the 1286 assize, and thus an illegitimate daughter) in fee tail, to Agnes' mother Joan (clearly John's mistress) for life, and then to Walter son of William of Bayfield (perhaps a brother of John) in fee simple. The 1286 assize, concerning lands in some of these villages and in other neighbouring villages shows that John's heirs were his sisters, Katharine and Mabel, which provides additional confirmation that Agnes and Thomas were both illegitimate, since Agnes at least was still then alive. Some of the lands (probably those which formed part of the lands settled in 1282) were found by the jury to have been acquired jointly by John and Agnes; others to have been acquired by John alone, and thus to have been inherited on his death by his sisters. John is also known to have acquired rents amounting to one hundred shillings a year owed for lands in the parishes of St. Giles Cripplegate, St. Sepulchre Newgate and Clerkenwell outside London from Edmund of Fulham (almost certainly the son and heir of the former Justice of the Jews, Robert of Fulham) and his wife Maud.[379] It seems probable that John's entry into Hauteyn's service is to be connected with his Norfolk origins and Hauteyn's own ties with the same county, even though Bayfield is not close to any of Hauteyn's Norfolk lands. Perhaps John came to his attention while he was sheriff of the county, and thus in contact with men from all over the county. If so, John would have been in his service for some years prior to 1273. He seems to have remained in Hauteyn's service up to the time of his death. In Trinity term 1284 he was still suing in the Exchequer of the Jews as one of its clerks,[380] but by the following Michaelmas term, he was dead. His executors were William of Middleton, the former Keeper of Rolls and Writs, and John of Berwick, a clerk in the queen's service, who was already Keeper of the Queen's Gold,[381] and thus also with responsibilities in the Exchequer of the Jews.[382]

It is difficult to know how far Bayfield is typical of his fellow clerks, and there is much more it would be nice to know even about him and his career. Of the other clerks mentioned on the rolls, we know little more of *Robert of Broughton* than that he was already serving as a clerk in the Exchequer of the Jews in 1279,[383] and that in 1286 he was entrusted by Ludham, presumably as Ludham's chief clerk, with writing the membrane whose entries were to match those on Hauteyn's rolls, and ended up in prison for doing so.[384] The *Simon of Creeton* mentioned as a former clerk of the court in Hilary term 1268,[385] is perhaps to be identified with the man of that name who was an usher in the main Exchequer in 1269;[386] while the *Hugh 'de Hengham'* mentioned as a clerk of the court in Trinity term 1280 and Trinity term 1286,[387] is probably to be identified with the man of the same name appointed a clerk of the London chirograph chest in 1274 and who was acting as a clerk of the main Exchequer in 1294 and 1299.[388] The *John of Battisford* mentioned as a former clerk of the Exchequer of the Jews in Michaelmas term 1273 is probably to be identified with the later royal justice of that name;[389] while the *John Bacon* mentioned as a clerk in Trinity term 1284 is perhaps to be identified with the man of the same name who was appointed Keeper of Rolls and Writs of the Common Bench in 1292.[390] Of others, we know even less. The *Bartholomew of 'Ginges'* mentioned as a clerk in Hilary term 1268 was almost certainly a clerk of Robert

[374] On membranes 8 and 8d of E 9/13 there appears beside some of the entries the annotation - 'Scribendum/scribenda sunt in rotulo J. de Bayfeud'.
[375] Above, p. 37.
[376] CP 25(1)/159/108, no. 144.
[377] CP 25(1)/160/113, no. 252.
[378] JUST 1/578, m. 45.
[379] CP 40/107, m. 115; CP 40/109, m. 117; JUST 1/544, m. 10.
[380] E 9/44, m.2d.
[381] E 159/57, m. 4.
[382] E 9/45, m. 6. At this stage William denied he was an executor, but he can later be found acting as one: E 159/60, m. 19 (1287).
[383] *EJ*, vi, no. 145. He was also suing as a clerk in 1280 and 1281: *EJ*, vi, nos. 275, 373, 438, 611, 781. In 1286 he acted as Ludham's attorney in a land plea in the London Hustings court: Corporation of London Records Office, Hustings Pleas of Land Roll 13, m. 6.
[384] Above, p.37.
[385] *EJ*, i, p. 172. See also *EJ*, ii, p. 162 and *EJ*, iii, p. 262.
[386] E 159/43, m. 8d.
[387] *EJ*, vi, no. 670; E 9/47, m. 8.
[388] *EJ*, ii, p. 81; E 159/67, m. 30d; E 13/23, m. 9.
[389] *EJ*, ii, p. 82.
[390] E 9/44, m. 2.

of Fulham;[391] *Henry of 'Strafford'* is specifically described as the clerk of master Henry de Bray in Michaelmas term 1283;[392] and the *Godfrey Rosamund,* mentioned as a clerk of Hauteyn in Michaelmas term 1284, was perhaps Bayfield's successor as Hauteyn's chief clerk.[393]

(iv) *The serjeants of the Exchequer of the Jews*

The serjeants of the Jewish Exchequer are, as a group, at least as obscure as the clerks, though again we know at least the names of several of them through incidental mentions on the plea-rolls, particularly through enrolments relating to litigation brought by them under the court's privilege jurisdiction.

Lawrence of the Exchequer can be found suing as a serjeant of the Exchequer of the Jews in 1273.[394] He was the hereditary usher not just of the Exchequer of the Jews but also of the Exchequer proper and of the Common Bench; and as such had the duty to keep order in each of the courts and was also responsible for the transmission of such of their orders as were of direct concern to the king, to the sheriffs and others concerned.[395] The duties, and the rights, of the ushers in the Jewish Exchequer seem normally to have been exercised through one or more deputies. The *Nicholas of Winchester* mentioned as a serjeant in 1266 was probably one such deputy;[396] the *Roger of Fleet* mentioned as a serjeant in 1280 and 1281 was certainly another.[397]

Other 'serjeants' are described as the serjeants of individual justices, and even when we find them using the privilege jurisdiction of the court, it may be wrong to conclude that their service to their master was one performed in the court and almost certainly wrong to conclude that their service was only performed there. *Hugh the trumpeter* may have blown his trumpet for Robert of Fulham when he was sitting in the Exchequer of the Jews, but must surely have also blown it for him elsewhere.[398] *John of Axbridge* is described in enrolments of 1281 and 1286 as the serjeant of Robert of Ludham.[399] He was probably already in Robert's service in 1274 when he was one of three men all associated with the court who stood surely for the outer sub-constable of the Tower of London.[400] John seems to have remained in Robert's service after the latter's disgrace and dismissal. In 1292 he was one of two sureties found by Robert in the Common Bench for a wager of law in denying a debt,[401] and in 1293 he was Robert's attorney for the making of the final concord on the sale of his Suffolk manor of Cookley.[402] John probably came, as his surname suggests, from Axbridge in Somerset. He can certainly be found acquiring property in the county in 1286,[403] though he also acquired other property the same year at Osmondiston in Norfolk, close to where some of his master's property interests lay.[404] John outlived his master and was still alive in 1301 when he was suing on a bond made in London in 1289 by Hugh de Brok for eight marks.[405] There seems to be only a single mention on the rolls of *William de Molins,* who is identified as a serjeant of muster Henry de Bray in an entry of 1283.[406]

A different kind of 'serjeant', the lawyer who spoke in court on behalf of individual litigants, is also found in the records of the Exchequer of the Jews. A Jewish serjeant, *Isaac of Southwark* was amerced in 1270 for being disavowed in what he had said as a serjeant (*narrator*) by his clients.[407] In a previous case of 1268 he had similarly been amerced for a 'false presentment', perhaps a disavowed count.[408] Another entry of 1270 shows him being excused an amercement as a 'serjeant of the Jews' (*serviens Judeorum*).[409] *Roger of Kinton* is mentioned in a number of entries in the plea rolls between 1270 and 1280 and several specifically identify him as a serjeant or former serjeant.[410] In one entry he is specifically described as the *serviens* of William of Middleton, the

[391] *EJ*, i, pp. 177-8. Fulham held land in the area of Essex of the 'Ginges' place names: above, p. 23. See also KB 26/206, m. 26.

[392] E 9/42, m. 8.

[393] E 9/45, m. 7.

[394] *EJ*, ii, pp. 99-100.

[395] T. Madox, *The History And Antiquities of the Exchequer* (London, 1711), pp. 718-23; *Cal. Inq. Post Mortem*, ii, no. 528.

[396] *EJ*, i, p. 135. Nicholas had been appointed a deputy usher of the main Exchequer in 1256, and is again mentioned as serving as such in 1268: Madox, *op. cit.*, p. 720.

[397] *EJ*, vi, no. 694: payment to Roger, as attorney of Lawrence, for the carrying of summonses; *EJ*, vi, no. 618: litigation brought by him as a serjeant of the Exchequer of the Jews; *EJ*, vi, no. 960: payment to Roger as serjeant of the Exchequer for carrying writs for the king to various counties of England. He is probably also the Roger the serjeant to whom various summonses were delivered, and who then transferred them to named messengers in *EJ*, vi, no. 703. In Hilary term 1282, the messengers included Simon of 'Beref', Roger Brocland, Richard of Ivingho, and Alan Motun: E 9/39, m. 2. In Lawrence of the Exchequer's inquisition post mortem of 1284 it is said that he had one deputy in the Exchequer of the Jews and received from him yearly for his fee 26 shillings and 8 pence: above, n. 395.

[398] *EJ*, i, p. 235.

[399] *EJ*, vi, no. 808; E 9/47, m. 5. ('Axeby' is clearly a clerical error).

[400] *EJ*, ii, p. 187.

[401] CP 40/92, m. 64d.

[402] CP 25(1)/216/42, no. 6.

[403] *Somerset Fines*, p. 265.

[404] CP 25(1)/160/113, no. 341.

[405] CP 40/136, m. 165. He is probably not the same as the John of Axbridge, vicar of Yeovil in Somerset, mentioned in litigation of 1291: CP 40/87, m. 50.

[406] E 9/43, m. 1.

[407] *Select Pleas*, pp. 53-4.

[408] *EJ*, i, p. 70. The original (E 9/9, m. 2d) reads: *'Et Isac de Suwerk' attornatus predicti Tony pro falsa presentacione in misericordia.'* Although described as his attorney, his function seems to have been that of a serjeant.

[409] *EJ*, i, p. 245.

[410] *EJ*, i, p. 262; *EJ*, ii, pp. 15, 77, 91, 110, 121, 143, 179, 213, 219, 233, 252; *EJ*, iii, pp. 148, 243; *EJ*, v, no. 99 (former serjeant); *EJ*, v, no. 232; *EJ*, vi, nos. 94, 122, 175, 332, 421, 428, 586, 677.

keeper of rolls and writs.[411] He may indeed have been his servant but, if so, he seems also to have been a serjeant in the other sense as well, to judge from a case of 1273, which does not describe him as a serjeant but does show him acting as one, seeking a 'salary' for service done to the earl of Gloucester and bringing an action for defamation against Samuel son of Aaron, who had alleged that he had taken six pence to trick a Christian in a plea involving forty marks.[412] There also survive two law reports of pleadings in unidentified cases probably in the Exchequer of the Jews from the later 1270s or 1280s. One gives no names to serjeants or justices; the other shows two other Christian serjeants pleading for the litigants.[413]

There remain a number of other serjeants of the Exchequer of the Jews mentioned in the records who cannot be assigned for certain to any of these groups.[414]

(v) *The Jewish officials of the Exchequer of the Jews*

During the 1230s and 1240s there are a number of references to the *presbiter Judeorum* as 'residing' or 'sitting' at the Exchequer of the Jews,[415] terms commonly used to refer to one of the officials of an institution fulfilling his official duties there. From further references to the *presbiter Judeorum* in 1249 and 1252 it can be deduced that at that time it was still considered that he possessed the status of a justice of the Exchequer of the Jews.[416] It was still remembered in 1273 that when Hagin son of master Mosse had become *presbiter Judeorum* in 1258 he had sworn 'to give faithful advice to the king's Justices [of the Jews] and to expound the king's rights'[417] and he was to claim in the same year that the council of Henry III had promised to pardon his tallage as a reward for the profits he had made for the king.[418] A series of entries on the plea-rolls in 1273-4 relating to the deaths of Sampson son of Meyr and his son Cresse at Farningham in Kent suggest that the *presbiter Judeorum* may have retained some functions at the Exchequer of the Jews in connection with the initiation of proceedings relating to the killings of Jews.[419] There is, however, no reference in this period to the *presbiter Judeorum* as 'sitting in' or 'residing at' the Jewish Exchequer or having the status of a Justice there and it seems reasonable to conclude from this that his role in the Exchequer of the Jews was much smaller than it had been earlier in the century. It is perhaps symptomatic of that diminution that when Hagin son of Deulecresse succeeded Hagin son of master Mosse as *presbiter Judeorum* in 1281 it was the Barons of the Exchequer and not the Justices of the Jews who were instructed to admit him to his office; and that the appointment was noted on the Exchequer memoranda roll for Easter term 1281 but not recorded on the surviving roll of the Exchequer of the Jews for the relevant term.[420]

When Aaron of York had been appointed *presbiter Judeorum* in 1236 it was ordered that the rolls of his predecessor be handed over to him;[421] and when his successor, Elias le Eveske, was appointed in 1243, orders were given not just for Aaron's rolls to be delivered to him, but that he be allowed to keep his own 'counter-roll' of proceedings in the Exchequer of the Jews thereafter.[422] It seems probable that both Aaron and Elias had employed Jewish clerks for the writing of their rolls, but the first specific mention of a Jewish clerk with responsibility not

[411] *EJ*, ii, p. 121.

[412] *Select Pleas*, pp. 70-1.

[413] These are to be published in either volume III or IV of my *The Earliest English Law Reports* as 75 Exc. Jews 1 and 72-86 Exch. Jews.1. The two justices mentioned in the second report are Hauteyn and Lovetot. Lovetot may be a mistake for Ludham, but it may also be that John de Lovetot, a Common Bench justice, sat in with Hauteyn in the Jewish Exchequer for the hearing of this case. The two serjeants mentioned are 'Bradeford', perhaps the Robert of Bradfield who is found as a serjeant in reports of cases in Bench and in Eyres during the 1270s and 1280s, and 'Gosfe', probably the Richard of Gosfield, who is found as a serjeant in reports of cases in the Common Bench and in Eyres from the 1270s to the late 1290s.

[414] e.g. (1) *Nigel of Chatham: EJ*, i, pp. 290, 306. He is probably the Nigel the serjeant also mentioned in *EJ*, ii, pp. 12, 48, 174, 243. See also E 159/50, m. 3; E 13/4, m. 2d; *EJ*, ii, p. 187; *EJ*, iii, p. 93; (2) *Roger of Folkestone: EJ*, vi, no. 389; (3) *William de la Hay:* E 9/42, m. 1d; E 9/44, m. 3d; (4) *John of London:* E 9/47, mm. 4, 8.

[415] *Close Rolls, 1234-7*, pp. 243, 408; *Close Rolls, 1242-7*, pp. 51, 163. On the *presbiter Judeorum* see Roth, *History of the Jews in England*, pp. 30-1, 112; Richardson, *English Jewry under Angevin Kings*, pp. 121-2.

[416] *Close Rolls, 1247-51*, pp. 163, 165 (together); *Close Rolls, 1251-3*, p. 271.

[417] *Select Pleas*, p. 73.

[418] E 159/47, m. 5.

[419] *EJ*, ii, pp. 44-5, 186, 249.

[420] E 159/54, m. 6: '*Baronibus pro Hagino filio Deulacres.* Sciatis quod ad instanciam carissime consortis nostre Alianore regine Anglie et per assensum communitatis Judeorum nostrorum Anglie volumus et concedimus pro nobis et heredibus nostris quod Haginus filius Deulacres judeus London' habeat et teneat tota vita sua officium presbiteratus Judeorum predictorum libere, quiete et integre cum omnibus pertinenciis, libertatibus et liberis consuetudinibus ad eundem presbiteratum pertinentibus sicut Haginus filius magistri Mossei quondam judeus London' defunctus vel alius ante ipsum officium illud prius tenuit, prout in litteris nostris patentibus quas inde habet plenius continetur. Et ideo vobis mandamus quod ipsum Haginum ad officium illud admittatis et ea que ad officium illud pertinent liberetis eidem habenda sicut dictus Haginus ea habuit in forma predicta. Teste me ipso apud Westm' .xviij. die Maii anno regni nostri nono'. For a transcript of the relevant Patent Roll entry see H.P. Stokes, *Studies in Anglo-Jewish History* (Jewish Historical Society, 1913), p. 247 (but reading in line 3 'instanciam' not 'instantians', in line 6 "Deulacres' not 'Deulecres', in line 15 'si quid' not 'si quis' (though this should be emended to 'si quis'), in lines 20-21 'Teste ut supra' for the whole sentence). The letters patent were also enrolled on a plea roll recording proceedings in the London hustings: Corporation of London Records Office, Hustings Pleas of Land Roll 10, m. 14.

[421] *Close Rolls, 1234-7*, p. 408.

[422] *Close Rolls, 1242-7*, p. 51.

just for the writing but for also for the custody of the *rotulus regis Judaicus*, the king's Jewish roll, (which must be the roll made for the *presbiter Judeorum*) is in November 1252, when Cresse son of master Mosse was mentioned as holding this post.[423] His immediate predecessor in that post may have been the Jewish convert, Henry of Winchester, appointed in October 1252, though this appointment may not have been effective. The terms of that appointment indicate that the plea-roll compiled for the *presbiter Judeorum* was in Hebrew and that the same clerk who was responsible for writing the roll was also responsible for writing starrs.[424] There is again mention of a plea-roll written in Hebrew in 1259;[425] and the Vives who was then responsible for it is perhaps to be identified with the Vives le Chantur who was rewarded in 1267 for his past service in the Exchequer of the Jews.[426]

During the late 1240s and early 1250s there were also a number of other Jewish clerks at work in the Exchequer of the Jews. *Jacob son of Flurye* was appointed a clerk there in April 1246;[427] is mentioned as holding office there in 1249 and 1251;[428] and was perhaps dismissed as the result of an accusation made against him by the *presbiter Judeorum* in 1252.[429] In 1249 *Abraham son Vives* was appointed a clerk of the Exchequer of the Jews and also as chirographer of the chest at London.[430] It is possible, though not certain, that one of these two clerks acted as the king's Jewish escheator. We hear of this position for the first time in July 1276, when *Benedict of Winchester* was appointed to it. The letters close notifying the Justices of the Jews of his appointment speak of the position as one which had been vacant since the death of Henry III, but also as though such an official had been a normal part of the staff of the Exchequer of the Jews prior to then. The escheator's duties were said to be in connection with lands and chattels coming into the king's ownership through the death or wrongdoing of individual Jews or for other reasons.[431] Presumably he was required to alert the Exchequer of the Jews to such death and forfeitures, and organize the local enquiries held into the possessions of the Jews concerned. Benedict of Winchester was also appointed in the same year as the Jewish collector of the queen's gold.[432] In 1252 *Jacob le Eveske* had been acting in that same capacity,[433] though he is also described at the same time as a clerk of the king.[434] Jacob is known to have held an unnamed position in the Exchequer of the Jews in 1249. Perhaps he was already then keeper of the queen's gold.[435] In 1274, the post was held by *Jacob of Oxford.* [436]

Money was paid at the Exchequer of the Jews in 1273 to master Elias and to Sampson son of Sampson the clerk, as though they were officials of the institution, but if so, the offices which they held are not now known.[437] There seem to be no later references to them or others - except for the persons already mentioned - as clerks or officials of the Exchequer of the Jews.

It seems reasonable to conclude, therefore, that although members of the Jewish community were not entirely excluded by this period from playing any role in the running of the Exchequer of the Jews, that role was much diminished by comparison with that played by members of the community in the 1240s and 1250s. The *presbiter Judeorum* had ceased to be regarded as an official of the Exchequer of the Jews; the Hebrew plea-roll had ceased, it seems, to be compiled; there ceases to be much evidence of Jewish clerks or officials active in the work of the Exchequer of the Jews. These changes are, it seems, not unconnected with the other changes that were taking place during this period and which worsened the position of members of the Jewish community in England. They are, like them, in a wider context, to be explained in terms of an increasing tide of anti-Jewish sentiment which was to culminate in the expulsion of the whole Jewish community from England in 1290.

423 *Close Rolls, 1251-3*, p. 271.

424 *Ibid.*, p. 164.

425 *Chartulary of the Priory of Boxgrove*, ed. L. Fleming (Sussex Record Soc., 59: 1960), p. 44.

426 *Close Rolls, 1264-8*, p. 285.

427 *Close Rolls, 1242-7*, p. 415.

428 *Close Rolls, 1247-51*, pp. 177-8.

429 *Close Rolls, 1251-3*, p. 233.

430 *Close Rolls, 1247-51*, p. 175.

431 C 54/93, m. 7 (=*Cal. Close Rolls, 1272-9*, pp. 302-3): '*Pro Benedicto de Winton' Judeo.* Rex justiciariis suis ad custodiam Judeorum assignatis salutem. Quia accepimus quod dominus Henricus rex pater noster habere solebat in scaccario suo Judeorum quendem judeum intendentem officio escaetarie de tenementis et catallis que ad ipsum patrem nostrum accidere deberent per mortem vel transgressionem Judeorum vel quacumque alia racione, et quod nos nullum judeum seu alium adhuc habemus nec habuimus post mortem ejusdem patris nostri qui officio predicto intendat, propter quod damnum non modicum hactenus sustinuimus, ut accepimus, nos, indempnitati nostre prospici volentes in hac parte, assignavimus Benedictum de Winton' judeum ad officium predictum exequendum in forma predicta. Et ideo vobis mandamus quod, accepto ab eodem sacramento corporali quod fideliter se habebit in officio predicto quamdiu steterit in eodem, ipsum Benedictum ad officium illud admittatis in forma predicta. Teste rege apud Westm' .xix. die Julii'.

432 E 159/50, m. 8d.

433 *Close Rolls, 1251-3*, p. 271.

434 *Ibid.*, p. 143.

435 *Close Rolls, 1247-51*, pp. 177-8.

436 E 159/48, m. 7.

437 *EJ*, ii, pp. 13, 48-52.

IV *The supervision of the Exchequer of the Jews*

How far was the Exchequer of the Jews subject to external scrutiny, supervision and control? Certain aspects of the work of the Exchequer of the Jews, in which it was only able to become engaged after receiving prior authorisation from the King through Chancery, have already been discussed.[1] This section will examine the various ways in which the Exchequer of the Jews was subject to the control and supervision of a different part of the government apparatus, the main Exchequer.[2]

(i) *The accountability of the Justices of the Jews to the Exchequer*

Although the evidence appears to indicate that in the early thirteenth century revenues arising out of the work of the Exchequer of the Jews or collected under its supervision were paid into, and retained in, a separate Treasury,[3] such moneys seem by mid-century to have been paid into the ordinary Exchequer of Receipt along with other royal revenues.[4] One consequence, however, of Henry III's grant of the Jewry of England and of all of its profits for a three year period in June 1262 to his son Edward,[5] seems to have been that these moneys ceased to be paid into the Exchequer of Receipt and were paid instead to receivers acting on Edward's behalf, perhaps to the Justices of the Jews themselves. The withdrawal of revenues collected by the Exchequer of the Jews from the Exchequer of Receipt appears to have continued even after the three year period was over, with some, and possibly all, of these revenues being received initially by the Justices of the Jews and only subsequently being paid over into the King's Wardrobe, not into the Exchequer of Receipt.[6] Early in 1269 the Justices of the Jews received an instruction to return to the practice of paying over all money received from fines, amercements and other issues of the Exchequer of the Jews to the treasurer and chamberlains of the Exchequer, with the money being earmarked for the works at Westminster, but the supposition was still that they and not the Exchequer of Receipt, would be the initial receivers of the money.[7] Since all, or at least a substantial proportion, of the profits of the king's Jewry had passed through the hands of the Justices of the Jews, it is hardly suprising to find the king, apparently on the advice of his council, ordering the Barons of the Exchequer late in 1268 to hear the accounts of the Justices of the Jews for the issues of the Jewry from the time of their appointment up to Martinmas 1268.[8] Renewed attempts were made in 1272 to secure accounts from all those Justices of the Jews who had held office since 1265.[9]

With the appointment of Hauteyn and Ludham as Justices of the Jews early in 1273 there appears to have been a return to the practice of all, or almost all, of the

[1] Above, pp. 11, 14.

[2] It should also be noted that there is no evidence from this period of the Exchequer of the Jews being placed under the general supervision of a particular individual with 'superior care' of the Jewry in England like Peter des Rivaulx in 1232 (*Cal. Charter Rolls*, i, p. 163) or John Mansel in 1261 (*Cal. Pat. Rolls, 1258-66*, p. 156).

[3] Richardson, *op. cit.*, pp. 136-7.

[4] The evidence for this is mainly negative. It is the absence of any authorisations for payments from a separate Jewish treasury. In 1250 the king clearly expected that it would be the treasurer and chamberlains who would be in receipt of income from the Exchequer of the Jews: *Close Rolls, 1247-51*, pp. 255-6.

[5] *Cal. Pat. Rolls, 1258-66*, p. 233. Edward subsequently granted his interest in the profits of the Jewry and of the Exchequer of the Jews to merchants from Cahors (*Ibid.*, pp. 263, 283) but seems to have recovered it by 1265, just in time to lose it again after his escape from the control of Simon de Montfort: *Close Rolls, 1264-8*, pp. 32, 52, 62.

[6] *Cal. Pat. Rolls, 1266-72*, p. 191. See also *EJ*, i, p. 149 (order for money to be paid directly into the wardrobe).

[7] *Cal. Pat. Rolls, 1266-72*, p. 317. For orders for money to be levied and paid over to the Justices issued after 1269 see *EJ*, i, pp. 265, 268, 269, 311, 312.

[8] *Close Rolls, 1268-72*, pp. 3-4 [= E 159/43, m. 4] (8 November 1268). The current justices were instructed to appear on 7 December 1268 to render their account. A former justice, William of Orlestone, was also told to be there: E 159/43, m. 4d. Another former justice, John le Moyne, appointed an attorney to render account for him during that same Michaelmas term: E 159/43, m. 18. The account had still not been heard in Easter term 1269 when an order was issued to enforce the appearance of Orlestone and he was allowed to appoint an attorney to render an account on his behalf: E 159/43, mm. 11d, 18d.

[9] E 159/46, mm. 7d, 8; E 159/47, mm. 2d, 3, 4d. No account has been traced. The latest reference to an attempt to secure one is an adjournment given to the former Justices from Easter to Michaelmas term in 1273.

revenues collected through the Exchequer of the Jews being paid directly into the Exchequer of Receipt.[10] It is therefore, at first sight at least, a little surprising to find Hauteyn and Ludham again being required in 1286 to render an account at the Exchequer of their period as Justices of the Jews.[11] It seems clear, however, from the record of proceedings against them that, although Hauteyn was being called to account for money allegedly received by him in 1283 when he had been acting on a special commission and not *ex officio* as a Justice of the Jews,[12] the main focus of interest in the accounting process was not on the moneys received by the Justices but on their stewardship of the bonds belonging to the king which had been lodged in the treasury of the Exchequer of the Jews.[13] At the beginning of their period as Justices Hauteyn and Ludham had been given the management and control of all of these royal assets of which a full inventory had just been made.[14] Their records ought to have contained a note of all subsequent additions to the Exchequer of Jews treasury and the authority by which any of the bonds was withdrawn, whether on payment or when granted to some third party or when shown to have been quitclaimed. The accounting process was to ensure that the Justices had managed the king's bonds honestly and not defrauded him of revenue through unauthorised withdrawals.[15]

There is no trace in the records of the last Justices of the Jews, Carleton and Leicester, being required to provide any similar account of their period as justices.

(ii) *The trial of Justices of the Jews for misconduct*

As well as being liable to render their accounts at the Exchequer, it was also at the Exchequer that the justices of the Jews were liable to be tried for any alleged misconduct while in office.[16] Both trials of master William of Watford for misconduct in 1272 were conducted by the Treasurer and Barons of the Exchequer and in the Exchequer, though for one of them they were reinforced by a number of justices from other royal courts.[17] The trial of Hauteyn and Ludham in 1286 was also conducted in the Exchequer by the Treasurer and Barons, though again they were 'reinforced', this time by the regent as well as by various members of the judiciary.[18] Both sets of trials were closely connected with the accounting of the Justices concerned: indeed, in the case of Hauteyn and Ludham it is difficult to distinguish their trial for misconduct from the hearing of their accounts. In Watford's case, the misconduct alleged was against private individuals but may have been tried when and where it was because it was normal practice to allow private individuals to make accusations of official misconduct at the same time as those liable to account were rendering their accounts at the Exchequer.[19]

(iii) *The transfer of cases from the Exchequer of the Jews to the Exchequer*

A less dramatic way in which the main Exchequer supervised and controlled the Exchequer of the Jews during the last quarter century of its existence was through the rehearing of individual cases which had previously been heard in the Exchequer of the Jews. This practice appears to have come into use only in and after the year 1267.[20] It led to the rehearing of over twenty cases by the Exchequer between 1268 and 1286. The cases reviewed in this way included litigation about title to land,[21] alleging detinue of chattels,[22] alleging various kinds of trespass including several relating to the alleged forgery of

[10] During 1273 and 1274 some small payments for writs and other payments in the nature of *oblata* were still being made to the justices and other officials of the Exchequer of the Jews: *EJ*, ii, pp. 11-13, 48-52, 102-5, 144-5, 173-4. For still later evidence of small sums being paid directly to the Justices and other officials see *EJ*, vi, nos. 647, 678, 957, 960. For receipt rolls of the main Exchequer of Receipt specifically devoted to income from the Exchequer of the Jews for this period see E 401/1574-1582.

[11] *Select Cases ... King's Bench*, vol. I, pp. clv-clix. Although the Exchequer was reinforced by outside justices for the hearing of the account it seems to have been the Treasurer and Barons whose primary responsibility it was to do so.

[12] Above, p. 36 and note 292.

[13] The whole process of accounting was probably initiated by an order of 1284 to the Justices of the Jews telling them to appear at the Exchequer on a day to be fixed by the Treasurer and Barons to inform them about debts owed to the King at the Exchequer of the Jews: *Cal. Close Rolls, 1279-1288*, p. 256.

[14] E 101/249/11.

[15] There is no evidence that master Henry de Bray was required to play any part in the process of accounting, despite his position as a Justice of the Jews.

[16] Charles Gross suggested in a paper on 'The Exchequer of the Jews of England in the Middle Ages' published in *Papers read at the Anglo-Jewish Historical Exhibition at the Royal Albert Hall, London, 1887* (London, 1888) (at p. 176) that the Exchequer of the Jews was merely a department of the great Exchequer and that its justices possessed the status of Barons of that institution. He cited no authority for either assertion. There is a reference on the Memoranda Roll for 1266-7 concerning the attack made on Robert of Fulham in Westminster Hall to Fulham and his fellow-Justices being *de gremio scaccarii* (E 159/42, m. 3d) but this is an isolated refence and seems to mean only that they had the status of Exchequer officials, not that of Barons.

[17] Above, pp. 33-35.

[18] Above, pp. 35-38.

[19] *Select Cases in the Exchequer of Pleas*, ed. H. Jenkinson and B.E.R. Fermoy (Selden Soc. 48: 1931), pp. xciii-xciv, cii-cviii.

[20] The earliest reference to the procedure seems to be in Michaelmas 1267 when Isaac of Warwick is recorded as paying ten bezants for a case between himself and William 'de Dunesle' in the Exchequer of the Jews to be heard and determined before the Treasurer and Barons of the Exchequer: E 159/42, m. 5; *EJ*, i, pp. 146-7, 151.

[21] E 159/43, m. 2 (cf. *EJ*, i, p. 147); E 159/59, m. 17d.

[22] E 159/42, m. 21d; E 159/46, m. 1 (cf. *EJ*, i, pp, 245, 310).

chirographs,[23] one privilege suit,[24] and pleas of debt,[25] and account.[26] Cases might be reviewed while still pending in the Exchequer of the Jews for allegedly excessive delays,[27] for alleged procedural errors,[28] or without cause shown.[29] They could also be evoked to the Exchequer after final judgment on the grounds of unspecified errors.[30] The normal procedure was for the Justices of the Jews to be summoned into the Exchequer to appear in person bringing with them the 'record and process' of the case being reviewed, probably the original rolls containing the relevant entries plus related writs.[31] Other members of the judiciary were also sometimes associated with the Treasurer and Barons for this aspect of their supervisory jurisdiction over the Exchequer of the Jews.[32] This review procedure is in marked contrast with the procedure normally followed when King's Bench reviewed cases originally heard in the Common Bench or in the Eyre. It normally heard such cases only after final judgment had been given and the justices concerned were not required to attend the review in person.

These different ways in which the Exchequer supervised the work of the Exchequer of the Jews are but part of a much broader picture of the subordination of the Exchequer of the Jews to the main Exchequer. Another clear indication of that subordinate status came with the enactment of the statute of Jewry of 1275. Despite its overwhelming importance for the Exchequer of the Jews no text of the statute was sent by Chancery to that institution. What happened instead was that a copy was sent to the Exchequer and that institution later instructed, almost as an afterthought, to make and send a copy on to the Exchequer of the Jews.[33]

23 E 159/43, m. 8 (cf. *EJ*, i, pp. 160-1); E 159/48, m. 9 (cf. *EJ*, ii, pp. 136, 138-9, 191, 196, 198); E 13/3, mm. 9d, 12d (cf. *EJ*, ii, pp. 139-40, 193-4, 200, 213-14, 218, 258 and *Select Pleas etc.*, pp. 83-4); E 13/3, m. 17 (cf. *EJ*, iii, pp. 22, 141); E 368/50, m. 1d (cf. *EJ*, ii, pp. 227, 229-30, 258, 298; *EJ*, iii, pp. 83, 148).

24 E 13/3, m. 5 and E 159/49, m. 2d (cf. *EJ*, ii, pp. 29, 40, 88-9, 96-8, 130, 195, 205, 211, 214, 230, 239).

25 *EJ*, i, p. 266 (cf. *EJ*, i, pp. 219, 221, 227); E 13/2, m. 9d and E 159/49, m. 13 (cf. *EJ*, ii, pp. 134, 253, 290-1; *EJ*, iii, pp. 152-3); E 159/49, m. 9d (cf. *EJ*, ii, pp. 2, 89, 231, 238); E 13/5, m. 18 and E 13/6, mm. 3, 10 (cf. *EJ*, i, pp. 188-90, 221, 281, 298-9; *EJ*, ii, pp. 6, 15, 91, 120, 260, 261, 285; *EJ*, iii, pp. 31-2, 68, 167, 259); E 13/9, mm. 14, 14d, 17, 19 (cf. *EJ*, vi, nos. 2, 49, 57, 76, 114, 119, 196, 197, 253, 344, 350, 665, 667, 671, 899, 901, 921, 923, 924, 925, 977); E 159/57, m. 4d.

26 Above, n. 20; E 159/50, m. 1 (cf. *EJ*, i, p. 266) cf. also two other pleas relating to allegedly unjustified measures to enforce the payment of debts: E 159/44, m. 5 (cf. *E.J.*, i, p. 227) and E 13/9, m. 8 and E 368/53, m. 8d. One 'case' evoked to the Exchequer related to the alleged failure of the Justices of the Jews to act on an order for the attermination of a debt: E 159/42, m. 21d.

27 E 159/42, m. 21d; E 13/3, m. 17.

28 E 159/43, mm. 2, 8; E 13/3, m. 5; ?E 13/5, m. 18.

29 E 13/9, m. 14.

30 The clearest examples are E 159/46, m. 1; E 159/50, m. 1.

31 For an entry which appears to envisage them bringing the original records relating to a case see E 159/42, m. 21d. Two entries appear to envisage them sending rather than bringing the relevant records: E 159/46, m. 1 and E 13/2, m. 9d.

32 *Cal. Close Rolls, 1272-9*, pp. 463-4 (and E 13/5, m. 18); E 13/9, m. 8. On at least one occasion a case removed out of the Exchequer of the Jews into the main Exchequer was subsequently handed over to one of the Justices of the Jews (Hauteyn) and one of the barons of the Exchequer (Cobham) to be determined: *Cal. Pat. Rolls, 1272-81*, pp. 188, 236. For the association of Ralph de Hengham, the chief justice of King's Bench, and William of Brunton, a puisne justice of the Common Bench, with the Justices of the Jews in 1283 to determine two related cases of particular difficulty see *Cal. Pat. Rolls, 1281-92*, p. 81.

33 E 159/50, m. 3d: 'Quia rex vult quod statuta que de Judaismo nuper fecit publicari et eis sub magno sigillo transmitti per justiciarios ad custodiam Judeorum assignatos teneantur et firmiter observentur, et ideo rex mandat baronibus quod statuta illa scribi et sigillo scaccarii predicti signari et ea sic scripta et signata prefatis justiciariis liberent etc.' It was also the Exchequer and not the Exchequer of the Jews that was entrusted with the enforcement of the 1269 statute of Jewry and in particular its provisions relating to fee-rents: *Close Rolls, 1268-1272*, p. 268; E 159/45, m. 8A.

V *The Records of the Exchequer of the Jews*

The main record of the activities of the Exchequer of the Jews is the series of plea rolls. From at least 1259 onward, and very possibly from the beginnings of the existence of the Exchequer of the Jews, separate plea rolls were made for each of the justices of the court.[1] In this respect, at least, the Exchequer of the Jews bears a closer resemblance to the main common law courts (the Common Bench, King's Bench and the Eyre), where a similar practice was followed, than to the main Exchequer, where only a single plea roll seems to have been compiled (by the chancellor of the Exchequer) and where Memoranda were recorded in only two sets of rolls compiled neither by nor for the Barons but by and for the two Remembrancers. At one time, proceedings in the Exchequer of the Jews had also been recorded in a counter-roll made for the *presbyter Judeorum*.[2] This is probably the same as the Hebrew plea roll mentioned in 1252 and 1259.[3] There is, however, no mention of such a roll being compiled in this last quarter-century of the existence of the Exchequer of the Jews and the practice of compiling such a roll had probably been discontinued in the early 1260s.

Internally, the plea rolls of this period are divided into a number of separate sections which can be characterised as follows

i) *pleas:* this is the section containing all entries relating to litigation in the Exchequer of the Jews other than litigation in which the king had either a direct or an indirect interest except for entries of essoins, the appointments of attorneys and adjournments *prece parcium*.

ii) *essoins:* a separate section from the time of the earliest surviving plea rolls recording formal excuses for non-appearance proffered on behalf of litigants.

iii) *attorneys and adjournments prece parcium:* from at least 1253 onwards there was a separate section on the rolls for the appointment of attorneys by litigants; by 1266 this section also contained a record of all adjournments of litigation made at the request of the parties.

iv) *starrs:* from at least 1244 onwards there was a separate section for the enrolment of all types of starr.

v) *memoranda:* by 1244 there was a separate section (not initially headed as such) containing entries of a more purely administrative nature plus all litigation of interest to the king.

Like other royal courts and departments the Exchequer of the Jews also kept as part of its records *writ files* containing all writs sent to or returned into the court. These included royal orders sent under the great seal to the Justices, which were the authority for various of their actions. They also included various writs issued in the king's name by the Exchequer of the Jews which had been returned into the court. Such writs were written by the clerks of the Justices and sealed with the seal of the Exchequer of the Jews,[4] which were sent out with orders to the addressee (normally the local sheriff) instructing him to take certain action and report back to the court on

[1] For evidence that in 1259 a separate roll was being made for each of the Justices see *Chartulary of the Priory of Boxgrove*, p. 44. The first term for which more than one roll survives is Trinity term 1273. These are now E 9/14 and 62. There are at least thirteen terms between 1273 and 1284 for which all or part of a second plea roll survives. For a full list of these and for an attempt to identify which were made for Hauteyn and which for his colleague Ludham see Appendix III. For Michaelmas term 1282 parts survive of three separate plea rolls. The third must have been made for master Henry de Bray.

[2] Such a roll is mentioned both in 1236 and in 1243: *Close Rolls, 1234-1237*, p. 408; *Close Rolls, 1242-1247*, p. 51.

[3] *Close Rolls, 1251-1253*, pp. 164, 271; *Chartulary of Boxgrove Priory*, p. 44.

[4] A separate seal of the Exchequer of the Jews is mentioned in 1244 and 1246: *EJ*, i, p. 60; *Close Rolls, 1242-1247*, p. 416. It was lost during the Barons' Wars and in 1267 the seal of Robert of Fulham, the senior justice, was being used on a temporary basis as a replacement for it: *EJ*, i, p. 148. It had been replaced by 1272 when it is mentioned in the inventory of the Treasury of the Exchequer of the Jews: E 101/249/15. This is presumably the seal which is referred to in the oath of the Christian chirographer of c. 1270 as being the seal known as the 'king's head' (*sigillo quod vocatur capud regis).* The complicated arrangements for mandates to be sent under the seal of the Exchequer of the Jews for sealing either in Chancery or in the main Exchequer which were prescribed in 1262 probably applied only during the period when the Exchequer of the Jews was in the hands of the Lord Edward and did not represent normal practice: *Close Rolls, 1261-4*, pp. 79-80.

what he had done. The Exchequer of the Jews was mainly interested in these reports which came into the court either endorsed on the writs themselves or attached to them, as the writs themselves instructed. This meant that the returns could be brief and succinct, for they did not need to rehearse the content of the writs on which they were endorsed or to which they were attached. Separate files or separate sections within files were allocated to royal orders under the great seal; to inquisitions returned into the court (writs requiring the holding of local jury inquiries returned with the jury's verdict); and to other writs returned into the court (*brevia placitabilia*).[5]

The Exchequer of the Jews also kept separate *Pipe Rolls* recording the accounts rendered by local sheriffs for those Jewish debts which were in the king's hands and which they had been required to collect. These rolls were similar to, though on a much smaller scale than, the Pipe Rolls of the great Exchequer and covered a number of years rather than just one.[6]

Despite the increased amount of care taken during this period to ensure that Justices and other officials of the Exchequer of the Jews handed in the records which had been in their custody when they left office,[7] a phenomenon also observable in the case of other courts during this period, almost the only records of the Exchequer of the Jews to survive are the plea rolls. Many even of these are now lost.[8] Despite the compilation of more than one plea roll each term no plea roll at all survives for almost half the terms when the Exchequer of the Jews is known to have held sessions during this period. The business of a further one-sixth of terms is recorded only on rolls which are clearly damaged or incomplete.[9] These losses are probably due to the normal archival hazards of fire, theft, water and rodents. One particular early fire that is known to have destroyed part of the records of this institution is that which took place on 29 March 1298 at the palace and abbey of Westminster.[10]

The document which tells us of this fire also provides valuable information as to where the records of the Exchequer of the Jews were then being held, the chapel of St Katharine in the infirmary of Westminster abbey. From there the surviving records were probably removed in the early 1320s to the Tower of London for the Stapledon array.[11] Most appear to have been returned to Westminster but, as was the case also with the plea rolls of the main common law courts, a certain number seem to have been left behind at the Tower.[12] It was only the plea rolls at the Tower that were known to or seen by William Prynne in the middle of the seventeenth century.[13] In the early nineteenth century the Exchequer of the Jews plea rolls then at Westminster were removed to the temporary repository at Carleton Ride and from there they were taken in a single box to the Stone Tower at Westminster Hall in 1847.[14] Between 1856 and 1858 these were again moved, this time to the new Public Record Office in Chancery Lane, from whence they have now been removed to what has now become The National Archives at Kew.[15]

When the first edition of the *List of Plea Rolls* was published in 1894 there were 47 rolls in the class of Exchequer of Jews Plea Rolls.[16] Between 1894 and 1910

5 *EJ*, ii, pp. 214-15. The *inquisiciones* were kept in termly sections or files: *EJ*, vi, nos. 43, 81, 682; the *brevia placitabilia* in return day sections or files: *EJ*, vi, no. 32.

6 A single membrane from such a roll for the counties of Bedfordshire and Buckinghamshire (which shared a single sheriff) covering the period 50 Henry III-2 Edward I is now E 101/249/17. The inventory of the Treasury of the Exchequer of the Jews made in December 1272 mentions two such rolls (*duo magni rotuli de diversis compotis vicecomitum*) plus two separate rolls of fines (*duo magni rotuli de finibus*): E 101/249/15. For further references to these rolls see *EJ*, ii, p. 272; *EJ*, iii, pp. 51-2.

7 For evidence that this concern achieved results see E 159/40, m. 4 (delivery to the justices in Jews in Michaelmas term 1265 by Robert of Creeping of one challenged charter plus writs and plea rolls for Easter and Trinity terms 1265); E 9/12, m. 4d (=*Select Pleas*, p. 68) (delivery to William of Middleton in Trinity term 1272 by William of Orlestone of plea rolls for Easter term 1258 and Hilary term 1266); E 159/47, m. 6 (delivery to the Justices of the Jews in Easter term 1273 by Ralph the son of Ralph of St Osyth's of one 'inventory' of the treasury of the Exchequer of the Jews and two plea rolls and for the prior measures to compel his appearance with these records see *EJ*, ii, p. 18); *EJ*, iii, pp. 274-5 (delivery to the Justices of the Jews and to Adam of Winchester in Trinity term 1276 of various records in the custody of William of Middleton).

8 Apart from a fragment of a Pipe Roll (above, note 6) and a small number of writs and returns which owe their preservation to the fact that they had been sent to Chancery and retained among its files. For examples of the latter see C 145/15, no. 13; C 145/17, no. 13; C 145/33, no. 3.

9 For full details see Appendix III. There were no proceedings in Easter term 1267: E 9/7, m. 1. Even so, the survival rate is much higher than for the period prior to 1265. This may in part be the consequence of the theft of records from the Exchequer of the Jews in 1260 (E 159/33, m. 10), but probably mainly reflects the much lower level of effort to ensure that records were handed into official custody during the earlier period.

10 C 260/14, no. 12. cf. *The History of the King's Works*, i, ed. R.A. Brown, H.M.Colvin and A.J. Taylor (London, 1963), p. 505.

11 On the Stapledon array see V.H. Galbraith, 'The Tower as an Exchequer record office in the reign of Edward II' in *Essays in Medieval History presented to T.F. Tout*, ed. A.G. Little and F.M. Powicke (Manchester, 1925), pp. 231-47.

12 The rolls in question appear to be the rolls which are now E 9/14 or 62, 37 or 66 and (possibly) 40B and 54.

13 W. Prynne, *A Short Demurrer to the Jewes Long Discontinued Barred Remitter into England* (London, 2nd. edition, 1656), part II, pp. 104-8, 93-6.

14 *Eleventh Annual Report of the Deputy-Keeper of Public Records* (1250), Appendix I, p. 24. In 1807 there were *rotuli Judeorum* of the reigns of king John and Henry III among the records in the Chapter House at Westminster: OBS 692, p. 37. It is not clear whether these included Plea Rolls or refers only to other records such as Receipt Rolls.

15 *Twentieth Annual Report of the Deputy-Keeper of Public Records* (1859), Appendix, p. 18.

16 OBS 696, p. 72.

the plea rolls which had remained at the Tower and which had then been mistakenly assigned to the classes of Curia Regis Rolls and De Banco Rolls were transferred to the class and four second rolls added from Miscellanea, bringing the total number of rolls in the class up to 56. The mistaken decision to combine some of these quite separate rolls recording proceedings of the same term, had reduced the number of rolls in the class to 48 by the time of the publication of the second edition of the *List of Plea Rolls* in 1910.[17] Additions from hitherto unsorted Miscellanea made between 1910 and 1933 brought the number of rolls up to 60 and in 1951 a further roll was transferred to this class from the class of Eyre etc. Rolls to which it had been mistakenly assigned.[18] In the mid 1970s further additions were made both to the class and to individual existing rolls from Miscellanea and the opportunity taken to separate out, as far as possible, the separate constituent elements of the composite rolls which had been created by the work of modern archivists. This brought the number of rolls in the class up to 69.[19] One further addition was made to the class in 1984 when an Exchequer of the Jews plea roll membrane was found in the class of Loose Membranes of Memoranda Rolls (E160).[20] The British Library also contains two rolls which have strayed out of official custody.[21]

[17] For fuller details of these additions and consolidations see Appendix IV.

[18] E 9/40B.

[19] For fuller details see Appendix IV.

[20] See Appendix IV.

[21] See Appendix III.

APPENDIX I

Justices of the Jews in office between Michaelmas term 1265 and Trinity term 1290

1. Robert of Fulham

appointment: Robert of Fulham and John le Moyne were not formally appointed until 5 December 1265 (*Cal. Pat. Rolls, 1258-66*, p. 517). Both were, however, already acting on 14 November 1265 (E 159/40, m. 4) and again on 24 November (*Cal. Pat. Rolls, 1266-72*, p. 191). They had probably acted for most, if not all, of Michaelmas term 1265.

dismissal: still in office in Hilary term 1272 (E 159/46, m. 6) but had been dismissed by 4 July 1272 (E 159/46, m. 7d). His final term in office was therefore either Hilary or Easter term 1272.

2. John le Moyne

appointment: see above under Robert of Fulham.

dismissal: probably removed from office towards the end of Hilary term 1266. When a standing order was made on 17 February 1266 for the payment of the annual fees of the Justices of the Jews it mentioned only Fulham and Esporun (*Cal. Liberate. Rolls, 1260-7*, pp. 200-1) and on the preceding 15 February he had been appointed as one of the two custodians of the see of Worcester (*Cal. Pat. Rolls, 1258-66*, p. 553). A roll made for him covering Hilary term 1266 (or possibly only part of that term) was in the possession of his successor, William of Orlestone, in 1272 (E 9/12, m. 4d).

3. Thomas Esporun

appointment: an undated appointment is recorded among the *communia* enrolled under Hilary term 1266 on the main Exchequer Memoranda Roll (E 159/40, m. 8). It was on 12 February 1266 that a replacement was appointed to a position he had held in the Exchequer of the Receipt, presumably because it had been vacated by his appointment as a Justice (*Cal. Lib. Rolls, 1260-7*, p. 198).

dismissal: master William of Watford was appointed to replace him on 20 January 1267 in time for the beginning of Hilary term (*Close Rolls, 1264-8*, p. 286). The order does not specifically remove Thomas from office and he seems in fact to have ceased acting as a Justice prior to this. A note on the bottom of a membrane of a plea roll for Trinity term 1266 (E 9/6, m. 3d) giving the names of the Justices suggests he had already ceased acting by then and a starr enrolled in Michaelmas term 1266 was said to have been enrolled before Orlestone and Fulham alone: *Starrs and Jewish Charters preserved in the British Museum, vol. I*, ed. I. Abrahams, H.P. Stokes and H. Loewe (Jewish Historical Society, 1930), p. 74 and cf. *Reading Abbey Cartularies I*, ed. B.R. Kemp (Camden 4th series, 31: 1986), no. 73, p. 89. A mandate enrolled on the Close Rolls in late December 1266 also refers to Orlestone and Fulham as though they were already by then the only serving justices: *Close Rolls, 1264-8*, p. 277.

4. William of Orlestone

appointment: was certainly acting as a justice by Trinity term 1266: E 9/6, m. 3d and V.D. Lipman, *The Jews of Medieval Norwich*, pp. 294-5 (July 1266). He was presumably appointed some time after 17 February 1266 as he is not mentioned in an order of that date for annual fees to be paid to the justices then in office: *Cal. Lib. Rolls, 1260-7*, pp. 200-1. On 27 October 1266 an order was given for the payment of a half-yearly fee to him in respect of Easter 1266: *Ibid.*, p. 242. In 1272 he surrendered a roll which had been made for John le Moyne in Hilary term 1266: E 9/12, m. 4d.

dismissal: was paid a half-yearly fee as a justice for Easter term 1268 (*Cal. Lib. Rolls, 1266-72*, no. 319) but by Michaelmas term 1268 was being described as a former justice: E 159/43, m. 4.

5. master William of Watford

appointment: was appointed to replace Thomas Esporun on 20 January 1267, in time for the start of Hilary term: *Close Rolls, 1264-8*, p. 286.

dismissal: still in office at the end of Hilary term 1272 since he attested a writ as a justice on 3 March 1272: *Cal. Inq. Misc.*, i, no. 396. He was under arrest and had almost certainly been removed from office by 10 July 1272: *Close Rolls, 1268-1272*, p. 492.

6. **William Pasket**

appointment: was acting as a justice by 7 May 1271 when he is so described in a starr of Manser son of Aaron enrolled on the rolls of the court *coram rege*: KB 26/201, m. 17.

dismissal: had ceased to be a justice by July 1272 when a scrutiny of the charters kept in the treasury of the Exchequer of the Jews on the Saturday before the feast of St Margaret (2 or 16 July) made in the presence of the Justices does not mention him: E 101/249/11.

7. **Fulk Peyforer**

appointment: was acting as a Justice by 15 July 1272: E 9/12, m. 4d.

dismissal: the death of Henry III on 16 November 1272 probably terminated his period of office.

8. **Ralph of St. Osyth's**

appointment: as Fulk Peyforer.

dismissal: as Fulk Peyforer, though it is possible that he predeceased Henry III (above, p. 32).

9. **Hamon Hauteyn**

appointment: was appointed on 27 or 28 January 1273: *Cal. Close Rolls, 1272-9*, p. 6; E 159/47, m. 4.

dismissal: was suspended from office on 28 June 1286, in the middle of Trinity term, but only definitively removed on 20 October 1286: *Sel. Cases in the Court of King's Bench, vol. I*, ed. Sayles, pp. clx-clix.

10. **Robert of Ludham**

appointment: as Hamon Hauteyn.

dismissal: as Hamon Hauteyn.

11. **master Henry de Bray**

appointment: was commissioned in October 1281 with Hauteyn and Ludham to open the chirograph chests and scrutinize them and transcribe the charters, starrs and muniments they contained with a view to levying what was owed to the king (probably on the bonds of fugitive and executed Jews). One of the three rolls was to go to the Exchequer, one to the Exchequer of the Jews and one to master Henry for delivery to the king: *Cal. Pat. Rolls, 1272-1281*, pp. 458, 459; E 159/55, m. 4. Payments made to him in November 1281 and in January 1282 in connexion with this work do not describe him as a justice of the Jews: C 62/58, m. 5; *Cal. Close Rolls, 1279-1288*, p. 146. However, in Easter term 1283 men described as a clerk and as a serjeant of master Henry are to be found suing in the Exchequer of the Jews under its privilege jurisdiction (E 9/43, m. 1; E 9/42, m. 8) and in a deed of 17 November 1283 he is described as a Justice of the Jews: *Cal. Close Rolls, 1279-88*, p. 146. The survival of parts of three plea rolls for Michaelmas term 1282 suggests that he was already then functioning as a Justice of the Jews: below, Appendix III.

dismissal: was paid as a Justice of the Jews between 12 and 15 Edward I (1283/4-1286/7): E 159/64, m. 16. From 24 February 1283 he also held the demanding position of escheator of England south of the Trent (*Cal. Pat. Rolls, 1281-92*, p. 58; *Cal. Fine Rolls*, i, p. 267) and a special commission issued to him on 10 August 1285 for the taking of recognisances of Christian debtors to Jews appears to imply that he was not then regarded as a Justice of the Jews (*Cal. Pat. Rolls, 1281-1292*, p. 128). He was, however, still being described as a Justice in December 1288 (E 13/12, m. 32d) and still possessed one of three keys to the treasury of the Exchequer of the Jews when arrested in 1290: E 159/66, m. 18.

12. **William of Carleton**

appointment: was paid a half-yearly fee as a Justice from Michaelmas 1286 onwards (C 62/63, m. 3) and was probably appointed when Hauteyn and Ludham were dismissed. He is already described as a Justice in a special gaol delivery session held at the Tower of London on 20 October 1286: JUST 3/36/1, m. 33.

dismissal: the last payment made to him was in respect of Michaelmas term 1290 when the Exchequer of the Jews ceased its operations: above, p. 2 and note 4.

13. **Peter of Leicester**

appointment: was paid a half-yearly fee as a justice from Michaelmas 1287: C 62/64, m. 4.

dismissal: as William of Carleton.

APPENDIX II

The trials of master William of Watford and his colleagues

I

E 159/46, m. 9

Lond' Midd' Essex'. In termino sancti Hillarii post mortem Pictavini filii Benedicti le Jofneue judei, qui debebat domino regi sexcies viginti libras, Robertus de Fuleham, magister Willelmus de Watford' et Willelmus Pasket [i]<tunc>[i] justiciarii ad custodiam Judeorum assignati, postquam Pictavinus le Fort et Isac de Norht', qui habent in uxores duas de filiabus et heredibus dicti Pictavini defuncti, finem fecerunt cum domino rege pro habendis catallis ejusdem defuncti, miserunt ad scaccarium quasdam cartas factas sub nominibus ipsius defuncti et quorundam christianorum inutiles ad recuperandum dictum debitum, propter quod barones de eodem scaccario injunxerunt eisdem justiciariis quod omnes cartas de debitis ipsius judei defuncti mitterent ad scaccarium, ut exinde eligere possent meliora debita ad opus domini regis pro debito suo; ita quod quadam die jovis fuit quedam pixis delata ad scaccarium coram thesaurario et baronibus per dictum Willelmum Pasket, Johannem le Ferrun et Johannem de Laufar' cirographarios christianos arche Lond' integra et cum una corigia integra et sigillata in anteriori parte ipius pixidis sigillo ejusdem Willelmi Pasket, qui tunc presens ibidem idem sigillum suum advocavit. Qua pixide coram eis aperta, invente fuerunt in ea decem et septem carte cum cera et una carta sine cera sub nominibus dicti judei et Johannis de Rocheford' militis de quodam debito quaterviginti et decem librarum, cujus data est decimo die Decembris anno regni regis terciodecimo, set suspiciosa fuit eo quod videbatur esse facta de novo percameno et quasi conculcata, confricata et inpulverata, et sic calumpniata fuit per Guidonem de Rocheford' tunc presentem, cujus avus fuit dictus Johannes de Rocheford', tanquam falsa, ut idem Wydo dicebat. Unde prefati barones, vocatis coram se dictis magistro Willelmo, Willelmo Pasket, Johanne et Johanne cyrographariis, Pictavino et Isac, Aron Crespin judeo cyrographario et Samueli serviente ipsius Aaron et prestito ab eis sacramento de veritate dicenda, examinaverunt eos singillatim de predicta carta suspecta. Et dictus magister Willelmus de Watford' recongnovit quod die veneris proxima ante dictum diem jovis quando scaccarium Judeorum claudi debuit, absente Roberto de Fuleham qui prius recesserat, orta fuit contentio inter ipsos et clericos de Judaismo pro quatuor denariis quod ipsi petebant pro deliberacione cujuslibet ipsarum decem et septem cartarum, et, commotus ex illa peticione injusta, posuit in ipsa pixide habente unam corrigiam de duabus peciis predicta .xvij. cartas tantum, et quod in nodo quod fuit in posteriori parte sigillavit eandem suo sigillo et in anteriori parte sigillo dicti Willelmi Pasket quasi eodem Willelmo invito set postmodum consenciente et eandem pixidem taliter sigillatam portavit secum eadem die in villam ad hospicium suum et fieri fecit ibidem per clericum suum quoddam breve domini regis et illud sigillo suo proprio sigillavit directum predictis cyrographariis, ut ipsam cum dictis decem et septem cartis tantum ponerent in predicta archa, mandans dicto Aaron quod ad se veniret et tradens ei eandem pixidem cum eodem brevi, set dicit quod de predicta carta calumpniata non debet esse suspectus eo quod pixis ille fuit in custodia ipsorum Aaron et Samuelis fere per octo dies. Idem vero Aaron juratus dicit se invite et per minas ipsius magistri recepisse ab eo illam pixidem et quod eam liberavit statim eidem Samueli deferendum dictis cyrographariis christianis, quia eadem hora oportuit ipsum exire villam cum Hagino domino suo. Dicit eciam quod recepit eam sigillatam sigillo Willelmi Pasket et cum una corrigia integra tantum. Et predictus Samuel juratus dicit illud idem. Et predicti Johannes et Johannes cyrographarii christiani jurati dicunt quod quando receperunt dictum pixidem deferendam ad scaccarium sigillata fuit sigillo dicti Willelmi Pasket et cum una corrigia integra, sicut predicti Aron et Samuel predixerunt. Dicit eciam idem Aaron quod, quando eam recepit, invenit in hospicio dicti magistri Willelmi dictos Pictavinum et Isac, ita quod suspicabatur sinistrum de illa pixide; ipsi autem Pictavinus et Isac jurati dixerunt quod de predicta suspecta carta nichil sciverunt nec per ipsam cartam aliquod debitum exigerunt nec exigere potuerunt.

Et quia postea in presencia thesaurarii et baronum de scaccario, Martini de Litlebir', Johannis de Cokefeud', Laurencii del Brok et aliorum domini regis fidelium per confessionem ipsius magistri Willelmi convictum est quod idem magister posuit in predicta pixide decem et septem cartas et pixidem illa sigillavit in parte posteriori sigillo suo et in parte anteriori sigillo Willelmi Pasket socii sui et pixidem illam [i]<cum predictis>[i] sigillis integris ad domum suam portavit et ibidem in absencia sociorum suorum [i]<et sine eorum assensu>[i] quandam litteram fieri fecit sub sigillo suo directam predictis cyrographariis ut eam ponerent in predicta archa, quod ei non licuit quia hujusmodi pixides liberande sunt secundum consuetudinem Judaismi cyrographariis christianis et non judeis cyrographariis, et non dicit quod aliquis alius posuit dictam cartam suspectam in dicta pixide quando habuit eam penes se nec quando fuit in custodia predictorum cyrographariorum, et preterea cum convictum est per predictos cyrographarios quod eam invenerunt sigillatam sigillo Willelmi Pasket tantum et cum una corigia integra et portata fuit ad scaccarium integra bene sigillata et cum una corrigia, sicut remansit quando magister Willelmus illam eodem sigillo signavit, et potuit amovisse sigillum suum proprium a posteriori parte ipsius pixidis, et non defendit se nec defendere potuit de predictis, consideratum est quod committeretur gaiole donec dominus rex aliud inde preceperit.

II

E 159/46, m. 9d

Suht'. Magister Willelmus de Watford', attachiatus ad respondendum Petro le Marchaunt filio Roberti de Mapeldorham de placito transgressionis, venit coram baronibus et idem Petrus similiter, qui queritur de eodem magistro Willelmo quod quando fuit justiciarius ad custodiam Judeorum assignatus nequiter, maliciose et ad exheredacionem ipsius Petri et per sedicionem prelocutam inter ipsum et Benedictum de Wynt' judeum scienter et sine assensu sociorum suorum justiciariorum posuit in thesauro domini regis quandam falsam cartam sine cera de debito .lxiiij. librarum factam sub nominibus dicti Roberti patris sui et Elye filii Chere judei et eandem cartam extraxit ab illo thesauro et per breve domini regis [i]<et>[i] liberavit eidem Benedicto judeo ponendam in archa cyrographariorum Judeorum apud Wynt', ita quod idem Benedictus ad sequelam suam habuit per vicecomitem seisinam terrarum, tenementorum, reddituum et catallorum predicti Petri in Mapeldorham a die sabbati [i]<proxima>[i] post Cineres anno etc. .lvj.º usque ad diem martis proximam ante festum sancti Barnabe apostoli anno eodem et eadem bona et catalla vastavit, ut in blado, equis, bobus et aliis, ad dampnum ipsius Petri ad valenciam .c. librarum. Et inde produxit sectam. Et quod hec predicta fecit verificabit per socios ejusdem magistri Willelmi et clericos de Judaismo tunc ibi presentes et alio modo secundum quod curia domini regis consideraverit.

Et predictus magister Willelmus defendit injuriam etc. et quicquid est contra pacem domini regis et omnem prodicionem et predictum dampnum. Et dicit quod predicta carta non est falsa set vera et bona, sicut illa que inventa fuit in thesauro domini regis et per ipsum et socios suos de eodem thesauro extracta et liberata predicto judeo per breve domini regis et de consensu sociorum. Et hoc paratus est verificare secundum quod curia domini regis consideraverit.

Et predictus Petrus dicit quod, desicut sequitur versus eum quod posuit predictam cartam in thesauro domini regis, sicut predictum est, et idem magister ad hoc non respondit nec respondere voluit, petit judicium de eo sicut de indefenso.

Et idem magister de posicione dicte carte in thesauro noluit plus dicere quam dixerat ante. Et quia barones consulte voluerunt procedere in dicto negocio datus est dies eidem magistro Willelmo a die sancti Michaelis in .xv. dies per manucapcionem contentam in memorandis ad faciendum quod de jure facere debebit. Et idem Petrus habet eundem diem ad idem. Quem diem uterque admisit.[1]

Postea venerunt ad eundem diem. Et peciit predictus Petrus quod idem magister responderet ad posicionem predicte carte in thesauro. Et respondit quod non posuit illam set quod tanquam vera et bona extracta fuit de thesauro de consensu sociorum suorum [et] liberata Benedicto predicto per breve regis. Et cum quesitum esset ab eodem Petro qualiter vellet verificare quod ipsa carta falsa est et quod idem magister tanquam [falsam][2] posuit eam in thesauro et quod eam liberavit dicto judeo sine assensu sociorum suorum respondit quod per illos qui tunc fuerunt justiciarios et [socios suos][3] et clericos et servientes ad scaccarium Judeorum et eciam per alios per quos rei veritas melius sciri poterit. Et predictus magister dixit quod ea que pro se proposuit similiter verificentur exceptis adversariis suis.[4]

Postea venit dictus Willelmus ad diem predictum coram etc. per manucapcionem predictam. Et quia tunc latenter recessit sine licencia baronum resummonita fuit [i]<loquela post mortem domini Henrici regis et>[i] mandatum fuit viceomiti Essex' quod distringeret eum per terras etc., set idem vicecomes venit et dixit quod non habuit laicum tenementum in balliva sua per quod potuit distringi, unde mandatum fuit episcopo Bathon' et Wellensi quod distringeret eum etc., ita quod haberet eum coram etc. a die sancti Martini in .xv. dies, qui returnavit quod sequestraverat ejus beneficium et quod ulterius inde nichil facere potuit eo quod inveniri non potuit in diocesa sua nec scivit ubi morabatur. Et ideo consideratum fuit quod scriberetur vicecomiti Sumers' in forma subscripta: 'Edwardus dei gracia etc. vicecomiti Sumers' salutem. Cum pluries mandaverimus Bathon' et Wellensi episcopo quod venire faceret coram baronibus nostris de scaccario apud Westm' magistrum Willelmum de Watford' clericum suum auditurus recordum et judicium suum de loquela que fuit in scaccario domini Henrici regis patris nostri inter Petrum de Mapeldorham querentem et ipsum Willelmum de quadam carta sub nominibus Roberti de Mapeldorham, patris predicti Petri, cujus heres ipse est, et Elye filii Chere judei facta, quam idem Willelmus dum fuit justicarius ejusdem

1 *there is a change of ink at this point*
2 *MS. reads* falsa
3 *MS. reads* socii sui
4 *there is a further change of ink at this point.*

<patris>[5] nostri ad custodiam Judeorum assignatus falso et in decepcionem curie ejusdem patris nostri posuit in archam thesauri ad exheredacionem ipsius Petri, ut dicitur, idem episcopus mandavit [i]<prefatis baronibus nostris in octabis sancti Martini quod beneficia predicti Willelmi que habuit in sua diocesa>[i] sequestravit et quod corpus ejus coram prefatis baronibus habere non potuit eo quod in sua diocesi non potuit inveniri. Et, quia cohercio ecclesiastica ulterius in clericos nostram curiam contumaciter contempnentes extendi non potest, tibi precipimus quod capias predictum Willelmum, si inventus fuerit in balliva tua, et eum in prisona nostra salvo custodias, ita quod habeas corpus ejus coram predictis baronibus apud Westm' in octabis sancti Hillarii ad respondendum tam nobis quam predicto Petro de predictis falsitate et decepcione. Et habeas ibi tunc hoc breve.'[6]

Postea habuit dictus vicecomes breve quod caperet corpus dicti Willelmi, ita quod haberet corpus ejus coram baronibus ad quindenam Pasche. Ad quem diem vicecomes returnavit per breve suum quod nec in domibus religiosis nec alibi in balliva sua potuit inveniri. Ita quod tunc mandatum fuit vicecomiti quod exigeret eum de comitatu in comitatum donec utlagetur vel veniat ad pacem regis et, si veniat ad pacem regis, quod capiat corpus ejus et salvo custodiat, ita quod eum coram prefatis baronibus habeat a die sancti Michaelis in .xv. dies ad respondendum tam regi quam predicto Petro tam de decepcione quam transgressione predicta.

[5] *repeated in MS.*

[6] *There is a further change of ink at this point*

APPENDIX III

List of Surviving Plea Rolls of the Exchequer of the Jews, 1219–1290

ABBREVIATIONS USED

For the terms

H Hilary
E Easter
T Trinity
M Michaelmas

For the business

A Attorney [appointments]
E Essoins
M Memoranda
MT Memoranda relating to tallage
P Pleas
PP Adjournments made at the request of the parties
R Recognizances
S Starrs

HENRY III

Year, Regnal Year and Term	Plea Roll reference	Contents of Roll	Where calendared or Printed	Additional Notes
1219M (3/4 Henry III)	E 9/1	P on mm. 1, 1d, 3, 3d (part) and ?4, 4d E on m. 2	*EJ*, i, pp. 1-9, 11-18; Cole, *Documents Illustrative of English History*, pp. 285-91, 293-5, 297-301	E 9/1 (covering this and the following three terms) is a single annual roll and not a later composite of originally separate rolls
1220H (4 Henry III)	E 9/1	P on mm. 3d (part), 5, 5d, 6, 6d E on m. 2d (part)	*EJ*, i, pp. 9-11, 18-30; *Select Pleas*, pp. 3-4; Cole, *Documents*, pp. 291-2, 295-6, 302-10	The membranes are probably not in their original order. Attorney appointments are included in the Plea section
1220E (4 Henry III)	E 9/1	P on mm. ?8, ?8d, 9, 9d E on m. 2d (part)	*EJ*, i, pp. 34-45; *Select Pleas*, pp. 5-7; Cole, *Documents*, pp. 292, 315-324	There is no Memoranda section and no Starrs are enrolled
1220T (4 Henry III)	E 9/1	P on mm. 7, 7d (part), 10, 10d E on m. 7d (part)	*EJ*, i, pp. 30-4, 46-55; *Select Pleas*, pp. 4-5; Cole, *Documents*, pp. 310-15, 324-32	
1244E (28 Henry III)	E 9/2	P on mm. 1, 2 (part), 2d, 3d E on m. 2 (part) S on m. 3 M on mm. 4, 4d (part)	*EJ*, i, pp. 55-70; *Select Pleas*, pp. 7-11	Although m. 4 and most of m. 4d contain Memoranda business they are not so headed. The remainder of m. 4d contains essoins for the morrow of Trinity (repeated in E 9/3 at m. 1d)
1244T (28 Henry III)	E 9/3	P on mm. 1, 1d (part), 2 (part), 3, 3d, 5, 5d, 6, 6d E on m. 4d (part) S on mm, 7, 7d (part) M on mm. 2 (part), 2d, 7d (part)	*EJ*, i, pp. 70-91	Again the material in the Memoranda section has no separate heading
1244M (28 Henry III)	E 9/4	P on mm. 1-1d, 3-5d E on m. 2 S on mm. 6-6d and 7 (part) M on mm. 2d, 7 (part)	*EJ*, i, pp. 91-112; *Select Pleas*, pp. 11-14	Again the material in the Memoranda section has no separate heading. Membrane 7d is blank
1253E (37 Henry III)	E 9/5	P on mm 3-6 E on m. 2 S on mm. 1-1d M on mm. 7-7d A on m. 8	*EJ*, i, pp. 130-19; *Select Pleas*, pp. 14-31	

Year, Regnal Year and Term	Plea Roll reference	Contents of Roll	Where calendared or Printed	Additional Notes
1266T (50 Henry III)	E 9/6	P on mm. 1d-2d E on m. 1 (part) S on m. 3 (part), 3d M on m. 3 (part) A and PP on m. 1 (part)	*EJ*, i, 130-9 (**excluding material added more recently to mm. 2-2d**); *Select Pleas*, pp. 31-6	mm. 1-2 are so numbered in a contemporary enumeration in roman numerals on the top left-hand side of their face; m. 3 is numbered 'vi' in this same enumeration. The tail of m. 3d has on it *Placita de scaccario Judeorum de termino sancte Trinitats anno regni regis Henrici filii regis Johannis quinquagesimo* and *Justiciarii: Willelmus de Orlaveston et Robertus de Fuleham*
1267T (51 Henry III)	E 9/7	P on mm. 1-1d and 2 (part) S on m. 3d (part) M on mm. 2 (part), 2d, 3, 3d (part)	*EJ*, i, pp. 139-54 (**excluding material added more recently to mm. 3-3d**); *Select Pleas*, pp. 36-8	
1267M (51/52 Henry III)	E 9/8	S on mm. 1-1d	*EJ*, i, pp. 154-7 (**excluding material added more recently**)	This single membrane is numbered 'iii' in a contemporary roman numeral enumeration
1268H (52 Henry III)	E 9/9	P on mm. 2-6d E on m. 1 S on mm. 10-12d M on mm. 7-9d A and PP on m. 1d	*EJ*, i, pp. 166-214; *Select Pleas*, pp. 38-48	mm. 2-6 are numbered 'j' to 'v'; mm. 7-9 'j' to 'iij' in two separate contemporary enumerations
1268E (52 Henry III)	E 9/10	P on mm. 1-1d	*EJ*, i, pp. 158-63	
1270E (54 Henry III)	E 9/11	P on mm. 1d (part), 2-6, 6d (part) E on m. 1 (part) S on mm. 8 (part), 8d M on m. 6d (part), 7-7d and 8 (part) A and PP on mm. 1-1d (part)	*EJ*, i, pp. 214-74; *Select Pleas*, pp. 51-62	mm. 3-8 are so numbered in a contemporary roman numeral enumeration; m. 9 is the original cover of the roll and on the foot of the dorse is a list of its contents and the date: *Essonia; Attornati; Prece Parcium; Placita; Memoranda et Starra de Scaccario Judeorum de termino Pasche anno regni regis Henrici filii regis Johannis quinquagesimo quarto*
1270T (54 Henry III)	E 9/61	P on mm. 1-1d	Not printed	
1271M (55 Henry III)	No surviving roll but for a transcript of an entry recording an agreement enrolled on a roll of this term see TCD MS. 524, f. 135r			

Year, Regnal Year and Term	Plea Roll reference	Contents of Roll	Where calendared or Printed	Additional Notes
1272E (56 Henry III)	BL Additional Roll 19,299	P on mm. 1-1d	*EJ*, i, pp. 274-82; *EJ*, iv, nos. 1-39; *Select Pleas*, p. 63	
1272T (56 Henry III)	E 9/12	P on mm. 2 (part), 2d-3d, 4 (part) E on m. 2 (part) M on mm. 4 (part) and 4d A and PP on m. 2 (part)	*EJ*, i, pp. 283-313; *Select Pleas*, pp. 63-70	mm. 2-4 are numbered 'j' to 'iij' in a contemporary enumeration
1272M (56 Henry III)	E 9/12	P on m. 1 (part) E on m. 1d (part) A and PP on mm. 1-1d (part)	*EJ*, i, pp. 313-16	Although now bound up with a roll of the previous term this probably belongs to a separate roll

EDWARD I

Year, Regnal year and term	Plea Roll reference	Justice for whom made	Contents of Roll	Where Calendared or Printed	Additional Notes
1273H (1 Edward I)	E 9/13	Ludham: see notes on mm. 8, 8d (*scribendum/scribenda sunt in rotulo J. de Bayfeud*)	P on mm. 2-4d E on m. 1 S on mm. 8-8d M on mm. 5-7d A and PP on m. 1d	*EJ*, ii, pp. 1-24; *Select Pleas*, pp. 70-6	
1273E (1 Edward I)	NONE SURVIVES				
1273T (1 Edward I)	E 9/14	?	P on mm. 1-3d, 14-16d E on m. 13 S on mm. 12-12d M on mm. 4-10, 11-11d A and PP on m. 13d	*EJ*, ii, pp. 71-6 (part only)	m. 10d is blank. The roll is not in its original order: mm. 13-16 were probably originally the first four membranes of the roll
	E 9/62	?	P on mm. 2-6 E on m. 1 S on mm. 15-16 M on mm. 7-14d, 17-17d A and PP on m. 1d	*EJ*, ii, pp. 24-71; *Select Pleas*, pp. 76-7	mm. 6d and 16d are blank
1273M (1/2 Edward I)	E 9/15	? Ludham	P on mm. 2-7 E on m. 1 S on mm. 12-12d M on mm. 8-10, 11-11d A and PP on m. 1d	*EJ*, ii, pp. 76-118; *Select Pleas*, p. 78	mm. 7d and 10d are blank
	E 9/56	? Hauteyn	P on mm. 1-6 M on mm. 7-8	Not printed or calendared	mm. 6d and 8d are blank
1274H (2 Edward I)	NONE SURVIVES				
1274E (2 Edward I)	NONE SURVIVES				
1274T (2 Edward I)	E 9/16	? Ludham	P on mm. 2-7d E on m. 1 S on mm. 13-13d M on mm. 8-12d A on m. 1d	*EJ*, ii, pp. 118-171; *Select Pleas*, pp. 62-3, 78-81	

Year, Regnal year and term	Plea Roll reference	Justice for whom made	Contents of Roll	Where Calendared or Printed	Additional Notes
1274M (2/3 Edward I)	E 9/17	?	P on mm. 7-13 E on m. 6 S on mm. 5-5d M on mm. 1-4d A on m. 6d	*EJ*, ii, pp. 171-215; *Select Pleas*, pp. 81-4	m. 13d is blank
1275H (3 Edward I)	E 9/18	?	P on mm. 2-7 E on m. 1 S on mm. 8-8d M on mm. 9-11d A and PP on m. 1d	*EJ*, ii, pp. 215-51; *Select Pleas*, pp. 84-6	m. 7d has a heading but is otherwise blank
1275E (3 Edward I)	E 9/19	?	P on mm. 1-3d E on m. 4 S on mm. 9-9d M on mm. 5, 6-8d A and PP on m. 4d	*EJ*, ii, pp. 251-82; *Select Pleas*, pp. 86-7	m. 5d is blank
	E 9/59	?	P on mm. 1-1d S on mm. 2-2d	Not calendared or printed	
1275T (3 Edward I)	E 9/20	?	P on mm. 15-20d E on m. 14 S on mm. 13-13d M on mm. 9-12d A and PP on mm. 14d MT on mm. 1-6, 7, 8	*EJ*, ii, pp. 282-317; *Select Pleas*, pp. 87-9	mm. 7d, 8d are blank
1275M (3 Edward I)	E 9/21	?	P on mm. 2-8d E on m. 1 S on mm. 14-14d M on mm. 9-13 A and PP on m. 1d MT on m. 13d	*EJ*, iii, pp. 1-82; *Select Pleas*, pp. 89-91	There is also a separate Memoranda roll for business relating to tallage from this term: E 101/249/20 (calendared in *EJ*, iv, nos. 22-271).
1276H (4 Edward I)	E 9/49	?	P on mm. 1-2 S on mm. 7-7d M on mm. 3-3d, 6-6d MT on mm. 4-5d	*EJ*, iii, pp. 82-112	m. 2d is blank
	E 9/58	?	M on mm. 1-1d	Not calendared or printed	E 9/60 is probably also from the same roll
	E 9/60	?	M on mm. 1-1d	Not calendared or printed	E 9/58 is probably also from the same roll

Year, Regnal year and term	Plea Roll reference	Justice for whom made	Contents of Roll	Where Calendared or Printed	Additional Notes
1276E (4 Edward I)	E 9/52	?	S on mm. 7-7d M on mm. 1-3, 4-4d MT on mm. 5-6d	*EJ*, iii, pp. 113-46	m. 3d is blank
1276T (4 Edward I)	E 9/22	?	P on mm. 2-10d E on m. 1 S on mm. 16-17d M on mm. 11-15d	*EJ*, iii, pp. 147-229; *Select Pleas*, pp. 91-2	m. 18 is a scrutiny of the chest at Hereford in 1276 and has wrongly been added to this roll
1276M (4/5 Edward I)	E 9/68	? Ludham	P on mm. 1-1d	Not printed or calendared	
	E 9/42	?	M on mm. 3-3d	*Select Pleas*, pp. 92-3 (**but otherwise not in print**)	membrane wrongly added to a roll belonging to Easter term 1283
1277H (5 Edward I)	BL Additional Roll 7218	? Hauteyn	P on mm. 2-5d E on m. 1 S on mm. 10-10d M on mm. 6-8d A and PP on m. 1d	*EJ*, iv, nos. 272-481; *Select Pleas*, p. 92	
	E 9/23 (one membrane only)	? Ludham	M on mm. 12-12d	*EJ*, iii, pp. 284-7	this membrane has mistakenly been added to a plea roll belonging to the following term
1277E (5 Edward I)	E 9/23 (remainder of roll)	?	P on mm. 2-6d E on m. 1 S on mm. 11-11d M on mm. 3-3d, 5-8d A and PP on m. 1d	*EJ*, iii, pp. 239-84; *Select Pleas*, pp. 93-5	mm. 12-12d belongs to a different roll from the preceding term
1277T (5 Edward I)	E 9/24	Hauteyn (see the note at the bottom of m. 8)	P on mm. 2-2d, 9-9d E on m. 1 S on mm. 11-11d M on mm. 3-3d, 5-8	*EJ*, iii, pp. 288-323; *Select Pleas*, pp. 95-100	m. 8d is blank
1277M (5/6 Edward I)	E 9/25	? Hauteyn	P on mm. 2-5d E on m. 1 S on m. 9 M on mm. 6-8 A and PP on m. 1d	*EJ*, v, nos. 1-169; *Select Pleas*, pp. 100-1	mm. 8d and 9d are blank

Year, Regnal year and term	Plea Roll reference	Justice for whom made	Contents of Roll	Where Calendared or Printed	Additional Notes
1278H (6 Edward I)	E 9/26	? Ludham	P on mm. 2-5d E on m. 1 S on mm. 8-8d M on mm. 6-7 A and PP on m. 1d	*EJ*, v, nos. 170-313; *Select Pleas*, pp. 101-3	m. 7d is blank
1278E (6 Edward I)	E 9/27	? Hauteyn (mm. 5d and 6d both have a large 'h' at the bottom)	P on mm. 3-7d E on m. 2 S on mm. 1-1d M on mm. 8-8d, 10-11d A and PP on m. 2d	*EJ*, v, nos. 314-484; *Select Pleas*, pp. 103-4	m. 9 belongs to a roll of Trinity term 1280
1278T (6 Edward I)	E 9/28	Hauteyn: mm. 4-4d record business heard locally before him and there are 'h's at the top of mm. 3 and 9, the bottom of mm. 2, 6 and 12 and at both top and bottom of mm. 8 and 11	P on mm. 2-5, 6-7d E on m. 1 S on mm. 12-12d M on mm. 9-11d A on m. 1d	*EJ*, v, nos. 485-6, 509-11, 527-69, 571-7, 581-724; *Select Pleas*, pp. 105-6	m. 5 is a schedule attached to m. 4
	E 9/63	Ludham	P on mm. 2-4, 5-9d E on mm. 1, 1d (part) M on mm. 10-13d A and PP on m. 1d (part)	*EJ*, v, nos. 487-508, 512-26, 570, 578-80 and variants printed in footnotes of 485-6, 509-11, 527-69, 571-7 and 581-711	m. 4d is blank; for the lower section of mm. 2-2d see E 9/57 below
	E 9/57	Ludham	P on mm. 1-1d	*E.J.*, v, nos. 530-3, 542-3 (variants printed in footnotes)	probably the lower section of E 9/63, mm. 2-2d
1278M (5/6 Edward I)	E 9/29	Hauteyn: m. 13 has an 'h' at the top	P on mm. 2-6d E on m. 1 S on mm. 13-14d M on mm. 7-12d A on m. 1d	*EJ*, v, nos. 725-919	
1279H (7 Edward I)	E 9/30	Ludham	P on mm. 2-3d E on m. 1 M on mm. 4-4d A on m. 1d S on m. 3d (one only)	*EJ*, v, nos. 920-972	

Year, Regnal year and term	Plea Roll reference	Justice for whom made	Contents of Roll	Where Calendared or Printed	Additional Notes
	E 9/50	Hauteyn: m. 1 has a large 'h' at both top and bottom	P on mm. 1-1d M on mm. 2-2d	*EJ*, v, nos. 920-972 (variants printed in footnotes)	
1279E (7 Edward I)	E 9/31	? Ludham	P on mm. 2-3 E on m. 1 S on mm. 3d, 5 M on mm. 4-4d A and PP on m. 1d	*EJ*, vi, nos. 1-68; *Select Pleas*, pp. 48-50	
	E 9/70	? Hauteyn	S on mm. 1-1d	*EJ*, vi, nos. 64-8 (variants printed in footnotes)	
1279T (7 Edward I)	E 9/32	? Hauteyn	P on mm.1d (part), 2-2d E on m. 1 M on mm. 3-3d A on m. 1d (part)	*EJ*, vi, nos. 146-64 (main text); *EJ*, vi, nos. 69-145 (variants printed in footnotes); *Select Pleas*, pp. 106-7	
	E 9/64	? Ludham	P on mm. 2-4 E on m. 1 S on m. 5 (part) M on mm. 5 (part) and 5d A on m. 1d	*EJ*, vi, nos. 69-145	m. 4d is blank
1279M (7/8 Edward I)	E 9/33	Hauteyn: m. 3 has an 'h' at the top	P on mm. 2-3 E on m. 1 S on mm. 7-7d M on mm. 4-6d A on m. 1d	*EJ*, vi, nos. 165-245	m. 3d is blank
1280H (8 Edward I)	E 9/34	Hauteyn: mm. 3, 4, 5d, 6 and 9 have the letter 'h' at the top; m. 2 has the same letter at the bottom	P on mm. 2-3d, 9-9d E on m. 1 S on m. 8 M on mm. 4-7d A and PP on m. 1d	*EJ*, vi, nos. 246-392; *Select Pleas*, pp. 107-9	m. 8d is blank
	E 9/65	Ludham	M on mm. 1-1d	*EJ*, vi, nos. 271, 308-335, 353 (variants printed in footnotes)	
1280E (8 Edward I)	E 9/35	Hauteyn: mm. 2, 3, 5, 6, 7, 9 and 10 have the letter 'h' at the top	P on mm. 2-5d E on m. 1 S on mm. 10, 10d (part) M on mm. 6-9d, 10d (part)	*EJ*, vi, nos. 393-523; *Select Pleas*, pp. 109-13	m. 1d is blank

Year, Regnal year and term	Plea Roll reference	Justice for whom made	Contents of Roll	Where Calendared or Printed	Additional Notes
1280T (8 Edward I)	E 9/36	?	P on mm. 2-5d E on m. 1 S on mm. 10-10d M on mm. 6-9d A and PP on m. 1d	*EJ*, vi, nos. 524-719	
	E 9/27 (one membrane only)	?	M on mm. 9-9d	*EJ*, vi, nos. 720-38	this membrane has been wrongly placed in a roll whose other membranes belong to Easter term 1278
1280M (8/9 Edward I)	E 9/53	? Hauteyn	M on mm. 1-1d	*EJ*, vi, nos. 739-78	
1281H (9 Edward I)	NO SURVIVING ROLL				
1281E (9 Edward I)	E 9/37	?	P on mm. 1, 1d, 2, 5 (part) E on m. 3 S on mm. 7-7d M on mm. 4-4d, 5 (part), 5d-6d A on m. 3d R on m. 8d	*EJ*, vi, nos. 779-1028 (variants printed in footnotes), 1029-1077; *Select Pleas*, p. 114	mm. 2d and 8d are blank; mm. 1 and 2 may belong to E 9/66
	E 9/66	?	P on mm. 1-3d E on m. 5 S on mm. 4-4d M on mm. 6-11d A and PP on m. 5d	*EJ*, vi, nos. 779-1028	E 9/37, mm. 1 and 2 may also belong to this roll
1281T (9 Edward I)	E 9/38	?	P on mm. 7-7d E on m. 6 S on mm. 9-9d M on mm. 1-5, 8-8d, 10, 11, 12-12d A on m. 6d	*EJ*, vi, nos. 1078-1245; *Select Pleas*, pp. 115-16	mm. 5d, 10d, 11d are blank; mm. 1, 2 and 12 may be part of a second roll for the same term
1281M (9/10 Edward I)	NO SURVIVING ROLL				
1282H (10 Edward I)	E 9/39	?Ludham	P on mm. 5-6d E on m. 8 S on mm. 1-1d, 7 (part) M on mm. 2-4d, 7 (part), 7d, 9-9d	*Select Pleas*, pp. 117-120; otherwise unprinted	m. 8d is blank

Year, Regnal year and term	Plea Roll reference	Justice for whom made	Contents of Roll	Where Calendared or Printed	Additional Notes
1282E (10 Edward I)	NO SURVIVING ROLL				
1282T (10 Edward I)	NO SURVIVING ROLL				
1282M (10/11 Edward I)	E 9/40A	?	P on mm. 1-2d, 8-8d E on m. 6 S on mm. 5, 10 M on mm. 3-4d, 5d, 7-7d, 9-9d A and PP on m. 6d	*Select Pleas*, pp. 120-4; otherwise unprinted	These membranes come from two separate rolls: m. 8 duplicates m. 1 and m. 10 is a partial duplicate of m. 5. Membrane 10d is blank
	E 9/40B	?	P on mm. 2-3d E on mm. 1, 1d (part) S on m. 5 M on mm. 4-4d, 5d, 6-7d A on m. 1d (part)	unprinted	
1283H (11 Edward I)	E 9/41	? Ludham or Bray	P on mm. 1-2d E on m. 5d S on m. 5 M on mm. 3-4d	*Select Pleas*, p. 124; otherwise unprinted	m. 4 has a note showing that it was originally the *secundus rotulus* of this roll; m. 5 has a note on it showing that it is the last of the five original membranes of the roll (*ultimus rotulus hujus termini et quinque rotuli sunt in universo*)
	E 9/51	Hauteyn: mm. 1, 2 are marked *Haut'* at the top	P on mm. 1-1d, 2 (part) M on m. 2 (part), 2d R on mm. 3-3d	unprinted	m. 3 may belong to a third roll of the same term
1283E (11 Edward I)	E 9/42	Hauteyn: m. 2 records an inquisition heard before him at the Tower	P on mm. 1-1d, 7-7d, 8 (part) S on m. 9 M on mm. 2-2d, 4-6d, 8 (part), 8d, 9d	*Select Pleas*, pp. 124-8; otherwise unprinted	for m. 3 of this roll see 1276M
1283T (11 Edward I)	E 9/43	?Bray	P on mm. 1, 2 M on mm. 3-5d	*Select Pleas*, pp. 129-130; otherwise unprinted	mm. 1d, 2d are blank
1283M (11/12 Edward I)	E 9/67	?	M on mm. 1-1d	unprinted	
1284H (12 Edward I)	NO SURVIVING ROLL				
1284E (12 Edward I)	NO SURVIVING ROLL				

Year, Regnal year and term	Plea Roll reference	Justice for whom made	Contents of Roll	Where Calendared or Printed	Additional Notes
1284T (12 Edward I)	E 9/44	Hauteyn (in part): mm. 1 and 5 are both marked 'h'	P on mm. 2-4d E on m. 1 S on mm, 8 (part), 8d M on mm. 5, 6-7d R on mm. 5d, 8d (part)	*Select Pleas*, pp. 130-3; otherwise unprinted	m. 1d is blank; m. 9 is the cover. Membrane 1 is marked as the first membrane (*primus rotulus*) and both mm. 2 and 3 are marked as the third membrane (*tercius rotulus*). Membrane 5 is wrongly ascribed to the ninth regnal year. There may be parts of two different rolls here
	E 9/54	?Ludham	P on mm. 2-7d E on m. 1 S on mm. 14-14d M on mm. 8-13d A on m. 1d	unprinted	
1284M (12/13 Edward I)	E 9/45	?	P on mm. 7-8d E on m. 2 S on mm. 1-1d M on mm. 3-6 A and PP on m. 2d	*Select Pleas*, pp. 133-4; otherwise unprinted	m. 6d is blank
1285H-M (13-13/14 Edward I)		NO ROLLS SURVIVE			
1286H (14 Edward I)	E 9/46	?	P on mm. 1-2d S on mm. 3-3d M on mm. 4-6d R on mm. 7-7d	unprinted	
	E 9/48	?	M on m. 1	unprinted	m. 1d is blank; this membrane may be part of E 9/46
1286H or 1286E (14 Edward I)	E9/69	?	S on mm. 1-1d	unprinted	
1286T (14 Edward I)	E 9/47	Hauteyn: mm. 4 and 5 are marked 'h'	P on mm. 2, 4-4d, 7-8d E on m. 1 S on m. 9 M on mm. 3-3d, 6 R on mm. 5, 5d, 9d	unprinted	mm. 1d, 2d and 6d are blank
1286M-1290M (14/15 Edward I-18/19 Edward I)	NO SURVIVING ROLLS But for transcripts of individual entries from the plea rolls of Easter term 1287 and Michaelmas term 1289 see BL MSS. Additional 46352, ff. 90v-91v and Cotton Julius D.ii, f. 182v and note that there is also a copy of an inquisition taken before the Justices of the Jews at Westminster in Trinity term 1290 in BL MS. Harley 79 at f. 1r				

APPENDIX IV

Archival History of the Plea Rolls of the Exchequer of the Jews now in the The National Archives (formerly the Public Record Office), 1894-2004

This appendix has been compiled from the following sources:

i) The copy of the first edition of volume IV of the PRO series of Lists and Indexes published in 1894 (*List of Plea Rolls*) formerly kept in the Public Search Room of the PRO and annotated for additions to and renumberings of the Plea Rolls between 1894 and 1910, now OBS 696.
ii) J. M. Rigg's *Select Pleas, Starrs and other Records from the Rolls of the Exchequer of the Jews* published by the Selden Society in 1901 as its vol. 15 and also by the Jewish Historical Society of England.
iii) The document repair register of the PRO for the period 1901-18, PRO 12/2.
iv) The second edition of volume IV of the PRO series of Lists and Indexes (*List of Plea Rolls*) published in 1910.
v) Annotations on the Plea Rolls.
vi) Personal knowledge.

E 9/1 Roll 1 in this class since 1894.

E 9/2 Roll 2 in this class since 1894.

E 9/3 Roll 3 in this class since 1894.

E 9/4 Roll 4 in this class since 1894.

E 9/5 (i) **membrane 1**: the one and only membrane of Roll 5 in 1894.
(ii) **membranes 2-8**: in 1894 formed Roll 6; probably united with the remainder of Roll 5 in September 1909.

E 9/6 (i) **membrane 1 and part of membrane 2**: formed Roll 7 between 1894 and c. 1910 when it was joined with membrane 3 of the roll and the roll received its current reference.
(ii) **part of membrane 2** was recovered from unsorted Miscellanea and added to the existing membrane 2 in 1975.
(iii) **membrane 3**: formed membrane 4 of Roll 8 between 1894 and c. 1910 when it was moved to its current position in this roll.

E 9/7 (i) **membranes 1 and 2**: formed Roll 9 between 1894 and c. 1910 but then joined with the current membrane 3 of this roll and received its present reference.
(ii) **membrane 3**: formed membrane 2 of Roll 8 between 1894 and c. 1910 when it was joined to membranes 1 and 2 of this roll under its current reference.

E 9/8 Between 1894 and c. 1910 was membrane 1 of a composite Roll 8. For the other membranes which then formed part of this roll see E 9/6, m. 3, E 9/7, m. 3 and E 9/10.

E 9/9 Included in the 1840 list of records in the Tower: *Second Report of the Deputy Keeper* (1841), Appendix II, p. 49; subsequently Tower Coram Rege Roll 38 and (by 1894) Curia Regis Roll 183. In about 1902 transferred to this class and became Roll 10. Given its current reference by 1910. The former **membrane 13** in this roll which had been added to it at a date not known was removed from it in 1979 and re-united with the remainder of membrane 1 of JUST 1/363 of which it had originally formed part.

E 9/10 Between 1894 and c. 1910 was membrane 3 of Roll 8; given its current reference by 1910.

E 9/11 Between 1894 and c. 1902 formed mm. 1-8 of Roll 10; thereafter mm. 1-8 of Roll 11. For the former **membrane 9** of this roll see E 9/61.

E 9/12 Between 1894 and c. 1902 Roll 11; renumbered Roll 12 c. 1902.

E 9/13 Between 1894 and c. 1902 Roll 12; renumbered Roll 13 c. 1902.

E 9/14 Between 1894 and c. 1910 Roll 14; renumbered Roll 15 c. 1902; shortly before 1910 became mm. 1-16 of a new composite Roll 14. Now again forms the whole of Roll 14. For the former mm. 17-33 which were removed from this roll in 1975 see E 9/62.

E 9/15 Between 1894 and c. 1902 Roll 15; renumbered Roll 16 c. 1902; renumbered again as Roll 15 by 1910. A Roll 15A of the same term was added to the class sometime between 1894 and c. 1902. This was renumbered as Roll 17 in c. 1902 but seems to have been added to Roll 15 by 1910. For the former membranes 8B and 13 of this roll see E 9/56.

E 9/16 Between 1894 and c. 1902 Roll 16; became Roll 18 between c. 1902 and c. 1910; renumbered Roll 16 by 1910.

E 9/17 Between 1894 and c. 1902 Roll 17; became Roll 19 between c. 1902 and c. 1910; renumbered Roll 17 by 1910.

E 9/18 Between 1894 and c. 1902 Roll 18; became Roll 20 between c. 1902 and c. 1910; renumbered Roll 18 by 1910.

E 9/19 Between 1894 and c. 1902 Roll 19; became Roll 21 between c. 1902 and c. 1910; renumbered Roll 19 by 1910.

E 9/20 Between 1894 and c. 1902 Roll 20; became Roll 22 between c. 1902 and c. 1910; renumbered Roll 20 by 1910.

E 9/21 Between 1894 and c. 1902 Roll 21; became Roll 23 between c. 1902 and c. 1910; renumbered Roll 21 by 1910.

E 9/22 Between 1894 and c. 1902 Roll 22; became Roll 24 between c. 1902 and c. 1910; renumbered Roll 22 by 1910. A nineteenth century label shows that the roll formerly consisted of only sixteen membranes. The additional membranes are the current mm. 10 and 18. Membrane 10 has the earlier sorting reference TG 41041 and was correctly added from Exchequer Miscellanea during the course of the nineteenth century; membrane 18 was also added during the course of the nineteenth century but was wrongly added to this roll.

E 9/23 Between 1894 and c. 1902 Roll 23; became Roll 25 between c. 1902 and c. 1910; renumbered as Roll 23 by 1910. Membrane 12 belongs to a roll of the following term.

E 9/24 Between 1894 and c. 1902 Roll 24; became Roll 26 between c. 1902 and c. 1910; renumbered Roll 24 by 1910.

E 9/25 Between 1894 and c. 1902 Roll 26; became Roll 28 c. 1902; renumbered as Roll 27 between c.1902 and c. 1910; renumbered Roll 25 by 1910.

E 9/26 Between 1894 and c. 1902 Roll 27; became Roll 29 c. 1902; renumbered Roll 28 between c.1902 and c. 1910; renumbered Roll 26 by 1910.

E 9/27 (i) **membranes 1-5**: between 1894 and c. 1902 were Roll 28; became Roll 30 c. 1902; renumbered Roll 29 between c. 1902 and 1910; renumbered Roll 27 by 1910.

(ii) **membrane 6**: between 1894 and c. 1902 membrane 2 of Roll 29; became membrane 2 of Roll 31 c. 1902 and membrane 2 of the renumbered Roll 30 between c. 1902 and c. 1910; had been added to its current Roll (but as membrane 7) by 1910; renumbered as membrane 6 of this roll in 1934.

(iii) **membrane 7**: between 1894 and c. 1902 was membrane 1 of Roll 29; became membrane 1 of Roll 31 c. 1902 and membrane 1 of the renumbered Roll 30 between c. 1902 and c. 1910; had been added to its current Roll but as membrane 6 by 1910; renumbered as membrane 7 of this roll in 1934.

(iv) **membranes 8-11**: between 1894 and c. 1902 were membranes 3-6 of Roll 29; became membranes 3-6 of Roll 31 c. 1902 and membranes 3-6 of the renumbered Roll 30 between c. 1902 and c. 1910; added to their current Roll under their current reference by 1910.

E 9/28 Between 1894 and c. 1902 Roll 30; became Roll 32 c. 1902; renumbered as Roll 31 between c.1902 and c. 1910; renumbered as Roll 28 by 1910. For the former **membranes 13-25** of this roll see E 9/63.

E 9/29 Between 1894 and c. 1902 Roll 25 (and wrongly dated as of Michaelmas 1277); became Roll 27 c. 1902; renumbered Roll 32 and later Roll 33 between c.1902 and c. 1910; renumbered Roll 29 by 1910.

E 9/30 Between 1894 and c. 1902 Roll 32; became Roll 34 c. 1902; renumbered Roll 35 between c. 1902 and c. 1910; renumbered Roll 30 by 1910.

E 9/31 Between 1894 and c. 1902 Roll 33; became Roll 35 c. 1902; renumbered Roll 36 between c. 1902 and c. 1910; renumbered Roll 31 by 1910.

E 9/32 Between 1894 and c. 1902 Roll 34; became Roll 36 c. 1902; renumbered Roll 37 between c. 1902 and c. 1910; by 1910 had become mm. 1, 3 and 6 of a new composite Roll 32. The membranes than added to this roll (mm. 2, 4, 5, 7, 8) were removed in 1975 to form a new E 9/64.

E 9/33 Between 1894 and c. 1902 Roll 31; became Roll 33 c. 1902; renumbered Roll 34 between c. 1902 and c. 1910; renumbered Roll 33 by 1910.

E 9/34 Roll 35 in 1894; became Roll 39 between c. 1902 and c. 1910; had become mm. 1-8 of Roll 34 by 1910. For the former **membrane 10** of this roll see E 9/65.

E 9/35 Roll 36 in 1894; became Roll 41 between c. 1902 and c. 1910; had become Roll 35 by 1910.

E 9/36 Roll 37 in 1894; became Roll 42 between c. 1902 and c. 1910; had become Roll 36 by 1910.

E 9/37 Roll 38 in 1894; became Roll 43 between c. 1902 and c. 1910; by 1910 had become mm. 1-10 of a new composite Roll 37. For the former **membranes 11-21** of this roll removed from it in 1975 see E 9/66.

E 9/38 Roll 39 in 1894; became Roll 46 between c. 1902 and c. 1910; had become Roll 38 by 1910.

E 9/39 Roll 40 in 1894; became Roll 47 between c. 1902 and c. 1910; had become Roll 39 by 1910.

E 9/40A Roll 41 in 1894; became Roll 48 between c. 1902 and c. 1910; had become Roll 40 by 1910; renumbered Roll 40A in 1951 when Roll 40B added to the class.

E 9/40B Justices Itinerant etc. Roll (JUST 1/) 738 until 1951 when transferred to this class.

E 9/41 (i) **membrane 1**: membrane 2 of Roll 42 in 1894 and of renumbered Roll 49 between c. 1902 and c. 1910, of renumbered Roll 41 by 1910; membrane renumbered in 1975.

(ii) **membrane 2**: membrane 3 of Roll 42 in 1894 and of renumbered Roll 49 between c. 1902 and c. 1910 and of renumbered Roll 41 by 1910; membrane renumbered in 1975.

(iii) **membrane 3**: membrane 5 of Roll 42 in

1894 and of renumbered Roll 49 between c. 1902 and c. 1910 and of renumbered Roll 41 by 1910; membrane renumbered in 1975.
(iv) **membrane 4**: added from unsorted Miscellanea in 1975
(v) **membrane 5**: membrane 1 of Roll 42 in 1894 and of renumbered Roll 49 between c. 1902 and c. 1910 and of renumbered Roll 41 by 1910; membrane renumbered in 1975.

E 9/42 Roll 43 in 1894; became Roll 50 between c. 1902 and c. 1910; had become Roll 42 by 1910.

E 9/43 Roll 44 in 1894; became Roll 51 between c. 1902 and c. 1910; had become Roll 43 by 1910.

E 9/44 Roll 45 in 1894; became Roll 52 between c. 1902 and c. 1910; had become Roll 44 by 1910.

E 9/45 (i) **membranes 1-7:** Roll 46 in 1894; became Roll 53 between c. 1902 and c. 1910; had become Roll 45 by 1910.
(ii) **membrane 8**: when first added to the class in 1914 was membrane 3 of Roll 51; transferred to its current reference in 1975.

E 9/46 (i) **membranes 1-3**: added to the class as Roll 46A between 1894 and 1902; renumbered Roll 54 between c. 1902 and c. 1910; by 1910 renumbered Roll 46
(ii) **membrane 4**: part of this membrane added to the class as Roll 55 c. 1926; the remainder recovered from unsorted Miscellanea when transferred to its current reference in 1975.
(iii) **membranes 5-7**: added from unsorted Miscellanea in 1975.

E 9/47 Roll 47 in 1894; became Roll 55 between c. 1902 and c. 1910; had become Roll 47 by 1910.

E 9/48 Added to the class after 1902 as Roll 48; became Roll 56 prior to 1910; had become Roll 48 by 1910.

E 9/49 Added in 1914 from Exchequer Miscellanea B.

E 9/50 Added in 1914 from Exchequer Miscellanea B.

E 9/51 (i) **membranes 1-2**: added to the class in 1914 from Exchequer Miscellanea B as mm. 1-2 of Roll 51
(ii) **membrane 3**: membrane 4 of Roll 42 in 1894 and of renumbered Roll 49 between c. 1902 and c. 1910 and of Roll 41 by 1910; transferred to its current reference in 1975
[for what was **membrane** 3 of Roll 51 between 1914 and 1975 see E 9/45, m. 8]

E 9/52 Added in 1914 from Exchequer Miscellanea B. Earlier sorting reference JR 8488.

E 9/53 Added in 1914 from Exchequer Miscellanea B. Earlier sorting reference TG 41032.

E 9/54 Formerly Coram Rege Roll, Edward I, no. 85 and Coram Rege Roll, no. 85. Transferred to this class between 1914 and 1926.

E 9/55 [No document currently bears this reference; for the document formerly bearing this reference see E 9/46, m. 4.]

E 9/56 (i) **membrane 1**: added from unsorted Miscellanea in 1975.
(ii) **membranes 2-5**: constituted mm. 1-4 of Roll 56 when first added to the class between 1926 and 1931 from unsorted Miscellanea; renumbered in 1975.
(iii) **membrane 6**: added from unsorted Miscellanea in 1975.
(iv) **membrane 7**: added to Roll 15 as membrane 8B in 1926; transferred to its current reference in 1975.
(v) **membrane 8**: added to Roll 15 as membrane 13 at an unknown date; transferred to this reference in 1975.

E 9/57 Added in 1931 from Plea Roll fragments.

E 9/58 Added in 1931 from Plea Roll fragments.

E 9/59 Added in 1933 from Plea Roll fragments.

E 9/60 Added in 1933 from Plea Roll fragments.

E 9/61 membrane 9 of Roll 10 in 1894 (which became Roll 11 c. 1902); transferred to this separate reference in 1975.

E 9/62 Formerly Chapter House De Banco Roll, no. 6 and then De Banco Roll, Edward I, no. 4; had become Roll 13 in this class by 1894 and was renumbered as Roll 14 c. 1902; mistakenly combined with what was then Roll 15 to form the composite Roll 14 by 1910 (of which it formed mm. 17-33); separated and given its own reference in 1975.

E 9/63 Formerly De Banco Roll, Edward I, no. 27 and De Banco Roll, no. 25. Transferred to this class between 1902 and 1910 and given the reference Roll 32; by 1910 mistakenly combined with the second roll of the same term as Roll 28 (of which it formed mm. 13-25); separated and given its own reference in 1975.

E 9/64 Added to the class between 1894 and 1902 as Roll 28A; between 1902 and 1910 renumbered as Roll 38; by 1910 merged with the second roll of the same term as mm. 2, 4, 5, 7 and 8 of Roll 32; separated and given its own reference in 1975.

E 9/65 Probably Roll 35A when added to the class between 1894 and 1902; renumbered as Roll 40 between 1902 and 1910; added to Roll 34 as m. 10 by 1910; separated and given its own reference in 1975.

E 9/66 Formerly De Banco Roll, Edward I, no. 42 and then De Banco Roll, no. 40. Transferred to this class as Roll 38A between 1894 and 1902. Between 1902 and 1910 renumbered as Roll 45; added to the second roll of the same term to form the composite Roll 37 (of which it was mm. 11-21); separated and given its own reference in 1975.

E 9/67 Added in 1975 from unsorted Miscellanea.

E 9/68 Added in 1977 from unsorted Miscellanea.

E 9/69 Added in 1979 from Exchequer Miscellanea B.

E 9/70 Added in 1984; formerly part of E 160/7.

APPENDIX V

Jewish Tallages and analogous payment, 1265-90: a preliminary list

In the revision of this list I have been fortunate in being able to use the work of Zefira Rokeah on the tallages of the 1270s which appears in Appendix II of her article on 'A Hospitaller and the Jews: Brother Joseph de Chauncy and English Jewry in the 1270s in *Jewish Historical Studies*, 34 (1994-6) at pp. 203-7 (hereafter Rokeah, Appendix II)

1. A **fine of £1,000** paid in 1269 for a three year respite for tallage, which bought off a tallage which was being prepared early in May 1269. Its grant was subject to the condition that a full tallage would still be payable if the king or the Lord Edward went on Crusade. It is not clear how the fine was allocated or collected. It may have been by the Jewish community itself.
References: *Close Rolls, 1268-72*, pp. 44, 50, 53-4, 55; *Cal. Pat. Rolls, 1266-71*, p. 345; E 159/43, mm. 12d, 13, 23

2. A **tallage of 6000 marks** for the expenses of the Lord Edward in going on crusade in 1270. Only 4,000 marks had been raised by the time of his departure and the remaining 2,000 marks was advanced by his uncle Richard of Cornwall on the security of the money still to be collected. The tallage (which was never called that) seems to have been collected by Hagin son of master Mosse and his brother Elias.
References: *Cal. Pat. Rolls, 1266-72*, pp. 545-6, 671, 716; *Cal. Pat. Rolls, 1272-81*, p. 4; E 159/47, m. 5; Rokeah, Appendix II, p. 203

3. A **tallage of 5000 marks** imposed apparently on the Jews of London alone in 1272. The money was apparently collected by the main Exchequer.
References: *Cal. Pat. Rolls, 1266-72*, pp. 660, 661; *Close Rolls, 1268-1272*, pp. 498-9; *Cal. Close Rolls, 1272-9*, pp. 199-200; E 401/1567; E 101/250/14; E 159/46, mm. 8d, 10; E 159/47, m. 4; Rokeah, Appendix II, p. 203

4. A **tallage of one third of the possessions of the Jews of England (including unliquidated obligations)** imposed at the end of 1273 or early in 1274 and perhaps in 1276 described as of the value of 25, 000 marks. The tallage was assessed by the Treasurer (brother Joseph de Chauncy) and Pain de Chaworth. The initial collectors (first mentioned in May 1274) were brother Stephen of Fulbourn and William of Middleton; in October 1274 Adam of Stratton joined them in a commission to collect arrears. In November 1274 in a similar commission brother Luke of Hammington replaced Stratton. Fulbourn had ceased to play an active roll in collection by early 1275 when he went to Ireland as bishop of Waterford and in May 1275 the justices of the Jews and William of Middleton (the keeper of rolls and writs) took over responsibility for collecting arrears. Middelton relinquished responsibility in July 1276 when appointed keeper of rolls and writs in the Common Bench and in June 1278 one final change was made, transferring responsbility for collecting the remaining arrears to the Treasurer and two of his colleagues as Barons of the Exchequer (John of Cobham and Philip of Willoughby).
References: *Cal. Pat. Rolls, 1272-81*, pp. 51, 52, 61, 62-3, 83, 84, 154, 163, 273; *Cal. Close Rolls, 1272-9*, pp. 83, 110, 144, 166-7, 176, 181, 264-5; E 159/48, m. 4; E 159/49, m. 4; E 159/50, m. 4; E 101/249/16, 18, 21; E 401/1568-1571, 1573; *E.J.*, iv, nos. 13-88; *E.J.*, ii, pp. 302-17; *E.J.*, iii, pp. 63-6, 95-104, 130-9; Rokeah, Appendix II, pp. 204-5, 205-6 (treats as two separate tallages)

5. A **fine of £1000** imposed or agreed in 1276.
References: *Cal. Fine Rolls, 1272-1307*, p. 61; *Cal. Close Rolls, 1272-1279*, p. 306; Rokeah, Appendix II, pp. 206-7

6. A **tallage of uncertain amount** of which the assessors were instructed to ensure a minimum of 3,000 marks and set a target of 4,000 marks imposed in 1277. The assessors were John of Cobham, Philip of Willoughby and William of Middleton. The same men were also named as collectors, though in February 1278 Middleton is to be found cooperating with Gregory of Rokesley in the collection of a recent Jewish tallage, which may be this one.
References: *Cal. Pat. Rolls, 1272-81*, pp. 211, 215; *Cal. Close Rolls, 1272-79*, pp. 392, 441; Rokeah, Appendix II, p. 207.

7. A **tallage of 3,000 marks** imposed in 1278. The assessors and collectors were the Treasurer, Walter de Helyon, John of Cobham and Philip of Willoughby

References: *Cal. Pat. Rolls, 1272-1281*, pp. 274, 282; *Cal. Close Rolls, 1272-1279*, p. 503.
[but perhaps the same as 6]

8. A **tallage of uncertain amount** assessed by Ralph of Sandwich, William of Carleton and Gregory of Ruxley in 1287. This may be the same as the Jewish tallage of which £889 14s 6d was paid into the wardrobe at some date between 1288 and 1290. Possibly to be identified with the fine of £12,000 made by the Jews of England and mentioned in a royal mandate of July 1290.
References: *Cal. Close Rolls, 1279-1288*, p. 456; E 159/61, m. 6d; E 159/63, m. 16d (I owe this reference to Professor Robert Stacey); E 401/1584-5; E 372/138, m. 26.

EASTER TERM, 7 EDWARD I [1279]

Exchequer of Jews, Plea Rolls Nos. 31 and 70 [E 9/31 and 70]

The main surviving roll for this term is E 9/31. A single membrane from a second roll was transferred to this class from E 160/7 by Dr M. Condon and given the number E 9/70. It supplies a second version of the following entries from Roll 31: 64 and 65 (on the face), 66, 67 and 68 (on the dorse, of which nos. 66 and 67 are written upside down). Significant differences from the version on Roll 31 are noted in the footnotes. At the bottom of the dorse is a note correctly recording that the membrane belongs to *Pascha anno .vij.º*

MEMBRANE 1

Essonia de quindena Pasche anno regni regis Edwardi septimo

(1)

Sutht'. Adam de Wynton' clericus versus Ricardum le Porter, Agnetem uxorem ejus et Ricardum filium ejus de placito transgressionis per Johannem de Alto Bosco.

Postea venit.

(2)

Warr'. Nicholaus de Hayles, attornatus abbatis de Bordesle, versus Regem et Johannem de Ba de placito debiti per Johannem Orgily.

Frater Willelmus de Cuerdale alter attornatus versus eosdem de eodem per Henricum de Toneworth.

In octabis sancti Johannis Baptiste. Affidaverunt.

(3)

Berk'. vetus est post prece parcium. Johannes de Newt' attornatus Bartholomei de Yhatinghdene versus Ricardum de Sutton de placito aquietacionis debiti per Walterum Bost.

Petrus de Trumpeton alter attornatus versus eundem de eodem per Adam Prodhom.

A die sancte Trinitatis in xv dies. Affidaverunt.

(4)

Oxon'. Robertus de Bodenton' attornatus Johannis Giffard versus Johannem de Scaccario de placito debiti unde jurata per Adam Prodhom.

Postea venit.

(5)

Suth'. vetus est. Laurencius de Netherhavene attornatus abbatis de Hyda Wynton' versus Regem de placito debiti per Johannem Swynebuk'.

vetus est. [e]<Ricardus de Forsterbiry>[e] alter attornatus versus eundem de eodem per Willelmum Prat.

(6)

Suth'. Johannes Edgar attornatus Willelmi filii Willelmi de Donstyle versus Regem de placito debiti per Johannem filium Roberti.

Ricardus de Forstesbiry alter attornatus versus eundem de eodem per Willelmum filium Johannis.

(7)

Oxon'. [e]<Willelmus>[e] [i]<Ricardus>[i] le Povere versus Belyam que fuit uxor Lumbardi de Oxon' judei de placito dotis per Johannem Scot.

In octabis sancti Johannis Baptiste. Affidavit.

(8)

Sampson de Wygorn' attornatus Vyves filii Abr' judei versus Johannem le Buler de placito debiti per Adam Prodhom.

Postea venit.

(9)

Nortff'. Non jacet quia breve dicit 'venire facias'. Ricardus Rust versus Abr' filium Deulecresse de Linc' judeum de placito debiti per Johannem Strut.

Radulfus Badok' versus eundem de eodem per Adam Prodhom.

Gilbertus Hole versus eundem de eodem per Johannem Scot.

(10)

Nicholaus Duredent versus Johannem de Monemuta de placito acquietacionis debiti per Johannem Fox.

Postea venit Nicholaus.

Essonia de tribus septimanis Pasche

(11)

Nortff'. Willelmus de Scothowe attornatus Samuelis de Norwyco versus Henricum de Hasting', Robertum de Crakeford', et Simonem de Ryston' de placito debiti per Johannem Pye.

In crastino sancti Johannis Baptiste. Affidavit.

Essonia de mense

(12)

Nortff'. Willelmus de Scothowe.[1]

[1] *This entry is unfinished.*

MEMBRANE 1 DORSE

Attornati, Prece Parcium

(13)

Cantebr'. Thomas Bacun ponit loco suo Stephanum de Croxton' vel Stephanum de Dykedale versus Reginaldum fiz le Fevre et alios in brevi de placito debiti et ammovet Johannem de Caam et alios quos prius etc.

(14)

Norff'. Hugo Hoche, custos terre et heredis Galfridi Wascelyn, ponit loco suo Simonem le Grys versus magistrum Walterum de la Mare de placito debiti.

(15)

Oxon'. Willelmus le Especer ponit loco suo Aaron filium Vyves judeum versus Adam Beneyt et Agnetem uxorem ejus de placito debiti.

Idem ponit loco suo eundem Aaron versus Wydonem filium Wydonis et [Margeriam][2] uxorem ejus de placito debiti.

(16)

Wylt'. Alexander de Dunho ponit loco suo Johannem Waryn versus Johannem et Thomam filios et heredes Roberti de Salusbur' de placito injuste detencionis cujusdam starri.

MEMBRANE 2

Placita de [Quindena][3] Pasche anno regni regis Edwardi septimo

(17)

Cantebr'. Thomas Bakun fecit venire Rogerum filium le Fevere de Croxton', tenentem quandam partem terrarum que fuerunt Ivonis Quarel, et exigit ab eo .xl. solidos de debitis predicti Ivonis, quos ei debet racione predictarum terrarum quas tenet etc.

Et predictus Rogerus venit et defendit etc. Et dicit quod non tenetur prefato Thome respondere de predictis .xl. solidis racione alicujus terre quam tenet de terris que fuerunt prefati Ivonis, quia nullam terram tenet que umquam fuit predicti Ivonis. Et de hoc ponit se super patriam.

Et prefatus Thomas per attornatum suum dicit quod tenet terras que fuerunt ejusdem Ivonis. Et de hoc ponit se [i]<similiter>[i] super patriam; unde preceptum est vicecomiti quod venire faciat .xij. probos etc., per quos etc., et qui nulla affinitate etc., a die sancte Trinitatis in .xv. dies ad recognoscendum etc.

Ad quem diem predictus Thomas venit et petit licenciam querendi melius breve. Ideo predictus Rogerus per attornatum suum eat inde sine die.[4]

(18)

Cantebr'. Thomas Bakun fecit venire Willelmum le Kepere et Johannam uxorem ejus, tenentes partem terrarum que fuerunt Ivonis Quarel, et exigit ab eis racione predictarum terrarum .xl. solidos de debito in quo prefatus Ivo tenebatur Hagino filio magistri Mossei.

Et prefati Willelmus et Johanna veniunt per attornatum suum et petunt diem premeditandi et habent a die sancte Trinitatis in xv dies.

<Idem Thomas fecit venire Robertum Alewyn', Cristianam [i]<de>[i] Maunz et Willelmum Gorge, tenentes quandam partem terrarum que fuerunt predicti Ivonis, et exigit ab eis racione predictarum terrarum etc., videlicet ab unoquoque eorundem .xl. solidos de debito predicto.

Et ipsi per attornatos suos venerunt et petunt diem premeditandi et habent a die sancte Trinitatis in xv dies.>[5] Ad quem diem essoniati fuerunt et habent diem a die sancti Johannis Baptiste in .xv. dies. Ad quem diem Willelmus le Kepere et Johanna uxor ejus et Robertus Alwyn veniunt et de porcionibus ipsos contingentibus vocant ad warantum Hugonem Saunzaver. Et preceptum est vicecomiti quod venire faciat predictum Hugonem ad acquietandum etc. a die sancti Michaelis in xv dies etc.[6]

Et ad quem diem Willelmus Gorge et Cristiana Maunz essoniati fuerunt et habuerunt diem a die sancti Johannis Baptiste in .xv. dies. Ad quem diem Willelmus Gorge venit et dicit quod ipse et Richolda uxor ejus feoffati sunt simul, sicut continetur in quadam carta quam protulit, sine qua Richolda non debet respondere et petit judicium de brevi. Dictus Thomas per attornatum suum non potuit hoc dedicere. Ideo [consideratum][7] est quod dictus Willelmus eat inde sine die de hoc brevi.

Et predicta Cristiana venit et dicit quod feoffata est sicut continetur in quadam carta quam protulit de terris quas tenet una cum filio suo qui non nominatur in brevi, sine quo non debet respondere, et petit judicium de brevi predicti Thome attornati Willelmi de Leyburn'. Judicium quod predicta Cristiana eat inde sine die.

(19)

Wilt'. Nicholaus Duredent per attornatum suum optulit se quarto die versus Johannem de Monemuth' de placito aquietacionis debiti. Et dictus Johannes non venit. Et preceptum fuit vicecomiti quod distringeret ipsum Johannem per terras etc., et quod de exitibus etc., et quod haberet corpus ejus coram etc. ad hunc diem ad respondendum etc. Et vicecomes mandavit quod predictus Johannes districtus est etc. et quod Johannes le Frye, Thomas le Teuke, Johannes de Mersche, Rogerus le Dunt et Walterus Faber manuceperunt ipsum Johannem, quem non habuerunt. Ideo in misericordia.

[2] *MS. reads* Mag'.

[3] *MS. reads* Quindecim.

[4] *Followed in MS. by a continuation of the following entry which has been copied into the wrong place. It has been transcribed here in what should have been its proper place.*

[5] *These words are repeated in MS.*

[6] *The remainder of this entry was wrongly added by the clerk to the preceding entry but has now been restored to its proper place.*

[7] *MS. reads* concessum.

Mandavit etiam quod exitus dictarum terrarum sunt dimidia marca. Et ideo preceptum est vicecomiti, sicut pluries, quod distringat predictum Johannem per terras etc. ut prius, et quod de exitibus etc., et quod habeat corpus ejus coram etc. in octabis sancte Trinitatis ad respondendum etc. et ad audiendum etc. de pluribus defaltis. Et vicecomes salvo custodiat etc. et habeat hic ad eundem diem [i]<hic>[i] predictos exitus et omnes alios exitus predictarum terrarum a tempore quo primo ei preceptum fuit etc.

(20)

Hereff'. Aaron filius Vyves per attornatum suum optulit se quarto die versus Johannem filium Walteri de Thornebur', tenentem quandam partem terrarum que fuerunt Willelmi Devereus, de placito debiti. Et ipse Johannes non venit. Et preceptum fuit vicecomiti quod ipsum distringeret per terras etc., et quod de exitibus etc., et quod haberet corpus ejus coram etc. ad hunc diem. Et vicecomes mandavit quod dictus Johannes nichil habet in comitatu suo. Et quia testatum est[8] quod satis habet in comitatu predicto per quod distringi potest, preceptum [i]<est>[i] eidem vicecomiti, sicut pluries, quod distringat etc., ita quod habeat corpus ejus [i]<coram>[i] etc. a die sancte Trinitatis in .xv. dies ad respondendum predicto judeo de placito predicto et ad audiendum etc. Et quia vicecomes male retornavit in misericordia. Condonatur ad instanciam Walteri de Redmerlegh'.[9]

(21)

Bed'. Preceptum fuit vicecomiti quod distringeret Ivonem Quarel per quendam redditum .c. solidorum quem percipit annuatim de Rogero de Nowers et Isabella uxore ejus, ita quod nec ipse etc., et quod de exitibus etc., et quod haberet corpus ejus coram etc. ad hunc diem ad respondendum Willelmo de Leyburn' una cum predictis Rogero et Isabella uxore ejus ac aliis tenentibus terrarum que fuerunt eiusdem Ivonis Quarel de placito debiti. Et predictus Ivo non venit. Et vicecomes mandavit quod prohibuit predictis Rogero et Isabelle ne aliquid reddant prefato Ivoni de predicto redditu donec etc., et quod non potuit facere venire ipsum Ivonem. Ideo preceptum est vicecomiti, sicut alias, quod distringat ipsum Ivonem per dictum redditum, ita quod nec ipse etc., et quod habeat corpus ejus coram etc. in octabis sancte Trinitatis ad respondendum etc. ut supra. Et vicecomes habeat coram etc. ad eundem diem omnes exitus de prefato redditu provenientes a tempore quo primo [i]<ei>[i] preceptum fuit quod inde respondeat.

Memoranda

(22)

Cantebr'. Johannes de Whatel, custos auri domine Alianore Regine Anglie matris Regis nunc, venit coram etc. et recognovit se recepisse de Willelmo Seman et sociis suis .xl. solidos, quos debuerunt de auro predicte Alienore regine. Et ideo preceptum est vicecomiti quod de demanda quam eis facit occasione etc. pacem habere permittat.

(23)

Aaron filius Vyves judeus recognovit per starrum quod recepit de Ricardo de Aumundevyle .xij. libras, .x. solidos et .xx. solidos pro una roba die quindene Pasche anno regni regis Edwardi septimo.

MEMBRANE 2 DORSE

(24)

Kanc'. Robertus de Monteny optulit se quarto die versus Thomam de Sandewyco de placito injuste detencionis averiorum. Et ipse non venit. Et preceptum fuit vicecomiti, sicut alias, quod non omitteret propter libertatem episcopatus Cant' quin eam etc. et destringeret ipsum Thomam per terras etc., ita quod nec ipse etc., et quod de exitibus etc., et quod haberet corpus ejus coram etc. Et vicecomes mandavit quod predictus Thomas districtus est, et quod Thomas Tankard, Hamo le Paye, Askerimus de Messeburgh', Robertus atte Ford manuceperunt ipsum Thomam, quem non habuerunt. Ideo in misericordia.[10] Judicium, sicut pluries, quod non omittat etc. et distringat predictum Thomam per terras etc., et quod habeat corpus ejus coram etc. a die sancte Trinitatis in .xv. dies ad respondendum etc., et ad audiendum judicium de pluribus defaltis.

(25)

Wyltes'. Thomas de Chelewarton' optulit se quarto die versus Johannem de Havering' quondam vicecomitem Suth' de placito transgressionis. Et ipse non venit. Et preceptum fuit vicecomiti, sicut alias, quod ipsum distringeret per terras etc. Et vicecomes mandavit quod habet breve regis quod omnes demandas super ipsum Johannem factas ponat in respectum usque ad instans parlyamentum, per quod de precepto predicto nichil actum est. Et preceptum est vicecomiti, sicut pluries, quod ipsum distringat per terras etc., ut prius, ita quod habeat corpus ejus coram etc. in octabis sancte Trinitatis [e]<in .xv. dies>[e] ad respondendum etc., et ad audiendum.

(26)

Linc', Not'. Preceptum fuit vicecomiti quod venire faceret coram etc. Mosseum filium Salomonis de Staunford' judeum ad respondendum Roberto de Brus et Hugoni filio Alani de Ryhale de Eyton' de placito aquietacionis debiti. Et ipse non venit. Et vicecomes mandavit quod predictus Mosseus non fuit inventus in balliva [sua][11] postquam breve ei venit, set manet apud Not'. Et ideo preceptum est vicecomiti Not' quod ipsum venire faciat coram etc. in octabis sancti Johannis

[8] *Followed in MS. by* et.

[9] *In the margin is written* misericordia condonatur.

[10] *The word* misericordia *is repeated in the margin.*

[11] *MS. reads* tua.

Baptiste ad respondendum prefatis Roberto et Hugoni de placito predicto.

(27)

Suth'. Godefridus le Clerck de Werldham optulit se quarto die versus Thomam Paynel de placito aquietacionis debiti. Et ipse non venit. Et preceptum fuit vicecomiti, sicut pluries, quod non omitteret propter libertatem episcopatus Wynton' quin eam etc. et salvo etc., per que etc., tam infra dictam libertatem quam infra hundredum de Aulton'; et si plures etc. ipsum per ea etc., ita quod de exitibus etc. a tempore quo primo etc., et quod haberet corpus ejus coram etc. ad respondendum predicto Godefredo de placito predicto. Et vicecomes mandavit quod salvo custodivit etc. terras et catalla per que etc. Et quod Johannis Pylgrim, Nicholaus de Cruce, Johannes de Cruce, Henricus Pynnok', Rogerus Prepositus et Radulfus de Aqua ipsum manuceperunt, quem non habuerunt. Ideo in misericordia. Et preceptum est vicecomiti, sicut pluries, quod salvo etc., ut prius, et si plures etc. a die sancte Trinitatis in .xv. dies ad respondendum etc. et ad audiendum etc.

(28)

Northt'. Willelmus Folyot et Ysabella uxor ejus, filia Stephani filii David de Esseby, venire fecerunt coram etc. Elenam la Zuche ad respondendum eis de placito quare eadem Elena racione quorundam debitorum per predictum David a magistro Elia judeo Lond' mutuatorum, que se emisse asserebat, sicut prefati [Willelmus][12] et Isabella dicunt, eandem Isabellam, cui terre et tenementa predicti David hereditarie descendebant, antequam dictus Willelmus eandem Isabellam desponsaverat de domibus et edificiis suis dehospitavit et in residuis terris et tenementis dicte Isabelle que fuerunt predicti David, ipsa Isabella non summonita, sine judicio se intrusit et ipsam Isabellam plenius ejecit et ejectam detinet, et domus infra capitale messuagium de Asseby David existentes extirpavit, fraxinos et alias arbores in eodem mesuagio crescentes abradicavit et boscum suum prostravit, vendidit et distruxit ad grave dampnum suum et exheredacionem suam manifestam et contra assisam et consuetudinem Judaismi.

Et prefata Elena venit et dicit quod non tenetur respondere prefatis Willelmo et Isabelle, nec ad breve suum, eo quod aliud breve regis de nova disseisina dependet coram Rogero Loveday et Johanne de Methyngham justiciariis assignatis de prefatis terris et tenementis. Et petit judicium si ad dictum breve debeat respondere, desicut dictum breve nove disseisine sit breve originale et placitatur usque ad assisam, et aliud breve [i]<est>[i] originale et novum breve ad quod hactenus responsum non est; et super hoc habent diem <usque diem>[13] lune proximo sequentem ad audiendum inde judicium suum. Ad quem diem partes venerunt et prefata Elena peciit judicium, ut prius; et prefati

[12] *MS. omits.*

[13] *These words are repeated in MS.*

Willelmus et Isabella petunt licenciam recedendi de brevi suo et perquirendi melius breve, et habent.

(29)

Suht'. Adam de Wynton' clericus fecit venire Ricardum le Porter, Agnetem uxorem ejus et Ricardum filium dicti Ricardi ad respondendum ei de placito transgressionis. Et queritur quod prefati Ricardus et alii noctanter vi et armis venerunt ad quemdam murum ipsius Ade in suburbio Wynton' et magnam partem ipsius prostraverunt et catalla ipsius Ade ad valenciam .xx. solidorum ceperunt et asportaverunt et alia enormia ei intulerunt ad dampnum ejusdem Ade .c. solidorum et contra pacem nostram etc.

Et prefatus Ricardus, cui concessum est respondere pro se ipso et [i]<dicta>[i] Agnete uxore ejus, venit [i]<et>[i] defendit etc. Et dicit quod non prostravit dictum murum ipsius Ade nec aliquod dampnum ei intulit sicut idem Adam dicit, et ad hoc ponit se super patriam.

Et quod dictum murum prostravit et alia enormia prefato Ade intulit etc., ut predicitur, ponit idem Adam similiter se super patriam. Et preceptum est vicecomiti quod venire faciat coram etc. a die sancte Trinitatis in .xv. dies .xij. probos et legales etc., per quos rei veritas etc.; et qui nulla affinitate etc., ad recognoscendum etc. Ad quem diem predictus Adam optulit se versus predictos Ricardum et Agnetem. Et ipsi non venerunt. Ideo ipsi Ricardus et Agnes in misericordia.[14] Et patria non venit. Et preceptum fuit vicecomiti quod eam venire faceret ad inquirendum, ut supra. Et vicecomes mandavit quod retornavit breve ballivis libertatis Wynton' et episcopatus Wynton', qui nichil inde fecerunt. Judicium quod non omittat etc., et venire faciat coram etc. inquisicionem a die sancti Michaelis in .xv. dies ad recognoscendum etc. Ad quem diem vicecomes mandavit quod breve sibi adeo tarde venit quod non potuit exequi. Judicium, sicut alias, quod non omittat etc. et venire faciat coram etc. inquisicionem in crastino Purificacionis etc.

(30)

Wygorn'. Vyves filius Aaron judeus per attornatum suum optulit se quarto die versus Rogerum de Mortuo Mari, tenentem terrarum que fuerunt Roberti de Clyfton', de placito debiti. Et dictus Rogerus non venit. Et preceptum fuit vicecomiti, sicut pluries, quod ipsum distringeret per terras etc., ita quod [haberet][15] corpus ejus coram etc. ad hunc diem ad respondendum etc. Et vicecomes mandavit quod dictus Rogerus districtus est, unde exitus terrarum suarum sunt dimidia marca; et quod Milo de Heleye, Johannes del Ake, Robertus de Monte et Willelmus Waryn manuceperunt ipsum Rogerum, quem non habent. Ideo in misericordia.[16] Judicium quod prefatus Rogerus distringatur per terras etc., ut prius, et quod habeat corpus ejus coram etc. in

[14] *The word* misericordia *is repeated in the margin.*

[15] *MS. reads* habeat.

[16] *The word* misericordia *is repeated in the margin.*

octabis sancti Johannis Baptiste ad respondendum etc., et ad audiendum; et vicecomes habeat ad eundem diem dimidiam marcam quam levavit de exitibus terrarum.

MEMBRANE 3

Placita de tribus septimanis Pasche et de mense anno regis Edwardi septimo

(31)

Nort'. Magister Walterus de la Mare fecit venire Hugonem Hochede, custodem heredis Galfridi filii Andree Wascelyn et tenentem terrarum que fuerunt ejusdem Galfridi, et exigit ab eo quindecim libras in quibus prefatus Galfridus tenebatur Cresseo filio magistri Elie per unum cyrographum .xv. librarum, unde altera pars est in archa cyrographariorum apud Lond', quod quidem debitum idem Walterus habuit ex dimissione Stephani de Cheynduit, cui prefatus Cresseus debitum illud dimisit.

Et prefatus Hugo venit per attornatum suum et petit diem premeditandi et habet a die sancte Trinitatis in .xv. dies.

(32)

Surr', Sussex'. Magister Elyas filius magistri Mossei judeus optulit se quarto [die][17] per attornatum suum versus Willelmum de Hastyng de placito debiti. Et ipse non venit. Et preceptum fuit vicecomiti quod salvo custodiret terras etc., et si plures etc., ita quod nec ipse etc., et quod de exitibus etc., et quod haberet <corpus>[18] ejus coram etc. ad hunc diem ad respondendum etc. Et vicecomes mandavit quod predictas terras etc. salvo custodivit et quod non habet plures etc., et quod Johannis Capenore de Nadderfeld, Anselmus de Lynde, Willelmus Attefeld, Alanus de Lynde, Walterus atteBech et Willelmus le Puke de eadem manuceperunt predictum Willelmum, quem non habent. Ideo in misericordia.[19] Judicium quod terre etc. salvo custodiantur etc., ita quod nec ipse etc., et quod de exitibus etc. a tempore quo primo etc., et quod habeat corpus ejus coram etc. a die sancti Johannis in .xv. dies ad respondendum etc., et ad audiendum etc. de pluribus defaltis. Et quia vicecomes non habuit nunc hic de Galfrido de Hokestepl' et Rogero le Bedle et aliis manucaptoribus predicti Willelmi quinque marcas ad quas amerciati fuerunt, sicut patet inter brevia ad hunc diem retornata, sicut ei preceptum fuit, ideo ipse vicecomes, videlicet Emerycus de Chauncels, in misericordia.[20]

(33)

Herff'. de mense. Preceptum fuit vicecomiti quod venire faceret coram etc. ad hunc diem Thomam filium Hamonis de Vyeleston', tenentem quandam partem terrarum que fuerunt predicti Hamonis, ad respondendum Mosseo filio Jacobi judeo de placito debiti. Et vicecomes mandavit quod predictus Thomas nullas habet terras in balliva sua seu tenementa, per quod de dicto precepto nichil actum est. Et quia testatum est quod satis habet etc. ideo preceptum est vicecomiti, sicut alias, in octabis sancte Trinitatis.

(34)

Kanc'. Preceptum fuit vicecomiti quod venire faceret coram etc. Johannem filium Hamonis de Vyeleston', tenentem quandam partem terrarum que fuerunt predicti Hamonis, ad respondendum Mosseo filio Jacobi de placito debiti. Et vicecomes mandavit quod breve regis retornatum fuit senescallo libertatis archiepiscopatus Cant', qui nichil inde respondet. Ideo preceptum est vicecomiti quod non omittat propter libertatem etc. quin eam etc. et venire faciat coram etc. in octabis sancte Trinitatis prefatum Johannem ad respondendum etc. de placito predicto.

(35)

Som', Dors'. Preceptum fuit vicecomiti, sicut pluries, quod non omitteret propter libertatem comitis Glouc' quin eam etc. et distringeret Johannem filium Willelmi Ruffigeray per terras et catalla sua, ita quod nec ipse etc., et quod de exitibus etc, et quod haberet corpus ejus coram etc. ad hunc diem ad respondendum Ricardo Loverle et Joscee uxori ejus de placito aquietacionis debiti. Et vicecomes mandavit quod preceptum fuit Waltero de la Lynde capitali ballivo de Westperot, qui ei respondit quod predictus Johannes non habet aliquid per quod possit distringi nisi quandam grangiam que inclusa est occasione predicta, et quod non potuit invenire manucaptores. Et ideo preceptum est vicecomiti, ut prius, quod non omittat propter libertatem predictam quin eam etc. et distringat predictum Johannem per terras etc., ut prius, ita quod habeat corpus ejus coram etc. a die sancte Trinitatis in .iij. septimanas ad respondendum etc. et ad audiendum etc. Et vicecomes, scilicet Johannes de Cormayles, in misericordia, eo quod non intravit dictam libertatem ad distringendum predictum Johannem, sicut ei preceptum fuit.

(36)

Surr', Sussex'. Preceptum fuit vicecomiti quod venire faceret coram etc. ad hunc diem .xij. probos et legales homines de comitatu suo, per quos etc., et qui nulla affinitate etc. attingant Willelmum de Hevere et Matillidem uxorem ejus vel Gamaliel de Oxon' judeum, ad recognoscendum etc. si prefati Willelmus et Matillis tenent .x. marcatas redditus que fuerunt Johannis de Kaumvyle et quas idem Johannes invadiare potuit, sicut predictus Gamaliel dicit, vel si iidem Willelmus et Matillis hujusmodi redditum non teneant nec aliquo tempore tenuerunt, sicut ipsi Willelmus et Matillis dicunt. Et vicecomes mandavit quod Walterus de

[17] *MS. omits.*

[18] *This word is repeated in MS.*

[19] *This word is repeated in the margin.*

[20] *The word* misericordia *is repeated in the margin but with below it the amount of the amercement* c solidi.

Wyford', Thomas de Lecchewille de Westmere, Thomas Aldewyne, Petrus atte Nasse, Thomas atte Hale, Gilbertus atte Hacche, Petrus le Moneth', Ricardus le Warner, Willelmus la persone, Gilbertus atte Rak', Ricardus Atterlynde, Gilbertus atte Dene, Robertus Henry, Johannes le Whyte et Willelmus Bolle districti sunt veniendi per terras et catalla, qui non veniunt. Ideo ipse Walterus et alii in misericordia. Et quia preceptum fuit vicecomiti quod ipse venire faceret .xij., sicut predicitur, et ipse non retornavit aliquos manucaptores ideo idem vicecomes, scilicet Emerycus de Chauncels, quia male retornavit, in misericordia.[21]

(37)

Oxon'. Preceptum fuit vicecomiti, sicut pluries, quod de terris et catallis Eadmundi filii Johannis de Glouc' fieri faceret octo libras .xiij. solidos et .iiij. denarios ad opus Ade de Stratton' de .xx. libris quas idem Adam in curia domini Henrici regis versus eundem Eadmundum de debitis Isak' de Suwerk' judei per consideracionem etc. recuperavit, ita quod denarios illos ad hunc diem haberet etc. eidem Ade solvendos. Et vicecomes mandavit quod mandaverat ballivis libertatis dominici domini regis in Wodestok' ad levandum dictos denarios, qui ei respondebant quod dictus Eadmundus nichil habet infra dictam libertatem unde aliqui denarii levari possint nisi tantummodo bladum viride crescens in terra. Ideo, sicut prius, a die sancti Michaelis in .xv. dies, ita quod denarios illos habeat et de blado illo et aliis catallis ipsius Eadmundi ad diem predictum.

(38)

Glouc'. Preceptum fuit vicecomiti, sicut pluries, quod de terris et catallis Eadmundi filii Johannis de Glouc' fieri faceret .x. libras ad opus Ade de Stratton' de .xx. libris quas idem Adam in curia domini Henrici regis coram etc. recuperavit versus ipsum Edmundum de debitis Isak' de Suwerk' judei etc., ita quod denarios illas haberet ad hunc diem eidem Ade solvendos. Et vicecomes mandavit quod dictus Eadmundus nichil habet in comitatu Glouc' unde aliqui denarii levari possunt nisi quandam terram apud Lassindon', quam abbas de Glouc' modo tenet et eam hoc anno inbladavit ante adventum hujus mandati. Ideo, sicut prius, a die sancti Michaelis in .xv. dies.

MEMBRANE 3 DORSE

(39)

Warr', London'. Magister Elias filius magistri Mossei et Aaron filius Vyves recognoverunt per starrum suum quod aquietaverunt Roberto Hasteng .xl. libras in quibus eis tenebatur reddendas terminis subscriptis, videlicet .xx. libras a die sancti Michaelis in unum mensem anno regis E. sexto et .xx. libras a die Pasche in unum mensem anno regis E. septimo, quia inde omnino recognoverunt se esse perpacatos de predictis .xl. libris terminis predictis de debitis in quibus ipsis judeis tenebatur. Et quod recognoverunt hoc littera sua hebrayca [sigillaverunt].

MEMBRANE 4

Memoranda de termino Pasche anno regni regis [Edwardi] septimo

(40)

Dors'. Johannes filius et heres Hamonis de Burton' venit coram etc. et protulit breve regis de magno sigillo in hec verba:. 'Edwardus etc. justiciariis suis ad custodiam Judeorum assignatis salutem. Cum Johannes filius et heres Hamonis de Burton' nuper defuncti teneretur Abr' Russel judeo nostro de Wilton' defuncto in diversis debitis occasione quorundam debitorum mutuorum, que prefatus Hamo a predicto judeo dudum receperat, sicut in carta ipsius Hamonis quam dictus judeus inde habuit et que in thesauro nostro existit plenius continetur, que quidem debita occasione mortis eiusdem judei capi fecimus in manum nostram, nos juxta provisionem et concessionem nostram quam nuper fecimus graciose christianis in Judaismo nostro indebitatis prefato Johanni subvenire volentes in hac parte, vobis mandamus quod, salvis eidem Johanni capitali mesuagio et medietate terrarum et tenementorum suorum et capitali domino servicio suo de terris et tenementis illis, eidem Johanni racionabiles terminos ad quos predicta debita nobis persolvere possit juxta extentam quam nuper inde fieri fecimus et vobis transmisimus habere faciatis, proviso quod ea que predicto judeo de debitis predictis soluta fuerunt predicto Johanni in dictis debitis allocentur. Teste me ipso apud Westm' .xvij. die Aprilis anno regni nostri septimo.' Per hoc breve, scrutata extenta de terris et tenementis que fuerunt Hamonis de Burton' que facta fuit per breve regis Edwardi nunc, sicut reperitur inter extentas factas termino sancte Trinitatis anno dicti regis quarto, que continet .xiij. libras, quinque solidos .xj. denarios obolum, de quibus subtractis .iij. solidis pro capitali mesuagio predicte terre et .x. libris sex denariis debitis comiti Cornubie per annum capitali domino feodi, restant .lxij. solidi .xj. denarii obulus. Concessum est Johanni filio et heredi predicti Hamonis quod solvat per annum domino regi ad scaccarium sancti Michaelis .xxxj. solidos .v. denarios obulum, incipiendo in quindenam sancti Michaelis anno predicti regis septimo, et sic de anno in annum ad eundem terminum donec persolverit totum debitum in quo predictus Hamo tenebatur predicto Abr', unde carta existit in thesauro regis, allocato eidem Johanni quod solvit de eadem debito, sicut racionabiliter monstrare poterit quod inde regi vel dicto judeo satisfecit. Et preceptum est vicecomiti quod ipsum decetero de predicto debito pacem habere permittat etc.

[21] *The word* misericordia *is repeated in the margin.*

(41)

Kanc'. Simon de Cray venit coram etc. die martis proxima ante festum Invencionis sancte Crucis et protulit .xx. solidos quos debet de debitis diversorum judeorum de termino Pasche. Qui denarii remanent in thesauro regis sub sigillo ejusdem Simonis ad opus Abr' filii magistri Elie.

(42)

Rotel', quattuor libri soluti in recepta regis. Reginaldus Tornehare solvit in recepta regis .iiij. libras de debitis Samuelis filii Sauloti et habet duas tallias.

(43)

Norff'. Preceptum fuit vicecomiti quod inquireret per sacramentum etc qui sunt tenentes terrarum et tenementorum que fuerunt Willelmi Oldeland' etc., et quid et quantum porcio singulorum tenencium valeat per annum in omnibus exitibus, salvo servicio dominorum feodi, et inquisicionem etc. scire faceret justiciariis etc ad hunc diem, et omnes quos etc. venire faceret coram etc. ad respondendum Regi una cum Johanne Cosyn, Roberto filio Rogeri, Ricardo Rust, Johanne de Badebrigg', Johanne Hachet, David de Blakeland', David Bene, Johanne Gerland', Ricardo de Paunton', Agnete Hachet, et Johanne de la More, [tenentibus][22] partes predictarum terrarum, qui eundem diem habent de .xx. libris quas debent Regi de debitis Salomonis filii Deulecresse judei occasione predictarum terrarum quas tenent. Et vicecomes mandavit quod Andreas Oldelond' tenet capitale mesuagium quod fuit Willelmi Oldelond' et .xv. acras terre arabilis in Elyngham et .v. acras prati in eadem villa. Et alii tenentes supradicti tenent de terris predictis secundum quod patet inter inquisiciones in hoc termino Pasche retornatas. Mandavit eciam vicecomes quod preter predictos tenentes sunt alii tenentes predictarum terrarum Willelmi Oldelond, videlicet Letya de Toft, Alexander Lytel, Willelmus le Mouner, [e]<Willelmus>[e] [i]<Gilbertus>[i] le Bole et Radulfus de Doddek', sicut continetur inter inquisiciones predictas. Et predicti Johannes Cosyn, Robertus filius Rogeri, Johannes Gorlond', David Bene, Ricardus Panton', Letya del Toft, Johannes de la More capellanus, David de Blakelond', Johannes de Badebrigge et Willelmus le Mouner per attornatos suos coram H. Hauteyn et R. de Ludham et per breve regis vicissiter attornatos venerunt. Et predictus Johannes Cosyn recognovit se tenere de terris predictis sex acras et dimidiam et inde vocat ad warantum de aquietacione [i]<dicti>[i] debiti Nicholaum de la Hale de porcione ipsum contingente de .v. acris et .iij. rodis. [Robertus][23] filius Rogeri dicit [se][24] <tenere>[25] duas acras de eisdem terris de quibus feoffatus fuit antequam dictus Willelmus Oldelond obligabatur in dicto debito. Johannes Gerland' dicit se tenere unam rodam terre et dimidiam de quibus feoffatus fuit ante etc. David [i]<Bene>[i] dicit se tenere duas acras et dimidiam de quibus feoffatus fuit ante etc. de una acra et dimidia, et de una acra vocat ad warantum predictum Nicholaum de la Hale. Ricardus Panton' dicit etc. unam acram terre de qua feoffatus fuit ante etc. Johannes de Badebrigge dicit se tenere dimidiam acram terre de qua feoffatus fuit [i]<ante>[i] etc. Johannes Hachet dicit se tenere unam acram terre de qua feoffatus fuit ante etc. Johannes de la More dicit se tenere unam acram prati de qua feoffatus fuit ante etc. Et Willelmus le Mouner venit et dicit quod non tenet nec aliquo tempore tenuit terram neque tenementum quod fuit predicti Willelmi Oldelond'. Et Alexander Lytel dicit quod tenet de eodem Willelmo Oldelond .iiij. acras terre et dimidiam in villenagium. Ideo preceptum est vicecomiti quod per sacramentum proborum etc., per quos etc., in pleno comitatu diligenter inquirat quibus diebus et annis Robertus filius Rogeri, Johannes Gerlond', David Bene, Ricardus Panton', Johannes Hachet, Johannes de la More capellanus et Johannes de Badebrigge vel eorum antecessores fuerunt de predictis terris etc. quas tenent, et si Willelmus Molendinarius teneat aliquam terram que fuit ejusdem Willelmi Oldelond', et inquisicionem etc. scire faciat justiciariis etc. a die sancte Trinitatis in .iij. septimanas etc. Et interim de dicta demanda pacem habere permittat.

Et quia vicecomes mandavit quod Ricardus le Carpenter de Elyngham, Willelmus le Wastelman de eadem, Ranulfus le Ko de eadem, Ricardus le Ko de eadem manuceperunt Andream Oldelond; et Johannes de la Bruere, Rogerus filius Johannis, Johannes le Tayllur et Herveus filius Philippi manuceperunt Ricardum Rust; et Walterus filius Johannis de Elyngham, Walterus le Clerck' de Attebrigge, Johannes filius Willelmi de Elyngham et Walterus del Wro manuceperunt Gilbertum le Bole; et Willelmus Beveryche de eadem, Alexander Norre, Rogerus filius Johannis Dod, et Johannes filius Elvered manuceperunt Radulfum de Doddek', tenentes terrarum predictarum, quos non habuerunt etc., ideo ipsi manucaptores in misericordia. Et preceptum est vicecomiti quod distringat predictos Andream et alios tenentes qui non venerunt, sicut patet inter inquisiciones hujus termini, per terras et catalla, ita quod nec ipsi etc., et quod de exitibus etc., et quod habeat corpora eorum coram etc. ad predictum diem ad respondendum Regi una cum supradictis de .xx. libris quas Regi debent de debitis Salomonis filii Deulecresse judei, et ad audiendum etc., et venire faciat ad eundem diem Nicholaum de la Hale ad warantizandum et aquietandum Johannem Cosyn de porcione ipsum contingente de dicto debito racione .v. acrarum et .iij. rodarum terre quas tenet de terris predictis et acquietandum David Bene de porcione ipsum contingente de eodem debito racione unius acre terre quam tenet de terris predictis.

22 *MS. reads* tenentes.

23 *MS. reads* Rogerus.

24 *MS. omits.*

25 *This word is repeated in MS.*

MEMBRANE 4 DORSE

(44)

Ebor'. Memorandum quod Andreas de Gramayre venit coram etc., et protulit .xij. marcas et dimidiam de debitis Joscei le Joefne judei et optulit pecuniam illam in recepta regis et non erat admissus propter retonsam monetam.

(45)

Norff'. Willelmus filius Willelmi de Blomvill' venit coram etc.[26]

(46)

Hereford'. Abbas de Reding' districtus ad respondendum Regi de porcione ipsum contingente de quinque marcis quas dominus Rex ab eo exigit racione terrarum et tenementorum que fuerunt Johannis filii Willelmi Aubyn, quas idem abbas tenet, de debitis Benedicti le Eskyrmisur. Et idem abbas venit et dicit quod non debet respondere de aliquo debito racione predictarum terrarum et tenementorum eo quod idem abbas feoffatus fuit de omnibus terris et tenementis predictis quas tenet que fuerent predicti Johannis per multum tempus antequam idem Johannes dictum debitum .v. marcarum a predicto judeo mutuasset, et de hoc ponit se super patriam. Ideo preceptum est vicecomiti quod in pleno comitatu per sacramentum etc. diligenter inquirat quo die et anno etc feoffatus fuit de terris etc., et inquisicionem etc. in octabis sancti Johannis Baptiste etc.

(47)

Hugo filius Otonis protulit breve regis in hec verba.: 'Edwardus etc. justiciariis suis ad custodiam Judeorum assignatis salutem. Sciatis quod, cum Stephanus de Cheynduit nuper dederit et concesserit dilecto et fideli nostro Hugoni filio Otonis manerium de Isenhampstede in comitatu Buk' cum pertinenciis, habendum et tenendum eidem Hugoni et heredibus suis, prout in carta ejusdem Stephani sibi inde confecta plenius continetur, nos eidem Hugoni pro laudabili servicio suo quod nobis impendit volentes graciam facere specialem concessimus sibi et heredibus suis pro nobis et heredibus nostris quod ipse et heredes sui occasione alicujus contractus initi inter predictum Stephanum et quoscumque judeos regni nostri occasione predicti manerii cum pertinenciis nobis vel heredibus nostris seu judeis quibuscunque in aliquibus debitis, mutuis, prestitis, penis, usuris, feodis aut demandis quibuscunque nullatenus teneantur nec in manerio predicto aut pertinenciis suis pro hujusmodi debitis, mutuis, prestitis, penis, usuris, feodis aut demandis quibuscumque ad mandatum nostrum vel justiciarorum nostrorum ad custodiam judeorum assignatorum ad opus nostrum vel ipsorum judeorum vel aliorum nomine ipsorum judeorum vel Judaismi nostri aut per vicecomitem aut alios quoscumque ministros nostros aliquatenus distringantur set in perpetuum sint quieti in forma predicta, salvis nobis et heredibus seu prefatis judeis recuperare nostro, si necesse fuerit, de debitis, mutuis, prestitis, penis, usuris et demandis hujusmodi in aliis terris et tenementis Stephani supradicti. Et ideo vobis mandamus quod in scaccario Judaismi nostri predicti sic fieri, observari et irrotulari faciatis. Teste me ipso apud Dunanemey .xxix. die Marcii anno regni nostri septimo.'

(48)

[e]<*Northt' vacat.* Aaron filius Vives venit coram etc. et recognovit se recepisse .vij. libras de Willelmo de Bray de debitis in quo idem Willelmus ei tenebatur.>[e]

Quia justiciarii non recordantur.

(49)

Linc'. Preceptum fuit vicecomiti quod per sacramentum proborum et legalium hominum de comitatu etc., per quos etc., diligenter inquireret quantum porcio singulorum tenencium terras et tenementa que fuerunt Gilberti de Benyngworth' in comitatu predicto, videlicet de terris et tenementis que[27] Henricus de Lacy comes Linc', prior de Bolyngton', prior de Ormesby, heres Willelmi de Holegate quondam majoris Linc', et Helewysa de Nevill' tenent de terris predictis.[28] Et vicecomes mandavit quod terre et tenementa que fuerunt predicti Gilberti sunt in diversis trethingis et in diversis wapentakiis et in diversis locis per diversas et multas parcellas, per quod propter brevitatem temporis super valore dictarum porcionum cerciorari non potuit, unde nichil actum est de precepto predicto. Et ideo preceptum est vicecomiti, ut prius, ut diligenter inquirat quantum porcio singulorum tenencium valeat per annum etc. salvo etc., et inquisicionem etc. scire faciat justiciariis etc. in octabis sancti Johannis Baptiste. Et preceptum fuit [i]<eidem>[i] vicecomiti quod distringeret predictos Henricum et alios tenentes predictarum terrarum per terras etc., et quod de exitibus etc., et quod habeat corpora eorum coram etc. a die Pasche in .xv. dies ad respondendum Regi una cum Johanne de Bathon' de .ccc. et .lx. libris quas Regi debent racione predictarum terrarum quas tenent de debitis Judaismi. Et ipsi non venerunt. Et vicecomes mandavit quod dicti Henricus et alii tenentes districti sunt, prout patet inter brevia nunc retornata. Et quod Henricus prepositus de Swaneton', Galfridus prepositus de eadem, Willelmus ad ecclesiam et Willelmus filius Roberti de eadem manuceperunt predictum Henricum de Lacy; et Simon de Askeby, Simon Faldetake, Andreas Breton et Hamo West de Barkeworth' manuceperunt priorem de Bolyngton; et quod Philippus West de Vitterby, Radulfus Wenegys de eadem, Alanus Tan de Ormesby et Willelmus le Mazam de eadem manuceperunt priorem de Ormesby; et quod Radulfus prepositus de Brinkyl', Willelmus Fayl de eadem, Willelmus Haryng et Ricardus de Norman' de eadem manuceperunt heredem Willemi

[26] *This entry is unfinished. For what seems to be the complete entry see below, no. 50.*

[27] *Followed by MS. by* fuerunt.

[28] *Followed in MS. by* Et vicecomes mandavit quod terre et tenementa predicta *which should have been marked for deletion.*

de Holegate; et quod Ricardus Page de Stretton, Ricardus Goscelyn, Rogerus Molendinarius et Johannes Felawe de eadem manuceperunt Helewysam de Nevill, quos non habuerunt. Ideo in misericordia.[29] Judicium quod prefati Henricus de Lacy et alii distringantur per terras etc., ita quod habeat corpora eorum coram etc. in octabis sancti Johannis Baptiste ad respondendum etc., et ad audiendum etc. Et vicecomes habeat ad eundem diem hic .xx. solidos quos habet de exitibus terrarum prioris de Bolyngton' et .xx. solidos quos habet de terris prioris de Ormesby et unam marcam quam habet de herede Willelmi de Holegate et dimidiam marcam quam habet de terris etc. Helewysie de Nevill'.

(50)

Nortff'. Willelmus filius Willelmi de Blomville venit coram etc. et protulit .xij. marcas et dimidiam quas debet Cresseo filio Cressei filii Gente et Aaron filio Vives judeis die veneris proxima ante mensem post Pascham nunc, que pecunia solvi debet a die P[asche] predicto in unum mensem. Et quia prohibitum est per regem quod debita judeorum judeis non solvantur dictum [est] prefato Willelmo per justiciarios quod non solvat denarios illos donec mandatum inde habuerit per eosdem.[30]

MEMBRANE 5

Starra de termino Pasche anno regni regis Edwardi septimo

(51)

Glouc'. Aaron filius Elie le Blund judeus recognovit per starrum suum quod Adam filius Johannis de Wylton' de Dymmok' et heredes et antecessores sui quieti sunt de ipso judeo et heredibus et antecessoribus suis de omnibus debitis, demandis et calumpniis in quibus eis unquam tenebantur a creacione seculi usque ad finem. Et si inveniatur carta, tallia vel aliquod aliud instrumentum in aliqua archa cyrographariorum Anglie vel extra idem judeus recognovit quod quieta sunt et nichil valoris.

(52)

Lond'. Magister Elias filius magistri Mossei judeus Lond' recognovit per starrum suum se recepisse quadraginta sex libras et unam marcam de Ada cissore domini Regis de termino Pasche anno regni regis Edwardi septimo de quodam fine quem fecit cum eodem judeo pro quibusdam debitis in quibus Willelmus de Hadestok' civis Lond' eidem judeo tenebatur.

(53)

Glouc'. Aaron filius Vives judeus recognovit per starrum suum quod recepit residuum quinquaginta marcarum de Mauricio de Berkel' de termino octabarum Pasche anno regni regis Edwardi septimo. Et idem Aaron tenetur allocare duodecim libras et dimidiam marcam in quinquaginta marcis quas idem Mauricius eidem judeo debet, reddendas ad octabas sancti Michaelis proximo futuras post Pascha predictum ad instanciam [i]<domini>[i] Edmundi filii domini Henrici illustris regis Anglie et spontanea voluntate hoc sigillavit predictus judeus littera ebrayca, quia plene satisfactum est predicto judeo ad instanciam predicti [i]<domini>[i] Edmundi.

(54)

Somers'. Aaron filius Vives judeus recognovit per starrum suum quod quietavit et quietum clamavit magistro Thome de Button' archidiacono Well' totum jus, clamium et calumpniam que habuit occasione .c. et duarum acrarum terre que fuerunt Willelmi de Middelton' debitoris ipsius judei, que fuerunt vadium ipsius judei pro quibusdam debitis sibi venditis per Josceum Salomonis, Salomonem filium ejus et Suetman filium Davyd judeos, sicut continetur in rotulis domini regis Edwardi, que quidem debita loquuntur sub nominibus Willelmi filii Roberti de Middelton' et eorundem judeorum, quia predicta debita sub nominibus predictorum judeorum sunt ipsius Aaron, sicut continetur in rotulis domini regis Edwardi in termino sancti Michaelis anno quinto incipiente, videlicet unum debitum .xx. marcarum sub nominibus predicti Willelmi et [i]<ipsius>[i] Joscei et unum debitum .xx. marcarum sub nominibus predicti Willelmi et predicti Salomonis, et unum debitum sexdecim marcarum sub nominibus predicti Willelmi et Joscei, et unum debitum .xl. librarum sub nomine predicti Swetman filii Davy. Et idem Aaron relaxavit et quietavit predicto magistro Thome et successoribus suis pro se et heredibus suis et pro predictis Josceo et Salomone et Swetman totum jus et demandam quod habuit versus eundem magistrum Thomam occasione predictorum debitorum sub nominibus predicti Willelmi et predictorum judeorum, scilicet pro centum et duabus acris terre cum pertinenciis quas predictus magister Thomas tenuit die confeccionis presentis starri. Acta die sancti Marcii evangeliste anno regis Edwardi septimo. Et hoc sigillavit pro se et heredibus suis predicto magistro Thome et heredibus et successoribus suis. Insuper recognovit idem Aaron quod tenetur acquietare, warantizare et defendere predicto archidiacono predictam terram contra omnes predictos judeos occasione predictorum debitorum et ad hoc obligavit omnia catalla sua mobilia et inmobilia.

(55)

Belassez filia Isac recognovit per starrum suum per testimonium Manseri filii Urselli et Samuelis filii Samuelis quod vendidit Aaron filio Vives quartam partem debiti Alexandri de Auno quod fuit Jacobi filii Salamonis viri sui, quod eundem Jacobum contigit post mortem patris sui, videlicet .xx. librarum. Et concedit quod dictus Aaron sit attornatus suus ad levandum et aquietandum totam predictam quartam partem dicti debiti que fuit

[29] *The word* misericordia *is repeated in the margin.*

[30] *Followed by only the marginal county,* Linc', *of another entry, left unfinished.*

predicti viri sui et ad faciendum totam voluntatem suam de tota predicta quarta parte in omnibus.

(56)

Lond', Essex'. Jacobus filius Hagini judeus recognovit per starrum suum quod dominus Willelmus Giffard et antecessores et heredes sui sunt quieti de ipso Jacobo et heredibus suis de omnimodis debitis, calumpniis et demandis ab inicio [seculi][31] usque ad Pentecosten anno regni regis Edwari septimo. Et si inveniatur carta, tallia vel aliquod instrumentum in archa cyrographariorum vel extra de aliquo debito sub nominibus predicti domini Willelmi vel alicujus antecessorum suorum et ipsius Jacobi, vult et concedit quod nichil valeat et pro nullo habeatur.

(57)

Warr'. Preceptum fuit vicecomiti quod per sacramentum proborum et legalium hominum extendi faceret terras et tenementa que abbas de Bordesl' recognovit se tenere de terris et temenentis que fuerunt Gilberti de Beinyngworth', et extentam illam scire faceret justiciariis etc. a die Pasche in .xv. dies. Et vicecomes mandavit quod inquiri fecit per sacramentum Willelmi de Wylecote, Simonis Brayn et aliorum, sicut patet inter inquisiciones hujus termini retornatas. Qui dicunt super sacramentum suum quod dictus abbas non tenet aliquas terras [nec][32] tenementa in comitatu Warr' que fuerunt predicti Gilberti de Beinyngworth', set predictus abbas tenet terras et tenementa que fuerunt de hereditate uxoris ipsius Gilberti que non debent pro debitis dicti Gilberti obligari et petit judicium ut exoneratus possit abire a peticione debiti dicti Gilberti. Et quia nullam mencionem fecit in recognicione sua de uxore dicti Gilberti set tantummodo recognovit se tenere quasdam partes terrarum et tenementorum que fuerunt predicti Gilberti, ista excepcio non debet ei valere nunc, dicendo se non esse tenentem predictarum terrarum et tenementorum, cum prius recognovit se esse tenentem predictarum terrarum et tenementorum, set quod sit coram justiciariis etc. a die sancti Michaelis in .xv. dies recepturus porcionem suam ipsum contingentem de debitis .ccclx. librarum in quibus dictus Gilbertus Regi tenebatur de debitis judaismi una cum Johanne de Baton' et aliis tenentibus terrarum et tenementorum predicti Gilberti quibus idem dies datur. Et quia vicecomes excessit tenorem precepti Regis, inquirendo de terris et tenementis uxoris predicti Gilberti et hoc retornavit, cum nullum inde habuerat preceptum, ideo ipse vicecomes, scilicet [blank] in misericordia.[33]

(58)

Suff'. Edmundus de Shardelawe, tenens terrarum que fuerunt magistri Roberti de Shardelawe, de quo Rex exigit .x. libras de debitis Deulecresse filii Aaron judei, venit coram etc. et vocat inde ad warantum Johannem de Heccham, nepotem et heredem predicti magistri Roberti, qui summoneatur in comitatu Suff' quod sit coram etc. in octabis sancte Trinitatis ad acquietandum predictum Edmundum de debito predicto.

(59)

Lond'. Memorandum quod Elias clericus vicecomitum London' venit coram etc. [i]<et>[i] reddidit compotum de tempore Radulfi le Fevre et Roberti de Araz quondam vicecomitum ejusdem et eciam de tempore Walteri le Engleys et Johannis Adryan vicecomitum similiter ejusdem civitatis et protulit .xxiiij. solidos .viij. denarios per diversas tallias et habet diem ad computandum a die sancti Michaelis in .xv. dies.

(60)

Robertus Revel venit coram etc., et solvit Benedicto filio Jacobi de Oxon' .ij. marcas in quibus eidem judeo tenebatur de termino sancti Michaelis anno sexto et de termino Pasche nunc et habet inde starrum judei dicti de acquietancia.

(61)

Memorandum quod Robertus de Dreyton' venit coram etc. et protulit .iiij. tallias de .iiij. libris per quas dicit se solvisse in recepta Regis de debitis Hagini filii magistri Mossei de extenta .xx. solidorum de termino sancti Michaelis anno regis Edwardi quinto, et de termino Pasche proximo sequenti .xx. solidos, de termino sancti Michaelis anno regis Edwardi sexto .xx. solidos, et de termino Pasche nunc .xx. solidos.

(62)

Nortff', Suff'. Hugo Pecche et Adam de Cretyng' milites venerunt coram etc. et recognoverunt se debere Hamoni Hauteyn .x. libras reddendas ei vel suo certo attornato a die sancti Johannis proximo futuro in .xv. dies. Et bene liceat eidem Hamoni se capere ad quemcumque ipsorum voluerit de toto predicto debito vel de parte, prout plenius continetur in quodam scripto obligatorio inter eos inde confecto et prout iidem Hugo et Adam recognoverunt coram justiciariis de Banco, prout patet in rotulis domini regis de Banco in termino Pasche anno regis Edwardi .vij. Et si in solucione predicta defecerunt, concedunt quod de terris et catallis suis fiant.

Postea dictus Hamo recognovit quod predicti Hugo et Adam satisfecerunt ei de predictis .x. libris et quieti sunt.

(63)

Linc'. Magister Elias filius magistri Mossei per attornatum suum venire fecit Adam de Hospitali et exigit ab eo .xv. libras de debito Mossei de Seynt Liz, quod liberatum fuit dicto Elie de thesauro Regis in recompensacione aliorum debitorum in quibus abbas et conventus de Stratford' ei tenebatur.

[31] *MS. omits.*

[32] *MS. reads* ne.

[33] *The word* misericordia *is repeated in the margin and the amount of the amercement* c solidi.

Dictus Adam per attornatum suum recognovit se debere de dicto debito undecim libras et dicit quod solvit de dicto debito .xv. librarum predicto Mosseo de Seynt Liz .iiij. libras, unde habet starrum suum, quod attornatus dicti Elie concedit bonum esse.

Et quia Robertus de Ludham justiciarius manucepit satisfacere de predictis .xj. libris, attornatus dicti Elie concessit diem solvendi usque ad quindenam sancti Michaelis.

MEMBRANE 5 DORSE

(64)

Norh'. Jacob le fiz Pey^{e}<n>^{e}tevyn et Beneyt <fiz>[34] <Peyntevyn>[35] de <Bed'>[36] judei venerunt coram etc. et recognoverunt starrum subscriptum in hec verba: 'Jeo, ky suy desuz <encel>[37] <reconeys>[38] pur mey et tesmoyngne pur ma mere Bele de Bed', jadis femme Peyntevyn le fiz Isac de Bed', ke nous avums lesse et vendu al honurable Gilbert de Clare, counte de <Glouc',>[39] et a ses heyrs et a ses assignez tut le dreyt et le cleym [e le][40] chalenge et obligement et le poer ke nus avyum ou aver poyum sur touz les dettes ke Willam de <Whyston'>[41] ou nul de ses auncestres deveyent al avaunt dist Peyntevyn mon pere ou a acun de ses auncestres del comencement del mound jeske al jour <de>[42] cest estarre fu fet, ceo est a saver .iiij. dettes,[43] une de dette de .xx. livres en le <noun del avant dit>[44] Willam de Whyst' et Peyntevyn mon pere, <dount>[45] le terme fu a la Tyffayngne le an .xlij. del regne nostre seignur ly rey H. fiz ly rey Johan; et une dette de .xx. livres en les nouns <de les avant diz>[46] Willam et Peyntevyn, <dount le terme>[47] de la paye fu a la Paske le an .xlij. del regne avant dit; et une dette de .lxxviij. livres et .vj. summes de furment en les nuns <des avant diz>[48] Willam et Peyntevyn a rendre .xxvj. livres et .ij. summes de furment a la fest seynt Nichole le an .xlij. del regne avant dit et .xxvj. livres et .ij. summes de furment a la Chaundelur suant, et .xxvj. livres et .ij. summes de furment al Hokeday suant; et [une dette de][49] cent souz de fe de anuele rente, dount les termes furent a les uytaves de la Pask' le an .xliij. del regne avant dit la meyte et a le seynt Michel suant apres lautre meyte, ceo est asaver .l. souz a checun terme, et issi de terme en terme, de an en an jeske a la fin del syecle. Totes <les avant dites>[50] furent en la huche nostre seygnur ly rey des <cyr' a>[51] Bed' ke fu tolue e arse par les enemys ly rey en tens de guere et tribulaciun. Totes les dettes avant dites enterement ove le gayn ke ilyat amunte jeske al jour ke cest estarre fu fet, ceo est asaver mil mars en chatel e en gayn, tut ceo avums nus lesse[52] al honurable counte avant dit et a ses heyrs e a ses assignez pur nus et pur noz heyrs e pur noz assignez vente perfite e estable e durable a touz jours cum dettes enterement dues et leles cum fetes de meyn de clerck' <cyr'>[53] jure al rey et receves de denz la huche de Bed' avantdite cum usage e dreyt de Juerye. E jeo grant pur mey e pur ma mere ke nus ne avums ren receu de totes les dettes avant dites, ne del chatel ne del gayngne, ne nient receverums ne ke nus ne avums [fet][54] al avant dit Willam ne a ses heyrs ne a ses assignez nul estarre de aquitaunce ne ne frums, si il ne seyt par le cunge et par le seu le honurable counte avaunt dit et par son comaundement. Et si nul jeu ou cresteyn aporte estar ou aquitaunce de les avant dites ou de partye de chatel ou del gayn el nun mon pere Peytevyn avant dit ou en noz nouns jeo coneys pur mey e pur ma mere ke il est faus et sumes obligez a prover e [averer][55] ke il est issi et abatre le anient par dreyt e usage de Juerye. E si <il y>[56] vient jeu ou cresteyn et cleyme dreit sur le avant dit counte [ou ses heirs ou ses heirs [ou][57] assignez par achesun de dettes avantdites sumis obligez, nus et noz heirs, a oster ly del avantdit counte e ses heirs e ses assignez sur no despenses. E si le avauntdit counte][58] mette nul despens par enchesun del cleym avant dit, totes ses despenses oveke le damage et la perte ke il averat par nostre defaute sumes tenuz, nus et noz heyrs, a fere luy restorer; et quel houre ke le avant dit counte voudra ke nus queriums bref le rey sur Willam le avant dit ou sur ses heyrs de somunce ou de destresce par dreit et usage de la Juerye, nous serroms prestz aquere le sur ses despenses. E nus sumes obligez a garauntyr et defendre al avant dit counte totes les avant dites dettes oveke [tot][59] le geyn en tote la manere ke est devise a luy e a ses heyrs e a ses assignez pur nus e pur nos heyrs et noz assignez encontre touz cels ki cleym i purrunt mettre pur Peytevyn mon pere ou pur nus. E totes les terres, rentes et tenemenz ke le avant dit Willam de Whyston' ad vendu a quel home ke il les ad vendu, ceo est asaver del jour ke les quatre dettes avant dites furent fetes, sumes obligez nus e noz heyrs a fere venir eus a play, quel hure ke le honurable counte avant dit voudra, ceo est asaver sur ses despenses, a respundre a luy sulom custome e usage de Jurye de tote

[34] filius *(over an erasure) 70.*
[35] Peytevin *70 (and so in the remainder of the entry as well).*
[36] Bedeford *70 (and so in the remainder of the entry as well).*
[37] ensele *70.*
[38] reconuse *70.*
[39] Gloucestre *70.*
[40] *Supplied from 70.*
[41] Wischeton' *70 (and so in the remainder of the entry as well).*
[42] ke *70.*
[43] *70 adds* icetes.
[44] nuns devantdiz *70.*
[45] ke *70.*
[46] devantdiz *70.*
[47] ke la soute *70.*
[48] devantdiz *70.*
[49] *Supplied from 70.*
[50] iceles dettes avantdites *70.*
[51] cyrograyfis en *70.*
[52] *70 adds* et vendu.
[53] de cerograferes *70.*
[54] *Supplied from 70.*
[55] *MS. reads* aver.
[56] ly *70.*
[57] *MS. omits.*
[58] *Supplied from 70.*
[59] *Supplied from 70.*

la porcion ke a eus apendra solom le pris e la value des teres, rentes e tenenenz ke els achaterunt puys ke noz dettes avant dites furent fetes. E ceste vente, warentye et defens avant dites avums obligez noz teres, rentes [i]<et>[i] chatels, moebles e non moebles. E jeo grant pur mey et tesmoyngne pur ma mere Bele avant dite ke les quatre dettes avant dites [sus][60] les nuns Willam de Whystan' et Peyt' avant diz furent enroulez en les roules Symun Passelewe quant il ala a enrouler partye de huches de Engletere et furent apurez en le tens Johan de Kauz, abbe de Burgh', dunke tresorer del Escheker. E totes les avant diz covenaunz a aver les fermes e estables al avant dit honurable counte e a ses heyrs e a ses assignez sumes tenuz nus e noz heyrs e noz assignez et totes les covenaunz ay jeo grante e ensele pur mey e pur ma mere Bele e pur noz heyrs e pur nos assignez. Cest estar fu fet lendemeyn del Hokeday le an .lij. del regne ly rey H. fiz ly rey Johan. E ceo ke jeo ay grante ay jeo ensele pur mey et tesmoigne pur ma mere Bele.

(65)

Lond'. Haginus filius magistri Mossei et Cok' filius ejus recognoverunt per starrum suum quod ipsi debent Roberto de Basyng' .lv. libras reddendas ad Pentecosten anno regni regis Edwardi septimo. Et pro eo invadiaverunt et obligaverunt omnia catalla, mobilia et inmobilia, ad capiendum de eisdem totum debitum supradictum vel ad quem eorum dictus Robertus se capere voluerit; et omnes expensas quas Robertus antedictus expendet ad levandum debitum supradictum dicti Hag' et Cok' tenentur ei reddere heredibus vel assignatis suis et eciam integre suo solo [sermone.][61] Et credatur dictus Robertus suo solo sermone. Et ad hoc [invadiaverunt et obligaverunt][62] ei omnia catalla mobilia et inmobilia. Et si dictum terminum preterierit dicto Roberto heredibus vel assignatis, recognoverunt se teneri domino Regi in duabus marcis auri et nihilominus non exonerentur de debito supradicto. Et hoc recognoverunt ex mera voluntate pro ipsis et heredibus et manibus eorum consignaverunt etc.

(66)

[Hereff'.][63] Radulfus Muschet [de comitatu Hertford'][64] venit coram etc. [et][65] recognovit [se][66] debere Aaron filio Vives judeo .l. marcas reddendas infra quinque annos, termino incipiente ad quindenam sancti Michaelis anno [regni][67] regis Edwardi septimo. Et tunc solvet [eidem][68] judeo .v. marcas, et ad quindenam Pasche proximo sequentem .v. marcas, et sic de anno in annum .x. marcas ad terminos supradictos quousque predicte .l. marce totaliter fuerint persolute. Et si terminos dicte solucionis <observaverit,>[69] dictus Aaron tenetur aquietare dictum Radulfum de uno debito .xxx. librarum cum lucro .iiij.^{xx} librarum inde emergente sub nominibus dicti Radulfi et Joscey filii Sauloti judei. Et, nisi fecerit, in nullo tenetur ipsum aquietare de predicto debito.

(67)

Not'. Walterus de Furneaus miles et Johannes de Furneaus, filius et heres ipsius Walteri, venerunt coram etc., et recognoverunt se debere Jacobo filio Hagini judeo .iiij.^{xx} libras, reddendas in octabis Purificacionis beate Marie anno [regni][70] regis Edwardi octavo .l. marcas et in quindena Pasche proximo sequenti .l. marcas, et in octabis sancti Michaelis proximo sequentibus .xx. marcas. Et, nisi fecerunt, concedunt quod de terris et catallis suis fiant etc.

<Et postea predictus Jacobus concessit et [a]ssignavit Johanni de Bosco, executori testamenti Petri de Sancto Petro, .xix. libras [percipiendas][71] de predicto debito .iiij.^{xx} librarum pro quadam recognicione .xix. librarum quas idem Jacobus recognovit se debere predicto Petro de Sancto Petro in termino sancti Michaelis anno regis Edwardi tercio incipiente quarto.>[72]

(68)

Memorandum quod Robertus de Hasteng' venit coram etc. et recognovit se debere Aaron filio Vives judeo .x. libras reddendas a die sancti Michaelis in unum mensem anno [regni][73] regis Edwardi septimo. Et, nisi fecerit, concedit quod de terris et catallis suis fiant etc.[74]

60 *MS. reads* sur.
61 *Supplied from 70. Left blank in original.*
62 *MS. reads* invadiavit et obligavit.
63 Hertf' *70.*
64 *Supplied from 70.*
65 *Supplied from 70.*
66 *Supplied from 70.*
67 *Supplied from 70.*
68 *Supplied from 70.*
69 servaverit *70.*
70 *Supplied from 70.*
71 *MS. reads* percipient'.
72 *70 omits but it also has the deleted entry: Warr'.* Robertus de Hasteng' recognovit se debere Aaron filio Vives judeo .x. libras reddendas a die sancti Michaelis in unum mensem anno regis Edwardi .vij. Et nisi etc.
73 *Supplied from 70.*
74 *At the bottom of membrane 5d is written* Essonia, Placita, Memoranda, Recogniciones et Starra de termino Pasche anno regis Edwardi septimo.

TRINITY TERM, 7 EDWARD I [1279]

Exchequer of Jews, Plea Rolls Nos. 32, 64 [E 9/32, 64]

There are two surviving plea rolls for this term. One was presumably made for Hamon Hauteyn, the senior justice, the other for Robert of Ludham, his colleague. Which roll was made for which justice is not now certain, but the hand of Roll 32 looks like the hand responsible for writing the other rolls believed to have been made for Hauteyn, so this is probably Hauteyn's roll. For some time prior to 1975, these two separate rolls, like a number of other similar pairs of rolls, were incorrectly joined up together to form a single composite roll. Roll 64 now contains the membranes which were numbered 2, 4, 5, 7 and 8 when they formed part of composite roll 32.

For the purposes of this edition, Roll 64, the fuller of the two rolls and the roll which survives in better condition, has been taken as the main text, although Roll 32, where it survives, sometimes provides a superior text. Significant variants in Roll 32 from the version given in Roll 64 are noted in the footnotes. At the end of the transcript of roll 64 will be found a transcript of those entries which occur only on Roll 32.

The order of the entries on Roll 32 is as follows:

Membrane 1 [similar heading to Roll 64, m. 1, though much of it has been lost through damage]
same as entries on m.1 of Roll 64 (nos. 69-78)
Membrane 1d [no heading now visible]
1st-3rd entries not in Roll 64 (printed below, nos. 146-8)
4th entry as 2nd entry on m.1d of Roll 64 (no. 80)
5th entry not in Roll 64 (printed below, no. 149)
6th entry as 3rd entry on m.1d of Roll 64 (no. 81)
Membrane 2 [same heading as Roll 64, m. 2]
1st-10th entries as 1st-10th entries on m. 2 of Roll 64 (nos. 82-91)
11th-12th entries as 1st-2nd entries on m. 2d of Roll 64 (nos. 92-3)
13th entry as 10th entry on m. 2d of Roll 64 (no. 101)
14th entry as 4th entry on m. 2d of Roll 64 (no. 95)
Membrane 2d [heading is 'Adhuc Placita']
1st-4th entries as 5th-8th entries on m. 2d of Roll 64 (nos. 96-9)
5th-6th entries not in Roll 64 (printed below, nos. 150-1)
Membrane 3 [heading is 'Memoranda de termino sancti Johannis Baptiste anno septimo']
1st-4th entries as 5th-8th entries on m. 5 of Roll 64 (nos. 132-5)
5th entry as 10th entry on m. 5 of Roll 64 (no. 137)
6th-17th entries not in Roll 64 (printed below, nos. 152-62)
Membrane 3d [no heading]
1st entry not in Roll 64 (printed below, no. 163)
2nd entry as 5th entry on m. 5d of Roll 64 (no. 144)

There are, therefore, no equivalent entries on roll 32 to the following entries on Roll 64: membrane 1d., 1st entry (no. 79); membrane 2d, 3rd entry (no. 94); 9th entry (no. 100); 11th entry (no. 102); all the entries on mm 3-4d (nos. 103-27); membrane 5, 1st-4th entries (nos. 128-131); 9th entry (no. 136); 11th entry (no. 138); 12th entry (no. 139); membrane 5d, 1st-4th entries (nos. 140-3); 6th entry (no. 145).

ROLL 64

MEMBRANE 1

Essonia de octabis sancte Trinitatis anno regni regis Edwardi septimo

(69)

Norhampt'. Elena la <Theuche>[1] versus Willelmum Foliot et [Isabellam][2] uxorem ejus de placito transgressionis per Henricum Hod.

Non jacet quia breve dicit 'attachiari facias.'

(70)

Sutht'. Laurencius de Netheravene, attornatus abbatis de Hyda, versus Regem de placito debiti per Willelmum Leching'.

Ricardus de <Frostbury>[3] attornatus versus eundem de eodem per Thomam de Cheylwarton'. A die sancti Johannis Baptiste in .xv. dies.

Johannes Edgar, attornatus Willelmi filii Willelmi de Dunstyghel', versus eundem de eodem per Willelmum de Bacham.

Ricardus de <Fortesber'>[4] alter attornatus versus eundem de eodem per Willelmum <Fot.>[5] A die sancti [Johannis] Baptiste in .xv. dies.

Essonia de quindena sancte Trinitatis

(71)

Cantbr'. Robertus Alwine, attornatus Willelmi le Kepere et Johanne uxoris ejus, Willelmi Gorge et Cristiane de [Mauns,][6] versus Thomam Bakun de placito debiti per Adam <Brodhond.>[7]

Idem Robertus versus eundem Thomam de eodem per Johannem Prat.

A die sancti Johannis Baptiste in .xv. dies. [Affidavit.][8]

(72)

Cant.' Rogerus le fiz le Fevere versus Thomam Bakun de placito debiti unde jurata [per Adam Prodhom. A die sancti Michaelis in .xv. dies, nisi H. Hauteyn vel R. de Lud[ham in]terim etc.

Affidavit.][9]

(73)

Norff. Simon le Gris, attornatus Hugonis Hochede custodis heredis et terre Galfridi Wascelin, versus magistrum Walterum de la Mare de placito debiti per Willelmum de Engham.

A die sancti Michaelis in .xv. dies. Affidavit.

(74)

Herfford'. Walter de Thornbur', custos Johannis filii Walteri de Thornbir', versus Aaron filium <Wives>[10] de placito debiti per Adam <Brodham.>[11]

(75)

Norff. Thomas de Aleby, attornatus Roberti de Crakeford', versus Samuelem de Norwico judeum de placito debiti per <Thomas de Plomstede.>[12]

Rogerus le <Corsun>[13] alter attornatus de eodem per Johannem de Kanc'.

Johannes de Wikemere <alter attornatus versus eundem de eodem per Adam Brodhom.>[14]

Michael de Naring' alter attornatus versus eundem de eodem per Adam <Brodhomme.>[15]

Judeus non venit. Ideo eant quieti et judeus in misericordia.

Essonia de octabis sancti Johannis Baptiste

(76)

Linc'. Willelmus <de Pincebek',>[16] attornatus Johannis de Bathon', versus <Henricum de Lacy comitem Linc'>[17] et alios in brevi de placito debiti per Johannem Herneys.

A die sancti Michaelis in .xv. dies. Affidavit. Henricus [de Lacy][18] et alii non venerunt.

Essonia de tribus septimanis sancti Johannis Baptiste

(77)

Herfford'. Rogerus de Burghulle vicecomes Herford' versus Gilbertum de Bosco de placito transgressionis per Rogerum [le][19] Palfreyman.

Non jacet quia <breve quod tunc sit ibi.>[20]

(78)

[Kanc'.] [21] Johannes filius et [heres][22] Johannis de la Teye versus Anteram que fuit [uxor][23] Vives filii magistri Mossei judei de placito debiti per Adam <Brodhom.>[24]

A die sancti Michaelis in .xv. dies. Affidavit.

[Ad quem diem non venit. Judicium quod distringatur per terras etc. in octabis sancti Johannis Baptiste.][25]

[1] Zuche *32*. [2] *MS. reads* Iosab'. [3] Fortesbyri alter *32*.
[4] Fortesbyri *32*. [5] Fort *32*.
[6] *MS. reads* Manus. Mauns *is the reading of 32*.
[7] Prodhom *32*. [8] *Supplied from 32*. [9] *Supplied from 32*.

[10] Vives *32*. [11] Prodom *32*.
[12] Clementem de Plumbsted' *32*. [13] Curcun *32*.
[14] attornatus ... styng' versus eundem Sam' de eodem per Johannem Prat *32*.
[15] Prodhom *32*. [16] Pinsebek *32*.
[17] *In 32 this name has been inserted over* Regem, *which has been marked for deletion.*
[18] *Supplied from 32*. [19] *Supplied from 32*.
[20] preceptum fuit quod fuisset ibidem ad eundem diem *32*.
[21] *Supplied from 32*.
[22] *MS. reads* Henricus; heres *is the reading of 32*.
[23] *Supplied from 32*. [24] Prodom *32*.
[25] *Supplied from 32*.

MEMBRANE 1 DORSE

(79)

Lond'. Hagin filius magistri Mossei ponit loco suo Isak' le Eveske versus Willelmum Heygaud' de placito debiti.

(80)

North'. Willelmus Foliot et Isabella uxor ejus ponunt loco suo <Willelmum de Whiston' vel Petrum de Whyston'>[26] vel Robertum de Aston' versus Elenam la Zuche de placito transgressionis <et quod ipsam Isabellam dehospitavit etc.>[27]

(81)

Norff'. Preceptum fuit vicecomiti quod per sacramentum proborum et legalium hominum diligenter inquireret quibus diebus et annis Robertus filius Rogeri, Johannes Garland', David Bene, Johannes Hachet, [Johannes][28] de la More capellanus, Johannes de <Baddebrigge>[29] et Ricardus de <Paunton'>[30] feoffati fuerunt de terris que fuerunt Willelmi <Hadelond>[31] quas tenent, [qui dicunt se feofatos fuisse antequam dictus Willelmus Holdelond' Salamoni filio Deulecresse judeo per cartam suam in .xx. libris obligaretur, ita quod de dicto debito ^{i}<respondere>^{i} non tenentur.][32] Et vicecomes mandavit quod inquisicionem inde fecit per sacramentum Roberti Carbonel, Nicholai filii capellani et aliorum christianorum, sicut patet inter inquisiciones hujus termini retornatas. Qui dicunt quod Robertus filius Rogeri tenet duas acras [terre][33] que fuerunt dicti Willelmi et de una acra feoffatus fuit die sancti Michaelis anno regni regis Henrici .xliiij.^{to}; et de alia acra feoffatus fuit die sancti Martini anno regni regis H. xlvij.^{to}. Johannes Garland tenet unam rodam et dimidiam et feoffatus fuit die dominica proxima post festum sancti Mathei anno regni ejusdem .xlv.^{to}. David Bene tenet unam acram terre et dimidiam et fuit inde feoffatus die martis proxima post Pascha anno regni ejusdem .xlij.^{o}. Johannes <Haget>[34] tenet unam acram terre et fuit inde feoffatus die Pentcostes anno ejusdem .xlj.^{o} Johannes de la More capellanus <tenet>[35] unam acram prati et inde fuit feoffatus die Pentecostes anno ejusdem .xlvj.^{to}. Johannes de Baddebrigge tenet unam acram terre et feoffatus fuit inde die Purificacionis beate Marie anno ejusdem .xlij.^{to} Ricardus Panton' tenet unam acram terre et fuit inde feoffatus die sancti Stephani anno ejusdem .xlj.^{o} Et dicunt quod Willelmus Holdelond' nunquam fuit seisitus de terris quas Willelmus le Mouner tenet. Ideo de dicto debito eat exoneratus. Et concessum est Gilberto Bule, qui solvit heredi dicti Willelmi <Holdelont'>[36] de redditu assiso per annum .ij. denarios, et Radulfo <le Doket,>[37] qui solvit eidem [heredi][38] [per annum][39] .j. denarium obolum, quod pro predicto debito de cetero non vexentur, set quod inde eant exonerati, quia pauperes et tam parum inde tenent.

Ricardus Rust, qui tres acras terre inde tenet, venit et de duabus acris terre vocat ad warantum Johannem Cosin per quandam cartam dicti Johannis inde eidem Ricardo confectam, quam porigebat coram etc. Et predictus Johannes per attornatum suum presens non potuit dedicere quin dictas .ij. acras eidem R. warantizare debet secundum tenorem carte sue predicte. Ideo consideratum est quod dictus Ricardus quantum ad dictas .ij. acras eat quietus et dictus Johannes Cosin inde oneratus. Et de tercia acra terre dicit se feoffatum fuisse antequam dictus Willelmus Holdelond' in dicto debito dicto judeo obligaretur, et petit hoc per patriam <verificari.>[40] Lucia de le <Toft>[41] similiter dicit se feoffatam fuisse ante confeccionem carte predicti debiti viginti librarum de una acra terre quam inde tenet, et petit hoc per patriam [ut supra][42] inquiri. [Concessum est eis.][43] Et preceptum est vicecomiti etc. quod per sacramentum etc. diligenter inquirat quibus diebus et annis feoffati fuerunt [de dictis .ij. acris terre,][44] et inquisicionem etc. [scire faciat][45] a die sancti Michaelis in .xv. dies etc.

Et preceptum fuit vicecomiti quod distringeret Andream Holdelond', tenentem quandam partem terrarum que fuerunt predicti Willelmi, per terras etc., et quod de exitibus etc., et quod haberet corpus ejus coram etc. a die sancte Trinitatis in tres septimanas ad respondendum Regi de porcione dicti debiti ipsum contingente occasione [terrarum que fuerunt dicti Willelmi quas tenet][46] etc. Et ipse non venit. Et vicecomes mandavit quod Ranulphus le Ko de Elingham, Willelmus Wastelman de eadem, Ricardus le Ko de eadem, et Willelmus Molendinarius de eadem manuceperunt predictum Andream, quem non habuerunt. Ideo [ipsi manucaptores][47] in misericordia. Et vicecomes non respondit de exitibus.

Preceptum fuit vicecomiti quod venire faceret Nicholaum de Hale, quem Johannes Cosin et David Bene vocaverunt ad warantum ut ipsos de porcione debiti predicti ipsos contingente acquieteret, sicut racionabiliter etc. Et ipse non venit. Et vicecomes mandavit quod Johannes Godman de Hengham, Rogerus Attehalle de eadem, Willelmus Underwode de eadem et Radulfus Attemor de eadem manuceperunt predictum Nicholaum, quem non habuerunt. Ideo in misericordia. Judicium quod predicti Andreas et Nicholaus distringantur per terras etc., [ita quod nec ipsi etc.,][48] et quod de exitibus etc., et quod habeat corpora eorum coram etc. a die sancti Michaelis in .xv. dies ad

[26] Rogerum de Triberge clericum *32*.
[27] *32 omits.* [28] *Supplied from 32.*
[29] Badbrige *32 (and so consistently hereafter in this entry).*
[30] Panton' *32*. [31] Holdeland' *32*. [32] *Supplied from 32.*
[33] *Supplied from 32.* [34] Hachet *32*. [35] *Repeated in MS.*
[36] Holdeland' *32*.
[37] de Loddon' *32*.
[38] *MS. reads* Henrico; heredi *is the reading of 32.*
[39] *Supplied from 32.* [40] inquiri *32*. [41] Thoft *32*.
[42] *Supplied from 32.* [43] *Supplied from 32.*
[44] *Supplied from 32.* [45] *Supplied from 32.*
[46] *Supplied from 32.* [47] *Supplied from 32.*
[48] *Supplied from 32.*

respondendum <etc.>[49] una cum Johanne Cosyn <et aliis in brevi>[50] qui habent eundem diem <etc.>[51]

Johannes Cosyn per attornatum suum fecit venire Nicholaum de la Hale et vocat <ipsum>[52] ad warantum quod ipsum <aquietet>[53] de porcione ipsum contingente de <predicto>[54] debito viginti librarum occasione <terrarum etc.>[55] que fuerunt [supradicti][56] Willelmi Holdelond', sicut continetur in quadam carta dicti Nicholai quam ei inde fecit et quam <protulit>[57] coram etc., in qua continetur quod predictus Nicholaus prefatum Johannem contra omnes homines acquietare, warantizare et defendere tenetur. Predictus Nicholaus venit coram etc., et recognovit dictam cartam <esse factum suum et warantizat dicto Johanni.>[58] Ideo consideratum est quod dictus Johannes quantum ad <porcionem ipsum inde contingente>[59] eat quietus [de dicto debito.][60] Et dictus Nicholaus inde respondeat etc.

David Bene per attornatum suum fecit venire [i]<pre>[i]dictum Nicholaum de la Hale et vocat ipsum ad warrantum quod ipsum acquietare debeat de porcione <etc.>[61] occasione unius acre terre etc. de terris predicti Willelmi [quam inde tenet;][62] et <protulit>[63] cartam ipsius Nicholai [coram][64] etc., in qua continetur quod dictus Nicholaus prefatum David acquietare, warrantizare et defendere tenetur contra omnes homines. Predictus Nicholaus venit coram etc. et <recognovit dictam cartam esse factum suum et ei>[65] warantizat. Ideo consideratum est quod dictus David de dicto debito [quo ad porcionem suam][66] eat quietus et dictus Nicholaus inde respondeat.

David de Blakeland' fecit venire eundem Nicholaum et ipsum vocat ad warrantum quod <ipsum acquietet etc. de debito predicto .xx. librarum occasione etc.>[67] et <protulit>[68] coram etc. [quandam][69] cartam dicti Nicholai, in qua continetur quod predictus Nicholaus <tenetur acquietare etc. predictum David.>[70] Predictus Nicholaus venit coram etc. et <recognovit predictam cartam esse factum suum et warrantizat etc.>[71] Ideo consideratum est quod predictus <Nicholaus inde respondeat.>[72]

Per inquisicionem factam coram vicecomiti etc., sicut patet inter inquisiciones hujus termini, quod Robertus filius Rogeri de Baconesthorp' feoffatus fuit de una acra terre, Johannes Garlaund' de una roda et dimidia, David Bene de una acra [dimidia terre,][73] Johannes Hachet de una acra terre, Johannes de la More capellanus de una acra prati, Johannes de Baddebrigge de una acra [terre,][74] Ricardus Panton' de una acra, et Ricardus Rust de una acra terre, sicut patet inter inquisiciones termini sancti Michaelis proximo sequentis [retornatas,][75] feoffati fuerunt [de predictis terris][76] priusquam Willelmus filius Henrici Holdel' in predictis viginti libris [Salomoni filio Deulecres judeo Norwyci][77] obligaretur, videlicet ante diem lune proximam post festum sancti Luce evangeliste anno regni regis Henrici .xlv.^{to} Ideo consideratum est quod ab <accione>[78] dicti debiti eant quieti. Et preceptum est vicecomiti quod ipsos inde pacem <etc.>[79]

Andreas Holdelond' et alii tenentes terrarum que fuerunt predicti Willelmi Holdelond' qui feoffati fuerunt post invadiacionem predicti debiti debent respondere de eodem debito, sicut continetur in termino sancti Michaelis proximo sequenti.

MEMBRANE 2

Placita de octabis sancte Trinitatis anno regni regis Edwardi vij^{o}

(82)

Hertff. Mosseus filius Jacobi de Oxon' judeus optulit se quarto die versus Thomam filium Hamonis de <Wieleston',>[80] tenentem quandam partem terrarum que fuerunt predicti Hamonis, de placito debiti. Et ipse non venit. Et preceptum fuit vicecomiti quod, <sicut alias, quod>[81] ipsum venire faceret. Et vicecomes mandavit quod <ballivus libertatis de Berkhamstede ei respondit quod>[82] Willelmus le Neueman de <Gatesdon'>[83] et Henricus filius Ricardi de eadem manuceperunt predictum Thomam, quem non habuerunt. Ideo in <misericordia.>[84] Judicium quod distringatur per terras etc., ita quod nec ipse etc., et quod

[49] Regi de predictis .xx. libris *32*.

[50] Roberto filio Rogeri, Johanne Garland, David Bene, Johanne Hachet, Johanne de la More capellano, Johanne de Badebrige, Ricardo Panton', Ricardo Rust, Lucia de le Thoft. David de Blakeland et Alexandro Kytel *32*.

[51] ad quindenam sancti Michaelis *32*.

[52] dictum Nicholaum *32*. [53] acquietare debet *32*.

[54] supradicto *32*.

[55] quinque acrarum dimidie et unius rode terre quas inde tenet *32*.

[56] *Supplied from 32*. [57] porrigebat *32*.

[58] suam et factum suum et devenit warantum dicti Johannis *32*.

[59] dictas quinque acras dimidiam et .j. rodam *32*.

[60] *Supplied from 32*. [61] dicti debiti ipsum contingente *32*.

[62] *Supplied from 32*. [63] porrigebat *32*.

[64] *Supplied from 32*.

[65] dictam cartam et factum suum cognovit et *32*.

[66] *Supplied from 32*.

[67] eum acquietare debet de porcione dicti debiti ipsum contingente occasione unius acre et dimidie terre quas inde tenet de terris dicti Willelmi *32*.

[68] porrigebat *32*. [69] *Supplied from 32*.

[70] prefatum David contra omnes homines acquietare, warrantizare et defendere tenetur *32*.

[71] dictam cartam et factum suum recognovit et warrantizat *32*.

[72] David de supradicto debito eat quietus et predictus Nicholaus inde respondeat *32*.

[73] *Supplied from 32*. [74] *Supplied from 32*.

[75] *Supplied from 32*. [76] *Supplied from 32*.

[77] *Supplied from 32*. [78] exaccione *32*.

[79] habere permittat. [Et si] quid ab eis predicta occasione ceperit id eisdem deliberet *32*.

[80] Vieleston' *32*. [81] *32 omits*. [82] *32 omits*.

[83] Gatesdene *32*.

[84] *The word* misericordia *is repeated in the margin.*

de exitibus etc., <et quod habeat corpus ejus coram etc.>[85] a die sancti Johannis Baptiste in .xv. dies <ad respondendum etc., et ad audiendum etc.>[86]

(83)

Kanc'. Mosseus filius Jacobi de Oxon' judeus optulit se quarto die versus Johannem filium Hamonis de <Vyeleston',>[87] tenentem quandam partem terrarum que fuerunt predicti Hamonis, de placito debiti. Et ipse non venit. Et preceptum fuit vicecomiti quod <non omitteret propter libertatem archiepiscopi Cant' quin eam etc. sicut alias, et>[88] venire faceret. Et vicecomes mandavit quod Willelmus de Burne et Radulfus de eadem manuceperunt predictum Johannem, quem non habuerunt. Ideo in misericordia. Judicium quod <non omittat etc. quod>[89] distringat [per terras][90] etc., ita quod nec ipse etc., et quod de exitibus etc., <et quod habeat corpus ejus coram etc.>[91] a die sancti Johannis Baptiste in .xv. dies <ad respondendum etc. et ad audiendum etc.>[92]

(84)

Northt'. Willelmus Foliot et Isabella uxor ejus per attornatum suum optulerunt se quarto die versus Elenam la <Thuche>[93] de placito transgressionis. Et ipsa non venit. Et preceptum fuit vicecomiti quod ipsam attachiari faceret, <ita quod haberet corpus ejus coram etc. ad hunc diem.>[94] Et vicecomes mandavit quod predicta Elena districta <fuit et quod>[95] nichilominus Radulfus <Fauk'>[96] de Esseby, Alanus Drake de eadem, Ricardus de Valencia <de eadem,>[97] et Willelmus in Angulo <de eadem>[98] manuceperunt <ipsam,>[99] [quam non habuerunt. Ideo in misericordia. Judicium quod distringatur per terras etc., et quod de exitibus etc.,][100] <et quod habeat corpus ejus coram etc.>[101] a die sancti Johannis Baptiste in. xv. dies <ad respondendum etc.>[102] et ad audiendum etc.

(85)

Suff'. Edmundus de <Sardelawe,>[103] tenens quandam partem terrarum que fuerunt magistri Roberti de <Sardeloue,>[104] de quo exiguntur decem [libre][105] ad opus Regis occasione <predictarum terrarum quas tenet,>[106] optulit se quarto die versus Johannem de Heccham, [heredem][107] predicti magistri Roberti, de placito aquietacionis debiti. Et ipse non venit. Et preceptum fuit vicecomiti quod ipsum venire faceret. Et vicecomes mandavit quod <Petrus le Charetter>[108] de Hegham, Johannes Gilot <de eadem,>[109] Johannes prepositus <de eadem,>[110] et Petrus <Rolande>[111] [de][112] eadem manuceperunt ipsum Johannem, quem non habuerunt. Ideo in misericordia.[113] Judicium quod distringatur per terras etc., <ita quod nec ipse etc.,>[114] et quod de exitibus etc., <et quod habeat corpus ejus coram etc.>[115] a die sancti Johannis Baptiste in .xv. dies <ad respondendum etc. et ad audiendum>[116] etc.

(86)

<*Wiltes'*.>[117] Nicholaus Duredent per attornatum suum optulit se quarto die versus Johannem de <Monemuth'>[118] de placito aquietacionis debiti. Et ipse non venit. Et preceptum fuit vicecomiti quod <terras et catalla etc. salvo custodiret etc., ita quod nec ipse etc., et quod de exitibus etc., et quod haberet corpus ejus coram etc. ad hunc diem ad respondendum etc., et quod haberet dimidiam marcam quam levari fecit de exitibus terrarum predicti Johannis, sicut significavit justiciariis a die Pasche ultimo preterito in .xv. dies>[119] etc. Et vicecomes mandavit quod breve regis adeo tarde sibi venit quod non potuit exequi <propter brevitatem temporis.>[120] Ideo, sicut [prius,][121] a die sancti Johannis Baptiste in .xv. dies etc.

(87)

<*Wiltes'*.>[122] Thomas de Chelwarton' optulit se quarto die versus Johannem de Haveringe <nuper vicecomitem Sutht'>[123] de placito acquietacionis debiti <Judaismi.>[124] Et ipse non venit. Et preceptum fuit vicecomiti, <sicut pluries,>[125] quod ipsum distringeret <per terras etc., et quod de exitibus etc., et quod haberet corpus ejus coram etc. ad hunc diem ad respondendum>[126] etc. Et vicecomes mandavit quod <postquam recepit istud breve regis quod dudum idem Johannes una cum bonis suis existit sub manucapcione demandam quam [i]<ei>[i] fecit de quibuscunque debitis aliis quam de debitis domini regis poneret in respectum usque ad parliamentum sancti Michaelis. Ideo nichil inde actum est. Et quia constat justiciariis etc. quod dictus Thomas non exigit aliquod debitum de prefato Johanne ad opus suum proprium, set quod eidem Thome debitam inde habere faciat allocacionem versus judeos predictos, ideo preceptum est ei, sicut pluries, a die sancti Johannis Baptiste in .xv. dies ad respondendum etc. et ad audiendum et quod vicecomes sit ibidem etc.>[127]

85 *32 omits.* 86 *32 omits.* 87 Vieleston' *32.*
88 ipsum *32.* 89 *32 omits.* 90 *Supplied from 32.*
91 *32 omits.* 92 *32 omits.* 93 Zuche *32.* 94 *32 omits.*
95 et *32.* 96 Faukes *32.* 97 *32 omits.* 98 *32 omits.*
99 dictam Elenam *32.* 100 *Supplied from 32.*
101 *32 omits.* 102 *32 omits.* 103 Skardelawe *32.*
104 Skardelawe *32.* 105 *MS. reads* libras. 106 etc. *32.*
107 *MS. reads* heres; heredem *32.* 108 Johannes *32.*
109 *32 omits.*

110 *32 omits.* 111 Kaban *32.* 112 *MS. omits.*
113 *The word* misericordia *is repeated in the margin.*
114 *32 omits.* 115 *32 omits.* 116 *32 omits.*
117 *32 omits.* 118 Monemue *32.*
119 ipsum distringeret *32.*
120 *32 omits.* 121 alias *32.* 122 *32 omits.* 123 *32 omits.*
124 *32 omits.* 125 *32 omits.* 126 *32 omits.*
127 post adventum brevis recepit aliud breve quod poneret in respectum usque ad parliamentum sancti Michaelis dictam demandam. Ideo sicut alias a die sancti Johannis in .xv. dies etc. *32.*

<*Placita de quindena Trinitatis*>[128]

(88)

<*Wylts'*.>[129] Rogerus de Ly et Angnes uxor ejus per attornatum suum optulerunt se quarto die versus [Hugonem][130] <le Guerysse,>[131] Eliam le Frye, Willelmum de Gardino, Ricardum de Ferle, Johannem de la <Wrmerde>[132] et Nicholaum de Neston' de placito transgressionis. Et ipsi non venerunt. Et preceptum fuit vicecomiti, sicut pluries, quod non omitteret propter libertates de Bradeford' et Chypham quin [eas][133] etc. et ipsos distringeret <per terras etc., ita quod [i]<nec >[i] ipsi etc., et quod de exitibus etc., et quod haberet corpora eorum coram etc. ad hunc diem.>[134] Et vicecomes mandavit quod <Hugo le Guerisse districtus est per terras etc., et sunt exitus .xvj. denarii, qui traditi sunt custodiendi Nicholao Fot, Thome Virly, Ricardo Pascelode et Waltero le Guerisse, qui manuceperunt predictum Hugonem;>[135] <et quod Elias le Frye eodem modo districtus est et quod Robertus le Frie, Robertus Doget, Willelmus Austin et Johannes le Parker manuceperunt predictum Eliam et sunt exitus .xij. denarii et traduntur predictis manucaptoribus, qui modo respondebunt;>[136] <et quod Willelmus de Gardino eodem modo districtus est et quod Willelmus Cokes, Willelmus Bord, Walterus de Browe, et Robertus de la Rewe manuceperunt predictum Willelmum et sunt exitus etc. .xv. denarii, qui traduntur predictis manucaptoribus;>[137] <et quod Ricardus de Farle et Johannes de la Wordemerde non sunt inventi, sicut prius;>[138] <et quod Nicholaus de Neston' districtus eodem modo, et quod Johannes Malger, Henricus Trendeboys, Philippus de Mockisham, et Robertus Doget manuceperunt predictum Nicholaum, et quod exitus sunt .xviij. denarii, de quibus predicti manucaptores respondebunt;>[139] quos non habuerunt. Ideo ipsi manucaptores in misericordia. Judicium quod <predicti Hugo, Elias, Willelmus, Ricardus, Johannes et Nicholaus>[140] distringantur <per terras etc., ita quod nec ipsi>[141] etc., et quod de exitibus etc., <et quod haberet corpora eorum coram etc.>[142] in octabis sancti Michaelis <ad respondendum etc. et ad audiendum etc.>[143]

[128] *There is no corresponding heading at this point in 32.*
[129] *32 omits.* [130] *Supplied from 32.* [131] de Gersie *32.*
[132] Wermode *32.* [133] *MS. reads* eam; eas *32.*
[134] *32 omits.*
[135] Nicholaus Fot, Thomas Virli, Ricardus Patelote et Walterus de Gersie manuceperunt dictum Hugonem *32.*
[136] Et quod Robertus le Frie, Robertus Dogit, Willelmus Austin et Johannes le Parkere manuceperunt dictam Eliam *32.*
[137] Et quod Willelmus de Gardino, Willelmus Colis, Willelmus Dord', Walterus Browe et Robertus de la Browe manuceperunt dictum Willelmum *32.*
[138] *32 omits.*
[139] Et quod Johannes Malger, Henricus Trudeboys, Philippus de Mokesham et Robertus Doget manuceperunt Nicholaum *32.*
[140] *32 omits.* [141] *32 omits.* [142] *32 omits.*
[143] *32 omits.*

(89)

Berk'. Preceptum fuit vicecomiti quod de bonis et catallis Johannis de Scaccario fieri faceret .x. marcas ad opus Johannis Gifford, quas nuper <per consideracionem curie etc. recuperavit pro dampnis etc. eidem Johanni Gifford per predictum Johannem illatis, ita>[144] quod denarios illos haberet coram etc. ad hunc diem etc. Et vicecomes mandavit quod <predictus Johannes de Scaccario nulla habet bona unde aliqui denarii levari possint nisi blada in terra crescencia.>[145] Ideo <preceptum est ei,>[146] sicut alias, a die sancti Michaelis in .xv. dies etc. <ad solvendum etc.>[147]

(90)

Sutht'. Adam de Winton' clericus optulit se quarto die versus Radulphum de Fraxino de placito debiti. Et ipse non venit. Et vicecomes mandavit quod retornavit breve ballivis libertatis <civitatis>[148] Winton', qui nichil inde fecerunt. Judicium quod non omittat <propter libertatem etc. quin eam etc. et venire faciat coram>[149] etc. a die sancti Johannis Baptiste <in .xv. dies ad respondendum.>[150]

(91)

Sutht'. <Godefridus le Clerk de Wordlham>[151] fecit venire Thomam Paynel ad aquietandum ipsum versus Benedictum de Winton' judeum de .xxxviij. libris, septem dolis cisere et sex quarteriis frumenti in quibus tenebatur predicto judeo per duas cartas que fuerunt in archa cyrographariorum[152] Winton' et de .x. libris in quibus tenebatur Lumbardo filio <predicti Benedicti judeo>[153] per unam cartam que fuit in predicta archa et omnibus debitis judeorum.

Predictus Thomas dicit quod non tenetur dicto Godefrido respondere de aliqua aquietacione debiti ad hunc diem eo quod predicti Benedictus et Lumbardus mortui sunt, nec dictus Godefridus districtus est pro aliquibus debitis <[in quibus][154] tenebatur>[155] predictis Benedicto et Lumbardo <et de hoc petit judicium.>[156] <Et quia predicta debita forisfacta sunt domino regi per feloniam predictorum judeorum nec adhuc per Regem exiguntur,>[157] consideratum est quod predictus Thomas inde eat sine die. Et preceptum est vicecomiti quod <inde habeat pacem etc. et districcionem manucaptoribus suis deliberet etc.>[158]

[144] in curia etc. pro dampnis etc. et *32.*
[145] nulla bona habet in balliva sua per que potest distringi *32.*
[146] *32 omits.* [147] *32 omits.* [148] *32 omits.*
[149] *32 omits.* [150] etc. *32.*
[151] Godefridus de Welham *32.*
[152] *32 adds* apud. [153] Benedicti *32.* [154] *MS. omits.*
[155] que debebat *32.* [156] *32 omits.*
[157] Et quia predicta debita sunt forisfacta regis *32.*
[158] ipsum in pace permittat etc. *32.*

MEMBRANE 2 DORSE

(92)

Kanc'. Robertus de Mounteney <per attornatum suum>[159] optulit se quarto die versus Thomam de [Sandwico][160] de placito injuste destriccionis averiorum [suorum.][161] Et ipse non venit. Et preceptum fuit vicecomiti quod ipsum distringeret <per terras etc., et quod de exitibus etc., et quod haberet corpus ejus coram etc. ad hunc diem.>[162] Et vicecomes mandavit quod <predictus Thomas>[163] habet litteras domini Regis de proteccione quod quietus sit de placitis et querelis usque ad quindenam sancti Michaelis eo quod stat in servicio domini Regis in partibus transmarinis senescalcie <Pontif'.>[164] Ideo ponitur in respectum usque ad <dictam quindenam sancti Michaelis eodem statu quo nunc.

Ad quem diem predictus non venit. Ideo, sicut alias, in quindena sancti Martini.>[165]

(93)

<*Surr' Sussex'*>[166] Prece parcium [dies][167] datus est Johanni de <Watele>[168] custodi auri domine <Regine matris Regis>[169] et Willelmo Herigaud usque ad quindenam sancti Johannis Baptiste de .c. et .xvj. libris quas idem Johannes ad opus dicte domine Regine de dicto Willelmo exigit de debitis Benedicti Crespyn judei.

(94)

Somers' Dors'. Preceptum fuit vicecomiti quod venire faceret Johannem de Assele ad respondendum Rogero de Kinton', servienti de scaccaro judeorum, de .x. solidis et .viij. denariis. Et vicecomes mandavit quod dictus Johannes nichil habet in comitatu Somers' neque Dors', per que possit distringi vel attachiari, set manet apud Bradeford' in comitatu Wilts'. Et, quia testificatum est per Willelmum de Becham quod habet terras et catalla in villa de Assele proper Baton' in comitatu Somers', preceptum est vicecomiti, sicut alias, quod venire faciat coram etc. dictum Johannem a die sancti Johannis Baptiste in tres septimanas ad respondendum predicto Rogero de dicto debito et ad audiendum judicium etc. et quod vicecomes sit ibi ad eundem diem ad audiendum judicium suum ex quo male retornavit breve inde [sibi][170] directum.

(95)

<*Lond' Hereff'*.>[171] Aron filius Vives [judeus][172] venire fecit coram etc. Johannem filium Walteri de <Thornbur',>[173] tenentem quandam partem terrarum que fuerunt Willelmi de Everous, et exigit ab eo occasione <predictarum terrarum quas tenet>[174] .xx. libras per [cyrographum][175] .cc. librarum sub nominibus predictorum Willelmi et Aaron confectum.

[Et][176] Walterus de Thornbir', custos Johannis de Thornbir' filii sui, venit. Et prece parcium habent diem usque quindenam sancti Michaelis.

(96)

Wiltes'. Preceptum fuit vicecomiti quod non omitteret propter libertatem de <Ambresbir'>[177] quin eam etc. et distringeret Willelmum de Derneford' per terras <et catalla etc. ad reddendum ad opus Regis .x. libras de debitis Aaron filii Vives, ita quod denarios illos haberet coram etc. ad hunc diem Regi solvendum.>[178] Et vicecomes mandavit quod <octo boves per quos predictum Willelmum prius distrinxit nondum venditi sunt qui bonam monetam haberent et nulla alia bona habet nisi blada in terra crescencia unde aliqui denarii levari possint.>[179] <Et>[180] preceptum est <predicto vicecomiti>[181] quod de predictis octo bobus <et aliis catallis potestati Willelmi>[182] fieri faceret predictas .x. libras, ita quod eas habeat coram etc. a die sancti Johannis Baptiste in tres septimanas <Regi solvendum.>[183]

(97)

Wiltes'. Preceptum fuit vicecomiti quod de bonis et catallis Johannis de Haveringe <nuper vicecomitis Suths'>[184] fieri faceret decem <marcas>[185] ad opus <Aaron filii Vives>[186] quas recognovit [coram etc.][187] se recepisse de Rogero de <Radingham>[188] de debitis dicti Aaron, <ita quod eas haberet ad hunc diem predicto judeo solvendas.>[189] Et vicecomes mandavit quod breve Regis de magno sigillo recepit, dum dictus Johannes cum bonis suis extitisset sub manucapcione, quod demandam eidem Johanni factam de quibuscumque debitis <quam de debitis Regis>[190] poneret in respectum usque ad proximum parleamentum sancti Michaelis. <Preceptum est vicecomiti,>[191] sicut alias, a die sancti Michaelis in unum mensem.

(98)

Kanc'. Antera que fuit uxor Vives filii magistri Mossei <judei per Isac le Eveske attornatum suum>[192] venire fecit Johannem, filium et heredem Johannis de la Teye, et exigit ab eo .xxxv. solidos de debito .lxx. solidorum in quibus dictus Johannes <de la Teye,>[193] pater predicti Johannis, tenebatur Sleme uxori Jornini de Cantuar'

[159] *32 omits these words.*
[160] *MS. reads* Sancwico; Sandwico *32*.
[161] *Supplied from 32.* [162] *32 omits.* [163] *32 omits.*
[164] de Puntif' *32*. [165] dictum diem etc. *32*.
[166] *32 assigns this entry to* Surr' *alone.*
[167] *Supplied from 32.* [168] Whatele *32*.
[169] A. Regine Anglie etc. *32*. [170] *MS. reads* tibi.
[171] *32 omits.* [172] *32 omits.* [173] Thorneber' *32*.

[174] etc. *32*. [175] *Supplied from 32.* [176] *Supplied from 32.*
[177] Aumbesber' *32*.
[178] etc. pro .x. libris etc. *32 (where all except the first word is interlined).*
[179] districit ipsum per octo boves quod adhuc vendere non potest, nec alia bona habet nisi in terra crescencia *32*.
[180] Ideo *32*. [181] *32 omits.* [182] *32 omits.* [183] *32 omits.*
[184] vicecomitis *32*. [185] libras *32*. [186] regis *32*.
[187] *Supplied from 32.* [188] Radenham *32*. [189] *32 omits.*
[190] *32 omits.* [191] Ideo *32*. [192] *32 omits.* [193] *32 omits.*

<judee, et qui prefate Antere assignati fuerunt de thesauro Regis in recompensacionem cujusdam debiti in quo Robertus de Wenden' tenebatur <eidem>[194] Antere, quos .xxx. et .v. solidos ei debet occasione dicte assignacionis et terrarum quas tenet que fuerunt predicti Johannis de la Teye patris sui.>[195]

[Et][196] predictus Johannes venit. Et dicit quod non est factum suum et petit diem premeditandi. Et habet a die sancti Johannis Baptiste in <tres septimanas.>[197]

<Ad quem diem dictus Johannes fuit essoniatus et habet diem a die sancti Michaelis in .xv. dies. Ad quem diem predictus Johannes venit et non potuit dedicere quin de eo pro patre suo scito satisfacere teneatur et petit terminos ad dictum debitum solvendum et habet ex concensu dicti Isac ad solvendum ad quindenam Pasche proximo sequentem .x. solidos, et ad quindenam sancti Johannis Baptiste proximo sequentem .x. solidos, et ad quindenam sancti Hillarii proximo sequentem .xv. solidos ad solucionem dictorum .xxxv. solidorum pro porcione dicti debiti ipsum contingente perficiendum. Et, nisi fecerit, concedit quod de terris et catallis suis fiant.>[198]

(99)

<Lond'>[199] Preceptum fuit constabulario quod attachiaret Hake de Cantuar' et Jorninum filium Abr' judeos ad respondendum Thome de Sancto Michaele de placito quod ipsum insultaverunt, verberaverunt <et maletractaverunt contra pacem>[200] etc., <ita quod habeat corpora eorum in crastino sancti Johannis.>[201] Et constabularius <nichil inde mandavit nec breve retornavit.>[202] Ideo, sicut alias, die lune proxima post translacionem sancti Thome [Martiris][203] etc.

(100)

Kanc'. Antera que fuit uxor Vyves filii magistri Mossei judea per Isac le Eveske attornatum suum fecit venire Thomam, [filium et heredem][204] Johannis de la Teye, et exigit ab eo .xxxv. solidos de quodam debito .lxx. solidorum in quibus dictus Johannes pater dicti Thome tenebatur Sleme uxori Jurn' de Cantuar' judei et qui prefate Antere assignati fuerunt de thesauro regis in recompensacionem cujusdam debiti in quo Robertus de Wendone tenebatur eidem Antere et quos ei debet occasione dicte assignacionis et terrarum quas tenet etc.

Predictus Thomas venit. Et dicit quod non est factum suum et petit diem premeditandi et habet a die sancti Michaelis in .xv. dies etc.

Ad quem diem predictus Thomas non venit. Judicium quod distringat per terras etc. in octabis sancti Andree. Ad quem diem predictus Thomas venit et dedicere non potuit dictum debitum quin inde satisfacere teneatur pro patre suo et petit terminos ad solvendum dictum debitum et habet ex concensu predicti Isac le Eveske ad solvendum ad quindenam Pasche .x. solidos et ad quindendam sancti Johannis Baptiste proximo sequentem .x. solidos, et ad quindenam sancti Hillarii .x. solidos ad solucionem dictorum .xxxv. solidorum pro porcione dicti debiti ipsum [contingente][205] perficiendum. Et, nisi fecerit, concedit quod de terris et catallis suis fiant.

(101)

<Sumers' Dors'>[206] Ricardus de Loverle et Joscea uxor ejus per attornatum suum optulerunt se quarto die versus Johannem filium <Willelmi>[207] Ruffrigeray de placito acquietacionis debiti. Et ipse non venit. Et preceptum fuit vicecomiti, <sicut pluries,>[208] quod non omitteret propter libertatem comitis Glouc' quin eam etc. et distringeret <per terras etc., ita quod nec ipse etc., et quod de exitibus etc., et quod haberet corpus ejus coram>[209] etc. Et vicecomes mandavit quod <predictus Johannes non fuit inventus in balliva sua post recepcionem brevis et quod>[210] nichil habet in balliva sua nisi <quendam tassum>[211] bladi, in quo extimantur sex quarteria frumenti et ordei, <quem>[212] cepit in manum Regis. Judicium quod <distringatur, ut prius, et quod habeat corpus ejus coram>[213] etc., a die sancti Michaelis in .xv. dies <ad respondendum etc. et ad audiendum etc.>[214]

(102)

Kanc'. Mosseus filius Jacobi per Isac le Eveske attornatum suum fecit venire Johannem filim Hamonis de Weyleston', tenentem quandam partem terrarum que fuerunt predicti Hamonis patris sui, et exigit ab eo .xx. libras de catallo occasione predictarum terrarum quas tenet que sunt vadium etc. per cyrographum .xl. librarum et .xl. libras de lucro.

Predictus Johanne venit et dicit quod [non][215] est factum suum et petit diem premeditandi et habet a die sancti Michaelis in .xv. dies.

Ad quem diem dictus Johannes fuit essoniatus et habet diem per essonium suum in crastino sancti Martini. Ad quem diem dictus Johannes venit et recognovit se esse tenentem partem terrarum que fuerunt predicti Hamonis et dicit quod plures sunt tenentes terrarum que fuerunt predicti Hamonis qui secum de predicto debito debent respondere in comitatibus Hertff' et Essex' et petit quod terre et tenementa que fuerunt predicti Hamonis extendantur ut possit de porcione sua respondere. Ideo preceptum est vicecomitibus Kanc' et Essex' quod extendi faciant etc. omnes terras et tenementa que fuerunt predicti Hamonis, videlicet quid et quantum etc.,

[194] *MS. reads* ejusdem.
[195] Et assignato de thesauro dicte Antere in recompensacionem etc. *32*.
[196] *Supplied from 32*. [197] .xv. dies *32*. [198] *32 omits*.
[199] *32 omits*. [200] *32 omits*. [201] *32 omits*.
[202] inde nichil fecit *32*. [203] *Supplied from 32*.
[204] *MS. reads* filius et heres.
[205] *MS. reads* contingit. [206] *32 omits*. [207] *32 omits*.
[208] *32 omits*. [209] *32 omits*. [210] *32 omits*.
[211] quoddam *32*. [212] quod *32*.
[213] salvo custodiat etc., ita etc., et quod de exitibus etc. Et quod habeat *32*.
[214] *32 omits*. [215] *MS. omits*.

et inquisicionem etc. scire faciant justiciariis etc. in octabis sancti Andree. Ad quem diem predicti Johannes et Mosseus veniunt. Et datus est dies prece parcium eo statu quo nunc usque ad quindenam Pasche.

MEMBRANE 3

Placita de tribus septimanis, in crastino et octabis sancti Johannis

(103)

Wigorn'. Wives filius Aaron optulit se quarto die versus Rogerum de Mortuo Mari de placito debiti. Et dictus Rogerus non venit. Et preceptum fuit vicecomiti, sicut pluries, quod distringeret dictum Rogerum per terras etc., et quod haberet corpus ejus coram etc., et quod haberet dimidiam marcam de exitibus terrarum predicti Rogeri prius inde levatam. Et vicecomes mandavit quod dictus Rogerus districtus ad respondendum de dicto placito et de exitibus predictis, et quod ballivi prefati Rogeri dictam districcionem replegiare nolunt nec aquietare, et quod nullus ausus est averia sua emere dicta occasione capta. Judicum, sicut prius, et quod vicecomes habeat dimidiam marcam de exitibus a die sancti Michaelis in .xv. dies.

(104)

Oxon'. Belya que fuit uxor Lumbardi de Crikelade judea, que tulit breve de placito dotis super Ricardum le Povre, non est prosecuta. Ideo ipsa Belya et plegii sui de prosequendo, silicet Mosseus de Neumarch et Isac gener Lumbardi, in misericordia.[216] Et idem Ricardus, qui presens fuit, inde sine die.

(105)[217]

Lond'. Joel de Bloye aurifaber fecit venire Cresseum filium Cressei judeum et queritur [quod][218] ei injuste detinet unum ciphum argenteum deauratum precii quinque marcarum, quem eidem judeo impingnoravit pro .xx. solidis, de quibus solvit eidem .xvj. solidos, et unde queritur quod cum [sepius][219] venisset ad domum dicti judei ad solvendum quatuor [solidos][220] residuos ad plenam solucionem predictorum .xx. solidorum faciendam eidem Cresseo, maliciose se absentavit in detencionem dicti vadii ad dampnum ipsius Joeli .xl. solidorum.

Cresseus venit. Et defendit vim etc. et recognovit se dictum ciphum recepisse in vadium pro .xlvj. solidis, de quibus recepit .xvj. solidos et restant triginta solidi solvendi de dicto debito.

Et prefatus Joel dicit quod non habuit super dictum vadium nisi .xx. solidos, sicut predictum est. Et de hoc ponit se super patriam.

Et judeus dicit quod non debet ponere se super patriam de catallo suo. Et quia recognovit se recepisse dictum vadium per partem debiti sibi restitutam consideratum est quod veritas in premissis inquiratur. Et preceptum [est][221] constabulario Turris Lond' quod venire faciat coram etc. die lune proxima post translacionem sancti Thome Martyris .xij. legales judeos et preceptum [est][222] vicecomitibus Lond' quod venire faciant ad eundem diem .xij. probos et legales homines de visneto vici sancti Laurencii qui nulla affinitate etc., ad recognoscendum etc.

Ad quem diem inquisicio venit per Johannem le Coffrere, Martinum le Botiler et alios christianos, sicut patet inter brevia hujus termini retornata, qui quidem christiani propter libertatem Lond' onerantur de veritate dicenda super sacramentum quod Regi fecerunt, et per Sampsonem de Staundon', Eliam de Cornhull' et alios judeos juratos, sicut patet inter brevia predicta. Qui dicunt super sacramentum suum quod cum prefatus Joel impignasset quoddam fermaculum aureum precii .viij. marcarum Cresseo filio Cressei pro .xlvj. solidos per manum Jocei Bundi, postea dictus Joel tradidit dicto judeo unum ciphum argenteum deauratum precii .v. marcarum pro predictis .xlvj. solidis et extraxit fermaculum predictum, et in partem solucionis predicti debiti idem Joel solvit prefato judeo .xvj. solidos tantum. Ideo consideratum est quod dictus judeus teneat vadium suum donec de .xxx. solidis qui ei aretro sunt fuerit satisfactum.

(106)

Wylts'. Nicholaus Duredent per attornatum suum optulit se [quarto die][223] versus Johannem de Monemuth' de placito aquietacionis debiti. Et ipse non venit. Et preceptum fuit vicecomiti, sicut alias, quod distringeret predictum Johannem per terras etc., et quod ea in manum domini regis salvo custodiret, ita quod nec ipse etc., et quod [de][224] exitibus etc., et quod haberet corpus ejus coram etc. Et vicecomes mandavit quod Thomas le Jeovene, Walterus le Leche, Walterus Faber, Johannes in Marisco, Simon le Leche, Walterus Burgeys, Rogerus Duc, Henricus Intesle, Fulco Meliore, Philippus Cyssor, Hugo filius Basilie et Henricus Mussel manuceperunt predictum Johannem, quem non habuerunt. Ideo in misericordia.[225] Judicium, sicut pluries, a die sancti Michaelis in .xv. dies ad respondendum etc. et ad audiendum etc. Et vicecomes habeat ad eundem diem .viij. solidos de exitibus terrarum predicti Johannis qui sunt in manibus manucaptorum de exitibus terrarum predicti Johannis.

(107)

Lond'. Thomas de Sancto Michaele querens et Hake de Cantuar' et Jorninus filius Abr' judei defendentes

216 *The word* misericordia *is repeated in the margin.*
217 Previously printed by Rigg in *Select Pleas*, pp. 106-7.
218 *MS. omits.* 219 *MS. reads* cepius.
220 *MS. reads* vel.

221 *MS. omits.* 222 *MS. reads* fuit. 223 *MS. omits.*
224 *MS. omits.*
225 *The word* misericordia *is repeated in the margin.*

concordati sunt sub hac forma, videlicet quod idem Thomas remisit eisdem judeis omnes transgressiones eidem per eos illatas a creacione seculi usque ad quindenam sancti Johannis Baptiste nunc. Et pro ista remissione iidem judei dant eidem [Thome][226] unam marcam ei solvendam ad festum sancti Petri Advincula. Et, nisi fecerint, consedunt quod de terris et catallis suis fiant. Et eciam dictus Jorninus manuepit pro dicto Hake quod satisfaciet prefato [Thome][227] ad idem festum.

(108)

Suff'. Edmundus de Sordesloue, de quo exiguntur ad opus Regis .x. libre debite Deulecresse filio Aaron occasione terrarum quas tenet que fuerunt magistri Roberti de Sardelewe, fecit venire Johannem de Hecham, nepotem et heredem dicti magistri Roberti, ad respondendum ei de placito quod ipsum acquietet de debito predicto; et protulit quandam cartam, in qua continetur quod ipsum defendere, acquietare et warantizare debet. Et predictus Johannes dedicere non potuit quin sit heres predicti magistri Roberti et quod dictum Edmundum de predicto debito .x. librarum acquietare debet secundum formam dicte carte. Et invenit manucaptores de satisfaciendo de toto predictarum .x. librarum a die sancti Michaelis in unum mensem, videlicet Nicholaum de Laffham, Alanum de Boclaund, Eadmundum de Skhardeloue et Henricum filium Willelmi de Sancto Eadmundo, qui omnes et singuli concedunt quod, si ad dictum diem prefatus Johannes de dicta pecunia non satisfecerit, de terris et catallis eorum fiat, nisi idem Johannes ad eundem diem sufficientem [acquietanciam][228] inde ostendere possit.

Ad quem diem dictus Johannes venit et [vocat][229] acquietanciam per rotulos de magno scaccario et per quasdam tallias quas protulit coram etc., quibus scrutatis et examinatis non constat quod aliqua solucio facta fuerit de debito .l. librarum predictarum. Ideo consideratum est quod dictus Johannes satisfaciat de predictis .x. libris ad presens et de residuis .xl. libris remanet obligatus nisi alios invenerit tenentes.

(109)

Norht'. Willelmus Foliot et Isabella uxor ejus optulerunt de quarto die versus Elenam la Zuche de placito transgressionis. Et ipsa non venit. Et preceptum fuit vicecomiti quod ipsam distringeret per terras etc., ita quod ipsa etc., et quod haberet corpus ejus etc. Et vicecomes mandavit quod Johannes de Schadewelle, Johannes de Rodeston', et Willelmus Godwine manuceperunt predictam Elenam, quam non habuerunt. Ideo in misericordia. Judicium, sicut alias, ita quod habeat corpus ejus coram etc. a die sancti Michaelis in tres septimanas ad respondendum etc. et ad audiendum etc.

(110)

Ebor'. Adam de Novo Mercato per attornatum suum optulit se quarto die versus Henricum de Luffenham de placito transgressionis. Et ipse non venit. Et preceptum fuit vicecomiti, sicut pluries, quod ipsum venire faceret. Et vicecomes mandavit quod Hugo prepositus de Saynton', Willelmus filius ejus, Matheus prepositus de eadem et Johannes Attebriggestones manuceperunt predictum Henricum, quem non habent. Ideo in misericordia.[230] Judicium quod distringat per terras etc., ita quod nec ipse etc., et quod de exitibus etc., et quod habeat corpus ejus coram etc. a die sancti Michaelis in .xv. dies ad respondendum etc. et ad audiendum etc.

(111)

Ebor'. Henricus de Luffenham pro pluribus deffaltis .v. marce.

(112)

Hereff'. Gilbertus de Bosco optulit se quarto die versus Rogerum de Burghull' vicecomitem Hereff' de placito transgressionis. Et ipse non venit. Et preceptum fuit ei quod fuisset hic ad hunc diem ad respondendum eidem Gilberto de eo quod .ix. boves suos vendidit pro .vj. marcis minus sufficienter contra statuta Regis. Et vicecomes mandavit [i]<quod non>[i] potuit venire propter adventum justiciariorum domini regis etc. et quod vendidit dictos boves pro .vj. marcis in pleno mercato in presencia serviencium predicti Gilberti. Et non plus potuit habere pro eis de bona moneta et vendicio dictorum bovum diucius differri non potuit propter brevitatem temporis contenti in quodam brevi regis sibi directo quod de bonis et catallis predicti Gilberti et aliorum fidejussorum fieri faceret .xv. marcas ad opus Johannis de Pecheford. Et preceptum est eidem Rogero vicecomiti Herff' quod sit coram etc. a die sancti Michaelis in .xv. dies ad respondendum etc. Et vicecomes sit etc.

(113)

Kanc'. Antera que fuit uxor Vyves filii magistri Mossei per attornatum suum optulit se quarto die versus Willelmum filium Ricardi de Bereacre et Thomam filium Willelmi de Rinchemere de Sheftingdon' de placito debiti. Et ipse non venit. Et preceptum fuit vicecomiti quod non omitteret propter libertatem archiepiscopi Cant' quin eam etc. et venire faceret predictos Willelmum et Thomam. Et vicecomes mandavit quod postquam recepit breve istud non fuerunt inventi in balliva sua nec aliquid habuerunt per quod possent distringi. Et quia testificatum est quod satis habent et manent in balliva sua preceptum est vicecomiti, sicut alias, a die sancti Michaelis in .xv. dies. Et vicecomes sit etc. ad audiendum etc. quare preceptum regis inde sibi directi non est secutus.

226 *MS. reads* Michaeli. 227 *MS. reads* Michaelis.
228 *MS. reads* acquietant. 229 *MS. reads* vic'.

230 *The word* misericordia *is repeated in the margin.*

MEMBRANE 3 DORSE

(114)

Ebor'. Preceptum fuit vicecomiti, sicut pluries, quod distringeret Rogerum de Mortuo Mari, Lucam de Chancy et heredes Henrici de Eyvile, tenentes quasdam partes terrarum que fuerunt Gilberti de Beningworthe per terras etc., et quod haberet corpora eorum etc. ad respondendum Regi una cum Johanne de Bathon', qui habuit eundem diem, de .ccclx. libris in quibus predictus Gilbertus Regi tenebatur de debitis judaismi. Et ipsi non venerunt. Et vicecomes mandavit quod Rogerus de Mortuo Mari districtus est [per catalla][231] ad valenciam .x. marcarum et tradita custodiendum Petro filio Lamberti de Bulburgh' et Ade servienti de eadem; et quod Ricardus filius Gerardi de Bulburgh', Johannes prepositus de eadem, Robertus filius Walteri de eadem et Gilbertus Dresey de eadem manuceperunt predictum Rogerum, quem non habuerunt. Ideo in misericordia.[232] Et quod Willelmus de Chauncy, heres Lucie de Chauncy, districtus est [per catalla][233] ad valenciam x. marcarum tradita custodiendum Petro filio Radulphi de Munketon' et Philippo clerico de eadem; et quod Hugo filius Walteri de Munkton', Johannes Cocus de eadem, Serlo molendinarius de eadem et Johannes le Fraunceys de eadem manuceperunt predictum Willelmum, quem non habuerunt. Ideo in misericordia.[234] Et quod heredes Henrici de Eyvile non sunt inventi. Judicium quod distringat, sicut pluries, per terras etc., et quod [habeat][235] corpora eorum coram etc. a die sancti Michaelis in .xv. dies ad respondendum etc. et ad audiendum etc.

(115)

Berks'. Inquisicio facta de bonis et catallis Lumbardi de Windes' judei mortui per sacramentum Thome Burnell', Reginaldi Coci et aliorum christianorum, Manseri de Norwyco, Joscei de North' et aliorum judeorum, sicut patet inter brevia hujus termini retornata. Qui dicunt super sacramentum suum quod idem Lumbardus habuit die quo egrotavit etc., ut in auro etc. .xx. libras, et quod Rex habuit inde quinque marcas pro inquisicione accleranda de statu suo pro transgressione sibi imposita pro retoncione monete et sic remanet .xv. marce; unde tercia pars Regi est quinque marce. Et Sarra que fuit uxor ipsius Lumbardi finem fecit pro predictis. Et de .xxij. solidis et octo denariis residuis concessum est eidem Sarre solvere incontinenti .ij. solidos .viij. denarios et ad Pascha proximo sequens .x. solidos et ad festum sancti Michaelis proximo sequens, videlicet anno regni regis E. .viij. .x. solidos. Et preceptum est vicecomiti Wiltes' quod de catallis viri sui mobilibus et inmobilibus liberam permittat administracionem etc. Postea predicta Sarra dedit Regi et ei assingnavit pro predictis .xx. solidis predictam cartam .lx. solidorum sub nominibus Thome de Winteburne et Rogeri Juvenis et predicti Lumbardi, ita quod, nisi dicti .xx. solidi levari possint de dicto debito .lx. solidorum, quod dicta Sarra inde Regi satisfaciet. Et concessum est eidem Sarre quod, si totum debitum lx [solidorum] levetur, tunc .xl. solidi inde liberentur eidem Sarre habendum per .v. marcas quas solvet Regi a die sancti Michaelis in .xv. dies per plegium Mossei de Clare et Isaak le Evesk judeorum. Postea inventa fuit quadam carta .lx. solidorum sub nomine Thome et sic est summa omnium catallorum .xviij. libre .viij. solidi; unde tercia pars Regis est .vj. libre .ij. solidi .viij. denarii, pro qua tercia parte Sarra que fuit uxor dicti Lumbardi assignat Regi unam cartam .c. solidorum sub nominibus Galfridi filii Galfridi de Cundy et dicti Lumbardi, quam eadem Sarra dicit esse in archa cyrographariorum de Devys'. Et concessit quod, nisi Rex habere possit .c. solidos de debito predicto, tunc illi .c. solidi leventur de residuis catallis suis.

(116)

Wylts'. Johannes de Havering, nuper vicecomes Suth', quia non venit ad compotum, sicut ei preceptum fuit, set recessit sine licencia, ideo pro contemptu in misericordia.[236]

(117)

Lond', Surr'. Isak de Suthwerk judeus venit coram etc. et dicit se amisisse quasdam partes cyrographorum debitorum suorum per latrones qui nuper domum suam fregerunt et dictas partes cyrographorum una cum aliis bonis suis asportaverunt et petit graciam et [auxilium][237] ad dicta debita sua levanda. Et concessum est ei quod debita sua nomine Regis summoneantur et leventur pro quarta parte que de dictis debitis levari poterit per brevia regis.

Debita Isak de Suwerk

Hereff'. Nicholaus de Wormel' debet eidem Isak .x. marcas.

Linc'. Henricus Futesadame de Staunff' debet eidem Isak .c. solidos.

Essex'. Johannes de Kamville debet eidem Isak .c. solidos.

Wyltes'. Johannes Wayse de Hunyton' debet eidem .x. libras.

Bed'. Jacon Wake debet eidem .iiij. marcas. Abbas de Warden' tenet terras.

Berk'. Willelmus Cocus de Suthwerk' debet eidem .c. solidos. De isto debito dat Regi medietatem.

Kanc'. Batholomeus Malemeins debet eidem .lx. solidos.

Surr'. Ricardus de Hadisham debet eidem .c. solidos.

Suss'. Ricardus filius Ricardi de Hadisham debet eidem .x. libras.

231 *MS. omits.*
232 *The word* misericordia *is repeated in the margin.*
233 *MS. omits.*
234 *The word* misericordia *is repeated in the margin.*
235 *MS. reads* habeas.
236 *The word* misericordia *is repeated in the margin.*
237 *MS. reads* aucilium.

Thomas Haumsard filius Jacobi Haumsard debet eidem .c. solidos, de quibus abbas de [Certeseye,][238] tenens quandam partem terrarum predicti Thome, satisfecit eidem Isak de .l. solidis pro medietate dicti debiti acquietanda. Jacobus Haumsard, frater predicti Thome, et Thomas Haron, tenentes quandam partem terrarum predicti Thome, distringantur pro .l. solidis qui adhuc restant de dicto debito.

Sweyn le Chalonner de Gueldeforde debet eidem .xx. solidos.
Normannus de Suwerk' debet eidem .xl. solidos.
Henricus Jukel debet eidem .ij. marcas.
Margeria de Camerwell' debet eidem .iiij. libras.

Robertus le Duc debet eidem .iiij. libras. Tenentes terras distringantur preter Johannem de Ludham qui quietus [est][239] de porcione ipsum contingente de dicto debito per starrum dicti Isak.

(118)

Linc'. Preceptum fuit vicecomiti quod per sacramentum proborum et legalium hominum diligenter inquireret quantum Henricus de Lacy comes Linc', prior de Bolington', prior de Ormesby, heredes Willelmi de Holegate quondam majoris Linc' et Helewysia de Nevile tenent de terris et tenementis que fuerunt Gilberti de Benyngworthe et quantum valeant per annum in omnibus exitibus salvis serviciis dominorum feodi. Et vicecomes mandavit quod inquiri fecit per sacramentum Radulphi Neuman de Kelingesholm', Oliveri Berner et aliorum, sicut patet inter inquisiciones hujus termini [retornatas.][240] Qui dicunt super sacramentum suum quod predictus Henricus tenet de terris et tenementis predictis in Halton' super Humbre viginti et novem bovatas terre in dominico et villani predicti Henrici tenent de terris et tenementis predictis triginta et septem bovatas terre cum toftis, quarum quelibet bovata valet per annum .viij. solidos. Idem Henricus tenet ibidem de redditu liberorum tenencium .xxv. solidos. Idem Henricus tenet ibidem de redditu cotariorum qui tenent ad voluntatem suam .xxx. solidos .iij. denarios per annum. Et idem Henricus tenet de terris predicti Gilberti in Parva Steping' unam carucatam terre que valet per annum in omnibus exitibus salvo servicio etc. centum solidos.

Summa .xxxiiij. libre .iij. solidi .iiij. denarii.

Juratores dicunt quod prior de Bollington' tenet de terris predicti Gilberti in villa de Freskans .xv. acras terre, .xiij. acras dimidiam prati et pasture et unum molendinum aquaticum cum tribus toftis que valent per annum in omnibus salvo etc. .lxv. solidos .iij. denarios. Juratores dicunt quod prior de Ormesby tenet de terris dicti Gilberti in villa de Fresken' .xl. acras terre, .xlix. acras prati et pasture, que valent per annum in omnibus exitibus salvo etc. .cxiij. solidos .vj. denarios. Item dicunt quod heredes Willelmi de Holegate quondam [majoris][241] Linc' ac Helewisia de Neville non tenent aliquas terras seu tenementa in comitatu predicto que fuerunt predicti Gilberti.

(119)

Linc'. Johannes de Baton', tenens quandam partem terrarum que fuerunt predicti Gilberti, de quo exigitur dictum debitum .ccclx. librarum, per essoniatorem suum optulit se quarto die versus Henricum de Lacy, priorem de Bolington', priorem de Ormisby, heredes Willelmi de Holegate et [Helewisam][242] de Nevile, tenentes quasdam partes terrarum que fuerunt predicti Gilberti. Et ipsi non venerunt. Et preceptum fuit vicecomiti quod ipsos distringeret per terras etc., ita quod nec ipsi etc., et quod de exitibus etc., et quod haberet corpora eorum coram etc. ad hunc diem, scilicet quindenam sancti Johannis Baptiste. Et vicecomes mandavit quod Walterus prepositus de Brocelby, Thomas Tundu de eadem, Thomas filius Margerie de eadem et Ricardus ad portam aule de eadem manuceperunt predictum Henricum, quem non habuerunt. Ideo in misericordia. Et quod Alanus de Waldingford in Ingham, Simon Modipas de eadem, Henricus inthelane de eadem et Alanus Tuthut de eadem manuceperunt priorem de Bolington'; et quod Philippus de Woterbi, Radulphus Wenges de eadem, Walterus Lommy de Ormesby et Alanus Can de eadem manuceperunt priorem de Ormesby; quos non habuerunt. Ideo in misericordia.[243] Et quod heredes Willelmi de Holegate et Helewysia de Nevile nullas terras tenent in predicto comitatu que fuerunt ipsius Gilberti, ideo de ipsis nichil actum est. Judicium quod distringat per terras etc., ut prius, et quod habeat corpora eorum coram etc. a die sancti Michaelis in .xv. dies etc. ad respondendum etc. et ad audiendum etc.

(120)

Hereff'. Mosseus filius Jacobi fecit venire Thomam filium Hamonis de Wyeleston', tenentem quandam partem terrarum que fuerunt Hamonis de Wieleston', et exigit ab eo .xl. libras per cyrographum .xl. librarum inter predictum Hamonem et predictum Mosseum confectum et .xl. marcas de lucro quas ei debet occasione terrarum etc.

Predictus Thomas venit et petit auditum brevis et habet. Et, audito brevi et lecto, petit judicium de brevi desicut non exigit per breve suum nisi .xx. libras et in querela sua exigit .xl. libras. Et quia in peticione sua non concordat cum brevi suo ideo consideratum est quod dictus Thomas eat inde sine die et predictus Mosseus in misericordia.[244]

[238] *MS. reads* Serteseye.
[239] *MS. omits.*
[240] *MS. reads* recognitas.
[241] *MS. reads* mercatoris.
[242] *MS. reads* Helewise.
[243] *The word* misericordia *is repeated in the margin.*
[244] *The word* misericordia *is repeated in the margin.*

MEMBRANE 4

Adhuc placita de termino Trinitatis

(121)

Preceptum fuit vicecomiti quod de bonis et catallis [Briani][245] de Gowyz fieri faceret .x. marcas ad opus Aaron filii Vyves quas idem Aaron per consideracionem curie etc. versus eundem [Brianum][246] recuperavit. Et vicecomes mandavit quod cepit in manum regis de bonis et catallis predicti Briani pro predictis .x. marcis decem boviculos precii .ij. marcarum et dimidie, quatuor asinos precii .viij. solidorum et sex mullones feni precii .xij. solidorum, ad quos vendendum adhuc nullum invenit emptorem. Ideo, sicut alias etc., quod de predictis boviculis, asinis et aliis bonis et catallis predicti [Briani][247] fieri faciat predictas .x. marcas, ita quod eos habeat coram etc. a die sancti Michaelis in .xv. dies etc.

(122)

Lond'. Rogerus de Kynton', serviens de scaccario etc., optulit se quarto die versus Galfridum de Specteshale rectorem ecclesie sancte Marie de Wellechichehaue de placito transgressionis. Et ipse non venit. Et preceptum fuit vicecomitibus Lond' quod ipsum venire facerent. Et vicecomites mandaverunt quod predictus Galfridus capellanus est et non habet laycum feodum per quod possit distringi. Ideo mandatum est episcopo Lond' quod ipsum venire faciat coram etc. a die sancti Michaelis in .xv. dies ad respondendum etc.

(123)

Lond'. Willelmus Beraud optulit se quarto die versus Milonem filium Jaconi de Ebor' judeum de placito transgressionis. Et ipse non venit. Et preceptum fuit constabulario Turris Lond' quod ipsum venire faceret. Et constabularius mandavit quod Benedictus de Ebor' et Benedictus de Reoun manuceperunt predictum Milonem, quem non habuerunt. Ideo in misericordia. Judicium quod distringat per terras etc., ita quod nec ipse etc., et quod de exitibus etc., et quod habeat corpus ejus etc. a die sancti Michaelis in .xv. dies ad respondendum etc. et ad audiendum etc.

(124)

Lond'. Idem Willelmus optulit se quarto die versus Benedictum filium magistri Elie de placito transgressionis. Et ipse non venit. Et preceptum fuit constabulario quod ipsum venire faceret. Et constabularius mandavit quod idem Benedictus non fuit inventus in balliva sua postquam recepit istud breve. Ideo, sicut alias, a die sancti Michaelis in .xv. dies etc.

(125)[248]

Sussex'. Johannes de Watele, custos auri domine Regine A. matris domini Regis et attornatus ejusdem domine Regine, fecit venire Willelmum Herigaud, filium et heredem Radulphi Herigaud, et exigit ab eo .cxvj. libras quas eidem domine Regine debet occasione terrarum quas tenet que fuerunt predicti Radulphi patris sui et que sunt vadium pro predicto debito secundum convencionem factam inter predictum Radulphum et Benedictum Crespyn judeum per cirographum quod predictus Johannes profert coram etc., et quod cyrographum eidem domine Regine liberatum fuit per manum Hagini filii magistri Mossei judei pro auro suo in quo Manserus filius Aaron ei tenebatur et quod debitum predictus Haginus recepit de thesauro Regis in recompensacionem quorundam debitorum in quibus Petrus de Maulay ei tenebatur, que quidem debita catalla fuerunt Johannis Giffard de dono regis Henrici.

Predictus Willelmus venit et petit visum cyrographi per quod exigit dictum debitum et habet. Et postea venit et dedicit dictum debitum et dicit quod non est factum suum nec patris ejus et hoc offert verificare etc.

Et dictus Johannes attornatus [i]<dicte>[i] Regine dicit quod hanc verificacionem non debet habere quia ponit se super rotulos de scaccario judeorum quod dictum debitum liberatum fuit pro bono debito et fideli. Et habent diem ad scrutandum dictos rotulos usque diem mercurii proximam ante festum sancte Margarete. Et scrutatis rotulis compertum est in rotulis Judaismi in anno regis Henrici .lv.^{to} in termino sancti Hillarii quod prefatus Willelmus [recognovit][249] dictum debitum .c. et .xvj. librarum tanquam debitum et factum predicti Radulphi patris sui et, facta hac recognicione, predicta Regina habuit breve secundum assisam judaismi de districcione super terras et tenementa ipsius Willelmi, cum idem Willelmus hoc dedicere non potuit. Et dicit quod dicta Regina per breve regis quod emanavit de scaccario judeorum habuit seisinam de terris et tenementis suis pro debito supradicto, et exitus eorundem habuit per biennium ad valenciam debiti supradicti et amplius, per quod non tenetur respondere de eodem debito nec pro eo debito distringi.

Et dictus Johannes dicit quod predicta Regina habuit seisinam de terris et tenementis predicti Willelmi et exitus eorundem recepit, quos allocavit eidem Willelmi in quodam debito quatraginta marcarum in quibus ei tenebatur de fine pro redempcione sua, sicut continetur in quodam scripto obligatorio de predicta summa quod predictus Johannes protulit coram justiciariis etc. Et quod dicti exitus allocati fuerunt eidem Willelmo in dicto fine redempcionis sue et non pro predicto debito Judaismi offert verificare per patriam.

Et dictus Willelmus dicit quod dicta domina regina habuit seisinam de terris et tenementis suis pro debito

[245] *MS. reads* Barani.
[246] *MS. reads* Barianum.
[247] *MS. reads* Bar'.

[248] *Compare the quite different version of this entry in Roll 32, below no. 151.*
[249] *MS. reads* recepit.

Judaismi supradicto, ut predictum est, et non pro redempcione sua nec aliquid allocatum fuit ei de exitibus predictarum terrarum per predictum tempus in redempcione sua set exitus earundem terrarum suarum dicta domina regina recepit pro debito Judaismi supradicto. Et de hoc ponit se super patriam.

Et quod exitus predictarum terrarum allocate fuerunt dicto Willelmi in fine redempcionis sue et non pro debito Judaismi supradicto dictus Johannes pro dicta domina Regina similiter ponit se super patriam. Et preceptum est vicecomiti quod venire faciat coram etc. in octabis sancti Andree .xij. tam milites etc.

Ad quem diem dictus Johannes pro Regina et dictus Willelmus per attornatum suum venerunt. Et inquisicio non venit. Et vicecomes mandavit quod omnes subscripti districti sunt per omnes terras et catalla sua ad veniendum ad hunc diem, videlicet Ricardus de Esburham, Walramus de Mucheaus, Ricardus le Waleys, Robertus Livet, Thomas de Padiham, Stephanus de Cotele, Johannes de Ferles, Robertus le Hosier, Ricardus le Knyth', Willelmus Gemesing', Thomas de Croteberch', Willelmus de Holmdale, Willelmus Ceffrey, Oliverus Heat, Simon Payn, Petrus de Edelescombe et Rogerus le Waleys. Et nullus venit. Judicium quod distringat per terras etc., ita quod nec ipsi etc., et quod de exitibus etc., et quod habeat corpora eorum coram etc. in octabis sancti Hillarii ad respondendum etc., et preter eos venire faciat ad eundem diem tot et tales etc., ne pro defectu etc. Et quia nullus eorum [venit][250] qui venire debuerat ad hunc diem ideo ipse vicecomes, scilicet Emericus de Cancellis, in misericordia,[251] quia insufficienter returnavit breve sibi inde directum.

Ad quem diem predictus Johannes et Willelmus optulerunt se et juratores non venerunt, sicut patet inter brevia termini sancti Hillarii proximo preterito returnata. Et preceptum est vicecomiti, sicut alias, in crastino Cinerum etc. Ad quem diem Johannes de Ferle, Willelmus de Holmdale, Willelmus Ceffrey, Oliverus Hevet, Robertus de North', Gilbertus de Bemergeton', Henricus de Langeport, Hamo atte Stock, Galfridus de Motington', Radulphus le Lungte, Johannes Russel, Johannes de Gotecote, Galfridus de Snateyngeshulle et Johannes de Bromham venerunt. Et, quia non fuit nisi unicus miles inter eos, datus est eis dies <a die Pasche in .xv. dies a die Pasche in .v. septimanas.>[252] Et preceptum est vicecomiti ut prius etc.

Ad quem diem inquisicio venit per Rogerum le Waleys, Rogerum de Leukenore et alios, sicut patet inter brevia de termino Pasche anno regis Edwardi .viij.° Qui dicunt super sacramentum suum quod predicta domina Regina habuit seisinam terrarum predicti Willelmi in comitatu Sussex', videlicet maneriorum de Ikelesham, Waudern', Dene et Beause pro debito Judaismi a die sancti Petri ad Vincula anno regis Henrici .lv.^to^ usque ad vigiliam Natalis Domini anno regis Edwardi secundo, scilicet per duos annos fere et dimidium, et exitus earundem terrarum nomine dicti judei per idem tempus percepit et consecutum fuit quantum perceptum per idem tempus; et si haberet seisinam aliarum terrarum suarum in aliis comitatibus pro predicto debito dicebant quod hoc ignorabant. Dicebant tamen quod dictum fuit in partibus suis quod [ipsa][253] habuit seisinam terrarum dicti Willelmi in comitatu [Sutht'][254] pro predicto debito. Ideo preceptum est vicecomiti [Sutht'][255] quod per sacramentum proborum etc. inquirat.[256]

Et ideo preceptum est vicecomiti Sussex' quod per sacramentum etc. inquirat quantum terre que fuerunt in manu prefate Regine valuerunt per annum in omnibus exitibus, salvo servicio etc. Et similiter preceptum est vicecomiti Sutht' etc. et inquisicionem etc. scire faciant justiciariis etc. a die sancti Johannis [Baptiste][257] in tres septimanas.

Ad quem diem vicecomes returnavit extentam predictarum terrarum, videlicet extentam de Icclesham Beause que fuerunt in manu predicte regine a die dominica proxima ante festum sancti Petri ad Vincula anno regis Henrici .lv.^to^ usque ad vigiliam Natalis Domini anno regni regis Edwardi secundo, videlicet per duos annos et .xxiij. septimanas, et valuerunt predicta maneria, sicut patet per extentam inde factam et returnatam in termino sancte Trinitatis anno regis Edwardi .viij., per predictum tempus centum quatraginta et .j. libras, .iiij. solidos obolum. Manerium de Walderne valuit per predictum tempus .xxj. libras, .vj. solidos, .ij. denarios quadrantem. Manerium de Dene valuit per idem tempus quatervinginti .iij. libras, .viij. solidos, .j. denarium. Summa extente predictorum maneriorum in comitatu Sussex' .cclv. libre, .xviij. solidi, .ij. denarii obulus quadrans. Manerium de Langestoke in comitatu Sutht' quod fuit in manu domine Regine a die Pasche anno regis Henrici .lv.^to^ usque ad festum sancti Barnabe apostoli anno regis predicti .lvj.^to^ valet per predictum tempus .xxx. libras, sicut continetur in extenta inde facta et returnata ut supra. Summa exituum predictorum maneriorum tam in comitatu Sussex' quam in comitatu Sutht' dum fuerunt in manum predicte Regine, sicut predictum est, .cc.iiij.^xx^ libre, .xviij. solidi, .iij. denarii, obulus quadrans, de quibus subtractis .cxvj. libris que exigebantur a prefato Willelmo ad opus prefate regine de debitis Judaismi in quibus Radulphus pater predicti Willelmi tenebatur per cartam que remanet in custodia Johannis Whatele custodis auri predicte regine, remanent de summa totali .clxix. libre, .xviij. solidi, .iij. denarii, obulus quadrans. Et ideo consideratum est quod predictus Willelmus de predictis .cxvj. libris sit quietus et quod

[250] *MS. omits.*

[251] *The word* misericordia *is repeated in the margin and the amount* c solidi *is written beneath.*

[252] *Neither of these dates is marked for deletion and it is unclear which is meant.*

[253] *MS. reads* ipse.

[254] *MS. reads* Sussex'.

[255] *MS. reads* Sussex'.

[256] *The remainder of this entry is to be found after no. 127 though there is nothing on the roll to indicate this.*

[257] *MS. omits.*

carta patris sui inde confecta liberetur eidem Willelmo quiete damnanda. Et quod habeat recuperare suum versus predictam Reginam de .clxix. libris, .xviij. solidis, .iij. denariis, obulo, quadrante, qui super sunt de exitibus terrarum suarum, ut patet supra, ultra .cxvj. libras que sibi allocantur in solucione supradicta. Et mandatum est Johanni de Whatele custodi auri predicte Regine quod habeat predicta cartam coram etc. a die sancti Michaelis in .xv. dies predicto Willelmo, ut predictum est, liberandam.

(126)

Sussex'.[258] Magister Elias filius magistri Mossei judeus per Isaac le Eveske attornatum suum optulit se quarto die versus Willelmum de Hasting' de placito debiti. Et ipse non venit. Et preceptum fuit vicecomiti, sicut pluries, quod salvo custodiret in manu regis terras etc., per quas etc., et plures etc., ita quod nec ipse etc., et quod de exitibus etc., et quod haberet corpus ejus coram etc. ad hunc diem. Et vicecomes mandavit quod returnavit breve regis inde sibi directum ballivis Johannis de Britannia de Hasting', qui nichil inde sibi respondunt. Et quia pluries preceptum fuerat vicecomiti quod non omitteret propter libertatem predictam quin eam etc. et nunc mandavit quod returnavit breve ballivis predictis eciam cum ingredi debuisset et .v. marcas levasse de manucaptoribus predicti Willelmi quas non levavit, ideo ipse vicecomes, scilicet Emerycus de Chaunci, in misericordia.[259] Et preceptum est vicecomiti, sicut pluries, quod non omittat propter libertatem etc. quin eam etc. et salvo custodiat etc., ut prius, et quod habeat corpus ejus coram etc. in crastino Animarum ad respondendum etc. et ad audiendum etc. de pluribus [defaltis.][260] Et quod vicecomes habeat secum ad eundem diem de manucaptoribus predicti Willelmi etc.

(127)

Lanc'. Magister Elias filius magistri Mossei judeus per Gamalielum de Oxon' attornatum suum optulit se quarto die versus Thomam de Regge de placito debiti. Et ipse non venit. Et preceptum fuit vicecomiti quod ipsum venire faceret ad hunc diem. Et vicecomes mandavit quod Willelmus de Walebi et Laurencius de Fonte mancuperunt ipsum Thomam, quem non habuerunt. Ideo in misericordia. Judicium quod distringat per terras etc., ita quod nec ipse etc., et quod de exitibus etc., et quod habeat corpus ejus coram etc. a die sancti Michaelis in .xv. dies ad respondendum etc. et ad audiendum etc.[261]

[membrane 4d is blank]

MEMBRANE 5

Starra et Memoranda de termino sancte Trinitatis anno regni regis Edwardi septimo

(128)

Buk'. Johannes de Merston' capellanus venit coram etc. et recognovit se debere Isak le Eveske judeo quatraginta solidos, reddendum eidem vel suo certo attornato in crastino Commemoracionis Animarum anno regis Edwardi .vij. Et, nisi fecerit, concedit quod de terris et catallis <suis fiant>[262] una cum dampnis, si quas occasione solucionis non facte etc. sustinuerit.

Postea venit predictus judeus et recognovit quod recepit predictos .xl. solidos et quod predictus Johannes inde quietus est.

(129)

Norht'. Martinus de Karon venit coram etc. et recognovit se debere Johanni de Axebrugge .xx. solidos pro uno equo reddendos a die sancti Michaelis in .xv. dies proximo futuro. Et, nisi fecerit, concedit quod de terris et catallis suis fiant etc.

(130)

Radulphus filius Jacobi de Shirley venit coram etc. et recognovit se debere Johanni de Axebr' quatraginta solidos reddendos a die sancti Michaelis in .xv. dies proximo futuro. Et, nisi fecerit, concedit quod de terris et catallis suis fiant.

(131)

Lond'. Sarra que fuit uxor Benedicti le Eveske judea venit coram etc. et recongnovit se vendidisse et dimisisse Gamalielo de Oxon' judeo unum debitum .xvij. marcarum sub nominibus Simonis de Hortheston' et ipsius Benedicti, unde terminus solucionis est in crastino Omnium Sanctorum anno regni regis Edwardi primo. Acta die veneris proxima post festum sancti Jacobi anno eodem. Ita quod idem Gamaliel possit inde in omnibus liberam habere administracionem tam de toto debito quam lucro inde emergente. Et preceptum est cirographariis Oxon' quod ipsum Gamalielum inde permittant etc.

(132)

<Lond'.>[263] Henricus [de][264] Evre, Ricardus de Evre et Johannes de <Whatham>[265] dant regi dimidiam marcam pro secta regis relaxanda de appello Bonef' de Cruce Roysia. Postea solverunt in recepta regis.[266]

[258] *The words* .c. marce *are written above this.*
[259] *The word* misericordia *is repeated in the margin.*
[260] *MS. reads* districcionibus.
[261] *This entry is followed by the continuation of no. 125.*
[262] *These words are repeated in MS.*
[263] *32 omits.*
[264] *Supplied from 32.*
[265] Waltham *32.*
[266] *In the margin (but only in 64) are the words* dimida marca; can' in recepta regis.

(133)

Bed' <*Buk'*>[267] Memorandum quod Hugo de Stapelford <quondam>[268] vicecomes [etc.][269] venit coram etc. et computavit de .c. xij. solidis et .viij. [denariis][270] de divercis amerciamentis per diversas particulas per .xl. tallias etc. <et>[271] soluti sunt in recepta regis.

(134)

Hunted'. <Radulphus>[272] de [Freskeney][273] venit coram etc. et recongnovit pro se et heredibus suis et tenentibus terrarum suarum ad quorumcumqe manus devenerunt se teneri Roberto de Ludham in quatraginta marcis, reddendum terminis subscriptis, videlicet ad Pascha anno regni regis Edwardi octavo quinque marcas et sic de anno in annum quinque marcas <per annum>[274] ad eundem terminum quousque etc. Et, nisi fecerit, concedit <pro se et heredibus suis et tenentibus terrarum suarum ad quorumcumque manus devenerint>[275] quod de terris et catallis suis <et heredum suorum>[276] et tenencium <predictorum>[277] fiant etc.

(135)

Wilts'. <Memorandum quod>[278] Hildebrandus de Lond' vicecomes etc. venit coram etc. et habet diem ad compotum etc. usque ad quindenam sancti Michaelis etc. <Postea habuit diem ad compotum etc. usque a die Purificacionis in .xv. dies.>[279]

(136)

Norff'. Concessum est Johanni filio Ricardi de Widewille de Greston' quod solvat Regi ad scaccarium judeorum duas marcas quas ab eo exigit de debitis in quibus idem Ricardus tenebatur Josceo filio Jacobi judeo ad terminos subscriptos, videlicet dimidiam marcam ad scaccarium sancti Michaelis proximo sequens et dimidiam marcam ad scaccarium Pasche proximo sequens, et residuum, videlicet .j. marcam, in anno sequente ad eosdem terminos.

Starra

(137)

Norff',<*Sussex'*>[280] Mosseus filius Jacobi <de Oxon'>[281] judeus recognovit per starrum suum et testatur pro Henna que fuit uxor Jacobi de Oxon' patris predicti Mossei quod Hamo Chevre et heredes et antecessores sui quieti sunt de predictis Mosseo <et>[282] Henna et heredibus et antecessoribus suis de duobus debitis, videlicet de uno debito .xx. librarum et de uno debito .xl. librarum sub nominibus predictorum Hamonis et Jacobi a creacione seculi usque ad finem et de omnibus aliis debitis et demandis que unquam debebantur per predictum Hamonem vel aliquem antecessorum suorum predicto Jacobo vel alicui antecessorum suorum a creacione seculi usque ad festum sancti Johannis Baptiste anno regni regis Edwardi sexto. Et si inveniatur carta, tallia vel aliquod aliud instrumentum sub nominibus predicti Hamonis vel predictorum judeorum vel sub nomine predicti Jacobi vel alicujus antecessorum suorum in archa cyrographariorum vel extra facta ante predictum diem predictus Mosseus recognovit quod quieta sunt et nichil valeant. Et hoc recognovit pro se et testatur pro Henna predicta. [Et][283] Cok Hagin filius Deulecres et Mosseus filius Jacobi de Oxon' et Cresseus filius Gente recognoverunt et testantur quod predicta Henna recognovit coram eis omnes predictas acquietaciones, <videlicet>[284] quod predictus Hamo quietus est de ipsa Henna de omnibus debitis in quibus umquam predictus Hamo vel aliquis antecessorum suorum tenebatur predictis Henne vel Jacobo vel alicui antecessorum suorum. Et hoc <singillaverunt>[285] litera <sua>[286] hebraica per preceptum ejusdem Henne.

(138)

Lond'. Preceptum fuit cyrographariis arche Lond' quod accederent ad archam etc. pro quibusdam negociis domini regis expediendis. Et iidem justiciarii veniant ad archam illam. Et justiciarii venerunt etc. et omnes cyrographarii venerunt preter Abr' Motun. Et ideo ipse Abr' pro contemptu in misericordia.[287]

(139)

Isac filius Elie de Linc', Meyr filius Jacobi de Ebor' judei Lond' venerunt coram etc. et manuceperunt quod Josceus de Shorham erit coram etc. a die sancti Michaelis in .xv. dies ad standum recto etc. et ad respondendum Regi de debitis in quibus ei tenetur.

MEMBRANE 5 DORSE

Adhuc Memoranda

(140)

Hereff'. Preceptum fuit vicecomiti quod per sacramentum proborum et legalium hominum diligenter inquireret quo die et quo anno abbas de Rading' feoffatus fuit de terris que fuerunt Johannis filii Willelmi Aubin quas tenet, qui Regi tenebatur in .v. marcis de debitis Benedicti le Eskermiser; et, si plures invenisset tenentes terrarum predictarum, eos venire faceret ad hunc diem ad respondendum Regi de predicto debito una cum abbate predicto. Et vicecomes mandavit quod inquisicio facta fuit coram eo per sacramentum Ricardi de Brumfeld', Henrici de Meneton et aliorum, sicut patet inter [inquisiciones hujus][288] termini retornatas. Qui

267 *32 omits.* 268 *32 omits.* 269 *32 omits.*
270 *Supplied from 32.* 271 qui *32.* 272 Ranulphus *32.*
273 *MS. reads* Feskeney'; *32 reads* Freskeni. 274 *32 omits.*
275 *32 omits.* 276 *32 omits.* 277 terrarum suarum *32.*
278 *32 omits.* 279 *32 omits.* 280 *32 omits.*
281 *32 omits.* 282 de *32.*

283 *Supplied from 32.* 284 *32 omits.* 285 sigillavit *32.*
286 *32 omits.* 287 *In the margin are the word* x libre.
288 *MS. reads* hujus inquisiciones.

dicunt super sacramentum suum quod predictus abbas feoffatus fuit de terris et tenementis que fuerunt predicti Johannis quas tenet die dominica proxima post festum sancti Michaelis anno regni regis Henrici .lvj.^{to} Et quod Rogerus de Clifford senior et Simon de Berton' capellanus tenent quasdam partes terrarum que fuerunt predicti Johannis. Et quia dictus abbas dicit se prius esse feoffatum quam dicta terra obligata esset judeo predicto et non constat adhuc justiciariis etc. qualis sit data carte per quam dicta terra obligatur datus est dies predicto abbati a die sancti Michaelis in tres septimanas etc. Et preceptum est vicecomiti quod venire faciat coram etc. predictos Rogerum et Simonem ad respondendum etc. una cum predicto abbate; et interim pacem etc.

(141)

Linc'. Preceptum fuit vicecomiti quod per sacramentum etc. diligenter inquireret que bona et catalla Josceus de Oxon' judeus mortuus habuit die quo egrotavit etc., et ad cujus manus dicta bona devenerunt post mortem dicti judei. Et vicecomes mandavit quod inquisicio facta fuit coram eo per Willelmum le Jeofne de Linc', Robertum le Especer de eadem et aliorum, sicut pater inter inquisiciones termini retornatas. Qui dicunt super sacramentum suum quod dictus Josceus habuit die etc. ut in auro, argento et aliis mobilibus extra archa ad valenciam .xx. solidorum et in terris et domibus et redditibus ad valenciam .xiiij. solidorum per annum, et non habuit plura bona etc. extra archa cyrographariorum; et dicunt quod predicta bona post mortem dicti judei devenerunt in manus Muriele uxoris ipsius Joscei.

(142)

Suth'. Prior sancti Johannis Jerusalem' in Anglia, abbas de Hida Wynton' et Willelmus filius et heres Willelmi de Dunsteyghel', qui habuerunt diem per essoniatores suos in quindena sancti Johannis Baptiste hic de .lxxj. libris que ab eis exiguntur ad opus Regis de debitis Elie filii Chere et Deulegard filii Elie judei Winton' defunctorum, protulerunt breve regis in hec verba: 'Edwardus etc. justiciariis suis etc. salutem. Ostensum est nobis ex parte dilectorum nobis in christo prioris [1]<sancti Johannis>[1] Jerusalem' in Anglia, abbatis de Hyda Winton' et Willelmi filii Willelmi, tenencium terrarum et tenementorum que fuerunt Willelmi de Donstyghl' defuncti, quod, cum idem Willelmus in aliquo debito in Judaismo nostro non teneretur die quo obiit, vos a predictis priore, abbate et Willelmo .lxxj. libras in quibus Elie filio Chere et Deulegard filio Elie quondam judeis Winton' defunctis tenebatur, ut asseritis, exigitis ad opus nostrum; volentes igitur super causa accionis plenius cerciorari, vobis mandamus quod secundum consuetudinem scaccarii judeorum nostri diligenter inquiratis utrum prefatus Willelmus eisdem judeis vel aliis teneretur in predicta pecunie summa et inde recognicionem aliquam fecerit in scaccario judeorum nostri necne, et, si recognicio inde ibidem facta fuerit, quo tempore, qualiter et quo modo; et inquisicionem illam nobis sub sigillis vestris mittatis et hoc breve. Teste me ipso apud Westm' .xxv. die Aprilis anno regni nostris septimo.' Per hoc breve preceptum est vicecomiti quod venire faciat coram etc. a die sancti Michaelis in unum mensem sex probos et legales christianos de comitatu suo, et sex legales judeos de Winton' ad recognoscendum etc.

(143)[289]

Not'. Walterus de Forneus miles et Johannes de Forneus, filius et heres ipsius Walteri, venerunt coram etc. et recognoverunt se debere Jacobo filio Hagini judeo quaterviginti libras, reddendum in octabis Purificacionis Beate Marie anno regis Edwardi .viij.^{o} .liij. marcas et in quindena Pasche proximo sequenti .xx. marcas. Et, nisi fecerint, concedunt quod de terris et catallis suis fiant, ad quorumcumque manus devenerunt.

Postea venit Jacobus filius Hagini et concessit et assignavit Johanni de Bosco executori testamenti Petri de Sancto Petro .xxx. libras percipiendas de prefato debito quaterviginti librarum quas idem Jacobus recognovit se debere prefato Petro, prout patet in termino sancti Michaelis anno regis Edwardi <primo incipienti quarto.>[290]

(144)

Suff'. Rogerus <Kiysterpeny>[291] et <Margareta>[292] Bernard de Donewico [de comitatu Suff'][293] <venerunt coram etc. et>[294] recognoverunt se debere Aaron filio [Wivs][295] .cl. quarteria frumenti, <reddenda ad festum sancti Michaelis anno regni regis Edwardi sexto vel pro quolibet quarterio dimidiam marcam ad eleccionem ipsius judei, sicut continetur in quodam scripto obligatorio inter eos confecto. Et, nisi fecerint, concedunt quod de terris et catallis suis fiant.>[296]

(145)

Lond'. Willelmus Beraud venit coram etc. et recognovit se debere Roberto de Brothton', clerico de scaccario, quatraginta solidos, reddendum inde medietatem in crastino sancte Margarete proximo futuro, et aliam medietatem ad quindenam sancti Michaelis proximo sequentem. Et, nisi fecerit, concedit quod de terris et catallis suis fiant etc.[297]

[289] *Compare no. 67.* [290] *Sic.* [291] de Kistepeny *32.*
[292] Margeria *32.* [293] *Supplied from 32.* [294] *32 omits.*
[295] Vives judeo *32.*
[296] vel dimidiam marcam etc., reddendum ad festum sancti Michaelis anno regis Edwardi sexto. Et nisi etc. *32*
[297] *At the bottom of this membrane is written* Essonia, Prece Parcium et Attornati, Placita, Memoranda et Starra de termino sancte Trinitatis anno regis Edwardi filii regis Henrici septimo.

ROLL 32
additional entries not found in Roll 64

MEMBRANE 1 DORSE

(146)

... [I] saac le Eveske versus Johannem de Vileston' de placito debiti.

... eundem ... de Vileston' de placito debiti.

(147)

... loco suo Simonem de Wyndes' [i]<vel Willelmum de Pentlo>[i] ...

Rogerum de Burghulle vicecomitem Hereff' de placito ....

(148)

[Prece] parcium datus est dies inter Walterum de Thornbery, custodem Johannis de Thornebyr', et Aaron filium Vyves judeum usque a die sancti Michaelis in .xv. dies.

(149)

Sussex'.Willelmus Hergaud ponit loco suo Alexandrum filium ... [versus] Reginam [matrem][298] Regis de placito debiti.

MEMBRANE 2 DORSE

(150)

Cresseus filius Cresei judeus attornatus Aaron filii Vives venit coram etc. et recognovit se recepisse de domino Mauricio de Berkele .xxxj. marcas et .xl. denarios de termino octabarum sancti Michaelis sequenti et idem Cresseus tenetur liberare dicto Mauricio starrum super hoc de aquietacione consignatum manu dicti Aaron filii Vives etc.

(151)[299]

Sussex'. Cum Willelmus Herigaud districtus fuisset pro centum et sexdecim libris de auro domine A. Regine Anglie matris Regis nunc in quibus Radulphus Herigaud, pater dicti Willelmi, tenebatur domino Regi de debito Benedicti Crespin judei, quod quidem debitum liberatum fuit dicte domine Regine pro auro etc., idem Willelmus venit in curia coram etc. et dicit quod non tenetur respondere de eodem debito [i]<eo>[i] quod non est factum dicti Radulphi patris sui et precise dedicit.

Et Johannes de Whatele thesaurarius predicte domine Regine venit et dicit quod dictus Willelmus in anno domini Henrici regis etc. .lv. [i]<in termino sancti Hillarii>[i] venit in curia coram etc. et recognovit predictum debitum centum et sexdecim librarum tanquam debitum et factum dicti Radulphi patris sui et super hac recognicione predicta domina Regina habuit breve secundum assisam Judaismi de districcione super terris et tenementis ipsius Willelmi pro predicto debito. Et petit quod rotuli de anno supradicto super ista recognicione scrutentur.

Et dictus Willelmus dicit quod domina Regina per breve regis quod emanavit de scaccario judeorum habuit seisinam de terris et tenementis ipsius Willelmi pro debito supradicto per biennium et fructus et exitus terrarum suarum habuit per predictum tempus ad valenciam dicti debiti et amplius, per quod non tenetur respondere de predicto debito nec pro eodem distringi etc.

Et predictus Johannes dicit quod predicta domina Regina habuit seisinam de terris et tenementis suis et exitus terrarum suarum in parte recepit tantum pro [i]<quadam>[i] redempcione quam fecerat, ut per quoddam scriptum liquet quod dictus Johannes protulit etc., et quicquid dicta domina Regina habuit de exitibus terrarum suarum allocatum fuit ei in debito in quo tenebatur dicte domine Regine pro redempcione predicta [i]<et non pro dicto debito.>[i] Et hoc offert verificare per patriam.

Et dictus Willelmus dicit quod dicta domina Regina habuit seisinam de terris et tenementis suis per breve domini regis de scaccario judeorum pro debitis Judaismum tangentibus et non pro aliquo alio debito in quo dicte domine Regine tenebatur pro aliqua redempcione eidem domine Regine facta. Et de hoc ponit se super patriam. Et dictus Johannes similiter. Ideo preceptum est vicecomiti.[300]

MEMBRANE 3

(152)

Essex'. Elias filius magistri Mossei judeus recognovit per starrum suum quod ipse recepit de domino Benedicto de Blakenham .xxv. libras de quodam debito .l. librarum unde terminus solucionis fuit ad Nativitatem sancti Johannis Baptiste anno regni regis Edwardi septimo; et de residuis .xxv. libris dedit dictus judeus eidem Benedicto terminum solucionis usque ad festum sancti Michaelis proximo venturum.

(153)

Linc'. Normannus filius Philippi de Arci et Philippus de Arci filius suus milites venerunt coram etc. et recognoverunt se debere Hagino filio Deulecres judeo, qui dicitur Cok Hagin, quatervigiinti et decem marcas, reddendum ad Mediam Quadragesimam anno regis Edwardi septimo .xx. marcas et in die sancti Botulphi proximo sequenti .xxxv. marcas et in octabis sancti Michaelis sequentibus .x. libras et ad Natale Domini proximo sequens .xx. marcas. Et, nisi fecerint, concedunt quod de terris et catallis suis fiant etc.

[298] *MS. reads* matris.

[299] *Compare the quite different version of this entry from Roll 64, above no. 125.*

[300] *In the margin is written* habent diem in quindena sancti Michaelis.

(154)

Linc'. Normannus filius Philippi de Arci et Philippus de Arci filius suus milites venerunt coram etc. et recognoverunt de debere Hagino filio Deulecres, qui dicitur Cok Hagin judeo, .l. libras sterlingi reddendas eidem judeo ad mediam Quadragesimam anno regni regis Edwardi septimo. Et, nisi fecerint, concedunt quod de terris et catallis suis fiant etc.

(155)

Sussex'. Loquela que [fuit][301] inter dominam Reginam et Willelmum Herigaud per breve regis patet in termino sancti Hillarii anno .lv.to et judicium inde sortitum etc.

(156)

Suff'. Johannes de Falesham de comitatu Suff' venit coram etc. et recognovit se debere domino Henrico de Winton' .xx. marcas, reddendum ad octabas sancti Edmundi regis anno octavo .v. marcas et ad Mediam Quadragesimam proximo sequentem .v. marcas, et ad festum Nativitatis sancti Johannis Baptiste sequens .v. marcas et ad festum sancti Michaelis sequens .v. marcas. Et, nisi fecerit, concedit quod de terris et catallis suis fiant etc.

Postea solvit et quietus est.[302]

(157)

Suff'. Idem Johannes venit coram etc. et recognovit se debere Thome filio domini Henrici de Winton' militis decem marcas, reddendum medietatem ad festum Purificacionis Beate Marie anno octavo et aliam medietatem ad Mediam Quadragesimam anno eodem. Et, nisi fecerit, concedit quod de terris et catallis suis fiant etc.

<Postea solvit et quietus est.>[303]

(158)

Essex'. Johannes le Rus de comitatu Essex' venit coram etc. et recognovit se debere magistro Elie filio magistri Mossei judeo .xxx. quarteria frumenti vel dimidiam marcam pro quolibet quarterio reddendum a die Pasche in .xv. dies anno regni regis Edwardi septimo. Et, nisi fecerit, concedit quod de terris et catallis suis fiant.

(159)

Rotel'. Petrus filius Radulphi de Grenham de comitatu Rotel' venit coram etc. et recognovit se debere magistro Elie filio magistri Mossei judeo .xl. quarteria frumenti vel dimidiam marcam pro quolibet quarterio, reddendum a die Pasche in .xv. dies anno regni regis Edwardi septimo. Et, nisi [i]<etc.,>[i] concedit quod de terris et catallis suis fiant etc.

Ista debita sunt Isaac filii ejus.

(160)

Leyc'. Willelmus de Whiston' recognovit se debere Aaron filio Vives .xv. saccos lane, reddendum medietatem ad Pascha anno septimo et aliam medietatem ad Nativitatem sancti Johannis Baptiste proximo sequentem. Et, nisi fecerit, concedit quod de terris et catallis suis fiant etc.

(161)

Lond'. Memorandum de testimonio quod fuit coram nobis qui subtus sigillamur. Die jovis in die Exaltacionis Sancte Crucis anno septimo venit coram nobis Slumne filia Jacobi que fuit uxor Sampsonis filii Vives judea et dixit quod <testes>[304] sui essemus et scribere et consignare et dare Vives filio Aaron in manu ejus pro eo quod ego concessi bona voluntate mea sine aliqua vi, recognovi quod vendidi dicto Vives omnia debita que fuerunt dicti Sampsonis avunculi sui viri mei omnia debita predicta cum exitibus in vendicione stabili inperpetuum. Et ex nunc sit sua potestas ut mea fuit et factum ejus sicut meum fuit acquietandi, perdonandi, dandi, invadiandi et cambiandi de omnibus debitis que dictus vir meus michi dimisit vel in parte et capiendum breve regis de districcione nomine meo sicut attornatus meus ad distringendum debitores dictorum debitorum et tenentes terrarum secundum assisam Judaismi. Et juravi in lege quod nichil recepi de predictis debitis in parte vel in toto nec recipiam decetero nec feci aliquod starrum, quietanciam vel perdonacionem nec faciam sine licencia dicti Vives nec queram occasionem ad elongandum ipsum de predictis debitis. Et similiter eadem Slema venit coram nobis et dixit et recognovit quod ista vendicio in publico asseratur et discoperiatur et quod non celetur. Et quod recognovit coram nobis rogavit quod sigillavimus jam sigillavimus, Samuel filius Joscei et Sampson filius Joscei.

(162)

Wiltes'. Willelmus Painel venit coram etc. et recognovit se debere Aaron filio Vives judeo centum quarteria frumenti, reddendum medietatem ad festum sancti Hillarii et aliam medietatem ad Pascha proximo sequens. Et, nisi fecerit, concedit quod de terris et catallis suis fiant etc.

(163)

Kanc'. Radulphus filius Radulphi de Grendon' venit coram etc. et recognovit se debere Aron filio Vives judeo in .cc. quarteria frumenti vel in dimidia marca argenti reddendum a die Pasche in unum mensem anno regni regis Edwardi octavo. Et, nisi fecerit, concedit quod de terris et catallis suis fiant etc.

301 *MS. omits.*

302 *The word* quietus *is repeated in the margin.*

303 This sentence has been added in a later ink. *The word* quietus *is repeated in the margin.*

304 *This word is interlined above* plegii *which is marked for deletion.*

MEMBRANE 3 DORSE

(164)

Not'. Walterus [i]<de>[i] Furneaus miles venit coram etc. et recognovit se debere Willelmo de Bixle pro Hagino filio magistri Mossei centum solidos, reddendum ad quindenam sancti Michaelis proximo futuram. Et, nisi fecerit, concedit quod de terris et catallis suis fiant etc.

[At the bottom of membrane 3 dorse on the left hand side are the deleted words *Hillarii septimo*; on the right hand side are the words *Trinitatis anno .vij.*^{o}]

MICHAELMAS TERM, 7/8 EDWARD I [1279]

Exchequer of Jews, Plea Rolls Nos. 33 [E 9/33]

This is a relatively small but well-written roll. The 'h' found at the top of membrane 3 suggests that it may have been made for Hamon Hauteyn.

MEMBRANE ONE

Essonia de octabis sancti Michaelis anno regni regis Edwardi septimo

(165)

Surr'. Robertus de Camerwell' versus Isac de Suwerk' judeum de placito debiti per Johannem de Appelton'.

Essonia de quindena sancti Michaelis

(166)

Surr'. Robertus de Camerwell' versus Isac de Suwerk' judeum de placito debiti per Johannem de Appelton'.

Non jacet quia breve dicit 'distringas'.

(167)

Lond'. Johannes Gylle versus Rosam que fuit uxor Samuelis judei de placito debiti per Johannem de Hoverhill'.

(168)

Kanc'. Johannes filius Hamonis de Vyeleston' versus Mosseum filium Jacobi judeum de placito debiti per Adam Prodhom.

Dies in crastino sancti Martini. Affidavit.

Essonia de mense

(169)

Walterus de la Barre versus Aaron filium Vives de placito debiti per Walterum Siward.

Non jacet quia breve dicit 'venire facias'.

(170)

Simon Gobiun versus Willelmum de Middelton' de placito debiti per Willelmum de Clavering'.

Non jacet quia breve dicit 'venire facias'.

In crastino sancti Martini

(171)

Robertus de Bockwell', tenens terrarum Margerie de Camerwell', quod est in servicio regis per Johannem de Appell'.

Non jacet quia breve exit pro rege.

De octabis sancti Martini

(172)

Elena la Zuche versus Willelmum Foliot et Isabellam uxorem ejus quod est in servicio regis de placito transgressionis per Adam Prodhomme.

Non jacet quia femina.

MEMBRANE 1 DORSE

Attornata

(173)

Oxon'. Sarra que fuit uxor Benedicti le Eveske ponit loco suo Isac le Eveske vel Sampsonem de Wigorn' versus Henricum de Schottebrok' de placito debiti.

Eadem Sarra ponit loco suo eosdem versus Henricum le Tuler de placito debiti.

(174)

Northt'. Willelmus Foliot et Isabella uxor ejus ponunt loco suo Willelmum de Whiston' vel Petrum de Whiston' versus Elenam la Zuche de placito transgressionis etc.

MEMBRANE 2

Placita de octabis sancti Michaelis anno regni regis Edwardi septimo

(175)

Per licenciam justiciariorum Rogerus de Kinton', serviens de scaccario etc., et Galfridus de Specteshale de placito transgressionis concordati sunt sub hac forma, quod predictus Rogerus remisit eidem Galfrido omnia debita et exacciones que erga ipsum exigere poterit usque ad hunc diem. Et pro hac remissione dictus Galfridus recognoscit se debere dicto Rogero .x. solidos, solvendum eidem in festo sancti Thome Apostoli proximo futuro. Et, nisi fecerit, concedit quod de terris et catallis suis fiant etc.

(176)

Somers'. Gamaliel de Oxon' judeus fecit venire Guydonem rectorem ecclesie de Bacwell', tenentem quandam partem terrarum que fuerunt Roberti de Bruthasse, et exigit ab eo .x. marcas quas ei debet occasione predictarum terrarum quas tenet per cyrographum .x. marcarum una cum lucro inde emerso ante statuta regis quod usura non curreret.

Predictus Guydo venit et dicit quod non est factum suum et petit diem premeditandi. Et habet in octabis sancti Hillarii.

(177)[1]

Deulecres filius Bonef' fecit venire Willelmum, filium et heredem Johannis de Wateville, et exigit .x. libras quas ei debet occasione etc. que fuerunt predicti Johannis patris sui per cyrographum .x. librarum, unde altera pars est in archa apud [blank] inter predictum Johannem et predictum judeum confectum.

Predictus Willelmus venit et dicit quod non est factum suum et petit diem premeditandi. Et habet in octabis sancti Hillarii.

(178)

Norff'. Isaac le Eveske optulit se .iiij. die versus Barthomeum de Acre, tenentem quandam partem terrarum que fuerunt Samuelis de Norwico, de placito debiti. Et ipse non venit. Et preceptum fuit vicecomiti quod ipsum venire faceret. Et vicecomes mandavit quod retornavit breve sibi directum ballivis libertatis Norwyc', qui nichil inde responderunt. Judicium quod non omittat propter libertatem predictam quin eam etc., et venire [faciat][2] coram etc. [predictum Bartholomeum][3] in crastino sancti Martini ad respondendum etc. et ad audiendum etc.

(179)

Norff'. Isaac le Eveske judeus optulit se .iiij. die versus magistrum Alanum de Freston', tenentem terrarum que fuerunt Samuelis de Norwyco, de placito debiti. Et ipse non venit. Et preceptum fuit vicecomiti quod ipsum venire faceret. Et vicecomes mandavit quod retornavit breve sibi inde directum ballivis libertatis Norwyc', qui nichil inde responderunt. Judicium quod non omittat propter libertatem predictam quin eam etc. et venire faciat predictum magistrum Alanum coram etc. in crastino sancti Martini ad respondendum etc.

(180)

Norff'. Idem Isaac optulit se .iiij. die versus Josceum filium Deulecres judeum de placito debiti. Et ipse non venit. Et preceptum fuit vicecomiti quod ipsum venire faceret. Et vicecomes mandavit quod dicti Isaac et Josceus concordati sunt. Et dictus Isaac totum dedicit. Ideo preceptum est vicecomiti quod dictum Josceum venire faciat in crastino sancti Martini ad respondendum etc.

1 *Compare to no. 187.*

2 *MS. reads* faceret.

3 *MS. reads* magistrum Alanum.

(181)

Oxon'. Sarra que fuit uxor Benedicti le [Eveske][4] optulit se .iiij. die versus Henricum le Teuler de Oxon' de placito debiti. Et ipse non venit. Et preceptum fuit vicecomiti quod ipsum venire faceret. Et vicecomes mandavit quod retornavit breve sibi inde directum ballivis libertatis Oxon', qui nichil inde fecerunt. Judicium quod non omittat propter libertatem predictam quin eam etc. et venire faciat coram etc. in octabis sancti Martini ad respondendum etc.

(182)

Oxon'. Eadem Sarra optulit se .iiij. die versus Henricum de Shotebrok', tenentem terrarum que fuerunt Simonis de Hordeston', de placito debiti. Et ipse non venit. Et preceptum fuit vicecomiti quod ipsum venire faceret. Et vicecomes mandavit quod Johannes Pynzun et Willelmus Fodyng' manuceperunt predictum Henricum, quem non habuerunt. Ideo in misericordia.[5] Judicium quod distringatur per terras etc., ita [quod][6] nec ipse etc., et quod de exitibus etc., et quod habeat corpus ejus coram etc. in octabis sancti Martini ad respondendum etc. et ad audiendum etc.

(183)

Suff'. Aaron filius Vives per attornatum suum optulit se quarto die versus Willelmum de Boclounde, tenentem terrarum que fuerunt Philippi de Boclounde, de placito debiti. Et ipse non venit. Et preceptum fuit vicecomiti quod ipsum venire faceret. Et vicecomes mandavit quod Willelmus Edward de Shadyngfelde, Willelmus de Stanham de eadem et Robertus de Gillyngham clericus manuceperunt predictum Willelmum, quem non habuerunt. Ideo in misericordia.[7] Judicium quod distringatur per terras etc. et quod de exitibus etc. et quod habeat corpus ejus etc. in crastino sancti Martini ad respondendum etc. et ad audiendum etc.

(184)

Linc'. Magister Elias filius magistri Mossei judeus per attornatum suum optulit se quarto die versus priorem de Turgarton', tenentem quandam partem terrarum que fuerunt Gerardi de Fanacurt, de placito debiti. Et ipse non venit. Et preceptum fuit vicecomiti quod ipsum venire faceret. Et vicecomes mandavit quod Walterus filius Ivonis de Schapwyk' et Ricardus ad furnum de Blaunkeneye manuceperunt predictum priorem, quem non habuerunt. Ideo in misericordia.[8] Judicium quod distringatur per terras etc., ita quod nec ipse etc., et quod de exitibus etc., et quod habeat corpus ejus etc. in octabis sancti Hillarii ad respondendum etc. et ad audiendum etc.

4 *MS. reads* Evske.

5 *The word* misericordia *is repeated in the margin.*

6 *MS. omits.*

7 *The word* misericordia *is repeated in the margin.*

8 *The word* misericordia *is repeated in the margin.*

MEMBRANE 2 DORSE

Adhuc Placita

(185)

Berk'. Ricardus de Sutton tenens terrarum que fuerunt Johannis Belet de Ingelflotbelet, a quo exiguntur .xx. libre ad opus Regis occasione terrarum que fuerunt dicti Johannis de debitis Bonevie de Neuber' judei, fecit venire Bartholomeum de Yhatinden' et vocat ipsum ad warantum quod eum aquietare debet de omnibus debitis dictam terram tangentibus; et porigebat quandam cartam dicti Bartholomei de dictis terris et tenementis in Ingelflotbelet eidem Ricardo confectam, in qua continetur quod dictus Bartholomeus dictum Ricardum contra omnes homines aquietare, warantizare et defendere debet etc.

Predictus Bartholomeus venit et dicit et recognoscit dictam cartam esse suam et factum suum warantizat. Ideo consideratum est quod dictus Ricardus de dicto debito .xx. librarum eat quietus et dictus Bartholomeus inde respondeat; qui Bartholomeus petit visum cyrographi per quod dictus Johannes dicto Bonevie judeo in dictis .xx. libris obligatur. Et habet diem ad illud cyrographum videndum usque ad quindenam sancti Hillarii. Et preceptum est vicecomiti quod eidem Bartholomeo de predictis .xx. libris interim pacem permittat etc.

(186)

Dors'. Johannes de Neuburg venit coram etc. et recognoscit se debere Mansero filio Aaron judeo quater viginti libras, reddendum duas marcas ad Pascha proximo futuro et duas marcas ad festum sancti Michaelis proximo sequens; et sic annuatim quatuor marcas ad eosdem terminos quousque dictas quaterviginti libras persolverit. Et, nisi fecerit, concedit quod de terris et catallis suis fiant etc. Et per istam recognicionem dictus Manserus concedit [quod acquietat][9] eundem Johannem versus Cressaundin filium Leonis de omnibus debitis que Henricus pater ipsius Johannis debuit eidem Cressandino. Postea dictus Manserus concedit quod, si dictus Johannes solverit a termino Pasche predicto in duos annos subsequentes viginti marcas, tunc quietus sit de debito predictarum quaterviginti librarum etc. Et dictus Manserus concedit quod dictus Johannes et antecessores sui quieti sint de omnibus debitis que unquam debebant dicto Mansero vel antecessoribus suis, exceptis debitis que idem Manserus vendidit Willelmo le Moyne a principio seculi usque ad festum sancti Andree anno regni regis Edwardi octavo per solucionem predictam.

[9] *MS. omits.*

MEMBRANE 3

Placita de octabis et quindena sancti Michaelis anno septimo[10]

(187)[11]

Essex'. Deulecres filius Leonis judeus fecit venire Willelmum, filium et heredem Johannis de Whatevyle, et exigit ab eo .x. libras occasione terrarum etc. que fuerunt predicti Johannis patris sui per cyrographum .x. librarum inter predictos Johannem et judeum confectum.

Predictus Willelmus venit et dicit quod non est factum suum et petit diem premeditandi et habet in octabis sancti Hillarii. Ad quem diem predictus Willelmus fuit essoniatus et habet diem in crastino Cinerum.

Ad quem diem predictus Willelmus venit et dictus Deulecres narrat versus eum ut prius et petit ab eo dictas .x. libras occasione ut supra. Et predictus Willelmus dicit quod non tenetur respondere dicto Deulecres de predicto debito eo quod non clamat aliquas terras seu tenementa hereditarie tenere de terris vel tenementis que fuerunt predicti Johannis patris sui, quia terras et tenementa que tenet in Hamsted' et Paunfeld' recuperavit per placitum inter ipsum et predictum Johannem patrem suum motum coram justiciariis domini regis de Banco anno regis Henrici .xlvj^{to}. Et postea predictus Johannes predictas terras et tenementa tenuit ad terminum vite sue per cyrographum inter eos ibidem levatum, cujus cyrographi partem suam protulit coram etc., ita quod dictus Johannes dictas terras vel tenementa predicto Deulecres invadiare non potuit. Et hoc offert verificare per curiam domini regis et habet diem a die Pasche in .v. septimanas.

Et predictus Deulecres dicit quod dictus Willelmus de dicto debito ei respondere tenetur eo quod terras et tenementa in Chelesham in comitatu Surr' que tenet predictus Johannes pater ejus obiit vestitus et seisitus ut in dominico suo. Et post obitum dicti Johannis predictus Willelmus dedit capitali domino illius feodi relevium et alia servitia que pertinebant ad terram predictam ut proximus heres predicti Johannis et hoc offert verificare per patriam.

Et predictus Willelmus dicit quod feoffatus fuit de terris et tenementis que tenet in Chelesham priusquam predictus Johannes pater ejus predicto Deulecres in dicto debito obligaretur et hoc petit verificari per patriam.

Et quod dictus Johannes obiit vestitus et seisitus, ut predictum est, et dictas terras et tenementa ei obligavit una cum aliis bonis suis predictus Deulecres similiter ponit se super patriam. Et preceptum est vicecomiti Surr' quod venire faciat coram etc. ad eundem diem .xij., tam milites quam alios etc., ad recognoscendum etc.

Membrane 3d is blank, except that at the bottom in a contemporary hand there is written *Michaelis anno*

[10] *On the left-hand side above this heading is the letter 'H'.*

[11] *Cf. no. 177.*

*septimo incipiente viij^o^*, and in what seems to a sixteenth century hand *Placita et Memoranda coram Justiciariis ad custodiam Judeorum.*

MEMBRANE 4

Memoranda de termino sancti Michaelis anno septimo

(188)

Ebor'. Preceptum fuit vicecomiti quod non omitteret propter libertatem de Osgodecros quin eam etc. et de bonis et catallis Hunfridi de Veyli fieri faceret vinginti quatuor marcas ad opus Willelmi de Middilton' clerici de scaccario Judeorum, ita quod denarios illos [haberet][12] coram etc. a die sancti Michaelis in. xv. dies predicto Willelmo ibidem liberandos. Et vicecomes mandavit quod predictus Hunfridus non habet terras nec catalla unde possint aliqui denarii levari, quia partem terrarum suarum vendidit, partem ad firmam commisit, ita quod nichil penes [se][13] retinuit et manens est cum familia sua ad domum persone de Thornovere ad custus dicte persone.

(189)

Kanc'. Preceptum fuit vicecomiti quod distringeret tenentes terrarum que fuerunt Stephani de Cresi per terras et catalla ad reddendum sibi ad opus Regis ducentas et quinquaginta libras quas Regi debent occasione predictarum terrarum quas tenent de debitis Hagini filii magistri Mossei judei et Vives fratris ejus, ita quod denarios illos haberet ad hunc diem coram etc. vel corpora tenencium etc. Et vicecomes mandavit quod breve sibi inde directum retornavit senescallo libertatis archiepiscopi qui nichil inde fecit. Judicium quod non omittat etc in octabis sancti Martini.

(190)

Northt'. Per breve regis de magno sigillo in hec verba: 'Edwardus dei gracia etc. justiciariis suis ad custodiam etc. assignatis salutem. Monstravit nobis Simon filius Radulphi de Trop quod, cum ipse sufficientem habeat aquietanciam de omnibus debitis in quibus dictus Radulphus pater ipsius Simonis dudum tenebatur Deulecres filio Aaron judeo, vos nichilominus dictum Simonem[14] pro quibusdam debitis in quibus dictus Radulphus prefato judeo tenebatur nobis solvendum per summonicionem scaccarii nostri distringi faciatis minus juste in ipsius Simonis dispendium non modicum et gravamen. Et quia prefatum Simonem indebite pregravari nolumus in hac parte vobis mandamus quod, inspectis starris et aquietanciis quas dictus Simon inde asserit se habere, si vobis legitime constare possit ipsum ad debita illa nobis solvenda aliquatenus non teneri, tunc ei super hoc plenam et celerem justiciam fieri faciatis secundum legem et consuetudinem Judaismi predicti. Teste me ipso apud Westm' .xvj. die Octobris anno regni nostri septimo.' facta fuit inquisicio per sacramentum Mossei de Clare, Jacobi le Clerc, Mossei Poteman, Gamalielum de Oxon', Diey le Eveske, Isac le Eveske, Sampsonis de Standon, Sam' de Ebor', Manserum de Norwic', Meir nepotis Leonis, Isac de Suwerk et Meyr nepotis Belassez judeorum Lond' super confeccione cujusdam starri quod dictus Simon protulit coram justiciariis etc. in hec verba: 'Omnibus hoc scriptum visuris vel audituris Benedictus filius Deulecres judeus London' salutem. Quia pro certo intellexi quod Radulphus filius Simonis de Trop' aquietavit se de patre meo de omnibus debitis que idem Raduphus debuit eidem patri meo a creacione seculi usque ad finem, et quod heredes dicti Raduphi similiter quieti sint de omnibus predictis debitis, ideo predictum Radulphum et heredes suos inde plene quieto.' Qui quidem judei jurati dicunt quod predictus Benedictus fecit dictum starrum et manu propria consignavit antequam captus fuit pro retonsione monete pro qua suspensus fuit et tempore quo habuit administracionem catallorum patris sui et quod predictum starrum est factum suum. Et quia constat justiciariis per inspeccionem rotulorum de termino sancti Hillarii anno regis Edwardi sexto quod unum debitum .ccxxxiij. librarum .vj. solidorum .viij. denariorum sub nominibus dicti Raduphi de Trop' et Deulecres filii Aaron liberatum fuit dicto Benedicto et carta inde transmissa fuit cyrographariis Lond' ad opus ipsius Benedicti, ita quod liberam inde [habuit][15] administracionem, et quod omnia debita sub nominibus predictorum Radulphi et Deulecres aquietati fuerunt tempore licito et debito, consideratum est quod dictus Simon, filius et heres dicti Radulphi, de dictis debitis et de dicta carta secundum tenorem dicti starri quietus sit in perpetuum. Et preceptum est cyrographariis quod dictam cartam ab archa extrahant et eam dicto Simoni quiete liberari faciant dampnandum etc.

(191)

Norff', Suff'. Preceptum fuit vicecomiti quod distringeret tenentes terrarum que fuerunt Stephani de Cresy per terras etc. ad reddendum sibi ad opus Regis ducentas et quinquaginta libras quas Regi debent occasione predictarum terrarum quas tenent de [debitis][16] Hagini filii magistri Mossei et Vives fratris ejus judeorum, ita quod denarios etc. coram etc. ad hunc diem vel corpora tenencium etc. Et vicecomes mandavit quod Robertus filius Rogeri et Robertus Hovel sunt tenentes quarundam parcium terrarum predicti Stephani, set non fuerunt inventi in balliva sua post adventum brevis, et districti sunt set per districcionem illam ab eis aliquos denarios levare non potest et quod adhuc non constat ei de aliis tenentibus. Ideo preceptum est ei quod distringat predic-

[12] *MS. reads* habeat.
[13] *MS. omits.*
[14] *Followed in MS. by* distringatis.

[15] *MS. reads* habeant.
[16] *MS. reads* debita.

tos Robertum filium Rogeri et Robertum Hovel et alios quos [invenerit][17] tenentes predictarum terrarum ad reddendum dictos denarios, et quod eos habeat coram etc. in octabis sancti Martini regi liberandos.

(192)

Suff'. Aaron filius Vives judeus venit coram etc. et recognovit quod Hugo Pecche quietus est de omnibus debitis et demandis que unquam dicto Aaron tenebatur a creacione seculi usque ad festum apostolorum Simonis et Jude anno regni regis Edwardi septimo. Et, [i]<si>[i] scriptum, obligacio vel recognicio super aliquo debito in quo dictus Hugo tenebatur dicto judeo ante predictum festum inventum fuerit in rotulis domini regis de scaccario judeorum vel alibi, concedit quod nichil valeant et pro vano et vacuo habeantur.

(193)

Kanc'. Preceptum fuit vicecomiti quod de bonis et catallis Andree de Elham fieri faceret ad opus Isaac le Eveske judei unam marcam quam idem Andreas coram justiciariis etc. recognovit se debere predicto Ysaac. Et vicecomes mandavit quod predictus Andreas nichil habet in balliva sua nisi quandam terram friscam et incultam. Et quia testificatum est coram etc. in termino sancte Trinitatis proximo preterito quod predictus Andreas habuit blada in terra crescencia, ideo preceptum est vicecomiti quod de dicto blado et aliis catallis predicti Andree fieri faciat predictam marcam et dimidiam marcam quam eidem Ysaac solvisse debuisset ad festum sancti Michaelis proximo preterito ad opus dicti Ysaac, ita quod denarios illos [habeat][18] coram etc. a die sancti Martini in quindecim dies eidem judeo liberandos, et quod vicecomes sit ibidem ad eundem diem ad audiendum etc. qualiter preceptum [e]<est>[e] inde sibi directum non fuit executus etc.

(194)

Hertef'. Preceptum fuit vicecomiti quod de bonis et catallis Johannis Gosham filii Ade Gosham de Berkhamstede et Thome de Flaunden filii Nicholai de Flaunden fieri faceret ad opus Jornini filii Abr' quadraginta marcas quas iidem Johannes et Thomas nuper in curia nostra coram justiciariis nostris etc. recognoverunt se debere predicto Jornino. Et vicecomes mandavit[19] quod non omittat propter libertatem predictam quin eam etc. et de bonis et catallis predictorum Johannis et Thome fieri faceret predictas .xl. marcas ad opus predicti judei, ita quod eas habeat coram etc.

(195)

Oxon', Berk'. Johannes de Sancta Helena venit coram etc. et recognovit se debere H. Hautein .c. solidos vel duos cignos, reddendum ad Purificacionem Beate Marie anno regis Edwardi octavo. Et, nisi fecerit, concedit quod de terris et catallis suis fiant etc.

MEMBRANE 4 DORSE

Adhuc Memoranda de termino sancti Michaelis

(196)

Linc'. Preceptum fuit vicecomiti, sicut pluries, quod distringeret Henricum de Lacy comitem Linc', priorem de Bolinton' et priorem de Ormesbi per terras etc., ita quod nec ipse etc., et quod de exitibus etc., et quod haberet corpora eorum coram etc. ad respondendum Regi una cum Johanne de Baton' de tricentis et sexaginta libris quas Regi debent occasione terrarum que fuerunt Gilberti de Beningworthe quas tenent de debitis judaismi. Predictus Johannes de Baton' per attornatum suum optulit se quarto die versus predictos Henricum, priorem de Bolinton' et priorem de Ormesby de predicto debito secum respondendo et ipsi non venerunt. Et vicecomes mandavit quod Willelmus prepositus de Halton', Gilbertus clericus de eadem, Gilbertus le serjaunt de eadem et Robertus filius Michaelis de eadem manuceperunt Henricum de Lacy, comitem Linc', quem non habuerunt. Ideo in <misericordia.>[20] Et quod Willelmus prepositus de Strubby, Andreas Nest de eadem, Simon Frannceys de Herdewik', et Simon de Askeby in eadem manuceperunt priorem de Bolinton' quem non habuerunt. Ideo in misericordia. Et quod Philippus le Meseger de Uterby, Walterus Gunny de Ormesby, Radulphus Wenges de eadem, et Willelmus filius Gode de eadem manuceperunt priorem de Ormesby, quem non habuerunt. Ideo in misericordia. Judicium, [i]<sicut>[i] pluries, quod predicti Henricus de Lacy[21] comes Linc', prior de Bolinton' et prior de Ormesby distringantur per terras etc., ita quod nec [ipsi][22] etc., et quod de exitibus etc., et quod habeat corpora eorum coram etc. in octabis sancti Andree ad respondendum Regi una cum Johanne de Baton', qui habet eundem diem, de predicto debito et ad audiendum etc. Et quod vicecomes sit ibidem ad eundem diem et ad audiendum judicium suum ex eo quod non respondet de exitibus etc.

(197)

Ebor'. Preceptum fuit vicecomiti quod distringeret Rogerum de Mortuo Mari, Willelmum de Chauncy et heredem Henrici de Cuille ad respondendum Regi una cum Johanne de Baton' de tricentis sexaginta libris de debitis Judaismi in quo Gilbertus de Beningeworth' tenebatur. Rogerus de Mortuo Mari et Willelmus de Chauncy venerunt et dicunt quod non tenent aliquas terras vel tenementa que fuerunt predicti Gilberti que invadiare potuit, set tenent quandam partem terrarum

[17] *MS. reads* invenerunt.
[18] *MS. reads* haberet.
[19] *Several words have been omitted here by the scribe.*
[20] *The word* misericordia *is repeated in the margin.*
[21] *Followed in MS. by* de.
[22] *MS. reads* ipse.

que fuerunt de hereditate Sarre uxoris dicti Gilberti et de hoc se ponunt super patriam. Et preceptum est vicecomiti quod venire faciat coram etc. in octabis sancti Andree .xij. probos et legales homines, tam milites quam alios, de comitatu suo ad recognoscendum super premissis veritatem et quod distringat, sicut pluries, heredem Henrici de Cuille per terras etc., ita quod nec ipse etc., et quod de exitibus etc., et quod habeat corpus ejus coram etc. in octabis sancti Andree ad respondendum, ut supra, et ad audiendum etc.

(198)

Cantebr'. Warinus de Hereford' venit coram etc. et recognovit se debere Aaron filio Vives judeo .xx. marcas, reddendum medietatem ad quindenam Pasche proximo futuram et aliam medietatem ad quindenam sancti Michaelis proximo sequentis. Et, nisi fecerit, concedit quod de terris et catallis suis fiant etc. Et pro recognicione predictarum .xx. marcarum dictus Aaron quietavit dicto Warino unam cartam .xx. marcarum sub nominibus Johannis de Scalariis de Badburgham et dicti Aaron et concedit dictus Aaron quod dicta carta extrahatur et dicto Warino liberetur quiete dampnata. Et preceptum est cyrographariis Lond' quod ad dictam archam accedant et dictam cartam extrahant et sibi liberent etc.

(199)

Cantebr'. Warinus de Heref' venit coram etc. et recognovit se debere Mansero filio Aaron judeo .xxx. marcas, reddendum ad quindenam Pasche proximo futuram .v. marcas et ad quindenam sancti Michaelis proximo sequentem .v. marcas et sic de anno in annum ad dictos terminos quousque dicte .xxx. marce plene persolvantur. Et per hanc recognicionem quietavit dicto Warino duas cartas de .xxxv. marcis sub nominibus Johannis de Scalariis de Badburgham et Abrahe filii Vives judei et concedit quod dicte carte extrahantur etc. Ideo preceptum est cyrographariis Lond' quod illas extrahant et dicto Warino liberentur dampnandum etc. Et, nisi dictus Warinus dictos denarios ad terminos supradictos solverit, concedit quod de terris et catallis suis fiant etc.

(200)

Suff'. Hugo Pecche miles venit coram etc. et recognovit se debere Hamoni Hautein sex marcas argenti reddendas ad festum sancti Andree proximo futurum. Et, nisi fecerit, concedit quod de terris et catallis suis fiant etc. Postea solvit.

(201)

Suff'. Robertus filius Roberti de Valoines miles [i]<et Adam de Cretinge miles>[i] venerunt coram etc. et recognoverunt se debere Hamoni Hautein viginti et quatuor libras sterlingorum reddendas a die Pasche proximo futuro in tres septimanas. Et, nisi fecerint, concedunt quod de terris et catallis suis fiant etc.

(202)

Suff'. Memorandum quod, [i]<cum>[i] Willelmus de Middilton' habuit unum cyrographum .x. librarum sub nominibus Willelmi de Monte Canisio de Edwardeston' et Mossei de Clare judei et unum cyrographum .xl. librarum sub nominibus Huberti de Monte Canisio filii Hugonis de comitatu Suff' et predicti Mossei in equali manu custodiendum, idem Willelmus de Middilton' per assensum predicti Willelmi de [Monte][23] Canisio et ipsius Mossei tradidit et liberavit eidem Mosseo predicta duo cyrographa in pleno scaccario. Et predictus Mosseus concessit eidem Willelmo de Monte Canisio quod, si solvat ei die sancti Eadmundi Confessoris anno regni regis Edwardi incipiente octavo decem marcas et ad Mediam Quadragesimam proximo sequentem decem libras et ad festum Nativitatis sancti Johannis Baptiste proximo sequens decem libras, tunc predicta duo debita sint quieta. Et, si idem Willelmus de Monte Canisio non solvat predictos denarios ad terminos predictos, quod idem judeus habeat recuperare suum de duobus debitis supradictis. Et duo starra que predictus Willelmus de Middilton' habuit inter predictos Willelmum de Monte Canisio et Mosseum confecta de predicto debito in pleno scaccario fuerunt dampnata.

(203)

Memorandum quod Manserus filius Abrahe judeus venit coram etc. et recognovit unam cartam sub nominibus Ricardi filii Benedicti de Tolesland' de comitatu Huntedon' et dicti Manseri de .x. marcis reddendis ad octabas sancti Michaelis anno regni regis Henrici .lv.^{to} Acta .xx. die Marcii anno predicto et unam .xx. librarum sub nominibus Walteri filii Willelmi de Bydele et dicti Manseri reddendarum ad Purificacionem Beate Marie anno regis Henrici .xlvj.^{to} Acta .xvj. die Decembris anno eodem, esse Aaron filii Vyves judei, que quidem carte fuerunt in manu Regis pro tallagio ipsius Manseri, videlicet pro magno tallagio viginti quatuor mille marcarum etc. Et quia compertum est per rotulos de scaccario etc. quod idem Manserus quietus est de eodem tallagio pro quo eadem debita capta fuerunt in manum Regis consideratum est quod dicte carte liberentur dicto Aaron et inde habeat administracionem etc. Et preceptum est cyrographariis Lond' quod easdem cartas admittant et in archa predicta reponant ad opus ipsius Aaron. Et super hoc idem Aaron recognovit coram etc. quod, si reperiatur in aliquibus rotulis de scaccario judeorum quod dictus Manserus teneatur in aliquibus debitis per tallagium predictum, idem Aaron recognovit de eodem respondere et ipsum inde aquietare etc.

[23] *MS. omits.*

MEMBRANE 5

Adhuc memoranda de termino Michaelis

(204)

Heref'. Preceptum fuit vicecomiti quod distringeret Nicholaum de Wormele per terras et catalla sua ad reddendum sibi ad opus Regis decem marcas de debitis Ysaac de Suuerk' judei vel quod haberet corpus dicti Nicholai etc. ad ostendendum inde acquietanciam. Et vicecomes mandavit quod Willelmus Canber, Johannes Hullard, Simon filius Hugonis, Johannes Fileberm manuceperunt predictum Nicholaum, quem non habuerunt. Ideo in misericordia.[24] Et preceptum est vicecomiti, sicut alias, quod distringat prefatum Nicholaum, ut prius, ita quod dictos denarios habeat coram etc. in crastino sancti Andree Regi solvendos.

(205)

Linc'. Preceptum fuit vicecomiti quod distringeret Henricum Foucedame per terras etc. ad reddendum sibi ad opus Regis decem libras [de debitis][25] Ysaac de Suuerk' judei, ita quod eas [haberet][26] coram etc. ad hunc diem Regi solvendas vel corpus predicti Henrici ad ostendendum inde acquietanciam. Et vicecomes mandavit quod postquam breve sibi venit non potuit inquiri per ballivos suos quod aliquis in balliva sua vocatur Henricus Foucedame. Et preceptum est ei, sicut alias, in crastino sancti Andree.

(206)

Surr' Sussex'. Preceptum fuit vicecomiti quod distringeret tenentes terrarum Ricardi de Hadisham per terras et catalla sua ad reddendum sibi ad opus Regis .c. solidos de debitis Ysaac de Swerk' judei vel quod haberet corpora predictorum tenencium ad ostendendum inde acquietanciam. Et vicecomes mandavit quod Willelmus de Hadesham, Ricardus atteHalle, Alanus filius Ricardi et Nicholaus atteGate manuceperunt Robertum, filium et heredem dicti Ricardi et tenentem terrarum ejusdem Ricardi, quem non habuerunt. Ideo in misericordia.[27] Et preceptum fuit vicecomiti quod distringeret tenentes terrarum Ricardi filii predicti Ricardi de Hadesham pro decem libris et nichil de dictis tenentibus respondet, ideo ipse vicecomes, scilicet Emericus de Chauncy, in misericordia.[28] Et preceptum fuit ei eodem modo quod distringeret tenentes terrarum Thome Haunsard pro .l. solidis. Et mandavit [quod][29] Jacobus Haunsard mortuus est et Thomas Harun tenens terrarum non est inventus, ideo de ipsis nichil actum est. Et eodem modo preceptum fuit quod distringeret tenentes terrarum Sweyn le Chaluner pro .xx. solidis. Et vicecomes mandavit quod retornavit breve ballivis libertatis Guldeford', qui nichil inde responderunt. Judicium quod non omittat etc. Et quod distringeret eodem modo tenentes terrarum Henrici Jukel pro .ij. marcis. Et vicecomes mandavit quod Willelmus de Suthebrok', Ricardus Ciffray et Thomas Atteuatre manuceperunt predictos tenentes, quos non habuerunt. Ideo in misericordia. Et quod distringeret tenentes terrarum Normanni de Swerk pro .xl. solidis. Et vicecomes mandavit quod Robertus Riknard, Ricardus Nicole, Simon Jollyng et Johannes Portir de Camerwell manuceperunt predictos tenentes, quos non habuerunt. Ideo in misericordia. Et quod distringeret tenentes terrarum Margerie de Cameruelle pro .iiij. libris. Et vicecomes mandavit quod Robertus Makeman, Galfridus Sturmy, Henricus Sammon et Ricardus Gingyve manuceperunt Robertum de Bekewelle, tenentem terrarum dicte Margerie, quem non habuerunt. Ideo in misericordia. Et quod distringeret tenentes terrarum Thome le Provvost de Bechach pro .xxviij. solidis. Et vicecomes mandavit quod retornavit breve ballivis libertatis archiepiscopi, qui nichil inde fecerunt. Judicium quod non omittat etc. Et quod distringeret tenentes terrarum Roberti le Duk pro .xl. solidis excepto Johanne de Ludham. Et vicecomes mandavit quod non sunt aliqui alii tenentes terrarum predictorum debitorum ad reddendum sibi ad opus Regis predictos denarios,[30] ita quod eos habeat coram etc. Regi solvendos vel corpora etc. in crastino sancti Andree.

(207)[31]

Wygorn'. Vicecomes Wigorn' habet diem ad computandum a die Pasche in unum mensem.

(208)

Rotel'. Simon filius Simonis et participes sui tenentes terrarum que fuerunt Willelmi Clive solverunt in recepta regis .x. solidos et inde habent talliam de debitis Aaron de Colec' judei.

(209)

Robertus de Dratton' solvit in recepta regis .xx. solidos et inde habet talliam de debitis Hagini filii magistri Mossei.

(210)

Leyc'. Thomas de Linc' solvit in recepta regis .xx. solidos de debitis patris sui.

(211)

Berk'. Sarra que fuit uxor Lumberti de Windes' solvit in recepta regis .ij. solidos .viij. denarios de fine.

(212)

Kanc'. Heres Danielis Bogge solvit in recepta regis dimidiam marcam de debitis judeorum.

24 *The word* misericordia *is repeated in the margin.*
25 *MS. omits.*
26 *MS. reads* habeat.
27 *The word* misericordia *is repeated in the margin.*
28 *The word* misericordia *is repeated in the margin.*
29 *MS. omits.*
30 *Something has been lost in copying at this point.*
31 *This entry and the following entries to no. 219 (except no. 215) are also to be found on membrane 5d in a different hand.*

(213)

Dors'. Johannes filius et heres Hamonis de Burton' solvit in recepta regis .xxxj. solidos .v. denarios obulum de debitis Abr' Russell'.

(214)

Ebor'. Thomas de Bereville solvit in recepta regis dimidiam marcam de debitis Isac Gabbay et Deudonis Crespin et unde habet talliam.

(215)

Josceus filius Sauloti solvit in recepta regis .xx. solidos de fine et inde habet talliam.

(216)

Warr'. Robertus Hayhard venit coram etc. et recognovit se debere magistro Elye et Aaron filio Vives judeis centum solidos reddendos ad festum Purificacionis Beate Marie proximo futurum. Et, nisi fecerit, concedit quod de terris et catallis suis fiant.

(217)

Hertf' Essex'. Henricus de Boclande venit coram etc. et recognovit pro se et heredibus suis se debere Aaron filio Vives judeo centum libras reddendas ad festum sancti Michaelis proximo futurum. Et, nisi fecerit, concedit quod de terris et catallis suis fiant etc.

(218)

Suth'. Johannes de Sancto Johanne miles venit coram etc. et recognovit se debere magistro Elie filio magistri Mossei sexcies viginti quarteria frumenti reddenda a die Pasche in .xv. dies vel pro quolibet quarterio .iiij. solidos. Et, nisi fecerit, concedit quod de terris et catallis suis fiant etc.

(219)

Midd'. Walterus de Saunford venit coram etc. et recognovit se debere magistro Elye filio magistri Mossei judeo et Isac le Eveske judeo quater viginti et octo marcas argenti, reddendum ad quindenam sancti Michaelis anno regni regis Edwardi octavo .xxij. marcas et ad quindenam Pasche sequentem .xj. marcas, et ad quindenam sancti Michaelis proximo sequentem .xj. marcas; et sic de anno in annum ad eosdem terminos donec dictum debitum quaterviginti et octo marcarum plene persolvatur. Et, nisi fecerit, concedit quod de terris et catallis suis fiant etc. Medietas istius debiti est Isac le Eveske judei. Et per istam recognicionem dicti judei recognoverunt quod dictus Walterus et heredes sui quieti sunt de omnibus debitis in quibus eisdem judeis tenebantur a principio seculi usque ad diem irrotulacionis, videlicet diem sancti Andree.

(220)

Thomas Painel et Andreas de Neville venerunt coram etc. et recognoverunt se debere Aaron filio Vives judeo .cc. quarteria frumenti vel pro quolibet quarterio dimidiam marcam argenti reddendum ad Pentecosten anno regni regis Edwardi octavo. Et, nisi fecerint, concedunt quod de terris et catallis suis fiant etc.

(221)

Derb'. Urianus de Sancto Petro venit coram etc. et recognovit se debere Cok' Hagini centum marcas, reddendum in quindenam sancti Hillarii proximo futuram .l. marcas et ad quindenam sancti Johannis Baptiste proximo sequentem .l. marcas. Et, nisi etc., concedit quod de terris et catallis suis fiant etc.

MEMBRANE 5 DORSE [32]

(222)

Wigorn'. Vicecomes Wigorn' habet diem computandi a die Pasche in unum mensem.

(223)

Roteland. Simon filius Simonis et participes sui, tenentes terrarum que fuerunt Willelmi Clyve, solverunt in recepta regis .x. solidos et inde habent talliam de debitis Aaron de Colecetre judei.

(224)

Robertus de Drayton' solvit in recepta regis .xx. solidos et inde habet talliam de debitis Hagini filii magistri Mossei.

(225)

Leyc'. Thomas de Linc' solvit in recepta regis .xx. solidos de debitis patris sui de debitis Judaismi.

(226)

Berk'. Sarra que fuit uxor Lumbardi de Wyndlesor judea solvit in recepta regis .ij. solidos .viij. denarios de fine.

(227)

Kanc'. Heredes Danielis Bagge solverunt in recepta regis dimidiam marcam de debitis Judaismi.

(228)

Dors'. Johannes filius et heres Hamonis de Borton' solvit in recepta regis .xxxj. solidos .v. denarios obulum de debitis Abr' Russell' judei Wilton'.

(229)

Ebor'. Thomas de Berneville solvit in recepta regis .vj. solidos .viij. denarios de debitis Ysac Gabay et Deudonis Crespin, unde habet talliam.

[32] *At the top of this membrane is the erased heading* Adhuc Memoranda de termino sancti Michaelis. *The first twelve entries duplicate nos. 207-19 (other than 215) on membrane 5.*

(230)

Warr' Leyc'. Robertus Haihard venit coram justiciariis etc. et recognovit se debere magistro Elye filio magistri Mossei et Aaron filio Vives judeis centum solidos reddendum eisdem judeis ad festum Purificacionis Beate Marie proximo futuro. Et, nisi fecerit, concedit quod de terris et catallis suis fiant.

(231)

Essex' Hertf'. Henricus de Boclaund venit coram justiciariis etc. et recognovit pro se et heredibus suis se debere Aaron filio Vives judeo centum libras reddendas eidem Aaron ad festum sancti Michaelis proximo futuro. Et, nisi fecerit, concedit quod de terris et catallis suis fiant etc.

(232)

Sutht'. Johannes de Sancto Johanne miles venit coram justiciariis etc. et recognovit se debere magistro Elie filio magistri Mossei judeo sexies viginti quarteria frumenti, reddendum eidem magistro Elye dictum frumentum a die Pasche in .xv. dies vel pro quolibet quarterio .iiij. solidos. Et, nisi fecerit, concedit quod de terris et catallis suis fiant etc.

(233)

Midd'. Walterus de Saunford recognovit se debere magistro Elye filio magistri Mossei et Isak le Eveske judeis Lond' quater viginti et octo marcas argenti, reddendum inde ad quindenam sancti Michaelis anno regni regis Edwardi octavo .xxij. marcas et ad quindenam Pasche proximo sequentem undecim marcas, et ad quindenam sancti Michaelis proximo sequentem undecim marcas; et sic de anno in annum ad eosdem terminos donec predictum debitum persolvatur. Et, nisi fecerit, concedit quod de terris et catallis suis fiant etc. Medietas istius debiti est Isak le Eveske.

(234)

Herf'. Preceptum fuit vicecomiti quod venire faceret coram etc. Rogerum de Clifford seniorem et Simonem de Beriton' capellanum, tenentes quasdam partes terrarum que fuerunt Johannis filii Willelmi Aubyn, ad respondendum Regi de quinque marcis de debitis Benedicti le Eskyrmishur una cum abbate de Rading', qui habuit eundem diem. Et vicecomes mandavit quod Hugo de Porhamel et Willelmus Lacy manuceperunt predictum Rogerum, quem non habuerunt. Ideo in misericordia. Et quod Rogerus Baret et Rogerus filius Petri manuceperunt predictum Simonem, quem non habuerunt. Ideo in misericordia. Judicium quod distringat per terras etc., ita quod nec ipsi etc., et quod de exitibus etc., et quod habeat corpora eorum coram etc. in quindenam sancti Hillarii ad respondendum etc. et ad audiendum etc.

(235)[33]

Linc'. Inquisicio de bonis et catallis Joscei de Oxon' defuncti per sacramentum Willelmi le Jefne de Linc', Roberti le Especer et aliorum christianorum et Isak de Provinz de Linc' et aliorum judeorum, sicut patet inter inquisiciones termini sancte Trinitatis retornatas anno .vij.º Qui dicunt super sacramentum suum quod predictus Joceus die quo egrotavit etc. habuit in mobilibus ad valenciam .xx. solidorum et in terris, domibus et redditibus etc. habuit ad valenciam .xxiiij. solidorum. Summa .xxxiiij. solidi; unde tercia pars Regi est undecim solidi et .iiij. denarii. Et predicta bona devenerunt ad manus Murielle que fuit uxor predicti Jocei. Et predicta Muriella finem fecit pro catallis predictis per Salomonem filium Crecey. Et habet diem ad solvendum predictos .xj. solidos et .iiij. denarios, videlicet medietatem ad quindenam Pasche proximo sequentem et [34]

MEMBRANE 6

Adhuc Memoranda

(236)

Per breve domini regis directum justiciariis etc. in hec verba: 'Edwardus dei gracia etc. justiciariis suis ad custodiam judeorum assignatis salutem. Sciatis quod concessimus karissime consorti nostre Alienore Regine Anglie omnia debita que Hagino judeo nostro Lond' debentur a quibuscumque debitoribus suis per cartas suas. Et ideo vobis mandamus quod cartas illas ab archa cyrographariorum judeorum nostrorum et a thesauraria nostra scaccarii extrahi et in quadam archa per se poni et prefate consorti nostre liberari faciatis ad debita illa levanda et recuperanda secundum legem et consuetudinem Judaismi nostri. Teste me ipso apud Westm' .xv. die Novembris anno regni nostri octavo.' liberantur Waltero de Kanc' thesaurario domine Regine debita subscripta, videlicet unum debitum viginti librarum sub nominibus Walteri de Furneus et Hagini filii magistri Mossei reddendum ad quindenam Omnium Sanctorum anno regis Edwardi primo, acta .xx. die Augusti anno eodem; et unum quadraginta librarum sub nominibus Ricardi de Tilleberi militis de comitatu Essex' et dicti Hagini reddendum a die Pasche in tres septimanas anno regis Henrici .lvj.to, acta .vij. die Aprilis anno eodem; et unum .lx. librarum sub nominibus Roberti de Ferar' comitis Derb' et dicti Hagini per annum usque ad finem seculi reddendum ad quindenam sancti Michaelis anno regis Henrici .xlviij.º, et sic de anno in annum ad eundem terminum etc. usque ad finem seculi, acta primo die Novembris anno regis Henrici eodem; et unum debitum .l. librarum sub nominibus Gilberti de Claypol de comitatu Linc' et ipsius Hagini, reddendum inde .xij. libras .x. solidos ad octabas sancti Martini in hyeme anno regis

[33] *Cf. No. 141.*
[34] *This entry is unfinished.*

Henrici .lvij.^{o} et .xij. libras et .x. solidos ad quindenam Pasche proximo sequentem, et .xij. libras et .x. solidos ad octabas sancti Martini in hyeme et .xij. libras et .x. solidos ad quindenam Pasche proximo sequentem, acta .ix. die Maii anno .lvj.^{to}; et unum centum et decem librarum sub nominibus Walteri de Furneus militis de comitatu Somers' et dicti Hagini, reddendum a die sancti Martini in unum mensem anno .lvij., acta .xij. die Julii anno .lvj.^{to}; et unum .xxx. librarum sub nominibus Willelmi de Engelfeld militis ^{i}<Oxon'>^{i} et dicti Hagini, reddendum inde medietatem ad quindenam sancti Michaelis anno .l.^{o} et aliam medietatem ad quindenam Pasche proximo sequentem, acta .xix. die Februarii anno .l.^{o}; et unum debitum .xxvij. librarum sub nominibus Willlelmi de Engelfeld militis de comitatu Oxon' et dicti Hagini reddendum ad quindenam Pasche anno .lj.^{o}, acta .xix. die Februarii anno .l.^{o}; et unum quatuor librarum sub nominibus Reginaldi de Morteng' et dicti Hagini, reddendum ad festum Omnium Sanctorum anno .xlvj.^{to}, acta .xxv. die Maii anno .xlv.^{to}; et unum .xij. librarum sub nominibus Galfridi de Scaudeford de comitatu Leyc' et dicti Hagini reddendum ad octabas sancti Michaelis anno .xliiij.^{to}, acta .xiij. die Aprilis anno eodem; et unum .xij. marcarum sub nominibus ipsius Galfridi et dicti Hagini reddendum ad octabas sancti Martini anno .xlv., acta .vj. die Octobris anno .xliiij.^{to}; et unum sexcies viginti librarum sub nominibus Willelmi de Windes' de comitatu Midd' et Willelmi de Windes' filii ejusdem Willelmi [et dicti Hagini][35] reddendum inde .xv. libras a die Pasche in unum mensem anno regis Henrici .lij.^{o} et .xv. libras a die sancti Michaelis in unum mensem proximo sequentem, et sic de anno in annum ad eosdem terminos .xxx. libras donec etc., acta .ix. die Octobris anno .lj.^{o}; et unum ducentarum et .l. librarum sub nominibus Willelmi de Muntchenesy militis domini de Edwardeston' de comitatu Suff' et dicti Hagini, reddendum inde .xxv. libras ad octabas sancti Johannis Baptiste anno regis Henrici .lij.^{o} et .xxv. libras ad octabas Natalis Domini proximo sequentes; et sic de anno in annum etc. .l. libras per annum ad eosdem terminos etc. donec etc., acta .xiij. die Februarii anno .lij.^{to}; et unum quatuor centum marcarum et .l. sub nominibus Johannis de Burgo militis filii Huberti de Burgo de comitatu Kanc', reddendum inde .l. marcas per annum, scilicet medietatem ad quindenam sancti Michaelis anno regis Henrici .lij.^{o} et aliam medietatem ad quindenam Pasche proximo sequentem, et sic de anno in annum etc. .l. marcas per annum ad eosdem terminos usque ad finem novem annorum proximo sequencium, acta .vij. die Marcii anno .lij.^{o}; et unum .lx. librarum sub nominibus Willelmi de Windes' militis de comitatu Midd' et Willelmi de Windes' filii ejusdem Willelmi et Reginaldi de Morteng' de eodem comitatu et dicti Hagini, reddendum inde .xij. libras ad quindenam Pasche anno .lij.^{o} et .xij. libras ad quindenam sancti Michaelis proximo sequentem et .xij. libras ad quindenam Pasche proximo sequentem et .xij. libras ad quindenam sancti Michaelis proximo sequentem et .xij. libras ad quindenam Pasche proximo sequentem, acta .ix. die Octobris anno .lj.^{o}; et unum .xx. librarum sub nominibus Johannis de Lymare militis de comitatu Not' et Radulphi de Lymare miltis de comitatu Linc' et dicti Hagini, reddendum a die sancti Johannis Baptiste in tres septimanas anno .lij.^{o}, acta .xxv. die Maii anno eodem; et unum centum et sex librarum sub nominibus Rogeri de Eyville militis de comitatu Warr' et dicti Hagini, reddendum inde .liij. marcas ad quindenam Pasche anno regis Henrici .xlvij.^{o} et .liij. marcas ad quindenam sancti Michaelis proximo sequentem et .liij. marcas ad quindenam Pasche proximo sequentem, acta .xvj. die Octobris anno .xlvj.^{o}; et unum tresdecim marcarum sub nominibus Philippi filii Bernardi de Boclonde militis de comitatu Hertford' et dicti Hagini, reddendum ad quindenam sancti Hillarii anno regis Henrici .xlv., acta .xix. die Augusti anno .xliiij.^{to}; et unum .l. librarum sub nominibus Radulphi Pyrot militis de comitatu Bed' et dicti Hagini, reddendum medietatem a die Pentecosten in unum mensem anno regis Henrici .liiij.^{o} et aliam medietatem a die sancti Michaelis in unum mensem proximo sequentem, acta .xxviij. die Octobris anno .liij.^{o}; et unum .xx. librarum sub nominibus Rogeri de Eyvill filii Roberti de Eyvill militis de comitatu Warr' et dicti Hagini, reddendum inde medietatem ad quindenam Pasche anno regis Henrici .xlviij.^{o} et aliam medietatem ad quindenam sancti Michaelis proximo sequentem, et sic de anno in annum etc. .xx. libras ad eosdem terminos usque ad finem seculi, acta .viij. die Novembris anno eodem; et unum .cc. marcarum sub nominibus Andree de Feugers filii Willelmi de Feugers militis de comitatu Ebor' et Willelmi Alaunzon filii Willelmi de Alaunzon militis de comitatu Linc' et dicti Hagini, reddendum ad quindenam Nativitatis sancti Johannis <Baptiste>[36] anno regis Edwardi primo, acta .x. die Februarii anno eodem; et unum .cc. librarum sub nominibus Ricardi de Tillebiri militis de comitatu Essex' et dicti Hagini, reddendum inde .xl. libras ad quindenam sancti Michaelis anno regis Edwardi primo et .x. libras ad quindenam Pasche proximo sequentem, et sic de anno in annum etc. .xx. libras ad eosdem terminos post predictas .xl. libras persolutas quousque dicte .cc. libre persolvantur, acta .xviij. die Junii anno regis Edwardi eodem; et unum quingentarum librarum sub nominibus Johannis le Ferun de London' et dicti Hagini, reddendum inde centum libras ad quindenam sancti Michaelis anno regis Edwardi primo et centum libras ad Pascha proximo sequens et centum libras ad festum sancti Michaelis proximo sequens et centum libras ad Pascha proximo sequens, et centum libras ad festum sancti Michaelis proximo sequens, acta .xvij. die Marcii anno eodem; et unum .xv. librarum sub nominibus Johannis filii Alani de Wolvrinton' militis de comitatu Buk' et dicti Hagini, reddendum ad quindenam Pasche anno regis Henrici

[35] *MS. omits.*

[36] *Repeated in MS.*

.lvij.° .xv. libras et .xv. libras a die sancti Michaelis in tres septimanas proximo sequentes, et sic de anno in annum etc. .xxx. libras per annum ad eosdem terminos usque ad finem octo annorum proximo sequencium, acta .xx. die Octobris anno .lvj.°; et unum .xx. librarum sub nominibus Johannis de Stavele de comitatu Ebor' et dicti Hagini reddendarum ad quindenam sancti Hillarii anno regis Henrici .lvij.°, acta .xxv. die Octobris anno regis Henrici .lvj.°; et unum .cc. librarum sub nominibus Walteri de Furneus militis de comitatu Somers' et dicti Hagini reddendarum a die sancti Martini in hieme in unum mensem anno regis Henrici .lviiij., acta primo die Septembris anno .lvj.°; et unum centum librarum sub nominibus Andree de Feugers filii Willelmi de Feugers militis de comitatu Ebor' et dicti Hagini reddendarum ad quindenam Pasche anno regis Edwardi primo, acta secundo die Februarii anno eodem; et unum quadraginta et octo librarum sub nominibus Stephani de Asschewell' de comitatu Hertf' et dicti Hagini reddendo inde .xxviij. libras ad quindenam sancti Michaelis anno regis Henrici .xlvij. et .xxj. libras ad quindenam sancti Johannis Baptiste proximo sequentem, acta .vj. die Augusti anno .xlvij.; et unum .lx. librarum sub nominibus Roberti de Drayton filii Alexandri de comitatu Noting' reddendarum ad octabas sancti Michaelis anno regis Henrici .lv., acta .xxvj. die Octobris anno .liiij.^{to}; et unum quaterviginti librarum sub nominibus Stephani de Cheinduyt militis de comitatu Hertford' et dicti Hagini reddendarum ad quindenam Pasche anno regis Edwardi primo, acta ultimo die Januarii anno eodem; et unum .ccl. librarum sub nominibus Stephani de Cressi militis filii Rogeri de Cressi militis de comitatu Norff' et dicti Hagini, reddendum medietatem ad Purificacionem Beate Marie anno regis Henrici .xlviij. et aliam medietatem ad Nativitatem sancti Johannis Baptiste proximo sequentem, acta .xx. die Junii anno .xlvij.°; et unum .cc. marcarum sub nominibus Roberti de Ferars comitis Derb' et dicti Hagini, reddendum medietatem ad quindenam Pasche anno regis Henrici .xlviij.° et aliam medietatem ad quindenam sancti Michaelis proximo sequentem, acta primo die Novembris anno eodem; et unum centum et .l. librarum sub nominibus eorundem Roberti et Hagini, reddendum medietatem ad Nativitatem sancti Johannis Baptiste anno regis Henrici .xlviij.° et aliam medietatem ad festum sancti Michaelis proximo sequens, acta .xvij. die Septembris anno .xlvij.°; et unum octoviginti librarum sub nominibus Ricardi de Tillebiri militis de comitatu Essex' et dicti Hagini, reddendum inde .x. libras ad quindenam Pasche anno regis Henrici .liij.° et .x. libras ad quindenam sancti Michaelis proximo sequentem, et sic de anno in annum etc. .xx. libras per annum ad eosdem terminos usque ad finem octo annorum proximo sequencium etc., acta etc. quarto die Junii anno regis Henrici .lij.°

Respice in tergo

MEMBRANE 6 DORSE

Aduc Memoranda de debitis Hagini liberatis dicto domino W. de Kanc'

et unum quingentarum librarum sub nominibus Ade de Novo Mercato militis de comitatu Ebor' et dicti Hagini reddendarum ad Mediam Quadragesimam anno regis Edwardi primo, acta .xxviij. die Januarii anno eodem; et unum quadringentarum librarum sub nominibus eorundem Ade et Hagini, reddendum inde .xxv. libras ad quindenam Pasche anno regis Henrici .lvj.^{to} et .xxv. libras ad quindenam sancti Michaelis proximo sequentem, et sic de anno in annum etc. .l. libras per annum ad eosdem terminos donec etc., acta .iij. die Augusti anno .lv.^{to}; et unum mille marcarum sub nominibus Radulphi de Kameys de comitatu Cantebr' et dicti Hagini, reddendum inde .l. marcas a die sancti Hillarii in unum mensem anno regis Edwardi secundo et .l. marcas a die Nativitatis sancti Johannis Baptiste in unum mensem proximo sequentem, et sic de anno in annum etc. centum marcas per annum etc. donec etc. acta .xvij. die Julii anno regis Edwardi primo; et unum debitum quingentarum et .l. marcarum sub nominibus Radulphi Morin filii Johannis Morin de comitatu Bed' et dicti Hagini, reddendum inde .cc. marcas ad Natale Domini anno regis Edwardi secundo et .cc. marcas ad quindenam sancti Michaelis proximo sequentem et centum libras ad quindenam sancti Michaelis proximo sequentem, acta .iij. die Maii anno regis Edwardi primo.

Summa cartarum .xxxvij.

MEMBRANE 7

Starra de termino sancti Michaelis anno regni regis Edwardi septimo

(237)

Lond'. Cresseus filius Cressei judeus recognovit per starrum suum, tanquam attornatus Aron filii Vyves, quod ipse recepit de Radulpho Musqet quinque marcas de termino quindene sancti Michaelis anno regis Edwardi .vij. Et idem Cresseus tenetur facere eidem Radulpho starrum predicti Aaron de acquietancia [predicti][37] debiti quinque marcarum.

(238)

Lond'. Magister Elias filius magistri Mossei judeus recognovit per starrum suum quod ipse recepit de Adam cissore domini regis sex libras et .j. marcam de termino sancti Michaelis anno regni regis Edwardi .vij., scilicet de quadam fine quem predictus Adam fecit cum predicto judeo pro se pro debitis in quibus Willelmus de Hadestoke civis London' eidem judeo tenebatur. Et hoc sigillavit.

[37] *MS. reads* predicto.

(239)

London'. Jacobus filius Hagini recognovit per starrum suum quod debet Henrico de Winton' militi .xxv. libras et quinque solidos, videlicet pro pannis quos ab eo emit, solvendas infra Natale Domini anno regni regis Edwardi octavo. Pro debito predicto dictus judeus liberavit dicto [i]<H.>[i] unum scriptum obligatorium sub nominibus Walteri de Furneaus et Johannis filii sui et dicti judei de quater viginti libris subtus sigillatum quas debuerunt eidem judeo pro mercandisis que ad eodem judeo emerunt, sicut irrotulatur in rotulis de scaccario judeorum, videlicet quod dictas quaterviginti libras perdonavit usque ad quaterviginti marcas per quod ipsi teneant terminum solucionis, sicut continetur in predicto scripto. Et sacramentum fecerit dictus judeus secundum legem judaicam quod non fecit aliquod starrum aquietancie seu aliquam aliam aquietanciam dictis Waltero vel Johanni nec faciet de toto debito vel parte sine licencia dicti Henrici. Et, si contingat quod in dicta solucione defecerit ad Natale Domini predictum, tunc obligat omnia bona et catalla et terras per totum ut possit eum per ea distringere usque ad plenam solucionem dicti debiti et idem judeus concessit dare domino regi dimidiam marcam auri si predictum terminum preterierit non soluta pecunia. Et sacramentum prestitit secundum legem affirmandi dicto domino Henrico et heredibus suis sive suis assignatis pro se et heredibus suis omnes convenciones predictas. Et quod recognovit hoc sigillavit per testimonium Hagini de Linc' et Meyr filii Bon'. Item idem judeus recognovit quod recepit .xv. solidos pro pannis quos emit de dicto Henrico.

(240)

Aaron filius Vives judeus recognovit per starrum suum quod recepit de Ricardo de Amundeville .xij. libras et .x. solidos de termino quindene sancti Michaelis anno regis Edwardi septimo per manum domini Rogeri de Pulesdon' de debitis in quibus idem Ricardus eidem judeo tenetur et .xx. solidis pro una roba etc.

(241)

Norff'. Aaron filius Vives, Cresseus filius Gente et Cresseus filius Cressei judei Lond' recognoverunt per starrum quod Willelmus de Blunville de comitatu Norff' et heredes sui quieti sunt de ipsis judeis et heredibus suis de omnibus debitis, demandis, plegiis et calumpniis in quibus dictus Willelmus eisdem judeis umquam tenebatur sub nominibus predictorum judeorum in archa cyrographariorum domini regis vel extra a creacione seculi usque ad finem; et eciam Willelmus de Blunvyle, filius et heres predicti Willelmi, et heredes sui quieti sunt de predictis judeis et heredibus suis de omnibus debitis, demandis et calumpniis in quibus predictis judeis tenebatur ante confeccionem presentis starri a creacione seculi usque ad finem. Et si inveniatur carta vel tallia, cirographum vel obligacio sub nominibus predicti Willelmi patris Willelmi de Blunvyle filii in archa cyrographariorum vel extra facta ante confeccionem presentis starri predicti judei recognoverunt quod quieti sint et nichil valeant. Acta die dominica proxima [post/ante][38] festum apostolorum anno regni regis Edwardi septimo.

(242)

Norff'. Samuel filius Isac de Norwic' et Isac de Warr' judei recognoverunt per starrum suum quod ipsi quietaverunt et quietum clamaverunt Roberto Baygnard, filio Roberti Baygnard militis, totum jus, demandam et calumpniam que habuerunt vel habere potuerunt super terris, redditibus cum pertinenciis quas predictus Robertus tenet in villa de Hauboys vel alibi que quondam fuerunt patris Petri de Hauboys, quondam debitoris predictorum judeorum, ita quod ipsi judei nec aliquis alius nec aliquis heredum suorum nec assignati pro ipsis aliquod debitum possint exigere vel calumpniare erga predictum Robertum Baygnard et heredes nec assignatos suos occasione predictarum terrarum vel reddituum cum pertinenciis quas predictus Robertus tenet, ut predictum est, pro nullo debito in quo predictus Petrus de Hautboys vel antecessores vel heredes sui tenebatur predictis judeis, antecessoribus vel heredibus suis facto ante confeccionem presentis starri a creacione seculi usque ad finem. Et si aliquis judeus vel judea aliquod debitum exigat de predicto Roberto vel heredibus vel assignatis suis occasione alicujus debiti in quo idem Robertus predictis judeis vel antecessoribus suis tenebatur eidem judei tenentur ipsos acquietare, warantizare et defendere contra omnes calumpniantes. Acta in quindena Pasche anno regni regis Edwardi quinto.

(243)

Aaron filius Vives recognovit per starrum suum quod ad instanciam domini Hamonis Hauteyn quietavit et quietum clamavit totum jus, demandam et calumpniam, obligacionem et potestatem et servicium que habuit vel habere potuit in manerio de Egeringe quod Walterus de Sterchesl' et Alicia uxor ejus tenent occasione alicujus debiti vel calumpnie que habuit vel habere potuit erga Willelmum Folyot venditorem dicti manerii a creacione seculi usque ad finem, ita quod nec ipse judeus nec heredes nec assignati sui [aliquid][39] exigere vel calumpniare possint super predictum Walterum vel Aliciam uxorem ejus vel heredes suos occasione predicti maneri de Ekering' racione alicujus debiti in quo dictus Willelmus Folyot eidem judeo tenebatur a creacione seculi usque ad finem, salvo tamen eidem judeo quod habeat recuperare suum de debitis in quibus idem Willelmus eidem judeo tenetur super aliis terris et catallis ipsius Willelmi. Acta in crastino Animarum anno regni regis Edwardi septimo.

[38] *MS. omits.*

[39] *MS. reads* aliquit.

MEMBRANE 7 DORSE

Adhuc Starra

(244)

Essex'. Aaron filius Vives judeus recognovit per starrum suum quod perdonavit et quietumclamavit venerabili viro domino Roberto Bathoniensi et Wellensi episcopo totum jus, clamium et calumpniam, potestatem et servicium que habuit vel habere potuit super manerium de Borham cum omnibus pertinenciis quod dictus venerabilis pater tenet die confeccionis presentis starri, ita quod nec idem Aaron, heredes seu assignati sui nichil potuerunt exigere seu calumpniari de predicto episcopo, [i]<heredibus et assignatis suis>[i] in predicto manerio cum pertinenciis occasione alicujus debiti in quo Robertus de Borham tenebatur dicto Aaron vel suis heredibus infra archa cyrographariorum vel extra sub nominibus dicti Roberti et Aaron et heredum suorum et eciam sub nominibus dicti Roberti et Samuelis filii Aaron [i]<et similiter sub nominibus dicti Roberti et Sampsonis filii Vives>[i] a principio seculi usque ad finem, quia dicti Sampson et Samuel vendiderunt dicto Aaron duo debita sub nominibus dicti Roberti et dictorum Sampsonis et Samuelis, videlicet unum debitum centum librarum et aliud centum solidorum. Et dictus Aaron et heredes sui tenentur aquietare dictum episcopum de dictis debitis sub nominibus predictorum Roberti, Sampsonis et Samuelis a principio seculi uque ad finem et de omnibus debitis in quibus dictus Robertus de Borham tenebatur dicto Aaron vel heredibus suis contra omnes calumpniantes versus dictum episcopum occasione debitorum supradictorum super manerium predictum a principio seculi usque ad finem, salvo dicto Aaron et heredibus suis suo recuperare versus alios tenentes terrarum que fuerunt dicti Roberti de Borham, videlicet priorem de Leghes et Robertum le Poer, die quo istud starrum factum fuit. Acta die dominica proxima ante festum sancti Nicholai anno regni regis Edwardi octavo.

(245)

Norff'. Magister Elias filius magistri Mossei judeus recognovit per starrum suum quod Edmundus de Illegh' [et][40] heredes sui quieti sunt de ipso, heredibus et pueris suis de omnibus debitis, plegiis, demandis, calumpniis factis ante Purificacionem Beate Marie anno octavo usque ad finem seculi, videlicet quia magister Adam de Hales aquietavit versus eundem magistrum de omnibus debitis predictis. Et, si inveniatur carta, tallia vel aliud instrumentum infra archa cyrographariorum vel extra facta ante predictum festum Purificacionis Beate Marie sub nominibus dicti Edmundi et predicti judei, concedit quod vana sint et nichil valeant. Et quod scripsit manu sua consignavit.

[40] *MS. omits.*

HILARY TERM, 8 EDWARD I [1280]

Exchequer of Jews, Plea Rolls Nos. 34, 65 [E 9/34 , 65]

There are two plea-rolls for this term, though of one, Roll 65, only a single membrane survives. The letter 'h' at the top of membranes 3, 4, 5d, 6, 9 and the bottom half of membrane 2 of Roll 34 suggests that this is the roll made for the senior justice, Hamon Hauteyn; the single membrane of Roll 65 probably, therefore, represents the surviving part of the roll of his fellow justice Robert of Ludham. This single membrane was probably initially numbered Roll 35A when it was added to the class between 1894 and 1902 but was renumbered as Roll 40 between 1902 and 1910. By 1910 it had been added to Roll 34 as membrane 10. It was restored in 1975 to its original state as the sole surviving membrane of a separate roll.

The entries on the recto of the single membrane of Roll 65 occur in exactly the same order as those on the recto of membrane 5 of Roll 34 [nos. 308-23]; the 1st-10th entries on the dorse of the membrane correspond to the 1st-10th entries on membrane 5d of Roll 34 [nos. 324-33]; the 11th entry corresponds to entry no. 271 on Roll 34; the 12th entry corresponds to entry no. 353 of Roll 34; the 13th and14th entries correspond to the 11th and 12th entries on m. 5d of Roll 34 [nos. 334-5]. Significant variants in the text of these entries in Roll 65 are noted in the footnotes. The heading of the recto of membrane 1 of Roll 65 is *Memoranda de termino sancti Hillarii anno regis Edwardi octavo;* the heading of the recto of m. 1d of Roll 65 is *Adhuc Memoranda.*

ROLL 34

MEMBRANE 1

Essonia de octabis sancti Hillarii anno regni regis Edwardi octavo

(246)

Devon'. Hunfridus Kael versus Johannem filium Bernardi de placito aquietacionis debiti per Ricardum de Monte Sorelli.

Non jacet quia breve dicit 'venire facias'.

(247)

Somers'. Philippus de Paunton', attornatus Guydonis persone de Bacwell', versus Gamalielum de Oxon' judeum de placito debiti per Johannem de Lyon'.

(248)

Essex'. Willelmus de Tunstede, attornatus Willelmi de Wateville, versus Deulecres judeum London' de placito debiti per Willelmum Fox.

MEMBRANE 1 DORSE

Attornata et Prece Parcium de termino sancti Hillarii

(249)

Lond'. Cresseus filius Gente ponit loco suo Sampsonem filium Isac judeum versus Walterum de la Linde de placito debiti.

(250)

Idem Cresseus ponit loco suo eundem versus Willelmum Margrete de placito debiti.

(251)

Leo filius Cressei ponit loco suo Sampsonem filium Isac versus Clerkin de Schoberi de placito debiti.

(252)

Norff'. Johannes de Hadessawe ponit loco suo Mattheum de Hadeswe versus[1]

(253)

Linc'. Prior de Bolyngton' ponit loco suo Rogerum de Ormesby vel Adam Prodhom versus Johannem de Bathon' de placito debiti.

MEMBRANE 2

Placita de octabis sancti Hillarii anno regni regis Edwardi octavo

(254)

Elena que fuit uxor Alani i<la>i Zuche attachiata ad respondendum Willelmo Foliot et Isabelle uxori ejus, filie David de Essebi, de placito transgressionis et compoti. Et unde queruntur quod, cum secundum legem et consuetudinem Judaismi tempore predecessorum regum Anglie et regis nunc usitatas nullus tenens terras vel tenementa in Judaismum per alium quam per se ipsum obligata de

[1] *The remainder of this entry is illegible and has probably been erased.*

terris et tenementis illis eici debeat nec judeus aliquis cui obligata fuerunt inde seisinam habere deberet pro debito ab eo mutuato quousque tenens ille in curia eorundem progenitorum regum Anglie vel curia regis nunc vocatus seu summonitus fuisset, ita quod judeus ille vel locum ejus tenens secundum legem Judaismi debitum hujusmodi per consideracionem curie predicte recuperaverit; et, si forte eidem judeo vel suo attornato debitum illud deberi contingerit, ita quod seisina terrarum et tenementorum sic obligatorum sibi fuerit adjudicata, non liceret eidem judeo vel cuiquam suo attornato vastum, destruccionem vel exilium facere de boscis, gardinis vel vivariis in hujusmodi tenementis existentibus nec christianum illum a domibus et edificiis suis eicere vel dehospitare, set tantummodo exitus inde provenientes percipere quousque debitum illud inde fuerit levatum et solutum, predicta Elena, asserens prefatum Alanum quondam virum suum et se quedam debita per predictum David a magistro Elya judeo London' mutuata emisse, ac si debita illa secundum legem et consuetudinem Judaismi confecta et petita fuissent, cum non sint, eo quod in cartis, tallis, cyrographiis inter christianos et judeos Anglie confectis debita illa non sunt annotata vel intitulata, prout oporteret secundum legem et consuetudinem Judaismi supradicta, per maliciam inter ipsos Alanum, Elenam et Elyam excogitatam in manerio de Esseby David se intrusit et ipsam Isabellam pretextu illius [fraudulentis][2] vendicionis sine consideracione curie ab eodem manerio ejecit et dehospitavit et eam ejectam et dehospitatam detinet, fraxinos et alios arbores in capitali mesuagio crescentes abradicavit, boscum suum prostravit, vendidit et distraxit et vivaria sua piscari fecit ad dampnum suum quingentarum librarum et exheredacionem suam manifestam et contra assisam et consuetudinem Judaismi supradicti.

Predicta Elena venit et defendit vim etc. et quando etc. Et dicit quod predicta Isabella de predicto manerio per eam numquam fuit ejecta nec aliquo modo a predicto manerio eici potuit, eo quod Alanus la Zuche quondam vir ipsius Elene seisinam et statum habuerit de predicto manerio de Essebi per consideracionem curie domini regis secundum assisam et consuetudinem Judaismi pro debito Judaismi, et illam seisinam et statum habuit et tenuit pacifice tota vita sua et post decessum ejus dicta Elena eandem seisinam et statum pacifice continuavit usque nunc.

Et predicti Willelmus et Isabella dicunt quod quoquomodo dictus Alanus seisinam et statum habuerit de predicto manerio secundum assisam Judaismi, dicta Isabella habuit seisinam et statum de eodem manerio antequam aliqua seisina adjudicata fuit dicto Alano per consideracionem curie domini regis secundum assisam Judaismi, et illam seisinam et statum continuavit quousque ejecta fuit per predictos Alanum et Elenam.

Et predicta Elena dicit quod dicta Isabella seisinam et statum de predicto manerio habere non potuit antequam dictus Alanus inde seisinam et statum habuit, eo quod dictus Alanus eandem seisinam et statum habuit secundum assisam et consuetudinem Judaismi pro debito Judaismi antequam dicta Isabella nata erat. Et hoc offert verificare.

Et predicti Willelmus et Isabella dicunt quod dicta Isabella seisinam et statum habuit de predicto manerio antequam dictus Alanus umquam inde seisinam et statum habuit secundum assisam Judaismi, eo quod statim post decessum David de Essebi avi sui intravit predictum manerium tanquam heres propinquior et seisinam et statum in eodem manerio habuit et tenuit quousque dicti Alanus et Elena ipsam ejecerunt. Et hoc petunt quod inquiratur. Et predicta Elena similiter. Ideo preceptum est vicecomiti.[3]

(255)

Midd'. Cresseus filius Gente fecit venire Willelmum Margarete, tenentem quandam partem terrarum que fuerunt Ade le Norreys, et exigit ab eo occasione etc. .xx. solidos de catallo et .c. solidos de lucro per cyrographum .xxx. solidorum inter predictos Adam et Cresseum confectum etc.

Predictus Willelmus venit et recognovit se esse tenentem quarundam terrarum que fuerunt predicti Ade et vocat inde ad warantum per auxilium curie magistrum hospitalis sancti Egidii; et habet diem in crastino Cinerum etc.

(256)

Norff'. Isac le Eveske judeus fecit venire magistrum Alanum de Freston', tenentem quandam partem terrarum que fuerunt Samuelis de Norwyco judei, et exigit ab eo .xx. libras occasione terrarum etc. per quoddam starrum inter predictos Samuelem et Isac confectum de quodam cyrographo triginta librarum, unde altera pars est in archa cyrographariorum apud Lond', ut dicit.

Predictus magister Alanus venit et dicit quod non est factum suum et petit diem premeditandi et habet a die Pasche in tres septimanas.

(257)

Essex'. Aaron filius Vyves fecit venire priorem de Legh', tenentem quandam partem terrarum que fuerunt Roberti de Borham, et exigit ab eo occasione terrarum etc. .xx. libras de catallo et quaterviginti libras de lucro inde emerso per cyrographum .c. librarum, unde altera pars est in archa cyrographariorum apud Lond' etc.

Predictus prior per attornatum suum [venit][4] et dicit quod non est factum suum et petit diem premeditandi et habet in crastino Cinerum etc. [5]

[2] *MS. reads* fraudulente.

[3] *This entry is unfinished.*

[4] *MS. omits.*

[5] *The following entries are recorded on a second membrane sewn to the bottom of that containing the previous entries. On the top left-hand side is the letter 'h'.*

(258)

Wilt', Suth'. Thomas de Chelwarton' per essoniatorem suum optulit se quarto die versus Johannem de Haveryng', quondam vicecomitem Sutht', de placito acquietacionis debiti. Et ipse non venit. Et preceptum fuit vicecomiti, sicut pluries, quod ipsum distringeret per terras etc., et quod haberet corpus eus coram etc. Et vicecomes mandavit quod retornavit breve inde sibi directum ballivis libertatis de Kynewarton', qui nichil inde fecerunt. Judicium quod non omittat propter libertatem etc. quin eam etc. et distringat etc. a die Pasche in .xv. dies etc.

(259)

Oxon'. Sarra que fuit uxor Benedicti le Eveske per attornatum suum optulit se quarto die versus Henricum de Shotebroke, tenentem quandam partem terrarum que fuerunt Simonis de Hordleston', de placito debiti. Et ipse non venit. Et preceptum fuit vicecomiti, sicut alias, quod ipsum distringeret per terras etc. Et vicecomes [i]<nichil>[i] mandavit inde nec breve retornavit. Ideo, sicut pluries, in crastino Cinerum etc. Et vicecomes sit etc.

(260)

Glouc'. Alexander de Aunou per essoniatorem suum optulit se quarto die versus Bartholomeum de Suthl' et Rogerum Barbastre, executores testamenti Johannis la Ware, de placito acquietacionis debiti. Et ipsi non venerunt. Et preceptum fuit vicecomiti quod ipsos venire faceret ad hunc diem etc. Et vicecomes nichil inde mandavit nec breve retornavit. Ideo, sicut alias, a die Pasche in .xv. dies etc., et vicecomes sit etc.

(261)

Hertf'. Simon Gubyun attachiatus ad respondendum Willelmo de Middelton' clerico etc. de placito debiti. Et unde queritur quod, cum dictus Simon ei dimisisset .vij.^{xx} acras terre cum pertinenciis in Stapelford' ad terminum sex annorum, Johanna de Patemere infra eundem terminum coram justiciariis itinerantibus in comitatu Hertf' recuperavit versus dictum Simonem dotem suam, in qua dote fuerunt .xiiij. acre terre seminate cum frumento ad custus dicti Willelmi infra terminum suum ad valenciam .vij. marcarum, de quibus dicto Willelmo non satisfecit ad dampnum suum .x. librarum. Et hoc offert verificare etc.

Predictus Simon venit et defendit vim etc. quando etc. Et dicit quod injuste queritur de eo, eo quod eidem Willelmo satisfecit pro valore predictarum .xiiij. acrarum terre per vesturam .xj. acrarum prati in recompensacionem dicti debiti. Et de hoc ponit se super patriam. Et predictus Willelmus dicit quod ei de hoc nondum satisfecit, et de hoc similiter ponit se super patriam. Ideo preceptum est vicecomiti quod venire faciat coram etc. in crastino Cinerum .xij. probos etc. de visneto de Stapelford' ad recognoscendum etc.

(262)

Lond', Suth'. Abraham filius Benedicti de Wynton' judeus fecit venire Sarram que fuit uxor Salomonis filii Belcote et exigit ab ea .xvj. libras quas ei tradidit custodiendas cito post festum sancti Michaelis anno regni regis Edwardi sexto ut in denariis numeratis, auro, argento et aliis jocalibus suis ad valorem predictarum .xvj. librarum, et quas ei unjuste detinet ad dampnum suum x librarum etc., et ad hoc producit sectam etc.

Predicta Sarra venit et defendit vim etc. et dicit quod nichil ab eo recepit custodiendum sicut versus eam narrat et hoc parata est facere etc. contra predictum Abraham et sectam suam, si quam habeat, secundum legem et consuetudinem Judaismi; et vadiat inde dicto Abrahe legem faciendam in crastino Cinerum. Plegii de lege, Isac de Suthwerk' et Willelmus de Waldeshef'.

(263)

Linc'. Omnes judei communitatis Linc' qui tulerunt breve super Petrum de Karlel', Willelmum de Karl', Ricardum le Wyte, Radulfum de Filingham, Johannem le Lung, Walterum de Conyngby, Henricum de Bamburg', Henricum Dudeman, Radulfum de Clentwyth', Hugonem de Sancto Botulpho, Henricum le Deygnus, Simonem filium Bate, Radulfum Russel et Dobbe Scabbard de transgressione etc. non sunt prosecuti. Ideo predicta communitas in misericordia.[6]

(264)

Cantebr'. Aaron filius Vyves optulit se quarto die versus Willelmum de Lindes', tenentem quandam partem terrarum que fuerunt Roberti de Heref', de placito debiti. Et ipse non venit. Et preceptum fuit vicecomiti quod ipsum venire faceret etc. Et vicecomes mandavit quod Simon filius Willelmi, Johannes Cassaundre et Willelmus filius Simonis Drury manuceperunt predictum Willelmum, quem non habuerunt. Ideo in misericordia.[7] Judicium quod distringatur per terras etc. a die Pasche in .xv. dies etc. ad respondendum etc.

(265)

Kanc'. Josceus de Shorham judeus optulit se quarto die versus Ricardum filium Hamonis de Dodinton', tenentem quandam partem terrarum que fuerunt Johannis filii Johannes de Hundeskull', de placito debiti. Et ipse non venit. Et preceptum fuit vicecomiti quod ipsum venire faceret. Et vicecomes mandavit quod retornavit breve inde sibi directum senescallo libertatis archiepiscopatus Cant', qui nichil inde fecit. Judicium quod non omittat propter libertatem etc. quin eam etc., et venire faciat coram etc. a die Pasche in .xv. dies.

(266)

Essex'. Aaron filius Vives optulit se quarto die versus Robertum le Poer, tenentem quandam partem terrarum

[6] *The word* misericordia *is repeated in the margin.*

[7] *The word* misericordia *is repeated in the margin.*

que fuerunt Roberti le Poer, de placito debiti. Et ipse non venit. Et preceptum fuit vicecomiti quod ipsum venire faceret etc. Et vicecomes mandavit quod dictus Robertus districtus est per quandam carucam junctam et aliam manucapcionem habere non potuit. Ideo preceptum est vicecomiti quod ipsum distringat per terras etc., ita quod nec ipse etc., et quod habeat corpus eius coram etc. a die Pasche in .xv. dies ad respondendum etc.

(267)

Ebor'. Manserus filius Manseri judeus, qui tulit breve super Hugonem filium Sibille et Nalle uxorem ejus de placito detencionis bonorum et catallorum, non est prosecutus. Ideo ipse Manserus et plegii sui de prosequendo, videlicet Isac filius Samuelis et Isac de Ebor' judei, in misericordia.[8]

MEMBRANE 2 DORSE

(268)

Memorandum quod tale breve [i]<regis>[i] emanavit de cancellaria baronibus et justiciariis etc. in hec verba: 'Edwardus dei gracia etc. baronibus et justiciariis suis ad custodiam judeorum etc. salutem. Quia dilectus et fidelis noster Hugo filius Otonis, senescallus hospicii nostri, remisit nobis proficuum cuneorum nostrorum quod ad ipsum spectat nomine feodi racione Ottonis, filii et heredis Thome filii Ottonis, infra etatem et in custodia sua existentis ex concessione nostra, nos eidem Hugoni graciam facere volentes concessimus ei omnia debita que Thomas de Chelwarton' per cartas suas debet quibuscumque judeis regni nostri in recompensacione feodi supradicti. Et ideo vobis mandamus quod omnes cartas seu obligaciones in archis cyrographariorum judeorum Judaismi nostri existentes per quas dictus Thomas quibuscunque judeis nostris in aliquibus debitis tenetur ab archis predictis extrahi et eidem Hugoni liberari faciatis in recompensacionem feodi predicti, ut idem Hugo debita predicta levari facere possit, prout de jure et secundum legem et consuetudinem Judaismi nostri fuerit faciendum. Teste me ipso apud Lindhurst .xx. die Januarii anno regni nostri octavo.'

(269)

Stanf'. Sente de Stanford' judeus venit coram etc. et manucepit Benedictum generum Sente judeum quod erit coram etc. quando et ubi etc. ad respondendum de .ix. libris, si Johannes Aurifaber de Stanf' probare poterit quod dictus Benedictus dictas .ix. libras habuit ex tradicione ipsius Johannis. Et idem Sente manucepit quod dictus Benedictus solvet Stephano de Paris' mercatori .xxj. libras quas similiter habuit ex tradicione dicti Johannis et que sunt dicti Stephani. Et insuper manucepit dictum Johannem quod erit coram etc. quando et ubi etc. ad standum recto etc.

Item idem Sente manucepit solvere .v. marcas pro Blaunche de Stanf' per quas eadem Blaunche finem fecit.

(270)

Heref'. Per breve domini Henrici regis de magno sigillo directum justiciariis suis ad custodiam judeorum assignatis in termino sancti Michaelis anno regni predicti domini Henrici incipiente .liij. in hec verba - 'Henricus dei gracia etc. justiciariis suis etc. salutem. Cum vicecomiti nostro Wigorn' mandavimus quod tam per sacramentum proborum et legalium hominum de comitatu predicto quam judeorum Wigorn', per quos rei veritas melius sciri poterit, diligenter inquirat que et quot catalla et debita Hake quondam judeus Wigorn' defunctus habuit die quo obiit tam in archa cyrographariorum nostrorum Wigorn' quam extra in comitatu predicto, et quod inquisicionem inde distincte et aperte factam sub sigillo suo vobis mittat, vobis mandamus quod, recepta et inspecta inquisicione illa, Goye que fuit uxor ipsius Hake racionabilem dotem suam que eam contingit de catallis et debitis predictis assignari faciatis, [i]<prout>[i] secundum legem et consuetudinem judaismi nostri fuent faciendum. Teste me ipso apud Ebor' .xxiij. die Septembris anno regni nostri .lij^{o}.' compertum est, prout patet inter inquisiciones retornatas coram prefatis justiciariis in termino sancti Michaelis anno .lij.^{o}, quod debita subscripta assignantur predicte Goye que fuit uxor predicti Hake in dotem suam, videlicet unum debitum .xlvj. librarum et .x. solidorum sub nominibus Roberti de Staff' et predicti Hake, et unum debitum duarum marcarum et dimidie sub nominibus Walteri le Gaunter et ipsius Hake, et unum debitum duarum marcarum et dimidie sub nominibus Walteri capellani et ipsius Hake, et unum .xl. solidorum sub nominibus Roberti Blundel et predicti Hake, et unum debitum quatuor librarum sub nominibus Laurencii de Wendleswrth' et ipsius Hake, et unum debitum novem marcarum sub nominibus Henrici de Penebregg' et predicti Hake, et unum debitum sex librarum et unius robe precii .j. marce sub nominibus predictorum Henrici et Hake. Et postea assignatur ei in dotem suam, prout constat per recognicionem Aaron filii Hake et Sampsonis filii Hake judeorum, unum debitum viginti marcarum sub nominibus Ade le Pinnere et dicti Hake. Summa .iiij.^{xx} .j. libre .xvj. solidi .viij. denarii. Et sic ei aretro sunt .xviij. libre .iij. solidi .iiij. denarii. Et postea per breve regis directum justiciariis in hec verba: 'Edwardus dei gracia etc. justicariis suis ad custodiam judeorum assignatis salutem. Cum dominus H. rex pater noster dudum post mortem Hake filii Diey judei Wygorn' Goye que fuit uxor ejusdem Hake assignari fecit secundum legem et consuetudinem Judaismi racionabilem dotem suam que eam contingit de bonis et catallis dicti viri sui, ac eidem Goye de dote illa juxta assignacionem predictam ad plenum satisfactum non fuerit ut dicit, vobis mandamus quod, scrutatis rotulis scaccarii nostri Judaismi, si vobis constare possit hujusmodi dotem eidem Goye de bonis et catallis predictis legitime assignatum fuisse sicut predictum est, tunc id quod ei [i]<inde>[i]

[8] *The word* misericordia *is repeated in the margin.*

aretro esse inveneritis prefate Goye de bonis et catallis predicti viri sui juxta assignacionem predictam habere faciatis secundum legem et consuetudinem Judaismi predicti, salvo semper jure nostro et indempnitate nostra undique prospecta in hac parte. Teste me ipso apud Winton' .xxvj. die Decembris anno regni nostri octavo.' assignantur eidem Goye debita subscripta, videlicet unum debitum .xxij. marcarum sub nominibus Walteri de Deverus domini de Bodenham et dicti Hake, et unum .xx. solidorum sub nominibus Walteri le Mire et ipsius Hake, et unum .xl. solidorum sub nominibus Roberti Blundell' militis de comitatu Salop' et predicti Hake; et concessum est quod ipsam inde liberam administracionem habere permittant. Et concessum est predictis Goye et suis attornatis quod habeant suum recuperare versus predictum Walterum de predicto debito, nisi starrum habeat vel partem cyrographi etc.

(271)

Oxon'. Inquisicio capta per vicecomitem Oxon' ad preceptum Regis de bonis et catallis Joscei filii Jacobi judei defuncti per Henricum Owein, Nicholaum le Orfevere et alios christianos etc., et Vives le Petit et alios judeos, prout patet etc. inter inquisiciones etc. Qui dicunt super sacramentum suum quod dictus Josceus habuit die quo egrotavit etc. in bonis, catallis, jocalibus etc. .x. libras, que devenerunt ad manus Mildegod que fuit uxor ipsius Jocei. Summa catallorum mobilium .x. libre.

Item in archa debita subscripta, videlicet unum debitum <trium marcarum et dimidie>[9] sub nominibus Ade de la Dunhale de comitatu Oxon' et Joscei filii Jacobi, reddendum in septimana Pasche anno regis Edwardo quarto. Acta die veneris proxima post festum sancti Dionisii anno tercio. Et unum debitum <duarum marcarum et dimidie>[10] sub nominibus Ricardi le Grei de Wanetynge de comitatu Berk' et predicti Joscei, reddendum die sancti Mathie apostoli anno .lvij. Acta die dominica in festo sancti Dionisii anno .lvj^{to}. Et unum <quatuor marcarum>[11] sub nominibus Nicholai Dewy de Oxon' et ipsius Joscei, reddendum die de la Hokeday anno regis Edwardi tercio. Acta die sancti Thome apostoli anno eodem. Item unum debitum <.xx. librarum>[12] sub nominibus Walteri de la Rivere et dicti Joscei.

Summa catallorum in archa cyrographariorum: .xj. libre.

Summa catallorum tam mobilium quam inmobilium .xxj. libre de puro, unde tercia pars Regis est .vij. libre; pro qua Rex capit se ad unum debitum .xx. librarum sub nominibus Walteri de la Rivere et dicti Joscei, et unum trium marcarum et dimidie sub nominibus Ade de la Dunhale et dicti Joscei. Et dicta Mildegod concedit quod, nisi Rex possit levare predictas septem libras de predictis debitis, quod Rex capiat se ad omnia debita sua quousque predicte septem libre levate fuerint. Et dicta Mildegod dat Regi omnia debita que inveniri possunt in aliquibus archis sub nominibus quoruncumque christianorum et dicti Joscei preter debita suprascripta etc.[13]

MEMBRANE 3

Adhuc placita de <octabis>[14] sancti Hillarii anno .viij.º[15]

(272)

Surr'. Johannes de Bayfeld', clericus de scaccario etc., optulit se quarto die versus Johannem de Clare, rectorem ecclesie de Blechingle, de placito debiti. Et ipse non venit. Et preceptum fuit vicecomiti quod distringeret Nicholaum episcopum Wynton', ita quod haberet corpus predicti Johannes clerici sui coram etc. ad hunc diem. Et vicecomes mandavit quod dictus episcopus districtus est per terras etc., et quod Willelmus le Parker de Fornham, Willelmus Trapes de eadem, Johannes Smalk' de eadem, et Johannes de la Gate de eadem manuceperunt ad habendum corpus dicti Johannis, quem non habuerunt. Ideo in misericordia.[16] Judicium quod salvo custodiat etc., et si plures etc., ita quod nec ipse etc., et quod de exitibus etc., ita quod habeat corpus prefati clerici sui in crastino Cinerum ad respondendum etc. et ad audiendum etc.

(273)

Norff', Suff'. Willelmus de Middleton', clericus de scaccario etc., optulit se quarto die versus Johannem de Lenn', burgensem de Sancto Edmundo, Johannem personam de Magna Henneye et Rogerum de Feltewell' de placito debiti. Et ipsi non venerunt. Et preceptum fuit vicecomiti quod non omitteret propter libertatem sancti Edmundi quin eam etc., et distringeret predictos Johannem, Johannem et Rogerum per terras etc., et quod haberet corpora eorum coram etc. ad hunc diem. Et vicecomes mandavit quod breve adeo tarde venit quod exequi non potuit. Judicium, sicut alias, quod non omittat etc. in crastino Cinerum etc., ad respondendum etc., et ad audiendum etc. Et quia dictum breve liberatum fuit dicto vicecomiti coram etc. super compotum suum post festum sancti Nicholai ultimo preteritum, ita

[9] *Interlined above this is* quietus per .xl. solidos. *In 65 the same thing is given in the body of the text by a further clause after the date of the bond* quod quidem debitum app[uratur ad ...].

[10] *Interlined above this is* quietus per duas marcas. *In 65 the same thing is given in the text by a further clause after the date of the bond* quod quidem debitum appuratur ad ...

[11] *Interlined above this is* totum.

[12] *In the margin is* ... centum solidos. *In 65 the same things is given by an addition after the dating clause of the bond* quod debitum appuratur ad centum solidos.

[13] *The dorse of the second, lower membrane of m. 2d is blank except for a note possibly of fourteenth century date at the bottom* Placita, Essonia et Memoranda de termino sancti Hillarii anno .viiij.º *and a contemporary note reading* H *and* Hilarii .viiij.º. *Below this are further jottings.*

[14] *Interlined above* termino *which is marked for deletion.*

[15] *In the left hand margin opposite this heading is written* h.

[16] *The word* misericordia *is repeated in the margin.*

quod execucionem dicti brevis bene potuit fecisse et non fecit, ideo ipse vicecomes, scilicet Willelmus de Redham, in misericordia.[17]

(274)

Norff'. Preceptum fuit vicecomiti quod de bonis et catallis Johannes de Heccham, Nicholai de Lafham, Alani de Boclond', Edmundi de <Shardelawe,>[18] et Henrici filii Willelmi de Sancto Edmundo, fieri faceret .x. libras quas recognoverunt se debere Regi de debitis Aaron filii Abrahe et quas solvisse debuerunt a die sancti Michaelis proximo preterito in unum mensem, et eas haberet ad hunc diem. Et vicecomes mandavit quod ipse recepit aliud breve pro ipso Johanne et aliis, cujus tenorem transmisit, per quod nichil inde fecit. Et quia constat justiciariis etc. per inspeccionem returni illius quod secundum mandatum nichil operatur contra primum set quod finxit maliciose hujusmodi returnum, eo quod barones de scaccario a quibus recepisse debuit preceptum ut ipsum Johannem et alios in pace permitteret non recordaverint hujusmodi preceptum, ideo ipse vicecomes, scilicet Willelmus de Redham, in misericordia.[19] Et ideo, sicut alias, in crastino Cinerum; et quod capiat ipsum Johannem et salvo custodiat, ita quod habeat corpus ejus coram etc. ad respondendum Regi de hoc quod recessit etc. contra fidem prestitam.

(275)

Lond'. Robertus de Broghton', clericus de scaccario etc., optulit se quarto die versus Johannem de Westemelle de placito debiti. Et ipse non venit. Et preceptum fuit vicecomitibus quod ipsum distringerent per terras etc., et quod haberent corpus ejus coram etc. ad hunc diem. Et vicecomes mandavit quod Alardus de Hundesdich', Galfridus de Fynchingfeld', Ricardus de Bukyngham et Ricardus le Bocbyndere manuceperunt predictum Johannem, quem non habuerunt. Ideo in misericordia.[20] Judicium, sicut alias, in crastino Purificacionis ad respondendum etc. et ad audiendum etc.

(276)

Essex'. Henna que fuit uxor Jacobi judea que tulit breve super Ricardum de Bereholte de placito debiti non est prosecuta. Ideo ipsa Henna et plegii sui de prosequendo, videlicet Samuel filius Jacobi et Samuel filius Belye judei Colec', in misericordia.[21]

(277)

Suth'. Dyey filius Abrahe optulit se quarto die versus Robertum de Mortuo Mari et Jocosam uxorem ejus de placito debiti. Et ipsi non venerunt. Et preceptum fuit vicecomiti, sicut pluries, quod ipsos distringeret per terras etc., et quod haberet corpora eorum coram etc. ad hunc diem. Et vicecomes mandavit quod Nicholaus de Cnolle, Willelmus Cragrast, Robertus le Gay, et Johannes Russell manuceperunt predictos Robertum et Jocosam, quos non habuerunt. Ideo in misericordia.[22] Judicium quod salvo custodiat etc., ita quod nec ipsi etc., et quod habeat corpora eorum coram etc. in crastino Cinerum ad respondendum etc.

(278)

Devon'. Johannes filius Bernardi optulit se quarto die versus Humfridum le Kayel de placito debiti. Et ipse non venit. Et preceptum fuit vicecomiti quod ipsum venire faceret ad hunc diem. Et vicecomes mandavit quod Henricus Sweynga et Alexander de Boteresdouneford' manuceperunt predictum Humfridum, quem non habuerunt. Ideo in misericordia.[23] Judicium quod distringatur per terras etc., ita quod nec ipse etc., et quod de exitibus etc., et quod habeat corpus ejus coram etc. in crastino Cinerum ad respondendum etc., et ad audiendum etc. de defaltis.

(279)

Wygam'. Vyves filius Aaron judeus optulit se quarto die versus Rogerum de Mortuo Mari, tenentem terrarum que fuerunt Roberti de Cliftone, de placito debiti. Et ipse non venit. Et preceptum fuit vicecomiti, sicut pluries, quod ipsum distringeret per terras etc., et quod haberet corpus ejus coram etc. ad hunc diem. Et vicecomes mandavit quod breve adeo tarde venit quod exequi non potuit. Ideo preceptum est ei, sicut pluries, a die Pasche in .xv. dies etc. ad respondendum etc. et ad audiendum etc.

(280)

Norff'. Isac le Eveske judeus optulit se quarto die versus Josceum filium Deulecres de placito debiti. Et ipse non venit. Et preceptum fuit vicecomiti, sicut pluries, quod ipsum venire faceret. Et vicecomes mandavit quod dictus Josceus infirmus est, ita quod nullam manucapcionem ab eo habere potuit. Ideo preceptum est ei, sicut pluries, in crastino Cinerum etc. ad respondendum etc. Et vicecomes sit etc.

(281)

Linc'. Cresseus filius Gente optulit se quarto die versus Walterum de la Lynde, tenentem quandam partem terrrarum que fuerunt Johannis Russel, de placito debiti. Et ipse non venit. Et preceptum fuit vicecomiti quod ipsum venire faceret ad hunc diem. Et vicecomes mandavit quod Willelmus filius Persone de Bradel', et Willelmus de Hauvyle de eadem manuceperunt predictum Walterum, quem non habuerunt. Ideo in misericordia.[24] Judicium quod distringatur per terras etc., ita quod nec ipse etc., et quod de exitibus etc., et quod habeat corpus ejus coram etc. a die Pasche in .xv. dies ad respondendum etc. et ad audiendum etc.

[17] *The word* misericordia *is repeated in the margin.*
[18] *MS. reads* Thardelawe.
[19] *The word* misericordia *is repeated in the margin.*
[20] *The word* misericordia *is repeated in the margin.*
[21] *The word* misericordia *is repeated in the margin.*
[22] *The word* misericordia *is repeated in the margin.*
[23] *The word* misericordia *is repeated in the margin.*
[24] *The word* misericordia *is repeated in the margin.*

(282)

Lond'. Cristiana Benorth' de Comenore optulit se quarto die versus Isac de Kaune judeum de placito compoti. Et ipse non venit. Et preceptum fuit constabulario Turris quod ipsum venire faceret. Et constabularius mandavit quod predictus Isac non manet in balliva sua, set apud Oxon'. Ideo preceptum est vicecomiti Oxon' quod ipsum venire faciat coram etc. a die Pasche in .xv. dies ad computandum etc.

(283)

Wyltes'. Alexander de Aunou optulit se quarto die per essoniatorem attornati sui versus Godefridum de Acre rectorem ecclesie de Rusteshal', unum executorum Johannis le War', de placito acquietacionis debiti. Et ipse non venit. Et preceptum fuit vicecomiti quod ipsum venire faceret ad hunc diem. Et vicecomes mandavit quod dictus Godefridus non habet laycum feodum neque catalla per que possit distringi. Ideo mandatum est episcopo Sarum' quod ipsum venire faciat coram etc. a die Pasche in .xv. dies ad respondendum etc.

(284)

Wygorn'. Pictavinus filius Aaron per essoniatorem suum optulit se quarto die versus Mauricium Baldewyn', Ricardum Maufras et Matillidem uxorem ejus de placito debiti. Et ipsi non venerunt. Et preceptum fuit vicecomiti quod ipsos venire faceret ad hunc diem etc. Et vicecomes mandavit quod Robertus Bonamy et Willelmus Pyrun manuceperunt predictum Mauricium; et quod Henricus Burrich' et Willelmus de Cumbrinton' manuceperunt predictos Ricardum et Matillidem, quos non habuerunt. Ideo in misericordia.[25] Judicium quod distringantur per terras etc., ita quod nec ipsi etc., et quod de exitibus etc., et quod habeat corpora eorum coram etc. a die Pasche in .xv. dies ad respondendum etc. et ad audiendum etc.

(285)

Wygorn'. Sampson filius Isac judeus optulit se quarto die versus Ricardum de Grimel', Willelmum de Pulnee, Johannem le Charpenter et Henricum Nosse de placito debiti. Et ipsi non venerunt. Et preceptum fuit vicecomiti quod ipsos venire faceret ad hunc diem. Et vicecomes mandavit quod Galfridus Baldewyne et Walterus Curteys manuceperunt Ricardum de Grimel', quem non habuerunt. Ideo in misericordia. Judicium quod distringatur per terras etc., ita quod nec ipse etc., et quod de exitibus etc., et quod habeat corpus ejus coram etc. a die Pasche in .xv. dies ad respondendum etc., et ad audiendum etc. Et vicecomes mandavit quod nullus invenitur in balliva sua qui vocetur Willelmus de Pulnee. Et quod Johannes le Charpenter et Henricus Nosse non sunt de comitatu Wygorn'.

[25] *The word* misericordia *is repeated in the margin.*

MEMBRANE 3 DORSE

Adhuc placita

(286)

Rotel'. Simon filius Simonis optulit se quarto die versus Emmam que fuit uxor Ranulfi de Tykesour', Eliam, Willelmum et Henricum filios ejusdem Rannulfi de Tykesor' de placito acquietacionis debiti. Et ipsi non venerunt. Et preceptum fuit vicecomiti quod ipsos venire faceret ad hunc diem. Et vicecomes mandavit quod Elias filius Ranulfi et Johannes Caleys manuceperunt predictam Emmam; et quod Henricus clericus de Tykesor' et Robertus filius Ranulfi manuceperunt predictum Eliam; et quod Henricus le Porter et Robertus le Leye manuceperunt predictum Willelmum, quos non habuerunt. Ideo in misericordia.[26] Et quod predictus Henricus plegios invenire contempsit. Judicium quod distringantur per terras etc., ita quod nec ipsi etc., et quod de exitibus etc., et quod habeat corpora eorum coram etc. a die Pasche in .xv. dies ad respondendum etc., et ad audiendum etc.

(287)

Norff'. Isac le Eveske optulit se quarto die versus Bartholomeum de Acre, tenentem partem terrarum que fuerunt Samuelis de Norwyco, de placito debiti. Et ipse non venit. Et preceptum fuit vicecomiti, sicut alias, quod non omitteret propter libertatem Norwyc' quin eam etc., et distringeret predictum Bartholomeum per terras etc., et quod haberet corpus ejus coram etc. ad hunc diem. Et vicecomes mandavit quod Andreas de Acre de Norwyco, Galfridus Trussebut de eadem, Nicholas le Mouner de eadem et Robertus Lecche de eadem manuceperunt predictum Bartholomeum, quem non habuerunt. Ideo in misericordia.[27] Judicium quod salvo custodiat etc., et si plures etc., et quod habeat corpus ejus coram etc. a die Pasche in .xv. dies ad respondendum etc. et ad audiendum etc.

(288)

Bed', Buk'. Cresseus filius Gente optulit se quarto die versus Ricardum Reynfrey, tenentem quandam partem terrarum que fuerunt Johannis Russell, de placito debiti. Et ipse non venit. Et preceptum fuit vicecomiti quod ipsum venire faceret. Et vicecomes mandavit quod Willelmus atte Stighele de Chesham et Walterus de Fonte de eadem manuceperunt predictum Ricardum, quem non habuerunt. Ideo in misericordia.[28] Judicium quod distringatur per terras etc., ita quod nec ipse etc., et quod de exitibus etc., et quod habeat corpus ejus coram etc. in crastino Cinerum ad respondendum etc. et ad audiendum etc.

[26] *The word* misericordia *is repeated in the margin.*
[27] *The word* misericordia *is repeated in the margin.*
[28] *The word* misericordia *is repeated in the margin.*

(289)

Lond'. Leo filius Cressei judeus optulit se quarto die versus Clerkinum generum Henrici de Shobyr', tenentem quandam partem terrarum et reddituum que fuerunt Henrici de Shobyr', de placito debiti. Et ipse non venit. Et preceptum fuit vicecomitibus quod ipsum venire facerent. Et vicecomites mandaverunt quod Johannes Perceval piscenarius et Rogerus Lambin piscenarius manuceperunt predictum Clerkinum, quem non habuerunt. Ideo in misericordia.[29] Judicium quod distringatur per terras etc., ita quod nec ipse etc., et quod habeant corpus ejus coram etc. in crastino Cinerum ad respondendum etc., et ad audiendum etc.

(290)

Sussex'. Preceptum fuit vicecomiti quod venire faceret inquisicionem inter A. Reginam Anglie matrem Regis et Willelmum Herigaud, videlicet Ricardum de Asseburnham, Walramum de Mounceals et alios, sicut patet inter brevia hujus termini retornata, et preter eos tot et tales etc. Et vicecomes mandavit quod Adam atte Rude de Asburnham, Rogerus Sperue de eadem, Johannes Provost de eadem, Petrus de Molendino, Ricardus Avice de eadem et Johannes de Neweland' de eadem manuceperunt predictum Ricardum; et quod Robertus atte Churche de Hurst, Simon de la Pende de eadem, Willelmus atte Spredate de eadem, Thomas le Mouner de eadem, Simon le Bedel de eadem, et Ricardus de Horseye de eadem manuceperunt Walramum de Mounceals, et quod Henricus Spendelove, Willelmus atte Styghel, Johannes de Pette, Walterus Spendelove, Johannes atte Neweboue de Syrle et Thomas atte Newebue manuceperunt predictum Robertum; et quod Johannes de Heygton', Rogerus de la Pette, Ricardus Pelliparius, Robertus Noreyc, Laurencius Ferle, Robertus de Hoghton' manuceperunt Johannem de Ferle; et quod Ricardus le Knyght est infirmus. Ideo de ipso sicut alias. Et quod Johannes le Daubur de Hastyng', Johannes filius Johannis clerici de eadem, Thomas filius Mabilie de eadem, Laurencius atte Watere de eadem, Willelmus le Fissere de Berham et Adam le Deckere de eadem manuceperunt Willelmum de Genesing'; et quod Johannes de Holindale, Robertus de Holindale, Henricus Redelere, Robertus Possere, Galfridus Skelkebrid et Gervasius le Mouner manuceperunt Willelmum de Holindale; et quod Brunyng le Lung de Ikelesham, Petrus Carpentarius de eadem, Johannes filius Roberti de eadem, Robertus de Broham de Gestling', Andreas le Carpenter de eadem et Ricardus de la Prok' de eadem manuceperunt Willelmum Geffray; et quod Ricardus le Coverur de Ikelesham, Robertus Ledelyn de eadem, Walterus le Kinngl' de eadem, Gilbertus Snoppe de Geseling', Batecok' Heved de eadem et Radulfus de Fonte de Pesemers manuceperunt Oliverum Heved; et quod Petrus de Hettlescumbe est infirmus; et quod Thomas atte Wode de Ruherefeld, Rogerus de Essendon', Thomas le Walays, Willelmus de Essesdon', Willelmus le Sperewe et Robertus de Essesdon' manuceperunt Rogerum le Waleys; et quod Ricardus atte Melle de Lutle Horsted, Johannes atte Don' de eadem manuceperunt Robertum de Worth'; et quod Robertus atte Mers et Johannes atte Mers manuceperunt Robertum atte Mers; et quod Galfridus le Bat de Bum' et Adam Melkenust de eadem manuceperunt Gilbertum de Boverington'; et quod Egidius de Lamport et Henricus Gunnyld manuceperunt Henricum de Lamport; et quod Ricardus de Glydewys de Burg' et Ricardus de Fonte Russ' manuceperunt Johannem de Papolesham; et quod Simon le Riche de Gestling' et Godefridus le Riche de eadem manuceperunt Hamonem de Stok'; et quod Simon de Sotyngton' et Galfridus de Parlington' manuceperunt Galfridum de Sotington'; et quod Robertus de Bochirse de Westfeld' et Rogerus de eadem manuceperunt Radulfum le Lung'; et quod Johannes le Clerk de Hurst et Willelmus atteFord de Hurst manuceperunt Johannem Russel, et quod Andreas de Eston' de Nyfeld et Thomas Sprot manuceperunt Johannem de Gotecumbe; et quod Robertus le Gerdelere de Brede et Robertus de Posterne de eadem manuceperunt Galfridum de Snottingheshill'; et quod Robertus de Glesye de Pesmers' et Walterus de Hetton' de eadem manuceperunt Simonem de Oxenbrug'; et quod Johannes de Tunstall' de Ikelesham et Adam de Lydyham de Brede manuceperunt Johannem de Bromham, quos non habuerunt. Ideo in misericordia.[30] Judicium, sicut alias, quod distringantur per terras etc., et quod habeat corpora eorum coram etc. in crastino Cinerum ad respondendum etc.

(291)

Norh'. Robertus de Brus et Hugo de Ryhale optulerunt se quarto die versus Mosseum filium Salomonis judeum de placito acquietacionis debiti. Et ipse non venit. Et preceptum fuit vicecomiti quod ipsum distringeret per terras etc., et quod haberet corpus ejus coram etc. Et vicecomes mandavit quod predictus Mosseus non habet terras neque catalla per que possit distringi; et quod corpus ejus est in prisona in castro Norht' pro diversis debitis in quibus Regi et Regine tenetur. Ideo preceptum est ei, sicut alias, a die Pasche in .xv. dies etc.

(292)

Cantebr'. Josceus filius Sauloti judeus, qui tulit breve de placito debiti super magistrum Petrum de Abendon', custodem domus scolarium de Merton', Nicholaum Moryz et alios in brevi, non est prosecutus. Ideo ipse judeus in misericordia.[31] Et predicti Petrus, Nicholaus et alii quantum ad hoc breve eant inde sine die.

(293)

Suth'. Jacobus Mawe attachiatus ad respondendum Regi et Sarre que fuit uxor Salomonis filii Belecote de placito detencionis catallorum. Et unde queritur quod, cum

[29] *The word* misericordia *is repeated in the margin.*

[30] *The word* misericordia *is repeated in the margin.*

[31] *The word* misericordia *is repeated in the margin.*

dictus Salomon vir ipsius Sarre esset in statu libere administracionis bonorum suorum antequem captus fuisset pro tonsura monete, tradidit dicto Jacobo .x. libras salvo custodiendas ad promocionem maritagii fil' dicti Salomonis, et cum dictus Salomon captus fuisset pro tonsura monete, precepit dicte Sarre uxori sue et Elkino fratri suo quod dictum Jacobum adducerent ad domum dicte Belcote et ei traderent bona sua in certo loco deposita in quadam puchea, ut in auro, argento et aliis jocalibus ad valenciam .xl. librarum, que ei per preceptum dicti Salomonis tradiderunt custodienda ad opus dicti Salomonis, Sarre et puerorum suorum et Abrahe filii Benedicti, qui partem inde habuit, ut in societate prius inter eos habita per recognicionem dicti Salomonis, et que bona et catalla de domo predicta [e]<Salamonis>[e] secum asportavit, et dicta Sarra post dampnacionem dicti Salomonis viri sui de jocalibus de diversis amicis suis propter inopiam suam ei datis tradidit eidem Jacobo salvo custodienda ad opus ejus quatuor zonas de serico cum argento barratas, .x. cocleara argentea, decem ciphos de mazero et unum tapetum de opere Wynt' precii .v. marcarum. Et predictis .x. libris et aliis jocalibus ad valenciam .xl. librarum et bonis et catallis suis post dampnacionem dicti Salomonis viri sui dicto Jacobo custodiendum traditis pro Rege et se petit hoc inquiri per christianos et judeos Wynton'.

Predictus Jacobus venit et defendit vim etc. quando etc. Et dicit quod de predictis .x. libris et aliis bonis et jocalibus ad valenciam .xl. librarum nec de bonis aliis, sicut versus eum narrat, nichil umquam recepit et de hoc ponit se super patriam. Et quod predicta bona et catalla ei tradita fuerunt custodienda, ut predictum est, predicta Sarra pro Rege et se similiter se ponit super patriam. Ideo preceptum est vicecomiti quod venire faciat coram etc. a die Pasche in tres septimanas sex probos et legales christanos et sex legales judeos de Wynt' ad recognoscendum etc. Et corpus predicti Jacobi interim committitur constabulario Turris etc.

MEMBRANE 4

Memoranda de termino sancti Hillarii. Anno viij°[32]

(294)

Lond'. Memorandum quod Nicholaus de Eketon' protulit coram etc. breve regis de magno sigillo patens in hec verba: 'Edwardus etc. omnibus ad quos presentes littere pervenerint salutem. Sciatis quod dedimus licenciam Mansero filio Aaron judeo Lond' vendendi Nicholao de Eketon' et Margerie uxori ejus quandam domum ipsius Manseri in vico de Bassingheshawe infra parochiam sancti Michaelis in civitate Lond', que quidem domus sita est inter terram dicti Nicholai que fuit quondam Hugonis le Noreys et domos Aaron filii Vyves judei, que eciam domus continet in longitudine .xxviij. ulnas, unum quarterium et sex pollices et in latitudine .iiij. ulnas et septem pollices et eciam .xvj. denariatas et obolatam annui redditus percipiendas de heredibus Willelmi de Manhale tanquam pertinentes ad domum predictam; et eciam quandam placeam in eodem vico simul cum muris lapideis super placeam illam sitis, que se extendit in latitudine inter terram que fuit quondam Sampsonis filii Abrahe de Hertf' in manu dicti Manseri nunc existentem et terram que fuit quondam Simonis le Fuster in manu prefati Nicholai existentem, que quidem placea continet .xxij. ulnas, unum quarterium et tres pollices versus stratam regis et in longitudine .xxvj. ulnas ad unum caput et ad aliud caput .xxix. ulnas simul cum quodam muro ibidem, qui se extendit versus boream, habendum et tenendum prefatis Nicholao et Margerie et heredibus et assignatis suis, prout in carta dicti Manseri prefatis Nicholao et Margerie inde confecta plenius continetur. Dedimus eciam licenciam prefatis Nicholao et Margerie predictos domum, placeam et muros cum pertinenciis a prefato Mansero emendi in forma predicta. In cujus rei testimonium has litteras nostras fieri fecimus patentes. Teste me ipso apud Westm' .xiij. die Novembris anno regni nostri septimo.'

Lond'. Idem Nicholaus per concessionem domini regis supradictam protulit cartam Manseri filii Aaron littera hebrayca signatam in hec verba: 'Sciant presentes et futuri quod ego Manserus filius Aaron judeus Lond' dedi, concessi et hac presenti carta mea confirmavi Nicholao de Eketon' civi Lond' et Margerie uxori sue pro quadam summa argenti quam mihi dederunt pre manibus in gersumam unam domum quam habui in parochia sancti Michaelis in Bassyeshawe sitam inter terram predicti Nicholai de Eketon' que fuit quondam Hugonis le Noreys et terram et domum Aaron filii Vyves, que continet in longitudine .xxviij. ulnas et quartam partem unius ulne et sex pollices versus orientem et in latitudine quatuor ulnas et septem pollices versus occidentem, una cum .xvj. denariatis et obulata annui et quieti redditus percipiendum ad quatuor anni terminos principales et consuetos de toto tenemento quod fuit quondam Willelmi de Manhale inter tenementum quod fuit quondam Maydengod de la Gyldhalle ex parte una et tenementum quod fuit quondam Ricardi Cissoris ex parte altera in supradicta parochia de Bassyeshawe, qui quidem redditus antedictus pertinet ad domum predictam. Dedi eciam predictis Nicholao et Margerie quandam placeam terre simul cum muris lapideis in illa placea sitis quam habui in eadem parochia, que continet in longitudine .xxvj. ulnas ad unum caput versus orientem et ad aliud caput .xxix. ulnas et extendit se in latitudine inter terram meam que fuit quondam Sampsonis [i]<filii Abrahe>[i] de Heref' et terram que fuit quondam Simonis Fuster que nunc est predicti Nicholai de Eketon' et continet .xxij. ulnas et quartem partem unius ulne et tres pollices versus regiam viam. Et bene licebit predictis Nicholao et Margerie et heredibus suis et assignatis ad ponendum corbellas in longo super murum qui est inter me predictum Manserum et ipsum

[32] *On the left hand side above the heading is the letter* h.

Nicholaum et ad edificandum super illum murum in longitudine .xij. ulnarum, excepto quod predicti Nicholaus et Margeria nec heredes sui nec assignati sui in muro illo detrimentum facere possint nec debent. Licebit eciam predictis Nicholao et Margerie et eorum heredibus et assignatis edificare versus partem suam super quendam murum lapideum juxta forinsecam meam cameram, qui quidem murus extendit se versus aquilonem et continet in latitudine tres ulnas et quartam partem unius ulne. Nec licebit mihi predicto Mansero nec heredibus meis nec assignatis nec eciam predictis Nicholao et Margerie nec eorum heredibus nec assignatis murum illum prostenere nec abradicare sine amborum nostrum consensu et assensu seu heredum nostrorum seu assignatorum; habendum et tenendum de me et heredibus meis vel meis assignatis predictis Nicholao et Margerie et heredibus suis et suis assignatis cuicumque seu quibuscumque et quandocumque dare, vendere vel legare vel assignare voluerint, libere, quiete, bene et integre, jure hereditario et in pace inperpetuum, reddendo inde annuatim capitalibus dominis feodi illius .xj. denarios terminis statutis et mihi et heredibus meis vel meis assignatis unum denarium ad Pascha pro omnibus serviciis, consuetudinibus et omnimodis aliis secularibus exaccionibus et demandis. Et ego predictus Manserus et heredes mei et assignati predictis Nicholao et Margerie et heredibus suis et assignatis predictam domum et predictum redditum et predictam placeam terre cum tota sua longitudine et latitudine simul cum muris predictis pro predicto servicio contra omnes gentes tam christianos quam judeos warantizabunt, acquietabunt et defendent inperpetuum. Et ut hec mea donacio concessio et presentis carte mee confirmacio stabilis et rata inperpetuum permaneat presentem cartam littera hebrayca signavi. Hiis testibus dominis H. Houteyn et R. de Ludham tunc justiciariis judeorum, Gregorio de Rokel' tunc majore Lond', Johanne Skyp et Roberto Herun cyrographariis arche cyrographariorum Lond', Willelmo Gratefyge, Nicholao le Gerdelere; Adam Cissore.'

(295)[33]

Norff'. Hugo Hothed venit coram etc. et recognovit se debere Roberto de Ludham .xl. solidos reddendum a die sancti Michaelis proximo futuro in .xv. dies. Et, nisi fecerit, concedit quod de terris et catallis suis fiant.

(296)

Surr', Sussex'. Willelmus de Hastyng' venit coram etc. et recognovit se debere Aaron filio Vyves .xiiij. marcas reddendum a die Pasche proximo futuro in .xv. dies. Et, nisi fecerit, concedit quod de bonis et catallis suis fiant.

(297)

Essex'. Thomas de Belhus venit coram etc. et recognovit se debere Aaron filio Vyves .xlv. libras, reddendum a die Pasche proximo futuro in .xv. dies .xv. libras et a die sancti Michaelis proximo sequenti in .xv. dies .xv. libras et a die Purificacionis beate Marie proximo sequenti in .xv. dies .x. libras et ad quindenam Pasche proximo sequentem .c. solidos. Et, nisi fecerit, concedit quod de terris et catallis suis fiant.

(298)[34]

Cantebr'. Willelmus de Royng' miles venit coram etc. et recognovit se debere Aaron filio Vyves .xij. marcas reddendum ei die Jovis proxima post Purificacionem beate Marie anno regis Edwardi .viij. Et, nisi fecerit, concedit quod de terris et catallis suis fiant.

(299)[35]

Cantebr'. Willelmus de Caam venit coram etc. et recognovit se debere Aaron filio Vyves .c. solidos reddendum ei .l. solidos ad Pentecosten anno regis Edwardi .viij. et .l. solidos ad festum Omnium Sanctorum proximo sequens. Et, nisi fecerit, concedit quod de terris et catallis suis fiant.

(300)[36]

Norff'. Willelmus filius Alexandri le Moygne venit coram etc. et recognovit se debere Aaron filio Vyves .lx. quarteria frumenti reddendum ad festum sancti Michaelis anno regis Edwardi .viij.^{o} vel pro quolibet quarterio dimidiam marcam ad eleccionem ipsius judei, prout continetur in quodam scripto obligatorio inter eos inde confecto. Et, nisi fecerit, concedit quod de terris et catallis suis fiant.

(301)

Surr'. Willelmus le Keu de Suthwerk' venit coram etc. et recognovit se debere Isac de Suthwerk' .iiij. marcas, reddendum inde .ij. marcas in crastino Cinerum proximo futuro, et .ij. marcas a die Pasche proximo sequenti in .xv. dies. Et, nisi fecerit, concedit quod de terris et catallis suis fiant.

(302)

Cant'. Willelmus de Stowe venit coram etc. et recognovit se debere Aaron filio Vyves .iiij.^{xx} marcas, reddendum ad terminos subscriptos, videlicet .xx. marcas a die Pasche proximo futuro in tres septimanas et .xx. marcas a die sancti Michaelis proximo sequenti in tres septimanas et .xx. marcas a die Purificacionis beate Marie proximo sequenti in .xv. dies et .xx. marcas a die Pasche proximo post in tres septimanas etc. Et, nisi etc.

(303)

Wilt'. Willelmus Paynel filius Willelmi Paynel venit coram etc. et recognovit se debere Aaron filio Vyves .xx.

[33] *This and the following two entries are marked for deletion with the note* quia alibi supra. *See below, nos. 358-60.*

[34] *This entry is also duplicated on m. 7d (see no. 361) but is not marked for deletion.*

[35] *This entry is also duplicated on m. 7d (see no. 362) but is not marked for deletion.*

[36] *This entry is marked for deletion with the words* vacat quia alibi. *See below no. 363.*

quarteria frumenti reddenda ei in septimana Pentecosten proximo futura vel pro quolibet quarterio dimidiam marcam ad eleccionem ipsius judei, sicut continetur in quodam scripto obligatorio inter eos inde confecto. Et, nisi fecerit, concedit quod de terris et catallis suis fiant.

(304)

Derb'. Urianus de Sancto Petro venit coram etc. et recognovit se debere Gamalieli de Oxon' judeo .xx. marcas, reddendum ei inde .x. marcas ad quindenam Pasche proximo futuram et .x. marcas ad quindenam sancti Johannis proximo sequentem. Et, nisi fecerit, concedit quod de terris et catallis suis fiant. Concedit eciam quod, si primum terminum predicte solucionis non observaverit, quod distringatur pro toto debito .xx. marcarum.

(305)

Essex'. Edmundus de Fulham venit coram etc. et recognovit se debere Henrico le Blund .xl. marcas eo quod sororem suam ducit in uxorem, reddendum inde a die Pasche proximo futuro in xv dies .v. marcas, et a die sancti Johannis Baptiste proximo sequenti in .xv. dies .v. marcas et a die sancti Michaelis in .xv. dies anno regni regis Edwardi nono .x. marcas et a die sancti Michaelis proximo sequenti in .xv. dies .x. marcas, et sic de anno in annum ad eundem terminum .x. marcas quousque etc. Et, nisi fecerit, concedit quod de terris et catallis suis fiant.

MEMBRANE 4 DORSE

(306)

Bed'. Nicholaus Passelewe, a quo exiguntur quinque marce ad opus Regis de debitis Leonis filii Jurnini de Norwyc' defuncti, per magistrum Simonem de Bed' attornatum suum venit coram etc., et dicit quod predictus judeus totum predictum debitum v. marcarum sibi perdonavit pro .ij. marcis, si eas solveret ante Natale Domini anno regis Edwardi tercio, et inde debuit ei fecisse bonum starrum acquietancie. Et hoc petit verificare per christianos et judeos. Et quia constat justiciariis etc. quod prefatus Nicholaus solvit in recepta regis .ij. marcas de dicto debito .v. marcarum termino predicto, de residuis .iij. marcis volentes certificari fecerunt venire coram eis Johannem Currey, Laurencium le Saer et alios christianos, Manserum le Pape, Eliam de Cornhull' et alios judeos, sicut patet inter brevia hujus termini retornata. Qui dicunt super sacramentum suum quod predictus Leo perdonavit tempore quo habuit liberam administracionem bonorum suorum prefato Nicholao dictum debitum .v. marcarum pro .ij. marcis solvendis ad Natale Domini anno supradicto, et quod eas liberavit in recepta regis, ut predictum est, et quod ei fecisse debuit bonum starrum de acquietancia dicti debiti pro predictis .ij. marcis. Ideo consideratum est quod dicta carta .v. marcarum predicto Nicholao liberetur quiete dampnanda in hec verba. 'Nicholaus Passelewe debet Leoni filio Jurnini judeo de Norwyco .v. marcas argenti reddendas ad diem sancti Hillarii anno regni regis Edwardi tercio. Acta die veneris proxima ante festum sancti Michaelis anno regis Edwardi secundo.' Que carta liberatur predicto Nicholao in pleno scaccario quiete dampnanda.

(307)

Derb'. Robertus de Perers, a quo exiguntur .xxxviij. libre ad opus Regis de debitis Joscei filii Bonefey judei Linc', tulit breve regis de magno sigillo in hec verba: 'Edwardus etc. justiciariis suis etc. salutem. Ex parte Roberti de Perers nobis est ostensum quod, cum ipse dudum Josceo filio Bonef' judeo Linc' obligatus fuisset in .xxxviij. libris per cartam suam que est in thesauro nostro ac idem judeus magnam partem dicti debiti de bonis et catallis ipsius Roberti per varias districciones super eum ea occasione factas levari fecerit, vos nichilominus eundem Robertum pro toto predicto debito distringi faciatis minus juste in ipsius Roberti dispendium non modicum et gravamen. Et quia predictum Robertum indebite pregravari nolumus in hac parte, vobis mandamus quod, inquisita super hoc modis omnibus quibus convenit plenius veritate, si vobis constare poterit legitime ita esse, tunc id quod in partem solucionis dicti debiti de terris et catallis prefati Roberti per predictum judeum levatum fuisse et nobis vel prefato judeo solutum esse inveneritis eidem Roberto in solucionem ejusdem debiti allocari et ei de residuo debiti illius solvendo racionabiles terminos juxta discrecionem vestram assignari faciatis. Teste me ipso apud Wynt' .vij. die Januarii anno regni nostri .viij.º' Et per hoc breve preceptum fuit vicecomiti Derb' quod per sacramentum etc. diligenter inquireret quantum ad opus dicti Joscei occasione predicti debiti .xxxviij. librarum in quibus predictus Robertus ei tenebatur de bonis et catallis ipsius Roberti levatum fuerit. Et vicecomes mandavit quod inquiri fecit in pleno comitatu coram eo per sacramentum Nicholai de Coveland', Johannis filii Simonis de Foston', Willelmi Wildegos de eadem, Walteri Achehard de eadem, Johannis Wace de Matkelay, Johannis Fucher de Bentelay, Thome de Ibole de eadem, Johannis Morel de Sutton', Roberti fratris ejus, Willelmi de Coveland', Ricardi de la Sale de Wyardeston' et Willelmi Brown de Boliston'. Qui dicunt super sacramentum suum quod ad opus dicti Joscei occasione dicti debiti .xxxviij. librarum per varias districciones levatum fuit de bonis et catallis predicti Roberti, videlicet de .xx. baconibus .lx. solidi, de .xvj. bobus .viij. libre, de una vacca .viij. solidi, de .xj. quarteriis et tribus bussellis frumenti .xlvij. solidi, de uno tasso pisarum .c. solidi, de uno tasso frumenti .iiij. libre, de uno tasso avene .xl. solidi et de bosco dicti Roberti vendito .xiij. libre .xvj. solidi .viij. d. Summa .xxxviij. libre .xx. denarii. Ideo per predictum mandatum et per inquisicionem inde captam, consideratum est quod predictus Robertus de predicto debito .xxxviij. librarum sit quietus. Que carta in thesauro regis inter cartas de magno tallagio inventa fuit in hec verba. 'Robertus de Perers miles debet Josceo filio

Bonefey judeo .xxxviij. libras reddendas ad octabas sancti Michaelis anno regis Henrici filii regis Johannis .xlvij. Acta die mercurii proxima ante festum sancti Barnabe apostoli anno eodem' et que carta liberata est eidem Roberto in pleno scaccario quiete dampnanda.[37]

MEMBRANE 5

Memoranda de termino sancti Hillarii anno regni regis Edwardi octavo

(308)

Kanc'. Preceptum fuit vicecomiti quod de terris[38] et catallis Roberti filii Ricardi de Shetingden' levari faceret ad opus Regis .xx. libras quas Regi debet de debitis <Joscei filii Salle,>[39] et denarios illos haberet coram etc. in octabis sancti Hillarii, vel corpus ejus ad ostendendum etc. Et vicecomes mandavit quod breve adeo tarde venit quod exequi non potuit. Ideo, sicut alias, in crastino Cinerum etc.

(309)

Kanc'. Preceptum fuit vicecomiti quod distringeret tenentes terrarum Stephani de Cresy ad reddendum sibi ad opus Regis .ccl. libras quas Regi debent occasione terrarum etc. de debitis Hagini filii magistri Mossei et Vyves fratris ejus, et denarios illos haberet coram etc. in octabis sancti Hillarii vel corpora tenencium ad ostendendum etc. Et vicecomes mandavit quod Rogerus de Northwode et Johannes episcopus Roff' sunt tenentes <predictarum terrarum>[40] [in comitatu predicto, quos invenit coram][41] etc. Et quia rex contulit Alianore Regine [Anglie][42] consorti sue omnia <debita>[43] predicti Hagini [que sunt in custodia Walteri de Kanc' custodis auri dicte regine][44] etc.

(310)

Kanc'. Preceptum fuit vicecomiti quod de terris et catallis Nicholai filii Bernardi fieri faceret ad opus Regis .xiij. libras quas Regi debet de debitis Aaron filii Joscei, ita quod denarios haberet coram etc. in octabis sancti Hillarii nunc vel corpus [predicti Nicholai ad ostendendum][45] etc. Et vicecomes mandavit quod breve adeo tarde venit quod exequi non potuit. Ideo, sicut alias, in crastino Cinerum etc.

(311)

Cantebr'. Preceptum fuit vicecomiti quod de terris et catallis Johannis Auvrey fieri faceret ad opus Regis .c. solidos quos Regi debet de debitis Mossei filii Jacobi, et denarios haberet coram etc. in octabis sancti Hillarii nunc vel corpus [predicti Johannis ad ostendendum][46] etc. Et vicecomes mandavit quod retornavit breve inde sibi directum ballivis libertatis Cantebr', qui nichil inde fecerunt. Judicium quod non omittat propter libertatem etc. quin eam [et de terris etc. levari faciat predictos .c. solidos, et eos habeat coram][47] etc. in crastino Cynerum etc.

(312)

Cantebr'. Preceptum fuit vicecomiti quod de terris tenencium terras Johannis le Rus <fieri>[48] faceret ad opus Regis .viij. libras quas Regi debent occasione [terrarum][49] etc. de debitis Mossei filii Isac, et denarios illos haberet coram etc. in octabis sancti Hillarii nunc vel corpora [predictorum tenencium ad ostendendum][50] etc. Et vicecomes mandavit quod retornavit breve inde sibi directum ballivis libertatis Cant', qui nichil inde responderunt. Judicium quod non omittat propter libertatem etc. quin eam etc. [et deferat etc.][51] in crastino Cinerum etc.

(313)

Ebor'. Preceptum fuit vicecomiti quod venire faceret coram etc. in octabis sancti Hillarii .xij. probos et legales homines de civitate Ebor' et .xij. legales judeos de eadem civitate ad recognoscendum etc. que bona et catalla Josceus le Joefne nepos Aaron habuit etc., ut in auro etc. Et vicecomes mandavit ballivis <Ebor'>[52] pro christianis, qui nichil inde fecerunt. Judicium quod non omittat propter libertatem etc. quin eam etc. [et venire faciat etc.][53] a die Pasche in .xv. dies etc. Et vicecomes mandavit quod Bonamicus gener Joscei, Josceus filius Bonamy, Deudone Crespin, Benedictus Crespyn, Isac le Evesk, Deudone le Fort, Mosseus de Colton', Leo de Scardeburg', Mosseus filius Bonefey et Isac filius Bonefey districti sunt ad veniendum ad diem in brevi contentum et quilibet eorum manucepit alium essendi ad diem in brevi contentum, et quod non sunt plures judei manentes in civitate Ebor'. Et nullus eorum venit. Ideo in misericordia.[54] Et preceptum est, sicut alias, a die Pasche in .xv. dies etc.

[37] *There follows an unfinished but uncancelled second version of no. 268 (down to the word* Chelwarton).

[38] *65 adds* redditibus.

[39] Salle filii Joscei judei *65*.

[40] terrarum predicti Stephani *65*.

[41] *Supplied from 65*.

[42] *Supplied from 65*.

[43] Bona et catalla *65*.

[44] *Supplied from 65*.

[45] *Supplied from 65*.

[46] *Supplied from 65*.

[47] *Supplied from 65*.

[48] levare *65*.

[49] *Supplied from 65*.

[50] *Supplied from 65*.

[51] *Supplied from 65*.

[52] predicte civitatis, scilicet Nicholaus de Seleby et Petrus de Saunton *65*.

[53] *Supplied from 65*.

[54] *The word* misericordia *is repeated in the margin.*

(314)

Heref'. Preceptum fuit vicecomiti quod distringeret Willelmum de Sholle, filium Willelmi de Sholle, per terras etc. ad reddendum sibi ad opus Regis .v. marcas [quos Regi debet occasione terrarum etc.][55] de debitis Sampsonis filii Isac, et denarios haberet coram etc. [in octabis sancti Hillarii][56] vel corpus [predicti Willelmi ad ostendendum acquietanciam][57] etc. Et vicecomes mandavit quod Adam de Malverne et Adam de Houeton' manuceperunt predictum Willelmum, quem non habuerunt. Ideo in misericordia.[58] Ideo [preceptum est ei,][59] sicut alias, a die Pasche in .xv. dies etc.

(315)

Warr'. Preceptum fuit vicecomiti quod de terris et catallis Henrici de Benygton' <fieri>[60] faceret ad opus regis .xxx. libras [quas Regi debet][61] de debitis Cressei filii magistri Elie; <et>[62] quod denarios [illos][63] haberet coram etc. in octabis sancti Hillarii nunc vel corpus [predicti Henrici ad ostendendum][64] etc. Et vicecomes mandavit quod dictus Henricus mortuus est et quod dictus Cresseus habuit seisinam medietatis terrarum predicti Henrici tempore quo ambo vixerunt per breve regis de extenta et partem suam tradidit hominibus predicte ville de Benygton', set si ad campi partem vel ad firmam hoc ignorat. Ideo preceptum est quod distringat predictos tenentes etc. pro predictis .xxx. libris, ita quod eas habeat coram etc. in crastino Cinerum etc.

(316)

Warr'. Preceptum fuit vicecomiti quod distringeret Robertum de Westcote ad reddendum sibi ad opus Regis .xx. marcas [quas Regi debet][65] de debitis Isac de Kaune, ita quod denarios haberet coram etc. <in <quindena>[66] sancti Hillarii vel corpus etc.>[67] Et vicecomes mandavit quod Radulfus de <Underwalle>[68] de Rokeby, Henricus Strery de eadem, Johannes filius Petri et Ranulfus filius Roberti manuceperunt predictum Robertum, quem non habuerunt. Ideo in misericordia.[69] Judicium, sicut <alias,>[70] a die Pasche in .xv. dies etc.

(317)

Linc'. Preceptum fuit vicecomiti, sicut pluries, quod distringeret tenentes terrarum Henrici Fusedame pro decem libris <ad opus Regis>[71] de debitis Isac de Suthwerk', et denarios haberet coram etc. ad hunc diem, vel corpora tenencium etc. Et vicecomes mandavit quod non potuit inquirere postquam breve sibi venit quod dictus Henricus umquam habuit terras in comitatu predicto nec qui debent esse tenentes [terrarum][72] predicti Henrici. [Et quia testatum est quod predictus Henricus habuit terras in Staunford', ideo preceptum est ei, sicut pluries, ... in crastino Cinerum etc.][73]

(318)

Surr', Sussex'. Preceptum fuit vicecomiti quod distringeret tenentes terrarum Henrici Jukel' pro .ij. marcis ad opus Regis de debitis Isac de Suthwerk'. Et vicecomes mandavit quod retornavit breve inde sibi directum ballivis libertatis archiepiscopi Cantuar', qui nichil inde <fecerunt.>[74] Et preceptum fuit ei quod distringeret tenentes terrarum Normanni de Suthwerk' pro .xl. solidis, et quod distringeret tenentes terrarum que fuerunt Roberti le Duk', ut supra, pro .xl. solidis. Et vicecomes mandavit quod retornavit breve ballivis libertatis predicte, qui nichil inde fecerunt. Et quod distringeret tenentes terrarum Thome Haunsard et Thome Harme pro .l. solidis. Et Thomas Harme venit coram etc. et recognovit se esse tenentem cujusdam partis terrarum predicte Thome, et dicit quod Johannes de Walington' tenet quandam partem predictarum terrarum et petit breve per auxilium curie ad faciendum predictum Johannem respondere cum [i]<eo de>[i] de predicto debito, et habet diem in crastino Cinerum. Et preceptum fuit vicecomiti quod distringeret Radulfum le Pelee, ut supra, tenentem quandam partem terrarum que fuerunt Galfridi Norman, pro .lx. solidis. Et vicecomes mandavit quod retornavit breve ballivis libertatis predicte, qui nichil inde fecerunt. Et quod distringeret priorem de Bermund', tenentem quandam partem terrarum que fuerunt Thome le Provost, pro .xxviij. solidis. Et vicecomes mandavit quod Johannes de Renham de Retherhethe, Adam filius Murielle de eadem, David de Balgham et Willelmus de ecclesia de eadem manuceperunt predictum priorem, quem non habuerunt. Ideo in misericordia. Et preceptum fuit ei quod non omitteret propter libertatem de Guldeford' quin eam etc. et distringeret tenentes terrarum que fuerunt Sweyn' le Chaloner pro .xx. solidis. Et vicecomes mandavit quod Walterus de Purbyk', subballivus Regine matris, habet de catallis predicti Sweyn' quatuor tapeta precii .x. solidorum et non permittit predicta tapeta extra libertatem predictam removeri. Judicium quod non omittat propter libertates predictas quin eas etc. et distringat predictos tenentes pro predictis debitis. Et quod distringat priorem de Bermund' per terras etc., ita quod denarios habeat coram etc. in crastino Cinerum etc.

55 *Supplied from 65.* 56 *Supplied from 65.*
57 *Supplied from 65.*
58 *The word* misericordia *is repeated in the margin. 65 adds here* Et mandavit quod breve sibi venit in vigilia sancti Hillarii et adeo tarde quod ulterius exequi non potuit.
59 *Supplied from 65.* 60 levari *65.* 61 *Supplied from 65.*
62 ita *65.* 63 *Supplied from 65.* 64 *Supplied from 65.*
65 *Supplied from 65.*
66 *Interlined above* octabis *which is marked for deletion.*
67 a die sancti Hillarii in .xv. dies vel corpus predicti Roberti ad ostendendum acquietanciam *65.*
68 Wnderwalle *65.*
69 *The word* misericordia *is repeated in the margin.*
70 pluries *65.*

71 quas Regi debet *65.*
72 *Supplied from 65.*
73 *Supplied from 65.*
74 responderunt *65.*

(319)

Surr', Sussex'. Prior de Reygate, de quo exiguntur .iiij. libre ad opus Regis de debitis Isac de Suthwerk' occasione terrarum etc. que fuerunt Johannis Patrik' de Pollesdon', optulit se quarto die versus Willelmum Herbert de Aylevehagth' et priorem de Merton', tenentes quandam partem terrarum que fuerunt predicti Johannis, de placito debiti occasione predictarum terrarum etc. Et ipsi non venerunt. Et preceptum fuit vicecomiti quod ipsos venire faceret ad hunc diem. Et vicecomes mandavit quod Gilbertus Herbert de Berkyng' et Johannes le Fughelere de eadem manuceperunt predictum Willelmum; et quod Willelmus de Aylevehagth' de Vecham et Robertus filius Hugonis de eadem manuceperunt Osbertum de Aylevehagth'; et quod Baro prepositus de Becham et Willelmus atte Playhull' manuceperunt priorem de Merton', quos non habuerunt. Ideo in misericordia.[75] Judicium quod distringantur per terras etc., ita quod nec ipsi etc., et quod de exitibus etc. et quod habeat corpora eorum coram etc. in crastino Cinerum ad respondendum etc. et ad audiendum etc.

(320)

Linc'. Preceptum fuit vicecomiti quod distringeret priorem de Spaldyng' et alios tenentes terrarum que fuerunt Johannis de Fulney pro .xxviij. libris ad opus Regis de debitis Abrahe filii Murielle [judei,][76] et quod denarios haberet coram etc. in quindena sancti Hillarii vel corpora etc. Et predictus prior per attornatum suum venit et dicit plures esse tenentes terrarum predicti Johannis, vicelicet Walterus Godard, Alanus rector ecclesie de <Shipsey,>[77] Robertus filius Johannis de Fulney miles et Thomas frater ejus. Et petit breve ad faciendum ipsos venire ad respondendum secum de predicto debito, et concessum est ei, ita quod sumptibus propriis pro Rege et pro se etc. ipsos prosequatur.

(321)[78]

Oxon'. Communitas judeorum Oxon' dat Regi .j. marcam pro habendo brevi quod vicecomes eos manuteneat etc.

(322)

Linc'. Preceptum fuit vicecomiti quod non omitteret propter libertatem Lancastr' quin eam etc. et distringeret tenentes terrarum que fuerunt magistri Thome de Quappelade ad reddendum sibi ad opus Regis .xlvj. libras, quas Regi debent occasione terrarum etc. de debitis Abrahe filii Murielle, et quod denarios haberet ad hunc diem. Et vicecomes mandavit quod breve adeo tarde venit quod exequi non potuit. Ideo, sicut alias, a die Pasche in .xv. dies etc.

[75] *The word* misericordia *is repeated in the margin.*

[76] *Supplied from 65.*

[77] Schybseye *65.*

[78] *Cf. no. 345.*

(323)

Derb'. Urianus de sancto Petro venit coram etc. et recognovit se debere domine Regine consorti domini Regis nunc .iiij.^{xx} marcas pro acquietacione .ij. debitorum .c. librarum sub nominibus Willelmi filii Willelmi de Meysham militis et Gamalielis de Oxon' judei que fuerunt in manus ipsius Regine per predictum Gamaielem, quas .iiij.^{xx} marcas idem Urianus solvet eidem Regine ad terminos subscriptos, videlicet ad quindenam Pasche proximo futuram .xx. marcas, et ad quindenam sancti Johannis proximo sequentem .xx. marcas, et ad quindenam sancti Michaelis proximo sequentem .xl. marcas. Et, nisi fecerit, concedit quod de terris et catallis suis fiant.

MEMBRANE 5 DORSE[79]

(324)

Cantebr'. Hugo Saunzaver, Willelmus le Kepere, Johanna uxor ejus et Robertus Aylwyne, qui vocaverunt dictum Hugonem ad warantum de porcionibus ipsos contingentibus de quodam debito .c. marcarum et .xx. librarum annui feodi in quibus Ivo Quarel tenebatur Hagino filio magistri Mossei judeo et quod quidem debitum dictus Haginus vendidit et dimisit Rogero de Leyburn' et quas porciones [de debito ipsos contingentes occasione terrarum etc.][80] Willelmus de Leyburn', filius et heres dicti Rogeri, per Thomam Bakun attornatum suum ab eis exigit, et Willelmus Gorge, Richolda uxor ejus et Christiana de Mauns, tenentes <quandam partem earundem>[81] terrarum <etc.,>[82] concordati sunt sub hac forma, videlicet quod predicti Willelmus et alii dabunt predicto Hugoni quatuor marcas reddendas ad festum sancti Michaelis anno regis .E. .viij^{o}. Et Willelmus le Kepere et Robertus Aylwyne pro se et heredibus suis et pro Willelmo Gorge et Richolda uxor ejus et Christiana de Mauns recognoverunt se debere satisfacere de dictis .iiij.^{or} marcis ad dictum terminum. Et pro predictis quatuor marcis predictus Hugo Saunzaver predictos Willelmum, Johannam, Robertum, Willelmum, Richoldam et Christianam et heredes suos versus predictum Willelmum de Leyburn' et Thomam Bakun attornatum suum penitus defendere et acquietare tenetur de porcionibus dicti debiti ipsos occasione terrarum <etc.>[83] contingentibus etc.

(325)

Wyltes'. Preceptum fuit vicecomiti quod venire faceret Johannem de Haveryng' quondam vicecomitem Sutht' ad respondendum de diversis debitis Judaismum

[79] *There is a letter* h *at the top of this membrane but no general heading.*

[80] *Supplied from 65.*

[81] quasdam partes predictarum *65.*

[82] a quibus dictus Thomas tanquam attornatus dicti Willelmi peciit porciones dicti debiti ipsos contingentes *65.*

[83] quas tenent que fuerunt predicti Ivonis ipsos *65.*

tangentibus de quibus respondisse debuerat tempore que fuit vicecomes comitatus predicti. Et vicecomes mandavit quod retornavit breve ballivis libertatis de Kynewarston', qui nichil inde fecerunt. Judicium quod non omittat propter libertatem etc. quin eam etc. et venire faciat etc. a die Pasche in .xv. dies ad computandum etc.

(326)

Oxon, Berk'. Preceptum fuit vicecomiti quod non omitteret propter libertatem de Rading' quin eam etc. et distringeret Simonem filium Nicholai de Chausey per terras etc. ad reddendum Regi octo marcas de debitis Isak de Kaune judei. Et vicecomes mandavit quod <Isac>[84] de Blaybir' et Willelmus le Provost de Chauseye manuceperunt predictum Simonem, quem non habuerunt. Ideo in misericordia.[85] Et quod distringeret Walterum Sachel de Radyng', ut supra, pro .x. libris. Et vicecomes mandavit quod Ricardus de Wytel' et Henricus Godding' manuceperunt predictum Walterum, quem non habuerunt. Ideo in misericordia.[86] Et quod distringeret tenentes terrarum que fuerunt Walteri de Flexeney pro <.xxxj.>[87] solidis. Et vicecomes mandavit quod retornavit breve [sibi inde directum][88] ballivis libertatis de Bampton', qui nichil inde fecerunt. Judicium quod non omittat etc., et distringat predictos Simonem, Walterum et tenentes <etc.>[89] Et habeat coram etc.

(327)

Kanc'. Preceptum fuit vicecomiti quod, nisi Robertus de Totyngden reddat Aaron filio Vyves judeo vel ejus nuncio .xx. libras quas ei debet per cyrographum .xx. librarum, unde altera pars est in archa [cyrographariorum][90] Lond', quod appreciari faceret omnia catalla ipsius Roberti [mobilia ad satisfaciendum de medietate catallorum predicto judeo;][91] et, si <catalla>[92] non sufficerent, [quod extendi faceret omnes terras et tenementa ipsius Roberti, salvo capitali mesuagio suo et servicio dominorum feodi, ut idem judeus medietatem terrarum et tenementorum habere possit pro debitis etc.][93] Et vicecomes mandavit quod catalla <ipsius Roberti appreciata fuerunt>[94] ad .xij. solidos et terre <etc. salvo>[95] etc. extenduntur ad .vj. solidos .ij. denarios obulum. Et preceptum est vicecomiti quod habere faciat eidem judeo seisinam medietatis terrarum [et tenementorum predictorum ut habere possit etc., salvo capitali mesuagio,][96] donec [inde debitum perceperit][97] etc.>[98]

(328)

Kanc'. Preceptum est vicecomiti quod habere faciat Mansero filio Ursi judeo vel ejus nuncio seisinam medietatis terrarum etc. Laurencii filii Gilberti Unwyn', salvo capitali mesuagio etc., que extenduntur ad .xxiiij. solidos, sicut patet inter inquisiciones hujus termini retornatas, pro .xl. solidis quos dictus Manserus a dicto Laurencio exigit per cyrographum .xl. solidorum, unde altera pars est in archa cyrographariorum apud Lond', ut dicitur, et ipsum [judeum][99] in seisinam [custodiat etc.][100]

(329)

Ebor'. Preceptum fuit vicecomiti quod de terris, [redditibus][101] et catallis Roberti de Wileby <fieri>[102] faceret ad opus Regis .xvj. libras [quos Regi debet][103] de debitis Joscei nepotis Aaron, et denarios illos haberet coram [etc.][104] in octabis sancti Hillarii nunc vel corpus [predicti Roberti ad ostendendum][105] etc. Et vicecomes mandavit quod breve [sibi inde directum][106] adeo tarde venit quod exequi non potuit. Ideo, sicut alias, a die Pasche in .xv. dies.

(330)

Linc'. Preceptum fuit vicecomiti quod de terris <etc.>[107] Roberti de Wileby fieri faceret ad opus Regis .xxiiij. libras [quas Regi debet][108] de debitis Joscei nepotis Aaron, et denarios haberet coram etc. in octabis sancti Hillarii vel corpus [predicti Roberti ad ostendendum][109] etc. Et vicecomes mandavit quod breve adeo tarde venit quod exequi non potuit. Ideo, sicut alias, a die Pasche in .xv. dies etc.

(331)

Heref'. Preceptum fuit cyrographariis christianis et judeis arche cyrographariorum Heref' quod ad archam predictam accederent et ab ea extraherent unam cartam .v. marcarum sub nominibus Johannis filii Willelmi Aubyn et Benedicti le <Eskermisur>[110] judei et eam haberent coram etc. a die sancti Hillarii in .xv. dies nunc. Et cyrographarii mandaverunt quod dicta archa signata fuit sigillo Walteri de Helyun, ita quod ad hunc diem nichil fieri potuit. Ideo, sicut alias, a die Pasche in .xv. dies.

84 *MS. reads* Willelmus.
85 *The word* misericordia *is repeated in the margin.*
86 *The word* misericordia *is repeated in the margin.*
87 .xxx. *65*.
88 *Supplied from 65*.
89 terrarum predicti Walteri de Flexeney ad reddendum sibi denarios supradictos *65*.
90 *Supplied from 65*.
91 *Supplied from 65. 34 has only* etc.
92 *65 omits.*
93 *Supplied from 65. 34 reads* etc. tunc extendi faceret terras etc.
94 sua mobilia appreciantur *65*.
95 redditus et tenementa, salvo capitali mesuagio suo *65*.
96 *Supplied from 65; 34 reads* etc.
97 *Supplied from 65*.
98 et tenementorum predictorum habere possit etc. salvo capitali mesuagio etc. donec inde debitum perceperit *65*.
99 *Supplied from 65*.
100 *Supplied from 65*.
101 *Supplied from 65*.
102 levare *65*.
103 *Supplied from 65*.
104 *Supplied from 65*.
105 *Supplied from 65*.
106 *Supplied from 65*.
107 et catallis *65*.
108 *Supplied from 65*.
109 *Supplied from 65*.
110 Eskermysur *65*.

(332)

Somers'. Rogerus de <Kynt',>[111] serviens [de scaccario][112] etc., optulit se quarto die versus Johannem de Asselegh' de placito debiti. [i]<Et ipse non venit.>[i] Et preceptum fuit vicecomiti, sicut pluries, quod ipsum venire faceret. Et vicecomes mandavit quod dictus Johannes non manet in balliva sua nec habet terras vel tenementa unde possit distringi. Et pluries testificatum est quod dictus Johannes habet terras et catalla in [villa de][113] Weston' [in balliva sua.][114] Ideo, sicut pluries, a die Pasche in .xv. dies ad respondendum etc.

(333)

Somers'. Preceptum fuit vicecomiti quod distringeret Ricardum Bisshop per terras etc. et quod haberet corpus ejus coram etc. [ad hunc diem][115] ad respondendum Regi de falsitate cujusdam brevis in decepcionem curie regis impetrati ad auferendum .xx. libras de manibus Regis per quandam falsam inquisicionem per ipsum Ricardum impetratam. Et ipse non venit. Et vicecomes mandavit quod Hugo de la Brok' de Somerton', Nicholaus Syward de eadem, Walterus de la Wythe de eadem, Nicholaus de la Brok' de eadem, Ricardus Lovewyne et Durandus le Gardiner de eadem manuceperunt predictum Ricardum, quem non habuerunt. Ideo in misericordia.[116] Judicium, sicut alias, quod distringatur per terras etc., <ita quod habeat corpus ejus coram etc.>[117] a die Pasche in .xv. dies ad respondendum etc.

(334)

Surr'. Ricardus Sweyn de Guldeford' venit coram etc. et recognovit se debere Isac de Suthwerk' judeo .j. marcam pro acquietacione habenda de uno debito .xx. solidorum sub nominibus <Sweyn'>[118] le Chaloner et predicti Isac, quam quidem marcam solvet eidem judeo in septimana Pasche proximo futura. Et, nisi fecerit, concedit quod de terris et catallis suis fiant.

(335)

Glouc'. Preceptum fuit vicecomiti, sicut pluries, quod de terris etc. Edmundi filii Johannis de Glouc' fieri faceret .x. libras ad opus Ade de Stratton' de .xx. libris quas idem Adam in curia domini H. regis versus eundem Edmundum recuperavit per consideracionem curie etc. de debitis Isac de Suthwerk'. Et vicecomes mandavit quod dictus Edmundus non habet aliqua bona nec catalla in balliva sua nisi quandam partem avene in grangia sua, per estimacionem .iiij. quarteria, et unam virgatam terre et terciam partem unius virgate in Lassendene[119] extra Glouc' et illam terram vendere non potest nec aliquem emptorem ad illam inveniret sine waranto securo. Ideo, sicut pluries, a die Pasche in .xv. dies etc.

MEMBRANE 6

Adhuc Memoranda[120]

(336)

Surr', Suss'. Preceptum fuit vicecomiti quod distringeret Johannem de Kameys per terras etc. pro mille marcis in quibus Radulfus de Kameys pater ejus tenebatur Hagino filio magistri Mossei, cujus debita Rex dedit Regine consorti etc., et denarios haberet coram etc. in quindena Purificacionis beate Marie eidem Regine solvendos vel corpus etc. Et vicecomes mandavit quod breve adeo tarde venit quod exequi non potuit. Et ex consensu W. de Kanc' attornati predicte regine dictus Johannes habet diem in crastino Cinerum.

(337)

Norff', Suff'. Walterus de Kanc' attornatus Regine consortis etc. fecit venire Gilbertum Pecche et exigit ab eo octingentas marcas ad opus predicte Regine de debitis Aaron filii Vyves et .cc. marcas pro .cccc. quarteriis frumenti et .ccc. marcas pro .xxx. saccis lane de debitis ejusdem Aaron, et .lx. marcas per unam cartam inter predictus Gilbertum et Aaron confectam etc., et que debita supradicta dictus Aaron concessit predicte Regine.

Predictus Gilbertus venit et dicit quod de predictus .cc. marcis pro predicto frumento et de .ccc. marcis pro predicta lana et .lx. marcis per predictam cartam petitis quietus esse debet per recognicionem octingentarum marcarum, reddendum inde eidem Aaron per annum .xl. marcas ad duos terminos, de quibus satisfecit eidem Aaron de tribus terminis jam inde preteritis. Et quia nullum starrum de acquietancia inde habet nec recognicionem aliquam coram justiciariis inde factam nisi dictum suum, consideratum est quod dictus Gilbertus pro toto supradicto debito etc.

(338)

Lond'. Idem Walterus fecit venire Mosseum filium Jacobi de Oxon' et exigit ab eo .xl. marcas quas recepit de quodam debito confecto sub nominibus Hamonis Chevere et Jacobi de Oxon' patris predicti Mossei, cujus debita Rex dedit Regine consorti etc.

Predictus Mosseus venit et dicit quod carta dicti debiti sub nominibus predictorum Hamonis et Jacobi ex mutuo suo et propriis suis denariis confecta fuit set eam posuit pro nomine suo sub nomine dicti Jacobi patris sui pre timore tallagii sui et aliarum occasionum et inde cepit starrum dicti Jacobi quod dicta carta et debitum in ea contentum suum fuit et cum omnes carte dicti Jacobi capte fuissent[121] in manum Regis et posite in thesauro

[111] Kinton *65*. [112] *Supplied from 65*.

[113] *Supplied from 65*. [114] *Supplied from 65*.

[115] *Supplied from 65*.

[116] *The word* misericordia *is repeated in the margin.*

[117] ita quod nec ipse etc. ... quod attachiari faciat dictum Ricardum, ita quod habeat corpus ejus coram etc. *65*.

[118] Sweghein *65*. [119] Lassendon' *65*.

[120] *The letter* h *is in the left-hand side opposite this heading*

[121] *Followed by* et posite *marked for deletion.*

regis pro tallagio suo predictam cartam ut suam propriam per dictum starrum et per recognicionem dicti Jacobi de predicto thesauro habuit deliberatam ad archam cyrographariorum Norht' per breve regis deferendum et ad liberam inde administracionem habendum. Et hoc ponit se super rotulos de scaccario judeorum de anno regis Edwardi quarto.

(339)

Lond'. Idem Walterus fecit venire magistrum Eliam filium magistri Mossei et exigit ab eo unam zonam de serico cum argento barrato precii sex marcarum.[122]

(340)

Essex, Hertf'. Preceptum fuit vicecomiti quod distringeret Willelmum de Monte Canisio de Eadwardeston' per terras etc. pro .ccl. libris quas debet Regine consorti de debitis Hagini filii magistri Mossei; et quod distringeret Philippum filium Bernardi, heredes vel tenentes terrarum suarum pro .xiij. marcis de debitis dicti judei; et quod distringeret Stephanum de Ayswell' militem, heredes et tenentes terrarum suarum pro .xlviij. libris de debitis ejusdem judei ad opus dicte Regine; ita quod denarios haberet coram etc. in quindenam Purificacionis nunc vel corpora predictorum etc. Et vicecomes mandavit quod omnia blada Willelmi de Monte Canisio in grangia existencia per quoddam breve de magno scaccario cepit pro .c..iiij^{xx}. marcis ad opus dicte Regine levandis et partem inde vendidit et partem vendicioni exposuit; et quod corpus dicti Willelmi post recepcionem istius brevis in balliva sua non fuit inventum; ita quod quantum ad dictum Willelmum de hoc brevi nichil actum est. Et quod Philippus filius Bernardi non habet terras neque tenementa in balliva sua. Et pro Stephano de Ayswell' retornavit breve inde sibi directum ballivis libertatis abbatis de Westm' in Ayswell', qui nichil inde fecerunt. Judicium quod non omittat propter libertatem etc. quin eam etc. ut prius. Et quod distringat predictum Willelmum et predictum Philippum, ut prius etc., ita quod denarios habeat coram etc. in quindena Pasche vel corpora etc.

(341)

Bed', Buk'. Preceptum fuit vicecomiti quod distringeret Radulfum Moryn filium Johannis Moryn, heredes et tenentes terrarum suarum per terras etc. pro quingenta et .l. marcis quas debet Regine consorti Regis de debitis Hagini filii magistri Mossei; et quod distringeret Johannem filium Alani de Wolrinton', heredes et tenentes terrarum suarum pro .xv. libris ad opus Regine etc. de debitis dicti judei; et quod distringeret Johannem de Wahull', heredes et tenentes terrarum suarum pro .xl. libris de debitis Cressaunt de Hanerberge ad opus dicte Regine; ita quod denarios haberet coram etc. ad hunc diem vel corpora etc. Et vicecomes mandavit quod breve inde sibi directum adeo tarde venit quod exequi non potuit. Ideo, sicut alias, a die Pasche in .xv. dies etc.

[122] *This entry is unfinished.*

(342)[123]

Lond'. Walterus de Kanc', attornatus Regine consortis, fecit venire Copinum de Troys mercatorem et exigit ab eo ad opus predicte Regine .v. anulos auri et tres anulos auri alios majores cum saphiris et aliis lapidibus preciosis precii .x. librarum, quas Jacobus de Oxon' judeus sibi tradidit custodiendum, cujus bona et catalla Rex dedit predicte Regine etc.

Predictus Copinus venit et recognovit se recepisse de catallis predicti Jacobi predictos anulos in vadium pro .xxij. solidis et sex denariis per talliam hac condicione quod, si aliquis dictam pecuniam cum dicta tallia sibi deferret, predictos anulos ei traderet, et postea Benedictus filius predicti Jacobi predictos .xxij. solidos .vj. denarios et dictam talliam sibi attulit et idem Jacobus dictos denarios recepit et predictos octo anulos predicto Benedicto tradidit et talliam inde confectam fregit.

Predictus Benedictus venit et defendit totum etc., et dicit quod predictos denarios cum dicta tallia inde confecta, sicut dictus Copinus dicit, ei non portavit nec dictos .viij. anulos recepit ab eo, nec eos vidit et hoc paratus est facere etc. secundum legem Judaismi et vadiat inde dicto Copino legem, quam statim fecit, de omnibus articulis prenominatis. Ideo consideratum est quod dictus Benedictus inde sit quietus et dictus Copinus de precio dictorum .viij. anulorum respondeat. Et quia dictus Copinus dicit quod predictos anulos quando ei impignorabantur pro predictis .xxij. solidis .vj. denariis vicinis suis monstravit, preceptum est vicecomitibus Lond' quod venire faciant coram etc. in crastino Cinerum .xij. probos etc. de warda Nicholai de Wynt' ad recognoscendum etc. Ad quem diem inquisicio venit per Willelmum de Bosco, Thomam Bonvyn et alios christianos, sicut patet inter brevia hujus termini retornata. Qui dicunt super sacramentum suum quod predicti octo anuli non valuerunt die quo impignorati fuerunt nisi duas marcas. Ideo consideratum est quod predictus Copinus satisfaciat predicte Regine de predictis .ij. marcis, et habet diem de consensu Walteri de Kanc' usque ad quindenam Pasche.

(343)

Lond'. Walterus de Kanc' attornatus Regine consortis Regis etc. fecit venire Nicholaum le Convers et exigit ab eo unum pycherum argenti et alia jocalia que fuerunt Jacobi de Oxon', que sibi tradidit custodiendum, ad valenciam .xx. librarum.[124]

Predictus Nicholaus venit et dicit quod nichil de predicto Jacobo recepit custodiendum, ut in auro etc. nec in aliis jocalibus quibuscunque, ex tradicione dicti Jacobi. Et de hoc ponit se super patriam. Ideo preceptum est vicecomitibus Lond' quod venire faciant coram etc. in crastino Cinerum .xij. etc. de vico de Fridaystrete ad recognoscendum etc. Ad quem diem dictus Nicholaus

[123] *Previously printed by Rigg in* Select Pleas, *pp. 107-8.*

[124] *The marginal note* Heref' *has been marked for deletion at this point.*

venit et inquisicio non venit. Ideo datus est dies eidem Nicholao a die Pasche in .xv. dies etc. Et preceptum est vicecomitibus, sicut alias etc., ad eundem diem ad recognoscendum etc.

(344)

Linc'. Preceptum fuit vicecomiti quod distringeret Johannem de Bathon', tenentem quandam partem terrarum que fuerunt Gilberti de Benyngworth', per terras etc. ad reddendum sibi ad opus Regis .cl. libras de porcione ipsum contingente de .ccclx. libris in quibus idem Gilbertus Regi tenebatur de debitis Judaismi, ita quod denarios illos haberet coram etc. ad hunc diem. Et vicecomes mandavit quod predictus Johannes non habet aliquid in balliva sua nisi quedam averia que appreciata sunt ad .xxiiij. marcas. Ideo preceptum est vicecomiti, sicut alias, quod de eisdem averiis et aliis bonis etc. a die Pasche in .xv. dies. Et preceptum est vicecomiti Norff' et Suff' quod distringat predictum Johannem pro .l. libris et eas habeat coram etc. ad eundem diem Regi etc.

(345)[125]

Oxon'. De communitate judeorum Oxon' pro brevi habendo ut manuteneatur marca.[126] Et preceptum est vicecomiti quod habeat coram etc. a die Pasche in tres septimanas Hake le Petyt od la playe judeum[127] ad respondendum de uno cipho argenteo furato in hospicio Walteri aurifabri in Oxon' et aliis transgressionibus etc.

(346)

Kanc'. Thomas de Regge venit coram etc. et recognovit se debere Gamalieli de Oxon' .iiij.^{xx} quarteria frumenti vel pro quolibet quarterio dimidiam marcam, reddendum eidem judeo medietatem ad Mediam Quadragesimam anno regni regis Edwardi octavo et aliam medietatem a die Pasche proximo sequentem in tres septimanas. Et, nisi fecerit, concedit quod de terris et catallis suis fiant etc.

MEMBRANE 6 DORSE

(347)

Lond'. Quia constat justiciariis etc. per inspeccionem rotulorum quod Gamaliel de Oxon' judeus satisfecit regi de tallagio pro quo debita sua capta fuerunt in manum [regis,][128] eadem debita restituta sunt eidem, videlicet: unum debitum .xx. librarum sub nominibus Alicie de Coston' et Matildis de Coston' et predicti Gam'; et unum debitum .l. librarum sub nominibus Willelmi de Lascel' et dicti judei; et unum debitum .x. librarum sub nominibus Alani de Kaynes et dicti judei; et unum debitum octo librarum sub nominibus Johannis Marcyen et dicti judei; et unum debitum .x. librarum sub nominibus Hugonis de Stanewell' et dicti judei; et unum debitum .xx. librarum sub nominibus Johannis de Patemere filii Johannis et dicti judei; et unum debitum .c. solidorum sub nominibus Galfridi de Herlet et dicti judei; et unum debitum .xij. librarum sub nominibus Johannis de Norwyc' filii Claricie et dicti judei; et unum debitum .xxx. librarum sub nominibus Willelmi de Lascel' et dicti judei; et unum debitum .c. solidorum sub nominibus Michaelis de Auverne et dicti judei; et unum debitum .xx. librarum sub nominibus Willelmi de Lascel' [et dicti judei,][129] et unum debitum .v. marcarum sub nominibus Reginaldi de Loffenham et dicti judei; et unum debitum .x. marcarum sub nominibus dicti Reginaldi et ipsius judei; et unum debitum .xxv. librarum sub nominibus Johannis de Caumvyle militis et dicti judei; et unum debitum .xl. marcarum sub nominibus Henrici de Novo Burgo de Halton' et dicti judei; et unum debitum .x. librarum sub nominibus Willelmi de Lascel' et dicti judei; et unum debitum .x. librarum sub nominibus Willelmi de Lascel' et dicti judei; et unum debitum .x. librarum sub nominibus Roberti de Aula et dicti judei; et unum debitum .c. solidorum sub nominibus Willelmi de Lascel', Willelmi de Funteynes et dicti judei; et unum debitum .c. solidorum sub nominibus predictorum Willelmi et Willelmi et dicti judei; et unum debitum .v. marcarum sub nominibus Radulfi filii Reginaldi clerici et dicti judei; et unum debitum .xl. solidorum sub nominibus Saeri de Gaergrave et dicti judei; et unum debitum .xv. librarum sub nominibus Johannis de Canvyle militis et dicti judei; et unum debitum .lx. librarum sub nominibus Willelmi filii Willelmi de Meysham et dicti judei, unde carta ejusdem debiti liberata fuit Uriano de Sancto Petro per Walterum de Kanc' custodem auri Regine consortis Regis quiete dampnanda; et unum debitum .xl. librarum sub nominibus predictorum Willelmi filii Wilelmi militis et judei, unde carta ejusdem debiti liberata fuit eidem Uriano per eundem W. de Kanc' quiete dampnanda. Et preceptum est cyrographariis Lond' quod predictas cartas non quietas admittant et in archa cyrographariorum reponant et dicto Gamalieli liberam inde habere permittant administracionem.

(348)

Cantebr'. Preceptum fuit vicecomiti quod non omitteret propter libertatem Cantebr' quin eam etc., et distringeret tenentes terrarum que fuerunt Johannis le Rus per terras etc. pro .iiij. libris ad opus Regis occasione terrarum etc. de debitis Mossei filii Isac, et denarios haberet coram etc. ad hunc diem vel corpora etc. Et vicecomes mandavit quod prior de Bernewell', magister hospitalis sancti Johannis, Ricardus filii Ricardi Laur', Ricardus Wombe, Alicia Godeman, Willelmus de Wilburham, Ricardus Bateman junior, fratres Sacci, Johannes But, Nicholaus Morice, Robertus de Madingle, priorissa de Swafham,

[125] *Cf. No. 316 above.*

[126] *The words* .j. marca *are repeated in the margin.*

[127] *Followed in MS. by* a die Pasche in tres septimanas *which should have been marked for deletion.*

[128] *MS. omits.*

[129] *MS. omits.*

Guydo de Mortuo Mari, Lucas Carettarius, Osbertus le Ferrun, Cecilia de Overe et Thomas de Clopton' sunt tenentes predictarum terrarum et manucapti ad veniendum ad diem in brevi contentum vel ad ostendendum etc.

Magister hospitalis sancti Johannis dicit quod non tenetur respondere de dicto debito eo quod feoffatus fuit de terris etc. de Ricardo patre dicti Johannis, ita quod dictus Johannes dictas terras etc. invadiare non potuit. Et hoc petit verificare etc. Ricardus filius Laurencii dicit quod feoffatus fuit de terris etc. antequam dictus Johannes dicto Mosseo obligaretur. Et hoc petit inquiri etc. Ricardus Wombe dicit similiter quod feoffatus fuit de terris etc. antequam idem Johannes dicto judeo obligaretur. Et hoc petit inquiri.

Willelmus de Wilburham vocavit ad warantum de porcione etc. per auxilium curie.

Ricardus Bateman junior vocavit ad warantum etc. per auxilium curie Hugonem heredem dicti Johannis. Nicholaus Morice vocavit ad warantum etc. predictum Hugonem. Johannes But vocavit ad warantum etc. Thomam le Merveylyus. Robertus de Madingle venit coram etc. et recognovit se esse tenentem de dimidia acra terre que fuit dicti Johannis et paratus est satisfacere de porcione sua etc. Osbertus le Ferrun venit et dicit quod non tenet aliquas terras vel tenementa que umquam fuerunt predicti Johannis. Et hoc offert verificare per patriam. Et vicecomes mandavit quod Andreas le Redere et Rogerus de Huntyngfeld manuceperunt priorem de Bernewell'; et quod Thomas Godeman et Robertus de Lundr' manuceperunt Aliciam Godeman; et quod Johannis Funtyngg' et Ricardus Peketo manuceperunt priorissam de Swaffham; et quod Ricardus Wombe et Henricus Thoneye manuceperunt Lucam Carettarium; et quod Johannes le Bever et Willelmus de Lundr' manuceperunt Ceciliam de Overe; et quod Willelmus Wilecok' de Clopton', Robertus Frankeleyn de eadem manuceperunt Thomam de Clopton', quos non habuerunt. Ideo in misericordia. Judicium quod distringat per terras etc., ita quod nec ipsi etc., et quod de exitibus etc., et quod habeat corpora eorum coram etc. a die Pasche in unum mensem ad respondendum etc., et ad audiendum etc. de defaltis. Et vicecomes mandavit quod Guydo de Mortuo Mari et fratres Sacci tenent partem predictarum terrarum etc. Et preceptum est ei, sicut alias, quod inquirat etc., et inquisicionem etc. a die Pasche in unum mensem etc.

(349)

Norff', Suff'. Preceptum fuit vicecomiti quod attachiari faceret Johannem de Hecham, ita quod haberet corpus etc. ad hunc diem ad respondendum Regi de hoc quod, cum ipse affidasset quod non recederet a civitate Lond' antequam satisfecisset Regi pro Edmundo de Shardelowe de .x. libris que ab eodem Edmundo exigebantur, de quibus eundem Edmundum acquietare debet,[130] et insuper preceptum fuit vicecomiti quod, si bona dicti Johannis non sufficerent ad dictum debitum levandum, tunc de bonis et catallis Nicholai de Lafham et Alani de Boclond' manucaptorum predicti debiti pro predicto Johanne, sicut continetur in termino sancti Michaelis proximo preterito, levari faceret predictas .x. libras etc. Et vicecomes mandavit quod retornavit breve inde sibi directum senescallo libertatis sancti Edmundi et idem senescallus respondit quod corpus predicti Johannis non fuit inventum post adventum brevis inde sibi directi, et quod cepit de averiis ipsius Johannis .iiij. boves et unum stottum precii .xl. solidorum, et de averiis predictorum manuceptorum cepit .xij. [blank in MS.] precii .vj. marcarum; et cum dicta averia inparcare voluisset quousque ea vendere posset, Johannes Sampson de Kerseya et Walterus prepositus de Heccham ballivi episcopi Elyensis in Heccham cum aliis ignotis de villenagio dicti episcopi predicta averia rescusserunt et illa duxerunt usque ad manerium dicti episcopi de Hecham et ibidem detinent etc. Ideo preceptum est vicecomiti quod non omittat propter libertatem etc. quin eam etc. et capiat predictos Johannem de Hecham, Johannem Sampson et Walterum prepositum et eos salvo custodiat etc., ita quod habeat corpora eorum coram etc. a die Pasche in .xv. dies ad respondendum Regi de contemptu predicto. Et quod inquirat per sacramentum proborum etc. qui fuerunt illi ignoti qui interfuerunt predicte rescussioni etc., et omnes quos inde culpabiles invenerit, capiat et salvo custodiat etc. ita quod habeat corpora eorum coram etc. ad eundem diem etc. ad respondendum etc.

130 *Some words seem to have been omitted ast this point by the clerk.*

(350)

Linc'. Preceptum fuit vicecomiti, sicut pluries, quod distringeret Henricum de Lacy comitem Linc', priorem de Bulington', priorem de Ormesby, heredes Willelmi de Holegate et Helewysiam de Nevyle, tenentes quandam partem terrarum que fuerunt Gilberti de Benygworthe, per terras etc. ad respondendum Regi una cum Johanne de Bathon', tenente quandam partem predictarum terrarum, de .ccclx. libris de debitis Judaismi. Et predicti Henricus, prior de Ormesby, heredes predicti Willelmi et Helewysia non venerunt.[131]

MEMBRANE 7

(351)

Stanf'. Inquisicio capta coram H. Hautein apud Staunford' die lune proxima post octabas Epiphanie de bonis et catallis Bonefey filii Bretonis, Isac filii Abrahe et Abrahe filii Manseri judeorum mortuorum, videlicet que bona et catalla iidem judei habuerunt ut in auro etc. die quo <egrotaverunt>[132] infirmitate qua <obierunt>[133] etc., per sacramentum Johannis de Burton', Andree Mor,

131 *This entry is unfinished.*

132 *MS. reads* egrotavit.

133 *MS. reads* obiit.

Galfridi de Sancto Botulpho, Willelmi de Bukes, Gilberti le Mercer, Willelmi le Norreis christianorum, et per sacramentum Elie de Denec', Sampsonis filii magistri, Deulecres filii Samuelis, Tovy filii Meyr, Aaron filii Meyr et Benedicti filii David judeorum. Qui dicunt super sacramentum suum quod Bonefey filius Bretonis habuit die quo etc. bona et catalla ad valenciam .xx. marcarum; item habuit unam domum in Staunf' in vico de Colgate que valet per annum, servicio capitalium dominorum salvo, dimidiam marcam; et devenerunt ad manus Belassez uxoris sue.

Item bona et catalla Isac filius [Abrahe][134] die quo etc. valebant .v. marcas et devenerunt ad manus Marone uxoris ipsius Isac. Dicunt eciam quod nichil habuit in archa cyrographariorum etc., unde tercia pars Regis .xxij. solidi .ij. denarii obulus.

Item Abraham filius Manseri nichil habuit in bonis etc. die quo etc. eo quod ante terminum mortis sue fere per quinque annos demens et incompos mentis sue fuit; tamen in archa cyrographariorum Stanf' habuit catalla etc.

Postea veniunt et dicunt quod Josceus Bonngos, et Meyr filius Isac judei mortui moriebantur in prisona apud Linc'; parum vel nichil habuerunt in bonis, tamen ea que habuerunt percepit rex per dominos Johannem Bek' et alios socios suos etc.

Elias Denec', Leo filius Mossei, Tovi filius Meyr et Bateman de Winton' judei manuceperunt Belassez que fuit uxor Bonefey filii Bretonis ad respondendum de tercia parte predictorum catallorum que fuerunt ipsius Bonefey viri sui; et ad appurandum debita in archa cyrographariorum in quindena sancti Hillarii. Eadem Belassez ponit loco suo Leonem filium Mossei judeum.

Idem Elias et alii manuceperunt Maronam que fuit uxor Isac filii Abrahe ad respondendum de tercia parte predictorum catallorum que fuerunt ipsius Isac viri sui. Et eadem Marona ponit loco suo predictum Leonem ad appurandum etc. a die sancti Hillarii in tres septimanas etc.

Summa catallorum Bonefey filii Bretonis extra archa cyrographariorum .xx. marce et dimidia.

Summa catallorum illius Bonefey infra archam .xxxviij. libre .xiij. solidi .iiij. denarii

Summa catallorum tam mobilium quam immobilium tam infra archam cyrographariorum quam extra: .lij. libre, .vj. solidi .viij. denarii, unde tercia pars Regi est .xvij. libre .viij. solidi .x. denarii obulus.

Que quidem debita infra archam sunt haec:

'Robertus filius Roberti le Fraunkhomme de Wyham debet Bonefey filio Bretonis .vj. marcas reddendas die sancti Michaelis anno regnis regis Henrici .lvj.$^{to.}$ Acta in crastino sancte Trinitatis anno eodem.' Et appuratur ad .xx. solidos.

'Hugo filius Roberti de Cathethorp' comitatus Linc' debet eidem .xij. marcas et dimidiam reddendum ad octabis Natalis Domini anno regni regis Henrici .lv.^{o} Acta die mercurii ante festum sancti Michaelis anno .liiij.^{o}' Et appuratur ad .ij. marcas.

'Simon de Ravenesfeld' de comitatu Ebor' debet eidem .xx. libras, reddendum .x. libras die sancte Marie in Augusto anno .lvj.^{to} et .x. libras die sancti Martini anno .lvij.^{o}. Acta die lune ante Natalem Domini anno .lvj.^{to}' Et appuratur ad .xl. solidos.

'Johannes de Veer de comitatu Northant' debet eidem .xx. libras reddendas ad octabas sancti Michaelis anno .lvj.$^{to.}$. Acta die mercurii in septimana Pentecosten anno .lvj.^{to}'

'Ricardus filius Arketel de Wodeford de comitatu Northt' debet eidem .vj. marcas reddendas ad octabis Pentecosten anno .liiij.^{to}. Acta die dominica ante Annunciationem beate Marie anno predicto.' Et appuratur ad .ij. marcas.

'Ricardus de Wodeford' debet eidem .xl. solidos reddendos ad clausum Pasche anno .lij.^{o}. Acta in crastino Cinerum anno predicto.'

'Johannes de Middelton' de Butelesbrok' de comitatu Rotel' debet eidem .xj. libras reddendo ad duos terminos, videlicet ad festum Nativitatis sancti Johannis Baptiste anno regni regis Edwardi tercio unam medietatem, et alteram ad quindenam sancti Michaelis sequentem. Acta die jovis in septimana Penosa anno eodem.'

Unde Rex capit se ad unum debitum .xx. librarum sub nominibus predictorum Johannis de Veer et predicti Bonefey, videlicet tam pro fine catallorum ipsius Bonefey quam Isac filii Abrahe. Et super hoc Belassez que fuit uxor predicti Bonefey et Marona que fuit uxor ipsius Isac concedunt quod, nisi predictum debitum .xx. librarum fuerit bonum, clarum et debitum satisfaciant domino Regi de catallis suis ad valenciam illius debiti.

(352)

Norhumbr'. Magister Adam de Denun venit coram etc. et recognovit se debere Willelmo de Middelton' rectori ecclesie de Bolum .iiij.^{xx} .xv. marcas pro fructibus ecclesie de Bolum ^{i}<de anno regis Edwardi .vij.^{o}>^{i} reddendum apud Novum Castrum super Tinam ad festum sancti Petri ad Vincula anno regni regis Edwardi octavo unam medietatem et ad quindenam sancti Michaelis proximo sequentem aliam medietatem. Et, nisi fecerit, concedit quod de terris et catallis suis fiant etc.

MEMBRANE 7 DORSE

Adhuc Memoranda

(353)

Ebor'. Inquisicio facta apud Ebor' per vicecomitem Ebor', per Willelmum Schirloke et alios christanos etc., et per Deudonem Crespin et alios judeos etc., prout patet inter inquisiciones etc., de catallis Bonefey filii Joscei judei mortui. Qui dicunt quod predictus judeus habuit die quo egrotavit etc. quinque marcas et dimidiam in denariis, et in aliis rebus, domibus et aliis mobilibus

[134] *MS. omits.*

quadraginta solidos et devenerunt ad manus Mossei filii ejus.

Summa catallorum mobilium .viij. marce et dimidia.

Item in archa cyrographariorum Subir' una carta quatuor marcarum sub nominibus Walteri filii Willelmi de Bradele de comitatu Suff', reddendum ad quindenam de Hokeday anno regis Henrici .xlvj.^{to} Acta .ix. die Aprilis anno predicto.

Summa catallorum tam mobilium quam immobilium .viij. libre .vj. solidi .viij. denarii, unde tercia pars Regis est .lv. solidi .vij. denarii, pro qua quidem tercia parte concessum est Mosseo filio predicti Bonefey quod solvat ad quindenam Pasche medietatem et ad quindenam sancti Michaelis proximo sequentem aliam medietatem sub pena dupli per plegium Isac le Eveske.[135]

Postea pro predicta tercia parte, videlicet .lviij. solidis .viij. denariis, rex capit predictum debitum .iiij. marcarum sub nominibus supradictorum Walteri et Bonafey; et residuum dicti finis, videlicet .v. solidos .iiij. denarios, solvet regi per plevinam predictam. Et predictus Mosseus concedit quod, nisi predictum debitum .iiij. marcarum sit bonum, clarum et debitum satisfaciet Regi de aliis catallis suis pro pecunia predicta .iiij. marcarum. Et preceptum est cyrographariis arche cyrographariorum Subbyr' quod habeant predictam cartam coram etc. a die Pasche in .iij. septimanas.

(354)

Lond'. Reginaldus de Laufare venit coram etc. et recognovit se debere Cresseo filio Cressei quatuor marcas, reddendas ad Nativitatem sancti Johannis Baptiste anno octavo. Et, nisi fecerit, concedit quod de terris et catallis suis fiant etc.

(355)

Essex'. Robertus filius Johannis de Simay venit coram etc., et recognovit se debere Aaron filio Vives judeo centum quarteria frumenti vel pro quolibet quarterio dimidiam marcam, reddendum ad Pentecostem anno regni regis Edwardi octavo. Et, nisi fecerit, concedit quod de terris et catallis suis fiant etc.

Postea venit idem judeus et recognovit totum predictum debitum esse quietum per starrum suum, sicut patet in termino Pasche anno regni regis Edwardi .viij.[o][136]

(356)[137]

Surr'. Johannes de Camoeys filius Radulfi de Cameys venit coram etc. et recognovit se debere Cok Hagin judeo .c. libras, reddendum [unam medietatem][138] a die Pasche in unum mensem [i]<anno regni regis Edwardi .viij.[o] et aliam medietatem ad festum sancti Petri ad vincula proximo sequens.>[i] Et nisi fecerit, concedit quod de terris et catallis suis, ad quoruncunque manus devenerunt, fiant etc.

(357)

Suff'. Adam de Cretinge miles venit coram etc. et recognovit se debere Waltero de Kanc' .x. marcas, reddendum a die Pasche in quindecim dies per plegium Hamonis Hautein et Willelmi de Say. Et, nisi fecerit, concedit quod de terris et catallis suis fiant etc., et eciam de terris predictorum plegiorum.

(358)[139]

Norff'. Hugo de Hocstede venit coram etc., et recognovit se debere Roberto de Ludham .xl. solidos reddendos a die sancti Michaelis in quindecim dies. Et, nisi fecerit, concedit quod de terris et catallis suis fiant etc.

(359)[140]

Surr'. Willelmus de Hasteng venit coram etc. et recognovit se debere Aaron filio Vives judeo .xiiij. marcas reddendas a die Pasche in .xv. dies. Et, nisi fecerit, concedit quod de terris et catallis suis fiant etc.

(360)[141]

Essex'. Thomas de Belhus venit coram etc., et recognovit se debere Aaron filio Vives judeo .xlv. libras, reddendum a die Pasche in .xv. dies .xv. libras, et die sancti Michaelis anno regni regis Edwardi octavo proximo sequenti .xv. libras, et a die Purificacionis beate Marie in .xv. dies sequenti .x. libras, et a die Pasche in .xv. dies sequenti centum solidos. Et, nisi fecerit, concedit quod de terris et catallis suis fiant etc.

(361)[142]

Cant'. Willelmus de Roynge miles venit coram etc., et recognovit se debere Aaron filio Vives judeo .xij. marcas, reddendum die jovis proxima post Purificacionem beate Marie anno octavo. Et, nisi fecerit, concedit quod de terris et catallis suis fiant etc.

(362)[143]

Cant'. Willelmus de Caam venit coram etc. et recognovit se debere Aaron filio Vyves judeo .c. solidos, reddendum inde .l. solidos ad Pentecosten anno octavo, et ad festum Omnium Sanctorum proximo sequens .l. solidos. Et, nisi fecerit, concedit quod de terris et catallis fiant etc.

(363)[144]

Willelmus filius Alexandri le Moine miles venit coram etc. et recognovit se debere Aaron filio Vives judeo .lx.

135 *The remainder of this entry has been added after the following two entries with marks to indicate where it belongs. It is omitted from 65.*

136 *This entry is followed by the second section of no. 353.*

137 *This entry seems to have been added later as the handwriting has been compressed to fit the available space.*

138 *MS. omits.*

139 *Another version of this entry is to be found on m. 4 (no. 295).*

140 *Another version of this entry is to be found on m. 4 (no. 296).*

141 *Another version of this entry will be found on m. 4 (no. 297).*

142 *Another version of this entry will be found on m. 4 (no. 298).*

143 *Another version of this entry will be found on m. 4 (no. 299).*

144 *Another version of this entry will be found on m. 4 (no. 300).*

quarteria frumenti, reddenda ad festum sancti Michaelis anno octavo vel pro quolibet quarterio dimidiam marcam. Et, nisi fecerit, concedit quod de terris et catallis suis fiant etc.

(364)

Robertus le Lung et Galfridus le Botoner manuceperunt Johannem de Richemund quod erit coram etc. die lune post quindenam Purificacionis beate Marie.

MEMBRANE 8

Starra de termino sancti Hillarii anno octavo

(365)

Mosseus de Clare recognovit per starrum suum quod Edmundus de Illegh' filius Ade de Illegh' militis et heredes sui sunt quieti de ipso [et] heredibus de omnibus debitis, demandis, plegiagiis que habuit vel habere potuit die confeccionis istius starri et de principio seculi usque ad diem confeccionis istius starri; ita quod nec ipse nec heredes sui possint aliquid exigere super dictum Edmundum [vel] heredes suos. Et si aliquis homo vel femina aliquid exigerit de predicto Edmundo vel heredibus suis occasione alicujus debiti quod umquam sibi debuit usque diem confeccionis istius starri tenetur [i]<contra omnes calumpniantes>[i] warantizare et defendere. Acta in quindena sancti Michaelis anno quinto.

(366)

Aaron filius Vyves judeus recognovit per starrum suum quod ipse concessit Willelmo Baldewyne de Stowe ad instanciam amicorum suorum quod, si ipse solvat eidem judeo quaterviginti marcas sterlingorum ad terminos subscriptos sine prorogacione alicujus termini, videlicet .xx. marcas a die Pasche in tres septimanas anno regni regis Edwardi octavo, et .xx. marcas a die sancti Michaelis in tres septimanas proximo sequenti et .xx. marcas [in crastino Purificacionis beate Marie proximo sequenti et .xx. marcas a die Pasche proximo sequenti in tres septimanas,][145] perdonat ipse predicto Willelmo omnia debita in quibus ei tenebatur a creacione seculi usque ad confeccionem presentis starri et tenetur ipsum aquietare de omnibus debitis in quibus Willelmus filius Gilberti et heredes sui unquam ei tenebantur vel Joceo filio Sauloti vel Sauloto patri suo a creacione seculi usque ad diem confeccionis presentis starri. Insuper tenetur acquietare predictum Willelmum Baldewyne de Josceo filio Sauloti de omnibus debitis in quibus idem Willelmus Baldewyne vel predictus Willelmus filius Gilberti tenebantur Josceo predicto vel Sauloto patri. Et, si predictus Willelmus Baldewyne non solvat predicto judeo predictas quaterviginti marcas ad terminos predictos, vel si pretierit unum predictorum terminorum, tunc nichil perdonat idem judeus predicto Willelmo de toto predicto debito in quo idem Willelmus Bald' vel Willelmus filius Gilberti ei tenentur vel Josceo filio Sauloti nec tenentur ipsum acquietare de debitis in quibus Willelmus filius Gilberti tenebatur predicto Sauloto. Et tunc bene liceat predicto Aaron et Josceo filio Sauloti habere suum recuperare de omnibus debitis suis erga predictum Willelmum Baldewyne in quibus Willelmus filius Gilberti predicto Sauloto tenebatur; salvo tamen quod idem Aaron tenetur allocare predicto Willelmo Baldewyne id quod ipse receperit de ipso de debitis in quibus Willelmus filius Gilberti tenebatur predicto Sauloto. Et, si predictus Willelmus Baldewyne velit quod predictus Josceus facit ei unum starrum, ita quod postquam predictus Aaron erit perpacatus de predictis denariis ad terminos predictos, tunc aquietabit predictum Willelmum de omnibus debitis in quibus ipse vel Willelmus filius Gilberti vel heredes sui tenebantur eidem Josceo vel predicto Sauloto patri suo, tunc tenetur idem Aaron facere eidem Willelmo habere starrum de predicto Josceo a die Pasche in tres septimanas post primam solucionem predicte pecunie. Acta in octabis Purificacionis beate Marie anno regni regis [Edwardi] octavo. Et predictus Aaron recognovit quod post solucionem predictarum .iiij.^{xx} marcarum ad terminos predictos per predictas convenciones, tunc tenetur ipse Aaron facere predicto Willelmo habere quoddam starrum plene acquietancie de se ipso et Josceo filio Sauloti de omnibus debitis in quibus Willelmus filius Baldewyne vel Willelmus filius Gilberti vel heredes eorum unquam tenebatur predictis Aaron, Josceo vel Sauloto a creacione seculi usque ad confeccionem presentis starri. Et predictus Willelmus Baldewyne concessit et recognovit omnes convenciones supradictas.

(367)

Derb'. Lond'. Gamaliel de Oxon' judeus recognovit per starrum quod ipse perdonavit et aquietavit Uriano de Sancto Petro, tenenti manerium de Eyton' in parochia de Duvebrigge, et heredibus et assingnatis suis totum jus clamium et demandam que habuit, habet vel habere potest in duobus debitis centum librarum in archa cyrographariorum Lond', videlicet unum debitum sexaginta librarum et unum debitum .xl. librarum sub nominibus Willelmi de Meysham junioris filii Willelmi de Meysham militis et ipsius Gamalielis, a creacione seculi usque ad finem, ita quod nec ipse judeus nec heredes sui nec aliquis assingnatus ejus aliquid possint exigere nec vendicare super predictum Urianum, heredes vel assingnatos suos nec super predictum manerium de Eyton' cum pertinenciis, ad cujuscumque manus devenerit, occasione predictorum duorum debitorum vel occasione alicujus alterius debiti sub nominibus predicti Willelmi et ipsius judei vel Meyr filii ipsius Gamalielis vel alterius judei vel judee a creacione seculi usque ad finem. Et, si inveniatur carta, tallia vel aliud instrumentum in aliqua archa cyrographariorum vel extra sub nominibus predicti Willelmi filii et ipsius Gamalielis vel Meyr filii ejusdem Gamalielis a creacione seculi usque ad finem, idem

[145] *MS. reads* in den' est. *See no. 507.*

Gamaliel recognovit quod quieta sint et nichil valeant. Insuper recognovit idem Gamaliel quod ipse nec Meyr filius ejus nec heredes eorum nec assingnati nec aliquis alius judeus nec judea pro eis nec per eos nec ipsi Gamaliel et Meyr nomine alterius judei vel judee exigere nec vendicare aliquid jus, demandam vel calumpniam super predictum Urianum nec heredes nec assignatos suos nec super predictum manerium de Eyton' cum pertinenciis, ad cujuscunque manus devenerit, occasione alicujus debiti quod Willelmus de Meysham miles debuit in aliqua archa cyrographariorum vel extra facti sub nominibus ejusdem Willelmi et ipsius Gamalielis vel Meyr filii sui vel sub nomine cujuscunque alterius judei vel judee; salvo tamen domino Regi jure suo et clamio super predictum Urianum de vinginti quinque libris de arreragiis tallagii ejusdem Gamalielis de quinquaginta libris de tallagio .v. mille marcarum de tempore domini regis Henrici, ita videlicet prout eadem jus et clamium irrotulantur in rotulis domini regis coram justiciariis ad custodiam judeorum assignatis, salvo eciam eidem Gamalieli suo jure et clamio de debitis suis super alios tenentes terras et redditus Willelmi de Meysham militis excepto predicto manerio de Eyton'. Et hoc starrum fecit [idem][146] Gamaliel coram Hamone Hauteyn et Roberto de Ludham tunc justiciariis judeorum et Waltero de Kanc' thesaurario domine Regine, per assensum et preceptum ejusdem Walteri sub nomine venerabilis domine Regine consortis domini Regis. Acta die lune ante festum sancti Petri in Cathedra anno regni regis Edwardi filii regis Henrici octavo.

(368)

Derb'. Lond'. Meyr filius Gamalielis recognovit per starrum suum totam acquietanciam prenominatam quam Gamaliel pater ejusdem Meyr fecit Uriano predicto, sicut predictum est, de debitis Willelmi de Meysham filii ejusdem Willelmi sub nomine Gamalielis patris sui et nomine suo et hoc sigillavit littera sua ebrayca pro se et heredibus suis ratum et stabile habituram.

MEMBRANE 8 DORSE
[blank]

MEMBRANE 9

Adhuc placita de termino sancti Hillarii et de in crastino Cinerum anno .viij.[147]

(369)[148]

Cantebr'. Belassez que fuit uxor Leonis filii Preciose fecit venire Rogerum de Cauz, tenentem quandam partem terrarum que fuerunt Willelmi de Bussey, et exigit ab eo .xv. libras per cyrographum .xxviij. librarum sub nominibus predictorum Willelmi et Leonis, reddendum ad festum Pentecosten anno regis Henrici .xlvij.°. Acta .iij. die Dec' anno eodem; et .x. libras de lucro.

Predictus Rogerus venit et dicit quod non est factum suum et petit diem premeditandi et habet a die Pasche in unum mensem etc.

(370)

Lond'. Leo filius Cressei judeus fecit venire Clerkinum generum Henrici de Shobyr', tenentem quandam partem terrarum que fuerunt predicti Henrici, et exigit ab eo .x. marcas quas ei debet occasione etc. per cyrographum .xv. librarum inter predictos Henricum et judeum confectum.

Predictus Clerkinus venit et defendit etc., et dicit quod non est factum suum, et petit diem premeditandi et habet a die Pasche in .xv. dies. Ad quem diem dictus Clerkinus non venit. Ideo distringatur etc. a die Pasche in .xv. dies etc.

(371)

Norff'. Johannes de Lenn', burgensis de Sancto Edmundo, attachiatus ad respondendum Willelmo de Middelton' clerico de scaccario etc. de placito debiti. Et unde queritur quod idem Johannes injuste ei detinet .xlv. marcas quas ei debet, sicut continetur in quodam scripto obligatorio sigillo dicti Johannis consignato quod dictus Willelmus protulit coram etc. ad dampnum suum .x. librarum etc.

Predictus Johannes venit et defendit vim etc. quando etc. et dicit quod nec ipse nec aliquis pro eo dictum scriptum obligatorium sigillo suo consignavit nec sigillum in dicto scripto appositum suum est. Et predictus Willelmus dicit quod, si se sola manu jurare voluerit quod impressio sigilli in dicto scripto apposita per se nec per aliquem de suis ibidem fuit apposita nec impressio sigilli sui est, ipsum de predicto debito .xlv. marcarum quietumclamet. Qui statim omnia predicta juravit. Ideo consideratum est quod dictus Johannes de dicto debito sit quietus et dictus Willelmus pro injusta peticione in misericordia.[149]

Idem Willelmus optulit se quarto die versus Johannem personam de Magna Henneye et Rogerum de Feltewelle de dicto placito. Et ipsi non venerunt. Et preceptum fuit vicecomiti quod ipsos distringeret per terras etc. et quod haberet corpora eorum coram etc. Et vicecomes mandavit quod predicti Johannes et Rogerus non sunt manentes in balliva sua nec aliquid habent in ea unde distringi possunt. Ideo de ipsis nichil actum est. Ideo preceptum est vicecomiti Cantebr' quod predictum Rogerum distringat per terras etc. a die Pasche in tres septimanas etc.

(372)

Norff'. Radulfus de Chattegrave et Emma uxor ejus per attornatum suum optulerunt se quarto die versus

146 *MS. reads* eidem.

147 *A letter* h *is written above this heading in the left hand margin.*

148 *Previously printed by Rigg in* Select Pleas, *p. 108*

149 *In the margin is written* misericordia condonatur per justiciarios.

Rogerum filium Thome Sygor de Oulton' et Katerinam uxorem ejus, Robertum Ernald, Robertum Whystan et Hugonem Tyrel de placito transgressionis. Et ipsi non venerunt. Et preceptum fuit vicecomiti quod ipsos attachiaret, ita quod haberet corpora eorum coram etc. ad hunc diem. Et vicecomes mandavit quod predictus Rogerus et alii gratis se subtraxerunt, ita quod post recepcionem hujus brevis non fuerunt inventi. Ideo preceptum est ei quod capiat predictum Rogerum et alios et salvo custodiat etc., ita quod habeat corpora eorum coram etc. a die Pasche in unum mensem etc.

(373)

Glouc'. Robertus de Broghton', clericus etc., optulit se quarto die versus Henricum de Berkele de placito debiti. Et ipse non venit. Et preceptum fuit vicecomiti quod ipsum venire faceret. Et vicecomes mandavit quod Gilbertus de la Bergh' de Ryston' et Hugo Ballard de eadem manuceperunt predictum Henricum, quem non habuerunt. Ideo in misericordia.[150] Judicium quod distringatur per terras etc., ita quod nec ipse etc., et quod habeat corpus ejus coram etc. a die Pasche in .v. septimanas ad respondendum etc. et ad audiendum etc.

(374)

Lond'. Cok' Hagyn judeus fecit venire Michaelem le Oynter et exigit ab eo unum ciphum de mazero precii .xl. solidorum quem ei tradidit custodiendum et quem ei injuste detinet ad dampnum suum .xx. solidorum etc.

Predictus Michael venit et defendit etc. et totum negat de verbo ad verbum et dicit quod nullum ciphum ab eo cepit, sicut versus eum narrat, et hoc paratus est facere secundum quod curia consideraverit etc. Et dictus Cok dicit quod dictum cyphum ei tradidit et hoc paratus est facere etc. Ideo consideratum est quod dictus Michael vadiat dicto Cok' legem,[151] et habet diem a die Pasche in .v. septimanas etc. Plegii de lege Robertus de Bradefeld' et Willelmus.[152]

(375)

Hereff'. Sampson de Wygorn' judeus optulit se quarto die versus Willelmum filium et heredem Willelmi de Sholle de placito debiti. Et ipse non venit. Et preceptum fuit vicecomiti quod ipsum distringeret per terras etc., et quod haberet corpus ejus coram etc. Et vicecomes mandavit quod Rogerus de Senewell[153] manuceperunt predictum Willelmum, quem non habuerunt. Ideo in misericordia. Et quod exitus terrarum sunt .ij. solidi, quos misit cum brevi. Judicium, sicut alias, quod distringat predictum Willelmum per terras etc., et quod habeat corpus ejus coram etc. a die Pasche in unum mensem ad respondendum etc. et ad audiendum etc.

(376)

Dyey filius Abrahe judeus optulit se quarto die versus Robertum de Mortuo Mari et Jocosam uxorem eius de placito debiti. Et ipsi non venerunt. Et preceptum fuit vicecomiti quod salvo custodiret terras etc. in manu regis etc., et si plures etc., et quod haberet corpora eorum coram etc. Et vicecomes mandavit quod Philippus de Farlegh', Walterus Germayn, Mattheus de Bosco, Robertus Futeware, Johannes le Careter et Henricus Vodecok' manuceperunt predictos Robertum et Jocosam, quos non habuerunt. Ideo in misericordia. Et quod exitus terrarum predicti Roberti sunt .xiij. solidi .iiij. denarii. Judicium, sicut alias, a die Pasche in tres septimanas ad respondendum etc. et ad audiendum etc. de pluribus defaltis. Et vicecomes sit etc. ad respondendum de omnibus exitibus a tempore quo primo <preceptum fuit etc.>[154]

(377)

Cresseus filius Gente judeus optulit se quarto die versus Henricum de Well', fratrem et heredem Roberti de Well', tenentem partem terrarum que fuerunt predicti Roberti, de placito debiti. Et ipse non venit. Et preceptum fuit vicecomiti quod ipsum venire faceret coram etc. ad hunc diem. Et vicecomes mandavit quod predictus Walterus le Keu Remes, Symon clericus de eadem manuceperunt predictum Henricum, quem non habuerunt. Ideo in misericordia. Judicium quod distringat per terras etc., ita quod nec ipse etc., et quod de exitibus etc., et quod habeat corpus ejus coram etc. a die Pasche in quinque septimanas ad respondendum etc. et ad audiendum etc.

(378)

Essex'. Willelmus de Middelton', clericus de scaccario etc., per attornatum suum optulit se quarto die versus Johannem personam de Magna Henneye de placito debiti. Et ipse non venit. Et preceptum fuit vicecomiti quod ipsum venire faceret coram etc. ad hunc diem etc. Et vicecomes mandavit quod predictus Johannes clericus est et non habet laycum feodum per quod possit distringi. Ideo preceptum est custodibus spiritualitatis episcopatus Lond' quod dictum Johannem distringant per bona sua ecclesiastica, ita quod habeant corpus ejus coram etc. a die Pasche in quinque septimanas ad respondendum predicto Willelmo de predicto placito.

(379)

Essex', Her[t]ford'. Haginus de Berkhamsted' judeus per attornatum suum fecit venire Robertum filium Nicholai de Flaunden', tenentem quandam partem terrarum que fuerunt Thome de Flaunden', et exigit ab eo .v. marcas quas ei debet occasione etc. per cyrographum .xij. marcarum, unde altera pars est in archa cyrographariorum Bed', ut dicit, et de lucro inde emerso.

Predictus Robertus venit et petit diem premeditandi; et habet a die Pasche in .v. septimanas.

[150] *The word* misericordia *is repeated in the margin.*
[151] *The word* lex *is written in the margin at this point.*
[152] *This entry is unfinished.*
[153] *Followed by a blank (with space for a second name) in MS.*

[154] *MS. reads* primorc'.

Idem Haginus fecit venire Radulfum Serle, tenentem quandam partem predictarum terrarum, et exigit ab eo quinque solidos occasione terrarum etc. per cyrographum supradictum etc. Predictus Radulfus venit et dicit quod non est factum suum et petit diem premeditandi et habet a die Pasche in .v. septimanas.

(380)

Essex'. Idem Haginus optulit se quarto die versus Rogerum Walram et Willelmum Arundel tenentes quandam partem terrarum que fuerunt Thome de Flaunden' de placito debiti. Et ipsi non venerunt. Et preceptum fuit vicecomiti quod ipsos venire faceret. Et vicecomes mandavit quod Radulfus Serle et Willelmus Constabularius manuceperunt predictum Willelmum, quem non habuerunt. Ideo in misericordia.[155] Et predicta Rosa nichil habet nisi .xxiiij. solidos annui redditus per quod possit distringi. Judicium quod distringantur per terras etc., ita quod nec ipsi etc., et quod de exitibus etc., et quod habeat corpora eorum coram etc. a die Pasche in .v. septimanas.

(381)

Oxon'. Henna filia Jospini judea per attornatum suum optulit se quarto die versus Henricum de Shotebroke, tenentem quandam partem terrarum que fuerunt Simonis de Ordeston'. Et ipse non venit. Et preceptum fuit vicecomiti, sicut alias, quod ipsum distringeret per terras etc., et quod haberet corpus ejus coram etc. ad hunc diem. Et vicecomes mandavit quod Johannes de la Porte de Ordeston' et Willelmus atte Grene de eadem manuceperunt predictum Henricum, quem non habuerunt. Ideo in misericordia.[156] Judicium, sicut pluries, quod distringat per terras etc., et quod habeat corpus ejus coram etc. a die Pasche in .v. septimanas ad respondendum etc., et ad audiendum etc.

(382)

Oxon', Berk'. Josceus de Walyngford' per attornatum suum optulit se quarto die versus Galfridum de Wauncy de placito debiti. Et ipse non venit. Et preceptum fuit vicecomiti quod ipsum venire faceret ad hunc diem. Et vicecomes mandavit quod Willelmus Urry de Chaldelworth' et Nicholaus de Hundeshawe manuceperunt predictum Galfridum, quem non habuerunt. Ideo in misericordia.[157] Judicium quod distringat per terras etc., ita quod nec ipse etc., et quod de exitibus etc., et quod habeat corpus ejus coram etc. a die Pasche in .v. septimanas.

MEMBRANE 9 DORSE

(383)

Oxon', Berk'. Sarra que fuit uxor Benedicti le Eveke judea per attornatum suum optulit se quarto die versus Henricum de [Shotebrok',][158] tenentem quandam partem terrarum que fuerunt Simonis de Ordeston', de placito debiti. Et ipse non venit. Et preceptum fuit vicecomiti, sicut pluries, quod ipsum distringeret per terras etc., et quod haberet corpus ejus coram etc. ad hunc diem. Et vicecomes mandavit quod Johannes de la Porte de Ordeston', Willelmus atte Grene de eadem, Johannes Jog de eadem et Johannes Cytot de eadem manuceperunt predictum Henricum, quem non habuerunt. Ideo in misericordia.[159] Judicium, sicut pluries, quod distringat per terras etc., ita quod nec ipse etc., et quod de exitibus etc., et quod habeat corpus ejus coram etc. a die Pasche in .v. septimanas ad respondendum etc., et ad audiendum etc.

(384)

Surr', Sussex. Thomas Harm optulit se quarto die versus Johannem de Walynton', tenentem quamdam partem terrarum que fuerunt Thome Haunsard' in parochia de Hocham, de placito acquietacionis debiti. Et ipse non venit. Et preceptum fuit vicecomiti quod ipsum venire faceret ad hunc diem. Et vicecomes mandavit quod Willelmus atte Brok' de Ocham et Willelmus de Cruce de eadem manuceperunt predictum Johannem, quem non habuerunt. Ideo in misericordia. Judicium quod distringat per terras etc., ita quod nec ipse etc., et quod de exitibus etc., et quod habeat corpus ejus coram etc. a die Pasche in .xv. dies ad respondendum etc., et ad audiendum etc.

(385)

Sumers', Dors'. Manserus filius Aaron judeus optulit se quarto die versus Robertum de Aketon et Johannam uxorem ejus, tenentes quamdam partem terrarum que fuerunt Johannis Bretasse, de placito debiti. Et ipsi non venerunt. Et preceptum fuit vicecomiti quod ipsos venire faceret coram etc. ad hunc diem. Et vicecomes mandavit quod breve sibi inde directum ad eo tarde venit quod non potuit exequi. Ideo, sicut alias, quod venire faciat coram etc. a die Pasche in unum mensem predictos Robertum et Johannam ad respondendum predicto Mansero de placito supradicto.

(386)[160]

Lond'. Floria que fuit uxor Ysac de Berkhamsted' optulit se quarto die versus Johannem Gylle de placito debiti. Et ipse non venit. Et preceptum fuit vicecomitibus quod ipsum venirent coram etc. ad hunc diem. Et vicecomites mandaverunt quod predictus Johannes non fuit inventus

155 *The word* misercordia *is repeated in the margin.*
156 *The word* misericordia *is repeated in the margin.*
157 *The word* misericordia *is repeated in the margin.*
158 *MS. reads* Stokebrok'.
159 *The word* misericordia *is repeated in the margin.*
160 *Previously printed by Rigg in* Select Pleas, *p. 108.*

in balliva sua post recepcionem istius mandati. Ideo preceptum est eis, sicut alias, a die Pasche in .xv. dies etc.

(387)[161]

Predicta Flora venire fecit Hugonem de Bolonya et exigit ab eo .xx. marcas argenti, unum ciphum argenteum et unam supertunicam sanguinei coloris furrati, precii quinque marcarum, que sibi et Agneti le Callestere matri uxoris ejus tradidit custodiendum, que bona et catalla post decessum dicte Agnetis ad manus dicti Hugonis devenerunt ut principali executori testamenti sui et que bona et catalla Regi et ei post dampnacionem dicti Ysac viri sui injuste detinet ad dampnum suum .x. marcarum etc., et petit hoc pro Rege et se inquiri per patriam.

Predictus Hugo venit et defendit vim etc. Et dicit quod de dicta Floria et viro suo nichil recepit ut in denariis et aliis catallis, sicut versus eum narrat, nec in presencia dicte Agnetis matris uxoris sue nec in absencia ejus, nec bona sua post obitum ejus ad manus suas devenerunt nec executor testamenti ejus est, et hoc offert verificare per patriam. Et predicta Floria quod dicta bona et denarii ad manus ejus devenerunt, ut predictum est, ponit se similiter super patriam. Ideo preceptum est vicecomitibus Lond' quod venire faciant coram etc. a die Pasche in .xv. dies .xij. etc. de visneto de Grascherich', et qui etc., et constabulario Turris Lond' quod venire faciat etc. ad eundem diem .xij. legales judeos, et qui etc., ad recognoscendum super sacramentum suum super premissis veritatem etc.

Ad quem diem inquisicio venit per Ricardum de Hormede, Willelmum de Boxle et alios christianos, Sampsonem de Ralee, Manserum Lewy et alios judeos, sicut patet inter brevia termini Pasche proximo sequentis retornata. Qui dicunt super sacramentum suum quod predictus Hugo nichil habuit nec recepit de bonis predictorum Ysac vel Florie nec predicta Agnes nisi tantummodo unam ollam eneam precii .xv. denariorum, unum lavatrum precii .x. denariorum, unam patellam veterem precii .vij. denariorum, unam supertunicam de cameloto precii .v. solidorum, unum linthiamen et unum tapetum precii .vj. denariorum et unum cyphum de mazere precii .xij. denariorum, que bona dicta Agnes recognovit coram justiciariis de bonis judeorum dampnatorum ad inquirendum deputatis[162] liberavit. Et ideo consideratum est quod dictus Hugo inde eat quietus et dicta Floria pro falso clamore in misericordia.[163]

(388)

Jospinus filius Salmonis, qui tulit breve regis super Samuelem de Arundel de injusta detencione catallorum, non est prosecutus versus eum. Ideo ipse Jospinus in misericordia.[164] Et Abraham filius Jospini et Mosseus filius Abrahe, plegii sui de prosequendo, quia non habuerunt predictum Jospinum, ideo in misericordia.

(389)

Surr'. Sussex. Rogerus de Folkeston', serviens de scaccario etc., optulit se quarto die versus Willelmum,[165] Matildam uxorem ejus et Henricum de Fixerigg' de placito debiti. Et ipsi non venerunt. Et preceptum fuit vicecomiti quod ipsos venire faceret coram etc. ad hunc diem. Et vicecomes mandavit quod Robertus de Cruce de Horcy' et Willelmus le Taylur' de Brustoue manuceperunt predictos Willelmum et Matillidam, quos non habuerunt. Ideo in misericordia. Et quod Robertus de Walesbergh' et Nicholaus de Welkenested' manuceperunt predictum Henricum de Fixerigg', quem non habuerunt. Ideo in misericordia. Judicium quod distringat per terras etc., ita quod nec ipsi etc., et quod de exitibus etc., et quod habeat corpora eorum coram etc. a die Pasche in .v. septimanas ad respondendum etc., et ad audiendum etc.

(390)

Devon'. Johannes filius Bernardi optulit se quarto die versus Humfridum le Kael de placito acquietacionis debiti. Et ipse non venit. Et preceptum fuit vicecomiti quod ipsum distringeret per terras etc., et quod haberet corpus ejus coram etc. ad hunc diem. Et vicecomes mandavit quod Walterus de Holecomb' et Johannes de eadem manuceperunt predictum Humfridum [quem non habuerunt. Ideo in misericordia. Judicium, sicut alias, quod distringat predictum Humfridum][166] per terras etc., ita quod nec ipse etc., et quod habeat corpus ejus coram etc. a die Pasche in .v. septimanas ad respondendum etc. et audiendum etc.

(391)

Surr'. Sussex. Willelmum le Waleys, qui tulit breve super Samuelem de Arundel et Floriam uxorem ejus judeos, non est prosecutus versus eos. Ideo ipse Willelmus in misericordia.[167] Et Willelmus de Staunle et Walterus de la Fenne, plegii sui de prosequendo, quia non habuerunt predictum Willelmum, ideo in misericordia.

(392)

Walterus de la Forde et Cristiana uxor ejus optulerunt se quarto die versus Cheram que fuit uxor Cressey filii magistri Elie de placito.[168]

[161] *Previously printed by Rigg in* Select Pleas, *pp. 108-9.*
[162] *Some words seem to have been omitted here.*
[163] *The word* misericordia *is repeated in the margin.*
[164] *The word* misericordia *is repeated in the margin.*
[165] *Sic in MS.*
[166] *MS. omits.*
[167] *The word* misericordia *is repeated* in the margin.
[168] *This entry is unfinished.*

EASTER TERM, 8 EDWARD I [1280]

Exchequer of Jews, Plea Roll No. 35 [E 9/35]

There is only a single surviving roll for this term. The presence at the top left hand of several membranes of the letter 'h' suggests that the roll was made for the senior justice of the Jews, Hamon Hauteyn.

MEMBRANE 1

Essonia de quindena Pasche anno regni regis Edwardi octavo

(393)

Suth'. Petrus le Neuman de Andevere versus Sarram que fuit uxor Salle de Wynton' judeam de placito debiti per Adam Prodom.

Robertus le Swengere de Andevere versus eandem Sarram de eodem.

(394)

Buk'. Johannes filius Walteri de Hadenham, tenens terrarum que fuerunt Hugonis Juvenal, versus A. reginam Anglie consortem regis de placito debiti per Adam Prodom.

Essonia de tribus septimanis Pasche

(395)

Norff'; vetus est. Johannes de Pilketon' attornatus magistri Alani de Freston' versus Isac le Eveske judeum de placito debiti per Walterum Gyle.

Johannes le Messager alter attornatus versus eundem de eodem per Willelmum Cressaundyn.

A die sancti Michaelis in .xv. dies. Affidavit.

(396)[1]

Bed'. Johannes Malerbe venit coram etc. et recognovit se debere Aron filio Vives centum summas frumenti vel pro qualibet summa dimidiam marcam, reddendum ad festum sancti Michaelis anno regni regis Edwardi octavo. Et, nisi fecerit, concedit quod de terris et catallis suis fiant etc.

(397)

Warr'. Robertus Hasteng miles de comitatu Warr' venit coram etc. et recognovit se debere Aron filio Vives et magistro Elye filio magistri Mossei .lxx. libras sterlingorum reddendum a die sancti Michaelis in unum mensem anno regni regis Edwardi octavo.

[1] *This and the following entry are written upside down at the bottom of the membrane and in a different hand.*

MEMBRANE 1 DORSE

[blank]

MEMBRANE 2[2]

Placita de quindena Pasche anno regni regis Edwardi octavo

(398)

Norff'. Isac le Evesk judeus Lond' venire fecit Bartholomeum de Acre, tenentem quandam partem terrarum que fuerunt Samuelis de Norvic, et exigit ab eo decem [libras][3] quas ei debet occasione predictarum terrarum que fuerunt dicti Samuelis quas tenet per quoddam starrum .xxx. librarum inter predictos Ysac et Samuelem judeos confectum, cujus altera pars est in archa cyrographorum Lond' ut dicit.

Predictus Bartholomeus venit et dicit quod non est factum suum et petit diem premeditandi, et habet diem in octabis sancte Trinitatis.

(399)

Ebor'. Adam de Novo Mercato per attornatum suum optulit se quarto die versus Henricum de Luffenham de placito transgressionis. Et ipse non venit. Et preceptum fuit vicecomiti quod non omitteret propter libertatem de Tykehull' quin eam etc., et distringeret predictum Henricum per terras etc., et quod haberet corpus ejus coram etc. Et vicecomes mandavit quod Gilbertus filius Roberti de Sutton' juxta Norton', Robertus le Long' de eadem, Johannes le Long' de eadem, et Ricardus Clusemane de eadem manuceperunt predictum Henricum, quem non habuerunt. Ideo in <misericordia.>[4] Judicium,[5] sicut alias, quod non omittat propter libertatem etc. in octabis sancte Trinitatis etc. ad respondendum etc

[2] *The letter 'h' is written a little to the left and above the heading to this membrane.*

[3] *MS. reads* librarum.

[4] *The word* misericordia *is repeated in the margin.*

[5] *Followed in MS. by* quod non, *which should have been marked for deletion.*

(400)

Heref'. Preceptum fuit vicecomiti quod distringeret Willelmum, filium et heredem Willelmi de Sholle, per terras etc. pro quinque marcis ad opus Regis de debitis Sampsonis filii Isac judei per cyrographum .xv. marcarum inter predictum Willelmum, patrem predicti Willelmi, et ipsum Sampsonem confectum in hec verba: 'Willelmus de Scholle de comitatu Heref' debet Sampsoni filio Isaac de Wigorn' judeo .xv. marcas, reddendum .vij. marcas et dimidiam in crastino Purificacionis Beate Marie anno regis Edwardi secundo, et in crastino clausi Pasche proximo sequenti .vij. marcas et dimidiam. Acta die Exaltacionis Sancte Crucis proximo ante predictos terminos', cujus debita capta sunt in manu Regis pro debitis in quibus idem Sampson tenetur Regi. Predictus Willelmus venit et habet diem usque diem lune etc.

(401)

Norht'. Mosseus filius Salomonis judeus pro pluribus defaltis versus Robertum de Brus et Hugonem de Ryhale de placito acquietacionis debiti in <misericordia.>[6]

Idem Mosseus filius Salomonis attachiatus ad respondendum Roberto de Brus et Hugoni de Rihale de placito aquietacionis debiti, et unde tanquam tenentes terras que fuerunt Petri filii Rogeri queruntur quod injuste districti sunt pro .lx. solidis in quibus dictus Petrus ei per cartam suam tenebatur, eo quod dictus Petrus dictos denarios ad diem sibi inter eos inde prefixum propter absenciam dicti Mossei secundum legem et consuetudinem Judaismi tradidit cyrographariis Stamf' custodiendum, ut diem suum observaret et quos denarios predictus Mosseus a dictis cyrographariis postea recepit, ita quod eos de dictis .lx. solidis omnino acquietare debet et cartam inde confectam deliberare, et non adhuc eam deliberavit ad dampnum eorum [blank] etc. Et hoc offerunt verificare per dictos cyrographarios etc.

Predictus Mosseus venit et defendit vim etc. Et dicit quod indorsatum fuit in dicta carta quod medietas dicti debiti fuit Sampsonis de Staunf' judei, qui Regi in .iiij. marcis tenebatur de magno tallagio anno regis Edwardi secundo, et per predictum indorsamentum dicta carta capta fuit in manum Regis et missa Lond' pro tallagio dicti Sampsonis. Et de dictis denariis cyrographario judeo predicto custodiendum traditis recepit medietatem, videlicet .xxx. solidos pro porcione dicti debiti ipsum inde contingente, et aliam medietatem dictum Sampsonem contingentem non recepit. Et hoc ponit super dictos cyrographarios.

Et predicti Robertus et Hugo quod omnes predictos denarios prefatis cyrographariis ad opus suum custodiendum traditis recepit, et secum detulit similiter se ponunt super patriam. Et preceptum est vicecomiti Linc' quod venire faciat coram etc. in octabis sancte Trinitatis predictos cyrographarios christianos et judeos ad recognoscendum etc.

[6] *The word* misericordia *is repeated in the margin.*

(402)

Linc'. Cresseus filius Gente optulit se quarto die versus Walterum de la Linde, tenentem quamdam partem terrarum que fuerunt Johannis Russel, de placito debiti. Et ipse non venit. Et preceptum fuit vicecomiti quod ipsum distringeret per terras etc., et quod haberet corpus ejus coram etc. ad hunc diem. Et vicecomes mandavit quod Galfridus Brande de Scaleby, Henricus Bonde de eadem, Willelmus frater ejusdem de eadem, et Walterus le Nayn de eadem manuceperunt predictum Walterum, quem non habuerunt. Ideo in <misericordia.>[7] Et sunt <exitus terrarum dicti Walteri .x. solidi.>[8] Judicium quod salvo custodiat etc., et si plures etc., et quod de exitibus etc., et quod habeat corpus ejus coram etc. in octabis sancte Trinitatis etc. ad respondendum et ad audiendum etc.. Et quod vicecomes habeat ad eundem diem dictos exitus.

(403)

Herf'.Johannes de la Heche optulit se quarto die versus Jacobum filium Sadek' et Sarram de Herf' judeos de placito compoti. Et ipsi per Sampsonem de Wigorn' attornatum suum veniunt et dicunt quod dicta Sarra nihil exigit de dicto Johanne et dicunt quo dictus Jacobus exigit de dicto Johanne de Hech' .xl. solidos per cyrographum .xl. solidorum, unde altera pars est in archa cyrographariorum Heref' ut dicit in hec verba: 'Johannes de la Heche de parochia de Lesire debet Jacobo filio Sadekin' .xl. solidos argenti solvendos eidem ad Natale Domini anno regni regis Edwardi quarto' sigillo dicti Johannis roboratum in vigilia sancti Johannis ante'.[9]

Predictus Johannes, qui presens fuit, dicit quod solvit predictis Jacobo et Sarre pro predictis .xl. solidis in denariis .lij. solidos .ii. denarios per .v. tallias quas protulit coram etc., continentes predictam pecunie summam, et unum equum precii .vij. solidorum et hoc offert verificare per patriam.

Et predictus Sampson attornatus predictorum Jacobi et Sarre dicit quod de predictis .xl. solidis nichil adhuc receptum est nisi tantummodo unus equus debilis de precio .iiij. solidorum et hoc similiter ponit se super patriam.

Et preceptum est vicecomiti quod venire faciat coram etc. in quindena sancte Trinitatis .vj. bonos et legales christianos de visneto de Heche et .vj. legales judeos de civitate Heref' et qui etc. ad recognoscendum super premissis veritatem etc. Et quia in quadam tallia scriptum fuit ebrayca littera quod dictus Jacobus recepit .v. solidos de lucro cum terminus solucionis dictorum .xl. solidorum post statutum regis fuit, preceptum est vicecomiti quod habeat corpora predictorum Jacobi et Sarre ad respondendum Regi de predicta transgressione et cetera.

[7] *The word* misericordia *is repeated in the margin.*

[8] *The words* exitus *and* x solidi *are repeated in the margin.*

[9] *This paragraph seems to have been left unfinished. The letters* .L. s *are written in the margin.*

(404)

Cantebr' Hunt'. Magister Walterus de la Mare optulit se quarto die versus Willelmum le Moyne de placito injuste detencionis catallorum suorum. Et ipse non venit. Et preceptum fuit vicecomiti quod ipsum venire faceret coram etc. ad hunc diem. Et vicecomes mandavit quod Thomas Lompe de Drayton' et Johannes de Colmwranch manuceperunt predictum Willelmum, quem non habuerunt. Ideo in <misericordia.>[10] Judicium quod distringat per terras etc., ita quod nec ipse etc., et quod de exitibus etc., et quod habeat corpus ejus coram etc. in octabis sancte Trinitatis ad respondendum etc., et ad audiendum judicium etc.

(405)

Cantebr'. Dell' que fuit uxor Jacobi judea Cant' optulit se quarto die versus Johannem le Maltere et Matillidam uxorem ejus de placito injuste detencionis catallorum. Et ipsi non venerunt. Et preceptum fuit vicecomiti quod ipsos venire faceret coram etc. ad hunc diem. Et vicecomes mandavit quod Johannes le Maltere, Poletere de Berkham, Henricus filius Martini de eadem, et Thomas de Parnes de eadem manuceperunt predictos Johannem et Matillidem, quos non habuerunt. Ideo in <misericordia.>[11] Judicium quod distringat per terras etc., ita quod nec ipsi etc., et quod de exitibus etc., et quod [habeat] corpora eorum coram etc. a die sancte Trinitatis in .xv. dies ad respondendum etc.

(406)

Surr', Suss'. Walterus de Wouburn optulit se quarto die versus Joelem de Gerston', Rogerum le Moyne et Laurencium de Baker' de placito debiti. Et ipsi non venerunt. Et preceptum fuit vicecomiti quod ipsos venire faceret etc. Et vicecomes mandavit quod Willelmus le Fik' de Blessingl' et Henricus le Peyntur de eadem manuceperunt predictum Joelem; et quod Ricardus Attegate de Blessingle et Reginaldus le Rus de eadem manuceperunt predictum Rogerum; et quod Willelmus le Crawe de Taunregge et Walterus le Blake de eadem manuceperunt predictum Laurencium; quos non habuerunt. Ideo in <misericordia.>[12] Judicium quod distringat per terras etc., ita quod nec ipsi etc., et quod de exitibus etc., et quod habeat eorum corpora coram etc. in octabis sancte Trinitatis ad respondendum etc. et ad audiendum etc.

(407)

Lond'. Johannes de Bayfeld, clericus de scaccario etc., optulit se quarto die versus Robertum de Laufar chaucer de placito debiti. Et ipse non venit. Et preceptum fuit vicecomitibus quod ipsum venire facerent coram etc. ad hunc diem. Et vicecomites mandaverunt quod Nicholaus de Cantebr' et Willelmus de Harewe mercer manuceperunt predictum Robertum quem non habuerunt.. Ideo in misericordia. Judicium quod distringant per terras etc., ita quod nec ipse etc., et quod de exitibus etc., et quod habeant corpus ejus etc. a die Pasche in .v. septimanas ad respondendum etc. et ad audiendum etc.

(408)

Lond'. Fluria que fuit uxor Isac de Berkamsted' optulit se quarto die versus Johannem Chelle de placito debiti. Et ipse non venit. Et preceptum fuit vicecomitibus quod ipsum venire facerent et distringerent per terras etc. et quod haberent corpus ejus coram etc. ad hunc diem. Et vicecomites mandaverunt quod breve adeo tarde venit quod exequi non potuerunt. Ideo, sicut alias, a die Pasche in .v. septimanas.

(409)

Somers'. Gamaliel de Ox' optulit se quarto die versus Guidonem rectorem ecclesie de Bacwell', tenentem quandam partem terre que fuit Roberti Britach', de placito debiti. Et ipse non venit. Et preceptum fuit vicecomiti quod ipsum distringeret per terras etc. et quod [haberet][13] corpus ejus coram etc. ad hunc diem. Et vicecomes mandavit quod Nicholas Atteregh' de Brafeld', Rogerus Atteheth' de eadem, Johannes Attewatre de eadem et Rogerus de Stallar' de eadem manuceperunt predictum Guidonem, quem non habuerunt. Ideo in misericordia. Judicium, sicut alias, quod distringat per terras etc. in octabis sancte Trinitatis etc.

(410)

Suth'. Sarra que fuit uxor Salle de Winton' per essoniatorem suum optulit se quarto die versus Petrum le Neuman et Robertum de Myngere de Andever, Willelmum Parkeday, Hugonem de Northerne, Robertum filium Roberti le Cutelir, Johannem de Arundel de Winton' de placito debiti et injuste detencionis catallorum. Et ipsi non venerunt. Et preceptum fuit vicecomiti quod ipsos venire faceret. Et vicecomes mandavit quod Stephanus Orpede, Hugo Cupping, Willelmus Hugge et Thomas Waldef' manuceperunt Petrum le Neuman; et quod Willelmus Ingulsir', Thomas de Bosco, Hugo le Parmenter et Henricus Godir manuceperunt Robertum Swingere; quos non habuerunt. Ideo in <misericordia.>[14] Judicium quod distringat per terras etc., ita quod nec ipsi etc., et quod de exitibus etc. Et quod habeat corpora eorum coram etc. a die sancte Trinitatis in .xv. dies ad respondendum etc. et ad audiendum etc. Et vicecomes mandavit quod retornavit breve inde sibi directum [pro] Roberto, Willelmo, Hugone et Johanne de Winton' ballivis libertatis Winton', qui nichil inde fecerunt. Judicium quod non omittat propter libertatem etc. quin eam et venire faciat ad eundem diem etc..

[10] *The word* misericordia *is repeated in the margin.*

[11] *The word* misericordia *is repeated in the margin.*

[12] *The word* misericordia *is repeated in the margin.*

[13] *MS. reads* habeat.

[14] *The word* misericordia *is repeated in the margin.*

MEMBRANE 2 DORSE

(411)

Oxon'. Sarra que fuit uxor Benedicti le Eweske per Gamalielem de Oxon' attornatum suum optulit se quarto die versus Henricum de Shotebrok', tenentem quandam partem terrarum que fuerunt Simonis de Ordeston', de placito debiti. Et ipse non venit. Et preceptum fuit vicecomiti, sicut pluries, quod ipsum distringeret per terras etc., et quod haberet corpus ejus coram etc. ad hunc diem. Et vicecomes mandavit quod Willelmus Attegrene de Ordeston', [e]<Willelmus>[e] Johannes ad portam de eadem, Johannes Scot, et Walterus le Bercher manuceperunt predictum Henricum, quem non habuerunt. Ideo in <misericordia.>[15] Judicium quod salvo custodiat etc., et si plura etc., et quod de exitibus etc., et quod habeat corpus ejus etc. a die sancte Trinitatis in .xv. dies ad respondendum etc. et ad audiendum etc.

(412)

Nortf'. Isac le Eweske judeus Lond' optulit se quarto die versus Josceum filium Deulecres de placito debiti. Et ipse non venit. Et preceptum fuit vicecomiti, sicut pluries, quod ipsum venire faceret coram etc. ad hunc diem. Et vicecomes mandavit quod dictus Josceus non fuit inventus in balliva sua post recepcionem brevis inde sibi directi. Judicium, sicut pluries, in octabis sancte Trinitatis ad respondendum etc.

(413)

Esseyx'. Aaron filius Vyves fecit venire Robertum le Poer, tenentem quandam partem terrarum que fuerunt Roberti de Borham, et exigit ab eo occasione etc. .xl. libras de catallo et centum et decem libras de lucro per unam cartam .c. librarum sub nominibus predicti Roberti de Borham et Sampsonis filii Vyves. Predictus Robertus venit et petit diem premeditandi et habet a die sancte Trinitatis in .xv. dies.

Predictus Aaron per breve predictum fecit venire priorem de Legh', tenentem quandam partem terrarum predictarum[16] que fuerunt predicti Roberti de Borham, et exigit ab eo occasione etc. viginti libras de catallo et .iiii.^{xx} libras de lucro per predictam cartam .c. librarum sub nominibus predicti Roberti et Sampsonis.

Predictus prior venit et bene recognoscit se esse tenentem cujusdam partis terrarum que fuerunt predicti Roberti, et dicit quod de predicto debito respondere non debet eo quod Johannes Reynger satisfecit predicto [e]<debito>[e] judeo de toto predicto debito per .xliij. libras sex solidos et octo denarios et quas idem Johannes solvit predicto judeo ad terminos dudum preteritos. Et de hoc ponit se super rotulos de scaccario judeorum de anno regis Henrici .lij.

Et predictus Aaron dicit quod nunquam hujusmodi recognicionem fecit nec predictum debitum predicto Johanni acquietavit, et hoc ponit se super eosdem rotulos. Et quia, scrutatis rotulis de annis .lj.^{o}, .lij. et .liij., non est inventa aliqua recognicio nec quieta clamancia predicti debiti facta predicto Johanni Rynger nec cuicumque alii, ideo consideratum est quod predictus Aaron recuperet versus predictum priorem tenentem cujusdam partis.

(414)

Lond'. Hamo le Keu, Adam le Bokeler, Johannes Nevreathon et Teynot le Bokeler attachiati ad respondendum Sampsoni de Wigorn' judeo de placito transgressionis et roberie, unde queritur quod, cum ipse ad hostium domus sue in parochia sancti Laurencii stetisset, predictus Hamo, Adam, Johannes et Teynot ad ipsum venerunt et denarios ad vinum ab eo exigerunt et valde stricte eum tenuerunt et per consensum eorum Reginaldus de Winchecumbe capucium suum de capite suo precii dimidie marce cepit et contra pacem domini regis secum maliciose asportarunt et adhuc detinent ad dampnum suum .xx. solidorum etc, et producit sectam.

Predictus Hamo, Adam, Johannes, Teynot defendunt vim etc. Et dicunt quod dictum Sampsonem non tenuerunt nec capucium dicti Sampsonis per consilium et voluntatem ipsorum asportatum fuit, sicut versus eos narrat, et hoc petunt inquiri per patriam.

Et dictus Sampson quod ipsum stricte tenuerunt et capucium suum precii dimidie marce, ut predictum est, captum fuit et asportatum maliciose et adhuc detentum ponit se similiter super patriam. Et preceptum est vicecomitibus Lond' quod venire faciant coram etc a die Pasche in .xv. dies .xij. de visneto dicti Sancti Laurencii etc., et qui etc., ad recognoscendum super premissis veritatem etc. Et preceptum [est constabulario][17] Turris Lond' quod venire faciat .xij. judeos ad eundem diem etc.

(415)

Cantebr'. Manserus filius Aaron venire fecit Henricum de Hwadon, tenentem terrarum que fuerunt Thome de Qwadon fratris sui, et exigit ab eo novem marcas quas debet ei occasione etc., per cyrographum novem marcarum sub nominibus predicti Thome et Abraham filii Jues confectum et que carta ei liberata fuit de thesauro regis in recompensacionem debitorum Johannis de Burgo in quibus ei tenebatur.

Predictus Henricus venit et recognovit se esse tenentem predictarum terrarum et non potuit dedicere quin de dicto debito satisfacere tenetur et per licenciam justiciarorum concordati sunt sub hac forma, videlicet quod, [i]<si>[i] predictus Henricus solvit predicto Mansero die lune proxima post mensem Pasche .xl. solidos et ad Penthecosten proximo sequentem .xl. solidos, tunc idem Manser eidem Henrico predictam cartam .ix. marcarum quietam deliberabit pro predictis sex marcis terminis predictis solvendis. Et, nisi predictus Henricus predictas

[15] *The word* misericordia *is repeated in the margin.*

[16] *Followed in MS. by* terrarum.

[17] *MS. omits.*

sex marcas predicto Mansero solverit, predictus Manserus totum predictum debitum novem marcarum versus prefatum Henricum recuperabit, salvo tamen quod si predictus Henricus aliquid predicto Mansero solverit de dicto debito, dictus Manserus in solucione dicte pecunie perficiendo allocabit.

(416)

Cant', Suff'. Willelmus de Midelton clericus etc. fecit venire Rogerum de Feltewell' ad respondendum ei de placito debiti, et exigit ab eo .xl. marcas quas ei debet pro bladis ecclesie de Wridelington' venditis Thome capellano de Wridelington' et quas predictus [Rogerus][18] concessit solvere eidem Willelmo pro predicto Thoma, et [profert scriptum][19] predicti Rogeri quod hoc testatur.

Et predictus Rogerus venit et dicit quod non tenetur predicto Willelmo in aliquo debito nec prefatum scriptum umquam ei fecit nec idem scriptum sigillo suo consignavit. Et predictus Willelmus dicit quod dictum scriptum sibi fecit et sigillo suo consignavit de predicto debito .xlv. marcarum pro vendicione dictorum bladorum. Et de hoc ponit se super patriam et predictus Rogerus similiter. Ideo preceptum est vicecomiti quod venire faciat coram etc. in octabis sancte Trinitatis etc. .xij. liberos et legales homines de visneto de Wridelington' etc., per quos etc., ad recognoscendum etc. Quia tam etc.

(417)

Cantebr'. Idem Rogerus recognovit se debere eidem Willelmo .xx. solidos de quodam alio debito solvendos in octabis sancte Trinitatis. Et, nisi fecerit, concedit quod de terris et catallis suis fiant.

(418)

Norff' Suff'. Ricardus de Cokefeld', custos heredis, terrarum et tenementorum que fuerunt Roberti de Norton', optulit se quarto die versus Herveum de Hegeset' et Henricum Brun de Sancto Edmundo, executores testamenti predicti Roberti, de placito acquietacionis diversorum debitorum et amerciamentorum que de dicto Ricardo exiguntur racione dicte custodie per summonicionem scaccarii etc. de tempore quo fuit vicecomes comitatuum predictorum.

Predictus Herveus venit et dicit quod habet Henricum Brun coexecutorem dicti testamenti sine quo non potest respondere. Et dictus Henricus non venit. Et preceptum fuit quod ipsum venire faceret. Et vicecomes mandavit quod Rogerus Dyke de Staunton', Gilbertus frater ejus, Rogerus Pelliparius de eadem, et Galfridus Sutor de eadem manuceperunt predictum Henricum, quem non habuerunt. Ideo in <misericordia.>[20] Judicium quod distringatur per terras etc., et quod habeat corpus ejus coram etc. a die sancte Trinitatis in .xv. dies ad respondendum etc., et eundem diem habet dictus Herveus etc.

[18] *MS. reads* Thomas.

[19] *MS. reads* ven' idem Willelmus.

[20] *The word* misericordia *is repeated in the margin.*

(419)

Norff'. Isac le Eveske optulit se quarto die versus Josceum filium Deulecres judeum de placito debiti. Et ipse non venit. Et preceptum fuit vicecomiti, sicut pluries, quod ipsum venire faceret. Et vicecomes mandavit quod dictus Josceus non fuit inventus in balliva sua postquam recepit dictum breve. Ideo, sicut pluries, a die sancti Johannis Baptiste in .xv. dies ad respondendum etc.

(420)

Hereff'. Joye que fuit uxor Isac filii Diey per attornatum suum optulit se quarto die versus Walterum filium Walteri de Everoys, tenentem terrarum predicti Walteri patris sui, de placito debiti. Et ipse non venit. Et preceptum fuit vicecomiti quod ipsum venire faceret. Et vicecomes mandavit quod Rogerus filius Reginaldi, Hugo Deveroys de Bodenham, Thomas Wydye et Rogerus de Everoys de Bodenham manuceperunt predictum Walterum, quem non habuerunt. Ideo in misericordia. Judicium quod distringatur per terras etc., et quod habeat corpus ejus coram etc. a die sancte Trinitatis in .xv. dies etc.

(421)

Somers'. Rogerus de Kynton', serviens in scaccario etc., optulit se quarto die versus Johannem de Asshele de placito debiti. Et ipse non venit. Et preceptum fuit vicecomiti, sicut pluries, quod ipsum venire faceret. Et vicecomes mandavit quod dictus Johannes districtus est per .v. acras terre et non fuit inventus in balliva sua post recepcionem istius brevis. Ideo, sicut pluries, etc. a die sancte Trinitatis in .xv. dies.

(422)

Oxon'. Cristiana Benorth de Comenore optulit se quarto die versus Isac de Kaune judeum de placito compoti et acquietacionis debiti. Et ipse non venit. Et preceptum fuit vicecomiti quod ipsum venire faceret. Et vicecomes mandavit quod Benedictus filius Aaron et Elias de Norht' manuceperunt predictum Isac, quem non habuerunt. Ideo in <misericordia.>[21] Judicium quod distringatur per terras etc., ita quod nec ipse etc., et quod habeat corpus ejus coram etc. a die sancte Trinitatis in .xv. dies ad respondendum etc..

(423)

Lond'. Walterus de la Forde et Cristiana uxor ejus optulerunt se quarto die versus Cheram que fuit uxor Cressei filii magistri Elie judei de placito injuste detencionis vadii. Et ipsa non venit. Et preceptum fuit constabulario quod ipsam distringeret per terras etc. Et constabularius mandavit quod Jacobus de Hamersteyn et Salomon le Waleys manuceperunt predictam Cheram, quam non habuerunt. Ideo in misericordia. Judicium,

[21] *The word* misericordia *is repeated in the margin.*

sicut alias, a die Pasche in .v. septimanas ad respondendum etc. Et constabularius habeat ad eundem diem .j. marcam de predictis manucaptoribus quia non habuerunt etc.

(424)

Kanc'. Per licenciam justiciariorum Simon de Craye querens et Gregorius de Rokesle, tenens quandam partem terrarum que fuerunt Willelmi de Mares in Senting', de placito debiti Judaismi concordati sunt sub hac forma, videlicet quod idem Simon remisit, concessit et omnino quietumclamavit in perpetuum pro se et heredibus suis Gregorio de Rokesle omnem accionem, calumpniam et demandam quas habuit vel aliquo modo habere potuit vel debuit erga eundem Gregorium occasione cujusdam annui feodi decem marcarum in quo idem Willelmus tenebatur Leoni filii Preciose et eciam occasione cujusdam debiti .lx. marcarum in quo idem Willelmus tenebatur eidem judeo per cartam suam, quod quidem debitum et feodum dictus Leo concessit et dimisit prefato Simoni, cujus concessionem et dimissionem dictus Henricus rex confirmavit per litteras suas patentes, prout patet in termino sancti Hillarii anno regis Henrici .liij. Et quod nec idem Simon, heredes vel assignati sui occasione predicti debiti et feodi a dicto Gregorio, heredibus vel assignatis suis vel quocumque predictas terras et tenementa tenente de cetero nichil potuerunt exigere vel vendicare in perpetuum. Et preterea predictus Simon concessit prefato Gregorio quod habeat eundem statum et idem recuperare versus Johannem de Mares, tenentem quandam partem terrarum que fuerunt predicti Willelmi de Mares in Senting', que idem Simon habuit versus predictum Gregorium et alios tenentes ante istam concessionem eidem Gregorio factam racione predictorum debiti et feodi. Et super hoc predictus Gregorius concessit quod predictus Johannes non distringatur pro predicto debito et feodo. Et preterea dictus Simon concessit quod carte que sunt in archa cyrographariorum de predicto debito et feodo sub nominibus predictorum Willelmi et Leonis extrahantur qualicumque hora seu tempore predictus Gregorius vel heredes sui voluerint ad voluntatem eorum sine aliqua contradiccione vel impedimento.

MEMBRANE 3

Adhuc placita de quindena Pasche et tribus septimanis anno .viij.[22]

(425)

Kanc'. Haginus de Bradested' judeus fecit venire Simonem le Foutrer de Bradested' et Gretam uxorem ejus et exigit ab eis unam zonam et tres anulos auri precii .ij. marcarum quos ei tradidit custodiendum et ei injuste detinent ad dampnum suum .xx. solidorum etc. et producit sectam etc.

Predicti Simon et Greta veniunt et defendunt vim etc. Et dicunt quod non tenentur ad hoc breve respondere eo quod uxor dicti Simonis vocatur Margareta et non Greta nomine baptismi. Et hoc offerunt verificare per patriam. Et dictus [Haginus][23] non potuit dedicere quin vocetur Margareta. Ideo consideratum est quod dicti Simon et Margareta quantum ad hoc breve eant sine die. Et dictus Haginus pro falso clamore in <misericordia.>[24]

Idem Haginus fecit venire Dulciam que fuit uxor Galfridi le Poyt et exigit ab ea bona et catalla ad valenciam .xl. solidorum que ei tradidit custodiendum et injuste detinet ad dampnum suum .xl. solidorum et ad hoc producit sectam.

Predicta Dulcia venit et dixit quod vocata est nomine baptismi Mabilia et hoc offert verificare per patriam. Et dictus judeus non potuit dedicere quin vocatur Mabilia. Et petit licenciam recedendi de brevi suo et habet. Et dicta Mabilia inde sine die.

(426)

Warr'. Ricardus de Turbervyle per attornatum suum optulit se quarto die versus Nicholaum Siffrewast de placito acquietacionis debiti. Et ipse non venit. Et preceptum fuit vicecomiti, sicut alias, quod ipsum venire faceret coram etc. Et vicecomes mandavit quod Walterus atte Forde de Eddriston' et Willelmus frater ejus de eadem manuceperunt predictum Nicholaum, quem non habuerunt. Ideo in misericordia. Judicium quod distringat per terras, ita quod nec ipse etc., et quod de exitibus etc., et quod habeat corpus ejus coram etc. in octabis sancte Trinitatis ad respondendum etc. et ad audiendum etc.

(427)

Lond'. Willmus de Mortuo Mari optulit se quarto die versus Benedictum filium magistri Elie judeum de placito injuste detencionis vadii. Et ipse non venit. Et preceptum fuit constabulario Turris Lond' quod ipsum venire faceret coram etc. ad hunc diem, a die Pasche in unum mensem. Et dictus constabularius mandavit quod dictus Benedictus non fuit inventus in balliva sua postquam breve inde sibi directum ad ipsum venit. Ideo, sicut alias, a die Pasche in .v. septimanas ad respondendum etc. Et constabularius sit etc..

(428)

Essex'. Rogerus de Kynton, serviens de scaccario etc., optulit se quarto die versus Hugonem de Culewrth' de placito debiti. Et ipse non venit. Et preceptum fuit vicecomiti quod ipsum distringeret per terras etc., et quod haberet corpus ejus coram etc. Et vicecomes mandavit quod Willelmus atte Dune de Horindon', Walterus Bacun de eadem, Robertus Hot de eadem et Nicholas

[22] *There is a letter* h *in the left hand marin opposite this heading.*

[23] *MS. omits.*

[24] *The word* misericordia *is repeated in the margin.*

Pleint' de eadem manuceperunt predictum Hugonem, quem non habuerunt. Ideo in <misericordia.>[25] Judicium, sicut alias, quod distringat per terras etc., et quod habeat corpus ejus coram etc. a die sancte Trinitatis in .xv. dies ad respondendum etc. et ad audiendum etc. Et vicecomes mandavit quod exitus terrarum predicti Hugonis sunt .v. solidi. Et preceptum est ei quod dictos exitus habeat coram etc. ad eundem diem etc.

(429)

Lond'. Walterus de la Ford et Cristiana uxor ejus fecerunt venire Cheram que fuit uxor Cressei filii magistri Elie filii magistri Mossei judeam et queruntur quod, cum dicta Cristiana invadiasset dicte Chere bona et catalla sua ad valenciam .c. solidorum pro .lx. solidis in vigilia sancti Jacobi anno regni regis .E. .v.^{to}, videlicet unum ciphum de mazero cum magno pede et quadam benda argenti precii .ij. marcarum, unam capam de perseto sine capucio cum monilibus de calsidon' precii .xx. solidorum, .xiij. cocleara argenti precii .xiij. solidorum, decem anulos auri precii .xxv. solidorum, sex firmacula argenti precii .ix. solidorum et unum tapetum de reyns precii .viij. solidorum, et post istam mutuacionem predicta Cristiana solvit prefato Chere in parte solucionis predictorum .lx. solidorum, videlicet in vigilia sancte Andree proximo sequenti per manus Roberti de Pelham .xl. solidos et in septimana Pasche proximo sequenti per manus Johannis Pyper .xix. solidos, et die Jovis proxima post clausum Pasche venit dicta Cristiana ad dictam Cheram et optulit ei .xij. denarios qui ei aretro fuerunt de predictis .lx. solidis et peciit visum vadii sucepti et optulit ei .xx. solidos de libera voluntate sua pro predicta mutuacione sibi facta etc., et predicta Chera dicit quod visum vadiorum suorum ei non faceret antequam ei solvisset .lij. solidos pro lucro et usura inde emersis post invadiacionem predictam. Et [pro][26] predictis lucro et usura predicta Chera prefata vadium et predictos .lix. solidos quos pro eisdem vadiis recepit adhuc injuste detinet ad dampnum predictorum Walteri et Christiane .x. librarum et contra statuta regis etc. Et hoc offerunt verificare etc.

Predicta Chera per attornatum suum venit et defendit vim etc.. Et dicit quod nulla bona, vadia seu catalla nec denarios de predicta Christiana recepit sicut versus eam narrat nec per manus dicte Christiane nec alicujus alterius per ipsam seu pro ea. Et hoc parata est facere secundum quod judea facere debet contra christianum secundum legem et consuetudinem Judaismi etc. se sola manu.

Predicti Walterus et Christiana dicunt quod dicta Chera ad legem faciendam esse non debet eo quod prompti sunt verificare quod dicta vadia detinet contra statuta regis etc. Et predicta Chera dicit quod hanc libertatem habent per cartam predecessorum regis Anglie.[27]

[25] *The word* misericordia *is repeated in the margin.*

[26] *MS. omits.*

[27] *This entry is unfinished.*

(430)

Norff' Suff'. Radulfus de Chattegrave et Emma uxor ejus optulerunt se quarto die versus Rogerum filium Thome Syger de Owerton, Katerinam uxorem ejus, Robertum Ernald, Robertum Whistan, Hugonem Tyrell' de placito transgressionis. Et ipsi non venerunt. Et preceptum fuit vicecomiti quod ipsos caperet et salvo custodiret, ita quod haberet corpora eorum coram etc. Et vicecomes mandavit quod predicti Rogerus filius Thome et alii supradicti querunt subterfugia, ita quod non possunt inveniri, et hoc maxime ad sustentacionem Radulfi de Ingleworth, quia per composicionem inter dictos Radulfum et Rogerum factam habet terras ipsius Rogeri, propter quod dictum est quod multociens tenet dictum Rogerum et alios occulte in domo suo que est de feodo <de>[28] Kerbrok'. Judicium quod vicecomes capiat predictum Radulfum una cum predicto Rogero et aliis et eos salvo custodiat etc., et quod habeat corpora eorum coram etc. in octabis sancte Trinitatis ad respondendum etc.

(431)

Suth'. Abraham filius Benedicti de Wynton' judeus optulit se quarto die versus Radulfum Bisshop de placito injuste detencionis catallorum. Et ipse non venit. Et preceptum fuit vicecomiti quod ipsum venire faceret. Et vicecomes mandavit quod retornavit breve inde sibi directum ballivis libertatis Wynton', qui nichil inde fecerunt. Judicium quod non omittat propter libertatem etc. quin eam etc. et venire faceret etc. a die sancti Johannis in .xv. dies ad respondendum etc.

(432)

Suth'. Idem Abraham per essoniatorem suum optulit se quarto die versus Radulfum Aurifabrum Sutht' et Johannem Moraund' aurifabrum Wynton' de placito debiti. Et ipsi non venerunt. Et preceptum est vicecomiti quod ipsos venire faceret. Et vicecomes mandavit quod retornavit breve inde sibi directum ballivis libertatum Wynton' et Sutht', qui nichil inde fecerunt. Judicium quod non omittat propter libertatem etc. quin eas etc. et venire faciat coram etc. a die sancti Johannis Baptiste in .xv. dies etc. predictos Radulfum et Johannem ad respondendum etc.[29]

(433)

Hereff'. Sampson filius Isac judeus fecit venire Willelmum de Sholle, filium et heredem Willelmi de Sholl, et exigit ab eo occasione etc. .x. marcas de catallo per cyrographum .x. marcarum, unde altera pars est in archa cyrographariorum Wygorn' ut dicit in hec verba: 'Willelmus de Sholle filius Willelmi de comitatu Heref' debet Sampsoni filio Isac .x. marcas reddendas crastino

[28] *This word is repeated in MS.*

[29] *This entry is followed by a partial duplicate of no. 450. It is marked for omission in the margin with the note* vacat quia alibi, *and at the end of the entry is the note* respice in rotulo sequenti.

diei clausi Pasche anno regis H. .lv.^{to} Acta die lune proxima post festum sancte Lucie ante predictum terminum etc.[30]

MEMBRANE 3 DORSE

(434)

Kanc'. Simon de Craye optulit se quarto die versus Gregorium de Rokesle, Willelmum Peyforer et Johannem de Mares, tenentes terrarum que fuerunt Willelmi de Mares, de placito debiti. Et predictus Willelmus Peyforer non venit. Et preceptum fuit vicecomiti quod ipsum venire faceret. Et vicecomes mandavit quod Jordanus atte Rede et Robertus atte Rede manuceperunt predictum Willelmum, quem non habuerunt. Ideo in <misericordia.>[31] Judicium quod distringatur per terras etc., et quod de exitibus etc., et quod habeat corpus ejus coram etc. in octabis sancte Trinitatis ad respondendum etc. et ad audiendum etc.

Predictus Simon et Gregorius concordati sunt per licenciam justiciarorum, sicut patet in rotulo precedenti.[32]

(435)

Essex'. Cresseus filius Gente per attornatum suum fecit venire Henricum de Well', fratrem et heredem Roberti de Well', tenentem quandam partem terrarum que fuerunt predicti Roberti, et exigit ab eo occasione etc. .xl. libras de catallo et .xl. libras de lucro per cyrographum .lxx. marcarum, unde altera pars est in archa cyrographariorum Colech', ut dicit, in hec verba: 'Robertus filius Thome de Well' militis debet Cresseo filio Gente judeo Lond' .lxx. marcas, reddendas ad festum sancti Michaelis anno regis Henrici filii regis Johannis .xlvj.^{to} Acta die sancti Georgii martiris anno eodem.'

Predictus Henricus venit et petit diem premeditandi et habet a die sancti Johannis Baptiste in .xv. dies etc.

(436)

Bod' Buh'. Cresseus filius Gente judeus fecit venire Ricardum Reynfrey, tenentem quandam partem terrarum que fuerunt Johannis Russel, et exigit ab eo .v. marcas de catallo et decem marcas de lucro occasione terrarum etc. per cyrographum .xx. librarum, unde altera pars est in archa cyrographariorum apud Lond', ut dicit, in hec verba.[33]

Predictus Ricardus venit et recognovit se esse tenentem quandam partem terrarum que fuerunt predicti Johannis et dicit quod plures sunt tenentes earundem terrarum qui secum de predicto debito debent respondere, videlicet Rogerus de Drayton Beauchamps, thesaurarius sancti Pauli, Willelmus de Beauchamps de Drayton.

Et preceptum est vicecomiti quod ipsos venire faciat coram etc. a die sancti Michaelis in .xv. dies ad respondendum etc. una cum predicto Ricardo, cui idem dies datus est.

(437)

Lond'. Jacobus de Stivynton fecit venire magistrum Eliam filium magistri Mossei judeum cum cyrographis etc. ad computandum cum eo de omnibus debitis. Predictus magister Elias per Isaac Poteman attornatum suum venit et exigit ab eo .xv. marcas per cyrographum .xv. marcarum etc. et lucrum.

Postea per licenciam justiciariorum predicti Jacobus et magister Elias concordati sunt sub hac forma, videlicet quod predictus Jacobus recognovit se debere eidem magistro Elie .xv. libras pro predicto debito .xv. marcarum et lucro inde emergente, reddendum inde a die sancti Johannis Baptiste proximo futuro in .xv. dies .c. solidos et a die sancti Michaelis proximo sequenti in unum mensem .c. solidos et a die Pasche proximo sequenti in unum mensem .c. solidos. Et per istam recognicionem predictus magister Elias recognovit quod, si predictus Jacobus predictas .xv. libras solverit ad terminos predictos, tunc predictus Jacobus et heredes sui quieti sunt de predicto debito .xv. marcarum et lucro emergente et de omnibus debitis et demandis que predictus magister Elias versus eum exigere poterit occasione aliquorum debitorum in quibus predictus Jacobus eidem magistro Elie tenebatur a creacione seculi usque ad festum sancti Johannis Baptiste anno regni regis E. octavo. Et, si predictus Jacobus predictas .xv. libras ad predictos terminos non solverit vel si aliquem predictorum terminorum infregerit, tunc idem magister Elias habeat suum recuperare integre de predicto debito .xv. marcarum et lucro etc.

(438)

Glouc'. Robertus de Broghton', clericus de scaccario etc., optulit se quarto die versus Henricum de Berkele de placito debiti. Et ipse non venit Et preceptum fuit vicecomiti quod ipsum distringeret per terras etc., et quod de exitibus etc., et quod haberet corpus ejus coram etc. Et vicecomes mandavit quod Walterus atte Orcheard de Duresle et Willelmus le Drivere manuceperunt predictum Henricum, quem non habuerunt. Ideo in <misericordia.>[34] Judicium quod salvo custodiat etc. terras etc., et si plures etc., et quod de exitibus etc., et quod habeat corpus ejus coram etc. a die sancti Johannis Baptiste in .xv. dies ad respondendum etc. et ad audiendum etc.

(439)

Oxon'. Henna filia Jospini judea per attornatum suum optulit se quarto die versus Henricum de Shottebroke, tenentem terrarum que fuerunt Simonis de Ordeston', de placito debiti. Et ipse non venit. Et preceptum fuit vicecomiti, sicut pluries, quod ipsum distringeret per terras

[30] *This entry is unfinished.*

[31] *The word* misericordia *is repeated in the margin.*

[32] *See no. 424.*

[33] *The wording is not given.*

[34] *The word* misericordia *is repeated in the margin.*

etc., et quod haberet corpus ejus coram etc. Et vicecomes mandavit quod breve adeo tarde sibi liberatum fuit quod exequi non potuit. Ideo, sicut pluries, quod distringatur per terras etc. et quod habeat corpus ejus coram etc. a die sancti Johannis Baptiste in .xv. dies ad respondendum etc. et ad audiendum etc.

(440)

Oxon' Berk'. Josceus de Walingford judeus, qui tulit breve de placito debiti super Galfridum de Wauncy, non est prosecutus. Ideo ipse Josceus et plegii sui de prosequendo, videlicet [blank] in <misericordia.>[35] Et preceptum fuit vicecomiti quod distringeret predictum Galfridum de Wancy per terras etc., et quod haberet corpus ejus coram etc. ad hunc diem ad respondendum predicto Josceo de placito debiti. Et ipse non venit. Et vicecomes mandavit quod Nicholaus de Hundeshawe de Chadelworth' et Radulfus Be Suthe Wode de eadem, Petrus Morter de eadem et Galfridus Eldeman de eadem manuceperunt predictum Galfridum, quem non habuerunt. Ideo in <misericordia.>[36]

(441)

Lond'. Margalicia que fuit uxor Samuelis le Blund per attornatum suum optulit se quarto die versus Michaelem le Oynter de placito injuste detencionis redditus. Et ipse non venit. Et preceptum fuit vicecomitibus Lond' quod ipsum venire facerent ad hunc diem coram etc. Et vicecomites mandaverunt quod predictus Michael jacet infirmus fere mortuus. Ideo de ipso nichil actum est. Ideo preceptum est vicecomitibus, sicut alias, a die sancte Trinitatis in .xv. dies etc.

(442)

Suff'. Rannulfus de Ludham optulit se quarto die versus Johannem filium Ricardi de Gunton de placito transgressionis. Et ipse non venit. Et preceptum fuit vicecomiti quod ipsum venire faceret. Et vicecomes mandavit quod Adam Slypet de Blundeston', Adam ballivus de Ludd', Ricardus de Foxton' et Willelmus Danyel de Blund' manuceperunt predictum Johannem, quem non habuerunt. Ideo in <misericordia.>[37] Judicium quod distringatur per terras etc., ita quod nec ipse etc., et quod de exitibus etc., et quod habeat corpus ejus coram etc. a die sancti Johannis Baptiste in .xv. dies ad respondendum etc. et ad audiendum etc.

(443)

Cantebr'. Aaron filius Vyves judeus fecit venire Willelmum de Lyndes', tenentem partem terrarum que fuerunt Roberti de Hereford', et exigit ab eo occasione predictarum terrarum etc. centum libras de catallo per duo cyrographa .vj.^{xx} librarum unde altere partes sunt in archa cyrographariorum Lond', ut dicit, et que cyrographa predictus Aaron habuit ex vendicione Benedicti filii Cok' judei.

Predictus Willelmus venit et petit diem premeditandi et habet a die sancti Johannis Baptiste in .xv. dies etc.

MEMBRANE 4

Adhuc placita de termino Pasche

(444)[38]

Walterus de Kancia fecit venire Adam de Novo Mercato et exigit ab eo tanquam attornatus Regine consortis Regis quadringentas et quadraginta libras quas debet prefate Regine de debitis Hagini filii magistri Mossei judei, cujus debita predicta Regina habet ex dono Regis etc.

Et predictus Adam venit et dicit quod Robertus Tybetot per breve regis de scaccario judeorum recepit de eo centum marcas, que sibi debent allocari in eodem debito. Et predictus Robertus, qui presens fuit, testatur se recepisse predictas centum marcas de predicto Adam, quas Rex sibi concessit per breve regis directum justiciariis etc. Et de residuo protulit quoddam starrum in quo continetur quod Haginus filius magistri Mossei perdonavit et quietavit Ade de Novo Mercato medietatem cujusdam debiti quadringentarum et quadraginta librarum sub nominibus ipsorum Ade et Hagini, et unum starrum in quo continetur quod dictus Haginus recepit quatuordecim marcas de predicto Adam de debitis in quibus ei tenetur, et unum starrum in quo continetur quod dictus Haginus recepit sex marcas de predicto Adam de debitis que ei debet; et de residuo dicit quod aliquo tempore dictus Haginus vendidit sibi quasdam domos in civitatibus Linc' et Ebor' quas Regina cepit in manum suam et eas hucusque retinuit antequam vocatus vel summonitus fuisset super hoc responsurus. Et petit quod predicta starra juxta quod purportant et valencia predictarum domorum sibi in predicto debito allocentur.

Et predictus Walterus venit et dicit quod prefatus Haginus nullum jus vel potestatem habuit vendendi predictas domos tunc temporis quando eas vendidit dicto Ade eo quod prius eas vendidit Stephano de Chenduyt, cujus jus prefata Regina habet modo, per quod vendicio illa nulla est et vana, nec videtur quod valencia illarum domorum sibi debeat allocari. Et de starris petit tempus quando confecta erant.

Et predictus Adam dicit quod predicta starra confecta erant circa festum sancti Michaelis anno regni regis Edwardi tercio.

Et predictus Walterus venit et petit judicium desicut in anno tercio omnia debita et catalla predicti Hagini capta fuerunt in manum regis et dictus Haginus inprisonatus, ita quod nullam administracionem seu potestatem habuit de debitis vel catallis suis, per quod perdonacionem vel quietacionem potuit facere de predictis debitis.

Et Haginus, qui presens fuit, venit et dicit quod idem

[35] *The word* misericordia *is repeated in the margin.*

[36] *The word* misericordia *is repeated in the margin.*

[37] *The word* misericordia *is repeated in the margin.*

[38] *Previously edited by Rigg in* Select Pleas, *pp. 109-10.*

Haginus debuit cuidam Odino mercatori et postea per licenciam domini regis deliberatus fuit a prisona, ita quod potuit loqui cum debitoribus suis et debita sua de eis recipere ad satisfaciendum predicto mercatori et starra de quietancia debitorum suorum juxta voluntatem suam facere, per quod videtur quod starra illa debent esse rata et firma. Requisitus predictus Haginus quod habet in manu sua de licencia quam habuit de Rege ad perdonandum et quietandum debita sua et idem Haginus nichil habuit seu protulit inde. Et quia atinctum est quod predicta starra que predictus Adam protulit facta fuerunt tempore quo predictus Haginus nullam administracionem seu potestatem habuit de suis debitis nec aliquo modo ea potuit tunc temporis perdonare seu quietare [i]<nec predictas domos vendere potuit,>[i] consideratum est quod predicta Regina habeat suum recuperare versus predictum Adam de predicto debito [i]<preter de predictis centum marcis,>[i] et predictus Adam suum recuperare versus predictum Haginum de tanta solucione predicti debiti quantam sibi fecit etc., et predictus Haginus, quia fraudulenter recepit predictos denarios, committitur prisone etc.

Postea venit predictus Adam et recognovit quod de debito quadringentarum et quadraginta librarum, allocatis sibi supradictis centum marcis et viginti marcis per duo starra, debet domine Regine consorti domini Regis .ccclx. libras de predicto debito; idem debet eidem Regine per unam cartam sub nomine suo et predicto Hagino .d. libras; et sic debet in universo de predictis duobus debitis octingentas et sexaginta libras, de quibus satisfaciet predicte domine Regine.

(445)

Norff'. Walterus de Kanc' fecit venire Oliverum de Ingham, tenentem quandam partem terrarum que fuerunt Bartholomei de Redham, et exigit ab eo tanquam attornatus Regine consortis Regis quingentas marcas de porcione ipsum contingente occasione terrarum quas tenet que fuerunt predicti Bartholomei de debitis Jacobi de Oxon' judei, cujus debita predicta Regina habet ex dono Regis.

Predictus Oliverus venit et dicit quod terre et tenementa que tenet de terris predicti Bartholomei ad plus extenduntur quam valent, et dicit quod terre et tenementa de Redham que fuerunt predicti Bartholomei non valent nisi octo libras et tamen extenduntur in absencia sua per emulos suos ad .xiij. libras .iiij. solidos .xj. denarios; et terre et tenementa ejusdem apud Lammesse non valent nisi quinque marcas que extenduntur ad .ix. libras .xv. solidos .vj. denarios obolum quadrans ad dampnum suum etc. Ideo concessum est ei quod iterum melius extendantur. Et predictus Oliverus per auxilium curie vocat ad warantum Bartholomeum de Redham, qui summoneatur in comitatu Norff'. Et preceptum est vicecomiti quod venire faciat coram etc. in octabis sancte Trinitatis predictum Bartholomeum ad acquietandum predictum Oliverum de predicto debito, sicut racionabiliter etc.

Ad quem diem predictus Oliverus essoniatus fuit versus predictam Reginam [e]<et predictum Bartholmeum>[e] de predicto placito, et per essoniatorem suum optulit se versus predictum Bartholomeum. Et predictus Bartholomeus non venit. Et preceptum fuit vicecomiti quod ipsum venire faceret ad hunc diem. Et vicecomes mandavit quod predictus Bartholomeus nichil habet in balliva sua per quod potest distringi nisi quoddam jumentum et quod corpus ejus non fuit inventum in balliva sua post recepcionem istius brevis. Et quia testificatum est coram etc. quod idem Bartholomeus habet terras et tenementa apud Meauton', per que non fuit districtus, preceptum est vicecomiti quod ipsum distringat per easdem terras etc., et quod habeat corpus ejus coram etc. die lune proxima post festum sancte Margarete ad respondendum etc. Ad quem diem predictus Oliverus venit et optulit se versus Reginam et predictum Bartholomeum. Et ipse Bartholomeus non venit. Et preceptum fuit vicecomiti quod ipsum distringeret per terras etc., et quod de exitibus etc., et quod haberet corpus ejus coram etc. ad hunc diem. Et vicecomes mandavit quod qualitercunque testificatum fuerit coram justiciariis etc. quod predictus Bartholomeus habeat terras apud Meauton' dicit tamen quod predictus Bartholomeus non habet terras nec tenementa in balliva sua que valent .v. solidos. Et petit quod hoc inquiratur. Et predictus Oliverus dicit quod qualitercunque vicecomes respondit pro predicto Bartholomeo quod non habet terras nec tenementa in balliva sua, dicit tamen quod die quo ipsum Bartholomeum vocavit ad warantum satis habuit unde ipsum acquietare potuit versus predictam Reginam, et petit quod hoc inquiratur. Ideo preceptum est vicecomiti quod per sacramentum etc. diligenter inquirat quas terras et tenementa predictus Bartholomeus habuit .viij. die Maii anno regni regis Edwardi .viij., et inquisicionem etc. scire faciat justiciariis etc. a die sancti Michaelis in .xv. dies etc. Et preterea predictus Oliverus dicit quod nimis oneratus esset de predictis quingentis marcis ab ipso petitis quia porcio sua non erit tanta si omnes terre et tenementa que fuerunt predicti Bartholomei extendantur, quia dicit quod plures sunt tenentes predictarum terrarum, videlicet domina Regina consors domini Regis, Willelmus Bardolf, Oliverus de Ingham, Bartholomeus de Somerton', Hugo Peverel, Ricardus de Hedersete, priorissa de Karhowe et Bartholomeus de Redham.

Predictus Walterus de Kanc' dicit quod predictus Oliverus, quicquid dicat, non facit nisi quandam dilacionem in dicto placito vocando predictum Bartholomeum ad warantum de acquietancia de dicto debito, et petit judicium de eodem Olivero eo quod non habet warantum suum de acquietancia predicti debiti, sicut ipsum vocavit. Et quia predictus Oliverus non habuit predictum Bartholomeum, sicut eum vocavit ad warantum, nec vicecomes ipsum in balliva sua invenire potuit nec aliquid habet ibidem per quod possit distringi secundum quod vicecomes bis retornavit, consideratum est quod dictus Oliverus de porcione ipsum contingente de toto debito in quo diversis judeis tenebatur predictus Bartholomeus quantum pertinet ad tantam terram quantam inde tenet predicte Regine pro porcione sua satisfaciat. Et quod predictus Oliverus habeat recuperare suum versus predictum Bartholomeum, si quod habere possit, per auxilium curie domini regis, et eciam quod omnes terre et tenementa que fuerunt predicti Bartholomei que sunt in manibus diversorum tenencium extendantur, videlicet quid et quantum valeant per annum etc., et extentam etc. a die sancti Michaelis in .xv. dies; et omnes quos tenentes etc. venire faciat ad eundem diem etc. ut tunc unusquisque pro porcione sua respondeat.

MEMBRANE 4 DORSE

(446)

Not'. Prior de Thurgarton, tenens quandam partem terrarum que fuerunt Gerardi filii Elie de Fanecurt, districtus ad respondendum Alianore Regine Anglie pro sexies viginti libris in quibus predictus Gerardus tenebatur Benedicto de Linc' judeo et quod debitum predictus Benedictus domine Regine assignavit pro auro suo.

Predictus prior venit et protulit starrum predicti Benedicti de acquietancia pro porcione dicti debiti dictum priorem contingente de dicto debito occasione quarundam terrarum quas tenet que fuerunt predicti Gerardi in quo continetur quod predictus Benedictus prefatum priorem de porcione ipsum inde contingente acquietare debet; et quod ipse et heredes vel assignati sui in predictis terris et tenementis que fuerunt predicti Gerardi nichil exigere poterunt vel vendicare occasione alicujus debiti in quo predictus Gerardus umquam prefato Benedicto tenebatur a creacione seculi usque ad finem.

Et Walterus de Kanc' attornatus predicte domine Regine recognovit et dicit quod invenit per starrum predicti Benedicti quod fecit in assignacione predicti debiti predicte Regine prefatum priorem occasione terrarum que fuerunt predicti Gerardi contingente [quietum esse debeat][39] et quod ad opus dicte domine Regine nichil exigit. Et ideo consideratum est quod predictus prior quantum ad peticionem prefate domine Regine eat quietus.

[The remainder of membrane 4d is blank.]

MEMBRANE 5[40]

Adhuc placita de termino Pasche anno .viij.

(447)[41]

Lond'. Benedictus filius magistri Elie judeus attachiatus ad respondendum Willelmo de Mortuo Mari de placito injuste detencionis catallorum. Et unde queritur quod, cum ipse invadiasset predicto Benedicto quedam bona et catalla sua ad valenciam .l. librarum die mercurii proxima ante festum apostolorum Simonis et Jude anno regni regis Edwardi .vij. in domo magistri Galfridi de Mortuo Mari pro viginti septem marcis quas ab eo mutuo recepit, que bona adhuc injuste detinet etc., videlicet, aurum ponderis duarum marcarum, duos anulos auri [e]<conjun>[e] cum saphiro conjunctos cum quadam cathena argenti, unum firmaculum auri, tres zonas de serico argento subaurato barratas, .xij. coclearia argenti, .ij. ciphos argenti platos et unum supercooperatorium de scarleto furratum de minuto ver' precii .l. librarum. Et ideo injuste etc. quia die dominica proxima ante festum purificacionis beate Marie proximo sequens venit predictus Willelmus ad predictum Benedictum et peciit visum vadiorum suorum promptus ad satisfaciendum pro vadiis predictis, et predictus Benedictus dixit quod vadia illa ei non ostenderet nisi aliquos denarios ei pre manibus solveret, et idem Willelmus incontinenti solvit eidem Benedicto .ij. marcas et dimidiam et postea peciit visum vadiorum suorum, et idem Benedictus dixit quod visum omnium vadiorum suorum ei ostendere non potuit eo quod predictum aurum ponderis .ij. marcarum vendidit pro .xxiiij. marcis et dimidia, de qua vendicione idem Willelmus bene fuit contentus et dicebat quod predictum debitum per easdem .xxiiij. marcas et dimidiam et per .ij. marcas et dimidiam, quas eidem Benedicto tunc solverat, erat eidem Benedicto plene satisfactum, et peciit residuum vadiorum suorum, et idem Benedictus ea reddere contradicebat et ea adhuc ei injuste detinet ad dampnum suum .c. librarum. Et hoc offert etc.

Predictus Benedictus venit. Et defendit vim etc. quando etc. Et recognovit se recepisse predictum aurum ponderis duarum marcarum per manus cujusdam Willelmi de Bauns ut pignus pro .xxiiij. marcis quas super dictum aurum mutuavit, et per licenciam predicti Willelmi predictum aurum vendidit pro .xxiiij. marcis et dimidia quas allocavit in debito supradicto, et insuper idem Benedictus bene recognovit quod omnia predicta vadia recepit set non tanti valoris quam predictus Willelmus dicit et ea adhuc preterquam aurum quod prius vendidit penes se habet, super quibus vadiis idem Benedictus dicit quod accommodavit predicto Willelmo cito post festum Purificacionis beate Marie ultimo preteritum .viij. marcas .iij. solidos .iiij. denarios et dicta vadia pro predictis denariis ut vadium suum juste retinet; et de duabus marcis et dimidia quas dictus Willelmus dicit se ei solvisse, dicit quod nichil inde recepit.

Et predictus Willelmus dicit quod predictas .ij. marcas et dimidiam eidem Benedicto solvit, ut predictum est, et dicit quod per predictas .ij. marcas et dimidiam et per .xxiiij. marcas et dimidiam quas recepit de predicto auro satisfactum est ei de .xxvij. marcis quas ab eo mutuo recepit, et dicit quod nullum denarium ab eodem judeo post festum Purificacionis beate Marie supradictum recepit, per quod nichil ei debet super vadia predicta que

[39] *MS. omits.*

[40] *The letter 'h' is written in the top left hand margin of this membrane above the heading.*

[41] *Previously printed by Rigg in* Select Pleas, *pp. 111-12.*

ei adhuc injuste detinet. Et de hoc ponit se super veredictum Galfridi de Saham, Willelmi le Fraunceys et magistri Elie patris predicti Benedicti qui convencioni et solucioni inter eos facta interfuerunt. Et predictus Benedictus dicit quod sibi accommodavit predictas .viij. marcas .iij. solidos et .iiij. denarios super vadia predicta et predictas .ij. marcas et dimidiam de predicto Willelmo non recepit, et de hoc ponit se similiter super predictos Galfridum, Willelmum et Eliam. Ideo preceptum est vicecomiti Cantebr' quod venire faciat coram etc. in octabis sancte Trinitatis predictos Galfridum et Willelmum; et constabulario Turris Lond' quod venire faciat ad eundem diem magistrum Eliam ad recognoscendum etc.

(448)

Surr'. Johannes de Bayfeld optulit se quarto die versus Johannem de Clare de placito quod reddat ei .c. solidos. Et ipse non venit. Et mandatum fuit custodi spiritualitatis episcopatus Lond' quod ipsum distringeret per bona sua ecclesiastica eo quod non habet laycum feodum. Et custos nichil inde mandavit nec breve returnavit. Ideo mandatum est episcopo Norwic' quod ipsum distringat per bona sua ecclesiastica, ita quod habeat corpus ejus coram [etc.][42] in quindena sancti Johannis Baptiste ad respondendum etc.

(449)

Essex'. Johannes de Bayfeld optulit se quarto die versus Philippum filium Andree de Halstede de placito debiti. Et ipse non venit. Et preceptum fuit vicecomiti quod ipsum distringeret per terras etc. Et vicecomes nichil inde mandavit nec breve retornavit. Ideo, sicut alias, in quindena sancti Johannis etc.

MEMBRANE 5 DORSE

Adhuc placita de termino Pasche

(450)[43]

Norff'. Johannes de Hadesagh' attachiatus fuit ad respondendum Johanni de Bayfeld', clerico de scaccario judeorum, de placito detencionis catallorum. Et unde idem Johannes de Bayfeld' queritur quod, cum ipse habuisset septem saccos lane, unum equum et viginti quinque anulos auri precii quater viginti marcarum reposita in domo predicti Johannis de Hadisagh' in villa de Kyneburle, idem Johannes de Hadisagh' cum familia sua cepit predicta catalla et ea distraxit pro voluntate sua et ea eidem Johanni de Bayfeld' detinet et reddere contradicit ad dampnum suum .cc. marcarum. Et inde producit sectam.

Et Johannes de Hadisagh' per attornatum suum venit. Et defendit vim etc. quando etc. Et dicit quod predictus Johannes de Bayfeld' nunquam hujusmodi catalla in domo sua habuit reposita nec aliqua catalla ipsius Johannis [i]<de Baifeld'>[i] per ipsum nec per familiam [i]<suam>[i] capta, distracta seu detenta fuerunt. Et de hoc ponit se super patriam. Et Johannes de Bayfeld' similiter. Ideo preceptum est vicecomiti quod venire faceret coram etc. a die sancte Trinitatis in quindecim dies .xij. etc. de visneto predicto, qui nulla affinitate etc., ad recognoscendum etc.[44] Quia tam etc.

Ad quem diem predictus Johannes de Hades' per attornatum suum venit. Et Johannes de Bayfeld fuit essoniatus. Et habent diem a die sancti Michaelis in .xv. dies. Ad quem diem predicti Johannes et Johannes venerunt. Vicecomes non retornavit breve. Ideo preceptum est vicecomiti quod venire faciat hic .xij. etc. in octabis sancti Hyllarii ad recognoscendum etc., nisi prius H. Hauteyn in partes illas venerit. Et concessum est hinc inde etc.

Et interim venit H. Hauteyn apud Norwyc' in crastino sancte Thome Martiris. Et predictus Johannes de Bayfeld' et Johannes de Hadisagh' per attornatum suum venerunt. Et inquisitio venit per Thomam le Clerk' de Kyneburl' et alios juratos, sicut patet inter brevia huic rotulo consuta.[45] Qui dicunt super sacramentum suum quod predictus Johannes de Bayfeld habuit [i]<predictam>[i] lanam et alia minuta catalla ad valenciam sexaginta marcarum et non amplius ad domum predicti Johannis de Hadisagh' in deposito et in custodia et potestate ipsius Johannis de Hadisagh'. Et dicunt quod sine licencia vel voluntate ipsius Johannis de Bayfeld [i]<et eo nesciente>[i] idem Johannes de Hadisagh' una cum quodam Matheo filio suo easdem sexaginta marcatas catallorum cepit et ea distraxit et voluntatem suam inde fecit. Et requisiti si aliquid de eisdem catallis postea ad manus predicti Johannis de Bayfeld' vel ad commodum suum devenit, dicunt quod non. Et super hoc datus est dies partibus de audiendo judicio suo in octabis sancti Hillarii.

Ad quem diem venerunt predictus Johannes de Bayfeld' et similiter Johannes de Addyshawe per attornatum suum et datus est eis dies in pleno scaccario de die in diem usque diem lune proximo sequentem. Ad quem diem predictus Johannes venit. Et predictus Johannes de Hadyshagh' non venit. Et predictus Johannes de Bayfeld' petit judicium suum etc. Et quia compertum est per predictam inquisicionem quod predictus Johannes de Hadyshag' habuit de catallis predicti Johannis de Bayfeld ad valenciam sexaginta marcarum que ei nondum reddidit etc. ideo consideratum est quod predictus Johannes [i]<de Baifeld'>[i] recuperet predictas sexaginta marcas versus predictum Johannem de Hadyshag' et dampna sua que taxantur per justiciarios ad centum solidos. Et ipse Johannes de Hadishag' in <misericordia>[46] pro injusta detencione. Et preceptum est vice-

[42] *MS. omits.*

[43] *This entry is partially duplicated on m. 3 where it is marginated also as belonging to Suffolk and marked for deletion: see note to no. 432 above. It is also partially duplicated on Roll 36 (the plea roll of the following term): below no. 615.*

[44] *The version on membrane 3d ends at this point.*

[45] *Although there are stitch-marks here the panel itself is now missing.*

[46] *The word* misericordia *is repeated in the margin.*

comiti quod de terris et catallis ipsius Johannis de Hadishag' fieri faciat predictos denarios et eos predicto Johanni de Bayfeld' sine dilacione liberari faciat. Et predictus Johannes de Bayfeld' pro falso clamore quoad residuum predictarum .iiij.^{xx} marcarum in misericordia. Et quia vicecomes nichil inde fecit. Ideo preceptum ei, sicut alias, quod de bonis et catallis fieri faciat predictos denarios, ita quod eos habeat coram etc. a die sancti Michaelis in quindecim dies.

MEMBRANE 6[47]

Memoranda de termino Pasche anno regni regis E. octavo

(451)

Linc'. Preceptum fuit vicecomiti, sicut alias, quod non omitteret propter libertatem Lanc' quin eam etc. et distringeret tenentes terrarum que fuerunt magistri Thome de Quappelade per terras etc. pro .xlvj. libris quas Regi debent occasione terrarum etc. de debitis Abrahe filii Murielis judei; et denarios haberet coram etc. ad hunc diem vel corpora tenencium ad ostendendum acquietacionem. Et vicecomes mandavit quod nulla bona seu catalla invenit super terras vel tenementa predicta, per que possit tenentes distringere. Et Willelmus filius Petri et Nicholaus filius Petri, tenentes quandam partem terrarum que fuerunt predicti Thome, per auxilium curie vocant ad warantum Edmundum de Quappelade, filium et heredem predicti magistri Thome, heredem magistri Thome de Alkerke, de porcionibus dicti debiti inde eos contingentibus occasione predictarum terrarum etc. Et Willelmus Wyn senior similiter vocat ad warantum de porcione ipsum contingente etc. Johannem filium Alani Milis de Quappelade et habent diem in octabis sancte Trinitatis.

(452)

Linc'. Preceptum fuit vicecomiti quod venire faceret coram etc. Walterum Godard, Alanum rectorem ecclesie de Schebesh', Robertum filium Johannis de Fulney militis et Thomam fratrem ejus, tenentes quandam partem terrarum que fuerunt Johannis de Fulney, ad respondendum Regi una cum priore de Spalding', tenente quandam partem earundem terrarum, de .xxviij. libris quas Regi debent occasione terrarum etc. de debitis Abrahe filii Murielis judei. Et predicti Robertus et Thomas filii Johannis de Fulne venerunt et vocaverunt ad warantum per auxilium curie de porcionibus ipsos contingentibus predictum priorem. Et predictus prior per attornatum suum venit et pro se et Waltero Godard et Alano rectore ecclesie de Shepeshe et aliis de toto predicto debito vocaverunt ad warantum[48] magistrum Eliam filium magistri Mossei judeum et habent diem in octabis sancte Trinitatis.

[47] *The letter* h *is written in the top left hand margin above the heading.*

[48] *Followed in MS. by a redundant* per.

(453)

Linc'. Preceptum fuit vicecomiti quod de terris et catallis Roberti de Wileby fieri faceret ad opus Regis .xxiiij. libras quas Regi debet de debitis Joscei nepotis Aaron, ita quod denarios haberet coram etc. ad hunc diem vel corpus etc. ad ostendendum etc. Et vicecomes mandavit quod Galfridus Corpel de Wileby, Willelmus prepositus de eadem, Willelmus Hug' de eadem, et Willelmus prepositus de Silkeby manuceperunt predictum Robertum ad ostendendum acquietacionem, quem non habuerunt. Ideo in misericordia. Et preceptum est vicecomiti, sicut alias, in octabis sancte Trinitatis etc.

(454)

Buk' Bed' Lond'. Memorandum quod Robertus Herun unus cyrographariorum Lond' protulit quandam cartam .x. marcarum sub nominibus Henrici de Merk' de comitatu Buk' et Jacobi filii Hagini judei in hec verba: 'Henricus de Merk' de comitatu Buk' debet Jacobo filio Hagini judeo .x. marcas reddendas a die Pasche in tres septimanas anno regni regis E. filii regis H. quarto. Acta .xxix. die Aprilis anno r. E. tercio.' Que carta liberata fuit in pleno scaccario Johanni de Whatele custodi auri Regine matris Regis pro debito dicti Jacobi in quo eidem domine Regine tenebatur pro auro suo.

(455)[49]

Lond'. Aaron filius Vyves judeus tulit breve regis de magno sigillo in hec verba: 'Edwardus etc. dilectis et fidelibus suis Johanni de Cobeham et justiciariis suis ad custodiam etc. et dilecto clerico suo Ade de Wynton' salutem. Cum Aaron filius Vyves judeus Lond' dederit et concesserit karissime consorti nostre Alianore Regine Anglie debita in quibus Gilbertus Pecche eidem judeo tenetur per cartas et obligaciones suas ac nos indempnitati ipsius judei prospici et sibi debitam recompensacionem debiti predicti fieri cupientes concesserimus eidem judeo quod de clarioribus debitis et obligacionibus judeorum dampnatorum vel aliorum judeorum in manu nostra existentibus vel que accidere contigerit in manum nostram quedam debita usque ad summam debiti in cartis et obligacionibus prefati Gilberti contenti in recompensacionem ejusdem debiti assignentur et debita illa ad opus ejusdem judei nomine nostro leventur et sibi liberentur, ita quod si aliquid dictorum debitorum in manu nostra existencium vel que in manum nostram accidere contigerit, ut predictum est, quietum inveniri contingat post liberacionem sibi factam, tunc [i]<eidem judeo>[i] aliquod debitum loco ejusdem assignari faciamus, vobis mandamus quod premissa fieri faciatis in forma predicta. Et quia accepimus quod postquam judeos regni nostri capi fecimus quedam false facte sunt acquietancie et eciam starra inter christianos et judeos, vobis mandamus quod, si contingat debitores quoscunque acquietancias vel starra aliqua debitorum quoruncumque coram vobis proferre, tunc nullam

[49] *Previously printed by Rigg in* Select Pleas, *pp. 112-13.*

quietanciam vel liberacionem hujusmodi debitoribus [allocatis,][50] quousque legittime vobis constare possit acquietancias vel starra illa fideliter et legittime fuisse facta secundum legem et consuetudinem [i]<scaccarii>[i] judeorum predicti. Teste me ipso apud Merleberg' .xxvj. die Februarii anno regni nostro octavo.'

(456)

Ebor'. Adam de Novo Mercato venit coram etc. et recognovit pro se et heredibus suis debere acquietare Robertum de Tybetot versus omnes homines, tam christianos quam judeos, de omnibus debitis, demandis et calumpniis que aliquo modo exigi poterunt super terras, redditus et tenementa que predictus Robertus habet in villa de Bentelay in comitatu Ebor' ex vendicione predicti Ade.

(457)

Linc'. Cum nuper cepisset Abbe Jordan judeum et in prisona detinuisset eo quod dicebatur quod quidam christianus venit ad domum dicti judei, secum deferens .vij. libras argenti, ad emendum platas de tonsura monete et propter timorem supervenientem fugit, dimittendo ibidem, et quia Mosseus filius Abrahe, Aaron filius Hake, Sampson filius Hake de Linc' et Abraham filius Benedicti manuceperunt predictum Abbe quod veniat coram etc. ad quindenam Pasche ad respondendum Regi et predicto christiano de predicta transgressione, preceptum fuit vicecomiti quod predictum judeum interim a prisona deliberet. Ad quem diem predicti manucaptores predictum Abbe non habuerunt. Ideo in <misericordia.>[51] Et preceptum fuit vicecomiti quod venire faceret predictum christianum ad hunc diem et dictas .vij. libras quas in domo dicti judei dimiserat. Et vicecomes mandavit quod dictus christianus vocatur Thomas de Ebor', set de dictis .vij. libris quod eas in dicta domo dimisit nichil tam per inquisicionem christianorum quam judeorum invenire potuit. Predictus Thomas de Ebor' venit et optulit se quarto die versus dictum judeum et petit auxilium curie ad dictos denarios suos versus dictum judeum recuperandum. Et preceptum est vicecomiti quod predictum judeum capiat et in prisona regis salvo custodiat etc., ita quod habeat corpus ejus etc. in octabis sancte Trinitatis ad respondendum etc.

(458)

Linc'. Preceptum fuit vicecomiti, sicut pluries, quod distringeret tenentes terrarum que fuerunt Henrici Fucedame per terras etc. ad reddendum sibi ad opus Regis[52] quas Regi deberet occasione etc. de debitis Isac de Sutwerk, et denarios illos haberet coram etc. a die Pasche in quindecim dies. Et vicecomes mandavit quod breve inde sibi directum adeo tarde venit quod exequi non potuit. Ideo, sicut pluries, in octabis sancte Trinitatis etc.

50 *MS. omits.*

51 *The word* misericordia *is repeated in the margin.*

52 *The amount has been omitted here.*

(459)

Nortf' Suff'. Preceptum fuit vicecomiti, sicut alias, quod non omitteret propter libertatem de Donewyc' quin eam etc., et de bonis et catallis Rogeri Custepeny et Margarete Bernard fieri faciat .x. libras ad opus Aaron filii Vyves, quas ei se debere recognoverunt etc., et denarios illos haberet coram etc. ad hunc diem. Et vicecomes mandavit quod nichil invenit de bonis dictorum Rogeri et Margarete unde denarii fieri possent nisi vendidisset domos eorum. Et quia testificatum est quod dictus Rogerus habet .viij. marcatas redditus in Donewycum et predicta Margareta habet similiter redditus et catalla ibidem, preceptum est vicecomiti, sicut pluries, quod non omittat etc. quin eam etc. et de predictis redditibus et aliis bonis etc. fieri faciat predictas .x. libras et eas habeat coram etc. in quindena sancte Trinitatis etc.

(460)

Hereff'. Preceptum fuit vicecomiti quod, assumptis secum cyrographariis christianis et judeis arche cyrographariorum Hereff', dictam archam aperiri faciat et ab eadem extraheret cartas subscriptas, videlicet .xxij. marcarum et dimidie sub nominibus Walteri Everoys et Isac filii Dyey; et unam .xx. solidorum sub nominibus Walteri le Mire et dicti Isac; et unam .v. marcarum sub nominibus Roberti filii Nicholai de Furch' et dicti Isac; et unam .xx. librarum sub nominibus Hugonis de Turbervile et dicti Isac; et unam .j. marce sub nominibus Hugonis filii Willelmi de Bles' et dicti Isac; et eas traderet predictis cyrographariis sub sigillo suo apud Westm' deferendum justiciariis ibidem liberandum etc. Et vicecomes mandavit quod predicti cyrographarii omnes predictas cartas per Ricardum le Usser unum eorum cyrographarium adhuc in eodem officio existentem miserunt apud Westm' in octabis sancti Michaelis anno regni Edwardi primo ibidem justiciariis liberandas per breve regis et est testis in brevi 'H. Hauteyn apud Westm' .ij.° die Augusti anno regni predicti primo.' Et quia predicte carte in thesauro regis inveniri non possunt nec constat dictis justiciariis quod dictus Ricardus eas ibidem liberavit, preceptum est vicecomiti quod venire faceret coram etc. predictum Ricardum in octabis sancte Trinitatis ad respondendum regi de predictis cartis etc.

(461)

Kanc'. Robertus de Ardre miles de comitatu Kanc' venit coram etc. et recognovit se debere Aron filio Vives judeo centum summas frumenti vel pro qualibet summa dimidiam marcam reddendas a die sancti Michaelis in unum mensem anno regni regis Edwardi octavo. Et, nisi fecerit, concedit quod de tenementis et catallis fiant etc.

(462)

Essex. Willelmus de Rammesden' venit coram etc., et recognovit se debere Meir filio Benedicti .xlv. summas frumenti vel pro quolibet quarterio dimidiam marcam, reddendum in quindena sancti Michaelis proximo futura .xxij. quarteria et dimidium, et ad Pascham anno regni regis Edwardi decimo .xxij. quarteria et dimidium. Et, nisi fecerit, concedit quod de terris et catallis suis fiant etc.

MEMBRANE 6 DORSE

(463)

Hunt'. Josceus filius Sauloti judeus solvit in recepta regis .xx. solidos de fine pro catallis Sauloti patris sui et habet inde talliam.

(464)

Hereff'. Preceptum fuit vicecomiti quod distringeret Nicholaum de Wormel' pro .x. libris ad opus Regis de debitis Isac de Suthwerk' etc. Et vicecomes venit et protulit inde .xx. solidos, et dixit quod plus ad presens de predicto Nicholao levare non potuit. Ideo, sicut alias, in octabis sancte Trinitatis etc.

(465)

Sutht'. Preceptum fuit vicecomiti quod distringeret tenentes terrarum que fuerunt Willelmi de la Berton' quondam senescalli sancti Swythini per terras etc. pro .c. solidis ad quos amerciatus fuit etc., et denarios haberet coram etc. ad hunc diem. Et vicecomes mandavit quod Nicholaus de la Berton' tenet terras dicti Willelmi et manucepit satisfaciendi de predictis .c. solidis ad hunc diem per Gervasium de Iwode, Johannem de Tatham, Johannem le Godegrom et Hugonem atte Pitte, qui predictum Nicholaum non habuerunt. Ideo in <misericordia.>[53] Judicium, sicut alias, quod distringatur per terras etc. in octabis sancte Trinitatis etc.

(466)

Oxon'. Preceptum fuit vicecomiti quod attachiaret Isaac le Petyt od la Playe judeum, ita quod haberet corpus ejus coram etc. ad respondendum Regi de quodam cipho argenti ponderis et valoris .xx. solidorum furato et asportato a domo Walteri Aurifabri et aliis transgressionibus etc. Et vicecomes mandavit quod Jacobus filius Samuelis et Elias filius Cressei manuceperunt predictum Isaac, quem non habuerunt. Ideo in misericordia. Judicium, sicut alias, in octabis sancte Trinitatis etc.

(467)

Oxon'. Preceptum fuit vicecomiti quod per summonicionem scaccarii fieri faciat de Jacobo filio Jacobi judeo .iiij. libras .x. solidos ad opus Regis ac quidam Jacobus filius Jacobi, asserens alium Jacobum filium Jacobi manentem in Oxon' in dicto debito Regi teneri, ideo preceptum est vicecomiti quod dictum Jacobum venire faciat coram etc. Et vicecomes mandavit quod breve adeo tarde sibi venit quod exequi non potuit. Et quia dictus Jacobus, qui tulit breve super alium Jacobum, non prosequitur breve suum, ideo preceptum est vicecomiti quod ipsum distringat per terras etc., ita quod habeat predictos denarios coram etc. in octabis sancte Trinitatis Regi solvendos.

(468)

Surr' Sutht'. Johannes de Sancto Johanne et Rogerus de Clifford junior venerunt coram etc. et recognoverunt se debere Roberto de Ludham duodecim marcas bone et legalis monete, reddendum ad quindenam sancti Michaelis proximo futuram. Et, nisi fecerint, concedunt quod de terris et catallis suis fiant.

(469)

Sutht'. Preceptum fuit vicecomiti quod venire faceret coram etc. ad hunc diem sex probos et legales homines de Wynton' et sex judeos ad recognoscendum etc. super particulis que Sarra que fuit uxor Salamonis filii Belecote judei Wynton' exigit versus Jacobum Mawe, sicut patet inter placita de termino sancti Hillarii ultimo preterito. Et venerunt Henricus de Peveneseye, Johannes de Sanden', Walterus Bonde, Ricardus Curry, Ricardus de Dummere et Adam Scot christiani; Jacobus le Lung, Josceus gener Cokerel et Bendictus filius Cressaunt judei venerunt. Et vicecomes mandavit quod Beycok' filius Bonamy et Josceus gener Cokerel manuceperunt Josceum de Kaleys, et quod Jacobus le Lung et Beycok filius Bonamy manuceperunt Abraham filium Cokerel; et quod Isaac de Wylton' et Abraham filius Cokerel manuceperunt Beycok' filium Bonamy; quos non habuerunt. Ideo in misericordia. Judicium quod distringantur per terras etc., ita quod nec ipsi etc., et quod de exitibus etc., et quod habeat corpora eorum coram etc. in octabis sancte Trinitatis ad recongnoscendum etc. una cum predictis christianis etc. Et venire faciat ad eundem diem tot et tales etc.

(470)

Buk'. Willelmus Barentyn' venit coram etc. et recognovit se debere Aaron filio Vyves .xxxij. marcas et dimidiam de quodam debito .c. marcarum in quo Paganus de Caturc' eidem Aaron tenebatur per scriptum suum, reddendum predictas .xxxij. marcas et dimidiam ad terminos subscriptos, videlicet centum solidos ad festum Pentecosten proximo futurum, et ad festum sancti Michaelis proximo sequens .c. solidos, et ad Pascha proximo sequens, scilicet anno regni Edwardi nono, .c. solidos et ad festum sancti Michaelis proximo sequens .c. solidos; et sic de anno in annum et termino in terminum ad duos terminos, scilicet ad festum sancti Michaelis et ad festum Pasche etc. quousque predicte .xxxij. marce et dimidia persolvantur. Et pro ista recognicione liberatur predicto Willelmo quoddam scriptum .c. marcarum sub nominibus Pagani de Caturc' et ipsius Aaron sub hac forma, videlicet quod, nisi Patricius de Caturc' solvat dicto Aaron dictas .x. libras infra festum sancte Trinitatis proximo futurum, tunc predictus Willelmus predictum scriptum .c. marcarum eidem Aaron retradere tenetur.

53 *The word* misericordia *is repeated in the margin.*

(471)

Norff'. Preceptum fuit vicecomiti quod de bonis et catallis Radulphi de Ingheworth' fieri faceret ad opus Hamonis Hautein .xl. solidos quos recognovit etc., et quod denarios haberet coram etc. Et vicecomes mandavit quod Robertus de Petra, ballivus ubi Radulphus habet terras, respondit sibi quod nulla bona seu catalla invenit unde denarii possunt levari nisi vendidisset terras dicti Radulphi. Et, quia testificatum est coram etc. quod predictus Radulphus satis habet in balliva sua unde predictos denarios levasse potuit, ideo dictus Robertus in misericordia.[54] Et preceptum est vicecomiti, sicut alias, in octabis sancte Trinitatis.

(472)

Hereff'. Preceptum fuit vicecomiti quod distringeret Aaron le Blund pro .c. solidis ad opus Regis pro bissantia de quodam debito .xl. librarum quod recuperavit versus Walterum de Balun coram etc. Et vicecomes mandavit quod predictus Walterus non solvit dicto Aaron nisi decem libras de quibus vicecomes misit .xx. solidos etc.

(473)

Surr' Sussex'. Preceptum fuit vicecomiti quod distringeret Robertum Lyvet, Willelmum Genesing, Rogerum le Waleys et Simonem de Oxenebrigg' per terras etc., ita quod haberet eorum corpora etc. a die Pasche in .xv.dies ad recognoscendum etc. in loquela que est inter dominam Reginam matrem Regis et Willelmum Herigaud una cum Johanne de Ferles, Willelmo de Holyngdale, Willelmo Geffray, Olivero Heved, Roberto de Worth', Gilberto de Beveryngton', Henrico de Lamport, Hamoni atteStock', Galfrido de Sottington', Radulpho le Lung, Johanne Russell, Galfrido de Snayteneshull', et Johanne de Bremham, quibus idem dies datur, et tot etc. tam milites etc. Et predicti Robertus et Willelmus et alii de novo appositi non venerunt. Et vicecomes mandavit quod Henricus Spendelove de Ferle, Robertus atteWelle de eadem, Johannes attePette de eadem, et Willelmus atteStyghele de eadem manuceperunt Robertum Lyvet; et quod Walterus le Fisshere de Hastyng' et Thomas le Carpenter de eadem manuceperunt Willelmum de Genesing'; et quod Willelmus atte Snyth' et Simon Crudde manuceperunt Hamonem Bonet; et quod Walterus Ordwyne et Nicholaus de Coppeden' manuceperunt Rogerum de Coverl'; et quod Ricardus le Keu et Walterus Syward manuceperunt Hugonem de Buscy; et quod Johannes le Berker et Johannes le Kyng' manuceperunt Nigellum de Brok'; et quod Galfridus Stygaunt et Robertus Lyngedey manuceperunt Radulphum de Stopham; et quod Johannes de Bernham et Walterus Cordel' manuceperunt Lucam de Vyenne; et quod Robertus Frewyne et Willelmus Syward manuceperunt Willelmum de Alta Ripa; et quod Willelmus le Turnur et Robertus Lypet manuceperunt Hugonem Saunzaver; quos non habuerunt. Ideo in misericordia.[55] Judicium quod distringatur per terras etc., ita quod nec ipsi etc., et quod de exitibus etc., et quod habeat corpora eorum coram etc. a die Pasche in .v. septimanas ad recognoscendum etc. una cum Rogero le Waleys, Simoni de Oxenebrigge, Rogero la Ware, Rogero de Leukenore, Roberto de Perpunt, Simoni de Perpunt, Johanni de Ferle, Willelmo de Holyngdale et aliis supradictis qui venerunt, quibus idem dies datur etc.

MEMBRANE 7[56]

Adhuc memoranda de termino Pasche anno .viij.

(474)

Norff'. Nicholaus filius Johannis de Stutevyle de Bedingham recognoscit se debere Johanni de Bayfeld' viginti libras, reddendum ei ad Pascham proximo futuram. Et, nisi fecerit, concedit quod de terris et catallis suis fiant.

(475)

Lond'. Inquisicio facta de bonis et catallis que fuerunt Dyei filii Abrahe judei defuncti per sacramentum Ade le Chazefor', Osberti le Pestur et aliorum christianorum, Cressei filii Gente, Jacobi le Clerk et aliorum judeorum, sicut patet inter inquisiciones hujus termini retornatas. Qui dicunt super sacramentum suus quod dictus Dyey die quo egrotavit etc. in bonis mobilibus ad valenciam .x. librarum et quasdam domos que valent per annum salvo servicio etc. .lxiij. solidos et .iiij. denarios.

Summa bonorum mobilium: .xiij. libre, .iij. solidi .iiij. denarii

Debita ejusdem Dyey

Willelmus la Thusch de comitatu Sutht' debet Dyey filio Abrahe .xx. marcas, reddendum .ij. marcas et dimidiam a die Natalis Domini in tres septimanas anno regni regis Henrici .xlvj., et .ij. marcas et dimidiam a die Nativitatis Beati Johannis Baptiste proximo sequenti in tres septimanas; et sic de anno in annum et termino in terminum reddendum ei .v. marcas per annum ad eosdem terminos quousque etc. Acta .viij. die Junii anno .xlv. Appuratur per Sarram que fuit uxor dicti Dyey, que finem fecit pro catallis predicti Dyey, ad .x. libras.[57]

Simon de Arderne miles de comitatu Derb' et Thomas de Folevyle de Reresby de comitatu Leyc' debent eidem judeo .xx. libras, reddendum in crastino Omnium Sanctorum anno regis Henrici .lvj.^{to} Acta .x. die Februarii anno .lv. Appuratur ad .xvj. libras per predictam Sarram.[58]

Willelmus de la Leye clericus et Reginaldus le Forester de comitatu Surr' debent eidem .x. marcas reddendas ad

[54] *The word* misericordia *s repeated in the margin with underneath it* xx solidi.

[55] *The word* misericordia *is repeated in the margin.*

[56] *The letter* h *is written in the top left hand margin across from the heading.*

[57] *In the margin is written* Quietum per .x. libras.

[58] *In the margin is written* Quietum per .xvj. libras.

quindenam Pasche anno regis Henrici .lv. Acta .xvj. die Octobris anno .liiij.^{to} Appuratur ad .v. marcas per predictam Sarram.[59]

Johannes filius David de comitatu Surr' debet eidem .iiij. libras reddendas ad festum sancti Michaelis anno regis Henrici .lvj.^{to} Acta .ix. die Octobris anno .lv. Et indorsatur quod medietas istius debiti est Bonamy filii Bonamy de Oxon'. Et appuratur ad .xx. solidos per predictam Sarram pars ipsius Dyey.[60] Et pars predicti Bonamy est Regis per forisfacturam ipsius Bonamy.

Walterus Wolleward clericus de comitatu Midd' debet eidem Dyey .v. marcas reddendas in octabis sancti Martini anno regis Edwardi tercio. Acta .xj. die Octobris anno eodem. Appuratur ad .iiij. marcas per predictam Sarram.[61]

Robertus de Percy de comitatu Ebor' debet Mosseo filio Jacobi de Oxon' .xv. libras reddendas ad quindenam sancti Michaelis anno regis Henrici .lv.^{to}. Acta ultimo die Junii anno eodem. Indorsatur quod medietas istius debiti est Dyey filii Abrahe. Pars dicti Dyey appuratur ad .ij. marcas.[62]

Hamo de Vyeleston' de comitatu Essex' debet eidem .xx. libras reddendas ad Pascham anno regis Henrici .lv. Acta .x. die Decembris anno eodem. Et indorsatur quod medietas istius debiti est Mossei filii Jacobi et appuratur pro parte dicti Dyey ad .x. libras. Istud debitum est Regine matris.

Johannes filius Willelmi de Bozal' debet eidem Dyey per recognicionem .xxv. libras. Appuratur ad .x. libras per predictam Sarram.

Summa catallorum .xliiij. libre, .vj. solidi, .viij. denarii.

Summa catallorum tam mobilium quam immobilium ut in terris, redditibus, cartis et obligationibus .lvij. libre, .x. solidi. Unde tercia pars Regis est .xix. libre, .iij. solidi, .iiij. denarii. Pro qua tercia parte Rex capit se ad unum debitum .xx. marcarum quod appuratur ad .x. libras per Sarram que fuit uxor dicti Dyey sub nominibus Willelmi la Thusche de comitatu Sutht' et ipsius Dyey et ad unum debitum .x. marcarum sub nominibus Willelmi de la Leye clerici de comitatu Surr', Reginaldi le Forester et ipsius Dyey, quod appuratur per predictam Sarram ad .v. marcas, et ad unum debitum .iiij. librarum sub nominibus Johannis filii David de comitatu Surr' et ipsius Dyey et indorsatur quod medietas istius debiti est Bonamy filii Bonamy de Oxon', que quidem medietas est Regis per forisfacturam ejusdem Dyey, et pars ipsius Dyey appuratur per predictam Sarram ad .xx. solidos; et ad unum debitum .v. marcarum sub nominibus Walteri Wolleward clerici de comitatu Midd' et ipsius Dyey, que appuratur per predictam Sarram ad .iiij. marcas; et ad medietatem cujusdam debiti .xv. librarum sub nominibus Roberti de Percy de comitatu Ebor' et Mossei filii Jacobi, que quidem medietas est ipsius Dyey per indorsamentum carte predicti debiti et appuratur medietas ipsius Dyey per predictam Sarram ad .ij. marcas et alia medietas est predicti Mossei. Summa: .xviij. libre, .vj. solidi, .viij. denarii. Et sic debet predicta Sarra domino Regi .xvj. solidos, .viij. denarios. Et postea concessum est eidem Sarre quod, si inveniatur aliquod debitum in archa cyrographariorum vel extra sub nominibus quorumcumque christianorum et ipsius Dyey vel aliquod aliud debitum, in quo idem Dyey habuit partem, quod ipsa infra annum exnunc computandum pro eisdem debitis finem facere possit sine calumpnia.

(476)

Bed'. Cum Robertus filius Willelmi Angh' de Sharpenho de comitatu Bed' teneretur Leoni filio Jornini judeo Norht' in decem libris argenti, reddendum inde .v. marcas ad octabas Pasche anno regis Edwardi tercio et .v. marcas ad octabas sancti Johannis Baptiste proximo sequentes et .v. marcas ad octabas sancti Michaelis proximo sequentes; quod quidem debitum captum fuit in manum regis pro diversis debitis in quibus idem Leo Regi tenetur, predictus Robertus solvit in recepta regis predictas .x. libras et ideo carta dicti debiti liberatur eidem Roberto in pleno scaccario quiete dampnanda.

(477)

Lond'. Isabella que fuit uxor Stephani Cissoris de parochia sancti Egidii extra portam de Cripelgate Lond' venit coram etc. pro se et heredibus et assignatis suis quietum clamasse magistro Elie filio magistri Mossei judeo et communitati judeorum Anglie totum jus et clamium quod habuit vel quoquo modo habere potuit in quadam placea terre cum pertinenciis racione dotis etc., quam quidem placea predictus Stephanus vir suus vendidit aliquo tempore predicte communitati; ita quod nec ipsa nec aliquis per ipsam in predicta placea terre cum pertinenciis decetero quicquam poterit exigere vel calumpniari.

(478)

Wiltes'. Datus est die Hildebrando de Lond' vicecomiti ad computandum etc. a die Pasche a die sancti Michaelis in .xv. dies.

(479)

Lond'. Manserus filius Aaron judeus protulit breve regis de magno sigillo in hec verba: 'Edwardus etc. justiciariis etc. et dilecto clerico suo Philippo de Wyleby salutem. Cum Manserus filius Aaron judeus Lond' teneatur nobis in .xl. libris pro arreragiis .c. marcarum in quibus idem Manserus nobis tenebatur pro medietate cujusdam domus in Lond' que fuit eschaeta nostra per mortem Benedicti filii Cok' judei nuper dampnati et quam predictus Manserus habet ex concessione nostra, vobis mandamus quod .xl. libras de clarioribus debitis dicti Manseri sine dilacione levari faciatis ad opus nostrum in satisfaccionem arreragiorum debiti supradicti, prout de jure et secundum legem et consuetudinem Judaismi

59 *In the margin is written* .v. marce.
60 *In the margin is written* .xx. solidi.
61 *In the margin is written* .iiij. marce.
62 *In the margin is written* .ij. marce.

nostri fuerit faciendum. Teste me ipso apud Bristoll' .xxiij. die Aprilis anno regni nostri octavo.'

(480)

Norff'. Radulphus Byl de Fyleby miles venit coram etc. et recognoscit se debere Aaron filio Vyves .x. libras, reddendum medietatem ad festum Omnium Sanctorum anno regis Edwardi .viij., et ad aliam medietatem ad Pascham proximo sequens. Et, nisi fecerit, concedit quod de terris et catallis suis fiant.

(481)

Lond' Johannes de Whatel', custos auri domine A. Regine matris Regis, venit coram etc. et recognovit quod satisfactum est predicte domine Regine de medietate cujusdam debiti .xx. librarum sub nominibus Hamonis filii Hamonis de Vyeleston' et Dyey filii Abr' judei et indorsatur in carta ejusdem debiti quod alia medietas istius debiti est Mossei filii Jacobi. Et idem Mosseus venit et recognovit quod satisfactum est sibi de medietate sua et quod predictum debitum quietum est, prout patet inter starra hujus termini. Et per istam recognicionem preceptum est cyrographariis arche cyrographariorum Lond' quod ad archam accedant et cartam dicti debiti .xx. librarum habeant coram etc. ad faciendum quod justiciarii etc.

MEMBRANE 7 DORSE

(482)

Suff'. Preceptum fuit vicecomiti quod attachiaret Johannem de Heccham, ita quod haberet corpus ejus coram etc. ad respondendum Regi eo quod contra fidem prestitam recessit de civitate Lond' sine licencia antequam satisfecisset Regi de .x. libris de debitis Aaron filii Abrahe, quas solvisse debuit pro Edmundo de Shardelawe pro quadam parte terrarum quas idem Edmundus tenet que fuerunt magistri Roberti de Shardelawe, cujus heres ipse Johannes est; et quod idem vicecomes levare faceret de bonis et catallis dicti Johannis dictas .x. libras et eas haberet coram etc. ad quindenam Pasche nunc solvendum. Postea vicecomes recepit quoddam breve de magno sigillo quod, accepta sufficienti securitate de predicto Johanne quod satisfaceret Regi ad quindenam Pasche de predictis .x. libris vel de sufficienti acquietacioni ostendendo, tunc poneret in respectum demandam quam facit eidem Johanni de predictis .x. libris usque etc. Et vicecomes mandavit quod Adam Topy de Wroxham, Reginaldus Polchod de eadem, Willelmus [blank] de eadem, Johannes atte Tunesende de eadem, Adam Thede de eadem, Adam Child de Bastwyk, Henricus Dabald de eadem, Robertus Albreth' de eadem, Adam Seful de Wroxham et Johannes Edwyne de Beston' manuceperunt predictum Johannem, quem non habuerunt. Ideo in misericordia.[63] Et preceptum est vicecomiti, sicut pluries, quod attachiaret ipsum Johannem, ita quod habeat corpus ejus coram etc. in octabis sancte Trinitatis ad respondendum Regi de transgressione predicta, et levari faciat de bonis et catallis predictorum manucaptorum et de catallis ipsius Johannis predictas .x. libras, ita quod eas habeat coram etc. ad hunc diem etc.

(483)

Ebor'. Petrus filius Radulphi de Seyl' de Comelesford', districtus per summonicionem de scaccario judeorum pro decem libris ad opus Regis de debitis Milonis de Roderham occasione terrarum quas tenet que fuerunt Petri filii Berardi de Comelesford', venit coram etc., asserens se esse quietum de omnimodis debitis que fuerunt ipsius judei per quoddam starrum lingua latina scriptum et littera ebrayca signatum quod protulit coram etc. in hec verba: 'Omnibus hoc scriptum visuris vel audituris Milo de Roderham judeus salutem in Domino. Noverit universitas vestra me omnino quietum clamasse Radulpho de Seyl' de Camelesford' et Willelmo et Waltero fratribus suis omnes terras et tenementa que ipsi christiani prenominati umquam emerunt de Petro filio Berardi de Camelesford' ab inicio mundi usque ad diem Conversionis sancti Pauli anno regni regis Henrici filii regis Johannis .xlviij. de omnibus debitis in quibus predictus Petrus vel aliquis antecessorum suorum umquam tenebantur mihi vel alicui judeo vel judee per cartam, talliam vel per aliquod aliud instrumentum. Et si aliqua carta, tallia vel aliud instrumentum nomine predicti Petri in Judaismo inveniatur ego Milo predictus judeus et heredes mei predictam terram et dictum tenementum ipsis Radulpho, Willelmo et Waltero et eorum heredibus tenemur warantizare et acquietare contra omnes judeos et judeas inperpetuum. In cujus rei testimonium hoc presens scriptum littera mea ebrayca consignavi.' Ideo justiciarii, volentes super predicto starro cerciorari, preceperunt constabulario Turris Lond' quod de judeis Ebor' tunc apud Lond' existentibus venire faceret coram eis tres legales judeos Ebor' et tres de Lond' ad recognoscendum etc. Qui veniunt per Manserum le Eveske, Dyey le Eveske, Cressaundyn, Isaac le Eveske, Isaac filium Benedicti, et Isaac de Ebor' judeos. Et dicunt super sacramentum suum predictum starrum lingua latina scriptum ex spontanea voluntate predicti Milonis fuisse confectum et manu sua in lingua ebrayca signatum. Ideo consideratum est quod dictus Petrus de porcione ipsum contingente de debito supradicto occasione terrarum etc. eat quietus. Et preceptum est vicecomiti quod ipsum in pace permittat. Et si quid etc.

(484)

Surr'. Preceptum est vicecomiti quod de bonis et catallis Johannis de Cameys fieri faceret decem libras ad opus Johannis de Bayfeld', clerici de scaccario etc., quas in curia regis recognovit etc. Et vicecomes mandavit quod Petrus Alayn capitalis ballivus [rapi][64] de Brembre et

[63] *The word* misericordia *is repeated in the margin.*

[64] *MS. reads* Radi'.

Adam le Justur capitalis ballivus de Arundel habent de averiis villanorum predicti Johannis ad valenciam predicti debiti, set idem Johannes nulla habet bona propria in balliva sua. Ideo preceptum est vicecomiti quod de illis averiis et aliis bonis predicti Johannis levari faciat predictas .x. libras, ita quod eas habeat coram etc. in octabis sancte Trinitatis etc.

(485)

Northt'. Ricardus de Waldegrave constabularius Turris Lond' venit coram etc. et recognovit se debere Johanni de Bayfeld' clerico etc. sex marcas pro Jurnino filio Abrahe judeo, reddendum inde .xl. solidos a die sancte Trinitatis in .xv. dies proximo futuro et .xl. solidos a die sancti Michaelis proximo sequenti in .xv. dies. Et, nisi fecerit, concedit quod de terris et catallis suis fiant.

(486)

Norff'. Willelmus de Hawerdyn, tenens quandam partem terrarum que fuerunt Willelmi de Milyers, venit coram etc. et recognovit se debere magistri Elie filio.[65]

(487)

Lond'. Poncius de la More mercator venit coram etc. et sine brevi exigit de Henna que fuit uxor Jahu judei dampnati unum picherum argenteum et unum ciphum argenteum precii quatuor librarum que ei injuste detinet, desicut in nullo debito ei tenetur.

Predicta Henna venit et dicit quod predicta jocalia de eo recepit set tempore capcionis judeorum dicta Henna tradidit Meyrot nepoti Belassez octodecim marcas et predictum ciphum que dictus Poncius ab ea exigit et Cressandino filio Leonis judeo predictum picherum et duas marcas argenti quas ab ea extorsit, dicendo quod Jahu frater ejus, qui pro transgressione monete suspensus fuit, tenebatur ei ex donacione sua in quinque marcis et hujusmodi tradiciones predictorum denariorum factas predicto Cressandino fecit in presencia Manseri la Pape. Ideo predictus Cressandinus committitur prisone et preceptum est constabulario etc. quod capiat predictum Meyrot.

(488)

Memorandum quod Henna que fuit uxor Jahu judei suspensi venit coram etc. et dicit quod Petrus de la Chaumbre recepit de predicto Jahu ante communem capcionem judeorum pro transgressione monete .viij. marcas.

MEMBRANE 8

Adhuc memoranda de termino Pasche anno octavo

(489)

Surr', Sussex'. Preceptum fuit vicecomiti, sicut pluries, quod distringeret Ricardum de Hadersham et tenentes terrarum suarum per terras etc., pro .c. solidis ad opus Regis; Ricardum filium ejus et tenentes terrarum suarum pro .x. marcis; priorem de Bermundes', tenentem quandam partem terrarum et reddituum que fuerunt Johannis de Kaumvile, pro .c. solidis; et quod non omitteret propter libertatem archiepiscopatus Cant' quin eam etc. et distringeret tenentes terrarum Henrici Jukel pro .ij. marcis, et tenentes terrarum Normanni de Suthwerk pro .xl. solidis et Radulphum Pelce, tenentem terrarum que fuerunt Galfridi Norman, pro .lx. solidis, et quod distringeret tenentes terrarum que fuerunt Roberti le Duk' pro .xl. solidis; quos quidem denarios Regi debent occasione terrarum etc. de debitis Isaac de Suthwerk judei, ita quod predictos denarios haberet coram etc. in quindena Pasche Regi solvendos. Et vicecomes mandavit quod Robertus de Hadersham, tenens terrarum que fuerunt Ricardi de Hadersham, districtus est et manucaptus habendi denarios ad diem in brevi contentum per Johannem atte Burne de Northfeld', Rogerum atte Hamme de eadem, Johannem le Venur de eadem, et Stephanum atte Bure de eadem, quem non habuerunt. Ideo in misericordia. Et quod Ricardus filius predicti Ricardi nichil habet in balliva sua nisi ad terminum vite [i]<uxoris>[i] sue. Et quod Willelmus de Bermundes' le Provost, Rogerus le Craus de Waddon', Willelmus Gerard de Dylewys, et Willelmus atte Flesche de eadem manuceperunt priorem de Bermund'; et quod Johannes Hardyng' de Chelesham, Johannes Ive de eadem, Johannes [i]<de>[i] Buckesel' de eadem et Johannes Kebbel de eadem manuceperunt Alanum atte Hethe, tenentem quandam partem terrarum que fuerunt Roberti le Duk'; et quod Robertus Underheld' de Chelesham, Johannes Hervy de eadem, Johannes Hamund de eadem, et Laurencius de la Plensengefeud de eadem manuceperunt Johannem de Radl', tenentem quandam partem terrarum que fuerunt Roberti le Duk'; quos non habuerunt. Ideo in misericordia.[66] Et vicecomes mandavit quod preceptum fuit Hugoni de Dynghyeton' ballivo de Suthwerk' pro tenentibus terrarum que fuerunt Henrici Jukel, qui nichil inde respondit nec pro aliquibus ballivam suam tangentibus. Et mandavit quod Henricus atte Welle de Effyngham, Thurbarnus le Clerc de eadem, Radulphus le Carpenter de eadem et Johannes le Carpenter de eadem manuceperunt Willelmum de Evere et Matillidem uxorem ejus, quos non habuerunt. Ideo in misericordia.[67] Et preceptum est vicecomiti, sicut pluries, etc. a die sancte Trinitatis in .xv. dies etc.

(490)

Surr' Suss'. Preceptum fuit vicecomiti quod distringeret Willelmum Herbert filium Stephani Herbert, Osbertum de Eylivehawe et priorem de Merton', tenentes quasdam partes terrarum que fuerunt Johannis Patrik' de Polesden', per terras etc. ad respondendum Regi una cum priore de Reygate, tenente quandam partem predic-

65 *This entry is unfinished.*

66 *The word* misericordia *is repeated in the margin.*

67 *The word* misericordia *is repeated in the margin.*

tarum terrarum, de quatuor libris de debitis Isaac de Suthwerk' etc. Predictus Willelmus Herbert et Osbertus venerunt coram etc. et protulerunt duo starra in quibus continebatur quod predicti Willelmus et Osbertus et heredes et assignati sui quieti sunt de dicto Isaac et heredibus suis et assignatis de porcione ipsos contingente de debito dictarum quatuor librarum occasione terrarum etc. que fuerunt predicti Johannis, salvo tamen jure domini Regis quod inde habet. Et compertum est per rotulos de appuramento etc. quod medietas illius debiti quatuor librarum est Regis. Ideo quesitum fuit a predictis Willelmo et Osberto quantum inde solverunt predicto Isaac, dicebant quod .ij. marcas et dimidiam. Ideo consideratum est quod predicti Willelmus et Osbertus solvant Regi predictas .ij. marcas et dimidiam et habent diem usque a die Pasche in .xv. dies ad solvendum predictas .ij. marcas et dimidiam. Et predictus Isaac pro Rege fecit venire priorem de Reygate et exigit ab eo .xx. solidos occasione predictarum terrarum etc. de catallo et .iiij. libras de lucro per cyrographum quatuor librarum, unde altera pars est in archa chirographariorum etc.

Predictus prior venit. Et recognovit se esse tenentem partis terrarum que fuerunt predicti Johannis et dedicere non potuit quin predictum debitum prefato judeo debeatur et petit extendi terras quas inde tenet que fuerunt dicti Johannis etc. Et preceptum est vicecomiti quod per sacramentum proborum et legalium hominum extendi faciat omnes terras etc., quid et quantum etc., et extentam etc. a die sancti Johannis Baptiste in tres septimanas.

Et vicecomes mandavit quod Willelmus Bruttegrave, Willelmus le Dux de Micham, Nicholas Peruld et Ricardus Cocus de eadem manuceperunt priorem de Merton', quem non habuerunt. Ideo in misericordia. Et sunt exitus terrarum predicti prioris per idem tempus .vj. solidi .viij. denarii de quibus Willelmus Rabel capitalis ballivus et predicti manucaptores respondebunt.

(491)

Norff'. Willelmus le Rede de Norwico qui tulit breve regis super Starr' de Norwico judeam de placito injuste detencionis catallorum non est prosecutus. Ideo ipse Willelmus pro se et plegiis suis de prosequendo in misericordia.

(492)[68]

Lond'. Johannes le Clerk aurifaber et Willelmus le Convers, fratres domus conversorum Lond', assingnati per breve regis ad colligendum chevagium judeorum Anglie anno regni regis Edwardi sexto per capita singulorum judeorum habencium etatem .xij. annorum et ultra, quod quidem chevagium dominus Rex concessit fratribus predicte domus, venerunt coram etc. et reddiderunt compotum suum de predicto chevagio etc.

[Iidem reddunt][69] compotum de .xj. libris .iij. solidis .ix. denariis de chevagio .dccc iiii^xx^. et .xv. judeorum per capita per diversa loca Anglie, sicut continetur in quadam cedula quam predicti Johannes et Willelmus liberaverunt predictis justiciariis, videlicet de singulis judeis .iij. denarios secundum statutum judeorum, et non respondent de chevagio judeorum Lond' nec Cantuar' de anno predicto, quia Hugo de Dyngneton' ipsum chevagium collegit et inde debet respondere, sicut patet inter inquisiciones hujus termini retornatas, per predictam cedulam etc.

Summa .xj. libre, .iij. solidi, .ix. denarii, quos liberaverunt Johanni de Sancto Deonisio custodi predicte domus in partem solucionis .xxix. librarum .iiij. solidorum et .iij. denariorum ad comparacionem capelle predicte domus faciendum ex concessione regis per breve regis de mangno sigillo et sic quieti fuerunt.

(493)

Ebor'. Preceptum fuit vicecomiti quod distringeret Robertum de Cave per terras etc. ad reddendum sibi ad opus Regis .xij. marcas et dimidiam quas Regi debet de debitis Isaac le Eveske judei et denarios illos haberet coram etc. a die Pasche in unum mensem Regi solvendos. Et vicecomes mandavit quod Alanus de Sancto Jacobo, Johannes de Brotton', Ricardus de Benlay, Ricardus de Topclyf' manuceperunt ad habendum corpus predicti Roberti ad satisfaciendum de denariis predictis, quem non habuerunt. Ideo in misericordia.[70] Et preceptum est vicecomiti, sicut alias, quod distringeret predictum Robertum pro predictis denariis, ita quod eos habeat coram etc. in quindena sancti Johannis Regi solvendum etc.

(494)

Glouc'. Preceptum fuit vicecomiti, sicut pluries, quod de bonis et catallis Edmundi filii Johannis de Glouc' fieri faceret .x. libras ad opus Ade de Strattone de .xx. libris quas idem Adam in curia domini H. regis patris regis Edwardi nunc coram etc. per consideracionem ejusdem curie recuperavit versus eundem Edmundum de debitis Isac de Suthwerk' judei, et denarios haberet coram etc. predicto Ade solvendos. Et vicecomes mandavit quod predictus Edmundus non habet bona nec catalla in balliva sua unde aliqui denarii levari possunt, set de feno et de blado in terris crescentibus fieri potuerunt in autumpno .c. solidi. Et preceptum est vicecomiti, sicut pluries, quod de feno et aliis bonis et catallis ipsius Edmundi fieri faciat predictos denarios, ita quod eos habeat coram etc. a die sancti Michaelis in .xv. dies predicto Ade liberandum.

(495)

Oxon' Berk'. Preceptum fuit vicecomiti, sicut pluries, quod de bonis et catallis predicti Edmundi fieri faceret .x. libras ad opus Ade de Straton' de .xx. libris quas idem Adam versus eundem Edmundum recuperavit, ut supra; et denarios haberet coram etc. ad eundem diem. Et vice-

[68] *Previously printed by Rigg in* Select Pleas, *p. 113.*

[69] *MS. reads* idem reddit.

[70] *The word* misericordia *is repeated in the margin.*

comes mandavit quod predictus Edmundus nichil habet in balliva sua nisi tantummodo dimidiam virgatam terre que jacet inculta pro diversis debitis que ab eodem Edmundo exiguntur ad opus Regis et aliorum quibus idem Edmundus tenetur. Ideo, sicut alias, a die sancti Michaelis in .xv. dies.

(496)

Kanc'. Preceptum fuit vicecomiti quod de bonis et catallis Andree de Elham fieri faceret ad opus Isac le Eveske .xxj. solidos .iiij. denarios quos idem Andreas recognovit etc., et denarios haberet coram etc. a die Pasche in .v. septimanas. Et vicecomes mandavit quod de bonis et catallis predicti Andree fieri fecit .x. solidos, quos non habuit coram etc. Ideo preceptum est ei quod eos habeat coram etc. in quindena sancti Johannis. Et vicecomes sit etc. Et quod residuum denariorum de bonis etc. levari faciat et eos habeat coram etc. ad eundem diem etc.

(497)

Surr'. Preceptum fuit vicecomiti quod venire faceret coram etc. a die Pasche in .v. septimanas .xij. tam milites etc. ad recognoscendum etc. si Willelmus de Whatevile feoffatus fuit de terris etc. in Chelesham antequam Johannes, pater ipsius Willelmi, se obligasset Deulecres filio Leonis judeo in .x. libris per cartam suam. Et vicecomes mandavit quod Rolandus de Acsted', Nicholaus Malemeyns, Thomas de Tycheseye, Robertus de Becwell', Rogerus de Chelesham, Ricardus filius Rogeri de eadem, Hubertus de eadem, Jacobus de Hesel', Willelmus Edward, Johannes Edward, Willelmus de Riscumbe, Ricardus de Horne, Egidius de Portle, Johannes de Acstede, Simon de Riscumbe, Willelmus atte Pende et Robertus de Northeton' manucapti sunt veniendi ad diem in brevi contentam. Et Rogerus de Chelesham, Ricardus filius Rogeri de eadem, Hubertus de eadem, Jacobus de Hesel', Willelmus Edwardus, Johannes Edward, Willelmus de Riscomb' et Simon de eadem venerunt. Et Rolandus et alii supradicti non venerunt. Et vicecomes mandavit quod Walterus atte Grave et Willelmus de Molendino manuceperunt predictum Rolandum; et quod Radulfus Carpentarius et Rogerus le Welhere manuceperunt Nicholaum Malem', et quod Willelmus de Strong' et Rogerus atte Park manuceperunt Thomam de Tyches'; et quod Thomas atte Regge et Rogerus Faber manuceperunt Robertum de Becwell; et quod Walterus atte Nobriht et Reginaldus atte Felde manuceperunt Rogerum de Horne; et quod [blank] le Fode et Thomas le Sone manuceperunt Egidium de Portle; et quod Alexander Smallheved et Galfridus Attecherche manuceperunt Johannem de Acsted; et quod Walterus Aylbryht et Henricus Edmund manuceperunt Willelmum atte Pende; et quod Walterus le Sone et Johannes de Redburn' manuceperunt Robertum de Northeton'; quos non habuerunt. Ideo in misericordia. Judicium quod predictus Rolandus et alii distringantur per terras etc., ita quod nec ipsi etc., et quod de exitibus etc., et quod habeat corpora eorum coram etc. in octabis sancti Johannis ad recognoscendum etc. una cum Rogero de Chelesham et aliis qui venerunt, qui habent eundem diem; et venire faciat tot et tales etc.

MEMBRANE 8 DORSE

(498)

Sussex'. Cum preceptum fuisset vicecomiti quod distringeret Simonem de Oxenbrige, Rogerum la Ware, Hamonem Bonet, Rogerum le Covert, Hugonem de Buscy, Nigellum de Brok', Willelmum de Alta Ripa et Hugonem Saunzaver per terras etc., et quod haberet corpora eorum etc. ad recognoscendum etc. una cum Rogero le Waleys, Rogero de Leukenore et aliis qui dictam recognicionem fecerunt, sicut patet inter brevia hujus termini returnata, si Regina mater Regis recepit exitus terrarum Willelmi Herigaud dum eas habuit in manu sua pro debitis Judaismi vel pro redempcione dicti Willelmi, sicut patet in placito inter eosdem in termino sancte Trinitatis anno regni regis Edwardi septimo. Et ipsi non venerunt. Et vicecomes mandavit quod Reginaldus de Stapel' de Beckel', Michael de Wodegate de eadem, Thomas Julyane de eadem, et Ricardus Julyane de eadem manuceperunt Simonem de Oxenebrige; et quod Robertus le Whyte de Isefeld', Willelmus atte Watere de eadem, Galfridus Depelake et Johannes atte Brigge de eadem manuceperunt Rogerum la Ware; et quod Simon Lullyng de Shetyngton', Adam Porteman de eadem, Galfridus atte Helde de eadem at Alanum de Totyngton' manuceperunt Robertum Bonet; et quod Willelmus le Parker de Sellinton', Willelmus le Burgeys de eadem, Robertus Kenteys de eadem et Ricardus Chepman de eadem manuceperunt Rogerum le Covert; et quod Michael prepositus de Kyngeston', Nicholaus Syward, Walterus le Bab et Robertus Cotel manuceperunt Hugonem de Buscy; et quod Johannes de Weston' de Launcyng', Johannes le Kyng' de eadem, Adam le Fraunc de eadem, et Robertus le Poer de eadem manuceperunt Nigellum de Brok'; et Johannes Horselere, Willelmus Saghhere, Henricus atte Strode, et Ricardus le Puller manuceperunt Willelmum de Alta Ripa; et quod Ricardus prepositus de Bygenevere, Willelmus atte Gate, Andreas le Mouner, et Willelmus Wysard manuceperunt Hugonem Saunzaver; quos non haberunt. Ideo in misericordia. Et Galfridus Snateyngeshull' et Johannes de Bromham, qui habuerunt eundem diem, non venerunt. Ideo in misericordia.

(499)

Norht'. Johannes de Morteyn, Willelmus de Nowers, Robertus de Kampania, Nicholaus de Wynehal', Robertus Barry, Robertus filius Alexandri, Henricus de Holecote, Simon Torpel, Willelmus de Catworth' et Petrus Barry de Herdewyck' manucapti de veniendo ad hunc diem ad recognoscendum etc. de placito transgressionis et compoti inter Elenam la Zusch' defendentem et

Willelmum Folyot et Isabellam uxorem ejus querentes non venerunt, sicut patet inter brevia hujus termini returnata. Ideo ipsi et manucaptores eorum in misericordia. Et vicecomes mandavit quod Johannes de Knapetoft et Galfridus le Lung de eadem manuceperunt Johannem de Morteyn; et quod Radulfus de Dudyngton in Cestre et Hugo le Bonde de eadem manuceperunt Willelmum de Noers, et quod Robertus le Eyr de Dodinton' et Ricardus Byesteton' de eadem manuceperunt Robertum de Kampania; et quod Robertus de Werkinton' et Ricardus Dundo manuceperunt Nicholaum de Wynehal'; et quod Radulfus le Despenser de Billing' et Henricus de Fonte de eadem manuceperunt Robertum Barry; et quod Simon le Noreys et Ricardus Lymbry manuceperunt Robertum filium Alexandri; et quod Ricardus le Mazun de Pydington' et Adam filius Duce de eadem manuceperunt Henricum de Holecote; et quod Nicholaus filius Roberti de Barton' et Willelmus Ketel de eadem manuceperunt Simonem Torpel; et quod Simon de Boseyate et Galfridus Evelong de eadem manuceperunt Willelmum de Catyworth'; et quod Adam Kelke de Hardewyk' et Adam Bullok' de eadem manuceperunt Petrum Barry; quos non habuerunt. Ideo in misericordia.[71] Et dicti Willelmus et Isabella petunt licenciam recedendi de brevi suo et querendi aliud breve et habent, sicut patet inter placita de termino sancti Hillarii proximo preterito.

MEMBRANE 9[72]

Adhuc memoranda de termino Pasche anno .viij.º

(500)

Warr', Leyc'. Sygonia filia Isac de Warr' judea, que tulit breve regis de placito injuste detencionis catallorum super Johannem de Chelemeresford', Johannem Pynne et alios in brevi, non est prosecuta versus eos. Ideo ipsa Sygonia et plegii sui de prosequendo, videlicet Abraham filius Mossei et Isac filius Mossei judei, in misericordia.[73] Et predicti Johannes, Johannes et alii non venerunt. Et preceptum fuit vicecomiti quod ipsos venire faceret. Et vicecomes mandavit quod Rogerus de Kynton' de Warr' et Nicholaus Cullebol' de eadem manuceperunt Johannem de Chelmereford, quem non habuerunt. Ideo in misericordia. Et predictus Johannes, quia non venit, ideo in misericordia. Et quod Thomas de la Mere de Warr' et Alexander le Fevre de eadem manuceperunt Johannem Pynne, quem non habuerunt. Ideo in misericordia.[74] Et dictus Johannes, quia non venit, in misericordia. Et quod Henricus le Serjaunt et Nicholaus Pullegreve non sunt inventi in balliva sua nec aliquid habent in ea per quod possint distringi.

(501)

Linc'. Genta filia Manseri judea, que tulit breve regis de placito debiti super Willelmum Blant, Adam filium Reginaldi le Neyr, Agnetem de Namby et Willelmum de Clay, non est prosecuta. Ideo ipsa Genta et plegii sui de prosequendo, videlicet Josceus filius Elie et Elias filius Deulecres judei, in misericordia. Et predicti Willelmus, Adam, Agnes et Willelmus non venerunt. Et preceptum fuit vicecomiti quod ipsos venire faceret. Et vicecomes mandavit quod Johannes le Parmenter de Linc' et Gilbertus Russel de eadem manuceperunt Willelmum Blant; et quod Osbertus de Greyby de Linc' et Ricardus Wlly de eadem manuceperunt predictum Adam; et quod Ricardus Stertopp' de Linc' et Robertus Gogan de eadem manuceperunt predictam Agnetem; et quod Thomas Bylton' de Linc' et Radulphus de Lounesdale de eadem manuceperunt Willelmum de Clay. Et predicti Willelmus, Adam, Agnes et Willelmus, quia non venerunt, pro defalta in misericordia.[75]

(502)

Linc'. Milkana filia Aaron judea, que tulit breve regis de placito debiti super Aliciam de Eyncurt, Johannem Bof de Cranewelle et Ricardum de Namby, non est prosecuta versus eos. Ideo ipsa Milkana et plegii sui de prosequendo, videlicet Manserus filius Joscei et Samuel filius Manseri, in misericordia. Et predicti Alicia, Johannes et Ricardus non venerunt. Et preceptum fuit vicecomiti quod ipsos venire faceret. Et vicecomes mandavit quod Robertus filius Avicie de Rouceby et Robertus filius Simonis de eadem manuceperunt predictam Aliciam; et quod Robertus filius Petri de Cranewelle et Adam filius Thome de eadem manuceperunt Johannem Bof; quos non habuerunt. Ideo in misericordia.[76] Et dicti Alicia et Johannes, quia non venerunt, ideo in misericordia. Et quod Ricardus de Namby nichil habet in balliva sua per quod possit attachiari. Ideo de ipso nichil actum est.

(503)

Suth'. Abraham filius Benedicti judeus de Wynton'[77] attachiatus ad respondendum Matildi Pruet de Wynton' de placito transgressionis et roberie, unde ipsum appellat. Et unde queritur quod, cum ipsa esset in pace dei et domini Regis Edwardi qui nunc est in civitate Wynton' die martis ante Pentecostes anno regni Regis predicti sexto et venisset in vicum qui vocatur Flesmongeresstrete ex opposito domus Isac le Lung judei ex parte occidentali et detulisset secum pannos et alia bona venalia circa horam diei terciam, venit predictus Abraham obviam eidem Matildi et eam ibidem verbis contumeliosis insultavit et ipsam per humeros cepit et ipsam verberavit, wlneravit et maletractavit contra pacem etc. et ipsam nequiter et felonice ad terram prostravit et, de hiis non tantum erat contentus, set felonice, ut felo et latro, de

[71] *The word* misericordia *is repeated in the margin.*

[72] *There is a letter* h *in the left-hand margin opposite this entry.*

[73] *The word* misericordia *is repeated in the margin.*

[74] *The word* misericordia *is repeated in the margin.*

[75] *The word* misericordia *is repeated twice in the margin.*

[76] *The word* misericordia *is repeated in the margin.*

[77] *Followed in MS. by* judeus.

ipsa cepit quoddam cornu bubale precii unius marce, quod quidem cornu Ricardus de Bosco ei tradidit ad vendendum et felonice ut fur et felo predictum cornu secum asportavit et adhuc penes se detinet ad grave dampnum suum .c. librarum. Et hoc parata est verificare secundum quod curia consideraverit etc.

Predictus Abraham venit et defendit vim etc. et quicquid est contra pacem etc. Et dicit quod non tenetur predicti Matildi nec ad appellum suum respondere, eo quod non specificat si baculo vel armis ipsam verberasset. Dicit eciam quod ad appellum roberie respondere non tenetur eo quod ipsa narrat versus ipsum de re aliena et non de re sua propria, nec aliquam assignat racionem qualiter inde possit habere proprietatem et petit judicium de appello. Et quia hujusmodi excepciones peremptorie sunt in appello consideratum est quod dicta Matillis per sectam suam versus predictum judeum nichil capiat per appellum suum predictum et quod predictus judeus quo ad appellum ipsius Matillidis eat quietus.

Postea quesitum fuit per justiciarios de predicto Abrahe quomodo de crimine sibi imposito de dicta roberia se vellet acquietare et ipse dicit quod predictam roberiam non fecit nec inde est culpabilis. Et de hoc ponit se super patriam. Ideo preceptum est vicecomiti quod venire faciat coram etc. a die sancti Johannis Baptiste in .xv. dies sex probos et legales christianos de Wynton' et sex legales judeos de eadem civitate qui nulla affinitate etc. ad recognoscendum etc.

MEMBRANE 9 DORSE

Adhuc memoranda

(504)

Cantebr'. Preceptum fuit vicecomiti quod per sacramentum etc. diligenter inquireret quid et quantum porcio prioris de Bernewelle, fratrum Hospitalis sancti Johannis et aliorum tenencium terrarum et tenementorum que fuerunt Johannis le Rus, sicut patet inter memoranda de termino sancti Hillarii proximo preterito, valeant per annum in omnibus exitibus etc. Et vicecomes mandavit quod subscripti sunt tenentes terrarum et tenementorum que fuerunt predicti Johannis le Rus per inquisicionem inde factam, sicut patet inter inquisiciones hujus termini returnatas, videlicet fratres Sacci tenent capitale mesuagium quod fuit predicti Johannis et valet per annum .x. solidos, de quo mesuagio Alicia que fuit uxor predicti Johannis tenet dotem suam.

Guydo de Mortuo Mari, rector ecclesie de Kyngeston', tenet inde unum mesuagium et valet .xxxiij. solidos .iiij. denarios. Debet .xv. solidos .iij. denarios.

Johannes But tenet inde unum mesuagium et valet per annum .xv. solidos. Debet .vij. solidos .iiij. denarios obulum.

Fratres Hospitalis sancti Johannis tenent inde .xv. acras terre arabilis que valent per annum .xv. solidos, tres acras prati que valent per annum .x. solidos et quatuor solidatas annui redditus. Debent .xiij. solidos .iij. denarios obulum.

Thomas de Clopton' et Agnes filia Andree Treweman tenent inde .iiij. solidatas redditus et unum caseum precii .iiij. denariorum. Debent .ij. solidos.

Priorissa et moniales de Swafham tenent inde dimidiam marcatam redditus. Debent .iij. solidos .j. denarium.

Alicia relicta predicti Johannis tenet inde in dotem .xiiij. acras terre arabilis et dimidiam acram prati et valent per annum .x. solidos.

Ricardus Wombe tenet inde .xx. acras terre arabilis et valent .xij. solidos. Debet .v. solidos .ij. denarios.

Ricardus Bateman junior tenet inde .ij. acras terre arabilis et unam acram prati et valent .iiij. solidos. Debet .xxij. denarios.

Willelmus de Wilburham capellanus tenet .j. acram terre arabilis que valet per annum .xij. denarios. Debet .v. denarios obulum.

Ricardus filius Ricardi Laur' tenet inde .xij. denariatas redditus. Debet .v. denarios obulum.

Hugo le Rus tenet inde .v. acras terre arabilis et valent per annum tres solidos. Debet .xvj. denarios obulum.

Lucas Carettarius tenet inde tres acras terre arabilis que valent per annum duos solidos. Debet .xj. denarios.

Willelmus de Pykering' tenet inde dimidiam marcatam redditus. Debet .iij. solidos .j. denarium.

Robertus de Madynghele tenet inde dimidiam acram terre et valet per annum .vj. denarios.

Prior de Bernewelle tenet inde .lx. acras terre arabilis et valent per annum triginta solidos et .ij. solidatas annui redditus. Debet .xiiij. solidos .viij. denarios.

Bartholomus Goygyn tenet inde .iij. acras et tres rodas terre arabilis et valent per annum .ij. solidos .viij. denarios. Debet .xv. denarios.

Robertus filius Andree Frede tenet .j. acram terre arabilis que valet per annum .xij. denarios. Debet .v. denarios obulum.

Simon filius Simonis Godeman tenet dimidiam acram terre arabilis et valet per annum .vj. denarios.

Matildis de Walda tenet inde .j. acram et dimidiam terre arabilis et valent per annum .xviij. denarios. Debet .viij. denarios.

Robertus custos capelle sancti Edmundi tenet inde tres acras et dimidiam terre arabilis et valent .iij. solidos .vj. denarios. Debet .xx. denarios.

Cecilia relicta Petri de Well' tenet inde .iiij. acras terre arabilis et valent per annum .iiij. solidos. Debet .xxij. denarios.

Ricardus Pet tenet inde dimidiam acram terre arabilis et valet per annum .vj. denarios.

Nicholaus Morice tenet inde tres acras terre arabilis et tres acras prati et valent per annum .viij. solidos .vj. denarios. Debet .iij. solidos .xj. denarios.

Dyonisia relicta Willelmi de Hunted' tenet .j. acram terre arabilis et valet .xij. denarios. Debet .v. denarios, obulum.

Osbertus le Ferrer tenet inde .j. acram terre arabilis et

valet per annum .xij. denarios. Debet .v. denarios, obulum.

(505)

Norht'. Ricardus de Colewrth' miles de comitatu Norht' venit coram etc. et recognovit se debere magistro Elye filio magistri Mossei judeo London' occies viginti quarteria frumenti vel pro quolibet quarterio dimidiam marcam, reddendo inde viginti quarteria ad quindenam Pasche ano regni regis Edwardi octavo, et quadraginta quarteria ad quindenam sancti Martini in hyeme proximo sequentem, et .xxx. et duo quarteria ad quindenam Pasche proximo sequentem, et .xxxij. quarteria ad quindenam sancti Martini in hyeme proximo sequentem. Et, nisi fecerit, concedit quod de terris et catallis suis fiant etc.

MEMBRANE 10[78]

Starra de termino Pasche anno regni regis Edwardi octavo

(506)

Lond'. Isac de Suthwerk judeus recognovit per starrum suum quod ipse quietavit et quietum clamavit Simoni Orpedeman de Lond' totum jus, clamium, demandam et calumpniam que umquam habuit vel habere potuit super omnes terras quas idem Simon emit de Henrico Jukel. Totum hoc quietavit et quietum clamavit, ita quod nec ipse judeus nec heredes sui quicquam exigere vel clamare poterunt versus predictum Simonem occasione predictarum terrarum a principio seculi usque ad finem.[79]

(507)

Derb'. Gamaliel de Oxon' judeus recognovit per starrum suum quod ipse recepit .x. marcas de Uriano de Sancto Petro de .xx. marcis quas idem Urianus eidem judeo debuit per recognicionem suam factam in rotulis domini regis ad scaccarium judeorum. Et dictus Gamaliel concedit quod predictus Urianus et heredes sui et tenentes terrarum suarum quieti sunt de ipso judeo et heredibus suis de predictis .x. marcis integre a creacione seculi usque ad finem.

(508)

Hereff'. Sampson filius Isac recognovit per starrum suum quod ipse recepit .xxiij. solidos de Willelmo filio et herede Willelmi de Sholle per manus Ade de Kyngeshemed' in crastino diei Animarum anno regni regis Edwardi sexto de debitis in quibus predictus Willelmus pater predicto judeo tenebatur. Idem Sampson recognoscit per starrum suum quod ipse recepit de Nicholao clerico thesaurarii pro Willelmo filio Willelmi de Sholle quarto die post diem Animarum anno regis Edwardi sexto .viij solidos de debitis in quibus Willelmus pater predicti Willelmi eidem judeo tenebatur.[80]

(509)

Idem Sampson recognovit per starrum suum quod ipse recepit .ij. marcas de Willelmo de Sholle filio Willelmi de Sholle de debitis in quibus dictus Willelmus pater predicti Willelmi predicto judeo tenebatur de porcione predicti debiti, videlicet a die Pasche in tres septimanas anno regni regis Edwardi octavo.

(510)

Cantebr'. Aaron filius Vyves recognovit per starrum suum quod ipse recepit .xx. marcas de Willelmo filio Baldewini de Stowe de termino trium septimanarum a die Pasche anno regni regis E. .viij. de quodam fine facto inter predictum Willelmum et ipsum Aaron de .iiij.^{xx} marcis secundum quod irrotulatur in rotulis domini regis etc.

(511)

Essex'. Aaron filius Vyves judeus recognovit per starrum suum quod Robertus de Symay quietus est de ipso judeo et heredibus suis de quodam obligacione .c. quarteriorum frumenti et de omnibus aliis debitis, demandis, calumpniis et plegiagiis in quibus idem Robertus eidem judeo umquam tenebatur a creacione seculi usque ad Mediam Quadragesimam anno regis Edwardi .viij. Et quod recognovit hoc sigillavit.

(512)

Cantebr' Lond'. Josceus filius Sauloti judeus recognovit per starrum suum quod, si Willelmus filius Baldewini de Stowe vel heredes vel assignati reddant Aaron filio Vyves vel heredibus vel assignatis suis .iiij.^{xx} marcas ad terminos subscriptos, videlicet .xx. marcas a die Pasche [in tres septimanas][81] anno regis Edwardi octavo, et .xx. marcas a die sancti [Michaelis][82] proximo sequenti in tres septimanas, et .xx. marcas in crastimo Purificacionis Beate Marie proximo sequenti et .xx. marcas a die Pasche proximo sequenti in tres septimanas, tunc post solucionem predictorum denariorum ad terminos predictos acquietavit ipse judeus et perdonavit pro se et heredibus et assignatis suis predicto Willelmo filio Baldewyni et heredibus et assignatis suis omnimoda debita in quibus predictus Willelmus filius Baldewini <vel Willelmus>[83] filius Gilberti vel Johannes filius Willelmi filius Gilberti umquam eidem Josceo tenebantur vel Sauloto patri ejusdem Joscei a creacione seculi usque ad diem confeccionis predicti starri. Et post solucionem predictarum .iiij.^{xx} marcarum ad terminos predictos persolutarum predicto Aaron vel heredibus vel assignatis suis, predictus Josceus super se recepit [faciendum][84] pro se et

[78] *There is a letter* h *in the left hand margin above this heading.*

[79] *There is a letter* r *in the margin opposite this entry.*

[80] *A letter* r *is written in the margin opposite this entry.*

[81] *MS. omits but see no. 366.*

[82] *MS. omits.*

[83] *These words are repeated in MS.*

[84] *MS. omits.*

heredibus et assignatis suis predicto Willelmo filio Baldewini unum starrum de acquietacione plena de omnimodis debitis in quibus dictus Willelmus filius Baldewini vel Willelmus filius Gilberti vel Johannes filius Willelmi filii Gilberti umquam eidem Josceo vel Sauloto patri suo tenebantur a creacione seculi usque ad diem confeccionis presentis starri. Et, si predictus Willelmus filius Baldewini non reddat predictas .iiij.^{xx} marcas predicto Aaron ad terminos predictos vel si pretereat unum predictorum terminorum, tunc non tenetur idem Josceus facere acquietacionem de debitis predictis in quibus Willelmus filius Baldewini predictus vel Willelmus filius Gilberti vel Johannes filius Willelmi filii Gilberti prenominati eidem Josceo vel Sauloto patri ejus tenebantur, et quod ipse Josceus habeat recuperare suum super predicta debita, ita tamen quod idem Josceus tenetur allocare predicto Willelmo filio Baldewini id quod solvit predicto Aaron in debitis predictis; ita tamen quod predicta allocacio non sit ei computata seu allocata nisi una vice. Acta .iij. die post Hokeday anno .viij.

(513)

War'. Aaron filius Vyves judeus recognovit per starrum suum quod recepit de Ricardo de Mundeville per manus Thome de Asel' duodecim libras et .x. solidos de termino quindene Pasche anno regis Edwardi .viij. de quodam debito quingentarum librarum in quo ei tenebatur.

Recognovit eciam quod recepit ab eodem Ricardo per manus ejusdem Thome .xx. solidos pro quadam roba in qua ei tenebatur de termino predicto et quod idem Ricardus tam de predictis [i]<.xij.>[i] libris et .x. solidis quam de predictis .xx. solidis pro predicta roba eidem plenarie satisfecit.

Idem Aaron recognovit se recepisse .xij. libras .x. solidos et .xx. solidos pro una roba in quibus ei tenebatur de predicto debito quingentarum librarum de termino quindene sancti Michaelis anno regis Edwardi .vij. incipiente .viij.

(514)

Lond' Midd'. Elias filius magistri Mossei judeus recognovit per starrum suum quod recepit de Ada cissore domini Regis .lxx. marcas ad quindenam Pasche anno regni regis Edwardi .viij, scilicet de fine quam fecit cum eo de debitis Willelmi de Hadestok' in quibus idem Willelmus eidem judeo tenebatur.

(515)

Essex'. Manserus filius Aaron recognovit per starrum suum quod Ricardus de Suthcherche et heredes et antecessores sui et assignati sui quieti sunt de ipso et heredibus et assignatis suis de quodam debito .xl. librarum sub nominibus predicti Ricardi et ipsius judei a creacione seculi usque ad finem et de omnibus aliis debitis, plegiagiis et calumpniis a creacione seculi usque ad Pentecosten anno regni regis Edwardi .viij.^{o} Et si inveniatur tallia, debitum vel carta vel aliquod aliud instrumentum in archa cyrographariorum vel extra sub nominibus predicti Ricardi et ipsius judei factum ante Pentecosten predictam idem judeus recognovit pro se et heredibus suis et assignatis quibuscumque quod quieti sint et nichil valeant.

(516)

Derb'. Elias filius magistri Mossei et Aaron filius Vyves judei recognoverunt per starrum suum quod ipsi receperunt de Radulpho de Shirlee decem marcas et dimidiam quas idem Radulphus eisdem judeis debuit solvere ad quindenam Pasche anno regni regis Edwardi .viij. et super predictos judeos est allocare predicto Radulpho prefatas .x. marcas et dimidiam in frumento quod idem Radulphus et Jacobus pater ejus eisdem judeis debent.

(517)

Kanc' Lond'. Mosseus filius Jacobi recognovit per starrum suum quod ipse quietavit et quietumclamavit Johanni filio Hamonis de Vyeleston' et heredibus et assignatis suis totum jus, demandam et calumpniam que habuit vel habere potuit super manerium de Vyeleston' cum pertinenciis in comitatu Kanc' occasione medietatis duorum debitorum, videlicet medietatis unius debiti .xl. librarum sub nominibus Hamonis filii Hamonis de Vyeleston' et ipsius Mossei, unde medietas fuit Dyey filii Abrahe, et medietatis unius debiti .xx. librarum sub nominibus predicti Hamonis et ipsius Dyey, que quidem medietas est ipsius Mossei, ita quod nec ipse Mosseus nec heredes suis nec aliquis assignatus ejus aliquid possint exigere nec calumpniari super predictum Johannem racione dicti manerii de Vyeleston' occasione predictorum debitorum a creacione seculi usque ad finem, nec racione aliquarum aliarum terrarum quas predictus Hamo umquam prius tenuit in comitatu Kanc' predicto, salvo tamen ipsi Mosseo et heredibus et assignatis suis quod ipse possit recuperare debita sua super alias terras et redditus que fuerunt predicti Hamonis extra comitatum Kanc'. Acta die mercurii proxima post festum sancti Dunstani anno regni regis Edwardi octavo. Et quod recognovit hoc sigillavit.

(518)

Kanc' Lond'. Mosseus filius Jacobi de Oxon' recognovit per starrum suum pro se et idem Mosseus et Isac le Eveske judei testantur et recognoscunt pro Sarra que fuit uxor Dyey filii Abrahe quod Johannes de Vyleston' et Thomas frater ejus et heredes eorum et assignati quieti sunt de ipsis Mosseo et Sarra et heredibus et assignatis suis de duobus debitis, scilicet de uno debito .xl. librarum sub nominibus Mossei filii Jacobi et Hamonis filii Hamonis de Vyeleston', et de uno alio debito viginti librarum sub nominibus dicti Dyei et ipsius Hamonis, et indorsatur in carta quod medietas ejusdem debiti est Mossei filii Jacobi et irrotulatur in rotulis de scrutinio et appuramento debitorum judeorum quod pars ipsius Dyey est A. Regine Anglie matris Regis nunc. De predictis duobus debitis prefati Johannes et Thomas et heredes et assignati eorum quieti sint de predictis Mosseo et Sarra et heredibus suis a creacione seculi usque ad finem et de omnibus aliis debitis et demandis in quibus predictus Hamo umquam tenebatur ipsis judeis a creacione seculi usque ad finem et de omnibus aliis debitis et demandis in quibus predicti Johannes et Thomas umquam tenebantur eisdem judeis a creacione seculi usque ad festum Ascensionis Domini anno regni regis Edwardi .viij. et de omnibus hujusmodi debitis quieti sunt. Et si inveniatur carta, tallia vel aliquod aliud instrumentum in archa cyrographariorum vel extra sub nominibus ipsorum Johannis et Thome vel Hamonis fratris eorum vel alicujus antecessorum suorum et predictorum Mossei et Dyey factum ante diem predictum ipsi judei recognoverunt et concesserunt quod quieta sint et nichil valeant. Et istud starrum factum fuit coram R. de Ludham tunc justiciario judeorum et per licenciam et preceptum Johannis de Whatel' tunc custodis auri predicte domine Regine matris domini Regis Edwardi. Et hoc recognovit predictus Mosseus pro se et sigillavit et una cum predicto Isac pro predicta Sarra testatur.

MEMBRANE 10 DORSE

(519)

Norht'. Aaron filius Vyves recognovit per starrum suum quod Galfridus de Suthorp' et heredes sui quieti sunt de eodem Aaron et heredibus suis de una obligacione .xx. saccorum lane in qua idem Galfridus tenebatur eidem Aaron et de omnibus aliis debitis et.[85]

[85] *This entry is unfinished. It is followed by the note* Radulphus Bel, Robertus de Hardres patent inferius.

(520)

Essex'. Ricardus de Tany miles venit coram [etc. et][86] recognovit [se debere][87] Aaron Fives centum et quatuor quarteria frumenti, reddendo [unam medietatem][88] ad Natale Domini anno regis Edwardi .ix. et aliam medietatem ad festum Nativitatis sancti Johannis Baptiste proximo sequens vel pro quolibet quarterio .xl. denarios. Et nisi etc.

(521)

Norff'. Jacobus filius Gilberti miles venit coram etc. [et recognovit se debere][89] Aaron filio Vives judeo .l. marcas, reddendo ad festum Omnium Sanctorum anno regis Edwardi .viij. Et nisi etc.

(522)

Bed'. Johannes Malerbe recognovit se [debere][90] eidem centum summas frumenti vel etc., reddendo ad festum sancti Michaelis anno Edwardi .viij.° Et nisi etc.

(523)

Warr'. Robertus Hasteng venit coram etc. et recognovit [se debere][91] eidem .lxx. libras, reddendo a die sancti Michaelis in unum mensem anno regis Edwardi .viij.° Et nisi etc.

[86] *MS. omits.*
[87] *MS. omits.*
[88] *MS. omits.*
[89] *MS. omits.*
[90] *MS. omits.*
[91] *MS. omits.*

TRINITY TERM, 8 EDWARD I [1280]

Exchequer of Jews, Plea Rolls No. 36 [E 9/36] and Membrane 9 of Plea Roll no. 27 [E 9/27]

A single membrane (m. 9) now attached to the Roll for Easter term 1278 (E 9/27) originally belonged to a roll of this term and is reproduced here immediately following Roll 36 (as entries no. 720 onwards). It is possible that it once formed part of Roll 36. However, the fact that it includes four entries (nos. 722, 729, 735 and 737) which are duplicated on Roll 36 (nos. 659, 686, 697 and 676) suggests that it probably comes from a second roll.

MEMBRANE 1

Essonia ad scaccarium judeorum de octabis sancte Trinitatis anno regni regis Edwardi octavo

(524)

Hereford'. Robertus de Morton' versus Joye que fuit uxor Hake de Wygorn' judeam de placito debiti per Willelmum Castelyn'.

Willelmus de Morton' versus eandem de eodem per Willelmum de Stafford'.

Philippus de Turbervile versus eandem de eodem per Johannem Luberd.

Hugo filius Rogeri versus eandem de eodem per Johannem Furthingg'.

Cristiana que fuit uxor Thome de Essington' versus eandem de eodem per Hugonem le Piper.

Non jacet quia breve 'venire facias'.

(525)

Wiltes'. Johannes de Havering' versus Thomam de Chelevarton' de placito acquietacionis debiti per Adam Prodom.

Postea predictus Johannes venit et optulit se versus predictum Thomam et predictus Thomas non venit. Ideo predictus Johannes sine die et predictus Thomas in misericordia.

(526)

Norff'. Oliverus de Ingham, qui Bartholomeum de Redham vocavit ad varrantum, versus Alienoram Reginam Anglie consortem Regis de placito debiti per Adam de Stubbingg'.

Idem Oliverus versus eundem Bartholomeum de placito acquietacionis debiti per Robertum de Ingham.

Die lune proxima ante festum sancte Margarete. Affidaverunt.

(527)

Cantebr'; vetus est. Rogerus de Feltevell versus Willelmum de Middleton' de placito debiti unde jurata per Johannem Russell'.

In crastino sancte Margarete. Affidavit.

(528)

Northt'. Jacobus de Bedeford' versus Johannem de Cheyne vicecomitem Bed' de placito debiti per Benedictum de Bed'.

Non jacet quia breve 'venire facias'.

(529)

Oxon'; vetus est. Sarra filia Mossei versus Thomam le Verrur de placito debiti per Sampsonem de Wygorn'.

In crastino sancte Margarete. Affidavit.

(530)

Somers'. Ricardus de Loverley, qui vocat ad warrantum Johannem Ruffrigeray versus Sampsonem filium Sampsonis et Gentam uxorem ejus, de placito debiti per Adam Mosse.

Jocea uxor ejusdem Ricardi de eodem per Johannem filium Henrici.

(531)

Northt'. Ysac le Evesk' judeus [Northt'][1] versus Walterum de Celleston' de placito debiti per Pyctavinum filium Sampsonis.

A die sancti Michaelis in .xv. dies. Affidavit.

(532)

Kanc'. Symon le Feutrer versus Haginum de [Bradested'][2] judeum de placito debiti per Johannem filium Willelmi.

(533)

Linc'. Magister Elyas filius Mossei judeus versus priorem de Spaulinges de placito acquietacionis debiti per Sampsonem de Wygorn'.

Essonia de quindena sancte Trinitatis

(534)

Northt'. Wives le Romanzur[3] versus Ricardum de Lilleburn' et alios in brevi de placito debiti per Ysaac filium Mossei.

Nullum breve.

[1] *MS. reads* Northm'. [2] *MS. reads* Badested'.
[3] *Interlined above this name is* querens.

(535)
Essex'. Robertus le Poyr versus Aaron filium Vives de placito debiti per Robertum filium Willelmi.
A die sancti Michaelis in .xv. dies. Affidavit.

(536)
Norff'. Johannes de Bayfeld' versus Johannem de Hadesagh' de placito injuste detencionis catallorum per Rogerum de Kington'.
A die sancti Michaelis in .xv. dies. Affidavit.

(537)
Lond'. Laurencius Aubyn versus Leonem filium Cressei judeum de placito debiti per Willelmum le Keu.
Habent diem prece parcium a die sancti Michaelis in .xv. dies. Affidavit.

(538)
Northt'. Symon le Baud constabularius castri Northt' versus Adam le Furmarier de placito transgressionis per Adam Prodom.
Johannes le Porter de eodem versus eundem per Ricardum filium Walteri.

(539)
Lond'. Michael le Oynter versus Margaliciam judeam de placito debiti per Adam Prodom.
Non jacet quia breve districcionis.

(540)
Cant'. Willelmus de Lyndes' versus Aaron filius Vives judeum de placito debiti per Ricardum le Serjaunt.
A die sancti Michaelis in .xv. dies.

(541)
Cantebr'. Walterus de la Howeys, attornatus Alicie que fuit uxor Simonis Godman, quam Nicholaus Morice vocavit ad warantum versus Regem et magistrum Eliam de placito debiti per Adam Brun.
In octabis sancti Michaelis. Affidavit.

(542)
Essex'. Henricus de Webleys versus Cresseum filium Gente judeum de placito debiti per Galfridum Royt.
A die sancti Michaelis in .xv. dies. Affidavit.

(543)
Sutht'. Abraham filius Benedicti judeus Vynton' versus Saram que fuit uxor Salomonis Vynton' judeam de placito debiti per Adam de Oxon'.
Non jacet quia habuit diem de die in diem.

Essonia de in crastino sancte Margarete

(544)
Linc'. Johannes Michel, attornatus Walteri de la [Lynde,][4] versus Cresseum filium Gente de placito debiti per Adam le Petur.

(545)
Lond'. Michael le Oynter versus Margaliciam que fuit uxor Samuelis le Blund de placito debiti unde jurata per Thomam le Messagir.

(546)
Kanc'. Stephanus Gerard versus magistrum Eliam filium magistri Mossei judeum de placito debiti per Willelmum de Assey.

(547)
Norht'. Alicia que fuit uxor Roberti Etewel versus Saram de Lond' judeam de placito injuste detencionis catallorum per Adam le Norman.

MEMBRANE 1 DORSE

Prece parcium et attornati

(548)
Essex'. Margareta uxor Ricardi de Quercu ponit loco suo Rogerum Bering versus Belehasez que fuit uxor Leonis filii Preciuse judeam de placito debiti.

(549)
Kanc'. Margareta uxor Simonis le Foutrer ponit loco suo Johannem filium Henrici vel Willelmum Boey [versus][5] Haginum de Bradestede judeum et Sapol' uxorem ejus de placito debiti.

(550)
Lond'. Rosa que fuit uxor magistri Samuelis de Lohun ponit loco suo Gamaliel de Oxon' versus Robertum de Bery de placito debiti.

(551)
Hertf'. Eadem Rosa ponit loco suo eundem Gamaliel versus Hugonem de Brok' de placito debiti.

(552)
Essex'. Ricardus de Quercu ponit loco suo Isak de Suwerk judeum versus Beleassez que fuit uxor Leonis filium Preciuse de placito debiti.

(553)
Essex'. Hugo filius Ricardi ponit loco suo Rogerum de Flete vel Rogerum de Schirburne versus Willelmum clericum de Halesford' et Willelmum Cristemasse de placito transgressionis.

(554)
Lond'. Rosa filia Abrahe ponit loco suo Jorninum filium Abrahe et Sampsonem de Vygorn' versus Willelmum filium Willelmi de Samford' de placito debiti.

[4] *MS. reads* Lyde.

[5] *MS. reads* vel.

(555)

Lond'. Belasset que fuit uxor Leonis filii Preciose ponit loco suo Meyr' nepotem Leonis versus Floriam filiam Benedicti de placito debiti.

Eadem Belasset ponit loco suo eundem Meyr versus Michaelem le Ceynturer et Gilbertum, tenentes terrarum que fuerunt Willelmi de Dunstaple, de placito debiti.

(556)

Kanc'. Stephanus Chicche ponit loco suo Laurencium filium Johannis versus Walterum Carbonell' de placito aquietacionis debiti.

(557)

Essex'. Willelmus de Clere de Alesford' ponit loco suo Willelmum de Tvynsted' versus Hugonem filium Ricardi de placito transgressionis.

MEMBRANE 2

Placita de octabis sancte Trinitatis anno regni regis Edwardi octavo

(558)

Linc'. Walterus de la Linde pro pluribus defaltis versus Cresseum filium Gente in misericordia.

Cresseus filius Gente venire fecit Walterum de la Lynde, tenentem quandam partem terrarum que fuerunt Johannis le Rus, et exigit ab eo .xx. marcas de catallo et .xx. marcas de lucro occasione terrarum etc. per cyrographum viginti librarum, unde altera pars est in archa cyrographariorum Lond', ut dicit, in hec verba: 'Johannes Russell' filius Willelmi de comitatu Bok' debet Cresseo filio Gente judeo viginti libras, reddendum ei ad festum sancti Laurencii anno regni regis Henrici filii regis Johannis .xlvj. Acta .xiiij. die Februarii anno predicto.'

Predictus Walterus venit et petit diem [premeditandi][6] et habet in crastino sancte Margarete.

(559)

Norht'. Willelmus Folyot et Isabella uxor ejus per attornatum suum optulerunt se quarto die versus Elenam la Thusche de placito dehospitandi et eciam de placito compoti. Et ipsa non venit. Et preceptum fuit vicecomiti quod ipsam venire faceret ad hunc diem. Et vicecomes mandavit quod Alanus Drake de Esseby, Willelmus in Angulo de eadem, Radulphus Faukes de Esseby et Hubertus Drake de eadem manuceperunt predictam Elenam, quam non habuerunt. Ideo in misericordia.[7] Judicium quod distringat per terras et catalla etc., ita quod nec ipsa etc., et quod de exitibus etc., et quod habeat corpus ejus coram etc. in crastino sancte Margarete ad respondendum etc. et ad audiendum etc.

(560)

Lond'. Idem Willelmus et Ysabella per attornatos suos optulerunt de quarto die versus magistrum Eliam de placito compoti. Et ipse non venit. Et preceptum fuit constabulario quod ipsum venire faceret coram etc. ad hunc diem etc. Et constabularius mandavit quod Ysac de Canc' et Abraham filius magistri Elie manuceperunt predictum magistrum Eliam, quem non habuerunt. Ideo in misericordia. Judicium quod distringat per terras etc., ita quod nec ipse etc., et quod de exitibus etc., et quod habeat corpus ejus etc. in crastino sancte Margarete ad respondendum etc. et ad audiendum etc.

(561)

Notht'. Alicia que fuit uxor Roberti Etevel per attornatum suum optulit se quarto die versus Saram de Lond' judeam Norht' de placito injuste detencionis vadiorum. Et ipsa non venit. Et preceptum fuit quod ipsam venire faceret coram etc. Et vicecomes mandavit quod Saulot le Petyt et Ysac filius Ysac de Northt' manuceperunt predictam Saram, quam non habuerunt. Ideo in misericordia. Judicium quod distringat per terras etc., ita quod nec ipsa etc., et quod de exitibus etc., et quod habeat corpus ejus coram etc. in crastino sancte Margarete ad respondendum etc. et ad audiendum etc.

(562)

Norht'. Ysac le Eveke judeus Northt' per attornatum suum optulit se quarto die versus Rogerum Kene et Murielam uxorem ejus et Ysabellam Peny de placito injuste detencionis catallorum. Et ipsi non veniunt. Et preceptum fuit vicecomiti quod ipsos venire faceret coram etc. ad hunc diem. Et vicecomes mandavit quod Willelmus de Neuport, Nicholaus Grull, Ricardus le Coliere et Walterus Faukes manuceperunt predictum Rogerum; et quod Radulphus de Houthon' et Willelmus Aunfrey manuceperunt Murielam uxorem ejus; quos non habuerunt. Ideo in misericordia. Judicium quod distringat per terras etc.[8]

(563)

Kanc'. Mabilia que fuit uxor Galfridi attachiata ad respondendum Hagino de Bradested' et Sipole uxori ejus de placito injuste detencionis catallorum. Et unde queruntur quod, cum conduxissent quamdam domum de dicta Mabilia per .v. solidos per annum et [recedere][9] debuissent de Bradested' per preceptum Regis et tradiderunt clavem predicte domus predicte Mabilie et bona et catalla sua in dicta domo existencia, videlicet tunicam, supertunicam, tapetum et alia catalla sua ad valenciam .xl. solidorum, fideliter custodiendum, predicta Mabilia predicta bona et catalla penes se injuste retinet ad dampnum suum .c. solidorum. Et ad hoc producunt sectam etc.

Predicta Mabilia venit et defendit vim etc. Et dicit

6 *MS. reads* premetandi.

7 *The word* misericordia *is repeated in the margin.*

8 *This entry is unfinished.*

9 *MS. reads* resedere.

quod de bonis et catallis predictorum Hagini et Sipole sicut versus eam narrant nichil recepit et hoc promta est verificare per patriam.

Et predicti Haginus et Sipola dicunt quod predicta Mabilia predicta bona et catalla recepit, ut predictum est, et quod de predictis bonis et catallis inventa fuerunt postea unum tapetum et unus ciphus cum benda de argento sine pede in manu predicte Mabilie ponunt se similiter super patriam. Et preceptum est vicecomiti quod venire faciat coram etc. in crastino sancte Margarete sex probos et legales homines de willa de Bradested', et qui nulla affinitate etc., ad recognoscendum super premissis veritatem etc. Ad quem diem jurata venit per Nicholaum Hughelyn, Johannem atte Halle et alios christianos, sicut patet inter brevia hujus termini retornata, qui dicunt super sacramentum suum quod predicta Mabilia habuit unum ciphum de mazero, precii octo denariorum, ex tradicione predictorum Hagini et Sipole, qui impignoratus fuit predictis judeis per quandam mulierem pro .iiij. denariis, quos .iiij. denarios predicta Mabilia recepit de predicta muliere et ei dictum ciphum pro predictis .iiij. denariis tradidit, sicut sepe consuevit vadia christianorum de dictis judeis recipere quando absentes erant et denarios super ea mutuatos a christianis recipere et vadia eorum eis deliberare et denarios inde receptos predictis judeis in reditu suo reddere, et quod habuit ex tradicione predictorum judeorum unum tapetum per quandam christianam pro .xij. denariis nullius valoris quia totum corrodebatur tineis, et predicta christiana illud acquietare noluit, quia nichil valuit, et predicta Mabilia nichil aliud habuit de bonis predictorum judeorum. Ideo consideratum est quod predicta judei recuperent versus predictam Mabiliam predictos .iiij. denarios et quod predicta Mabilia de aliis bonis que predicti judei ab ea peciebant eat quieta etc.

(564)

Kanc'. Iidem Haginus et Sipola venire fecerunt Margaretam uxorem Simonis le Foutrer et petunt ab ea unam zonam et tres anulos aurei precii duarum marcarum quod tradiderunt custodiendum et injuste detinet ad dampnum suum [centum][10] solidorum et inde producunt sectam.

Predicta Margareta venit. Et dicit quod sine predicto Simone viro suo respondere non debet, sub cujus custodia ipsa est, et datus est ei dies respondendi in crastino sancte Margarete ad respondendum predictis judeis una cum predicto Simone viro suo de placito predicto. Et preceptum fuit vicecomiti quod venire faceret coram etc. ad hunc diem. Et vicecomes mandavit quod Petrus de Lake, Ricardus Purs, Dic' de Bywindle et Thomas Sutor de Bradested manuceperunt predictum Simonem, quem non habuerunt. Ideo in misericordia. Judicium quod distringat per terras etc., ita quod nec ipse etc., et quod habeat corpus ejus coram etc. ad eundem diem ad respondendum et ad audiendum etc.

Ad quem diem predicti judei exigunt de predictis Symone et Margareta predictam zonam et .iij. anulos aurei precii .ij. marcarum injuste detenta, ut supra, ad dampnum suum .xl. solidorum et producunt sectam etc.

Predicti Symon et Margareta per attornatos suos veniunt. Et dicunt quod nichil ab eisdem judeis recepit. Et de hoc ponunt se super patriam.

Et predicti judei dicunt quod predicta bona ab eis receperunt et hoc ponunt se super sacramentum predicte Margarete ... [11]quod eam habeat in propria persona sua coram etc. a die sancti Michaelis in tres septimanas et vicecomiti quod venire faciat ad eundem diem sex probos et legales homines ad recognoscendum super premissis veritatem etc.

(565)

Cantebr'. Thomas Rust de Swafham venit coram etc. et recognovit se debere Willelmo de Middleton' clerico etc. decem libras reddendas ad festum sancti Petri ad Vincula anno octavo. Et, nisi fecerit, concedit quod de terris et catallis suis fiant etc.

MEMBRANE 2 DORSE

(566)

Buk'. Cok Hagin venire fecit Johannem filium Walteri de Hadenham, tenentem terrarum et tenementorum que fuerunt Galfridi le Juvene, et exigit ab eo .xvj. libras de catallo et lucrum inde emergens ante statuta regis occasione terrarum etc. per cyrographum .xvj. librarum, unde altera pars est in archa cyrographariorum.

Predictus Johannes venit et petit diem premeditandi et habet in octabis sancti Michaelis.

(567)

[*Northt'.*][12] Johannes de Chedney optulit se quarto die versus Jacobum filium Belie de Bed' judeum de placito debiti. Et ipse non venit. Et preceptum fuit vicecomiti quod ipsum venire faceret coram etc. ad hunc diem. Et vicecomes mandavit quod Benettus de Celario de Northt', Saulot le Petyt de Northt' manuceperunt predictum Jacobum, quem non habuerunt. Ideo in misericordia. Judicium quod distringat per terras etc., ita quod nec ipse etc., et quod de exitibus etc., et quod habeat corpus ejus coram etc. in crastino sancte Margarete ad respondendum etc. et ad audiendum etc.

(568)

Surr' Sussex'. Gamaliel de Oxon' judeus optulit se quarto die versus Thomam de Rugg' de placito debiti. Et ipse non venit. Et preceptum fuit vicecomiti quod ipsum venire faceret coram etc. ad hunc diem. Et vicecomes mandavit quod Everard de Bracstede et Willelmus Pakyn manuceperunt predictum Thomam, quem non

[10] *MS. reads* sentum.

[11] *Some words seem to have been omitted here but there is no gap in the MS.*

[12] *MS. reads* Notht'.

habuerunt. Ideo in misericordia.[13] Judicium quod distringat per terras etc., ita quod nec ipse etc., et quod de exitibus etc., et quod habeat corpus ejus etc. coram etc. in crastino sancte Margarete ad respondendum etc. et ad audiendum etc.

(569)

Cant' Hunt'. Magister Walterus de la Mare optulit se quarto die versus Willelmum le Moyne de placito injuste detencionis catallorum. Et ipse non venit. Et preceptum fuit vicecomiti quod ipsum distringeret per terras etc., et quod haberet corpus ejus coram etc. Et vicecomes mandavit quod Johannes filius Galfridi de Sautre, Nicholaus prepositus de eadem manuceperunt predictum Willelmum, quem non habuerunt. Ideo in misericordia.[14] Judicium quod salvo custodiat etc., et si plures etc., ita quod nec ipse etc., et quod de exitibus etc., et quod habeat corpus ejus coram etc. in crastino sancte Margarete ad respondendum etc. et ad audiendum etc.

(570)

Essex'. Hugo filius Ricardi optulit se quarto die versus Willemum clericum de Halesford' et Walterum Cristemasse de placito transgressionis. Et ipsi non venerunt. Et preceptum fuit vicecomiti quod ipsos venire faceret coram etc. Et vicecomes mandavit quod retornavit breve sibi inde directum ballivo libertatis hundredi de Tendring', qui nichil inde respondit. Judicium quod non omittat etc. et venire faciat coram etc. in crastino sancte Margarete ad respondendum predicto Hugoni de placito supradicto etc.

(571)

Surr'. Isac de Suwerk' judeus fecit venire Robertum de Hadresham, filium et heredem Ricardi de Hadresham, tenentem quandam partem terrarum que fuerunt ipsius Ricardi, et exigit ab eo occasione etc. .x. marcas per quoddam cyrographum quod protulit in hec verba: 'Sciant universi quod Ricardus de Hadresham de comitatu Surr' debet Isac de Suwerk judeo .x. marcas reddendum ei medietatem ad festum sancte Margarete anno regni regis Edwardi secundo, et aliam medietatem ad quindenam sancti Michaelis proximo sequentem. Acta .vj. die Junii anno eodem.' Unde altera pars est in archa cyrographariorum apud Lond' etc.

Et predictus Robertus venit. Et dicit quod Ricardus de Hadresham, pater ipsius Roberti, nunquam tenebat predicto judeo in predicto debito .x. marcarum, set dicit quod Ricardus filius predicti.[15]

(572)

Essex'. Belasset que fuit uxor Leonis filii Preciose venire fecit Ricardum de Quercu et Margeriam uxorem ejus, tenentes quasdam partes terrarum que fuerunt Baldewyni [Fillol,][16] et exigit ab eis decem libras de catallo et decem libras de lucro occasione terrarum etc. per cyrographum decem librarum, unde altera pars in archa Lond', ut dicit, in hec verba: 'Baldewynus [Fyllol][17] de comitatu Essex' debet Leoni filio Preciose judeo decem libras, reddendas ad festum Omnium Sanctorum anno regni regis Henrici filii regis Johnnis .lvj. Acta decimo die Junii anno regni regis predicti .lv.'

Predicti Ricardus et Margeria per attornatos suos venerunt et pecierunt diem premeditandi et habent a die sancti Michaelis in .xv. dies.

MEMBRANE 3

(573)

[This entry is a duplicate of no. 596 on membrane 4 and is marked for deletion with the note *vacat quia alibi*. There are only minor differences between them].

(574)

Norff'. Radulphus de Ingeworth' attachiatus ad respondendum [Radulpho de Chattegrave et Emme uxori ejus][18] de placito trangressionis. Et unde queruntur quod, cum essent in seisina de terris et tenementis que Rogerus de Owlton' filius Thome Sygor de Owlton' habuit in villa de Owlton' ex hereditate vel quocumque alio modo habere potuit ex dimissione predicti Rogeri per recognicionem coram justiciariis etc. factam in termino sancti Michaelis anno regni regis Edwardi sexto incipienti septimo usque ad terminum .xvj. annorum proximo sequencium pro .x. marcis de quibus predicti Radulphus et Emma predictum Rogerum acquietaverunt versus Josceum filium Deulecres judeum, die dominica in Media Quadragesima anno regni regis Edwardi octavo, dum predicti Radulphus et Emma uxor ejus cum familia perdhendinarent apud Norwic', clausis hostiis et fenestris domorum suarum in Owlton', venit predictus Radulphus de Ingeworth' cum familia sua una cum predicto Rogero et aliis ignotis et fenestras predictorum domorum fregit, in domos illas intravit et ostia aperuit, bona et catalla predictorum Radulphi et Emme in eisdem domibus inventa extra predictos domos ejecit et quamdam domum ad stabulam et vaccariam deputatam prostravit et contra pacem domini regis vendidit et asportavit et de .xij. acris ad hanc [seisonam][19] seminandum impedivit et eos extra seisinam predictarum terrarum et domorum detinuit a die dominica predicta usque ad diem sabbati proximam post festum sancte Trinitatis proximo sequentem, ad dampnum suum .xx. librarum etc. Et producunt sectam.

Predictus Radulphus de Ingeworth' [venit.][20] Et

[13] *The word* misericordia *is repeated in the margin.*

[14] *The word* misericordia *is repeated in the margin.*

[15] *This entry is unfinished.*

[16] *MS. reads* Fillos.

[17] *MS. reads* Fyllos.

[18] *MS. reads* predictis Radulpho et Emme uxori ejus. *See above nos. 372 and 430 and below no. 604.*

[19] *MS. reads* seisinam.

[20] *MS. reads* vinit.

deffendit vim etc. Et dicit quod fenestras domorum predictorum Radulphi et Emme in villa de Owlton' non fregit nec ibidem cum predicto Rogero et aliis ignotis venit nec domos suos intravit, prostravit nec vendidit, nec ad terram suam seminandam impedimentum fecit seu alia mala eis fecit. Et de hoc ponit se super patriam.

Et quod predicta dampna superius dicta eis fecit predicti Radulphus et Emma ponunt se similiter super patriam. Et preceptum est vicecomiti quod venire faciat coram etc. a die sancti Michaelis in .xv. dies .xij. probos et legales homines de visneto de Owlton', et qui nulla affinitate etc., ad recognoscendum super premissis veritatem etc.

(575)[21]

Essex'. Willelmus de Monte Caniso de Edwardeston' per attornatum suum optulit se quarto die versus Johannem filium Johannis de Patemere et alios ignotos complices suos de placito transgressionis etc. Et ipse non venit. Et preceptum fuit vicecomiti quod predictum Johannem caperet et in prisona salvo custodiret, ita quod haberet corpus ejus coram etc. a die sancti Johannis Baptiste in .xv. dies. Et vicecomes mandavit quod Osbertus de Ponte, Jacobus de Opwike, Ricardus de Holdere et Willelmus Fraunceys manuceperunt predictum Johannem, quem non habuerunt. Ideo ipsi manucaptores in misericordia.[22] Et preceptum fuit predicto vicecomiti quod predictum Johannem caperet et in prisona salvo custodiret, ita quod haberet corpus ejus coram etc. ad hunc diem, et eum predictis manucaptoribus commisit, ideo ipse vicecomes, videlicet [blank], in misericordia.[23] Et preceptum fuit eidem vicecomiti quod...[24]per inquisicionem coram eo factam per breve predictum de ignotis qui venerunt ad manerium de Patemere cum predicto Johanni in auxilium ad ejiciendum predictum Willelmum et suos de predicto manerio invenit quod Philippus de Patemere, Ricardus le Normand, Johannes de Catesby, Andreas de Catesbyr', Philippus Maskerel, Gilbertus le Berker, Johannes de Mildeby et Alanus Levesone venerunt ad predictum manerium de Patemere cum predicto Johanne set nichil asportaverunt nec devastaverunt, ut dicta inquisicio dicit; et quod nullus eorum post recepcionem brevis sibi inde directi inventus fuit in balliva sua. Judicium quod [capiat][25] predictum Johannem et predictos Philippum, Ricardum et alios supradictos, et in prisona salvo custodiat, ita quod habeat corpora eorum coram etc. a die sancti Michaelis in .xv. dies ad respondendum predicto Willelmo de transgressione predicta, et quod salvo custodiat terras etc., ita quod nec ipsi etc., et quod de exitibus eorundem Regi respondeat ad diem supradictum etc.

[21] *There is a mark like the five on a dice beside the top part of this entry in the margin.*

[22] *The word* misericordia *is repeated in the margin.*

[23] *The word* misericordia *is repeated in the margin.*

[24] *Some words have evidently been omitted at this point by the scribe but there is no gap in the MS.*

[25] *MS. reads* capias.

(576)

Ebor'. Thomas de Bereville optulit se quarto die versus Deudonem Crespin judeum de placito debiti. Et ipse non venit. Et preceptum fuit vicecomiti quod ipsum distringeret per terras etc., et quod haberet corpus ejus coram etc. ad hunc diem. Et vicecomes mandavit quod Ysac filius Sampsonis, Aaron filius Mossei, Ysac filius Samuelis et Peres filius Ysace manuceperunt predictum Deudonem, quem non habuerunt. Ideo in misericordia.[26] Judicium, sicut alias, quod distringat per terras etc., ita quod nec ipse etc., et quod de exitibus etc., et quod habeat corpus ejus coram etc., in octabis sancti Michaelis ad respondendum etc., et ad audiendum etc.

(577)

Devon'. Johannes filius Bernardi per attornatum suum optulit se quarto die versus Humfridum le Kael de placito debiti. Et ipse non venit. Et preceptum fuit vicecomiti, sicut pluries, quod ipsum distringeret per terras etc., et quod haberet corpus ejus coram etc. ad hunc diem. Et vicecomes mandavit quod predictus Hunfridus districtus est per sex boves, .viij. juvencula et .lx. oves. Et quod Adam de Holecumbe et Lucas de eadem manuceperunt predictum Hunfridum, quem non habuerunt. Ideo in misericordia. Judicium quod salvo custodiat etc., et si plures etc., ita quod nec ipse etc., et quod de exitibus etc., et quod habeat corpus ejus etc. coram etc. a die sancti Michaelis in tres septimanas ad respondendum etc. et ad audiendum etc.

(578)

Kanc'. Stephanus Chyche burgensis Cantuar', tenens terrarum que fuerunt Gwydonis de Bussey, venire fecit per breve regis de compoto Mosseum le Petyt judeum Cantuar'. Et predictus Mosseus venit et exigit de predicto Stephano .viij. libras occasione predictarum terrarum quas tenet que fuerunt predicti Gwydonis per cyrographum octo librarum inter predictum Gwydonem et predictum Mosseum factum, unde altera pars est in archa cyrographariorum Cantuar'.

Predictus Stephanus venit et recognovit se esse tenentem predictarum terrarum et per auxilium curie vocat ad warantum Walterum de Carbonir civem Lond' ad ipsum de predicto debito acquietandum, sicut racionabiliter etc. Et preceptum est vicecomitibus Lond' quod venire faciant coram etc. die lune proxima ante festum sancte Margarete predictum Walterum ad acquietandum etc.

Ad quem diem predictus Stephanus venit et protulit coram etc. quandam cartam in qua continetur quod predictus Walterus ipsum acquietare, warantizare et defendere debet contra omnes homines, christianos et judeos. Predictus Walterus venit et factum suum recognoscit et warantizat. Ideo consideratum est quod predictus Stephanus de dicto debito eat quietus et dictus Walterus inde remaneat oneratus. Et predictus Walterus dicit quod plures sunt tenentes terrarum que fuerunt

[26] *The word* misericordia *is repeated in the margin.*

predicti Gwydonis sine quibus respondere non tenetur et habet diem a die sancti Michaelis in .xv. dies etc.

(579)

Berk'. Sara que fuit uxor Benedicti le Eveke per attornatum suum optulit se quarto die versus Henricum de Schothebrok', tenentem terrarum que fuerunt Simonis de Ordeston', de placito debiti. Et ipse non venit. Et preceptum fuit vicecomiti quod salvo custodiret etc., et si plures etc. ipsum distringeret etc., et quod haberet corpus ejus coram etc. Et vicecomes mandavit quod terre, redditus et catalla predicti Henrici, per que districtus fuit, salvo custodiuntur in manu Regis et sunt exitus terrarum dicti Henrici .v. solidi; et quod dictus Henricus stat in servicio comitis Cornubie et non [i]<fuit>[i] inventus in balliva sua post recepcionem brevis sibi inde directi, ideo non fuit manucaptus veniendi ad hunc diem. Judicium, sicut alias, quod salvo custodiat in manu Regis terras etc., et si plures etc., ita quod nec ipse etc., et quod de exitibus etc., et quod habeat corpus ejus coram etc. a die sancti Martini in .xv. dies ad respondendum etc. et ad audiendum etc.

(580)

Oxon'. Gywa filia Elie judea, que tulit breve regis de placito debiti super Cheram que fuit uxor Mossei de Warr', non est prosecuta versus predictam Cheram. Ideo ipsa Gywa et plegii sui de prosequendo, videlicet Abraham filius Henne et Ysac filius Ermine, in misericordia.[27]

(581)

Surr'. Deulecres filius Leonis optulit se quarto die versus Willelmum de Watevile de placito debiti, unde jurata. Et predictus Willelmus per attornatum suum venit et jurata non venit. Et preceptum fuit vicecomiti quod distringeret Rolandum de Acstede, Nicholaum Malemeyns et alios dicte jurate, sicut inter brevia hujus termini retornata, per terras etc., et quod haberet corpora eorum coram etc. ad hunc diem. Et vicecomes mandavit quod breve sibi inde directum adeo tarde venit quod non potuit exequi. Judicium, sicut alias, quod distringat predictos Rolandum, Nicholaum et alios per terras etc., ita quod nec ipsi etc., et quod de exitibus etc., et quod habeat corpora eorum coram etc. in crastino sancte Margarete ad recognoscendum etc. Et preceptum est [thesaurario,][28] baronibus et camerariis de scaccario quod habeant ad eundem diem per unum ex eis quemdam pedem cyrographi quem predictus Willelmus coram etc. vocavit esse levatum inter dictum Willelmum et Johannem patrem suum de manerio de Hamsede et Paumfeld' in comitatu Essex', ita quod predicto judeo pro predicto Johanne patre suo de aliquo debito respondere non deberet occasione predictorum maneriorum. Et predicti Willelmus et Deulecres habent eundem diem.

27 *The word* misericordia *is repeated in the margin.*

28 *MS. reads* tesaurario.

MEMBRANE 3 DORSE

(582)

Wiltes'. Adam de Winton', clericus de scaccario, optulit se quarto die versus Willelmum Sturdi de Kenele de placito debiti. Et ipse non venit. Et preceptum fuit vicecomiti, sicut alias, quod non omitteret propter libertatem de Werwedon' quin eam etc. et distringeret predictum Willelmum per terras etc., et quod haberet corpus ejus coram etc. ad hunc diem. Et vicecomes mandavit quod Henricus Lende, Everard Gaunt, Johannes le Fraunkeleyn et Nicholaus de Wike manuceperunt predictum Willelmum, quem non habuerunt. Ideo in misericordia.[29] Judicium, sicut pluries, quod non omittat etc., et distringat predictum Willelmum per terras etc., ita quod nec ipse etc., et quod de exitibus etc., et quod habeat corpus ejus coram etc. a die sancti Michaelis in .xv. dies ad respondendum etc. et ad audiendum etc.

(583)

Essex'. Rosa filia Abrahe judea venire fecit Johannem Sperwe, tenentem quamdam partem terrarum que fuerunt Walteri filii Willelmi de Saunford', et exigit ab eo .xl. solidos quos ei debet occasione etc. per cyrographum .xxx. librarum inter predictos Willelmum et Rosam factam, unde altera pars est in archa cyrographariorum apud Subbyr', ut dicit.

Predictus Johannes venit et petit diem premeditandi et habet in octabis sancti Michaelis.

Eadem Rosa fecit venire Nicholaum Sperwe, tenentem quandam partem terrarum que fuerunt predicti Walteri, et exigit ab eo .x. solidos quos ei debet occasione etc. per cyrographum supradictum.

Predictus Nicholaus venit et petit diem premeditandi et habet in octabis sancti Michaelis.

Eadem Rosa fecit venire Willelmum de Dedemore, tenentem quamdam partem terrarum predictarum, et exigit ab eo decem solidos quos ei debet occasione etc. per cyrographum supradictum.

Predictus Willelmus venit et petit diem premeditandi et habet in octabis sancti Michaelis.

Eadem Rosa fecit venire Radulphum de Tyndovorr', tenentem quandam partem predictarum terrarum, et exigit ab eo .x.solidos quos ei debet occasione etc. per cyrographum supradictum.

Predictus Radulphus venit et petit diem premeditandi et habet in octabis sancti Michaelis.

Eadem Rosa fecit venire Galfridum de Fratribus, tenentem quandam partem terrarum predictarum, et exigit ab eo quinque marcas quas ei debet occasione etc. per cyrographum supradictum.

Predictus Galfridus venit et petit diem premeditandi et habet in octabis sancti Michaelis.

Eadem Rosa fecit venire Willelmum atte Lentande, tenentem quandam partem terrarum predictarum, et

29 *The word* misericordia *is repeated in the margin.*

exigit ab eo unam marcam quam ei debet occasione etc. per cyrographum supradictum .xxx. librarum.

Predictus Willelmus venit et petit diem premeditandi et habet in octabis sancti Michaelis.

Predicta Rosa optulit se quarto die versus Johannem de Ros, tenentem quamdam partem predictarum terrarum, de placito debiti. Et ipse non venit. Et preceptum fuit vicecomiti quod ipsum venire faceret coram etc. ad hunc diem. Et vicecomes mandavit quod Elyas Wynter et Galfridus Neuman manuceperunt predictum Johannem, quem non habuerunt. Ideo in misericordia.[30] Judicium quod distringat per terras etc., ita quod nec ipse etc., et quod de exitibus etc., et quod habeat corpus ejus coram etc. in octabis sancti Michaelis ad respondendum etc. et ad audiendum etc.

(584)

Norff'. Johannes de Bayfeld', clericus etc., fecit venire Johannem de Clare, rectorem ecclesie de Holesle, ad respondendum ei de placito quod ei reddat .c. solidos quos ei debet et injuste etc., sicut racionabiliter etc. Et unde idem Johannes de Bayf' queritur quod, cum die dominica proxima ante festum sancti Barnabe Apostoli anno regni regis Edwardi quinto apud Lond' convenisset inter ipsos Johannem et Johannem quod idem Johannes de Bayfeld' haberet omnia blada et fena ecclesie predicti Johannis de Clare de Holesle tunc in terris parochie illius existencia pro decem et novem marcis sterlingorum quas ei solvit pre manibus et, si contigeret ipsum Johannem de Bayfeld' aliquod impedimentum, dampnum vel gravamen sustinere, per quod eadem blada et fena colligere, habere et de eisdem disponere pro voluntate sua non posset, tunc idem Johannes de Clare eidem Johanni de Bayf' restitueret omnia hujusmodi dampna et jacturas; ac prefatus Johannes de Bayfeld' apud Holesle de Lond' transmisisset [Robertum][31] filium Hugonis garcionem suum ad predicta blada colligenda in autumno subsequenti, venerunt ballivi domini regis per preceptum ejusdem regis et ex parte Willelmi prioris de Wymundham et Walteri de Grancourt tunc vicecomitis Norff' et Suff' tunc collectorum decime in subsidium Terre Sancte concessarum infra comitatus predictos apud Holesle et blada decimarum ecclesie predicte in campis de Holesle diversimode ceperunt et arestaverunt et distraxerunt [pro arreragiis][32] decimarum de tribus primis annis de ecclesia predicta debitarum, ita quod per defectum solucionis quam idem Johannes de Clare inde fecisse debuerat perierit; et preter hoc parochiani racione suspensionis et interdicte in eadem ecclesia illati [i]<et per multum tempus continuati>[i] et aliarum contencionum inter ipsum rectorem et parochianos suos habitarum decimas suas racionabiliter debitas de fructibus suis retinuerunt et de proventibus earum decimarum quas idem Johannes de Bayfeld' percipere debuerat racione vendicionis predicte sibi providerunt de quodam capellano celebrante in capella R. comitis [Marescalli][33] apud Halesd' quousque predictus Johannes de Bayfeld' ad predictos priorem et vicecomitem accessit et predicta blada que remanserunt post districcionem predictam deliberari fecit; unde dicit quod inde deterioratus est et dampnum habet ad valenciam .c. solidorum. Et inde producit sectam etc.

Et predictus Johannes de Clare venit. Et defendit vim etc. Et dicit quod predictus Johannes de Bayfeld' per defectum solucionis predictarum decimarum seu occasione alicujus sequesti, interdicti vel suspensionis predicte ecclesie vel eciam pro aliqua contencione inter predictum Johannem de Clare et parochianos suos mota nullum dampnum, impedimentum vel gravamen habuit. Et de hoc ponit se super patriam. Et Johannes de Bayfeld' similiter. Ideo preceptum est vicecomiti quod venire faciat coram etc. in octabis sancti Michaelis .xij. etc. de visneto de Holesle qui nulla affinitate etc., nisi H. Hauteyn vel R. de Ludham etc., quia tam etc., ad recognoscendum quod dampnum et gravamen Johannes de Bayfeld' sustinuit de predictis bladis occasione decimarum predictarum non solutarum in subsidium Terre Sancte et occasione interdicti, suspensionis et sequestri ecclesie et fructuum ad eandem de jure spectancium et occasione contentionum inter ipsum rectorem et parochianos suos habitarum.

(585)[34]

Essex' Hertf'. Walterus de Kanc', attornatus Regine Anglie consortis Regis, venire fecit Johannem de Aswelle, filium et heredem Stephani de Aswelle militis de comitatu Hertf', et exigit ab eo quadraginta et octo libras et .viij. quarteria frumenti quas debet prefate Regine occasione predictarum terrarum quas tenet que fuerunt predicti Stephani patris sui de debito Hagini filii magistri Mossei judei, cujus debita predicta Regina habet de dono Regis etc. per cyrographum .xlviij. librarum .viij. quarteriorum frumenti in hec verba: 'Sciant universi quod Stephanus de Aswelle de comitatu Hertf' debet Hagino filio magistri Mossei judeo .xlviij. libras .viij. quarteria frumenti, reddendum inde .xxvij. libras et octo quarteria frumenti ad quindenam sancti Michaelis anno regni regis Henrici .xlvij. et .xxj. libras ad quindenam sancti Johannis Baptiste proximo sequentem. Actum sexto die Augusti anno .xlvij.'

Predictus Johannes venit. Et dicit quod non tenetur prefate domine Regine de predicto debito .xlviij. librarum et octo quarteriorum frumenti respondere eo quod predictus Haginus, de cujus debito dictum debitum exigitur ad opus predicte domine Regine, dum fuit in plena potestate bonorum et debitorum suorum et habuit inde liberam administracionem et tempore quo illud facere potuit, vendidit et dimisit predictum debitum .xlviij. librarum et octo quarteriorum frumenti sub

[30] *The word* misericordia *is repeated in the margin.*

[31] *MS. reads* Roberto.

[32] *MS. reads* arreragiis pro.

[33] *MS. reads* Harescalli.

[34] *This entry is repeated on membrane 5d of this roll (no. 616). Neither version is marked for cancellation. There are no significant differences between them.*

nominibus predicti Stephani patris sui et predicti Hagini magistro Godefrido episcopo Wygorn', cui idem Johannes de toto predicto debito satisfecit, et protulit coram justiciariis etc. quamdam litteram predicti episcopi patentem sigillo suo auttentico signatam, in qua continetur quod predictus Johannes prefato episcopo satisfecit de predicto debito .xlviij. librarum octo quarteriorum frumenti, quod debitum idem episcopus habuit ex vendicione et dimissione predicti Hagini, ita quod nec ipse episcopus nec aliquis pro eo aliquid versus predictum Johannem, filium et heredem predicti Stephani, occasione predicti debiti exigere seu calumpniare poterit. Et quia constat justiciariis etc. per inspexionem rotulorum de appuramento et scrutinio de scaccario judeorum quod dictum debitum per predictum Haginum vendebatur predicto episcopo tempore licito et debito, tempore quo debita sua vendere potuit et quod predictus Johannes satisfecit predicto episcopo de predicto debito, sicut patet per litteram predicti episcopi quam protulit coram etc., ut supradictum est, ideo consideratum est quod predictus Johannes, filius et heres predicti Stephani, de predicto debito .xlviij. librarum et octo quarteriorum frumenti sit quietus, et quod predicta carta inde confecta eidem Johanni liberetur quiete dampnata. Et mandatum est Waltero de Kancia custodi auri predicte Regine quod predicto Johanni predictam cartam deliberet quiete dampnatam etc.

(586)

Essex'. Rogerus de Kyngton', serviens de scaccario etc., optulit se quarto die versus Hugonem de Coleworth' de placito debiti. Et ipse non venit. Et preceptum fuit vicecomiti quod distringeret per terras etc., et quod haberet corpus ejus coram etc. ad hunc diem. Et vicecomes mandavit quod Willelmus Onderdoune de Horndone, Walterus Messor de eadem, Robertus Hoky de eadem et Thomas Bardewade de eadem manuceperunt predictum Hugonem, quem non habuerunt. Ideo in misericordia.[35] Judicium, sicut alias, quod distringat per terras etc., ita quod nec ipse etc., et quod de exitibus etc., et quod habeat corpus ejus coram etc., a die sancti Michaelis in .xv. dies ad respondendum etc. et ad audiendum etc. Et quinque solidos quos misit cum brevi quos levari fecit de exitibus terrarum predicti Hugonis in dominica Pasche proximo preterita solvit predicto Rogero in partem solucionis debiti a predicto Hugone petiti de gracia justiciariorum et sic vicecomes inde quietus est.[36]

[35] *The word* misericordia *is repeated in the margin.*

[36] *In the margin is written* .v. solidi de exitibus. Vicecomes solvit predicto Rogero.

MEMBRANE 4

Adhuc placita de octabis et quindena sancte Trinitatis anno regni regis Edwardi octavo

(587)

Ebor'. Adam de Novo Mercato optulit se quarto die versus Henricum de Luffenham de placito transgressionis de debitis judeorum. Et ipse non venit. Et preceptum fuit vicecomiti, sicut pluries, quod non omitteret propter libertatem de Tykehull' quin eam etc. et distringeret predictum Henricum per terras etc., et quod haberet corpus ejus coram etc. ad hunc diem. Et vicecomes mandavit quod breve sibi inde directum nimis tarde venit. Et ideo nichil inde fecit. Et testatum est quod dictum breve sibi liberatum fuit multo tempore ante quam illud retornavit, ita quod dictum breve exequi potuisset si voluisset. Ideo ipse vicecomes, scilicet Ranulphus de Acre, in misericordia.[37] Judicium, sicut pluries, quod non omittat etc., et quod distringeret predictum Henricum per terras etc., ita quod nec ipse etc., et quod de exitibus etc., et quod habeat corpus ejus coram etc. ad quindenam sancti Michaelis ad respondendum etc. et ad audiendum etc.

(588)

Idem Aron[38] optulit se quarto die versus Mosseum filium Mossei de Clare judeum de placito debiti. Et ipse non venit. Et preceptum fuit vicecomiti quod ipsum venire faceret coram etc. Et vicecomes mandavit quod Manserus filius Abrahe et Judas filius Ysac manuceperunt predictum Mosseum, quem non habuerunt. Ideo in misericordia. Judicium quod distringat per terras etc., ita quod nec ipse etc., et quod de exitibus etc., et quod habeat corpus ejus coram etc., a die sancti Michaelis in .xv. dies ad respondendum etc. et ad audiendum etc.

(589)

Lond'. Margalicia que fuit uxor Samuelis le Blund judea per attornatum suum venire fecit Michaelem le Oynter et exigit ab eo unam marcam, quam ei debet pro conduxione cujusdam domus quam ab ea conduxit ad terminum quatuor annorum, per quoddam scriptum obligatorium inter eos confectum ad festum sancti Michaelis anno regni regis Edwardi septimo per quatuor marcas per annum in parochia sancti [blank], et unde ei predictam marcam solvisse debuerat ad Natale Domini anno regni regis Edwardi octavo et non solvit, set ei predictam marcam adhuc injuste detinet ad dampnum suum .c. solidorum etc. Et protulit quoddam scriptum inter eos inde confectum etc.

Predictus Michaelis venit. Et defendit vim etc. quando etc. Et [i]<dicit quod>[i] injuste ab eo predictam marcam exigit eo quod sepe ad dictam Margaliciam venit et optulit ei predictam marcam, ita quod ei bona sua in

[37] *In the margin is written* misericordia vicecomitis.

[38] *Sic.*

dicta domo existencia deliberaret ad valenciam unius marce et amplius, ut in meremio, lapidibus et aliis bonis suis que in predicta domo dimisit quando dicte Margalicie clavem predicte domus retradidit quam ab eo recepit, et quod predicta bona sua modo predicto adhuc penes se detinet hoc offert verificare per patriam.

Et predicta Margalicia quod predictam marcam ei non optulit solvendam nec aliqua bona de bonis suis pro predicta marca penes se habet posuit se similiter super patriam. Et preceptum est vicecomitibus Lond' quod venire faciant coram etc. in crastino sancte Margarete sex probos et legales homines de parochia sancti [blank] et constabulario Turris Lond' quod venire faciat coram etc. ad eundem diem sex legales judeos, et qui nulla affinitate etc., ad recognoscendum super premissis veritatem etc.

(590)

Kanc'. Simon de Crey optulit se quarto die versus Willelmum Peyforer, tenentem quandam [partem][39] terrarum que fuerunt Willelmi de Mareys. Et ipse non venit. Et preceptum fuit vicecomiti quod ipsum distringeret per terras etc., et quod haberet corpus ejus coram etc. Et vicecomes mandavit quod Gilbertus Godgrom, Johannes Attegare de Ealdinge, Walterus Baylf et Ricardus de Pympe manuceperunt predictum Willelmum, quem non habuerunt. Ideo in misericordia.[40] Judicium quod distringat, sicut alias, per terras etc., ita quod nec ipse etc., et quod de exitibus etc., et quod habeat corpus ejus coram etc. in crastino sancte Margarete ad respondendum etc. et audiendum etc.

(591)

Cantebr'. Belia que fuit uxor Jacobi judea optulit se quarto die versus Johannem le Saltere et Matillidem uxorem ejus de Linton' de placito debiti. Et ipsi non venerunt. Et preceptum fuit vicecomiti quod ipsos distringeret per terras etc., et quod haberet corpora eorum coram etc. Et vicecomes mandavit quod Michael le Fevre de Linton', Henricus Tyrel de eadem, Thomas le Greyte de eadem et Lucas le Peotur de eadem manuceperunt predictos Johannem et Matillidem, quos non habuerunt. Ideo in misericordia.[41] Judicium, sicut alias, quod distringat per terras etc., ita quod nec ipsi etc., et quod de exitibus etc., et quod habeat corpora eorum coram etc. a die sancti Michaelis in .xv. dies ad respondendum etc. et ad audiendum judicium etc.

(592)

[*Norff'*][42]*Suff'*. Dic' de Cocfeld, custos heredis et terrarum que fuerunt Roberti de Nortone, per attornatum suum optulit se quarto die versus Henricum Brun de Sancto Edmundo, executorem testamenti predicti Roberti, de placito acquietacionis debiti. Et ipse non venit. Et preceptum fuit vicecomiti quod ipsum distringeret per terras etc., et quod haberet corpus ejus coram etc. ad hunc diem. Et vicecomes mandavit quod Nicholaus de Bedingfeud, Stephanus filius Benedicti clerici de Sancto Edmundo, Willelmus Enterun de eadem et Johannes de Bribos de eadem manuceperunt predictum Henricum, quem non habuerunt. Ideo in misericordia.[43] Judicium, sicut alias, quod distringat per terras etc.., ita quod nec ipse etc., et quod de exitibus etc., et quod habeat corpus ejus coram etc. a die sancti Michaelis in .xv. dies ad respondendum etc. et ad audiendum etc.

(593)

Heref'. Aaron filius Vives judeus optulit se quarto die versus Johannem filium Walteri de Tayrnbyr', tenentem quandam partem terrarum que fuerunt Willelmi Deveros, de placito debiti. Et ipse non venit. Et preceptum fuit vicecomiti quod ipsum distringeret per terras etc., et quod haberet corpus ejus coram etc. ad hunc diem. Et vicecomes mandavit quod Ricardus le Notar et Ricardus de la More manuceperunt predictum Johannem, quem non haberunt. Ideo in misericordia.[44] Judicium, sicut alias, quod distringat per terras etc., ita quod nec ipse etc., et quod de exitibus etc., et quod habeat corpus ejus coram etc. a die sancti Michaelis in .xv. dies ad respondendum etc. et ad audiendum etc. Et vicecomes mandavit quod exitus sunt .iiij. solidi, qui liberantur clericis pro percameno emendo ad summoniciones inde scribendas.[45]

(594)

Northt'. Gywa filia Vives le Romaunsur judea per attornatum suum optulit se quarto die versus Ricardum de Longevile et Aliciam uxorem ejus, Gilbertum le Peyntur, Matillidem uxorem ejus, Willelmum le Peyntur generum predicti Gilberti, Henricum Passelewe, Johannem de Campedene, Johannem Belhunt, Ricardum de Bedeford', Ysabellam uxorem ejus, Agnetem que fuit uxor Thome filii Alexandri et Walterum Passelewe filium Henrici Passelewe de placito transgressionis. Et ipsi non venerunt. Et preceptum fuit vicecomiti quod ipsos venire faceret coram etc. Et vicecomes mandavit quod Galfridus le Wyse et Hugo le Fraunceys manuceperunt Ricardum de Longevile et Aliciam uxorem ejus, et quod Ricardus le Marechal et Willelmus Walmod manuceperunt Gilbertum le Peyntur et Matildam uxorem ejus, et quod Henricus Marsil et Robertus filius Fulconis manuceperunt Willelmum le Peyntur, et quod Ricardus de le Hulle et Walterus de Bromton manuceperunt Henricum Passelewe, et quod Willelmus le Catur junior et Willelmus Soft manuceperunt Johannem de Campedene, et quod Adam de Cogeho et Walterus de Pelevile manuceperunt Johannem Belaunt, et quod Walterus le Bakere et

39 *MS. omits.*

40 *The word* misericordia *is repeated in the margin.*

41 *The word* misericordia *is repeated in the margin.*

42 *MS. reads* Noff'.

43 *The word* misericordia *is repeated in the margin.*

44 *The word* misericordia *is repeated in the margin.*

45 *In the margin is written* exitus .iiij. solidi qui solvantur clericis pro percameno ad summoniciones inde scribendas.

Johannes Edyman manuceperunt Agnetem que fuit uxor Thome filii Alexandri, et quod Johannes de Duston et Johannes Ediman manuceperunt Walterum Passelewe, et quod Walterus le Bakere et Hugo Brun manuceperunt Ricardum de Bedef' et Ysabellam uxorem ejus, quos non habuerunt. Ideo ipsi manucaptores in misericordia.[46] Judicium quod distringat per terras etc., ita quod nec ipsi etc., et quod de exitibus etc., et quod [habeat][47] corpora eorum coram etc. in octabis sancti Michaelis ad respondendum etc. et ad audiendum etc.

(595)

Heref'. Samuel filius Jossei judeus per attornatum suum optulit se quarto die versus Manserum filium Jossei et Gentam uxorem ejus judeos de placito debiti. Et ipsi non venerunt. Et preceptum fuit vicecomiti quod ipsos venire faceret coram etc. ad hunc diem. Et vicecomes mandavit quod Mosseus de Glouc' et Leo de Wygorn' manuceperunt predictos Mosseum et Gentam, quos non habuerunt. Ideo in misericordia. Judicium quod distringat per terras etc., ita quod nec ipsi etc., et quod de exitibus etc., et quod habeat corpora eorum etc. a die sancti Michaelis in .xv. dies ad respondendum etc. et ad audiendum etc.

(596)[48]

Heref'. Joye que que fuit uxor Ysac filii Dyey judea per attornatum suum optulit se quarto die versus Robertum de Morton', Willelmum de Morton', Philippum de Turbervile, Hugonem filium Reginaldi et Cristianam que fuit uxor Elye de Eglynton' de placito debiti. Et ipsi non venerunt. Et preceptum fuit vicecomiti quod ipsos venire faceret coram etc. ad hunc diem. Et vicecomes mandavit quod Willelmus de Morton' et Ricardus de Colcome manuceperunt Robertum de Morton, et quod Robertus de Roubur' et Nicholaus de Morton manuceperunt Willelmum de Morton, et quod Ricardus filius Galfridi et Hugo filius Reginaldi manuceperunt Philippum de Turberville et quod Hugo filius Reginaldi et Ricardus filius Galfridi manuceperunt Cristianam que fuit uxor predicti Elye et quod Ricardus filius Galfridi et Philippus de Turbervile manuceperunt Hugonem filium Reginaldi, quos non habuerunt. Ideo in misericordia.[49] Judicium quod distringat per terras etc., ita quod nec ipsi etc., et quod de exitibus etc., et quod habeat corpora eorum coram etc. in octabis sancti Michaelis ad respondendum etc. et ad audiendum etc.

(597)

Not'. Alanus de Appelbi, qui tulit breve Regis de compoto super Hennam que fuit uxor Abrahe <le>[50] Prestre judeam, optulit se quarto die versus predictam Hennam. Et ipsa non venit. Et preceptum fuit vicecomiti quod ipsam venire faceret coram etc. Et vicecomes mandavit quod predicta Henna est in prisona regis pro .lx. marcis in quibus Regi tenetur de fine suo, ita quod nullam manucapcionem invenire potuit, nec ad diem in brevi contentum venire. Ideo preceptum est vicecomiti, sicut alias, quod eam venire faciat coram etc. a die sancti Michaelis in .xv. dies ad computandum cum predicto Alano etc. et quod predicto Alano de predicto debito interim pacem habere permittat etc.

46 *The word* misericordia *is repeated in the margin.*
47 *MS. reads* habeas.
48 *This entry is duplicated at the top of membrane 3 (above, no. 573) where it is marked for deletion. There are only minor differences between the two enrolments.*
49 *The word* misericordia *is repeated in the margin.*
50 *MS. repeats.*

MEMBRANE 4 DORSE

(598)

Suff' Cantebr'. Willelmus de Middelton' per attornatum suum optulit se quarto die versus Rogerum de Feltewelle de placito debiti, unde jurata. Et predictus Rogerus essoniatus fuit et habuit diem per essoniatorem suum in crastino sancte Margarete. Et jurata non venit et preceptum fuit vicecomiti quod ipsam venire faceret coram etc. Et vicecomes mandavit quod unusquisque subscriptorum manucaptor alterorum essendi coram etc. ad hunc diem ad recognoscendum veritatem de placito inter predictum Willelmum et Rogerum, videlicet Willelmus le Bray de Elvedene, Ricardus Brutin de Frekenham, Johannes Marham de eadem, Johannes le Wyte de Heringewelle, Robertus Passelewe de Hecham, Rogerus de Hunedene de eadem, Johannes Heved de Berton', Henricus de Molendino de Wridelington', Willelmus de Fertho de Mildenhale, Thomas Lorence de eadem, Johannes Gosselyn de Croswelle, Rogerus clericus de eadem, Radulphus de Suthet de eadem, Ricardus Wyger de eadem, Robertus filius Ydaine de Ikelingham, Alexander Folet de eadem. Et nullus eorum venit. Ideo ipsi in misericordia.[51] Judicium quod distringat per terras etc., ita quod nec ipsi etc., et quod de exitibus eorundem etc., et quod habeat corpora eorum coram etc. in crastino sancte Margarete ad recognoscendum super premissis veritatem.

(599)[52]

Essex'. Jacobus de Stiventon', qui tulit breve regis super Ricardum de Harlawe de placito acquietacionis debiti, non est prosecutus versus predictum Ricardum. Ideo ipse Jacobus et plegii sui de prosequendo, videlicet Johannes de Patemere et Philippus de Patemere, in misericordia.[53] Et preceptum fuit vicecomiti quod venire faceret coram etc. predictum Ricardum. Et vicecomes mandavit quod Adam de Bassingburn' et Ricardus le Cachepol de Harlawe manuceperunt predictum Ricardum, quem non habuerunt. Ideo in misericordia.[54]

51 *The word* misericordia *is repeated in the margin.*
52 *There is a mark in the margin with five spots like those on the face of a dice.*
53 *The word* misericordia *is repeated in the margin.*
54 *The word* misericordia *is repeated in the margin.*

(600)

Oxon'. Sarra filia Mossei judea optulit se quarto die versus Thomam le Verrur de placito injuste detencionis catallorum. Et ipse non venit. Et preceptum fuit vicecomiti quod ipsum venire faceret coram etc. Et vicecomes mandavit quod retornavit breve sibi inde directum ballivis liberatis ville Oxon', qui nichil inde fecerunt. Judicium quod non omittat propter libertatem predictam quin eam etc. et venire faciat coram etc. in crastino sancte Margarete predictum Thomam ad respondendum predicte Sarre de predicto placito etc.

(601)

Oxon'. Sarra Dunekan optulit se quarto die versus Ysac de Kaune et Gentam uxorem ejus de placito debiti. Et ipsi non venerunt. Et preceptum fuit vicecomiti quod ipsos venire faceret coram etc. Et vicecomes mandavit quod predictus Ysac non fuit inventus in balliva sua post recepcionem brevis sibi inde directi et quod predicta Genta gravi infirmitate detenta fuit, ita quod nullus eam manucapere voluit habere corpus ejus coram etc. Et quia testificatum est quod predictus Ysac manet in balliva sua preceptum est eidem vicecomiti, sicut alias, quod venire faciat coram etc. in crastino sancte Margarete predictos Ysac et Gentam ad respondendum predicte Sarre de predicto placito. Et vicecomes sit ibidem etc.

(602)[55]

Warr'. Ricardus de Turbervile, filius et heres Johannis de Turbervile, venire fecit Nicholaum Siffrewast et petit quod ipsum acquietet de quinque marcis ad quas predictus Johannes pater predicti Ricardi amerciatus fuit ad scaccarium judeorum pro comptemptu dum fuit vicecomes Bed' et Buk' et quas quinque marcas predictus Nicholaus, dum fuit vicecomes predictorum comitatuum, recepit de predicto Johanne patre suo per quamdam talliam contra predictum Nicholaum scriptam de predictis quinque marcis quam protulit coram etc.

Predictus Nicholaus venit et dicit quod ignorat utrum predictas quinque marcas recepit an non et petit diem consulendi cum clericis suis de recepcione predicta et habet diem in crastino sancte Margarete.

(603)

Lond'. Prior de Spaulinges venire fecit magistrum Elyam filium magistri Mossei et petit quod ipsum acquietet versus Regem de viginti octo libris que ab eo et aliis tenentibus terrarum Johannis de Folnhey exiguntur et protulit quoddam starrum in quo continetur.[56]

(604)

Norf'. Hugo Tyrel attachiatus ad respondendum Radulpho de Chategrave et Emme uxori ejus de placito transgressionis, et unde queruntur [quod,][57] cum essent in seisina terrarum et tenementorum que Rogerus filius Thome Sygor de Colton' habuit in villa de Colton' ex commissione predicti Rogeri facta coram justiciariis etc. ad festum sancti Michaelis anno regni regis Edwardi [i]<sexto incipienti>[i] septimo usque ad terminum sexdecim annorum proximo sequencium pro acquietacione facienda versus Josseum filium Deulecres judeum de decem marcis, de quibus ipsum acquietarunt, et plenam et [pacificam][58] seisinam inde habuerunt usque diem sancti Stephani anno regis Edwardi octavo, qua die predictus Hugo una cum predicto Rogero et Katerina uxore ejus, Roberto Ernald et aliis ignotis ad procuracionem predicti Rogeri venerunt ad domum predictorum Radulphi et Emme, quam habuerunt per predictam concessionem, et eosdem Radulphum et Emmam et eorum familiam a predicta domo una cum aliis prenominatis et aliis ignotis ejecit, wlneravit et eos ejectos detinet usque diem mercurii proximam post Purificacionem Beate Marie, quo die habuerint reseisinam per breve regis, et eciam de bonis et catallis eorundem Radulphi et Emme in predictis terris et tenementis inventis vastum et vendicionem una cum prenominatis fecit et eis alia enormia intulit ad dampnum suum decem marcarum et contra pacem regis. Et ad hoc producit sectam.

Predictus Hugo venit. Et deffendit vim etc. Et dicit quod ad domum dictorum Radulphi et Emme die sancti Stephani predicto non venit cum predicto Rogero et aliis nec moram ibidem fecit nec dampnum, vastum, vendicionem bonorum suorum seu aliquod malum vel enormia eis fecit vel intulit sicut versus eum narrant. Et hoc petit verificare per patriam. Et quod predicta dampna superius dicta una cum predicto Rogero et aliis sicut predictum est eis fecit predicti Radulphus et Emma ponunt se similiter super patriam. Et preceptum est vicecomiti quod venire faciat coram etc. a die sancti Michaelis in .xv. dies .xij. probos et legales homines de visneto de Owlton, et qui nulla affinitate etc., ad recognoscendum super premissis veritatem etc.

(605)

Cant'. Johannes de Camoys venit coram etc. et recognoscit se debere Arnaldo Chykot .lix. libras .iij. solidos .iij. denarios, reddendum inde .x. libras et .xvj. solidos ad festum sancte Margaret anno octavo et residuum, videlicet .xlviij. libras, .viij. solidos, .iiij. denarios ad festum sancti Bartholomei proximo sequens. Et, nisi fecerit, concedit quod de terris et catallis suis fiant etc.

MEMBRANE 5

Adhuc placita

(606)

Essex', Hertf'. Elias de Donecastre judeus optulit se quarto die versus Philippum de Stanburne de placito debiti. Et ipse non venit. Et preceptum fuit vicecomiti

[55] *There is mark in the margin with five spots arranged like the spots on the face of a dice.*

[56] *This entry is unfinished.*

[57] *MS. omits.*

[58] *MS. reads* passecam.

quod ipsum venire faceret coram etc. ad hunc diem. Et vicecomes mandavit quod Radulphus le Enveise de Stanburne et Rogerus Schalegray manuceperunt predictum Philippum, quem non habuerunt. Ideo in misericordia.[59] Judicium quod distringat per terras etc., ita quod nec ipse etc., et quod de exitibus etc., et quod habeat corpus ejus coram etc. a die sancti Michaelis in .xv. dies ad respondendum etc. et ad audiendum etc.

(607)

Somers', Dors'. Ricardus de Loverley et Joscea uxor ejus per attornatos suos optulerunt se quarto die versus Johannem filium Willelmi Ruffrigeray de placito acquietacionis debiti. Et ipse non venit. Et preceptum fuit vicecomiti, sicut pluries, quod predictum Johannem distringeret per terras etc., et quod haberet corpus ejus coram etc. ad hunc diem. Et vicecomes mandavit quod Robertus le Voghel, Robertus Hunfrei, Rogerus de Bole et Ricardus Hunfrei de Tyntenhulle manuceperunt predictum Johannem, quem non habuerunt. Ideo in misericordia.[60] Judicium, sicut pluries, quod distringat per terras etc., ita quod nec ipse etc., et quod de exitibus etc., et quod habeat corpus ejus coram etc. a die sancti Michaelis in .xv. dies ad respondendum etc. et ad audiendum etc.

(608)

Sutht'. Sara que fuit uxor Salomonis de Wynton' judea fecit venire Petrum le Neyweman et Robertum le Swyngare de Andevere et exigit ab eis viginti et tres libras quas eis una cum predicto Salomone quondam viro suo ad festum sancti Michaelis anno regni regis Edwardi .vj. apud Andevere fideliter custodiendum ad opus ipsorum Salomonis et Sarre tradidit antequam predictus Salomon captus fuit pro tonsura monete, pro qua transgressione dampnatus fuit, ut predicti Petrus et Robertus predictas .xxiij. libras eis redderent quando eas ab eisdem Petro et Roberto exigerent, quas eis hucusque injuste detinent ad dampnum suum .x. marcarum, et hoc petit verificari per patriam.

Predicti Petrus et Robertus veniunt et defendunt vim etc. et dicunt quod nichil receperunt in villa de Andevere nec alibi de bonis et catallis predictorum Salomonis vel Sare custodiendum nec in denariis nec in denaratis. Et de hoc ponit se super patriam. Et preceptum est vicecomiti quod venire faciat coram etc. a die sancti Michaelis in .xv. dies .xij. probos et legales homines de villa de Andevere et sex legales judeos de civitate Wynton', et qui etc., ad recognoscendum super premissis veritatem.

(609)

Nortff'. Willelmus de Midd', clericus de scaccario nostro judeorum, optulit se quarto die versus Thomam de Stivekeye de placito quod reddat ei .c. et .xiij. solidos quos ei debet de arreragiis compoti sui et injuste etc. Et ipse non venit. Et preceptum fuit vicecomiti quod venire faceret eum hic ad hunc diem. Et vicecomes nichil inde fecit set mandavit quod priusquam ei illud breve venit, dictus Thomas feoffavit Willemum de Styvekeye, filium et heredem suum, de toto tenemento suo etc. Ideo preceptum est vicecomiti quod distringat terras et tenementa que idem Thomas tenuit tercio die Junii hoc anno, et quod de exitibus etc. et quod habeat corpus ejus hic in octabis sancti Michaelis etc. Et unde etc.

(610)

Midd'. Aron filius Vives judeus optulit se quarto die versus Willelmum de Cumbe, tenentem quamdam partem terrarum que fuerunt Roberti Haron, de placito debiti. Et ipse non venit. Et preceptum fuit vicecomiti quod ipsum venire faceret. Et vicecomes mandavit quod retornavit breve sibi inde directum ballivis libertatis abbatis de Westm', qui nichil inde fecerunt. Judicium quod non omittat propter libertatem predictam etc., et venire faciat coram etc. a die sancti Michaelis in .xv. dies predictum Willelmum ad respondendum predicto Aron de predicto placito etc.

(611)

Glouc'. Robertus de Brokton', clericus de scaccario etc., optulit se quarto die versus Henricum de Berkele de placito debiti. Et ipse non venit. Et preceptum fuit vicecomiti quod salvo custodiret in manu regis terras etc., et si plures terras etc., et quod haberet corpus ejus coram etc., ad hunc diem. Et vicecomes mandavit quod Thomas Wauri de Durseleye et Hugo le Chaliner de eadem manuceperunt predictum Henricum, quem non habuerunt. Ideo in misericordia.[61] Et sunt exitus terrarum predicti Henrici dimidia marca. Judicium, sicut alias, quod salvo custodiat terras etc., ita quod nec ipse etc., et quod de exitibus etc., et quod habeat corpus ejus coram etc. a die sancti Michaelis in .xv. dies ad respondendum etc. et ad audiendum etc.

(612)

Suff'. Ranulphus de Ludham optulit se quarto die versus Johannem de Goneton' et Thomam Moryng' de placito transgressionis. Et ipsi non venerunt. Et preceptum fuit vicecomiti quod ipsos venire faceret coram etc. Et vicecomes mandavit quod predicti Johannes et Thomas districti sunt per averia sua, set corpora [i]<eorum non>[i] fuerunt inventa postquam breve sibi venit. Judicium quod salvo custodiat in manu regis predicta averia, et si plura etc., et quod ipsos distringat per terras etc., ita quod nec ipsi etc., et quod de exitibus etc., et quod habeat corpora eorum coram etc. a die sancti Michaelis in .xv. dies ad respondendum et ad audiendum etc.

(613)

Lond'. Jospinus filius Salomonis de Merlebergh' fecit venire Ricardum de Karleton' pistorem et Agnetem uxorem ejus, et exigit ab eis unum mantellum de bluetto

[59] *The word* misericordia *is repeated in the margin.*

[60] *The word* misericordia *is repeated in the margin.*

de miniver var' furatum et unam peciam russeti precii .ij. marcarum, que catalla eis tradidit custodiendum et que ei injuste detinent ad dampnum suum .xx. solidorum etc.

Predicti Ricardus et Agnes veniunt. [Et][62] defendunt vim etc. et dicunt quod de predicto Jospino predictum mantellum seu predictam peciam russeti non receperunt et de hoc ponunt se super patriam. Et quod predicta bona receperunt ut predictum est predictus Jospinus ponit se similiter super patriam.

Et preceptum est vicecomitibus quod venire faciant coram etc. a die sancti Michaelis in tres septimanas sex probos et legales homines de visneto de Colchereche et Cornhulle. Et preceptum est constabulario Turris Lond' quod venire faciat coram etc. ad eundem diem sex legales judeos de visneto de Colchereche, et qui nulla affinitate etc., ad recognoscendum super premissis veritatem etc.

(614)

Essex'. Hugo filius Ricardi venire fecit Willelmum clericum de Halefforde et queritur de eo quod[63]

(615)[64]

Norff'. Johannes de Hadisagh' attachiatus fuit ad respondendum Johanni de Bayfeld', clerico de scaccario etc., de placito detencionis catallorum. Et unde queritur quod, cum idem Johannes de Bayfeld' septem saccos lane, unum equum precii .xxx. solidorum et .xxv. anulos auri et alia bona ad valenciam quater viginti marcarum habuisset reposita in domo predicti Johannis de Hadisagh' in Kyneburle [i] <ad Pentecosten anno regni regis nunc septimo,>[i]predictus Johannes de Hadisagh' cum familia sua predicta catalla cepit, distraxit et ea predicto Johanne de Bayfeld' reddere contradicit ad dampnum suum .cc. marcarum, et inde producit sectam.

Predictus Johannes de Hadishagh' per attornatum suum venit. Et deffendit vim etc. Et dicit quod [i]<predictus Johannes de Bayfeld nunquam aliqua>[i] catalla [e]<nunquam>[e] in domo sua [e]<fuerunt>[e] [i]<habuit>[i] reposita nec ipse [i]<nec aliquis per ipsum aliqua>[i] catalla ipsius Johannis [i]<de Bayfeld cepit nec>[i] distraxit, et de hoc ponit se super patriam. Et predictus Johannes de Bayfeld similiter. Ideo preceptum est vicecomiti quod venire faciat coram etc. a die sancte Trinitatis in .xv. dies .xij. etc. de visneto predicto ad recognoscendum etc. Ad quem diem predictus Johannes de Bayfeld fuit essoniatus et Johannes de Hadeshagh' per attornatum suum venit et habuit diem a die sancti Michaelis in .xv. dies. Ad quem diem vicecomes non retornavit breve. Ideo preceptum est ei, sicut alias, quod venire faciat inquisicionem hic [i]<a die>[i] in octabis sancti Hilarii, nisi prius H. Hauteyn ad partes illas venerit.

[61] *The word* misericordia *is repeated in the margin.*

[62] *MS. omits.*

[63] *This entry is unfinished.*

[64] *This entry is a partial duplicate of one on membrane 5d of Roll 35, the plea roll for Easter term this year: see above, no. 450.*

MEMBRANE 5 DORSE

(616)

[This is a second version of no. 585 without significant differences from it]

(617)

Cantebr' Surr'. Walterus de Kanc', attornatus domine Regine Anglie consortis Regis, venire fecit Johannem de Camoys, filium et heredem Radulphi de Cameys, et exigit ab eo mille marcas quas debet prefate Regine occasione terrarum quas tenet que fuerunt predicti Radulphi patris sui de debito Hagini filii magistri Mossei judei, cujus debita predicta Regina habet de dono Regis etc.

Predictus Johannes non venit.[65]

(618)

Sutht'. Rogerus de Flitte, serviens de scaccario etc., optulit se quarto die versus Johannem atte Mersse de Andevere et Stephanus atte Mulle de Clatford' de placito debiti. Et ipsi non venerunt. Et preceptum fuit vicecomiti quod ipsos venire faceret coram etc. Et vicecomes mandavit quod Hugo Cupping et Robertus le Fevre manuceperunt predictum Johannem; et quod Robertus le Moneir et Henricus Howelle manuceperunt predictum Stephanum, quos non habuerunt. Ideo in misericordia.[66] Judicium [i]<quod>[i] distringat per terras etc., ita quod nec ipsi etc., et quod de exitibus etc., et quod habeat corpora eorum coram etc. a die sancti Michaelis in .xv. dies ad respondendum etc. et ad audiendum judicium etc.

Placita de crastino sancte Margarete

(619)

Northt'. Willelmus Folyot et Ysabella uxor ejus per attornatos suos optulerunt se quarto die versus Elenam la Zuche et magistrum Eliam judeum de placito transgressionis et compoti. Et predicta Elena non venit. Et preceptum fuit vicecomiti quod ipsam distringeret per terras etc. et quod haberet corpus ejus coram etc. Et vicecomes mandavit quod Radulphus Faukes de Esseby, Alanus de Hunte de eadem, Robertus Trigge de eadem, Henricus le Clerk de eadem, Alanus Drake de eadem et Hilbertus Trigge de eadem manuceperunt predictam Elenam, quam non habuerunt. Ideo in misericordia. Judicium quod salvo custodiat in manu regis terras etc., ita quod nec ipsa etc., et quod de exitibus a primo tempore etc., et quod habeat corpus ejus coram etc. a die sancti Michaelis in tres septimanas ad respondendum etc., et ad audiendum etc. Magister Elias per attornatum suum venit et dicit quod sine dicta Elena, que juncta est in dicto placito, respondere non debet, et datus est ei dies a die sancti Michaelis in tres septimanas ut supra.

[65] *This entry is unfinished.*

[66] *The word* misericordia *is repeated in the margin.*

(620)

Kanc'. Simon de Crey optulit se quarto die versus Willelmum Peyforer, tenentem quamdam partem terrarum que fuerunt Willelmi de Mareys, de placito debiti. Et ipse non venit. Et preceptum fuit vicecomiti quod ipsum distringeret per terras etc., et quod haberet corpus ejus coram etc. ad hunc diem. Et vicecomes mandavit quod Gilbertus Godegrom, Johannes atte Gate, Johannes serviens et Hugo serviens manuceperunt predictum Willelmum, quem non habuerunt. Ideo in misericordia.[67] Judicium quod vicecomes salvo custodiat in manu regis terras etc., et si plures terras etc., ita quod nec ipse etc., et quod de exitibus a primo tempore etc., et quod habeat corpus ejus coram etc. a die sancti Michaelis in tres septimanas ad respondendum etc. et ad audiendum etc.

(621)

Oxon' Berk'. Jospinus filius Salomonis de Marleberg' optulit se quarto die versus Avegaye que fuit uxor Jacobi Crespyn judeam et Haginum filium Abrahe judeum de placito debiti. Et ipsi non venerunt. Et preceptum fuit vicecomiti quod ipsos venire faceret coram etc. Et vicecomes mandavit quod predicta Avegaye non fuit inventa in balliva sua, set moram facit apud Lond' vel Bristoll', ut dicitur. Et quia [testificatum][68] est coram etc. quod manet apud Oxon', preceptum est ei quod venire faciat coram etc. a die sancti Michaelis in tres septimanas predictam Avegaye ad respondendum predicto Jospino de predicto placito. Et quod vicecomes sit ibidem etc. Et vicecomes mandavit quod pro predicto Hagino retornavit breve sibi inde directum ballivis libertatis Wallingford', qui nichil inde fecerunt. Judicium quod non omittat propter predictam libertatem etc. et venire faciat coram etc. ad eundem diem predictum Haginum ad respondendum predicto Jospino de predicto placito etc.

(622)

Ebor'. Jorninus filius Deudonis Crespyn' judeus, qui tulit breve Regis super Radulfum de Rubeo Monte de placito injuste detencionis, non est prosecutus versus eum. Ideo Jorninus et plegii sui de prosequendo, videlicet Josseus filius Sampsonis et Meyr filius Ys', in misericordia.[69] Et preceptum fuit vicecomiti quod venire faciat coram etc. ad hunc diem predictum Radulphum de Rubeo Monte. Et ipse non venit. Et vicecomes mandavit quod Ricardus de Arundel et Elias frater ejus manuceperunt predictum Radulphum, quem non habuerunt. Ideo ipse Radulphus et predicti plegii sui de veniendo in misericordia.[70]

[67] *The word* misericordia *is repeated in the margin.*
[68] *MS. reads* testifacatum.
[69] *The word* misericordia *is repeated in the margin.*
[70] *The word* misericordia *is repeated in the margin.*

(623)

Kanc'. Petekoc filius Davyd judeus optulit se quarto die versus Johannem filium et heredem Johannis Payn de placito debiti. Et ipse non venit. Et preceptum fuit vicecomiti quod ipsum venire faceret coram etc. ad hunc diem. Et vicecomes mandavit quod breve sibi adeo tarde venit quod non potuit exequi. Ideo preceptum est ei, sicut alias, quod eum venire faciat coram etc. a die sancti Michaelis in .xv. dies ad respondendum predicto judeo de predicto placito etc.

(624)

Surr' Sussex'. Gamaliel de Oxon' judeus optulit se quarto die versus Thomam de Rugg' de placito debiti. Et ipse non venit. Et preceptum fuit vicecomiti quod ipsum distringeret per terras etc., et quod haberet corpus ejus coram etc. ad hunc diem. Et vicecomes mandavit quod Johannes de Suntthinges capitalis ballivus rapi de Hastinghes, Everard de Stok', Willelmus Baky, Robertus Ballard manuceperunt predictum Thomam, quem non habuerunt. Ideo in misericordia.

Judicium quod salvo custodiat in manu regis terras etc., et si plures terras etc., ita quod nec ipse etc., et quod de exitibus etc., et quod habeat corpus ejus coram etc. a die sancti Michaelis in tres septimanas ad respondendum etc. et ad audiendum etc.

(625)

Buk'. Robertus de Ludham optulit se quarto die versus Willelmum capellanum de Quenton' de placito transgressionis. Et ipse non venit. Et preceptum fuit vicecomiti quod ipsum venire faceret coram etc. ad hunc diem. Et vicecomes mandavit quod retornavit breve sibi inde directum ballivis libertatis Walingeford', qui nichil inde responderunt. Judicium quod non omittat propter libertatem predictam etc. et venire faceret coram etc. a die sancti Michaelis in unum mensem predictum Willelmum ad respondendum predicto Roberto de predicto placito etc.

(626)

Linc'. Willelmus et Nicholaus filii Petri, qui vocaverunt Edmundum de Quappelade, filium et heredem Thome de Quappelade, ad warantum de porcionibus ipsos contingentibus occasione quarundem parcium terrarum que fuerunt magistri Thome de Quappelade, quam porcionem Rex ab eis exigit de quodam debito .xlvj. librarum in quibus idem magister Thomas tenebatur Abrahe filio Murielle judeo, optulerunt se quarto die versus predictum Edmundum de placito acquietacionis debiti predicti. Et ipse non venit. Et predictum fuit vicecomiti quod ipsum venire faceret coram etc. ad hunc diem. Et vicecomes mandavit quod Lambertus filius Galfridi de Quappelade et Petrus filius Semanni de eadem manuceperunt predictum Edmundum, quem non habuerunt. Ideo in misericordia. Judicium quod distringat per terras etc., ita quod nec ipse etc., et quod de exitibus etc., et quod habeat corpus ejus coram etc. a die sancti Michaelis in tres septimanas ad acquietandum predictos Willelmum et Petrum de porcionibus ipsos contingentibus de quibus ipsos acquietare debet ut dicunt etc.

(627)

Linc'. Willelmus Hwyn et Matilda uxor ejus venire fecerunt Johannem filium Alany Miles de Quappelade et petunt quod ipsos acquietet de porcione quam rex ab eis exigit occasione cujusdam partis terrarum quas tenent que fuerunt magistri Thome de Quappelade de quodam debito .xlvj. librarum in quo predictus magister Thomas tenebatur Abrahe filio Murielle judeo, et protulerunt coram etc. cartam predicti Johannis in qua continetur quod predictos Willelmum et Matildam warantizare, acquietare et defendere debet etc.

Predictus Johannes venit et predictam cartam esse factum suum recognovit et devenit warantum predictorum Willelmi et Matilde de predicta porcione et ulterius per auxilium curie regis vocat ad warantum Edmundum de Quappelade, filium et heredem Thome de Quappelade, ad ipsum et predictos Willelmum et Matildam acquietandum de porcione predicta de qua ipsos acquietare debet ut dicit. Et preceptum est vicecomiti quod venire faciat coram etc. a die sancti Michaelis in tres septimanas predictum Edmundum ad aquietandum predictum Johannem de predicta porcione etc.

MEMBRANE 6

Adhuc memoranda[71]

(628)[72]

Aron filius Vives judeus venit coram etc. et recognovit quod omnia debita in quibus Gilbertus Pecche tenebatur eidem Aron per cartas, obligaciones, recogniciones irrotulatas vel quocunque alio modo a creacione seculi usque die mercurii proxima post festum sancti Johannis Baptiste anno octavo sunt Alienore Regine Anglie consortis Regis etc. Et quia idem Gilbertus satisfecit predicte Regine de omnibus debitis que eadem Regina habet ex dimissione predicti Aron preter de octingentis marcis quas dictus Gilbertus debet predicte Regine per predictam dimissionem prefate Regine per prefatum Aron factam, [ut][73] Walterus de Kanc' custos auri prefate Regine plenius testatur, predictus Aron concessit facere predicto Gilberto starrum suum de quietancia omnium predictorum debitorum preter de predictis octingentis marcis. Et idem Gilbertus in pleno scaccario venit et recognovit se teneri predicte Regine in predictis octingentis marcis reddendis ad terminos contentos super obligacione earundem octingentarum marcarum etc. irrotulata. Et predictus Aron concessit quod nichil possit exigere de predictis octingentis marcis versus dictum Gilbertum.

(629)

Norff' Suff'. Memorandum quod Johannes filius Henrici de Hecham, a quo exigebantur .x. libre de debito Aron filii Abrahe judei, quod quidem debitum datum fuit Henrico de Lenn' per Benedictum filium Cok', unum heredum predicti Aron, venit coram etc. et solvit predicto Henrico decem marcas. Et de residuis quinque marcis predictus Henricus concessit eidem quod solvat ei illas quinque marcas in octabis sancti Hillarii proximo sequentibus. Et, nisi fecerit, concedit quod de terris et catallis etc.

(630)

Memorandum quod Walterus de Kanc' custos auri Alienore Regine Anglie venit coram etc. et protulit literam.[74]

(631)

Hereford'. Walterus filius Walteri Deveroys venit coram justiciariis etc. et recognovit se debere Sampsoni de Wygorn' judeo [attornato][75] Joye matris sue sexdecim marcas, reddendum inde octo marcas ad quindenam sancti Michaelis anno regni regis Edwardi octavo, et octo marcas ad festum Purificacionis beate Marie proximo sequens. Et, nisi fecerit, concedit quod de terris et catallis suis fiant.

(632)

Abraham filius Benedicti judeus venit coram etc. et finem fecit pro x bessanciis pro secta Regis relaxata de roberia cujusdam cornu quod fuit Matillidis Pruet, de quo eadem Matillis ipsum Abraham appellavit et in appello suo defecit.[76]

(633)

Norff'. Walterus de Monci venit coram etc. et recognovit se debere Hamoni Hauteyn pro Adam de Cretinge centum solidos reddendos ad festum sancti Michaelis proximo futurum. Et, nisi fecerit, [concedit][77] quod de terris et catallis suis fiant etc.

(634)

Berk'. Concessum est Bartholomeo de Yatindene quod de .xx. libris quas Regi debet occasione terrarum et tenementarum que fuerunt Johannes Belet in Ingeflot Belet, quas terras et tenementa Ricardus de Sutton' modo tenet ex dimissione predicti Bartholomei, cujus warrantus ipse

[71] *In the left hand margin above and below the heading are the marginated county headings* Northt'; Buk'.

[72] *This entry is marked for deletion with the marginal notes* vacat *and* quia plenius inter memoranda hujus termini. *See below, no. 657.*

[73] *MS. reads* et.

[74] *This entry is unfinished.*

[75] *MS. reads* attornatum.

[76] *The words* x bissancia *are repeated in the margin.*

[77] *MS. reads* consedit.

est, de debito Bonavie de Neubur' judei, quod solvat per annum decem marcas ad duos terminos, videlicet ad scaccarium sancti Michaelis proximo futurum quinque marcas, et ad scaccarium Pasche proximo sequens quinque marcas, et sic de anno in annum, termino in terminum ad eosdem terminos decem marcas donec predicte viginti libre plene persolvantur etc.

(635)

Willelmus de Gouiz venit coram justiciariis etc. et recognovit se debere Roberto de Ludham quinquaginta solidos reddendos eidem Roberto in crastino Animarum anno regni regis Edwardi octavo. Et, nisi fecerit, concedit quod de terris et catallis suis fiant.

(636)

Preceptum fuit cyrographariis arche cyrographariorum Lond' quod ad archam accederent et ab archa extraherent unam cartam quadraginta librarum sub nominibus Gilberti Pecche militis de comitatu Cantebr' et Aron filius Vives judei, ita quod eam haberent coram etc. die veneris proxima post festum Nativitatis sancti Johannis Baptiste nunc. Ad quem diem Robertus Heron unus cyrographariorum venit et protulit coram etc. predictam cartam .xl. librarum in hec verba: 'Sciant universi quod ego Gilbertus Pecche miles de comitatu Cantebr' debeo Aaron filio Vyves judeo quadraginta libras sterlingi, reddendas a die sancti Michaelis in unum mensem anno regni regis Edwardi tercio. Acta .xxviij. die Aprilis anno eodem.' Que quidem carta in pleno scaccario per predictum breve domine Regine in presencia Walteri de Kanc' tunc attornati predicte domine Regine per [licenciam][78] et voluntatem ipsius Walteri et per consensum, recognicionem et concessionem predicti Aaron predicto Gilberto liberatur quiete dampnata.

(637)

Hereford'. Willelmus le Moyne venit coram etc. et recognovit quod debet Aaron filio Vives judeo decem et novem libras et .x. solidos etc. ad quindenam sancti Michaelis anno regni Edwardi octavo. Et nisi etc.

(638)[79]

Suth'. Thomas Paynel [debet[80]] eidem et Andree de <Nevile>[81] .cc. quarteria frumenti reddenda ad festum Pentecosten anno octavo vel etc. Et nisi etc.

(639)[82]

Devon'. Urianus de Morsel' venit coram etc. et recognovit se debere eidem .c. quarteria frumenti reddenda ad quindenam sancti Michaelis anno octavo. Et nisi etc.

[78] *MS. reads* licensiam.

[79] *There is a better version of this entry on the dorse of this same membrane: see below, no. 650.*

[80] *MS. omits.*

[81] *This name has been corrected from* Neulonde.

[82] *There is a better version of this entry on membrane 7: see below, no. 658.*

(640)

Surr'. Johannes de Wauton' venit coram etc. et recognovit se debere Aron filio Vives judeo .cc. quarteria frumenti [i]<vel dimidiam marcam pro qualibet summa,>[i] reddenda ad festum Omnium Sanctorum anno regni regis Edwardi octavo vel pro quolibet quarterio dimidiam marcam. Et, nisi etc., concedit quod de [i]<terris et catallis suis fiant etc.>[i]

(641)

Suff'. Ricardus Pecche recognovit se debere eidem .x. marcas reddendas in quindena sancti Michaelis. Et nisi etc.

(642)

Northt'. Willelmus de Bray venit coram etc. et recognovit se debere Aron filio Vyves .lxx. marcas, reddendas in crastino Animarum. Et, nisi fecerit, concedit quod de terris et catallis suis fiant etc.

(643)

Buk'. Willelmus Blaket venit coram etc. et recognovit se debere Roberto de Ludham .xl. solidos reddendos in crastino Animarum. Et, nisi fecerit, concedit quod de terris et catallis suis fiant etc.

(644)

Oxon'. Patricius Chaward venit coram etc. et recognovit se debere eidem .x. libras reddendas ad festum sancti Edwardi Regis anno regis Edwardi octavo. Et nisi etc.

(645)

Glouc'. Memorandum quod Mokke le Blund venit coram etc. et recognovit se nichil posse exigere vel aliquo modo vendicare in quodam debito .l. marcarum, et in uno debito .xx. librarum sub nominibus Johannis de Eville et Elye le Blund, que quidem debita liberata fuerunt Salomoni Buntyng judeo suspenso in recompensacionem debiti. Et magister Elyas filius magistri Mossei, qui presens fuit et terciam partem habuit de predicto debito .l. marcarum, [i]<recognovit>[i] quod nichil potest exigere de predicta tercia parte [i]<et>[i] quod predictus Johannes quietus est de predicta tercia parte. Et Aron filius Vives, cui due partes predicti debiti .l. marcarum et predictum debitum .xx. librarum liberantur in recompensacionem, recognovit quod, si predictus Johannes solvat sibi septem marcas in octabis sancti Martini et ad festum [i]<sancte>[i] Trinitatis proximo sequens septem marcas et ad octabas sancti Martini quietanciam monstraverit de residuo, tunc quietus sit, [sinon][83] idem Johannes solveret predictas .xiiij. marcas ad predictos terminos ut predictum est et residuum predictorum debitorum, videlicet duas partes predicti debiti .l. marcarum, et totum debitum .xx. librarum, juxta quod quietancias suas monstrabit.

[83] *MS. reads* sindum?

MEMBRANE 6 DORSE

(646)

Heref'. Preceptum fuit vicecomiti quod distringeret Nicholaum de Wormele per terras etc. ad reddendum sibi ad opus Regis .viij. marcas et dimidiam quas Regi debet de debito Ysac de Sutwerk' judei, que aretro fuerunt de .x. marcis in quibus eidem judeo tenebatur. Et vicecomes mandavit quod de feno et pastura predicti Nicolai levari fecit .xx. solidos quos misit una cum brevi sibi inde directo, de quibus solvit in recepta regis .v. solidos per talliam, que est in custodia predicti Ysac, et in pleno scaccario solvit predicto Ysac .xv. solidos et sic predictus vicecomes [i]<inde>[i] quietus est. Et eciam habet starrum predicti Ysac de acquietancia de predictis viginti solidis.

(647)

Heref'. Nicholaus de Wormelegh' solvit in recepta Regis .v. solidos de debito Ysac de Suthwerk' judei et inde habet talliam, que est in custodia dicti Ysac.

(648)

London' Kanc'. Sampson filius Isac judeus venit coram etc. et protulit quoddam scriptum obligatorium .xxx. quarteriorum frumenti, in quibus Mauricius filius Gilberti de Chiselherst de comitatu Kanc' tenetur Aron Crespin judeo, asserens se illud scriptum invenisse. Et quia predictus judeus dampnatus est, scriptum illud capitur in manum regis quousque discussum fuerit etc. Postea dictus Mauricius, perpendens scriptum illud sic captum esse in manum regis, [venit][84] et dicit quod scriptum illud factum suum est, set dicit quod non tenetur per predictum scriptum nisi tantummodo in .xl. solidis. Et de hoc vocat ad warantum rotulos de termino sancti Michaelis anno regis Edwardi sexto incipiente septimo. Et quia, inspectis rotulis de termino predicto, compertum est ita esse, consideratum est quod predictus Mauricius quietus sit de predicto debito per predictos .xl. solidos quos postea solvit justiciariis etc. Et liberatur clericis pro scriptura summonicionum et extractarum etc. Et dictum scriptum liberatur eidem Mauricio etc.

(649)

Norff'. Cum Johannes de Teyvile tenebatur Ysac filio Deulecres judeo Norwyc' in uno debito .vj. marcarum et in alio debito .iiij. marcarum, idem Johannes in pleno scaccario solvit eidem judeo .ix. marcas. Et idem judeus concessit quod idem Johannes et heredes sui sunt quieti de predictis duobus debitis quandocumque ei unam marcam solvat residuam. Et preceptum est cyrographariis Norwyc' quod, quandocumque predictus Johannes solverit eidem Ysac predictam marcam residuam, dicto Johanni predictas duas cartas deliberant quietas dampnatas.

[84] *MS. omits.*

(650)[85]

Sutht'. Thomas Painel miles et Andreas de Nevile venerunt coram etc. et recognoverunt per scriptum suum obligatorium se debere Aron filio Vives judeo Lond' .cc. quarteria frumenti reddenda eidem Aron ad festum Pentecosten anno regni regis Edwardi octavo, vel dimidiam marcam pro quolibet quarterio. Et, nisi fecerint, concedunt quod de terris et catallis suis fiant etc. et unusquisque eorum obligatur in solidum.

(651)

Lond'. De Samuel de Ebor' de fine pro transgressione .iii. bissancia per plegium Manseri filii Aron.[86]

(652)

Sutht'. Preceptum fuit vicecomiti quod distringeret Nicholaum de la Berton', tenentem terrarum que fuerunt Willelmi de la Berton', per terras etc. ad reddendum sibi ad opus Regis .c. solidos quos Regi debet occasione etc. de debito predicti Willelmi de diversis amerciamentis ad que amerciatus fuit ad scaccarium judeorum, et denarios illos haberet coram etc. Regi solvendum. Et vicecomes mandavit quod retornavit breve sibi inde directum ballivis libertatis prioratus sancti Swithini Wynton', qui nichil inde fecerunt. Judicium quod non omittat propter predictam libertatem quin eam etc., et distringat predictum Nicholaum ad reddendum sibi ad opus Regis predictos .c. solidos, et eos habeat coram etc. in crastino sancte Margarete Regi solvendum.

(653)

Oxon'. Preceptum fuit vicecomiti quod venire faceret coram etc. sex probos et legales homines de willa Oxon' et sex legales judeos de eadem villa ad recognoscendum super sacramentum suum que bona et catalla Samuel' de la Venele judeus defunctus, Belaset que fuit uxor Salomonis de Alecetre, Hictecote soror ejus et Floria Tapay ad fidem Christianitatis converse habuerunt die quo etc., ut in auro, argento etc., et ad quorum manus etc. Et vicecomes mandavit quod retornavit breve sibi inde directum pro predictis sex christianis ballivis libertatis ville Oxon', qui nichil inde responderunt. Judicium quod non omittat propter libertatem predictam etc. et venire faciat coram etc. in crastino sancte Margarete sex probos et legales homines de villa predicta ad recognoscendum super sacramentum suum una cum Benedicto filio Benedicti, Dydde filio Belye, Ysac filio Jacobi, Abrahe filio Benedicti, Benedicto filio Milonis et Milone filio Leonis, quibus eundem diem dedimus ad recognoscendum super premissis veritatem etc.

(654)

Kanc'. Memorandum quod Mosseus filius magistri Aron judeus venit coram etc. et dixit se amisisse partes

[85] *There is another inferior version of this entry on the face of this same membrane: see above, no. 638.*

[86] *The words* iij bissancia *are repeated in the margin.*

quinque cartarum subscriptarum, videlicet unius carte .lx. solidorum sub nominibus Jacobi le Rus et ipsius Mossei, unde terminus solucionis est ad Pascham anno regni regis Henrici, Acta .xxix. die Decembris anno .liiij., et unius .viij. librarum sub nominibus Gwydonis de Brusell' filii Walteri et ipsius Mossei, unde terminus solucionis est ad festum sancti Michaelis anno regni regis Edwardi tercio, Acta quinto die marcii anno eodem, et unius .xij. marcarum sub nominibus Alani filii Thome de Meriston' et ipsius Mossei reddendum in octabis Pasche anno regis Henrici .lvii., Acta octavo die Februarii anno regis Henrici .lvj., et unius .iiij. librarum sub nominibus Willelmi la Wheyte et ipsius, unde terminus solucionis est ad festum sancti Mathei anno regni regis Edwardi tercio, Acta ultimo die Septembris anno eodem, et unius .xl. solidorum sub nominibus Stephani de la Le filii Thome de Everinge et ipsius Mossei, unde terminus solucionis est ad festum Omnium Sanctorum anno regis Henrici .lv., Acta tercio die Octobris anno .liij.

(655)

Lond'. Robertus Boxhorn captus per inquisicionem captam per vicecomitem London' pro decisione cujusdam burse cuiusdam judei in quo fuerunt .xl. solidi et obligaciones etc. Et committitur prisone in Turri Lond'.

(656)

Heref'. Walterus de Stone, Willelmus del Haye manuceperunt Ricardum le Husser, unum ex cyrographariis Her', quod erit coram etc. die veneris ante quindenam sancti Johannis Baptiste.

MEMBRANE 7

Adhuc Memoranda

(657)

Per breve domine Regine consortis Regis etc. in hec verba. 'Alienora dei gracia etc. Aron filio Vives judeo Lond' statum vite melioris. Cum nuper nobis dederis omnia debita in quibus dominus Gilbertus Pecche tibi tenebatur, ac idem dominus Gilbertus nobis plene satisfecerit de eisdem, tibi mandamus quatinus dicto domino Gilberto habere facias quietanciam, prout justum fuerit, de omnibus debitis supradictis, ad que quidem faciendum tibi tenore presencium liberam concedimus facultatem. In cujus rei etc. has litteras nostras fieri fecimus patentes. Dat' apud Westm' .vj. die Junii anno regni domini regis octavo.'

Lond'.[87] Aron filius Vyves judeus venit coram etc. in pleno scaccario et recognovit quod omnia debita in quibus Gilbertus Pecche tenebatur eidem Aron per cartas, recogniciones, obligaciones irrotulatas vel quocumque alio modo a creacione seculi usque ad diem mercurii proximam post festum sancti Johannis Baptiste anno octavo sunt Alienore Regine Anglie consortis Regis etc. Et quia idem Gilbertus satisfecit predicte Regine de omnibus debitis que eadem Regina habet ex dimissione predicti Aron preter de octingentis marcis quas idem Gilbertus debet prefate Regine per predictam dimissionem, exceptis quinquaginta et quatuor marcis quas predictus Aron recepit juxta terminos contentos super recognicione predictarum octingentarum marcarum ante predictam dimissionem et exceptis viginti et sex marcis quas predicta Regina recepit allocandis in predictis octingentis marcis, prout Walterus de Kanc' custos auri prefate regine plenius testatur, predictus Aron concessit facere predicto Gilberto starrum suum de quietancia omnium predictorum debitorum preter de predictis octingentis marcis exceptis .liiij. marcis sibi solutis ante predictam dimissionem prefate Regine factam.

Et idem Gilbertus in pleno scaccario venit et recognoscit se teneri prefate Regine in predictis octingentis marcis, exceptis predictis .liiij. marcis solutis predicto Aron ante predictam dimissionem et .xxvj. marcis solutis prefate Regine juxta terminos recognicionis predictarum octingentarum marcarum irrotulate, quas quidem octingentas marcas exceptis predictis .liiij. marcis solutis predicto Aron et .xxvj. marcis solutis prefate Regine ut predictum est, idem Gilbertus reddet ad terminos contentos super recognicione predictarum octingentarum irrotulata. Et predictus Aron concessit quod nichil poterit exigere versus predictum Gilbertum vel heredes suos de predictis octingentis marcis nec de aliis debitis supradictis inperpetuum in forma predicta etc.[88]

Aron filius Vyves recognovit per starrum suum quod Gilbertus Pecche et Johannes filius ejus sunt quieti de ipso et heredibus suis de tribus obligacionibus et uno debito, videlicet de una obligacione .xxx. saccorum lane precii sacci .x. marcarum et de duabus obligacionibus, videlicet una de .ccc. quarteriis frumenti sub nominibus predictorum Gilberti, Johannis et Aron et de una de .c. quarteriis frumenti precii quarterii dimidie marce sub nominibus predictorum Gilberti et Aron, et de uno debito .lx. marcarum quod fuit in archa cyrographariorum Lond' die confeccionis istius starri, et ista debita et obligaciones facte fuerunt ante festum sancti Johannis Baptiste anno octavo, et a principio seculi usque ad finem. Et insuper recognovit quod nec ipse nec heredes sui [i]<aliquid>[i] poterunt exigere vel vendicare super ipsum occasione unius [i]<debiti>[i] octingentarum marcarum quod irrotulatur in rotulo domini Regis pro eo quod illud debitum dimisit domine Regine consorti Regis etc. exceptis .liiij. marcis quas idem Aron recepit ante predictam dimissionem. Et si inveniatur carta, tallia vel

[87] *An earlier version of this part of the entry is to be found on membrane 6 where it is marked for omission: above, no. 628. There are significant differences between the two versions. Ther final paragraph is also found on membrane 6: above, no. 636.*

[88] *The name* Pecche *is written in large letters about half way down this paragraph of the entry. It is also written again near the top of the next paragraph.*

aliud instrumentum excepto debito predictarum octingentarum marcarum quod dimisit prefate Regine et exceptis .liiij. marcis quas idem Aron recepit ante predictam dimissionem sub nominibus predictorum Gilberti et Aron facta ante festum sancti Johannis Baptiste predictum quod quieta sint et nichil valeant etc. Acta in crastino sancti Johannis Baptiste anno octavo.

Et per breve domine Regine supradictum, preceptum est cyrographariis arche cyrographariorum Lond' quod ad archam accedant et ab eadem extrahant unam cartam .xl. librarum sub nominibus Gilberti Pecche militis de comitatu Cant' et Aron filii Vyves, ita quod eam habeant coram etc. die veneris proxima post festum Nativitatis sancti Johannis Baptiste nunc. Ad quem diem Robertus Heyrun unus cyrographariorum etc. venit et protulit coram etc. predictam cartam xl librarum in hec verba: 'Sciant universi quod ego Gilbertus Pecche miles de comitatu Cant' debeo Aron filio Vyves judeo .xl. libras sterlingorum, reddendum a die sancti Michaelis in unum mensem anno regni regis Edwardi tercio. Acta .xxviij. die Aprilis anno eodem.' Que quidem carta in pleno scaccario per predictum breve domine Regine in presencia Walteri de Kanc' tunc attornati predicte domine Regine per licenciam et voluntatem ipsius Walteri et per consensum, recognicionem et concessionem predicti Aron predicto Gilberto liberatur quiete dampnata etc.

(658)[89]

Devon'. Warinus de Morcell' miles de comitatu Devon' recognovit se debere Aron filio Vives .c. quarteria frumenti, reddenda ad quindenam sancti Michaelis vel pro quolibet quarterio dimidiam marcam. Et nisi fecerit, concedit quod de terris et catallis suis fiant etc.

(659)

Oxon'. Henricus de Schottebrok' de comitatu Berk' venit coram etc. et recognovit se debere Aron filio Vyves judeo .x. marcas reddendas ad festum Omnium Sanctorum anno regni regis Edwardi octavo. Et idem Aron concedit quod, si reddat sibi ad eundem terminum sex marcas, tunc perdonet ei residuum. Et, nisi fecerit, concedit quod predicte decem marce de terris et catallis suis fiant etc. Ad quem diem idem Henricus solvit predictas sex marcas. Et est quietus de dictis x marcis.

Idem Henricus venit coram etc. et recognovit se debere eidem Aron quinquaginta libras et .xij. quarteria frumenti, reddendum ad quindenam sancti Michaelis anno regni regis Edwardi octavo .xij. libras .x. solidos et tria quarteria frumenti, et ad Purificacionem beate Marie proximo sequentem .xij. libras .x. solidos et tria quarteria frumenti, et ad festum Nativitatis sancti Johannis Baptiste proximo sequens .xij. libras .x. solidos et tria quarteria frumenti, et ad quindenam sancti Michaelis proximo sequentem .xij. libras .x. solidos et tria quarteria frumenti. Et, nisi fecerit, concedit quod de terris et catallis suis fiant etc. Et per istam recognicionem predictus Aron recognovit se debere quietare predictum Henricum de uno debito .l. marcarum in quo [i]<dictus Henricus>[i] tenebatur Benedicto de Winton' judeo, quod quidem debitum dictus Aron habet in recompensacionem quorundam debitorum in quibus Regina consors Regis etc. eidem tenebatur.

MEMBRANE 7 DORSE

Adhuc memoranda

(660)

Surr'. Johannes de Wauton' venit coram etc. et recognovit se debere Aron filio Vyves judeo .cc. quarteria frumenti vel pro quolibet quarterio dimidiam marcam, reddenda in festo Omnium Sanctorum anno octavo. Et, nisi fecerit, concedit quod de terris et catallis suis fiant etc.

(661)[90]

Memorandum quod Galfridus de Suthorp', Willelmus de Albeny, Willelmus Botevileyn, Robertus de la Hyde, et Stephanus de Hopwrth' manuceperunt Johannem de Cameys quod erit coram etc. in vigilia sancte Margarete ad respondendum de debitis que erga ipsum potuerunt exigi occasione Judaismi. Ad quem diem venit. Ideo quieti.

(662)

Lond'. Thomas le Tanur de London' venit coram etc. et recognovit se debere Leoni filio Cressei judeo .x. quarteria frumenti, reddenda a die Natalis Domini in octo dies anno regni regis .ix., vel pro quolibet quarterio dimidiam marcam. Et, nisi fecerit, concedit quod de terris et catallis suis fiant etc.

(663)

Kanc'. Preceptum fuit vicecomiti quod de bonis et catallis Thome de la Teye fieri faceret .x. solidos ad opus Antere que fuit uxoris Vives filii magistri Mossei de triginta quinque solidis quos eidem Antere se debere recognovit coram etc., et quod denarios illos haberet coram etc. in octabis sancte Trinitatis prefate Antere solvendum. Et vicecomes mandavit quod predictus Thomas nulla bona seu catalla habet unde denarii predicti fieri possint ante autumpnum. Et ideo preceptum est ei, sicut alias, quod predictos denarios de blado et aliis bonis predicti Thome in autumpno fieri faciat et eos habeat coram etc. in octabis sancti Michaelis prefate Antere liberandum etc.

(664)

Linc'. Preceptum fuit vicecomiti quod venire faceret coram etc. cyrographarios christianos et judeos arche cyrographariorum Stamf' ad recognoscendum veritatem si Petrus filius Rogeri tradiderit eis sexaginta solidos ad

[89] *There is another version of this entry on membrane 6: above, no. 639.*

[90] *This entry is repeated below on memrane 8 (no. 679).*

opus Mossei filii Salomonis judei in quibus ei per cartam suam tenebatur et si predictus Mosseus predictos denarios postea ab eis recepit, ita quod predictum Petrum pro predictis denariis de dicto debito acquietare deberet, vel si predictus Mosseus non recepit nisi medietatem predictorum debitorum pro porcione dicti debiti ipsum inde contingente, quia medietas illius debiti fuit Sampsonis judei Stamf', prout in carta indorsatur, cujus partem non recepit ut dicit. Et vicecomes mandavit quod ballivi comitis Warr' de Stamf' non permittunt ipsum ingredi predictam villam ad execucionem dicti brevis faciendam. Et ideo preceptum est ei quod, assumpto secum sufficienti posse predicti comitatus, si necesse fuerit, predictam villam ingrediat et venire faciat predictos cyrographarios coram etc. in octabis sancti Michaelis ad recognoscendum super premissis veritatem et, si quos resistentes invenerit in hac parte, eos attachiari faciat, ita quod habeat corpora eorum coram etc. ad eundem diem ad respondendum Regi de transgressione predicta etc.

(665)

Linc'. Preceptum fuit vicecomiti quod salvo custodiret terras, redditus et catalla per que destrixit Henricum de Lacy comitem Linc', priorem de Ormesby, heredes Willelmi de Holegate quondam majoris Linc', Helevisam de Neivile, tenentes quandam partem terrarum et tenementorum que fuerunt Gilberti de Beningeworth', et si plures etc., quod haberet corpora eorum coram etc. in octabis sancte Trinitatis ad respondendum Regi una cum Johanne de Batonia, tenente quamdam partem terrarum que fuerunt predicti Gilberti, qui habuit eundem diem, de .ccclx. libris in quibus predictus Gilbertus Regi tenebatur de debitis Judaismi. Et vicecomes mandavit quod breve sibi inde directum sibi venit in vigiliam sancte Trinitatis, ita quod propter brevitatem temporis exequi non potuit. Ideo preceptum est ei, sicut alias, quod salvo custodiat etc., et si plures etc., ut supra, et quod de exitibus a primo tempore etc. et quod habeat corpora eorum coram etc. in octabis sancti Michaelis ad respondendum Regi de predicto debito una um predicto Johanne de Batonia, cui idem dies datur.

Et preceptum fuit vicecomiti quod venire faceret coram etc. ad hunc diem Hawisiam de Beningeworth', abbatem de Revesby, Willelmum de Ros, abbatem de Nuysom, Lambertum filium Hugonis de Bussey, Johannem Abr', Ricardum de Molton', Willelmum de Snellesland, Ricardum de Otteby, Robertum Otteby et Robertum Doun, tenentes quasdam partes terrarum que fuerunt predicti Gilberti, in octabis sancti Michaelis ad respondendum Regi una cum Johanne de Batonia, tenente quamdam partem terrarum predicti Gilberti, cui eundem diem dedimus de debito supradicto. Et vicecomes mandavit quod breve sibi inde directum adeo tarde venit quod exequi non potuit. Et preceptum fuit vicecomiti, sicut alias, quod ipsos venire faciat in octabis sancti Michaelis.

Et preceptum fuit eidem vicecomiti quod venire faceret coram etc. ad hunc diem .xij. tam milites quam alios probos et legales homines de visneto de Beningeworth' ad recognoscendum super sacramentum suum si abbas de Bolington' [tenet][91] aliquas terras vel tenementa que fuerunt predicti Gilberti, ut Johannes de [Batonia][92] dicit, vel non, ut predictus prior dicit. Et vicecomes mandavit quod breve sibi inde directum adeo tarde venit quod exequi non potuit. Et ideo preceptum est ei, sicut alias, quod ipsos venire faciat in octabis sancti Michaelis.

Et preceptum fuit eidem vicecomiti quod per sacramentum proborum et legalium hominum de comitatu suo diligenter inquireret qui sunt tenentes terrarum et tenementorum que fuerunt Gilberti de Beningeworth', qui Regi in dicto debito de debitis Judaismi tenebatur, et quid et quantum porcio singularum tenencium valerent per annum in omnibus exitibus etc. Et inquisicionem illam etc. scire faceret justiciariis etc. a die sancte Trinitatis in .xv. dies etc. Et vicecomes mandavit quod terre et tenementa que fuerunt predicti Gilberti sunt in diversis trehyngis, ita quod propter brevitatem temporis execucio brevis sibi inde directi fieri non potuit etc. Et ideo preceptum est ei, sicut alias, quod ipse inquirat qui sunt tenentes et quid porcio singularum valeat etc. Et inquisicionem illam scire faciat justiciariis etc. in octabis sancti Michaelis.

(666)

Linc'. Preceptum fuit vicecomiti, sicut pluries, quod [de terris, redditibus et catallis][93] Roberti de Wilebi levare faceret .xxiiij. libras ad opus Regis de debito Jossei nepotis Aaron judei et denarios illos haberet coram etc. in octabis sancte Trinitatis justiciariis liberandum ad faciendum inde etc. Et vicecomes mandavit quod breve sibi inde directum sibi venit in vigiliam sancte Trinitatis, ita quod propter brevitatem temporis exequi non potuit. Et preceptum est ei, sicut pluries, quod predictos denarios de terris, redditibus et catallis predicti Roberti levare faciat et eos habeat coram etc. a die sancti Michaelis in .xv. dies eisdem justiciariis liberandos ad faciendum inde etc.

(667)

Ebor'. Preceptum fuit vicecomiti, sicut pluries, quod distringeret heredem Henrici de Evyle, tenentem quamdam partem terrarum que fuerunt Gilberti de Beningeworth', per terras etc., et quod haberet corpus ejus coram etc. in octabis sancte Trinitatis ad respondendum Regi una cum Johanne de Batonia, tenente quamdam partem terrarum que fuerunt predicti Gilberti, qui habuit eundem diem, de .ccclx. libris in quibus prefatus Gilbertus Regi tenebatur de debito Judaismi. Et vicecomes mandavit quod retornavit breve sibi inde directum ballivo libertatis de Aynsti, qui nichil inde respondit. Judicium quod non omittat propter libertatem predictam

[91] *MS. reads* tenens.
[92] *MS. reads* Botonia.
[93] *MS. reads* distringat terras, redditus et catalla.

quin eam etc. et distringat heredem predicti Henrici per terras etc., ita quod nec ipse etc., et quod de exitibus etc. et quod habeat corpus ejus coram etc. in octabis sancti Michaelis ad respondendum etc. et ad audiendum etc.

MEMBRANE 8

Adhuc memoranda

(668)

Heref'. Preceptum fuit vicecomiti quod venire faceret Ricardum le Usser, unum ex cyrographariis arche cyrographariorum Heref', ad respondendum Regi de septem cartis quas de predictis cyrographariis sociis suis recepit ad portandum apud Westm' ad festum sancti Michaelis anno regni regis Edwardi primo ibidem in thesaurum ponendum sub nominibus diversorum christianorum et Ysac filii Diey judei, videlicet unam cartam .xxij. marcarum et dimidie sub nominibus Walteri Devros et Ysac filii Diey judei, et unam .xx. solidorum sub nominibus Walteri le Myre et dicti Isac, et unam .v. marcarum sub nominibus Roberti filii Nicholai de Furches et dicti Ysac, et unam .xx. librarum sub nominibus Hugonis de Turbervile et dicti Ysac, et unam .xl. solidorum sub nominibus Walteri le Myre de Elington et dicti Ysac, et unam .xx. solidorum sub nominibus Radulfi Erenke de Heref' et dicti Ysac, et unam .j. marce sub nominibus Hugonis filii Willelmi de Bles et dicti Ys'.

Predictus Ricardus venit coram etc. et recognovit se recepisse de sociis suis cyrographariis arche predicte predictas septem cartas sub sigillis eorum portandum apud Westm' ibidem justiciariis liberandum ad ponendum in thesaurum Regis per breve regis quod habuit in archa cyrographariorum predicta pro warranto, et eas apud Westm' sub sigillis predictorum cyrographariorum portavit post festum Purificacionis beate Marie anno regni regis predicti Edwardi secundo, et ibidem eas liberavit ad ponendum in predictum thesaurum Regis. Et quia nichil pro se habuit nisi dictum suum quod eas ibidem liberavit committitur prisone donec de eisdem cartis respondeat.

Postea finem fecit cum Rege pro predicta transgressione per .c. solidos, ita videlicet quod, si predictas cartas infra quindenam Pasche proximo futuram invenire poterit vel aliquam aliam acquietanciam inde interim habere possit, tunc quietus sit versus Regem de predictis .c. solidis. Et, si dictas cartas vel acquietanciam inde tunc non habuerit, solvat Regi predictos .c. solidos pro transgressione predicta.[94] Et quod extunc quietus sit pro predictis .c. solidis de transgressione predicta et quod decetero non calumpnietur de septem cartis predictis, et quod Rex recuperat debita supradicta versus supradictos debitores per rotulos de scrutinio qui sunt in thesauro Regis ad scaccarium judeorum.

[94] *The words* c solidi *are repeated in the margin.*

(669)

Lond'. Johannes le Mareschal' de Grascherech venit coram etc. et recognovit se debere Aron filio Vives judeo .xxx. solidos, reddendum ei inde ad festum sancti Michaelis proximo futurum .v. solidos, et ad Natale Domini proximo sequens .v. solidos, et ad Pascha proximo sequens .v. solidos, et ad Nativitatem sancti Johannis Baptiste proximo sequentem .v. solidos, et ad festum sancti Michaelis proximo sequens .v. solidos, et ad Natale Domini proximo sequens .v. solidos. Et, nisi fecerit, concedit quod de terris et catallis suis fiant etc. Et hanc recognovit predicto Aron pro quodam debito in quo idem Johannes tenebatur Ysac de Berkhamsted' judeo nuper dampnato, quod debitum idem Aron habet in recompensacionem quorundam debitorum in quibus Gilbertus Peche ei tenebatur.

(670)

Devon'. Warinus de Morcell' venit coram etc. et recognovit pro se et heredibus et tenentibus terrarum suarum teneri Hugoni de Hengham, clerico de scaccario judeorum, in quatuor marcatis annui redditus tota vita ipsius Hugonis quousque eidem Hugoni provisum fuerit per ipsum Warinum vel heredes suos in ecclesiastico beneficio ad valenciam quadraginta marcarum vel in decem libratis terre, reddendum predictas quatuor marcas ad duos anni terminos, videlicet ad festum sancti Michaelis duas marcas, et ad Pascha duas marcas. Et, nisi fecerit, concedit quod de terris et catallis et tenentibus terrarum suarum leventur etc.

(671)

Ebor'. Preceptum fuit vicecomiti, sicut pluries, quod venire faceret coram etc. in octabis sancte Trinitatis .xij. tam milites quam alios probos et legales homines etc., et qui nulla affinitate etc., attingant Willelmum de Chaunci, Rogerum de Mortuo Mari vel Johannem de Batonia, ad recognoscendum super sacramentum suum si predictus Willelmus et Rogerus tenent aliquas terras vel tenementa que fuerunt Gilberti de Beningeworth', ut Johannes de Batonia dicit, vel non, ut predicti Willelmus et Rogerus dicunt. Et vicecomes mandavit quod retornavit breve sibi inde directum ballivis libertatis de Aynsti, qui nichil inde responderunt. Judicium quod non omittat propter libertatem predictam quin eam etc. et venire faciat .xij. tam milites quam alios coram etc. in octabis sancte Trinitatis ad recognoscendum super premissis veritatem.

(672)

Northt'. Preceptum fuit vicecomiti quod venire faceret coram etc. apud Westm' ad hunc diem sex legales judeos de hiis qui temporibus preteritis moram fecerunt apud Warr' ad recognoscendum super sacramentum suum si Mossekinus de Warr' judeus nuper pro transgressione monete suspensus habuisset quoddam mesuagium in willa Warr' ex vendicione Johannis de la Porte, Johannis Martin vel Alicie filie Philippi le Gaoler, quod mesuagium predicta Alicia clamat esse liberum maritagium suum, ita quod posset esse eschaeta Regis per mortem predicti judei, vel quod dictus Mossekinus dictum mesuagium non habuit de predictis Johanne, Johanne et Alicia nisi ad terminum annorum qui preteriit, ut predicta Alicia dicit. Et Saulot le Petyt manucepit Sampsonem le Bacheler, et quod Vives le Romansors et Jacobus de Bed' manuceperunt Mosseum filium Avegaye et quod Vives le Romansor et Cresseus filius Sare manuceperunt Ysac le Eveske et quod Jacobus de Bed' et Saulot le Petit manuceperunt Samuel filium Judas et quod Samuel filius Sare et Saulot le Petit manuceperunt Benne le gendre [blank], quos non habuerunt. Ideo in misericordia.[95] Judicium quod distringat per terras etc., ita quod nec ipsi etc., et quod de exitibus etc., et quod habeat corpora eorum coram etc. a die sancti Michaelis in .xv. dies ad recognoscendum una cum Saulot le Petit, qui habet eundem diem super premissis veritatem etc.

(673)

Warr'. Preceptum fuit vicecomiti quod venire faceret coram etc. .xij. probos et legales homines de villa Warr' ad recognoscendum super sacramentum suum si Mossekinus de Warr' judeus nuper pro transgressione monete suspensus habuisset quoddam mesuagium in villa Warr' ex vendicione Johannis de la Porte, Johannis Martin seu Alicie filie Philippi le Gaoler, quod mesuagium predicta Alicia clamat esse liberum maritagium suum, ita quod posset esse eschaeta Regis per mortem predicti judei, vel quod dictus Mossekinus dictum mesuagium non habuit de predictis Johanne, Johanne et Alicia nisi ad terminum annorum qui preteriit, ut prefata Alicia dicit. Et nullus de duodecim venit. Et vicecomes mandavit quod Johannes Molf de Warr', Walterus filius ejus de eodem manuceperunt Henricum Andreu, et Willelmus Andreu et Willelmus atte More et Johannes Swan manuceperunt Philippum le Noricesone, et quod Radulphus Waterman et Johannes Eremitte manuceperunt Robertum Christofore, et quod Ricardus Pestour et Vincencius Colewile manuceperunt Galfridum de Pype, et quod Willelmus Wysdom et Johannes Coleman manuceperunt Ricardum Greneheye, et quod Ricardus Donwan et Willelmus Porkere manuceperunt Hugonem le Bedel, et quod Ivo le Webbe et Johannes Suam manuceperunt Henricum Album fabrum, et quod Ricardus Suift et Philippus Boucher manuceperunt Johannem de Pylardinton, et quod Willelmus Pinzoun et Radulphus Paty manuceperunt Clementem le Tanour, et quod Willelmus le Ventouser et Thomas frater ejus manuceperunt Willelmum Lyun, et quod Galfridus Werkman et Thomas Ayil manuceperunt Coleman ultra aquam, et quod Thomas Chapeleyn et Johannes Bor manuceperunt Robertum le Teytourer, et quod Reginaldus Cosman et Johannes the Walche manuceperunt Johannem Hairoun, et quod Stephanus Ragale et Galfridus Poucher manuceperunt Rogerum de Kyngton' de Warr', et quod Hugo le Bedel de Warr' et Galfridus Pype manuceperunt Johannem de Coventre, et quod Ricardus de Hailton' et Alanus del Slou manuceperunt Robertum Dorment; quos non habuerunt. Ideo in misericordia.[96] Judicium quod distringat per terras etc., ita quod nec ipsi etc., et quod de exitibus etc., et quod habeat corpora eorum coram etc. a die sancti Michaelis in .xv. dies ad recognoscendum super premissis veritatem.

(674)

Northt'. Preceptum fuit vicecomiti quod venire faceret coram etc. Freynildum le Weydur ad respondendum Regi de duobus pannis integris de burnetto et perseti precii .ix. marcarum, qui devenerunt ad manus ejus ex tradicione Mossei filii Avegaye judei, qui bona sua forisfecit Regi pro transgressione monete. Et ipse Freynildus non venit. Et vicecomes mandavit quod Walterus de Wahull' et Johannes le Marschal pelliparius manuceperunt predictum Freynildum, quem non habuerunt. Ideo in misericordia.[97] Judicium quod distringat per terras etc., ita quod nec ipse etc., et quod de exitibus etc., et quod habeat corpus ejus coram etc. a die sancti Michaelis in .xv. dies ad respondendum Regi de predictis duobus pannis et ad audiendum etc.

MEMBRANE 8 DORSE

(675)

Lond'. Johannes Schypt unus cyrographariorum Lond' venit coram etc. et detulit unam cartam quindecim librarum sub nominibus Willelmi de Langeford' militis de comitatu de Warr', Walter <de Rodebi de comitatu>[98] Oxon', et Diey filii Abrahe judei in hec verba: 'Willelmus de Langeford miles de comitatu Warr' et Walterus de Rodeby de comitatu Oxon' debent Diey filio Abrahe judeo quindecim libras, reddendas ad festum sancti Petri ad vincula anno regni regis Henrici filii regis Johannis .lv. Acta sexto die Februarii anno eodem.' Et quia constat justiciariis etc. per rotulos de appuramento quod predicta carta est Regine Anglie matris Regis pro auro suo in quo idem Diei predicte Regine tenebatur, ideo predicta carta liberatur Johanni de Whatel' custodi auri predicte Regine matris Regis in pleno scaccario.

Idem Johannes Schypt detulit unam cartam quadraginta et octo marcarum sub nominibus Johannis de Bachiworth filii Rogeri de comitatu Hertf' et Vives filii magistri Mossei judei in hec verba. 'Sciant universi quod Johannes de Bacheworth' filius Rogeri de comitatu Hertf' debet Vives filio magistro Mossei judeo quadraginta et octo marcas reddendas ei ad Nativitatem sancti Johannis Baptiste anno regni regis Henrici filii regis Johannis .liiij. Acta .x. die Junii anno .liij.', quam cartam Aron filius Vives habuit de thesaurario Regis in recompensacionem aliorum debitorum in quibus Rex ei tenebatur, sicut patet

95 *The word* misericordia *is repeated in the margin.*

96 *The word* misericordia *is repeated in the margin.*

97 *The word* misericordia *is repeated in the margin.*

98 *These words are repeated in MS.*

inter memoranda termini sancti Hillari anno regni regis Edwardi quinto, et nunc dicta carta restituta est et ponitur in thesauro Regis.

(676)

Lond'. Meyr filius Jacobi attachiatus ad respondendum Henne que fuit uxor Jahu judei dampnati de placito injuste detencionis catallorum. Et unde queritur quod, cum ipsa ei tradidisset .xij. marcas de catallis predicti Jahu quondam viri sui, et .vj. marcas de debitis suis per amicos suos ei post dampnacionem dicti Jahu viri sui collatis et unum ciphum argenti, quem Poncius de Mora invadiavit predicto Jahu dum vixerat precii .xxx. solidorum, et [i]<unum>[i] mantellum de camelleto precii .xx. solidorum et unam rochettam precii unius marce fideliter custodiendum, predictos denarios et bona sua ei injuste detinet et reddere contradicit ad dampnum suum .xx. marcarum. Et petit inquiri.

Predictus Meyrot venit et defendit vim etc. Et dicit quod predictas .xij. marcas que sibi tradidisse dicit de denariis predicti Jahu quondam viri sui dampnati, sex marcas de denariis suis propriis per amicos sibi collatis post mortem dicti Jahu, dictum ciphum, mantellum vel rochetam de dicta Henna non recepit. Et de hoc ponit se super patriam.[99]

(677)

Somers'. Rogerus de Kington optulit se quarto die versus Johannem filium Reginaldi de Assele de placito debiti. Et ipse non venit. Et preceptum fuit vicecomiti quod salvo custodiret [i]<terras>[i] etc., et si plures etc., et quod haberet corpus ejus coram etc. ad hunc diem. Et vicecomes mandavit quod Walterus le Neth' de Claverton', Willelmus de Wynton' de eadem, Willelmus atte Nasse de eadem, et Johannes Fraxino de eadem manuceperunt predictum Johannem, quem non habuerunt. Ideo in misericordia. Judicium, sicut alias, quod salvo custodiat etc., et si plures etc., ita quod nec ipse etc., et quod de exitibus etc., et quod habeat corpus ejus coram etc. a die sancti Michaelis in .xv. dies ad respondendum etc. et ad audiendum etc.

(678)

Surr'. Thomas Harm solvit in recepta regis .vj. solidos .viij. denarios de debitis Ysac de Suthwerk' judei, et inde habet talliam que est in manu dicti Ysac.

(679)[100]

Surr'. Memorandum quod Galfridus de Suthorp', Willelmus de Albeny, Willelmus Botevileyn, Robertus de la Hyde et Stephanus Hopworth' manuceperunt Johannem de Cameys quod erit coram etc. in vigilia sancte Margarete ad respondendum de debito que erga ipsum potuerunt exigi occasione Judeismi. Ad quem diem venit. Ideo predicti plegii sui de predicto plegagio sunt quieti.

(680)

Derb'. Henricus de Norwyco clericus Walteri de Kanc' attornati domine Regine consortis Regis venit coram etc. et recognovit se recepisse de Uriano de sancto Petro viginti marcas in partem solucionis quaterviginti marcarum quas idem Urianus recognovit se debere predicte domine Regine occasione quarundam parcium terrarum que fuerunt Willelmi de Meysham quas tenet de quindena sancte Trinitatis.

(681)

Cantebr'. Thomas Rust venit coram etc. et recognovit se debere Willelmo de Middelton' clerico etc. decem libras reddendas ad festum sancti Petri ad vincula anno octavo. Et, nisi fecerit, concedit quod de terris et catallis suis fiant etc.

(682)

Northt'. Preceptum fuit vicecomiti quod per sacramentum proborum et legalium hominum tam christianorum quam judeorum diligenter inquireret que bona et catalla Antera filia Fauntekin de Bedeford' judea habuit die quo egrotavit infirmitate [qua][101] obiit, ut in auro, argento etc. Et vicecomes mandavit quod inquisicionem inde fecit per sacramentum Ricardi de Haddon', Ade le Fevre et aliorum christianorum, Mossei filii Avegoye, Mossei filii Salomonis et aliorum judeorum, sicut patet inter inquisiciones hujus termini retornatas. Qui dicunt super sacramentum suum quod predicta Antera habuit die quo egrotavit etc. in manu sua .ij. solidos et .iij. denarios et in manu Hawisie Losunch .ij. solidos, qui devenerunt ad manus Hugonis de Kandale quando vendidit bona judeorum apud Northt' dampnatorum. Dicunt eciam quod predicta Antera habuit unum mantellum de viridi precii .ij. solidorum, et unam tunicam de viridi precii .xx. denariorum que vendebantur pro predicto precio, qui denarii, videlicet .ij. solidi et .xx. denarii, devenerunt ad manus Micke filie ejusdem Antere. Summa .iij. solidi .viij. denarii, unde tercia pars Regis est .xv. denarii, quos predicta Micka solvit in [recepta][102] regis et inde habet talliam, exceptis .iiij. solidis et .iij. denariis quos Hugo de Kandale recepit de bonis predicte Antere, ut jurati dicunt, quando vendidit bona judeorum dampnatorum Northt'.

(683)

Lond'. Cum Henna Capyun relicta Elie judei dampnati implacitasset coram justiciariis etc. Meir filium Jacobi de quadam pecunie summa que fuit predicti Elie, et ipse Meir condempnatus fuisset in .xix. marcis, ut patet inferius, per inquisicionem inde factam, et liberatus fuisset constabulario Turris Lond' in prisona custodiendum donec de eisdem denariis Regi satisfaceret. Et postea concessum est eidem Meyr quod omnia debita sua nomine Regis leventur et de primis denariis inde

[99] *This entry is unfinished.*

[100] *This entry is the same as one on membrane 7d (above, no. 661).*

[101] *MS. reads* quo.

[102] *MS. reads* recepcione.

levatis Regi solventur donec de predictis .xix. marcis Regi sit satisfactum. Et post satisfaccionem predictam Regi factam residua debitorum suorum eidem Meir ut catalla sua liberentur. Et preceptum est constabulario Turris Lond' quod corpus predicti Meir a prisona deliberet, non ei occasione predicta inferat molestiam aut gravamen. Et preceptum est cyrographariis arche cyrographariorum Lond' quod ad archam predictam accedant et ab ea extrahant omnes cartas et alia instrumenta que in ea invenire potuerunt sub nominibus diversorum christianorum et dicti Meir et eas habeant coram etc.

Postea finem fecit per .xl. solidos pro dicto concelamento, levandum de predictis catallis.[103]

(684)

Northt'. Preceptum fuit vicecomiti quod venire faceret coram etc. Willelmum de Pelevile et Margaretam uxorem ejus ad respondendum Regi de .xj. anulis aurei, tribus firmaculis aurei precii .vij. marcarum, uno cipho argenti precii .xl. solidorum et de .xl. solidis in denariis, quos receperunt de bonis Ysac Lond' judei pro transgressione monete dampnati; et quod venire faceret ad eundem diem Adam de la Fermerie ad respondendum Regi de .ij. ciphis argenteis precii .xxx. solidorum, et de aliis jocalibus que fuerunt predicti judei precii .vij. marcarum. Et predicti Willelmus et Margareta non venerunt. Et vicecomes mandavit quod Willelmus de Pelevile languidus est, ita quod ad hunc diem venire non potuit, sicut ballivi ville North' sibi responderunt, et quod Robertus de Leyc' et Warinus filius Ade North' manuceperunt Margaretam uxorem predicti Willelmi, et quod Walterus de Sivelesho et Willelmus Anketil de North' manuceperunt predictum Adam, quos non habuerunt. Ideo in misericordia.[104] Judicium quod distringat per terras etc., ita quod nec [ipsi][105] etc., et quod de exitibus etc. Et quod habeat [corpora eorum][106] coram etc. a die sancti Michaelis in .xv. dies ad respondendum Regi de predictis bonis et jocalibus et ad audiendum judicium etc.

(685)

Wiltes'. Preceptum fuit vicecomiti quod distringeret tenentes terrarum Henrici de Borle ad reddendum sibi ad opus Regis .iiij. libras quas Regi debent occasione etc. de debitis Ysac de Sobbyry judei et denarios illos haberet coram etc., vel corpora predictorum tenencium ad ostendendum inde etc. Et vicecomes mandavit quod ballivus libertatis de Chippenham sibi respondit quod Johannes de Borle tenet terras que fuerunt Henrici de Borle et quidam Henricus mercator, Johannes filius eius, Johannes de Lond', Rogerus Elis, Johannes Elis, Robertus Osegod et Johannes de Chiverden' manuceperunt predictum Johannem de Borle ad ostendendum vel faciendum etc., quem non habuerunt. Ideo in misericordia.[107] Judicium quod Johannes de Borle distringatur per terras etc. ad reddendum vicecomiti ad opus Regis predictas .iij. libras occasione etc., et quod denarios illos habeat coram etc. a die sancti Michaelis in .xv. dies Regi solvendum etc.

MEMBRANE 9

Adhuc memoranda

(686)

Surr'. Rosa que fuit uxor magistri Samuelis de Loun venit coram etc. et recognovit se recepisse de Johanne de Cameys, tenenti quamdam partem terrarum que fuerunt Roberti le Savage, per manum Nicholai le Gras vicecomitis Surr' .xl. solidos in partem solucionis [debiti][108] quindecim librarum sub nominibus Roberti le Savage et Aron [de][109] Ebor', quod quidem debitum liberatum fuit eidem Rose pro dote.

(687)

Lond'. Aron filius Vives et alii judei Lond' protulerunt breve regis de magno sigillo thesaurario et baronibus de scaccario in hec verba: 'Edwardus de gracia etc. thesaurario et baronibus suis de scaccario salutem. Mandamus quod, assumptis vobiscum justiciariis nostris[110] ad custodiam judeorum assignatis, audiatis querimonias et peticiones Aron filii Vives et aliorum judeorum singulares et generales et per consilium eorundem justiciariorum eisdem faciatis quod vobis videritis expedire. Et si aliqua dubia fuerint que per vos et per ipsos nequeant expedire sub sigillis vestris nobis una cum vestro consilio rescribatis. Teste me ipso apud Langeleye .xv. die Julii anno regni nostri octavo.'

(688)

Lond'. Preceptum fuit vicecomitibus quod distringerent Thomam Capuneshors de Candelwrstrete per terras et catalla sua pro .xij. marcis quas Regi debet de debito Aron de la Rye judei suspensi, et denarios illos haberet coram etc. ad hunc diem vel corpus predicti Thome ad ostendendum etc. Ad quem diem predictus Thomas venit et predictum debitum recognovit per quoddam scriptum ei inde ostensum quod dicto Aron inde fecit et nichil de solucione dicti debiti habuit. Ideo consideratum est quod predictus Thomas de predicto debito satisfaciat Aron filio Vives judeo, qui dictum debitum habet de thesauro Regis in recompensacionem aliorum debitorum in quibus Rex eidem Aron tenetur; et habet terminos ad dictas .xij. marcas solvendum, videlicet sex marcas ad festum Omnium Sanctorum anno regni regis Edwardi octavo et sex marcas ad festum sancti Johannis Baptiste

103 *The final sentence of this entry has been added later.*
104 *The word* misericordia *is repeated in the margin.*
105 *MS. reads* ipse.
106 *MS. reads* corpus ejus.
107 *The word* misericordia *is repeated in the margin.*
108 *MS. omits.*
109 *MS. omits.*
110 *Followed in MS. by* judeorum.

proximo sequens. Et, si defecerit in solucione primi termini, concedit quod statim post predictum terminum non observatum quod totum predictum [debitum][111] de terris et catallis suis fiat etc. Et predictus Aron habet quoddam scriptum dicti Thome obligatorium de predicto debito, quod scriptum eidem Thome post solucionem dictorum denariorum sibi factam deliberet quietum [dampnatum][112] etc.

(689)

Oxon' Berk'. Preceptum fuit vicecomiti quod de bonis et catallis Johannis de Scaccario fieri faceret ad opus Johannis Giffard .iiij. libras .xij. solidos .iiij. denarios quos idem Johannes Giffard versus predictum Johannem de Scaccario coram etc. per consideracionem [curie][113] Regis recuperavit pro dampnis suis. Et vicecomes mandavit quod predictus Johannes de Scaccario non habet bona nec catalla nisi blada in terra cressencia. Ideo preceptum est ei, ut pluries, quod de predictis bladis et aliis catallis predicti Johannis fieri faciat predictas .iiij. libras .xij. solidos .iiij. denarios et eos habeat coram etc. a die sancti Michaelis in .xv. dies predicto Johanni Giffard solvendos etc.

(690)

Norff' Suff'. Preceptum fuit vicecomiti, sicut pluries, quod non omitteret propter libertatem Donwyci etc. , et de redditibus et aliis catallis Rogeri Cristepeny et Margerie Bernard' fieri faceret ad opus Aron filii Vyves judei .x. libras quas iidem Rogerus et Margeria recognoverunt coram etc. et denarios illos haberet coram etc. eidem judeo solvendum. Et vicecomes mandavit quod nullus terminus solucionis redditus predictorum Rogeri et Margerie erit ante festum sancti Michaelis proximo futurum. Ideo preceptum est ei quod de redditu termini sancti Michaelis proximo futuri et aliis catallis predictorum Rogeri et Margerie fieri faceret predictas decem libras et eas habeat coram etc. in octabis sancti Michaelis predicto judeo solvendas etc.

(691)

Oxon'. Preceptum fuit vicecomiti quod non omitteret propter libertatem ville Oxon' quin eam etc. et venire faceret coram etc. ad hunc diem sex probos et legales homines de villa predicta ad recognoscendum super sacramentum suum una cum Benedicto filio Benedicti, Dudde filio Belye, Ysac filio Jacobi, Abrahe filio Benedicti, Benedicto filio Milonis et Milone filio Leonis judeis, qui habuerunt eundem diem, que bona et catalla Samuel de la Venele judeus mortuus, Beleasset que fuit uxor [Salomonis][114] de Alcestr', Hyghtecote soror ejus et Floria Tapay que fuit [uxor][115] Salomonis de Brubrok' judee ad fidem Christianam converse habuerunt etc. Ad quem diem Willelmus le Teler, Oliverus le Taylur, Willelmus de Medeburn', Thomas le Werrur, Johannes le Waleys et Johannes de Thame christiani [i]<et>[i] supradicti judei venerunt coram etc. Et omnes sex christiani predicti pauperes fuerunt et judei insufficientes ad predicta bona per sacramentum eorum pro Regi inquirenda. Ideo ipse vicecomes, scilicet [blank], in misericordia quia predictos christianos et judeos ad predicta facienda insufficientes venire fecit.[116] Et preceptum est vicecomiti, sicut alias, quod non omittat etc. et venire faciat coram etc. a die sancti Michaelis in tres septimanas sex christianos de ditioribus et discretioribus ville Oxon' et sex judeos de ditioribus et discretioribus ville predicte ad recognoscendum super sacramentum suum super premissis veritatem.

(692)

Ebor'. Preceptum fuit vicecomiti quod venire faceret coram etc. apud etc. a die sancti Michaelis in .xv. dies Mauricium de Osegate pissenarium Ebor' ad respondendum Regi de tribus ciphis argentii precii .iij. marcarum et dimidie et aliis bonis et catallis ad valenciam .x. marcarum que fuerunt Manseri de Jaron judei.

(693)

Linc'. Preceptum est eodem modo quod venire faceret ad eundem diem Gentam Pickethen et Joyam filiam ejus ad respondendum de .vij. anulis aureis precii .iij. marcarum et de sex marcis in denariis numeratis de catallis Urcelli filii Joscei judei.

(694)

Memorandum quod liberantur clericis pro .xxij. summonicionibus scribendis .ij. marce et eisdem clericis pro percameno emendo ad dictas summoniciones intus scribendas .iiij. solidi. Item eisdem clericis pro percameno .ij. solidi. Et liberantur Rogero de Flete, attornato Laurencii de Scaccario, pro summonicionibus portantibus .j. marca de denariis Simonis de Crey, qui assignantur magistro Elie.

(695)

Buk'. Walterus Bonet de Quenton' venit coram etc. et recognovit se debere Roberto de Ludham .ix. marcas bone et nove monete reddendas ad festum sancti Martini proximo sequens. Et, nisi fecerit, [concedit][117] quod de terris et catallis suis fiant etc.

(696)

Devon'. Warinus de Morsele de comitatu Devon' venit coram etc. et recognovit per scriptum suum se teneri Cresseo filio Cressei judeo in .l. quarteriis frumenti boni et mundi vel pro quolibet quarterio dimidiam marcam, reddendum in domo ipsius judei Lond' [ad][118] festum Natalis Domini anno regni regis Edwardi nono. Et, nisi fecerit, concedit quod de terris et catallis suis fiant etc.

[111] *MS. reads* terminus. [112] *MS. reads* dampnatam.
[113] *MS. omits.* [114] *MS. omits.* [115] *MS. omits.*

[116] *In the margin is written* c solidi vicecomes.
[117] *MS. reads* consedit.
[118] *MS. reads* a.

(697)[119]

Warr'. Johannes de Weston attachiatus ad respondendum Regi de .xlij. solidis in quibus tenebatur Ysac filio Joscei judeo nuper pro transgressione monete regis dampnato per quandam talliam .xlij. solidorum inter eos inde confectam, ut dicitur, que tallia eidem Johanni coram justiciariis etc. monstrata fuit etc.

Predictus Johannes venit et dicit quod in nullo debito predicto Ysac tenebatur nec per dictam talliam nec sine tallia sive per aliquod aliud instrumentum, et de hoc ponit se super patriam. Et preceptum est vicecomiti Warr' quod venire faciat coram etc. a die sancti Michaelis in .xv. dies sex probos et legales homines de villa Warr', et qui etc. Et preceptum fuit vicecomiti North' quod venire faciat coram etc. ad eundem diem sex legales judeos de hiis qui pre temporibus istis manere solebant apud Warr' ad recognoscendum super premissis veritatem.

(698)

Kanc'. Preceptum fuit vicecomiti quod distringeret tenentes terrarum que fuerunt Thome filii Thome Bigod per terras et catalla sua ad reddendum sibi ad opus Regis .xx. libras de debito Manseri filii Aron et denarios illos haberet coram etc. ad hunc diem. Et vicecomes mandavit quod retornavit breve sibi inde directum camerariis de Middelton, qui nichil inde fecerunt. Judicium quod non omittat propter predictam libertatem etc. et distringat predictos tenentes per terras etc. ad reddendum sibi ad opus Regis predictos denarios et eos habeat coram etc. a die sancti Michaelis in .xv. dies Regi solvendum vel corpora predictorum tenencium ad ostendendum etc.

(699)

Suff'. Ricardus Peche venit coram etc. et recognovit se debere Aron filio Vives judeo decem marcas reddendas in quindenam sancti Michaelis proximo sequentem. Et, nisi fecerit, concedit quod de terris et catallis suis fiant. Et, si idem Ricardus solvat eidem Aron predictas. x. marcas ad predictam quindenam sancti Michaelis, idem Aron concedit quod ille .x. marce allocentur Henrico de Chaddesle in solucione quam idem Henricus facere tenetur eidem Aron ad festum sancti Martini proximo futurum.

MEMBRANE 9 DORSE

(700)

Memorandum quod moneta retonsa super diversos judeos attachiata per diversas particulas diversis temporibus ponderis .lxj. solidorum .iij. denariorum remanet in custodia justiciarorum de quo pondere debent respondere.

(701)

Lond'. Johannes Skyp, unus cyrographariorum Lond', venit coram etc. et protulit per breve regis unam cartam triginta librarum sub nominibus Nicholai filii Radulphi Musard de comitatu Glouc' et Diei filii Abrahe judei in hec verba 'Sciant universi quod Nicholas filius Radulphi Musard de comitatu' Glouc' debet Diei filio Abrahe judeo triginta libras, reddendum inde .x. libras ad festum Omnium Sanctorum anno regni regis Edwardi secundo, et .x. libras a die Pasche in unum mensem proximo sequenti, et .x. libras a die sancti Michaelis proximo sequenti in unum mensem. Acta .xxv. die Februarii anno eodem.'

(702)

Cantebr'. Cum Johannes filius et heres Johannis Avered de Cantebr' et alii tenentes terrarum que fuerunt predicti Johannis districti fuissent pro .c. solidis ad opus Regis reddendum, quod debitum magister Elias filius magistri Mossei recepit de thesauro Regis in recompensacionem debitorum in quibus abbas de Stratford ei tenebatur, venit predictus Johannes et tulit breve regis de magno sigillo in hec verba: 'Edwardus dei gracia etc. justiciariis suis ad custodiam judeorum assignatis salutem. Monstravit nobis Johannes filius Johannis Awerd quod, cum [idem][120] Johannes Awered teneretur Mosseo filio Jacobi Crespyn judeo de Colecestr' defuncto in centum solidis, de quibus [idem][121] Johannes Awered predicto Mosseo plenarie satisfecit, sicut per starrum predicti Mossei quod predictus Johannes filius Johannis inde habet et quod vobis ostendere poterit plenius apparet, vos nichilominus predictos centum solidos a predicto Johanne filio Johannis, pro eo quod nos post mortem ipsius Mossei debita que eidem Mosseo die quo obiit debebantur una cum quibusdam aliis debitis Judaismi nostri magistro Elie judeo Lond' assignavimus, ad opus ipsius magistri Elie exigi et ipsum ea occasione graviter distringi faciatis ad ipsius dampnum non modicum et gravamen. Nolentes autem predicto Johanni filio Johannis injuriam fieri aud ipsum indebite pregravari in hac parte, vobis mandamus quod per sacramentum proborum et legalium hominum tam christianorum quam judeorum diligentem inquisicionem inde faciatis, et, si per inquisicionem illam inveneritis quod predictus Johannes Awered de predictis centum solidis satisfecerit Mosseo predicto, tunc ipsum Johannem filium Johannis super demanda quam ei ea occasione fieri faciatis pacem habere et quietum esse faciatis. Teste me ipso apud Odyham .xxviij. Junii anno octavo.' Per hoc breve preceptum est vicecomiti Cantebr' et Hunt' quod venire faceret coram etc. in crastino sancte Margarete .xij. probos et legales homines de villa Cantebr' et sex legales judeos de villa Hunt', et constabulario Turris Lond' quod venire faceret sex legales judeos de [e]<villa>[e] [i]<civitate>[i] Lond' ad certificandum justiciarios etc. super acquietanciam dictorum centum solidorum et confectionem dicti

[119] *No. 735 below appears to be a second enrolment of the same case.*

[120] *MS. reads* iidem.

[121] *MS. reads* iidem.

starri quod dictus Mosseus fecit Johanni Awred patri predicti Johannis et si illud starrum fecit tempore quo habuit liberam administracionem bonorum suorum et si illud littera sua ebrayca sigillavit, quod starrum predictus Johannes protulit coram etc. in hec verba: 'Ysac le fiz le prestre et Mosseus filius Jacobi Crespyn recognoverunt per starrum suum quod Johannes Awred et heredes sui quieti sunt de ipsis judeis et antecessoribus suis de omnibus debitis, calumpniis et demandis in seculo a creatione seculi usque ad finem. Et quod ipse Johannes et heredes sui quieti sunt de ipsis judeis et heredibus suis a creacione seculi usque ad festum sancti Andree anno regni regis Henrici filii Regis Johannis .xxvij. Et quod recognoverunt hoc sigillaverunt etc.' Et inquisitio venit per Johannem de Sancto Edmundo, Rogerum de Elmam et alios christianos de villa Cantebr', Josceum filium Sauloti et alios judeos de villa Hunt', Meyr nepotem Leonis, Ysac le Eveske et alios judeos de civitate Lond', sicut patet inter brevia hujus termini retornata, qui dicunt super sacramentum suum quod predictum starrum est factum predicti Mossei et manu sua propria littera ebreyca sigillatum et quod illud starrum fecit tempore quo habuit liberam administracionem bonorum suorum et quod predictus Johannes filius et heres predicti Johannis Awred' debet esse quietus de predictis centum solidis per predictum starrum.

Et ideo consideratum est quod predictus Johannes filius et heres predicti Johannis Awred quietus sit de predicto debito centum solidorum et quod carta predicti debiti eidem Johanni liberetur quieta dampnata. Et preceptum est cyrographariis christianis et judeis arche cyrographariorum Lond' quod ad archam predictam accedant et ab ea extrahant predictam cartam et eam predicto Johanni deliberent quietam dampnatam etc. Et preceptum est vicecomiti quod de predicto debito centum solidorum eidem Johanni de cetero pacem habere permittat etc.

(703)

Memorandum de summonicionibus dirigendis vicecomitibus subscriptis, videlicet

una summonicio vicecomiti Ebor' que sic incipit: 'De Adam de Bullingbrok', quia non est prosecutus.'

una summonicio directa fuit vicecomiti North' que sic incipit: 'De Meyr filio Sampsonis pro se et plegiis suis, quia non est prosecutus.'

una summonicio directa fuit vicecomiti Warr' et Leyc' que sic incipit: 'De Aron filio Deulecres, quia non est prosecutus.'

una summonicio directa fuit vicecomiti Norhumbr' que sic incipit: 'De Ricardo le Knoyce de Bradeford' et Roberto le Folur, quia non habuerunt.'

una summonicio vicecomiti Not' et Derby que sic incipit: 'De Willelmo Frauncpel et Roberto de Rolleston', quia non habuerunt.'

una summonicio vicecomiti Rotel' que sic incipit: 'De Petro filio Stephani et Stephano Blary, quia non habuerunt Gehob.'

una summonicio dirigenda vicecomiti Surr' que sic incipit: 'De Johanne de Hastinge, quia non est executus.'

una summonicio dirigenda vicecomiti Suth' que sic incipit: 'De Ricardo le Pestur et Ricardo le Parmenter, quia non habuerunt.'

una summonicio dirigenda vicecomiti Wiltes' que sic incipit: 'De Ricardo de Combe, Ada Matte, Johanne Lucas et Waltero Danfyn, quia non habuerunt.'

una summonicio dirigenda vicecomiti Devon' que sic incipit: 'De Ricardo Bissop et Rogero de Wodewell.'

una summonicio dirigenda vicecomiti Sumers' et Dors' que sic incipit: 'De Johanne de Neubergh', pro licencia concordandi.'

Iste quinque summoniciones liberate fuerunt Rogero servienti etc. et eas liberavit Rogero le Messagir in presencia R. de Ludham.

una summonicio dirigenda vicecomiti Wygorn' que sic incipit: 'De Alexandro filio Milonis de Clifton, Symoni de Sawell' et Nicholao le Turnur, quia non habuerunt.'

una summonicio dirigenda vicecomiti Heref' que sic incipit: 'De Rogero Ketel et Reginaldo de Lecton, quia non habuerunt.'

una summonicio dirigenda vicecomiti Oxon' et Berk' que sic incipit: 'De Johanne Pathorn et Radulpho Fabro de Shweymbrok'.

Que summoniciones liberate fuerunt Rogero servienti etc. et eas liberavit Ade predicto in presencia R. de Ludham.

(704)

Norff'. Cum Josceus filius Isac et Mosseus filius Jacobi de Norwico judei capti fuissent pro quibusdam platis de stagno fundatis, de quibus suspicio oriebatur ut de retonsura monete fuissent, que sunt de puro stagno, et insuper testatum est per vicecomitem Norff' quod dicte plate non fuerunt invente super predictos judeos set super quendam hominem extraneum qui attachiatus fuit per ballivos prioris Norwic' cum predictis platis, qui asserebat se habuisse de predictis judeis ad se excusandum, consideratum est quod predicti judei eant inde quieti.

(705)

Essex'. Laurencius de Scaccario venit coram etc. et recognovit se debere Aron filio Vives judeo centum solidos [i]<de debitis que ei debet>[i] reddendos ad quindenam sancti Michaelis. Et, nisi fecerit, concedit [quod][122] de terris et tenementis suis fiant etc.

(706)

Lond'. Preceptum fuit constabulario quod clamari faciat per duo vel tria sabbata per scolas judeorum quod, si aliquis judeus vel judea aliquod debitum exigere posset de Gilberto Pecche de debito suo proprio vel antecessorum suorum, tunc esset coram etc. in crastino sancte Margarete nunc cum cyrographis etc. ad computandum etc. Et constabularius mandavit quod nullus judeus vel

122 *MS. omits.*

judea aliquid ab eo exigit preter quam Aron filius Vives qui exigit .xxiiij. quarteria frumenti, ... robam sed ea non exigit ... neque ...

Eodem modo preceptum fuit eidem constabulario pro Roberto de Ludham quod clamari faciat quod si aliquis etc. tunc esset coram etc. ad eundem diem cum cyrographis etc. ad computandum etc. Et constabularius mandat quod proclamacio facta fuit et nullus exigit etc.[123]

MEMBRANE 10

(707)

Wiltes'. Sweteman filius Licorice judeus Wynton' pro se et Muriella filia Samuelis uxore sua recognovit per starrum suum quod ipse remisit et quietum clamavit Ricardo le Mareschal, heredibus et assignatis suis totum jus, demandam et calumpniam que habuit in quadam domo in villa Marlebergh' cum omnibus pertinenciis suis, unde mete predicte domus sunt magnus vicus versus partem australem et terra Alicie Tressor versus partem borealem et se extendit usque ad terram Radulfi le Mareschal versus partem occidentalem; ita quod nec ipse nec uxor sua nec heredes sui nec assignati sui aliquid calumpniare possint versus predictum Ricardum occasione predicte domus. Testibus Willelmo filio Hugonis custode castri Marleberg', Petro Lynenazs senescallo predicte ville, Johanne Bruning et Willelmo Fabro tunc [prepositis][124] ejusdem ville, Rogero Baron et Ricardo de Culewrth' tunc servientibus ejusdem ville, Willelmo Harvast, Nicholao Ayldwine et multis aliis. Et hoc starrum ei fecit pro se, uxore sua predicta et heredibus suis die mercurii proxima post festum sanctorum apostolorum Philippi et Jacobi anno regni regis Edwardi filii regis Henrici octavo. Et hoc starrum fecit per voluntatem domine Regine matris Regis Edwardi et per voluntatem suam propriam sine aliqua vi ad instanciam predicte domine Regine. Et quod recognovit hoc sigillavit.

(708)

Buk'. Manser filius Aron judeus recognovit per starrum suum quod Alexander de Sywardeshull' filius Roberti et heredes sui et tenentes terrarum suarum quieti sunt de ipso judeo et heredibus suis et antecessoribus suis de omnibus debitis, querelis et calumpniis et de omnibus obligacionibus factis sub nominibus predicti Alexandri et predicti judei et irrotulatis coram justiciariis ad custodiam judeorum assignatis, et eciam de omnibus debitis et obligacionibus tam irrotulatis quam non irrotulatis et de omnibus aliis debitis, querelis et calumpniis sub nominibus predictorum Alexandri et judei a creacione seculi usque ad quindenam sancti Johannis Baptiste anno regni regis Edwardi octavo.

[123] *At the bottom of the membrane in a contemporary hand is written* Terminus sancte Trinitatis Anno .viij.

[124] *MS. reads* prepositi.

(709)

Suff'. Mosseus de Clare judeus recognovit per starrum suum quod Willelmus de Monte Canisio de Edwardeston' et heredes sui quieti sunt de ipso judeo et heredibus suis de uno debito sub nominibus predictorum Willelmi et Mossei de .x. libris unde carta est in archa cyrographariorum apud Subir' et de omnibus aliis calumpniis, recognicionibus irrotulatis et non irrotulatis coram justiciariis ad custodiam judeorum assignatis et de omnibus aliis debitis factis ante festum sancti Johannis Baptiste anno regis Edwardi octavo. Et quod recognovit hoc idem sigillavit.

(710)

Glouc'. Aaron filius Vives judeus Lond' recognovit per starrum suum quod Mauricius de Berkele et Thomas filius ejusdem Mauricii et heredes sui quieti sunt de ipso judeo et heredibus suis de omnibus debitis, demandis, calumpniis et obligacionibus in quibus eidem Aaron unquam [tenebantur][125] que facta fuerunt ante festum Nativitatis Sancti Johannis Baptiste anno regni regis Edwardi octavo. Ita quod quieti sunt a creacione seculi usque ad finem de omnibus debitis, demandis, calumpniis et obligacionibus supradictis.

(711)

Aaron filius Vives recongovit per starrum suum quod Willelmus Paynell' et heredes sui quieti sunt de eo et heredibus suis de omnibus debitis, calumpniis, plegiis, obligacionibus et recognicionibus a principio seculi usque ad quindenam sancti Johannis Baptiste anno regni regis Edwardi octavo. Et si inveniatur carta, tallia, obligacio, recognicio vel aliud instrumentum sub nominibus predictorum Willelmi et Aaron facta ante predictum terminum concedit quod vana sint et nichil valeant etc.

(712)

Vives filius Aaron venit etc. et recognovit per starrum suum quod Willelmus Paynell' et heredes sui quieti sunt de ipso et heredibus suis de omnibus debitis, plegiis, calumpniis, obligacionibus, recognicionibus et omnibus demandis in quibus ei tenebatur a creacione seculi usque ad quindenam sancti Johannis Baptiste anno regni regis Edwardi octavo. Et si inveniatur carta, tallia, obligacio, recognicio, vel aliquod aliud instrumentum sub nominibus predictorum Willelmi et Vives facta ante predictum terminum concedit quod vana sunt et nichil valeant etc.

(713)

Essex'. Vives filius Mossei judeus recognovit per starrum suum quod Ricardus de Cornherde miles et heredes sui quieti sunt de ipso judeo et heredibus suis de uno debito octo librarum sub nominibus predictorum Ricardi et Vives, unde pars in qua cera dependet est in archa cyrographariorum apud Colec'. Et si aliqua alia carta sub

[125] *MS. reads* tenebatur.

nominibus predictorum Ricardi et Vives facta ante festum sancte Trinitatis anno regni regis Edwardi octavo inveniatur in aliqua archa domini Regis idem judeus recognovit quod quieta sit et nichil valeat.

(714)

Kanc'. Isac le Eveke judeus recognovit per starrum suum et testatur pro Antera que fuit uxor Vives filii magistri Mossei tanquam attornatus ipsius Antere quod Johannes de la Teye de Helham et heredes et assignati sui quieti sunt de ipsa Antera et Isac et heredibus suis de quodam debito sexaginta et decem solidorum sub nominibus predicti Johannis et Sleme que fuit uxor Jurnini de Cantuar', quod quidem debitum liberatum fuit eidem Antere de thesauro Regis; de predicto debito prefatus Johannes et heredes sui sunt quieti a creacione seculi usque ad finem. Et recognovit eciam quod Johannes et Thomas fratres et filii predicti Johannis de la Teye quieti sunt de predictis debitis et de quadam recognicione facta predicte Antere de .lxx. solidis, que quidem recognicio facta fuit sub nominibus predictorum Johannis et Thome et ipsius Antere [irrotulata][126] in rotulis justiciariorum domini regis de scaccario judeorum occasione predicti debiti, et de predicto debito quieti sunt ijdem Johannes et Thomas et heredes sui de predicta Antera a creacione seculi usque ad Gulam Autumpni anno regni regis Edwardi .viij. Et si inveniatur carta, pars vel aliud instrumentum sub nominibus predictorum Johannis et Thome et ipsius Antere in archa cyrographariorum vel extra facta ante diem predictum, idem judeus recognovit et testatur pro predicta Antera quod quieta sint et nichil valeant. Et quod recognovit pro predicta Antera hoc sigillavit per preceptum ipsius Antere. Et si aliquis homo vel femina veniat et calumpnietur aliquid super predictos Johannem vel Thomam occasione predicti debiti .lxx. solidorum idem Isac recognovit quod ipsi et heredes suis tenentur warantizare et defendere contra omnes calumpniantes. Et predicta Antera venit et recognovit omnia premissa in forma predicta.

(715)

Suff'. Mosseus de Clare judeus recognovit per starrum suum quod Hubertus de Monte Canisio de Holton' et heredes sui et tenentes terrarum suarum quieti sunt de ipso judeo et heredibus suis de uno debito .xl. librarum sub nominibus predictorum Huberti et Mossei unde carta est in archa cyrographariorum Subir' et de omnibus aliis debitis, querelis sub nominibus predictorum Huberti et Mossei a creacione seculi usque ad finem.

(716)

North' Lond'. Aaron filius Vives judeus recognovit per starrum suum quod quietavit et quietumclamavit Stephano de Cornhull' et heredibus et assignatis suis totum jus, demandam et calumpniam que habuit vel habere potuit super manerio de Sutthorp' in comitatu North' cum omnibus pertinenciis suis, quod manerium predictus Stephanus modo tenet de dimissione Galfridi de Suthorp' debitoris predicti Aaron et eciam totum jus, demandam et calumpniam que habuit vel habere potuit occasione cujusdam obligacionis viginti saccarum lane sub nominibus predictorum Galfridi de Suthorp' et Aron et omnium aliarum obligacionum in quibus idem Galfridus eidem Aron tenebatur a creacione seculi usque ad Pentecosten anno regni regis Edwardi filii regis Henrici octavo. Et idem Aron tenetur aquietare predictum Stephanum et heredes et assignatos suos contra omnes calumpniantes versus eundem Stephanum occasione alicujus obligacionis in qua idem Galfridus eidem Aron tenebatur a creacione seculi usque ad Pentecosten anno predicto. Acta die dominica proxima post Assencionem Domini anno regni regis Edwardi octavo.

(717)

Lond' Norht'. Aaron filius Vives judeus recognovit per starrum suum quod recepit de Stephano de Cornhull' sexaginta libras sterlingorum quas mihi debuit super quedam vadia que fuerunt in manu thesaurarii de Templo custodienda occasione maneri de Suthorp de quo idem Stephanus modo habet seisinam ex dimissione Galfridi de Suthorp, ita quod nec ipse Aron nec heredes nec assignati sui non possint aliquid exigere seu calumpniare versus predictum Stephanum, heredes vel assignatos suos occasione predictarum .lx. librarum nec occasione alicujus debiti in quo idem Galfridus eidem Aron tenebatur a creacione seculi usque in crastinum Translacionis Beati Thome Martiris anno regni regis Edwardi filii regis Henrici octavo.

MEMBRANE 10 DORSE

(718)

Essex'. Rosa filia Abr' [i]<le Jeofne>[i] per testimonium Mossei de Doggestrete et Abrahe filii Benedicti recognovit quod quietavit et quietumclamavit totum jus, clamium, calumpniam que habuit vel habere potuit super tribus acris terre, una acra prati in villa de Magna Saunford, de qua quidem terra et prato Walterus filius Willelmi de villa predicta seisivit Willelmum de Hasteng'. Postea quietavit et quietumclamavit predicto Waltero et Willelmo filio Radulphi de Geddeleston' quod ipsa non possit calumpniari super terram et pratum antedicta occasione alicujus debiti quod predictus Walterus ei debuit a principio seculi usque ad finem et per rogatum Philippi de Wyleby dicta Rosa quietavit predicto Willelmo predicta terram et pratum etc.

(719)

Essex'. Deulecres filius Leonis judeus recognovit per starrum suum quod Johannes de Whatevile et heredes sui et tenentes terrarum et heredes et assignati eorum quieti sunt de ipso judeo et heredibus et assignatis et de

[126] *MS. reads* irrotulatis.

quodam debito decem librarum sub nominibus ipsius et predicti Deulecres et de omnibus aliis debitis, demandis et calumpniis factis ante confeccionem presentis starri a principio seculi usque ad finem, ita quod ipse Deulecres nec heredes nec assignati sui exigere possint aliquod debitum nec calumpniam super predictum Johannem nec super tenentes terrarum suarum nec super heredes eorum nec assignatos a principio seculi usque ad finem. Et si inveniatur carta, tallia vel aliquod aliud instrumentum in archa cyrographariorum vel extra sub nominibus predicti Johannis et ipsius Deulecres facta ante confeccionem presentis starri idem judeus recognovit quod quieta sint et nichil valeant inperpetuum. Acta in crastino sancte Margarete anno regni regis Edwardi filii regis Henrici octavo coram justiciariis ad custodiam judeorum assignatis. Recognovit insuper predictus judeus quod si aliquis homo vel femina calumpnietur aliquod debitum versus predictum Johannem vel heredes suos vel tenentes terrarum suarum occasione cujusdam debiti decem librarum predictarum super ipsum judeum est ipsos warantizare, defendere et acquietare contra omnes calumpniantes etc.

ROLL 27

MEMBRANE 9

Adhuc memoranda

(720)

Berk'. Petrus de Aston', burgensis de Rading', venit coram etc. et recognovit se debere Roberto de Ludham pro decimis garbarum et feno ecclesie de Quenton', quas idem Robertus eidem Petro concessit et dimisit sexaginta et quinque marcas quas idem Petrus eidem Roberto solvet ad terminos subscriptos, videlicet .x. marcas die sancti Andree apostoli proximo futuro, et .xxx. marcas die sancti Johannis Baptiste proximo sequenti, et viginti et quinque marcas a die sancti Michaelis proximo sequenti in .xv. dies. Et, nisi fecerit, concedit quod de terris et catallis suis fiant etc.

(721)

Lond'. Cum Benedictus filius Cok' detulisset breve regis de magno sigillo justiciariis etc. directum, sicut continetur in termino sancti Hillarii anno regni regis Edwardi sexto, quod retentis ad opus Regis de clarioribus debitis de debitis ejusdem Benedicti tunc in thesauro Regis existentibus usque ad summam arreragiorum in quibus Regi tenebatur et quod de residuis debitis suis et antecessorum suorum, quorum heres ipse fuerat, et pro quibus ipse finem fecerat, habito compoto de predictis arreragiis et retentis ad opus Regis de clarioribus debitis suis usque ad summam arreragiorum predictorum, liberate fuerunt eidem Benedicto in quadam pixide sub sigillo capitis de scaccario judeorum .xxxviij. carte sub nominibus diversorum christianorum et predicti Benedicti ac quorundam antecessorum suorum cyrographariis arche cyrographariorum Lond' mittende in eandem archam reponendum. Et cum ipse Benedictus easdem cartas sic signatas per licenciam justiciariorum tradidisset Aron filio Vives pro sexaginta solidis, quibus tunc multum indigebat, postea quedam carta predictarum cartarum sub nominibus Radulphi de Thortp' de comitatu Norht' et Deulecres filii Aron judei de .ccxxxiij. libris .vj. solidis .viij. denariis, habita inde inquisicione per breve regis de magno sigillo, sicut continetur in termino sancti Hillarii anno regni regis Edwardi octavo, liberata fuit in pleno scaccario Symoni filio et heredi predicti Radulphi quieta dampnata, et prefatus Aron .xxvij. cartas que remanserunt in predicta pixide sub predicto sigillo post predictam cartam quietam et dampnatam liberavit justiciariis etc. in pleno scaccario et sic inde quietus est.

(722)

Berk'. Henricus de Schotebroke de comitatu Berk' venit coram etc. et recognovit se debere Aron filio Vives judeo .x. marcas reddendas ad festum Omnium Sanctorum anno regni regis Edwardi octavo. Et idem Aron [concedit][127] quod, si reddat sibi ad eundem terminum sex marcas, tunc perdonat ei residuum. Et, nisi fecerit, concedit quod predicte .x. marce de terris et catallis suis fiant etc.

Idem Henricus venit coram etc. et recognovit se debere eidem Aron quinquaginta libras et .xij. quarteria frumenti, reddendum ad quindenam sancti Michaelis anno regni regis Edwardi octavo .xij. libras .x. solidos et .iij. quarteria et ad festum Nativitatis sancti Johannis Baptiste proximo sequens .xij. libras .x. solidos et .iij. quarteria frumenti, et ad quindenam sancti Michaelis proximo sequentem .xij. libras .x. solidos et .iij. quarteria frumenti.[128] Et, nisi fecerit, concedit quod de terris et catallis suis fiant etc. Et per istam recognicionem predictus Aron recognovit se debere quietare predictum Henricum de uno debito .l. marcarum in quo dictus Henricus tenebatur Benedicto de Wynton' judeo, quod quidem debitum dictus Aron habet in recompensacione quorundam debitorum in quibus Regina consors Regis etc. eidem tenebatur.

(723)

Lond'. Rosa que fuit uxor magistri Samuelis de Loun' venit coram etc. et recognovit se recepisse per manum Nicholai le Gras vicecomitis Surr' quadraginta solidos de Johanne de Cameys, tenente terras que fuerunt Roberti le Sauvage, de quodam debito .xv. librarum sub nominibus Roberti le Sauvage et Aron de Ebor', quod quidem debitum liberatum fuit eidem Rose pro dote etc.

[127] *MS. reads* consedit.

[128] *The fourth term has been omitted.*

(724)

Lond'. Jorninus filius Abrahe dat Regi .j. bissancium ut Ysac de Suthwerke jurat super quinque libros Moysy quod Sara que fuit uxor Salamonis de Winton' judei dampnati non promisit Abrahe filio Benedicti de Wynton' judeo medietatem .xxiij. librarum quas de Petro le Neweman et Roberto le Swyngare de Andevere exigit, si eas recuperare versus eos contigerit pro lege dicto Abrahe vadiata de .xvj. libris quas ab ea peciit relaxanda. Et dictus Ysac presens statim juravit. Ideo dictus Jorninus in dicta bissancia condempnatus.[129]

(725)

Oxon'. Preceptum fuit vicecomiti quod attachiari faceret Ysac le Petyt od la playe, ita quod haberet corpus ejus coram etc. ad respondendum Regi de uno cipho argenteo precii .xx. solidorum furato in domo Walteri de Oxon' aurifabri et de aliis transgressionibus sibi per justiciarios inponendis etc. Et vicecomes mandavit quod predictus Ysac detentus est in prisona in castro Oxon' pro auro Regine consortis Regis, ita quod nullos invenire potuit manucaptores veniendi ad hunc diem. Ideo preceptum est vicecomiti, sicut pluries, quod attachiat predictum Ysac et corpus ejus habeat coram etc. in octabis sancti Michaelis ad respondendum Regi de predicta transgressione.

(726)

Salop'. Preceptum fuit vicecomiti quod de bonis et catallis Rogeri Springhose, Rogeri Tyrel, Johannis Baskervile, Gilberti de Bosco et Walteri Tirel fieri faceret .xxv. marcas ad opus Johannis de Picheford', que ei aretro sunt de .xx. marcis annuatim reddendis de debito .ccxl. marcarum pro plegio Willelmi Deveroys, ut dicit, et denarios illos haberet coram etc. a die sancte Trinitatis in .xv. dies predicto Johanni solvendos. Et vicecomes mandavit quod breve sibi inde directum adeo tarde venit quod exequi non potuit. Et preceptum est ei, sicut pluries, quod de bonis et catallis predictorum Rogeri et aliorum fieri faciat predictas .xxv. marcas, et illas habeat coram etc. a die sancti Michaelis in .xv. dies predicto Johannis solvendos etc.

(727)

Cant'. Preceptum fuit vicecomiti quod de bonis et catallis tenencium terras que fuerunt Johannis le Rus de Cant' levari faceret ad opus Regis .iiij. libras quas Regi debuit occasione predictarum terrarum etc., et quas Rex nuper per consideracionem curie sue coram etc. versus eosdem tenentes recuperavit de debito Mossei filii Ysac judei, et denarios illos haberet coram etc. ad hunc diem. Et vicecomes mandavit quod retornavit breve sibi inde directum majori et ballivis ville Cantebr', qui nichil inde fecerunt. Judicium quod non omittat propter libertatem predictam quin eam etc., et levari faciat de bonis et catallis predictorum tenencium predictas .iiij. libras, et eas habeat coram etc. in octabis sancti Michaelis Regi solvendas etc.

(728)

Surr'. Preceptum fuit vicecomiti quod distringeret Robertum de Backewell', tenentem quandam partem terrarum que fuerunt Margerie de Kamerwelle, per terras etc. ad reddendum sibi ad opus Regis .iiij. libras quas Regi debet etc. occasione etc. de debito Isac de Suthwerk judei, et denarios illos haberet coram etc. Regi solvendos. Et vicecomes mandavit quod predictus Robertus districtus est per .viij. boves de precio .iiij. librarum. Et preceptum est vicecomiti quod distringat predictum Robertum per predictos .viij. boves et alia bona sua ad reddendum sibi ad opus Regis predictas .iiij. libras, ita quod eas habeat coram etc. in octabis sancti Michaelis Regi solvendas etc.

(729)

Surr' Sussex. Preceptum fuit vicecomiti quod distringeret tenentes terras Ricardi filii Ricardi de Hadresham per terras etc. ad reddendum sibi ad opus Regis .x. libras quas Regi debent occasione etc. de debito Ysac de Suthwerk judei, et quod non omitteret propter libertatem archiepiscopatus Cantuar' quin eam etc. et distringeret eodem modo tenentes terras que [fuerunt][130] Henrici Jukel pro .ij. marcis, et distringeret tenentes terras Normanni de Suthwerke pro .xl. solidis, et quod distringeret Radulphum le Pelee, tenentem terras que fuerunt Gilberti fratris Normanni, pro .xl. solidis, et quod distringeret tenentes terras que fuerunt Roberti le Duke pro .xl. solidis, et quod distringeret tenentes terras Ricardi Hadresham senioris pro .c. solidis, et quod distringeret tenentes terras et redditus Johannis de Cammeys pro .c. solidis, quos Regi debent occasione [i]<etc.>[i] de debito predicti Ysac. Et vicecomes mandavit quod terre et tenementa que fuerunt Ricardi filii Ricardi de Hadresham sunt in manu Hugonis de Hengeham et jacent inculte et nichil invenit super terras predictas postquam breve sibi venit. Et quod tenentes terras Henrici Jukel districti sunt per .ij. equos precii .ij. marcarum. Et quod Normannus de Suthwerke non habuit nisi quandam domum in Suthwerke, quam Salerna que fuit uxor ejusdem Normanni tenet, per quam districta est. Et quod Radulphus le Pelee nichil habet in balliva sua nisi quoddam mesuagium in Suthwerke per quod districtus est et corpus ejus post recepcionem brevis non fuit inventum. Et quod Willelmus de Hevere et Matilda uxor ejus, tenentes redditus Johannis de Cammoys, districti sunt per averia sua ad valenciam .c. solidorum. Et preceptum fuit vicecomiti quod [per] predicta bona et alia catalla predictorum tenencium predictos tenentes distringat ad reddendum sibi ad opus Regis predictos denarios, et quod habeat coram etc. in octabis sancti Michaelis Regi solvendum etc. Et nichil respondit de tenentibus terras Ricardi de Hadresham senioris, ideo ipse vicecomes ...[131]

[129] *The words* .j. bissancia *are repeated in the margin.*

[130] *MS. omits.*

[131] *This sentence appears to be unfinished.*

Et preceptum fuit vicecomiti eodem modo quod distringeret priorem de Bermondes', tenentem quandam partem terrarum que fuerunt Thome le Provost, pro .xxviij. solidis ad opus Regis de debito predicti Ysac. Predictus prior venit et dicit quod injuste distringitur pro predictis .xxviij. solidis eo quod non tenet aliquas terras seu tenementa que fuerunt predicti Thome. Et predictus Ysac presens est et [dicit][132] quod nescit utrum predictus prior tenet aliquas terras vel tenementa que fuerunt predicti Thome vel non, et dicit quod non wlt ulterius versus predictum priorem pro predicto debito .xxviij. solidorum [prosequi].[133] Et ideo consideratum est quod predictus prior inde eat quietus et dictus Ysac etc.

(730)

Wiltes'. Preceptum fuit vicecomiti sicut pluries quod non omitteret propter libertatem de Kinewarston' quin eam etc., et de bonis et catallis Johannis <de>[134] Haverynge fieri faceret .x. marcas ad opus Aaron filii Vives judei, quas idem Johannes recognovit coram etc. se recepisse de Rogero de Radengham de debito dicti Aaron, et denarios illos haberet coram etc. ad hunc diem judeo solvendos. Et vicecomes mandavit quod de bonis et catallis predicti Johannis levari fecit .xl. solidos, quos solvit eidem Aaron in pleno scaccario; inde habet respectum de residuo usque ad quindenam sancti Michaelis. Et preceptum est vicecomiti quod predicto Johanni de predicto debito interim pacem habere permittat etc.

(731)

Essex Hertf'. Preceptum fuit vicecomiti quod non omitteret propter libertatem sancti Albani quin eam etc. et de bonis et catallis Mathei Nowel fieri faceret .vj. marcas ad opus Aron filii Vives et denarios illos haberet coram etc. ad hunc diem eidem Aron solvendos. Et vicecomes mandavit quod de bonis et catallis predicti Mathei levari fecit .xl. solidos quos solvit predicto Aron in pleno scaccario.

MEMBRANE 9 DORSE

(732)

Ebor'. Preceptum fuit vicecomiti, sicut alias, quod distringeret Robertum de Cave per terras etc. ad reddendum sibi ad opus Regis .xij. marcas et dimidiam quas Regi debet de debito Ysac le Eweske judei, et denarios illos haberet coram etc. ad hunc diem. Et vicecomes mandavit quod retornavit breve sibi inde directum ballivis libertatis sancti Petri, qui nichil inde fecerunt. Judicium quod non omittat propter predictam libertatem etc., et distringat predictum Robertum per terras etc. ad reddendum sibi ad opus Regis predictas .xij. marcas et dimidiam et eas habeat coram etc. a die sancti Michaelis in .xv. dies Regi solvendas etc.

[132] *MS. reads* disit. [133] *MS. omits.* [134] *MS. repeats.*

(733)

Wiltes'. Preceptum fuit vicecomiti quod distringeret Johannem Wase de Henton' per terras etc. ad reddendum sibi ad opus Regis .x. libras de debito Ysac de Suthwerk judei, et denarios illos haberet coram etc. Regi solvendas. Predictus Johannes venit coram etc. et dicit quod numquam tenebatur predicto Ysac in aliquo denario set Johannes Wase filius Nicholai, qui cepit terras cum uxore sua in villa de Palton' extra Merleberge, tenetur predicto Ysac in predicto debito. Et preceptum est vicecomiti quod venire faciat coram etc. a die sancti Michaelis in .xv. dies predictum Johannem Wase filium Nicholai Wase ad respondendum Regi una cum predicto Johanni Wase de Henton' de predictis .x. libris, cui idem dies datur etc.

(734)

Warr'. Preceptum fuit vicecomiti quod distringeret Robertum priorem domus sancti Sepulchri de Warr' per terras etc. ad reddendum sibi ad opus Regis quinque marcas, et quod distringeret eodem modo Radulphum de Lymesy pro .iiij. libris, Ricardum de Brommesgrave celerarium de Ken' pro .lx. solidis, Thomam Balance pro .xx. solidis, Theobaldum de Nevile pro .xl. solidis, Thomam de Cherlecote pro .xx. solidis, Johannem de Westone pro .xlij. solidis, Rogerum Dunhale pro .xx. solidis, Willelmum Fukerham et Willelmum le Esquier de Cherlecote pro .xxiiij. solidis, Robertum de Brule pro .x.solidis, Willelmum de Bereford' pro .xviij. solidis, Petrum de Leyc' pro .xl.solidis, Willelmum de Preston' pro .v. solidis, Petrum le Porter pro .vj. solidis .viij. denariis, Johannem de Wodeford' pro .xliiij. solidis, Johannem Rubeum de Alne pro .vj. solidis .viij. denariis, et Willelmum le Heyr de Heselowe pro .xiij. solidis .iiij. denariis, quos Regi debent de debitis Ysac filii Jossei judei dampnati, et denarios illos haberet coram etc. Regi solvendos vel corpora predictorum Roberti et aliorum ad ostendendum etc. Et vicecomes mandavit quod Thomas de Salterwyde in Warr', Johannes le Rour de eadem, Ricardus Greyve de eadem et Ricardus super le Hulle de eadem manuceperunt predictum Robertum priorem etc., et quod Henricus Payn de Solihulle, Henricus le Bedel de eadem, Henricus Godeholde de eadem et Johannes Adthelistan de eadem manuceperunt Radulphum de Lymesy; et quod Ricardus de Bremmisgrave canonicus est domus castri de Kenilworth' et non habet terras nec tenementa propria per que possit distringi, ideo de ipso nichil actum est; et quod Willelmus Gunnilde de Assehorne, Stephanus filius Alani de eadem, Johannes de Lockisle de eadem et Ricardus frater ejus de eadem manuceperunt Thomam Belance; et quod Willelmus atte Welle de Budibrocke, Willelmus Gulet de eadem, Henricus de Stodleye de Stratford et Robertus Swolonkocke de Stodlehye manuceperunt Theobaldum de Nevile; et quod Ricardus Hardinge de Haselleye, Robertus Hoddespicke de eadem, Henricus prepositus de eadem et Johannes de Aula de eadem manuceperunt Thomam de Cherlecote; et quod Rogerus de Dunhale,

Willelmus Fukeham, et Willelmus le Esquier de Cherlecote non sunt inventi in balliva sua nec aliquid habent in ea, per que possint distringi; et quod Robertus Love de Cotton', Thomas Warner de eadem, Henricus de Stodleye de Stratforde et Robertus de Stodleye manuceperunt Robertum de Bruly; et quod Willelmus juxta aquam de Bereford', Johannes Scheyle de eadem, Willelmus Edwyne de eadem et Simon juxta aquam de eadem manuceperunt Willelmum de Bereforde; et quod Petrus de Leyc' clericus est et non habet laycum feodum per quod possit distringi; et quod Willelmus de Prestone et Petrus le Porter <ignoti sunt>[135] et non sunt inventi in balliva sua nec aliqui tales; et quod Willelmus Gernoune de Wodeforde, Symon prepositus de eadem, Henricus de Stodleye et Robertus de Stodleye maunceperunt Johannem de Wodeforde; quos non habuerunt. Ideo in misericordia. Judicium quod distringat per terras etc. ad reddendum vicecomiti ad opus Regis predictos denarios et eos habeat coram etc. a die sancti Michaelis in .xv. dies Regi solvendos vel corpora predictorum debitorum ad ostendendum etc. Et insuper mandavit quod Johannes le Rede et Willelmus le Eyr de Hoselevere nichil habent in balliva sua per que possint distringi.

(735)[136]

[*Warr'.*][137] Johannes de Westone attachiatus ad respondendum Regi de .xlij. solidis in quibus tenebatur Ysac filio Joscei judeo nuper pro transgressione monete Regis [dampnato][138] per quandam talliam .xlij. solidorum inter eos confectum, ut dicitur, que tallia eidem Johanni coram justiciariis etc. monstrata fuit etc.

Predictus Johannes venit. Et dicit quod in nulla debito predicto Ysac tenebatur nec per predictam talliam nec sine tallia sive per aliquod aliud instrumentum et de hoc ponit se super patriam. Et preceptum est vicecomiti Warr' quod venire faciat coram etc. a die sancti Michaelis in .xv. dies sex probos et legales homines de villa Warr' et qui etc. Et preceptum est vicecomiti Norht' quod venire faciat coram etc. ad eundem diem sex legales judeos de hiis que pre temporibus istis manere solebant apud Warr' ad recognoscendum super premissis veritatem etc.

(736)

Bed'. Preceptum fuit vicecomiti quod distringeret Alinam, Johannam filias Jacobi Wake, Robertum Coke, Lucam de Astone, Willelmum Pidefische, Walterum Ordwy, Ricardum Sukeline, Johannem de Boweles, Walterum Glene et Johannem Stevenache, tenentes terras que fuerunt Jacobi Wake, per terras et catalla sua ad reddendum sibi ad opus Regis quatuor marcas quas Regi debent occasione predictarum terrarum etc. de debitis Ysac de Suthwerke judei, et denarios illos haberet coram etc. vel corpora predictorum tenencium ad ostendendum etc.

Et Robertus Coke, Walterus Ordwy et Ricardus Sukelinge venerunt et recognoverunt se esse tenentes quarundam parcium terrarum que fuerunt predicti Jacobi et prompti sunt satisfacere Regi de porcione ipsos contingente de debito supradicto. Et habent diem ad porciones suas inde [recipiendas][139] a die sancti Michaelis in .xv. dies.

Lucas de Astone venit et dicit quod Robertus le Corveser antecessor suus, qui terras quas dictus Lucas modo tenet emit de dicto Jacobo, et feofatus fuit inde multo tempore antequam dictus Jacobus predicto Ysac per cartam suam in dicto debito obligaretur. Et preceptum est vicecomiti quod per sacramentum proborum et legalium hominum diligenter inquirat quo die et quo anno predictus Robertus feofatus fuit de terris et tenementis que idem Lucas modo tenet que fuerunt predicti Jacobi; et inquisicionem illam scire faciat justiciariis etc. a die sancti Michaelis in .xv. dies.

Et Alina et Johanna filie Jacobi, Willelmus Pidifisch, Johannes de Boweles, Walterus Glene et Johannes de [Stevenache][140] non venerunt. Et vicecomes mandavit quod terre illorum penitus jacent frisse, per quod non sunt manucapti neque districti veniendi ad hunc diem. Et preceptum est ei quod ipsos distringat ad reddendum sibi ad opus Regis predicto denarios et eos habeat coram etc. ad eundem diem vel corpora predictorum [tenencium][141] etc.

(737)

Lond'. Meyr filius Jacobi attachiatus ad respondendum Regi una cum Henna que fuit uxor Jahu judei pro transgressione monete dampnati de .xxviij. marcis quas eadem Henna recepit de Poncio de la More pro vadio quod idem Poncius predicto Jahu invadiavit ante quam predictus Jahu captus fuit pro retonsura monete Regis pro qua suspensus fuit et pro qua transgressione [predicte][142].xxviij. marce quas prefatus Poncius solvit predicte Henne sunt Regi forisfacte.

Predicta Henna venit et dicit quod non recepit de predicto Poncio pro vadio quod predicto Jahu quondam viro suo invadiavit nisi .xix. marcas quas tradidit predicto Meyr salvo custodiendas etc.

Predictus Meir venit et recognovit se recepisse de predictis denariis per manum predicte Henne decem marcas quas idem Jahu ei assignavit custodiendas ad promocionem filii predicti Jahu et quod non plures denarios inde recepit ponit se super patriam. Et patria venit per Manserum filium Aron, Cok' filium Hagini, Gamaliel de Oxon', Ysac le Eveske, Sampsonem de Rayley, Elis de Cornhull, Dyey le Eveske, Josceum de North', Manserum la Pape, Abraham Gurgayn, Manserum le Eveske et Sampsonem de Hereford', qui dicunt super sacramentum suum quod predicta Henna recepit de predicto Poncio .xxviij. marcas pro vadio predicto Jahu, ut predictum est, invadiato, de quibus .xix. marce devenerunt ad manum predicti Meyr ex

135 *MS. repeats.* 136 *Cf. no. 697.* 137 *MS. omits.*
138 *MS. reads* dampnati.

139 *MS. reads* recipientes. 140 *MS. reads* Sevenache.
141 *MS. reads* tenensium. 142 *MS. reads* predicti.

tradicione predicte Henne, videlicet decem marce quas predictus Meyr prius recognovit se recepisse et .ix. marce quas predicta Henna ei tradidit de quibus nullam recognicionem fecit. Et quod predicta [Henna] penes se retinuit .ix. marcas de predictis .xxviij. marcis et eas concelavit. Et quia predictus Meyr predictas decem marcas de bonis predicti Jahu judei dampnati recepit, ut recognovit, et predictas .ix. marcas concelabat, sicut convictum est per juratores predictos, post communem inhibicionem per Regem inde factam quod nullus bona seu catalla judeorum dampnatorum sub periculo vite, membrorum et amissionis omnium bonorum suorum [concelaret][143] set eam monstraret certis personis ad hoc deputatis ad certum tempus inde provisum, ideo consideratum est quod omnia catalla predicti Meyr sunt Regi forisfacta et corpus ejus committitur constabulario Turris Lond' custodiendum in prisona donec Rex voluntatem suam de eo mandaverit. Et predicta Henna committitur constabulario de Turri London' in prisona custodienda donec Regi de predictis .ix. marcis et concelamento earundem satisfecerit etc.

(738)

Linc'. Memorandum quod Abr' Culle per consideracionem curie regis etc. abjuravit villam Linc' a die lune proxima ante festum sancti Petri ad Vincula in septem annis sequentibus pro transgressione monete, nisi interim graciam habuerit de domino Rege.

143 *MS. reads* conselaret.

MICHAELMAS TERM, 8/9 EDWARD I [1280]

Exchequer of Jews, Plea Roll No. 53 [E 9/53]

This is a single but relatively long membrane of memoranda from a Roll whose other membranes do not survive. It is not certain for which of the court's justices it was made.

MEMBRANE 1

Adhuc memoranda de termino sancti Michaelis anno regni regis Edwardi octavo

(739)

Norht'. Preceptum fuit vicecomiti quod distringeret Willelmum de Pelvile et Margeriam uxorem ejus per terras etc. ad respondendum Regi de diversis bonis et catallis que fuerunt Isac de Lon' judei dampnati que devenerunt ad manus ipsorum Willelmi et Margerie. Et vicecomes mandavit quod predictus Willelmus mortuus est et quod Willelmus de Upton' et Reginaldus filius Gervasii le Laver manuceperunt predictam Margeriam, quam non habuerunt. Ideo in misericordia. Judicium, sicut alias, quod distringat per terras etc., ita quod nec ipa etc., et quod de exitibus etc., et quod habeat corpus ejus coram etc. a die sancti Martini in .xv. dies ad respondendum etc. et ad audiendum etc. Et preceptum est vicecomiti quod venire faciat coram etc. ad eundem diem executores testamenti predicti Willelmi ad respondendum Regi una cum predicta Margeria de predictis bonis et catallis etc.

(740)[1]

Not'. Ranulphus de Huntyngfelt de comitatu Not' venit coram etc. et recognovit se debere Aaron filio Vyves judeo .c. quarteria frumenti, reddendo ad quindenam Purificacionis Beate Marie anno regni regis Edwardi nono.

(741)

Kanc'. Thomas Chycche de Kanc' venit coram etc. et recognovit se debere Aaron filio Vyves judeo .iij. marcas et dimidiam, reddendo ad Pentecosten anno regni regis Edwardi nono .xv. solidos .vj. denarios et ad festum sancti Michaelis proximo sequens .xv. solidos .vj. denarios et ad festum Pentecosten anno regni regis Edwardi decimo .xv. solidos .viij. denarios. Et, nisi fecerit, concedit quod de terris et catallis suis fiant etc.

[1] *This entry is marked for omission with the words* vacat quia alibi. *The marginal country has been altered, perhaps to or from* Norf'.

(742)

Kanc'. Thomas Chyche venit coram etc. et recognovit se debere Aaron filio Vyves sex marcas pro Willelmo le Duk de Kanc', reddendo unam marcam ad Pascham anno regni regis Edwardi nono; et ad festum sancti Johannis Baptiste proximo sequens unam marcam; et ad festum sancti Michaelis proximo sequens unam marcam; et ad Natale Domini anno regni regis Edwardi decimo unam marcam; et ad Pascham proximo sequens unam marcam; et ad festum sancti Johannis Baptiste proximo sequens unam marcam. Et, nisi fecerit, concedit quod de terris et catallis suis fiant etc.

(743)

Kanc'. Thomas Chyche venit coram etc. et recognovit pro Gilberto de Arderne se debere Aaron filio Vyves .xxvij. solidos, reddendo inde ad festum sancti Hillarii anno regni regis Edwardi nono .ix. solidos et ad Pascham proximo sequens .ix. solidos, et ad festum Nativitatis Sancti Johannis Baptiste proximo sequens .ix. solidos. Et, nisi fecerit, concedit quod de terris et catallis suis fiant etc.

(744)

Kanc'. Willelmus de Pouton' et Ricardus de Pouton' frater ejus recognoverunt se debere Batemin Benedicto .xx. quarteria frumenti vel pro quolibet quarterio dimidiam marcam reddendo ad Pascham anno nono. Et, nisi fecerint, concedunt quod de terris et catallis suis fiant.

(745)

Sussex'. Preceptum fuit vicecomiti, sicut pluries, quod de terris et catallis Johannis de Camoys fieri faceret centum solidos quos idem Johannes de Cameys recognovit se debere Johanni de Bayf', ita quod illos centum solidos haberet coram etc. Et vicecomes mandavit quod levavit centum solidos et eos liberavit Johanni de Bayfeld'. Et quia constat justiciariis quod per istud breve nullos denarios liberavit predicto Johanni de Bayfeld' seu per aliud breve sibi prius directum et retornatum in termino sancte Trinitatis proximo preterito, sicut satis liquet per retornum suum proprium indorsatum in eodem brevi de predictis .x. libris 'solvit ei centum solidos et non amplius', propter quod de istis residuis centum solidis levandis mandatum domini regis non est executus ipse vicecomes in misericordia, scilicet Nicholaus le Gras.[2] Et preceptum ei, sicut pluries, in octabis sancti Martini.

(746)

Warr'. Thomas Balaunce venit coram justiciariis etc. et recognovit se debere Samueli filio Joscei .j. marcam, reddendo inde dimidiam marcam ad octabas sancti Martini et dimidiam marcam ad octabas sancti Hillarii anno regni regis Edwardi nono. Et, nisi fecerit, concedit quod de terris et catallis suis fiant etc. Et pro hac recognicione idem Samuel concedit quod predictus Thomas quietus sit de omnibus debitis in quibus idem Thomas tenebatur Isac filo Joscei fratri suo judeo dampnato per talliam, ita quod ipse Samuel nec aliquis pro eo aliquid decetero exigere possit. Ad quas octabas sancti Martini Aaron filius Vyves venit coram etc. et recognovit se recepisse de predicto Thoma dimidiam marca pro predicto Samueli.

(747)

Warr'. Radulphus de Lymesi miles venit coram justiciariis etc. et recognovit se debere Samueli filio Joscei judeo sex marcas in quibus tenebatur Mosseo de Warr' filio Joscei fratri suo judeo dampnato per quoddam scriptum obligatorium inter predictos Radulphum et Mosseum judeum confectum reddendo eidem Sam' a die Pasche in .xv. dies. Et, nisi fecerit, concedit quod de terris et catallis suis fiant etc.

(748)

Oxon' Berk'. Johannes Alisoundre venit coram justiciariis etc. et recognovit se debere Josceo filio Abrahe judeo .xx. solidos et Johannes Hereward de Thacham venit coram etc. et recognovit se debere eodem Josceo .xx. solidos, reddendo eidem judeo ad octabas Purificacionis Beate Marie anno regni regis Edwardi nono. Et, nisi fecerint, concedunt quod de terris et catallis suis fiant etc.

(749)[3]

Kanc'. Willelmus Peverel pro Radulpho filio Henrici de la Wodegate venit coram justiciariis etc. et recognovit se debere Aaron filio Vyves .c. solidos, reddendo .ij. marcas et dimidiam in octabis Pasche anno regni regis Edwardi nono et ad festum sancti Johannis Baptiste proximo sequens .ij. marcas et et dimidiam et ad festum sancti Michaelis proximo sequens .ij. marcas et dimidiam. Et, nisi fecerit, concedit quod de terris et catallis suis fiant etc.

(750)

Oxon'. Henricus Symeon venit coram etc. et recognovit se debere Aaron filio Vyves .lx. solidos, reddendo .xx. solidos ad festum sancti Hyllarii anno regni regis Edwardi nono, et ad Pascha proximo sequens .xx. solidos, et ad festum sancti Michaelis proximo sequens .xx. solidos. Et, nisi fecerit, concedit quod de terris et catallis suis fiant etc.

(751)

Essex'. Preceptum fuit vicecomiti quod appreciari faceret omnia catalla Rogeri de Assewell' mobilia et extendi faceret omnes terras et tenementa predicti Rogeri, excepto capitali mesuagio suo etc. Et vicecomes mandavit quod catalla predicti Rogeri mobilia appreciata fuerunt ad .xj. solidos et terre ejusdem Rogeri, videlicet .clx. acre terre arabilis, [extenduntur] ad quinque marcas, acra ad .v. denarios. Preceptum est vicecomiti quod seysinam medietatis catallorum et predictarum terrarum habere faciat Isac filio Urselli judeo vel ejus nuncio pro .iiij. libris in quibus ei tenetur per cyrographum .xij. librarum, unde altera pars est in archa cyrographariorum Colecestr', ut dicit etc.

(752)

Essex'. Memorandum quod terre Johannis Carnice excepto capitali mesuagio suo, videlicet due acre terre arabilis, medietas terrarum predicti Johannis, extenduntur ad .viij. denarios per annum, sicut patet inter inquisiciones hujus termini retornatas. Et preceptum est vicecomiti quod Vives filio Mossei de Clare judeo vel ejus nuncio habere faciat seisinam medietatis predictarum terrarum pro .iiij. marcis in quibus idem Johannes predicto judeo tenetur per cyrographum nostrum etc.

(753)

Lync'. Preceptum fuit vicecomiti quod non omitteret propter libertatem de Bollyngbrok quin eam etc. et de terris et catallis Henrici le Coylter fieri faceret valorem unius sacci bone lane de Lyndes' de partibus de Kyrkeby et illum liberaret Johanni de Bayfeld' etc. Et vicecomes nondum levavit nisi medietatem ejusdem lane, ut Johannes dicit. Ideo preceptum est vicecomiti quod non omitteret etc. et quod de terris et catallis ipsius Henrici levari faciat valorem medietatis predicte lane, et eam habeat coram etc. in crastino sancti Nicholai predicto Johanni liberandum etc.

(754)

Suff' Essex'. Eadmundus de Hemegrave miles de comitatu Suff', Robertus le Norreys et Johannes de Walkefare de comitatu Essex' venerunt coram etc. et recognoverunt se debere Aaron filio Vyves judeo ducentas marcas, reddendo ad quindenam Pasche anno regni regis Edwardi nono. Et, nisi fecerint, concedunt quod de terris et catallis suis fiant etc. et quod idem Aaron capiat se ad quemcumque illorum Edmundi, [Johannis][4] et [Roberti][5] voluerit de toto predicto debito vel parte ejusdem debiti. Et per hanc recognicionem idem Aaron

2 *The word* misericordia *is repeated in the margin.*
3 *Cf. No. 774 below.*
4 *MS. reads* Johannes.
5 *MS. reads* Robertus.

concedit quod post decessum ipsius Johannis Walkefare predicti Edmundus, Robertus et eorum heredes quieti sint de predicto debito, salvo suo recuperare versus heredes, tenentes terrarum dicti Johannis vel alterum eorum. Et si iidem Edmundus et Robertus decesserint ante predictum Johannem vel post, ipsi Edmundus et Robertus et eorum heredes quieti sint de toto predicto debito. Et quod idem Aaron habeat suum recuperare versus predictum Johannem vel heredes et tenentes terrarum suarum, si idem Johannes decessit ante solucionem predicti debiti.

(755)

Norff'. Jordanus Foliot et Willemus Foliot venerunt coram justiciariis etc. et recognoverunt se debere Aaron filio Vyves judeo .x. saccos lane, reddendo eidem Aaron a die Pasche in .xv. dies anno regni regis Edwardi nono vel pro quolibet sacco .x. marcas et est in eleccionem predicti judei se capere de toto predicto debito vel [partem][6] predicti debiti, utrum voluerit, ad predictum Jordanum vel predictum Willelmum. Et, nisi fecerint, concedunt quod de terris et catallis suis fiant etc.

(756)

Wygorn'. Preceptum fuit vicecomiti quod distringeret Symonem de Throkemerton' et Willelmum Jordan de Norton' per terras ad reddendum sibi ad opus Regis .v. marcas quas Regi debent de debitis Isac filii Leonis de Polet judei dampnati; et quod distringeret Johannem de Bradecote eodem modo pro .iiij. marcis quas Regi debet de debitis Mossei filii Leonis judei dampnati; et denarios illos haberet coram etc. ad hunc diem. Et vicecomes mandavit quod retornavit breve sibi inde directum balliivis libertatis episcopi de Oswaldeslawe pro predictis Simone et Johanne, qui nichil inde fecerunt. Judicium quod non omittat propter libertatem predictam etc. et distringat predictos Willelmum et Johannem per terras etc. pro predictis denariis, et eos habeat coram etc. in octabis sancti Hyllarii Regi solvendum etc. Et vicecomes mandavit quod de bonis et catallis Willelmi Jordan levari fecit .j. marcam quam idem vicecomes, videlicet Thomas de Neuton', in pleno scaccario solvit Aaron filio Vyves judeo et sic inde quietus est et quam marcam idem Aaron recepit in partem solucionis et recompensacionis debitorum in quo Gilbertus Pecche ei tenebatur etc.[7] Et preceptum est eidem vicecomiti quod distringat predictum Willelmum una cum predicto Simone ad reddendum sibi ad opus Regis residuum predicti debiti ab ipsis petiti, ut supra etc.

(757)

Memorandum quod Belya que fuit uxor Jacobi de Glouc' venit coram etc. et liberavit Johanni de Watel' custodi auri Regine matris Regis pro auro suo duo debita, unum centum solidorum sub nominibus Johannis de Berclyve et Belie de Glouc', et aliud .v. marcarum sub nominibus Willelmi de Middilton' et dicte Belye. Et predicta Belya concedit quod, nisi predicta debita sunt bona et clara, quod dicta Regina habeat recuperare suum versus eandem Belyam de aliis catallis suis de debitis in quibus predicte domine Regine pro auro suo tenebatur.

[6] *MS. omits.*

[7] *In the margin is written* pro Willelmo Jordan .j. marca soluta quam Aaron filius Vyves recepit ut infra.

MEMBRANE 1 DORSE

(758)

Sutht'. Johannes de Insula venit coram etc. et recognovit se debere Aaron filio Vyves judeo .xxx. saccos lane vel .x. marcas pro quolibet sacco, reddendo eidem judeo infra mensem Pasche anno regni regis Edwardi nono. Et, nisi fecerit, concedit quod de terris et catallis suis fiant etc.

(759)

Essex'. Magister Henricus Sampson clericus venit coram etc. et recognovit se debere Aaron filio Vyves judeo London' .xxx. quarteria frumenti vel dimidiam marcam pro quolibet quarterio, reddendo eidem judeo a festo Purificacionis Beate Marie Virginis anno regni regis Edwardi nono. Et, nisi fecerit, concedit quod de terris et catallis suis fiant etc.

(760)

Surr'. Johannes de Wauton' venit coram etc. et recognovit se debere Aaron filio Vyves judeo quadraginta libras, reddendo eidem judeo a festo Purificacionis Beate Marie in .xv. dies. Et, nisi fecerit, concedit quod de terris et catallis suis fiant etc.

(761)

Oxon'. Willelmus de la Ryvere venit coram etc. et recognovit se debere Aaron filo Vyves judeo .lxiij. marcas, reddendo inde eidem judeo ad .xv. Pasche anno regni regis Edwardi nono .xxv. marcas et ad festum sancti Nicholai anno regni regis Edwardi decimo .xxiij. marcas. Et, nisi fecerit, concedit quod de terris et catallis suis fiant etc. Et per istam recognicionem dictus Willelmus quietus est de duobus debitis in quibus tenebatur Isac de Polet et Bonevye de Oxon' [judeis][8] dampnatis, videlicet de uno debito .iiij.^{xx} quarteriorum frumenti sub nominibus dictorum Willelmi de Isac; et de uno debito .lx. quarteriorum frumenti sub nominibus predictorum Willelmi et Bonevye, sicut continetur in rotulis de scaccario judeorum de recognicionibus, que quidem debita assignantur predicto Aaron per regem in recompensacionem debitorum in quibus Gilbertus Pecche eidem Aaron tenebatur etc.

(762)

Sussex'. Rogerus la Warre filius Johannis la Warre miles venit coram etc. et recognovit se debere Aaron filio Vyves

[8] *MS. reads* judei.

judeo pro quibusdam debitis in quibus tenebatur Aaron Crespin et Isac le Eveske judeis dampnatis, que quidem debita assignantur eidem Aaron filio Vyves in recompensacionem etc., et pro .xx. marcis quas recepit de eodem Aaron de mutuo, centum et sexdecim marcas reddendo ad quindenam Pasche anno regni regis Edwardi nono. Et, nisi fecerit, concedit quod de terris et catallis suis faint etc. Et per istam recognicionem predictus Rogerus quietus est de predictis debitis in quibus tenebatur predicto Aaron Crespin et Isac le Eveske et .xx.marcis de mutuo. Idem Aaron habet litteram obligatoriam predicti Rogeri de dicto debito centum et sexdecim marcarum que, facta solucione dicti debiti, debet adnichilari.

(763)

Oxon'. Willelmus de Skelbrok' venit coram etc. et recognovit se debere Aaron filio Vyves judeo .v. marcas et decem solidos, reddendo ad festum sancti Martini anno regni regis Edwardi octavo. Et, nisi fecerit, concedit quod de terris et catallis suis fiant etc.

(764)

Warr'. Robertus de Hasteng' de comitatu Warr' venit coram etc. et recognovit se debere magistro Elia filio magistri Mossei et Aaron filio Vyves judeis seccies viginti libras sterlingorum, reddendo die sancti Hyllarii anno regni regis Edwardi nono. Et, nisi fecerit, concedit quod de terris et catallis suis fiant etc.

(765)

Suff'. Simon filius Petri de Ryssingge, Johannes Crowe miles et Johannes de la Hen venerunt coram etc. et recognoverunt se debere Aaron filio Vyves judeo .xxiiij. libras reddendo eidem Aaron quinquaginta solidos ad quindenam Pasche anno regni regis Edwardi nono, et quinquaginta solidos ad quindenam sancti Michaelis proximo sequentem, et sic de anno in annum, termino in terminum centum solidos per annum ad eosdem terminos donec predicte .xxiiij. libre persolvantur. Et licet predicto Aaron se capere ad quemcumque illorum voluerit de toto predicto debito vel parte dicti debiti. Et, nisi fecerint, concedunt quod de terris et catallis suis fiant etc.

Et predictus Simon de Ryssingge nomine suo tantummodo fecit predicto Aaron quoddam scriptum obligatorium de quodem debito quod prefatus Aaron penes se habet. Et pro ista recognicione venit predictus Aaron coram etc. et liberavit predicto Simoni unam cartam .xxiiij. librarum sub nominibus predicti Simonis et Abrahe filii Deulecres judei, quam cartam predictus Aaron habuit de thesauro in recompensacionem etc. in pleno scaccario quiete dampnatam etc.

(766)

Kanc'. Rogerus de Thoketon' venit coram etc. et per scriptum obligatorium recognovit se teneri Mancero filio Aaron judeo Lon' in sexcies viginti quarteriis frumenti precii cujuslibet quarterii dimidie marce, reddendo predicta sexviginti quarteria frumenti ad terminos subscriptos, videlicet .xxx. quarteria ad festum Nativitatis Sancti Johannis Baptiste annno regni regis Edwardi nono, et .xxx. quarteria ad Natale Domini proximo sequens; et sic de anno in annum usque ad plenariam solucionem tocius frumenti predicti vel valorem. Et, nisi fecerit, concedit quod de terris et catallis suis fiant etc.

(767)

Wyltes'. Preceptum fuit vicecomiti quod venire faceret coram etc. Johannem Wasce filium Nicholai Wace, qui habet terras in villa de Paulton' extra Marleberge, ad respondendum Regi una cum Johanne Wayce de Heynton' de decem libris que Regi debentur de debito Isac de Suwerk' judei. Et Johannes Wace de Heynton', qui se dicit in predicto debito non teneri, venit et optulit se versus predictum Johannem filium Nicholai Wace. Et ipse non venit. Et vicecomes mandavit quod retornavit breve sibi inde directum ballivis libertatis de Salkel', qui nichil inde fecerunt. Judicium quod non omittat propter libertatem predictam etc. et venire faciat coram etc. a die sancti Martini in .xv. dies predictum Johannem filium Nicholai Wasce ad respondendum Regi etc. una cum predicto Johanne Wasce de Heynton', qui habet eundem diem de eodem debito etc.

(768)

Wiltes'. Preceptum fuit vicecomiti quod distringeret Johannem de Burle, tenentem terrarum que fuerunt Henrici de Burle, per terras etc. ad reddendum sibi ad opus Regis .iiij. libras quas Regi debet occasione terrarum etc. de debitis Isac de Sobber' judei, et denarios illos haberet coram etc. vel corpus predicti Johannis ad ostendendum etc. Et vicecomes mandavit quod Rogerus Chis, Hugo Pyge, Henricus Mercator et Rogerus Dicun, Johannes Elys et Ricardus Dybbe manuceperunt predictum Johannem, quem non habuerunt. Ideo in misericordia.[9] Et preceptum est vicecomiti, sicut alias, quod distringat predictum Johannem per terras etc. ad reddendum sibi predictas .iiij. libras et eas habeat coram etc. a die sancti Martini in .xv. dies Regi solvendum etc.

(769)

Memorandum quod Robertus de Wymton' clericus vicecomitis [Linc'][10] venit in pleno scaccario et solvit .v. marcas de decem marcis quas recognivit se levasse de bonis et catallis Ade del Hospital de debito magistri Nicholai de Wadyngham per summonicionem scaccarii judeorum et residuum, videlicet .v. marcas, solvet ad scaccarium Pasche. Et preceptum est vicecomiti quod ipsum Adam in pace permittat etc.

(770)

Somers' Dors'. Preceptum fuit vicecomiti quod de bonis et catallis Briani de Gouyz, tenentis quandam partem

9 *The word* misericordia *is repeated in the margin.*
10 *MS. reads* Lenc'.

terrarum que fuerunt Willelmi de Middelton', fieri faceret ad opus Aaron filii Vyves judei decem marcas quas idem Aaron per [consideracionem][11] curie regis versus predictum Brianum recuperavit et denarios illos haberet coram etc. Et vicecomes mandavit quod retornavit breve sibi inde directum ballivis libertatis Glaston' et Somerton', qui nichil inde responderunt. Judicium quod non omittat propter libertates predictas etc. et de bonis et catallis predicti Briani fieri faciat predictas decem marcas et eas habeat coram etc. predicto judeo solvendum.

(771)

Kanc'. Willelmus Payforer miles venit coram justiciariis etc. et recognovit se debere Johanni de Goshalm pro acquietacione Judaismi quam ei fecit decem marcas, reddendo in crastino Beate Katerine Virginis anno regni regis Edwardi nono, sicut continetur in quodam scripto obligatorio, quod predictus Johannes penes se habet de predicto debito. Et, nisi fecerit, concedit quod de terris et catallis suis fiant etc.

(772)

Oxon'. Rogerus de Martivaus tulit breve regis de magno sigillo in hec verba: 'Edwardus dei gracia etc. justiciariis suis ad custodiam judeorum assignatis salutem. Cum magister Rogerus de Martivaus dudum per scriptum suum Bonevite quondam judeo nostro Oxon', qui pro transgressione monete nostre suspensus fuit, in viginti marcis, quas idem judeus ei mutuaverat, se obligavit, ac ipse eidem judeo novem marcas in partem solucionis debiti illius solverit et solucionem inde factam legittime probaverit coram nobis, et Aaron filius Vyves judeo Edmundi fratris nostri, cui bona et catalla que fuerunt predicti Bonevite tanquam nobis forisfacta concessimus, et qui inter bona et catalla scriptum illud habet ex concessione predicta, de residuo ejusdem debiti satisfacere sit paratus, sicut dicit, vobis mandamus quod, vocato coram vobis prefato Aaron, si predictus Rogerus eidem Aaron de residuo debiti predicti satisfacere voluerit, tunc ipsum judeum ad restitucionem scripti illius dicto Rogero facere, prout justum fuerit, compellatis et, facta eidem judeo de residuo debiti predicti plena solucione, eundem Rogerum de toto debito predicto quietum esse faciatis. Teste me ipso apud Westm' .vj. die Novembris anno regni nostri octavo.'

(773)

Kanc'. Willelmus Peverel recognovit se debere Aaron filio Vives.[12]

(774)[13]

Kanc'. Willelmus Peverel pro Radulpho filio Henrici de la Wodegate recognovit se debere Aaron filio Vives .c. solidos, reddendo .ij. marcas et dimidiam in octabis Pasche anno regis Edwardi nono, et ad festum sancti Johannis Baptisthe proximo sequens .ij. marcas et dimidiam, et ad festum sancti Michaelis proximo sequens .ij. marcas et dimidium.

(775)

Warr'. Robertus de Hasteng recognovit se debere eidem Aaron et magistro Elia occies viginti libras, reddendo die sancti Hillarii anno nono.

(776)

Wilt'. Willelmus Paynel recognovit se debere eidem Aaron et magistro Elia .cc. quarteria frumenti vel dimidiam marcam etc., reddendo in septimana Pasche anno regis Edwardi nono. Et nisi etc.

(777)

Norht'. Willelmus de Duston recognovit eidem .xxx. libras, reddendo in quindenam Pasche anno regis Edwardi nono.

(778)

Linc'. Prior de Spalding recognovit eidem .viij. libras, reddendo medietatem ad Pascham proximo futurum et aliam medietatem ad festum sancti Michaelis proximo sequens.

On the attached cover is *Essonia .viij. E. j* and below in a contemporary hand is written *Essonia Placita et Memoranda in scaccarium judeorum anno regni regis Edwardi filii regis Henrici viij. Michaelis.*

[11] *MS. reads* consuetudinem.

[12] *This entry is unfinished.*

[13] *Compare no. 749.*

EASTER TERM, 9 EDWARD I [1281]

Exchequer of Jews, Plea Rolls Nos. 37 and 66 [E 9/37 and 66]

There are two surviving rolls for Easter term 1281. One must have been made for the senior justice, Hamon Hauteyn, and the other for his colleague, Robert of Ludham, but it is uncertain which is which. For some time prior to 1975 these two separate rolls plus a single membrane from a roll for the following Trinity term were united in a single composite Roll 37. In 1975 they were again separated into their constituent parts. Membranes 11-21 of the composite roll now form Roll 66 and membrane 5 of that roll is now membrane 12 of Roll 38. Membranes 1-4 of Roll 37 retain their original references: membranes 6-10 are now membranes 5-9 of Roll 37.

For the purposes of this edition Roll 66, the fuller of the two rolls, has been taken as the main text with any significant variants from the version given in Roll 37 noted in the footnotes. At the end of the transcript of Roll 66 will be found a transcript of such entries as are found only in Roll 37.

The headings and contents of the individual membranes of Roll 37 is as follows:

membrane 1: *Adhuc de termino Pasche anno regni regis nono*
entries 1-6: no overlap with entries on Roll 66 and all printed below as nos. 1029-34
entry 7: no. 986 as printed from Roll 66, membrane 10

membranes 1d and 2: no heading
no overlap with entries on Roll 66 and all printed below as nos. 1035-61

membrane 2d: blank

membrane 3: *Essonia ad scaccarium judeorum de quindena Pasche anno regni regis E. nono*
entries 1-3: nos. 878-80 as printed from Roll 66, m. 5
entry 4: not on Roll 66 and printed below as no. 1062

membrane 3d: no heading
no overlap with entries on Roll 66 and all printed below as nos. 1063-7

membrane 4: *Memoranda de termino Pasche anno regis E. nono*
entry 1: not on Roll 66 and printed below as no. 1068
entry 2: no. 932 as printed from Roll 66, m. 7d
entries 3-4: nos. 990-1 as printed from Roll 66, m. 10
entry 5: not on Roll 66 and printed below as no. 1069
entries 6-7: nos. 992-3 as printed from Roll 66, m. 10
entries 8-10: nos 906-8 as printed from Roll 66, m. 6d
entry 11: no. 922 as printed from Roll 66, m. 7
entry 12: not on Roll 66 and printed below as no. 1070

membrane 4d: *Adhuc memoranda*
entry 1: no. 995 as printed from Roll 66, m. 10d
entries 2-4: not on Roll 66 and printed below as nos. 1071-3 [though note that these entries seem to belong to Trinity term]

membrane 5: *Placita de termino Pasche anno regni regis E. nono*
entries 1-3: nos. 941-3 as printed from Roll 66, m. 8
entry 4: no. 985 as printed from Roll 66, m. 10
entry 5: no. 944 as printed from Roll 66, m. 8
entries 6-7: nos. 946-7 as printed from Roll 66, m. 8

membrane 5d: *Adhuc memoranda*
entries 1-7: nos. 949-55 as printed from Roll 66, m. 8d

membrane 6: *Memoranda de termino Pasche Pasche anno regni regis E. nono de quindena*
entries 1-8: nos. 1001-1008 as printed from Roll 66, m. 11
entry 9: no. 1010 as printed from Roll 66, m. 11
entry 10: no. 1011 (cancelled entry) as printed from Roll 66, m. 11 or no. 909 as printed from Roll 66, m. 6d

membrane 6d: *Adhuc memoranda de quindena Pasche*
entry 1: no. 1012 as printed from Roll 66, m. 11
entry 2: no. 1014 as printed from Roll 66, m. 11d
entries 3-8: nos. 1016-21 as printed from Roll 66, m. 11d
entry 9: no. 810 as printed from Roll 66, m. 2

membrane 7: *Starra de termino Pasche anno regni regis E. nono*
entries 1-10: nos. 846-55 as printed from Roll 66, m. 4
entry 11: not on Roll 66 and printed below as no. 1074
entry 12: no. 858 as printed from Roll 66, m. 4
entry 13: not on Roll 66 and printed below as no. 1075
entry 14: no. 856 as printed from Roll 66, m. 4
entries 15-17: nos. 866-8 as printed from Roll 66, m. 4d

membrane 7d: *Adhuc starra de termino Pasche anno regni regis E. ix^o^* [1]
Single entry: no. 871 as printed from Roll 66, m. 4d

membrane 8: *Recogniciones de termino Pasche anno regis E. nono*

[1] *At the bottom of this membrane is the contemporary note* Rotuli de termino Pasche anno regni regis E. nono, nono, nono, nono, nono.

entries 1-2: not on Roll 66 and printed below as nos. 1076-7
entries 3-4: nos. 1024-5 as printed from Roll 66, m. 11d
entry 5: no. 919 as printed from Roll 66, m. 7
entry 6: no. 931 as printed from Roll 66, m. 7d
entry 7: no. 934 as printed from Roll 66, m. 7d
entries 8-9: nos. 936-7 as printed from Roll 66, m. 7d

membrane 8d: blank

There are no equivalent entries on Roll 37 to the following entries on Roll 66

membranes 1-1d: all entries [nos. 779-805]

membrane 2: nos. 806-09, 811

membranes 2d, 3 and 3d: all entries [nos. 812-45]

membrane 4: nos. 857, 859-61

membrane 4d: nos. 862-5, 869-70, 872-7

membrane 5: no. 881

membranes 5d and 6: all entries [nos. 882-905]

membrane 6d: nos. 910-12

membrane 7: nos. 913-18, 920-1, 923-7

membrane 7d: nos. 928-30, 933, 935, 938-40

membrane 8: nos. 945, 948

membrane 8d: nos. 956-8

membranes 9 and 9d: all entries [nos. 959-80]

membrane 10: nos. 981-4, 987-9

membrane 10d: nos. 994, 996-1000

membrane 11: nos. 1009, 1013

membrane 11d: nos. 1015, 1022-3, 1026-8

ROLL 66

MEMBRANE 1

Adhuc placita de termino Pasche anno regni regis Edwardi nono

(779)

Buk'. Agnes que fuit uxor Johannis le Sauvage per breve regis de compoto fecit venire Aliciam de Luton' et Willelmum filium ejus tenentes duas virgatas terre in villa de Hertwell' de terris dicte Agnetis pro .xj. libris .iij. solidis de porcione ipsam Agnetem contingente de quodam debito .xl. marcarum in quo Willelmus de Hertwelle tenebatur Mosseo filio Isac judeo per cartam suam, cujus judei dicti Willelmus et Alicia attornati sunt, quousque etc., et petit quod cum ea computent eo quod multo magis receperunt de exitibus predictarum terrarum quam de jure deberent; et petit ab eis restitucionem dictarum terrarum cum pertinenciis et id quod ultra predictam summam .xj. librarum .iij. solidorum inde receperunt occasione porcionis ipsam de dicto debito contingentis.

Predictus Willelmus de Luton' venit et dicit quod nichil de dicta terra tenet nec aliquid inde tenere clamat, vivente predicta Alicia matre sua. Et predicta Alicia venit et dicit quod dictam terram tenet pro debitis in quibus predictus Willelmus de Hertwell' predicto Mosseo tenebatur ex dimissione domine A. regine Anglie consortis regis nunc ad voluntatem ejus, sine qua respondere non potest; et protulit inde litteram domine regine patentem, in qua continetur quod dictas terras dicte Alicie commisit quamdiu sibi placuerit. Et dictum est prefate Agneti quod sequatur versus predictam dominam Reginam, si sibi viderit expedire, ad graciam suam super hiis optinendam.

(780)

Suff'. Herveus de Heggesete et Ricardus de Kokefeld', executores testamenti Roberti de Norton', optulerunt se quarto die versus Henricum Brun, coexecutorem dicti testamenti, de placito acquietacionis debiti. Et ipse non venit. Et preceptum fuit vicecomiti, sicut pluries, quod non omitteret propter libertatem sancti Edmundi quin eam etc. et distringeret predictum Henricum per terras etc., et quod haberet corpus ejus coram etc. Et vicecomes mandavit quod Johannes Faber de Sancto Edmundo, Hugo de Cressyngham, Johannes de Ryseby de Sancto Edmundo, Walterus le Keu de Pakenham, Rogerus le Ko de eadem, Johannes de More de eadem, Johannes Buk' de Ryseby et Rogerus le Taylur de eadem manuceperunt predictum Henricum, quem non habuerunt. Ideo in misericordia.[2] Judicium, sicut pluries, a die sancti Johannis Baptiste in .xv. dies.

(781)

Suff'. Robertus de Broghton', clericus de scaccario etc., optulit se quarto die versus Adam filium Willelmi de Houton' de placito debiti. Et ipse non venit. Et preceptum fuit vicecomiti quod ipsum venire faceret. Et vicecomes mandavit quod predictus Adam clericus est et non habet laycum feodum per quod possit distringi. Ideo mandatum est episcopo Norwyc' quod ipsum venire faciat etc. a die sancte Trinitatis in .xv. dies etc.

(782)

Norff', Suff'. Robertus de Ludham optulit se quarto die versus Bartholomeum Flehund de placito compoti. Et ipse non venit. Et preceptum fuit vicecomiti quod ipsum venire faceret. Et vicecomes mandavit quod predictus Bartholomeus non fuit inventus in balliva sua post

[2] *The word* misericordia *is repeated in the margin.*

recepcionem istius brevis. Ideo, sicut alias, a die sancte Trinitatis in .xv. dies.

(783)

Norff'. Suff'. Johannes de Axebrigge optulit se quarto die versus Leticiam que fuit uxor Walteri Esman de Magna Gernem' et Johannem filium et heredem dicti Walteri de placito debiti. Et ipsi non venerunt. Et preceptum fuit vicecomiti quod ipsos venire faceret. Et vicecomes mandavit quod Johannes filius Walteri Aysman de Gernem', Nicholaus Everard de Ormesby, Willelmus Abbot de eadem et Henricus le Wylde de eadem manuceperunt predictam Leticiam; et quod Radulfus Franceys de Gernem', Reginaldus Aysman de eadem, Galfridus de Wykhampton' et Robertus del Chaump de eadem manuceperunt predictum Johannem; quos non habuerunt. Ideo in misericordia.[3] Judicium quod distringat per terras etc., ita quod nec ipsi etc., et quod de exitibus etc., et quod habeat corpora eorum coram etc. a die sancte Trinitatis in .xv. dies ad respondendum etc., et ad audiendum etc.

(784)

Norff'. Isac de Storteford' judeus, qui tulit breve regis de placito injuste detencionis catallorum super Johannem Bonde, Thomam de la Hagh', Margeriam uxorem ejus, Simonem le Toteler, et Isabellam que fuit uxor Rogeri le Rus, non est prosecutus versus eos. Ideo ipse pro se et plegiis suis de prosequendo in misericordia.[4]

(785)

Kanc'. Johannes Malemeyn [i]<filius et heres Henrici Malemeyns>[i] optulit se quarto die versus Rogerum de Tylemanston, Loram uxorem ejus et Nicholaum le Bret, executores testamenti Henrici Malemeyns, de placito aquietancie debiti. Et ipsi non venerunt. Et preceptum fuit vicecomiti quod salvo custodiret etc. terras etc., et quod haberet corpora eorum coram etc. ad hunc diem. Et vicecomes mandavit quod senescallus libertatis archiepiscopatus Cant', cui istud breve retornatum fuit, respondit quod Willelmus de Tydindon', Radulfus Textor, Andreas de Tylemanston', Henricus le Peyntur, Robertus frater ejus et Andreas Stace manuceperunt predictos Rogerum et Loram et Nicholaum, quos non habuerunt. Ideo in misericordia. Judicium, sicut alias, quod salvo custodiat etc. et quod habeat corpora eorum coram etc. in octabis sancte Trinitatis ad respondendum etc. et ad audiendum etc. Et nulli sunt exitus predictarum terrarum etc.

(786)

Essex. Johannes de Karmvyle, qui tulit breve regis de placito debiti super Eliam de Pelheye, Radulfum filium Fulconis et alios in brevi, non est prosecutus versus eos. Ideo in misericordia.[5]

(787)

Glouc'. Alexander de Authno optulit se quarto die versus Johannem, filium et heredem Bartholomei de Sully, et executores predicti Bartholomei, quondam coexecutoris testamenti Johannis la Ware, de placito acquietancie debiti. Et ipsi non venerunt. Et preceptum fuit vicecomiti quod ipsos venire faceret. Et vicecomes mandavit quod breve inde sibi directum adeo tarde venit quod exequi non potuit. Ideo, sicut alias, in octabis sancte Trinitatis. Et Godefridus de Acre, qui presens fuit, et Rogerus Barbastre,[6] coexecutores testamenti predicti Johannis, per essoniatorem suum habent eundem diem de eodem placito.

(788)

Linc'. Saunte de Linc' judeus optulit se quarto die versus Brianum de Herdeby de placito debiti. Et ipse non venit. Et preceptum fuit vicecomiti, sicut alias, quod ipsum distringeret per terras etc., et quod haberet corpus ejus coram etc. a die Pasche in unum mensem nunc. Et vicecomes mandavit quod Willelmus prepositus de Querington', Alexander filius Simonis de eadem, Radulfus filius Radulfi de eadem, et Robertus ad Portam Ecclesie manuceperunt predictum Brianum, quem non habuerunt. Ideo in misericordia.[7] Judicium quod salvo custodiat terras etc., et si plures etc., et quod de exitibus etc. a tempore quo primo etc. Et quod habeat corpus ejus coram etc. a die sancti Johannis Baptiste in .xv. dies ad respondendum etc., et ad audiendum etc. Et sunt exitus terrarum predicti Briani .xx. solidi. Et preceptum est vicecomiti quod eos habeat coram etc. ad hunc diem.

(789)

Linc'. Saunte de Linc' judeus optulit se quarto die versus Debbe filium Johannis de Thornhawe et Agnetem uxorem ejus de placito debiti. Et ipsi non venerunt. Et preceptum fuit vicecomiti, sicut alias, quod ipsos distringeret per terras etc. et quod haberet corpora eorum coram etc. ad hunc diem. Et vicecomes mandavit quod Thomas Oxebely de Linc', Johannes de Thornhawe de eadem, Hugo de Bliton' de eadem, et Thomas de Bliton' de eadem manuceperunt predictos Dobbe et Agnetem, quos non habuerunt. Ideo in misericordia.[8] Judicium quod salvo custodiat etc., et si plures etc., et quod de exitibus etc. et quod habeat corpora eorum coram etc. a die sancti Johannis Baptiste in .xv. dies ad respondendum etc. et audiendum etc. Et nulli sunt exitus etc.

(790)

Bed', Buk'. Benedictus de Bed' et Belya de eadem judei optulerunt se quarto die versus Warinum de Dene et Simonem de Perteshull' de placito debiti. Et ipsi non venerunt. Et preceptum fuit vicecomiti quod ipsos distringeret per terras etc. et quod haberet corpora eorum coram etc. ad hunc diem. Et vicecomes mandavit

[3] *The word* misericordia *is repeated in the margin.*
[4] *The word* misericordia *is repeated in the margin.*
[5] *The word* misericordia *is repeated in the margin.*
[6] *Followed in MS. by* per essoniatorem.
[7] *The word* misericordia *is repeated in the margin.*
[8] *The word* misericordia *is repeated in the margin.*

quod Radulfus le Noreys de Dene et Galfridus Batecok' de eadem manuceperunt Warinum de Dene; et quod Flor' ballivus de Eynden et Henricus de Fraxino manuceperunt Simonem de Perteshull', quos non habuerunt. Ideo in misericordia.[9] Judicium, sicut alias, quod distringat per terras etc., et quod habeat corpora eorum coram etc. a die sancti Johannis Baptiste in .xv. dies ad respondendum etc., et ad audiendum etc.

(791)

Warr'. Ricardus de Turbervyle optulit se quarto die versus Nicholaum Syfrewast de placito acquietancie debiti. Et ipse non venit. Et preceptum fuit vicecomiti, sicut alias, quod salvo custodiret terras etc. et quod haberet corpus ejus coram etc. ad hunc diem. Et vicecomes mandavit quod omnes terre etc. per que distrinxit predictum Nicholaum salvo custodivit etc. set nichil respondit de exitibus [i]<nec de manucaptoribus.>[i] Ideo ipse vicecomes, scilicet [blank], in misericordia. Et mandavit quod predictus Nicholaus habet plures terras in balliva sua infra libertatem honoris Leyc' et retornavit breve ballivis libertatis predicte, qui nichil inde responderunt. Judicium quod non omittat propter libertatem etc. quin eam etc. et salvo custodiat etc. et quod habeat corpus ejus coram etc. a die sancti Johannis Baptiste in .xv. dies ad respondendum etc., et ad audiendum etc.

(792)

Oxon', Berk'. Sampson de Wygorn' optulit se quarto die versus Ricardum le Porter de castro Oxon' de placito transgressionis. Et ipse non venit. Et preceptum fuit vicecomiti quod ipsum distringeret per terras etc. et quod haberet corpus ejus coram etc. ad hunc diem. Et vicecomes mandavit quod predictus Ricardus amotus est de custodia porte castri Oxon' et amplius non moratur in balliva sua nec corpus ejus fuit inventus in balliva sua post recepcionem brevis. Ideo, sicut alias, a die sancti Johannis Baptiste in .xv. dies etc.

MEMBRANE 1 DORSE

Adhuc Placita

(793)

Oxon'. Josceus de Newebery judeus, qui tulit breve regis super Basiliam que fuit uxor Ricardi de la Wyke de placito debiti, non est prosecutus versus eam. Ideo in misericordia.[10] Et Jacobus filius Mildegode et Josceus filius Abrahe, plegii sui de prosequendo, quia non habuerunt predictum Josceum, in misericordia.[11]

(794)

Oxon'. Meyr de Brug' judeus, qui tulit breve regis super Thomam le Orfevre de Oxon' de placito transgressionis, non est prosecutus versus eum. Ideo in misericordia.[12] Et Salomon de Bristoll' et Benedictus de Norwyco, plegii sui de prosequendo, quia non est prosecutus in misericordia.[13]

(795)

Oxon'. Abraham filius Dyey judeus, qui tulit breve regis super Johannem de Langheton de placito transgressionis, non est prosecutus versus eum. Ideo ipse Abraham pro se et plegiis suis de prosequendo in misericordia.[14]

(796)

Oxon'. Henricus de Shotebroke, tenens quandam partem terrarum que fuerunt Simonis de Ordeston', optulit se quarto die versus Hugonem filium et heredem predicti Simonis de placito debiti. Et ipse non venit. Et preceptum fuit vicecomiti quod ipsum venire faceret etc. Et vicecomes mandavit quod returnavit breve inde sibi directum ballivis Willelmi de Valence de Schrivenham, qui nichil inde fecerunt. Judicium quod non omittat propter libertatem etc., et venire faciat coram etc. predictum Hugonem in crastino sancti Johannis Baptiste ad respondendum etc.

(797)

Ebor'. Mosseus filius Urselli optulit se quarto die versus Jacobum de Lexynton' de placito acquietance debiti. Et ipse non venit. Et preceptum fuit vicecomiti <quod>[15] ipsum venire faceret. Et vicecomes mandavit quod Johannes Knot et Willelmus de Tocwyth manuceperunt predictum Jacobum, quem non habuerunt. Ideo in misericordia.[16] Judicium quod distringat per terras etc., ita quod nec ipse etc., et quod de exitibus etc., et quod habeat corpus ejus coram etc. a die sancti Michaelis in .xv. dies ad respondendum etc. et ad audiendum etc.

(798)

Lond'. Manserus filius Aaron judeus optulit se quarto die versus Deuteytum Guylelme, tenentem partem terrarum que fuerunt Ade de Novo Mercato, de placito debiti. Et ipse non venit. Et preceptum fuit vicecomitibus Lond' quod ipsum venire facerent etc. Et vicecomes mandavit quod Clerekinus filius Lini [i]<et>[i] Tholustan' de Florenc' mercator manuceperunt predictum Deuteytum, quem non habuerunt. Ideo in misericordia.[17] Judicium quod distringat per terras etc., ita quod nec ipse etc., et quod habeant corpus ejus coram etc. in octabis sancte Trinitatis etc. ad respondendum etc., et ad audiendum etc.

[9] *The word* misericordia *is repeated in the margin.*
[10] *The word* misericordia *is repeated in the margin.*
[11] *The word* misericordia *is repeated in the margin.*
[12] *The word* misericordia *is repeated in the margin.*
[13] *The word* misericordia *is repeated in the margin.*
[14] *The word* misericordia *is repeated in the margin.*
[15] *MS. repeats.*
[16] *The word* misericordia *is repeated in the margin.*
[17] *The word* misericordia *is repeated in the margin.*

(799)

Sutht'. Rogerus de Flete, serviens de scaccario etc., optulit se quarto die versus Johannem atte Mershe de Andevere de placito debiti. Et ipse non venit. Et preceptum fuit vicecomiti, sicut alias, quod ipsum distringeret per terras etc., et quod haberet corpus ejus coram etc. Et vicecomes mandavit quod Robertus le Mouner, Thomas Fromund', Walterus le Tryl', Henricus Senat, Henricus Auvile et Galfridus Syfrich' manuceperunt predictum Johannem, quem non habuerunt. Ideo in misericordia.[18] Judicium, sicut pluries, quod distringat per terras etc., et quod habeat corpus ejus coram etc. in crastino sancti Johannes Baptiste ad respondendum etc. et ad audiendum etc.

(800)

Sutht'. Pucele que fuit uxor Deules' de Basing' judea optulit se quarto die versus Walterum atte Brigge de Basynge, Blissotam uxorem ejus, Johannem Sauvage de Basingstoke et Johannem de Haywode de placito debiti et injuste detencionis catallorum. Et ipsi non venerunt. Et preceptum fuit vicecomiti quod ipsos venire faceret ad hunc diem. Et vicecomes mandavit quod Henricus Crede, Radulfus le Beste, Ricardus Crocard et Willelmus Wytfet manuceperunt predictos Walterum et Blissotam, quos non habuerunt. Ideo in misericordia.[19] Judicium quod distringat per terras etc., ita quod nec ipsi etc., et quod de exitibus etc., et quod habeat corpora eorum coram etc. a die sancte Trinitatis in .xv. dies ad respondendum etc., et ad audiendum etc. Et vicecomes mandavit quod Johannes le Sauvage et Johannes de Haywode non fuerunt inventi in balliva sua post recepcionem istius brevis. Ideo, sicut alias, ad eundem diem etc.

(801)

Rotel'. Elias de Denecastre et Belassez uxor eius optulerunt se quarto die versus Ricardum, filium et heredem Johannis de Middelton', de placito debiti. Et ipse non venit. Et preceptum fuit vicecomiti quod ipsum venire faceret ad hunc diem etc. Et vicecomes mandavit quod Ricardus Erl de Bissebroc et Jordanus ad Crucem de eadem manuceperunt predictum Ricardum de Middelton', quem non habuerunt. Ideo in misericordia.[20] Judicium quod distringat per terras etc., ita quod nec ipse etc., et quod de exitibus etc., et quod habeat corpus ejus coram etc. in octabis sancti Johannis Baptiste ad respondendum etc., et ad audiendum etc.

(802)

Surr'. Gamaliel de Oxon' judeus optulit se quarto die versus Willelmum de Hevre et Matildam uxorem ejus, tenentes quosdam redditus qui fuerunt Johannis de Kaumvyle, de placito debiti, unde inquisicio. Et prediciti Willelmus et Matilda veniunt et inquisicio non venit. Ideo datus est dies partibus a die sancte Trinitatis in .xv. dies. Et preceptum fuit vicecomiti quod distringeret Johannem de Bures et alios juratores dicte inquisicionis per terras etc., sicut patet inter brevia hujus termini retornata. Et vicecomes mandavit quod Johannes le Strut et Ricardus Godsweyn manuceperunt Johannem de Bures; et quod Johannes le Bult et Ricardus le Coc manuceperunt Hugonem de la Lane; et quod Ricardus de la Hoke et Johannes Chalvesfles manuceperunt Johannem le Frilend; et quod Robertus le Fowel et Ricardus le Scut manuceperunt Walterum le Scut; et quod Johannes atte Laneende et Willelmus atte Lanende manuceperunt Radulfum Symund; et quod Nicholaus Kupping' et Johannes le Kak manuceperunt Robertum le Kake; et quod Petrus le Tollere et Petrus le Rede manuceperunt Petrum le Blench; et quod Gilbertus atte Wode et Radulfus atte Wode manuceperunt Henricum atte Wode; et quod Henricus le Leche et Johannes Symple manuceperunt Thomam le Leche; et quod Walterus Beneyt et Thomas le Leche manuceperunt Petrum le Moyne; et quod Willelmus Bolle et Willelmus de Westm' manuceperunt Gilbertum le Cartere; et quod Radulfus le Chechere et Willelmus Chiverel manuceperunt Thomam Aldwyne; et quod Willelmus de Slifeld' et Willelmus Clericus manuceperunt Thomam Attehale; quos non habuerunt. Ideo in misericordia.[21] Judicium, sicut alias, quod distringat per terras etc. et quod habeat corpora eorum coram etc. a die sancte Trinitatis in .xv. dies ad recognoscendum etc., et ad audiendum etc. Et nulli sunt exitus, prout vicecomes significavit.

(803)

Hertff'. Prior Sancte Trinitatis Lond', tenens quandam partem terrarum que fuerunt Roberti de la Rokele, attachiatus ad respondendum Belassez que fuit uxor Leonis filii Preciose de placito debiti una cum Ricardo de la Rokele tenente quandam partem predictarum terrarum, qui habuit eundem diem, non venit. Ideo predictus prior in misericordia pro pluribus defaltis.[22] Et Johannes Kamp', Johannes Derkesale, Johannes de aqua de Brath' et Thomas de Aqua, plegii predicti prioris de veniendo, quia ipsum non habuerunt sicut manuceperunt, in misericordia.[23] Et sunt exitus terrarum dicti prioris .v. solidi, de quibus vicecomes respondebit.

Willelmus Paynot, tenens quandam partem predictarum terrarum, attachiatus pro eodem placito non venit. Ideo ipse Willelmus pro pluribus defaltis in misericordia.[24] Et Stephanus de Wabbadon' de Pelham, Ricardus Haldon de eadem, Ricardus Atte Heye et Robertus Rangho manuceperunt predictum Willelmum, quem non habuerunt. Ideo in misericordia.[25] Et sunt

18 *The word* misericordia *is repeated in the margin.*
19 *The word* misericordia *is repeated in the margin.*
20 *The word* misericordia *is repeated in the margin.*
21 *The word* misericordia *is repeated in the margin.*
22 *The word* misericordia *is repeated in the margin.*
23 *The word* misericordia *is repeated in the margin.*
24 *The word* misericordia *is repeated in the margin.*
25 *The word* misericordia *is repeated in the margin.*

exitus terrarum dicti Willelmi .ij. solidi, de quibus vicecomes respondebit etc.

Willelmus Bercarius attachiatus pro eodem placito ut supra non venit. Ideo in misericordia.[26] Et Willelmus de la Rokele de Bordisden', Ricardus de la Rokele, Petrus de Hormade et Ricardus le Here manuceperunt predictum Willelmum, quem non habuerunt. Ideo in misericordia.[27] Et nulli sunt exitus terrarum dicti Willelmi.

Willelmus de la Rokele attachiatus pro eodem, ut supra, non venit. Ideo in misericordia.[28] Et Willelmus de Bordisden', Petrus de Hormade, Ricardus le Hore et Ricardus de la Rokele manuceperunt Willelmum de la Rokele, quem non habuerunt. Ideo in misericordia.[29]

(804)

Norht'. Josceus filius Sauloti judeus fecit venire Johannem le Megre, tenentem quandam partem terrarum que fuerunt Henrici le Escot, et exigit ab eo .xx. solidos de catallo quos ei debet occasione terrarum etc. per cyrographum, unde altera pars est in archa cyrographariorum Lond' ut dicit.

Et predictus Johannes venit et petit auditum brevis; et, lecto brevi, non exigit per breve nisi .xviij. solidos, et dictus Johannes petit inde judicium. Et quia predictus Josceus non concordat in peticione cum brevi suo, ideo consideratum est quod predictus Johannes quantum ad hoc breve eat sine die; et predictus Josceus pro superflua peticione in misericordia.[30]

Johannes le Megre pro pluribus defaltis in misericordia.[31]

(805)

Idem Josceus optulit se quarto die versus Adam le Mazerer, tenentem quamdam partem terrarum que fuerunt predicti Henrici, de placito debiti. Et ipse non venit. Et preceptum fuit vicecomiti, sicut alias, quod ipsum distringeret per terras etc., et quod haberet corpus ejus coram etc. Et vicecomes mandavit quod Adam nichil habet in balliva sua per quod possit distringi nisi quandam parvam domum que vix sufficit ad redditum capitalis domini nec fuit inventus in balliva sua post recepcionem istius brevis. Ideo, sicut alias, a die sancti Johannis in .xv. dies etc.

MEMBRANE 2

Adhuc placita de termino Pasche anno regis Edwardi ix°

(806)

Surr', Sussex. Josceus filius Vyves et Samuel Motun judei, qui tulerunt breve regis de placito transgressionis super Robertum le Talyur de Northyham et Johannem de la Porte, non sunt prosecuti. Ideo predicti judei in misericordia.[32] Et Mosseus de Doggestrate et Sampson de Sydyngburn', plegii sui de prosequendo, quia non habent, in misericordia.[33]

(807)

Bed', Buk'. Hugo de Culeworth' per attornatum suum optulit se quarto die versus Walterum de Gayton' de placito acquietancie debiti. Et ipse non venit. Et preceptum fuit vicecomiti quod non omitteret propter libertatem Leyc' quin eam etc. et de bonis et catallis dicti Walteri fieri faceret ad opus Regis .xx. libras de quibus acquietare deberet predictum Hugonem per recognicionem etc. de debitis Benedicti de Linc' judei, et denarios haberet coram etc. in crastino Ascensionis Domini nunc. Et vicecomes mandavit quod predictus Walterus nichil habet in balliva sua citra autumpnum de quo aliqui denarii levari possint. Et preceptum est, sicut alias, quod non omittat etc. a die sancti Michaelis in .xv. dies etc.

(808)

Lond'. Johannes de Axebrigge, serviens Roberti de Ludham, optulit se quarto die versus Walterum de Oxon' alutarium de placito transgressionis. Et ipse non venit. Et preceptum fuit vicecomitibus quod ipsum venire facerent etc. Et vicecomes mandavit quod Willelmus de Undelye et Walterus de Staundon' manuceperunt predictum Walterum, quem non habuerunt. Ideo in misericordia.[34] Judicium quod distringat per terras etc., et quod habeat corpus ejus coram etc. in octabis sancti Johannis Baptiste ad respondendum etc. et ad audiendum etc.

(809)

Leyc'. Preceptum fuit vicecomiti quod distringeret Gerardum de Hamelton' et tenentes terrarum suarum ad reddendum Regi .x. libras de debitis Elie filii Manseri judei dampnati. Et Rogerus de Somervyle, tenens terrarum que fuerunt dicti Gerardi, venit coram etc. et recognovit se debere de dicto debito .vij. libras, que assignantur Aaron filio [Vives][35] in recompensacionem [etc.,][36] quas recognovit se recepisse; et de residuis .lx. solidis habuit aquietanciam per starrum dicti judei quod idem judeus fecit dicto Gerardo tempore quo habuit liberam administracionem bonorum suorum. Et hoc petit verificare. Et preceptum fuit vicecomiti quod venire faciat coram etc. a die sancti Michaelis in .xv. dies sex probos et legales homines de villa Staunff' et sex legales judeos de eadem villa ad recognoscendum etc. Et quia constabularius Staunff' returnum brevis regis admittere recusat nec vicecomitem ingredi permittit, facta fuit inquisicio per Haginum filium Bateman de Staunff',

[26] *The word* misericordia *is repeated in the margin.*
[27] *The word* misericordia *is repeated in the margin.*
[28] *The word* misericordia *is repeated in the margin.*
[29] *The word* misericordia *is repeated in the margin.*
[30] *The word* misericordia *is repeated in the margin.*
[31] *The word* misericordia *is repeated in the margin.*
[32] *The word* misericordia *is repeated in the margin.*
[33] *The word* misericordia *is repeated in the margin.*
[34] *The word* misericordia *is repeated in the margin.*
[35] *MS. omits.*
[36] *MS. omits.*

Benedictum Bonamy et Samuelem de eadem, Isac le Evesk' et Saulot' le Petit judeos Lond'. Qui dicunt super sacramentum suum quod starrum quod Rogerus de Somervyle protulit coram etc. in hec verba 'Elias filius Manseri recognovit per starrum suum quod recepit .lx. solidos de quodam debito .x. librarum quod est sub nominibus Gerardi de Hamelton' et predicti Elie filii Manseri in archa cyrographariorum apud Staunff' et quod dictos denarios recepit die sancti Michaelis anno regis Edwardi vj^{to}' fuit factum dicti Elie tempore quo habuit liberam administracionem bonorum suorum quia fuit ante capcionem judeorum Anglie pro transgressione monete. Ideo consideratum est quod predictus Rogerus de dicto debito .x. librarum sit quietus, et carta ejusdem debiti liberatur eidem Rogero quiete dampnata.

(810)

Norff'. Cum Alicia que fuit uxor Clementis de <Poringlond'>[37] districta fuisset pro .xl. solidis ad opus regis de debito Gente que fuit uxor Dyey filii Deulecres, eadem Alicia venit et clamat habere quietanciam de predicto debito per quoddam starrum coram etc. in hec verba: 'Jacobus filius Jurnini et Senior le Eveske judei testantur quod Gente de Glouc' concedit quod Alicia que fuit uxor Clementis de Poringlond' et heredes sui quieti sunt de ipsa et heredibus suis de omnibus demandis, calumpniis et plegiagiis a creacione seculi usque ad Pentecosten anno regis Edwardi quarto. Et si aliquis judeus homo vel femina aliquid exigat vel calumpnietur versus predictam Aliciam occasione alicujus debiti quam eidem Gente debebat a principio seculi usque ad predictum festum Pentecostes super predictam Gentam est acquietare defendere et warantizare. Et quod eadem Genta spontanea voluntate recognovit, predicti judei testantur et sigillaverunt.' Et quod istud starrum est factum predicte Gente et tempore quo habuit liberam administracionem de bonis et catallis suis illud fecit, petit quod inquiratur. Ideo preceptum est vicecomiti quod venire faciat coram etc. [in octabis sancte Trinitatis][38] <sex probos et legales homines et sex legales judeos>[39] de civitate Norwyc' ad recognoscendum etc., nisi interim H. Hauteyn etc. Postea capta fuit dicta inquisicio apud Norwyc' die martis proxima post festum sancte Trinitatis per Simonem le Palmer, Isac filium Joscei et alios. Qui dicunt super sacramentum suum quod predictum starrum est factum ipsius Gente et per voluntatem ipsius factum fuit tempore quo habuit liberam administracionem bonorum suorum. Ideo datus est dies ei ad audiendum judicium suum in octabis sancte Trinitatis. Ad quem diem predicta Alicia venit per Willelmum de <Gelverton'>[40] attornatum suum et petit judicium suum. Et quia constat per predictam inquisicionem quod predicta Alicia quieta est de predicto debito per predictum starrum quod est factum ipsius Gente et debito tempore factum, consideratum est quod predicta Alicia de predicto debito .xl. solidorum recedat quieta. <Et quod carta dicti debiti ei liberetur quiete dampnata.>[41]

(811)

Norff', Suff'. Ricardus Ille tulit breve regis de magno sigillo in hec verba: 'Edwardus etc. justiciariis suis ad custodiam judeorum assignatis salutem. Monstravit nobis Ricardus Ille quod, cum ipse dudum per scriptum suum se obligaret Isac filio Benedicti judeo, qui pro transgressione monete nostre suspensus fuit, in .xl. quarteriis frumenti eidem reddendis in solucionem octo librarum quas idem judeus pro eo solvisse debuerat Martino del Hill quondam mercatori Burdeg' defuncto, cui idem Ricardus in eodem debito tenebatur, ac idem judeus de debito illo prefato mercatori nichil solverit nec ipsum Ricardum juxta convencionem inter eos factam inde acquietaret, vos nihilominus predictas octo libras vice predicti frumenti tanquam nobis inter cetera bona et catalla que fuerunt dicti judei forisfactas a prefato Ricardo ad opus nostrum exigi et ipsum ea occasione distringi faciatis minus juste. Et quia ei injuriari nolumus in hac parte vobis mandamus quod, audita super hoc querela prefati Ricardi et veritate inde plenius inquisita, si vobis legittime constare possit ita esse tunc ab exaccione quam prefato Ricardo fieri faciatis pro predicto debito desistentes ipsum inde quietum esse faciatis, districcionem si quam eidem Ricardo ea occasione fieri feceritis relaxantes eidem. Teste me ipso apud Westm' .vj. die Novembris anno regni nostro octavo.' Per hoc breve preceptum est vicecomiti quod venire faciat coram etc. .xij. probos et legales homines, per quos etc., a die sancti Michaelis in tres septimanas, nisi R. de Ludham prius etc., ad recognoscendum etc. Et interim coram predicto R. capta fuit inquisicio inde per sacramentum Johannis le Bulur, Henrici le Day, Joscei de Dereham, Radulfi de Dunton', Willelmi Thebaud, Thome Caune, Rogeri Fidyen, Rogeri le Bulur, Huberti le Taverner, Johannis de Sybeton, Walteri Ade et Gilberti le Taverner. Qui dicunt super sacramentum suum quod predictus Ricardus Ille obligavit se predicto judeo in predictis .xl. quarteriis frumenti per sic quod idem judeus ipsum acquietaret erga predictum Martinum de predictis .viij. libris. Et dicunt quod predictus judeus ipsum inde non acquietavit nec eidem mercatori aliquem denarium pro ipso Ricardo solvit. Dicunt enim quod priusquam predictus mercator in partes Anglie venisset, predictus judeus captus fuit et imprisonatus pro transgressione monete pro qua suspensus fuit.

MEMBRANE 2 DORSE

(812)

Kanc'. Preceptum fuit vicecomiti quod de bonis et catallis Andree de Elham fieri faceret ad opus Isac le Eveske judei Lond' .xviij. solidos quos ei debet per

[37] Poringlong *37*.
[38] *Supplied from 37*.
[39] .vj. christianos, .vj. judeos *37*.
[40] Helverton *37*.
[41] *37 omits.*

recognicionem etc. Et vicecomes [mandavit quod][42] nulla habet bona vel catalla unde aliqui denarii fieri possint citra autumpnum. Ideo preceptum est ei, sicut alias, in octabis sancti Michaelis etc.

(813)

Hereff'. Preceptum fuit vicecomiti quod de terris et catallis Nicholai Wrmel' fieri faceret ad opus Regis .v. marcas quas Regi debet de debitis Isac de Suthwek' judei; et denarios haberet coram etc. Et vicecomes venit et protulit dimidiam marcam et dicit quod citra autumpnum plures denarios levare non potest,[43] de quibus solvit in recepta regis .xx. denarios unde habet talliam et dicto Isac solvit .v. solidos unde habet starrum. Et sic dictus vicecomes inde quietus est. Et preceptum est, sicut alias, a die sancti Michaelis in .xv. dies etc.

(814)

Lond'. Preceptum fuit vicecomitibus quod de bonis et catallis Rogeri de Wynton' clerici fieri facerent ad opus Isac le Eveske .l. solidos, qui ei aretro sunt de .c. solidis quos recognovit etc. pro Waltero de Saunford', et denarios haberent etc. Et vicecomites mandaverunt quod predictus Roger districtus est per bona et catalla sua nec nullum invenerunt adhuc emptorem. Ideo, sicut alias, a die sancti Johannis in .xv. dies etc.

(815)

Kanc'. Willelmus de Poton' venit coram etc. et recognovit per scriptum suum obligatorium se debere Elie filio Cressei filio Gente .xxx. quarteria frumenti [i]<vel dimidiam marcam pro quarterio,>[i] reddendo in crastino Exaltacionis Sancte Crucis anno regis Edwardi .ix.^{o}. Et, nisi fecerit, concedit quod de terris et catallis suis fiant. Postea dictus judeus venit et recognovit predictum debitum esse quietum.

(816)

Hereff'. Preceptum fuit viecomiti quod de terris et catallis Willelmi Deveroys, Rogeri Springehose, Rogeri Tyrel, Johannis de Baskervyle, Gilberti de Bosco et Walteri Tyrel fieri faceret ad opus Johannis de Pyccheford .xij. marcas que ei aretro sunt de .xx. marcis annuis de quodam debito .cc. et .xl. marcarum quas eidem Johanni debent per recognicionem etc. Et vicecomes mandavit quod de bonis et catallis Willelmi Deveroys levare fecit .v. marcas quas liberavit Mathulino attornato dicti Johannis et sic inde quietus est. Et mandavit quod Rogerus Springhose, Johannes de Baskervile et Walterus Tyrel nichil habent in balliva sua per quod etc. Et quod Gilbertus de Bosco manet infra libertatem Leomenistr' et ballivi ejusdem libertatis nichil inde respondent. Judicium quod non omittat etc. a die sancti Johannis in .xv. dies etc.

[42] *MS. omits*

[43] *Followed by* citra autumpnum.

(817)

Salop'. Preceptum fuit vicecomiti quod de bonis et catallis predictorum Willelmi, Rogeri et aliorum supradictorum fieri faceret ad opus dicti Johannis .xxv. marcas que sibi restant de dicto debito, et denarios haberet coram etc. Et vicecomes [i]<nichil>[i] mandavit nec breve inde retornavit. Ideo sicut alias a die sancti Johannis Baptiste in .xv. dies. Et vicecomes sit etc.

(818)

Norff'. Preceptum fuit vicecomiti quod per sacramentum proborum etc. de visneto de Harpele extendi faceret omnes terras et tenementa que Johannes de Harpele, abbas de Crek', Reginaldus rector ecclesie de Massingham, Willelmus Stag', David de la Grene, Adam Bonet, Robertus de Suanting' de Houton', Hugo de la Mare de Massingham et Odo filius Willelmi de Harpele tenent de terris et tenementis que fuerunt Willelmi filii Gilberti de Harpele, quid et quantum etc., et extentam etc. scire faceret justiciariis etc. Et vicecomes mandavit quod Johannes de Harpele tenet inde quatuor acras terre et valent per annum .ij. solidos; abbas de Crek tenet .j. acram et valet per annum .vj. denarios; rector ecclesie de Massingham tenet .ij. acras et j rodam et dimidiam terre et valent per annum .xij. denarios; item Willelmus Stag' tenet inde .iiij. acras et dimidiam et .j. rodam et valent per annum .ij. solidos .iiij. denarios; David de la Grene tenet inde .ij. acras et dimidiam et .j. rodam et valent per annum .xv. denarios; Adam Bonet tenet inde .ij. acras et tres rodas et valent per annum .xj. denarios; Robertus de Suatingh' tenet .iiij. acras et dimidiam et valent per annum .xviij. denarios; item Hugo de la Mare de Massingham tenet inde tres acras et dimidiam et valent per annum .vj. denarios; item Odo filius Willelmi de Harpele tenet .j. rodam et dimidiam et valent per annum .iij. denarios; Robertus Quityng tenet inde dimidiam acras et dimidiam rodam et valent per annum .j. denarium; Simon Nosse tenet .j. rodam terre et valet per annum .j. denarium; Willelmus de Harpele tenet tres acras et valent per annum .xviij. denarios; Johannes filius Willelmi de Harpele tenet inde .j. mesuagium et .ix. acras terre et dimidiam et valent per annum .ij. solidos; et quod venire faceret ad eundem diem predictos tenentes etc. ad respondendum Regi una cum Johanne de Harpele, qui habuit eundem diem, de .xx. libris quas Regi debet occasione terrarum predictorum de debitis Abrahe filii Deulecres judei.

Predicti Johannes de Harpele et alii tenentes veniunt et non dedicunt quin sint tenentes predictarum terrarum et vocant ad warrantum Johannem, filium et heredem Willelmi de Harpele, quod ipsos inde acquietare debet etc. Predictus Johannes, qui presens fuit, dicit quod non habet unde de predictis .xx. libris Regi possit satisfacere, cum non teneat de terris seu tenementis predictis nisi unum mesuagium et sex acras et dimidiam terre arabilis valoris supradicti; et petit quod predicti tenentes cum eo proporcionentur ad reddendum dictum debitum. Et predicti tenentes dicunt quod predictus Johannes satis habet de terris et tenementis predicti Willelmi patris sui unde ipsos acquietare potest, et petunt quod inquiratur. Et predictus Johannes dicit quod non habet unde ipsos acquietare possit et petit similiter quod inquiratur. Et preceptum est eidem Johanni et aliis tenentibus predictarum terrarum quod sequantur breve ad faciendum inquisicionem etc. in octabis sancti Johannis Baptiste ad recognoscendum etc., qui nullum breve exequebantur. Ideo consideratum est quod predicte .xx. libre inter eosdem tenentes proporcionentur, et quod prosequantur versus predictum Johannem quem vocant ad warantum quando sibi viderint expedire. Postea extenta terrarum et tenementorum Johannis filii Willelmi de Harpele in termino sancti Michaelis anno regis Edwardi .ix. incipiento .x.° retornata est et extenduntur terre et tenementa illa ad .viij. solidos .j. denarium. Et dictus Johannes et alii tenentes proporcionentur etc. in termino sancti Michaelis proximo sequenti, sicut patet ibidem inter memoranda etc.

MEMBRANE 3

Placita ad scaccarium judeorum de termino Pasche anno regis Edwardi nono. De Quindena Pasche.

(819)

Stuht'. Magister Radulfus salsarius domini regis optulit se quarto die versus Simonem de Wynton' et Beatriciam uxorem ejus de placito acquietancie redditus. Et ipsi non veniunt. Et preceptum fuit vicecomiti quod non omitteret propter libertatem prioratus Wynton' quin eam etc., et venire faceret coram etc. ad hunc diem predictos Simonem et Beatriciam. Et vicecomes mandavit quod Johannes atte Linnachre, Robertus de Cruce, Alexander atte Linnakere et Adam Leche manuceperunt predictos Simonem et Beatriciam, quos non habuerunt. Ideo in misericordia.[44] Judicium, sicut alias, quod non omittat etc., et distringat predictos Simonem et Beatriciam per terras etc., ita quod nec ipsi etc., et quod de exitibus etc. et quod habeat corpora eorum coram etc. in octabis sancte Trinitatis ad respondendum etc. et ad audiendum etc.

(820)

Suth'. Abraham filius Benedicti de Wynton' judeus optulit se quarto die versus Edmundum de Sutton' de placito transgressionis. Et ipse non venit. Et preceptum fuit vicecomiti quod ipsum venire faceret coram etc. ad hunc diem. Et vicecomes mandavit quod Willelmus Mogg' et Johannes Palmere manuceperunt predictum Edmundum, quem non habuerunt. Ideo in misericordia.[45] Judicium quod distringat per terras etc., ita quod nec ipse etc., et quod de exitibus etc., et quod habeat corpus ejus coram etc. in octabis sancte Trinitatis ad respondendum etc. et ad audiendum etc.

[44] *The word* misericordia *is repeated in the margin.*

[45] *The word* misericordia *is repeated in the margin.*

(821)

Norht'. Saulotus le Petit judeus et Blassa uxor ejus attachiati ad respondendum Ade de la Fermerye et Matilde uxori ejus de placito transgressionis et detencionis catallorum. Et unde queruntur quod, cum predicta Matilda venisset ad domum predictorum Sauloti et Blisse uxoris ejus die mercurii proxima ante festum Purificacionis beate Marie anno regni regis Edwardi octavo ad rogatum dicte Blisse pro quibusdam vasis argenteis venalibus emendum et secum detulisset sex marcas ad vasa illa legalia emendum, prefata Blissa porrexit predicte Matilde quasdam platas ex argento conflatas que suspecte fuerunt quod essent de retonsura monete, et, cum dicta Matilda hujusmodi mercimonia emere recusaret, predicta Blissa et alii judei ignoti predictam Matildam ceperunt, oppresserunt et predictas sex marcas ei abstulerunt et adhuc detinent ad dampnum suum centum solidorum et contra pacem etc. Et hoc offerunt etc.

Predicti Saulotus et Blissa veniunt et defendunt vim etc. et totum negant de verbo ad verbum, et dicunt quod predicta Matilda ad domum dicti Sauloti ad rogatum Blisse uxoris sue non venit ad aliquid ibidem emendum nec aliquid ab ea ibidem captum fuit seu oppressa fuit et hoc petunt quod inquiratur. Et predicti Adam et Matilda dicunt quod predictas sex marcas de dicta Matillide ceperunt et ipsam oppresserunt quia dictas platas emere recusavit et extra domum suam ipsam ejecerunt, sicut predictum est, et hoc petunt similiter quod inquiratur. Et preceptum est vicecomiti quod venire faciat coram etc. in octabis sancte Trinitatis sex probos et legales homines de villa Norht' et sex legales judeos, per quos etc., ad recognoscendum etc. Postea per licenciam justiciariorum concordati sunt sub hac forma, videlicet quod predictus Adam pro se et Matillide uxore sua perdonavit et remittit omnes exacciones, calumpnias et demandas quas habuit versus predictos Saulotum et Blissam uxorem ejus occasione dicte transgressionis seu detencionis catallorum seu quacumque alia causa usque diem lune proximam post festum sancti Luce evangliste. Et pro hac perdonacione et remissione dant predicti Saulotus et Blissa eidem Ade et Matillidi uxori ejus .lx. solidos, reddendo inde in vigiliam Natalis Domini anno regis Edwardi decimo quadraginta solidos et ad festum Purificacionis Beate Marie proximo sequens viginti solidos. Et, nisi fecerint, concedunt quod de terris et catallis suis fiant.

Iidem Saulotus et Blissa pro predicta transgressione in misericordia.[46]

(822)

Norht'. Belya que fuit uxor Pictavini judea per attornatum suum fecit venire Simonem filium Radulfi de Throp et exigit ab eo quinquaginta marcas occasione terrarum etc. que tenet que fuerunt predicti Radulfi patris sui, cui tradidit bona et catalla sua ad valenciam dictarum .l. marcarum et ea detinet ad dampnum suum etc.

[46] *The word* misericordia *is repeated in the margin.*

Predictus Simon venit et dicit quod est infra etatem et petit judicium si debeat respondere dum sit in custodia et infra etatem de aliquo debito patris sui. Et consideratum est quod non respondeat infra etatem et quod de hoc brevi [i]<interim>[i] eat sine die.

(823)

Linc'. Johannes Feg optulit se quarto die versus Haginum de Linc' judeum de placito compoti. Et ipse non venit. Et preceptum fuit vicecomiti quod ipsum distringeret per terras etc., et quod haberet corpus ejus coram etc. Et vicecomes mandavit quod Benedictus le Prestre, Elias filius Benedicti de Lond', Leo filius Sampsonis et Manser de Brauncegate manuceperunt predictum Haginum, quem non habuerunt. Ideo in misericordia.[47] Judicium, sicut alias, quod distringat per terras etc., et quod de exitibus etc., et quod habeat corpus ejus coram etc. in octabis sancte Trinitatis ad respondendum etc., et ad audiendum etc. de pluribus defaltis.

(824)

Hereff'. Sarra la Veve judea optulit se quarto die versus Lucam de Bergeveny, Dyonisiam uxorem ejus, Robertum de Daytesal et Agnetem uxorem ejus de placito injuste detencionis catallorum. Et ipsi non venerunt. Et preceptum fuit vicecomiti quod non omitteret propter libertatem Heref' quin eam etc., et ipsos venire faceret coram etc. ad hunc diem. Et vicecomes mandavit quod Willelmus Godknave et Reginaldus filius Marie manuceperunt predictum Lucam; et quod Henricus filius Dame et Johannes Hocche manuceperunt predictum Robertum; quos non habuerunt. Ideo in misericordia.[48] Judicium, sicut alias, quod non omittat etc. et distringat predictos Lucam et Robertum per terras etc., ita quod nec ipsi etc., et quod de exitibus etc., et quod habeat corpora eorum coram etc. in octabis sancte Trinitatis ad respondendum etc., et ad audiendum etc. Et quia vicecomes nichil respondit pro Dyonisia uxore dicti Luce nec pro Agnete uxore predicti Roberti, ideo ipse vicecomes, scilicet Rogerus de Burghull, in misericordia.[49]

(825)

Hereff'. Willelmus de la Haye optulit se quarto die versus Johannem Litfot de placito acquietancie debiti, et versus Thomam Hering' de Hereford' de placito quod ei reddat quoddam starrum de acquietancia debiti. Et ipsi non venerunt. Et preceptum fuit vicecomiti quod ipsos venire faceret ad hunc diem. Et vicecomes mandavit quod returnavit breve inde sibi directum ballivis libertatis de Heref', qui nichil inde fecerunt. Judicium quod non omittat propter libertatem etc., et venire faciat in octabis sancte Michaelis etc.

(826)

Hereff'. Johannes filius Eyr qui tulit breve regis super Hake de Brug' et Simonem generum dicti Hake de placito compoti petit licenciam recedendi de brevi suo et habet versus predictum Hake. Et predictus Hake, qui presens fuit, inde sine die.

Idem Johannes optulit se quarto die versus predictum Simonem de placito compoti. Et ipse non venit. Et preceptum fuit vicecomiti quod ipsum venire faceret. Et vicecomes mandavit quod Isac de Kaumpeden et Haginus de Webbele manuceperunt predictum Simonem, quem non habuerunt. Ideo in misericordia.[50] Judicium quod distringat per terras etc. et quod de exitibus etc., et quod habeat corpus ejus coram etc. in octabis sancte Trinitatis ad respondendum etc. et ad audiendum etc.

(827)

Kanc'. Jurninus filius Abrahe judeus optulit se quarto die versus Thomam de Ho et Johannem Russel de placito transgressionis. Et ipsi non venerunt. Et preceptum fuit vicecomiti quod ipsos distringeret per terras etc., et quod de exitibus etc., et quod haberet corpora eorum coram etc. ad hunc diem. Et vicecomes mandavit quod returnavit breve inde sibi directum ballivis civitatis Roff', qui nichil inde fecerunt. Judicium quod non omittat propter libertatem etc. quin eam etc. et distringat predictos Thomam et Johannem per terras etc., et quod habeat corpora eorum coram etc. in octabis sancte Trinitatis ad respondendum etc., et ad audiendum etc.

(828)

Kanc'. Gamaliel de Oxon' judeus optulit se quarto die versus Stephanum Gerard de placito debiti. Et ipse non venit. Et preceptum fuit vicecomiti, sicut alias, quod ipsum venire faceret. Et vicecomes mandavit quod Willelmus Erminard et Galfridus Lambert manuceperunt predictum Stephanum, quem non habuerunt. Ideo in misericordia.[51] Judicium quod distringat per terras etc., ita quod nec ipse etc. et quod de exitibus etc., et quod habeat corpus ejus coram etc. in octabis sancte Trinitatis ad respondendum etc. et ad audiendum etc.

(829)

Norff'. Johannes de Bayfeld per attornatum suum optulit se quarto die versus Reginaldum de Bynetre, Radulfum filium ejus et Henricum de Swanton' capellanum, executores testamenti magistri Thome de Bynetre, de placito debiti. Et ipsi non venerunt. Et preceptum fuit vicecomiti quod ipsos venire faceret. Et vicecomes mandavit quod returnavit breve inde sibi directum[52] Johanni de Fraxino, ballivo domini Johannis le Mareschal' de hundredo de Eynesford', qui nichil inde respondet. Judicium quod non omittat propter libertatem etc. quin eam etc. et

[47] *The word* misericordia *is repeated in the margin.*
[48] *The word* misericordia *is repeated in the margin.*
[49] *The word* misericordia *is repeated in the margin.*
[50] *The word* misericordia *is repeated in the margin.*
[51] *The word* misericordia *is repeated in the margin.*
[52] *Followed in MS. by* ballivo *which is marked for deletion.*

venire faciat coram etc. predictos Reginaldum, Radulfum et Henricum in octabis sancte Trinitatis ad respondendum etc.

(830)

Norff'. Hamo Hautein optulit se quarto die versus Johannem de Ryseby de placito compoti. Et ipse non venit. Et preceptum fuit vicecomiti, sicut pluries, quod ipsum venire faceret etc. Et vicecomes mandavit quod Adam filius Willelmi de Riseby, Rogerus Daniel de eadem, Rogerus Seward de eadem et Normannus filius Ade de eadem manuceperunt predictum Johannem, quem non habuerunt. Ideo in misericordia.[53] Judicium quod distringat per terras etc., ita quod nec ipse etc., et quod de exitibus etc., et quod habeat corpus ejus coram etc. in octabis sancte Trinitatis ad respondendum etc., et ad audiendum etc.

(831)

Norff'. Idem Hamo optulit se quarto die versus Adam le Especer [i]<de>[i] Lenn' de placito detencionis catallorum. Et ipse non venit. Et preceptum fuit vicecomiti quod non omitteret propter libertatem Roberti de Tatesal' quin eam etc., et venire faceret coram etc. ad hunc diem. Et vicecomes mandavit quod Eudo Cissor de Lenne, Willelmus de Lenne, Ricardus de Walton' de eadem, et Galfridus de Lamburn' de eadem manuceperunt predictum Adam, quem non habuerunt. Ideo in misericordia.[54] Judicium, sicut alias, quod non omittat propter libertatem etc. quin eam etc. et distringat per terras etc., et quod de exitibus etc., et quod habeat corpus ejus coram etc. ad respondendum etc. et ad audiendum etc.

(832)

Norff'. Radulfus de Chattegrave et Emma uxor ejus optulerunt se quarto die versus Rogerum filium Thome Syger de Owelton', Katerinam uxorem ejus et Robertum Ernald de placito transgressionis. Et ipsi non venerunt. Et preceptum fuit vicecomiti, sicut pluries, quod ipsos caperet et in prisona salvo custodiret, ita quod haberet corpora eorum coram etc. ad hunc diem etc. Et vicecomes mandavit quod predicti Rogerus, Katerina et Robertus non fuerunt inventi in balliva sua post recepcionem brevis. Ideo, sicut pluries, in octabis sancte Trinitatis etc.

(833)

Buk'. Josceus filius Joscei judeus per attornatum suum optulit se quarto die versus Ricardum de Wycumbe et Aliciam uxorem ejus de placito detencionis catallorum. Et ipsi non venerunt. Et preceptum fuit vicecomiti quod ipsos venire faceret. Et vicecomes mandavit quod returnavit breve inde sibi directum ballivis libertatis de Walyngf', qui nichil inde fecerunt. Judicium quod non omittat propter libertatem etc. quin eam etc. et venire faciat coram etc. in octabis sancte Trinitatis predictos Ricardum et Aliciam ad respondendum etc.

(834)

Essex. Abbas de Straff' pro pluribus defaltis versus magistrum Eliam in misericordia.

Magister Elias filius magistri Mossei per attornatum suum fecit venire abbatem de Stratford', tenentem quandam partem reddituum qui fuerunt Johannes le Rus, et exigit ab eo centum solidos occasione predictorum reddituum quos tenet qui fuerunt predicti Johannis, qui fuit vadium etc. secundum convencionem factam inter predictum Johannem et ipsum judeum per quoddam scriptum obligatorium.

Predictus abbas venit et petit diem premeditandi et habet in octabis sancti Michaelis.

MEMBRANE 3 DORSE

Adhuc placita de quindena Pasche

(835)

Norff'. Hugo de Chategrave et Emma uxor ejus optulerunt se quarto die versus Hugonem Tyrel et Radulfum de Ingheworth de placito transgressionis, unde jurata. Et ipsi non venerunt nec inquisicio venit. Et preceptum fuit viecomiti quod inquisicionem illam venire faceret coram etc. Et vicecomes mandavit quod Willelmus de Bosco de Blicling, Johannes Keye de eadem, Michaelis Lune de eadem, et Willelmus ad ecclesiam de eadem manuceperunt Thomam Bercham; et quod Johannes ad ecclesiam de Blicling, Johannes Keye de eadem, Robertus Ath... de eadem et Rogerus atte Montem de eadem manuceperunt Willelmum de Bosco; et quod Robertus Cok' de Blicling, Rogerus Cabbel de eadem, Reginaldus Weselinngh' de eadem et Robertus de Causton' de eadem manuceperunt Johannem ad ecclesiam; et quod Johannes Attehil de Blicling, Robertus Atteholf de eadem, Robertus Konyng' de eadem et Henricus Koning' de eadem manuceperunt Willelmum ad ecclesiam; et quod Willelmus de Holecroft de Itering, Ricardus Pistor de eadem, Willelmus Waryn de eadem et Walterus Joye de eadem manuceperunt Willelmum filium Eustachii; et quod Thomas de Itering', Willelmus Barth' de eadem, Willelmus Thomas de eadem et Adam Labbe de eadem manuceperunt Radulfum filium Ade; et quod Willelmus Tropet de Itering', Johannes Tropet de eadem, Godewynus Sheperd et Radulfus Carman de eadem manuceperunt Hugonem Attegrene; et quod Willelmus Brussel de Wykemere, Ricardus Goderich de eadem, Willelmus filius Ricardi de Wykemere et Willelmus Mercator de eadem manuceperunt Thomam Jay; et quod David le Muncy de Heydon', Robertus Skyrth', Ricardus Grut de eadem et Walterus Grut de eadem manuceperunt Everardum Levelok', et quod David le Muncy de Keydon', Walterus Grut de eadem, Hugo filius Matillidis de eadem et Simon [filius] Wlvive

[53] *The word* misericordia *is repeated in the margin.*

[54] *The word* misericordia *is repeated in the margin.*

de eadem manuceperunt Rogerum de Mortof; et quod Godefridus de Horsford' de Corpesty, Walterus Fles de eadem, Simon Habbe de eadem, Rogerus de Holowod de eadem manuceperunt Radulfum Godes; et quod Radulfus Godes de Corpesty, Simon Habbe de eadem et Rogerus de Holewod' de eadem et Walterus Fles de eadem manuceperunt Godefridus de Horsford; et quod Johannes Sping' de Calethorp, Thomas Jap de eadem, Robertus Spink' de eadem, et Robertus filius Letenc' de eadem manuceperunt Johannem Palewyc; et quod Johannes Tauke de Aleby, Andreas Brithmer de eadem, Johannes de Glanville de eadem et Adam Leman de eadem manuceperunt Robertum Grym; quos non habuerunt. Ideo in misericordia. Judicium quod predicti Thomas, Willelmus, et alii supradicti distringantur per terras etc., ita quod nec ipsi etc., et quod de exitibus etc., et quod habeat corpora eorum coram etc. in octabis sancte Trinitatis ad recognoscendum etc.

(836)

Essex'. Meyr de Oxon' optulit se quarto die versus Laurencium Hardel, tenentem terrarum que fuerunt Jolani de Cokham, de placito debiti. Et ipse non venit. Et preceptum fuit vicecomiti quod ipsum venire faceret. Et vicecomes mandavit quod Robertus Crakebon de Terling' et Elias Vado de eadem manuceperunt predictum Laurencium, quem non habuerunt. Ideo in misericordia.[55] Judicium quod distringat per terras etc., ita quod nec ipse etc., <et quod de exitibus etc.,>[56] et quod habeat corpus ejus coram etc. in octabis sancte Trinitatis ad respondendum etc. et ad audiendum etc.

(837)

Wyltes'. Bonefey de Crickelade judeus per essoniatorem suum optulit se quarto die versus Philippum Put, Robertum le Bird, Clementem Crek', Johannem Pascy, Ricardum Wither, Thomam le Mercer, Johannem Salveyn, Petrum de Gormenill', Robertum Seylfeste, David le Fevere, Adam del Pillor', Johannem de la Rochele, Johannem le Key, Willelmum de Neyvill', Radulfum de Gardino, Robertum de Eldebef et Johannem de Merston', Johannem Tregoz de placito debiti. Et ipsi non venerunt. Et preceptum fuit vicecomiti quod ipsos venire faceret. Et vicecomes mandavit quod retornavit breve sibi inde directum ballivis libertatum de Wurth' et Malmesber', qui nichil inde responderunt. Judicium quod non omittat propter predictas libertates etc., et venire faciat coram etc. in octabis sancte Trinitatis predictos Robertum, Robertum et alios supradictos ad respondendum predicto judeo de predicto placito etc.

(838)

Wyltes'. Josceus de Merlebergh' judeus optulit se quarto die versus Johannem Brunyng' le Joefne, filium Johannis Brunyng, et Ricardum Coleword' de Marlebergh' de placito transgressionis. Et ipsi non venerunt. Et preceptum fuit vicecomiti quod ipsos venire faceret coram etc. Et vicecomes mandavit quod retornavit breve sibi inde directum ballivis libertatis de Merlebergh', qui nichil inde fecerunt. Judicium quod non omittat propter predictam libertatem etc. et venire faciat coram etc. in octabis sancte Trinitatis predictos Johannem et Ricardum ad respondendum predicto judeo de predicto placito etc. Postea ad instanciam domine Regine matris Regis quietumclamavit predictum Ricardum de transgressione predicta per licenciam justiciariorum.

(839)

Linc'. Johannes filius Alani Miles de Quappelade, quem Willelmus Wyn et Matillis uxor ejus per auxilium curie vocaverunt ad warantum, et idem Johannes per auxilium ejusdem curie vocavit ad warantum Eadmundum de Quappelad' et eum venire fecit et petit quod ipsum aquietet de porcione ipsum contingente de quodam debito quadraginta et sex librarum, que porcio de Willelmo Vyn et Matillide uxore ejus, cujus warantus ipse est, exigitur ad opus Regis occasione unius acre et unius rode terre arabilis que fuerunt magistri Thome de Quappelade de debito Abrahe filii Murielle judei, sicut continetur in quadam carta quam predictus Johannes protulit coram etc., quam Thomas de Quappelade, pater predicti Eadmundi, fecit Alano Myles patri predicti Johannis quod ipsum, heredes et assingnatos suos contra omnes homines aquietare debet, defendere et warantizare.

Predictus Eadmundus venit et recognovit predictam cartam esse factum predicti Thome patris sui et ei warantizat. Ideo consideratum est quod dictus Eadmundus de porcione predictos Johannem, Willelmum Wyn et Matillidem uxorem ejus occasione predicte unius acre et unius rode terre de dicto debito contingente remaneat oneratus. Et predicti Johannes, Willelmus et Matillis, qui predictum Johannem vocaverunt ad warrantum, sint inde quieti. Et preceptum est vicecomiti quod predictos Johannem, Willelmum et Matillidem pacem habere permittat. Et si quid etc.

(840)

Linc'. Radulfus filius Rogeri le Champeneys venire fecit Eadmundum de Quappelade, filium et heredem Thome de Quappelade, et petit quod ipsum aquietet de porcione ipsum et Mariam matrem ejus de quodam debito .xlvj. librarum contingente occasione duodecim acrarum terre arrabilis quas tenent de terris que fuerunt magistri Thome de Quappelade, que porcio dicti debiti ab eis exigitur ad opus Regis de debitis Abrahe filii Murielle judei, et protulit cartam Thome de Quappelade patris sui, cujus heres ipse est, in [qua][57] continetur quod ipsum aquietare debet etc.

Predictus Eadmundus venit et recognovit predictam cartam esse factum predicti Thome patris sui et ei warantizat. Ideo consideratum est quod dictus Eadmundus de

[55] *The word* misericordia *is repeated in the margin.*

[56] *These words are repeated in MS.*

[57] *MS. reads* quo.

porcione predictos Radulfum et Mariam matrem ejus occasione predictarum .xij. acrarum terre de dicto debito ipsos contingente remaneat oneratus. Et predicti Radulfus et Maria inde sint quieti. Et preceptum est vicecomiti quod predictis Radulfo et Marie pacem habere permittat etc. Et si quid etc.

(841)

Cantebr'. Johannes atte Beche optulit se quarto die versus Josceum Batecok' judeum de placito debiti. Et ipse non venit. Et preceptum fuit vicecomiti quod ipsum venire faceret ad hunc diem. Et vicecomes mandavit quod Jacobus filius Mossei et Isac filius Abrahe de Norwyc' judei manuceperunt predictum Josceum, quem non habuerunt. Ideo in misericordia.[58] Judicium quod distringat per terras etc., et quod habeat corpus ejus coram etc. a die sancte Trinitatis in .xv. dies ad respondendum etc.

(842)

Cantebr'. Willelmus de Middelton' clericus de scaccario etc. optulit se quarto die versus Willelmum Godwey, Adam Aylmer, Willelmum filium Ade Aylmer et Simonem le Tregetur de Saham de placito transgressionis. Et ipsi non venerunt. Et preceptum fuit vicecomiti quod ipsos distringeret per terras etc., et quod haberet corpora eorum coram etc. ad hunc diem. Et vicecomes mandavit quod Adam Aylmer de Saham, Simon le Tregetur de eadem, Willelmus Attebernes de eadem et Johannes atte Mere de eadem manuceperunt Willelmum Godwy, et sunt exitus terrarum predicti Willelmi .vj. denarii; et quod Willelmus Godewy de Saham, Simon le Tregetur de eadem, Simon Aylmer de eadem, et Johannes Eustachius manuceperunt Adam Aylmer et sunt exitus terrarum dicti Ade .vj. denarii; et quod Adam Aylmer de Saham, Ricardus filius Rogeri de eadem, Johannes filius Johannis de eadem et Willelmus Godewy de eadem manuceperunt Simonem le Tregetur; quos non habuerunt. Ideo in misericordia.[59] Et sunt exitus terrarum dicti Simonis .vj. denarii. Judicium, sicut alias, a die sancte Trinitatis in .xv. dies etc. ad respondendum etc., et ad audiendum etc.

(843)

Oxon'. Josceus filius Sauloti judeus optulit se quarto die versus Willelmum de Charney de placito debiti. Et ipse non venit. Et preceptum fuit vicecomiti quod ipsum venire faceret etc. Et vicecomes mandavit quod Ricardus Banastre et Willelmus Halfrens manuceperunt predictum Willelmum, quem non habuerunt. Ideo in misericordia.[60] Judicium [quod] distringat per terras etc., et quod habeat corpus ejus coram etc. a die sancte Trinitatis in .xv. dies ad respondendum etc., et ad audiendum etc.

(844)

Devon'. Jacobus de Mouns, tenens quandam partem terrarum que fuerunt Baldewini de Wayford', optulit se quarto die versus abbatem de Bocfast, tenentem quandam partem terrarum que fuerunt predicti Baldewini, de placito acquietancie debiti. Et ipse non venit. Et preceptum fuit vicecomiti quod ipsum venire faceret. Et vicecomes mandavit quod Johannes le Skynnere et Robertus Corby manuceperunt predictum abbatem, quem non habuerunt. Ideo in misericordia.[61] Judicium quod distringat per terras etc., et quod de exitibus etc. et quod habeat corpus ejus coram etc. a die sancti Johannis Baptiste in .xv. dies ad respondendum etc. et ad audiendum etc.

(845)

Devon'. Petrus de Grenham optulit se quarto die versus Warinum de Sechevyle, quondam vicecomitem Devon', de placito ejeccionis de manerio de Weborneford. Et ipse non venit. Et preceptum fuit vicecomiti quod ipsum distringeret per terras etc., et quod de exitibus etc., et quod habeat corpus ejus coram etc. Et vicecomes mandavit quod retornavit breve inde sibi directum ballivis Rogeri le Merchaunt in Wyterygg', qui nichil inde respondent. Judicium quod non omittat propter libertatem etc. in octabis sancte Trinitatis etc.

MEMBRANE 4

Starra de termino Pasche anno regni regis Edwardi filii regis Henrici Nono

(846)

Warr'. Aaron filius Vyves judeus recognovit per starrum suum se recepisse de Ricardo de Amundeville milite duodecim libras et decem solidos de termino quindene Pasche anno regni regis Edwardi nono. Et <idem judeus tenetur>[62] allocare predictos denarios in debito in quo predictus Ricardus ei tenetur. Recognovit eciam quod recepit de predicto Ricardo viginti solidos pro una roba in qua idem Ricardus eidem judeo tenebatur ad eundem terminum. Et idem judeus recognovit se recepisse predictos denarios per manum Rogeri de <Pyvelesdon>[63] militis. Et quod recognovit, hoc idem sigillavit.

(847)

Kanc'. Aaron filius Vyves judeus recognovit per starrum suum quod Willelmus Godefrey et heredes sui quieti sunt de ipso judeo et heredibus suis de uno debito decem librarum sub nominibus predicti Willelmi et Avegaye que fuit uxor Salle de Cantuar', quod debitum liberatum fuit predicto Aaron de thesauro domini regis, a creacione

58 *The word* misericordia *is repeated in the margin.*
59 *The word* misericordia *is repeated in the margin.*
60 *The word* misericordia *is repeated in the margin.*
61 *The word* misericordia *is repeated in the margin.*
62 super ipsum judeum est *37*.
63 Pvylisdon' *37*.

seculi usque ad finem. Concedit eciam predictus judeus quod predictus Willelmus Godefrey quietus est de quadam recognicione de decem libris quam predictus Willelmus eidem judeo fecit, sicut irrotulatur in rotulis domini regis coram justiciariis ad custodiam judeorum assignatis, a creacione seculi usque a die Pasche in unum mensem anno regis Edwardi nono. Et quod recognovit hoc idem sigillavit.

(848)

Sussex'. Aaron filius Vyves judeus recognovit per starrum suum se recepisse de Rogero la Ware viginti et novem marcas de quindena termini Pasche anno regis Edwardi nono de quadam recognicione centum et sexdecim <marcarum>[64] quam <ei>[65] fecit coram justiciariis ad custodiam judeorum assignatis. <Recognovit eciam idem judeus quod recepit>[66] ab eodem Rogero sex solidos pro uno quarterio frumenti. Et quod recognovit hoc idem sigillavit.

(849)

Hertford'. Aaron filius Vyves judeus recognovit per starrum suum quod Willelmus le Enveyse et heredes sui quieti sunt de ipso judeo et heredibus suis de omnibus debitis, demandis calumpniis, plegiagiis, obligacionibus et recognicionibus factis ante tres septimanas Pasche anno regis Edwardi nono a creacione seculi usque ad finem. Et si inveniatur carta, tallia vel aliquod aliud instrumentum sub nominibus predictorum Willelmi et Aaron in archa cyrographariorum vel extra factum ante terminum predictum, idem Aaron recognovit quod quieta sunt et nichil valeant.

(850)

Wygorn'. Manserus filius Joscei judeus recognovit per starrum suum quod Robertus Aleyn, filius et heres Willelmi Aleyn, de villa de Wyz et heredes sui quieti sunt de ipso judeo et heredibus et assignatis [i]<suis>[i] de omnibus debitis, demandis, calumpniis et plegiagiis in quibus ei umquam tenebatur a creacione seculi usque ad Pentecosten anno regni regis Edwardi filii regis Henrici nono. Et si inveniatur carta, tallia vel aliquid aliud instrumentum in archa cyrographariorum vel extra sub nominibus predicti Roberti vel Willelmi patris sui et predicti Manseri facta ante predictum terminum Pentecostes, idem judeus recognovit quod quieta sint et nichil valeant.

(851)

Essex'. Magister Elias filius magistri Mossei judeus recognovit per starrum suum quod Willelmus <de Aumbely>[67] et heredes sui quieti sunt de ipso et heredibus suis de omnibus debitis, demandis et calumpniis a creacione seculi usque ad le Hokeday anno regni regis Edwardi nono. Et predictus Willelmus et Robertus filius Walteri, dominus de Wodeham. et heredes eorum quieti sunt de ipso judeo de quadam obligacione ducentarum marcarum sub nominibus ipsorum Willelmi et Roberti et predicti magistri Elie a creacione seculi usque ad finem. Et predictus judeus recognovit quod ipse vel heredes sui nichil poterunt exigere vel calumpniare super predictum Robertum occasione alicujus debiti in quo predictus Willelmus de Aumbely eidem judeo umquam tenebatur a creacione seculi usque ad finem.

(852)

Hereford'. Aaron filius Vyves judeus recognovit per starrum quod recepit de Willelmo de Everoys decem libras per manum Walteri Tyrel de termino trium septimanarum Pasche anno regni regis Edwardi nono de quodam debito in quo ei tenebatur.

(853)

Kanc'. Aaron filius Vyves judeus recognovit per starrum suum quod Robertus Germeyn et heredes sui quieti sunt de ipso judeo et heredibus suis de quodam debito decem solidorum in quibus ei tenebatur per recognicionem factam coram justiciariis nostris ad custodiam judeorum assignatis,[68] quod [i]<eidem>[i] Aaron liberatum fuit de thesauro domini regis, a creacione seculi usque ad finem. Idem eciam Aaron concedit quod predicti justiciarii liberari faciant cartam predicti debiti decem solidorum predicto Roberto quietam dampnatam.

(854)

Ebor'. Deudone Crespyn judeus recognovit per starrum suum quod Ranulphus de Middelton' et heredes sui quieti sunt de ipso judeo et heredibus [i]<suis>[i] de omnibus debitis, demandis, calumpniis et plegiagiis in quibus idem Ranulphus eidem judeo umquam tenebatur a creacione seculi usque ad finem. Et si inveniatur carta, tallia vel aliquod aliud instrumentum in archa cyrographariorum vel extra sub nominibus predictorum Ranulphi et Deudon' idem judeus recognovit quod quieta sunt et nichil valeant. Acta a die Pasche in tres septimanas anno regni regis Edwardi filii regis Henrici nono.

(855)

Essex'. Meyr filius Benedicti judeus recognovit per starrum suum quod Willelmus de Raumesden' et heredes sui quieti sunt de ipso judeo et heredibus suis de quadam obligacione quadraginta et quinque quarteriorum frumenti facta sub nominibus ipsorum Willelmi et Meyr. Et si inveniatur carta, [i]<obligacio,>[i] tallia vel aliquod aliud instrumentum in archa cyrographariorum vel extra sub nominibus ipsorum Willelmi et Meyr facta a creacione seculi usque a die Pasche in tres septimanas anno regni regis Edwardi filii regis Henrici nono, idem

[64] solidorum *37*. [65] michi *37*. [66] Recepi eciam *37*.
[67] Aumbelyn *37*.

[68] *Followed in 66 by the redundant* quodam debito decem solidorum *and in 37 by the redundant* de quodam debito decem solidorum.

judeus recognovit quod quieta sunt. Acta a die Pasche in tres septimanas anno regni regis Edwardi predicti nono.

(856)

[*Hereford'.*][69] Manserus filius Aaron judeus recognovit per starrum suum quod Johannes de Gatesden' et heredes sui quieti sunt de ipso judeo et heredibus et assingnatis suis de quodam debito sexaginta quarteriorum frumenti in quibus ei tenebatur per scriptum suum obligatorium, prout continetur in rotulis domini regis nunc, et de omnibus aliis debitis, demandis, calumpniis, plegiagiis et omnibus aliis rebus factis sub nominibus predictorum Johannis et Manseri. Et si inveniatur aliquod debitum vel obligacio irrotulata in rotulis domini regis vel extra sub nominibus predictorum Johannes et Manseri, idem Manserus recognovit quod quieta sint et nichil valeant.

(857)

Warr'. Aaron filius Vyves judeus recognovit per starrum suum quod quietavit Willelmum dominum de Bysshopesdon' de quadam obligacione sexaginta quarteriorum frumenti facta sub nominibus predictorum Willelmi et Aaron a creacione seculi usque ad finem, et de omnibus aliis debitis et demandis factis ante Pascham anno regni regis Edwardi filii regis Henrici nono, ita quod ipse et heredes sui inde quieti sint a creacione seculi usque ad finem, et eciam de decem marcis in quibus mihi tenebatur ante Pascham predictam a creacione seculi usque ad finem.

(858)

Glouc'. Aaron filius Vyves judeus recognovit per starrum suum quod recepit de Johanne filio Hugonis de Clifford' [.xxiiij. marcas][70] a die Pasche in unum mensem anno regni regis Edwardi filii regis Henrici nono. Et per predictam recepcionem idem judeus liberavit eidem Johanni quoddam scriptum obligatorium .iiij.^{xx} quarteriorum frumenti.

(859)

Linc'. Elias de Denecastre judeus venit coram etc. et recognovit [i]<hoc>[i] starrum subscriptum littera latina scriptum: 'Ego qui sum subtus sigillatus recognosco veram recognicionem quod Alexander Lucas et heredes sui et assignati sunt quieti de me et heredibus meis et meis assignatis de una carta .xx. librarum que est in archa Stamford' in suo nomine et meo et in nomine Andree Arketil, Isak' Lucas, Johannis le Flemang', Henrici de Akele, Johannis Plouman, Johannis Appotecar', et de omnibus aliis debitis et chalengiis que possunt interogari in nomine suo et meo ab initio seculi usque ad festum nativitatis sancti Johannis Baptiste anno regni regis Edwardi filii regis Henrici quinto. Et si judeus vel judea, cristianus vel cristiana veniat aliquid interogari predicto Alexandro aut heredibus suis aut suis assingnatis per scriptum vel per talliam vel per aliud instrumentum factum in suo nomine vel meo ante terminum supradictum manucapio pro me et heredibus meis et meis assingnatis aquietare, warantizare et defendere predictum [i]<Alexandrum>[i] et heredes suos et assingnatos. In cujus rei testimonium presens scriptum littera mea ebrayca sigillavi.' Et idem Elias de Denecastre sigillatur in starro isto littera ebraica.

[69] *This should probably have been* Hertford'.

[70] *Supplied from 37.*

(860)

Hertford', Buk'. Aaron filius Vyves judeus recognovit per starrum suum quod Hugo de Brok' et heredes sui quieti sunt de ipso Aaron et heredibus suis de omnibus obligacionibus et debitis in quibus umquam eidem judeo tenebatur a creacione seculi usque ad festum Pentecosten anno regni regis Edwardi filii regis Henrici nono. Et si inveniatur aliqua obligacio vel aliquod debitum sub nominibus predictorum Hugonis et Aron factum ante predictam diem idem judeus recognovit quod pro nullo habeantur et nichil valeant.

(861)

. . . . judeus recognovit per . . . . et perdon' . . . . Alano de Freston' archidiacono Norff' et heredibus et assingnatis suis totum . . . . magistrum Alanum ocasione dictarum . . . . idem magister . . . Isak' de Norwyc', ita quod nec predictus Isak' nec heredes . . . .vel assingnatos suos occasione cujusdam starri cujusdam debiti . . . .finem. Et si aliquis judeus vel judeo aliquid calumpri' . . . .k' tenetur ipsos warantizare et defendere . . . . m anno regni regis Edward filii regis Henrici nono.

MEMBRANE 4 DORSE

Adhuc Starra

(862)

Linc', Essex'. Elias de Denecastre judeus recognovit per starrum suum quod Philippus de Stamburn et heredes sui quieti sunt de ipso judeo et heredibus suis de omnibus debitis, calumpniis, plegiagiis, recognicionibus, depositis in quibus eidem Elie umquam tenebatur vel que idem Elias eidem Philippo umquam commisit custodiendum a creacione seculi usque a die Pasche in quinque septimanas anno regni regis Edwardi nono. Et si inveniatur carta, tallia vel aliud instrumentum in archa cyrographariorum vel extra sub nominibus predictorum Philippi et Elie factum ante confeccionem istius starri, idem Elias recognovit quod quieta sint et nichil valeant.

(863)

Hertford'. Aaron filius Vyves judeus recognovit per starrum suum quod Henricus junior de Bockeland', qui non est miles, filius Henrici de Bokland', qui non est miles, et heredes sui quieti sunt de ipso Aaron et heredibus suis de quadam obligacione .cc. quarteriorum frumenti sub nominibus ipsorum Henrici et Aaron, unde terminus solucionis predicte obligacionis fuit ad festum Pentecosten anno regni regis Edwardi filii regis Henrici nono a creacione seculi usque ad finem. Et quod recognovit hoc idem sigillavit.

(864)

Leyc'. Aaron filius Vyves judeus recognovit per starrum suum quod Benedictus de Rolleston' et heredes sui quieti sunt de ipso Aaron et heredibus suis de quadam obligacione octo saccorum lane in quibus ei tenebatur reddendo a die Pasche in unum mensem anno regni regis Edwardi filii regis Henrici nono a creacione seculi usque ad finem et de omnibus aliis debitis demandis, plegiagiis, calumpniis in quibus idem Benedictus eidem Aaron umquam tenebatur a creacione seculi usque ad Pentecosten anno supradicto. Et si inveniatur carta, tallia vel aliquod aliud instrumentum in archa cyrographariorum vel extra sub nominibus predictorum Benedicti vel Aaron factum ante terminum predictum, idem judeus recognoscit quod quieti sint et nichil valeant.

(865)

Oxon'. Berk'. Isac de Kaune judeus recognovit per starrum suum quod Symon de Ordeston' et heredes sui quieti sunt de ipso judeo et heredibus suis de quodam debito .xx. librarum sub nominibus predictorum Symonis et Isac, unde altera pars est in archa cyrographariorum Divis', et de omnibus aliis debitis, demandis et calumpniis in quibus idem Symon unquam eidem judeo tenebatur ante confeccionem istius starri a creacione seculi usque ad finem. Acta die jovis proxima ante festum sancti Petri ad Vinculam anno regni regis Edwardi filii regis Henrico quarto. Et quod recognovit hoc idem sigillavit.

(866)

Lond', Warr'. Magister Elias filius magistri Mossei et Aaron filius Vyves judei [London'][71] recognoverunt per starrum suum se recepisse de Roberto <Hasteng'>[72] .cc. libras a die Pasche in unum mensem anno regis Edwardi .ix.^{o}. Et pro solucione predicta et pro aliis solucionibus factis ante festum Pasche predictum, iidem judei recognoverunt quod predictus Robertus tenuit omnes [i]<terminos>[i] suos preteritos, sicut continetur in starro quod dictus Robertus habet de eisdem judeis, usque ad predictum mensem Pasche; ita quod dicti judei nec heredes eorum aliquid calumpniari seu exigere poterunt de predicto Roberto nec heredibus suis occasione predictarum .cc. librarum nec racione alicujus termini elapsi de predictis terminis in starro quod dictus Robertus habet in manu sua de dictis judeis tali condicione quod, si dictus Robertus reddat dictis judeis omnes denarios quos eis debet ad terminos venturos, sicut continetur in starro predicto. Et pro predictis .cc. libris predicti judei acquietaverunt predictum Robertum et heredes suos de una obligacione .c. .iiij.^{xx} librarum sub nominibus ipsius Roberti et predictorum judeorum et de .xx. libris in quibus dictus Robertus tenebatur dictis judeis ad predictum terminum Pasche. Et quod recognoverunt hoc sigillaverunt.

(867)

Warr'. Aaron filius Vyves et Jacobus filius Hagini recognoverunt per starrum suum se recepisse de Radulfo de Lymesy [milite][73] .xij. marcas de quindena termini sancti Michaelis anno regis Edwardi quinto. Et tenenetur allocare predictos denarios in debito quod irrotulatur in rotulis ad scaccarium judeorum de quadam obligacione que est ad Novum Templum sub nominibus predictorum Radulfi, Aaron et Jacobi.

(868)

Warr'. Aaron filius Vyves et Jacobus filius Hagini recognoverunt per starrum suum se recepisse de Radulfo de Lymesy .x. marcas de quindena termini Pasche anno regis Edwardi sexto. Et super ipsos judeos est allocare predictas .x. marcas in debito in quo eis tenetur, sicut irrotulatur in rotulis domini regis de quadam obligacione que est ad Novum Templum.

Iidem Aaron et Jacobus recognovenunt per starrum suum se recepisse de Radulfo de Lymesy .x. marcas de quindena termini sancti Michaelis anno regis Edwardi sexto. Et super ipsos est allocare predictas .x. marcas in debito in quo eis tenetur, sicut irrotulatur in rotulis domini regis de quadam obligacione que est ad Novum Templum.

Iidem Aaron et Jacobus recognoverunt per starrum suum se recepisse de Radulfo de Lymesy .x. marcas de quindena termini Pasche anno regis Edwardi septimo. Et super ipsos est allocare predictas .x. marcas in debito in quo eis tenetur, sicut irrotulatur in rotulis domini regis de quadam obligacione que est ad Novum Templum.

Iidem Aaron et Jacobus recognoverunt per starrum suum se recepisse de Radulfo de Lymesy .x. marcas de quindena termini sancti Michaelis anno regis Edwardi septimo. Et super ipsos est allocare predictas .x. marcas in debito in quo eis tenetur, sicut irrotulatur in rotulis domini regis in predicta obligacione que est ad Novum Templum.

Iidem Aaron et Jacobus recognoverunt per starrum suum se recepisse de predicto Radulfo .x. marcas de quindena Pasche anno regis Edwardi octavo. Et super ipsos est allocare predictas .x. marcas in debito in quo eis tenetur, sicut irrotulatur in rotulis domini regis de predicta obligacione que est ad Novum Templum.

Iidem Aaron et Jacobus recognoverunt per starrum suum se recepisse de eodem Radulfo .x. marcas de termino quindene sancti Michaelis anno regis Edwardi octavo. Et super ipsos judeos est allocare predictas .x. marcas in debito in quo eis tenetur, sicut irrotulatur in

[71] *Supplied from 37.* [72] de Hasting' *37.*

[73] *supplied from 37.*

rotulis domini regis de dicta obligacione que est ad Novum Templum.

Iidem Aaron et Jacobus recognoverunt per starrum suum se recepisse de predicto Radulfo .x. marcas de termino quindene Pasche anno regis Edwardi nono. Et super ipsos judeos est allocare predictas .x. marcas in debito in quo eis tenetur, sicut irrotulatur in rotulis regis de dicta obligacione que est ad Novum Templum sub nominibus predictorum predictorum Radulfi, Aaron et Jacobi.

(869)

Kanc'. Aaron filius Elie judeus recognovit per starrum suum quod Johannes filius Reginaldi de Cornhulle, heredes et assignati sui quieti sunt de ipso judeo, heredibus et assignatis suis de una obligacione .xxx. quarteriorum frumenti et alia obligacione .xx. quarteriorum frumenti a creacione seculi usque ad finem, et de omnibus aliis debitis, demandis et calumpniis in quibus idem Johannes vel antecessores sui umquam tenebantur eidem judeo vel antecessoribus suis a creacione seculi usque ad Pentecosten anno regis Edwardi nono. Et si inveniatur carta, tallia vel aliquod aliud instrumentum sub nominibus dicti Johannis vel antecessorum suorum infra archa cyrographariorum vel extra factum ante festum Pentecostes predictum, dictus judeus recognovit quod quieta sint et nichil valeant. Et quod recognovit hoc sigillavit.

(870)

Bed', Buk'. Magister Elias filius magistri Mossei judeus recognovit per starrum suum quod Milo de Hastyng' et heredes sui quieti sunt de ipso et heredibus suis de quadam obligacione duorum saccorum lane sub nominibus predictorum Milonis et Elie, et de omnibus aliis debitis, demandis et calumpniis factis sub nominibus predictorum Milonis et Elie[74] ante Pascham anno regis Edwardi nono. Et hoc sigillavit.

(871)

Ebor'. <Iwetta>[75] filia Joscei uxor Deudone filii Benedicti Crespyn rogavit David filium Meyr et Isac filium Josue le Evesk et Judam filium Deudonis ut testificarentur pro ea quandam vendicionem de quadam domo in Ebor' quam vendidit Cok' filio Aaron judeo London. Deudone maritus Jowette, Jurninus filius dicti Deudone recognoverunt per starrum suum eandem vendicionem eidem fecisse per bonam vendicionem et firmam. Et dicta Jowetta recognovit quod quietavit et quietum clamavit predicto Cok' totum jus et clamium que habuit vel habere potuit in dicta domo occasione dotis sue quam clamat in dicta domo cum pertinenciis suis que fuit predicti Deudone viri sui in vico de Coningstrete in parochia sancti Martini.[76] Que domus sita est in Conygstrete et extendit se versus partem orientalem usque ad curiam Stephani le Tywelur et versus partem occidentalem usque ad vicum regis qui vocatur Conygstrete et versus partem australem inter domum que fuit Benedicti filii Joscei et domum Benigmyn' judei versus partem borealem. Et [i]<idem>[i] recognoverunt idem Deudone et Jorninus filius ejus quod vendiderunt predicto Cok' totum jus suum et clamium que habuerunt vel habere poterunt, sicut predictum est superius, per easdem metas. Et quod decetero predictus Cok' vel nuncius ejus possit recipere seisinam de dicta domo cum pertinenciis suis ad faciendum inde voluntatem suam. Et si aliquis christianus vel judeus, frater vel soror, christianus vel judeus, calumpniari voluerit super predictam domum cum pertinenciis super ipsos judeos est warantizare, acquietare et defendere predictum Cok', reddendum sibi et heredibus suis unam rosam per annum et regi duos denarios quasi de socagio et capitali domino feodi dimidiam marcam per annum pro omnibus serviciis dictam domum tangentibus. Et predicti judei predictum Cok' per predictum servicium warantizare, acquietare et defendere debent contra regem et reginam et omnes homines christianos et judeos. Pro qua warantizacione acquietacione et defensione dedit prefatus Cok' predictis judeis .c. marcas. Et ad istam defensionem, warantizacionem et acquietacionem fideliter observandum obligant omnia bona sua mobilia et inmobilia ubicumque fuerint inventa. Et idem Jorninus filius Deudone concedit quod quoddam starrum quod Deudone pater suus ei fecit de predictis domibus cum pertinenciis ab archa cyrographariorum Ebor' extrahatur et predicto Cok' liberetur. Et preceptum est cyrographariis quod ad archam accedant et ab ea extrahant starrum predictum et predicto Cok' vel ejus attornato liberare faciant.

(872)

Ebor'. Benedictus filius magistri Mossei judeus recognovit per starrum suum quod quietavit et perdonavit Roberto Tybetot, heredibus et assignatis suis totum jus, demandam et calumpniam que habuit vel habere potuit super manerium de Benetele et manerium de Arkezey cum omnibus pertinenciis suis que fuerunt Ade de Novo Mercato; ita quod nec ipse Benedictus nec heredes nec assignati sui calumpniari possint versus predictum Robertum, heredes vel assignatos suos super predicta maneria cum pertinenciis suis nec super aliquam partem quam predictus Robertus tenuit die confeccionis hujus starri que fuit predicti Ade occasione alicujus debiti quod predictus Adam ei debuit per cartam vel [per] aliquod aliud clamium a creacione seculi usque ad finem. Et istud starrum factum fuit die mercurii proxima ante Pentecosten anno regis Edwardi nono.

(873)

Ebor'. Magister Elias filius magistri Mossei judeus recognovit per starrum suum quod quietavit et perdonavit Roberto Tybetot totum jus, demandam et calumpniam que umquam habuit vel habere potuit super Benetele et Arkele cum pertinenciis suis que Adam de

[74] *Followed in MS. by* factis.

[75] Juetta *37 (and subsequently).*

[76] *The version in 37 ends at this point.*

Novo Mercato ei dimisit, ita quod nec ipse Elias nec heredes sui exigere vel calumpniari possint aliquid super predicta duo maneria cum pertinenciis suis occasione alicujus debiti quod Adam de Novo Mercato umquam ei debuit. Acta die mercurii proxima ante Pentecosten anno regis Edwardi nono.

(874)

Ebor'. Manserus filius Aaron judeus recognovit per starrum suum quod quietavit et perdonavit Roberto Tybetot, heredibus et assignatis suis totum jus, demandam et calumpniam quas habuit vel habere potuit super maneria de Benetele et Arkele cum omnibus pertinenciis suis que fuerunt Ade de Novo Mercato, ita quod nec ipse Manserus nec heredes nec assignati sui aliquid calumpniare poterunt versus predictum Robertum, heredes vel assignatos suos super predicta maneria cum pertinenciis suis nec super aliquam terram quam predictus Robertus tenuit die confeccionis istius starri que fuit predicti Ade occasione alicujus debiti quod predictus Adam ei debuit per cartam vel per aliquod aliud clamium a creacione seculi usque ad finem. Et istud starrum factum fuit die mercurii proxima ante Pentecosten anno regis Edwardi nono.

(875)

Essex'. Abraham filius Isac judeus recognovit per starrum suum quod vendidit et dimisit Egidio de Garderoba, heredibus et assignatis suis unum debitum .xx. librarum, quod debitum est sub nominibus Manseri filii Aaron et Saeri filii Guydonis de Hay' de comitatu Essex, unde terminus soluccionis fuit ad quindenam sancti Michaelis anno regis Edwardi primo, et acta carte primo die Septembris anno predicto, unde pars in qua cera dependet est in archa cyrographariorum Lond' et irrotulatur in rotulis domini regis ad scaccarium judeorum quod dictum debitum est suum per recognicionem dicti Manseri. Et eciam recognovit quod vendidit dicto Egidio, heredibus et assignatis suis quoddam aliud debitum .iiij. librarum sub nominibus predictorum Saeri et Abrahe quod est in archa Lond', acta carte die Purificacionis Beate Marie anno regis Edwardi tercio, et tota predicta duo debita et omne clamium quod inde exire poterit et quantum inde emerserit sine aliqua relaxacione totaliter et integre vendidit predicto Egidio, heredibus et assignatis suis vendicione firma et stabili et quod decetero de predictis duobus debitis sit posse predicti Egidii sicut posse suum in eisdem debitis prius et factum dicti Egidii in omnibus sicut factum suum erat inde prius. Et licitum sit predicto Egidio predicta duo debita recipere, acquietare, perdonare, vendere, et dare in toto et in parte et capere breve districcionis nomine dicti judei sicut attornatus ejus in toto vel in parte sub expensis predicti Egidii secundum legem et consuetudinem Judaismi. Et idem Abraham juravit quod nichil de predictis duobus debitis recepit nec recipiet nec aliquod starrum acquietancie fecit predicto Saero nec faciet sine licencia et voluntate dicti Egidii; et quod non possit impetrare per se vel per alium aliquam causam in prorogacionem predictorum debitorum versus predictum Egidium, heredes vel assignatos suos vel de parte dicti debiti. Et omni tempore quando idem Egidius voluerit quod faciat predicto Saero, heredibus vel assignatis suis starrum acquietancie predictorum debitorum, super ipsum judeum est facere bonum et stabile secundum legem et consuetudinem Judaismi; et super ipsum judeum est warantizare, defendere et acquietare predictum Egidium, heredes et assignatos suos predicta duo debita ut vera et debita et clara facta secundum legem et consuetudinem Judaismi. Et super ipsum Abraham est et heredes suos warantizare, acquietare et defendere predictum Egidium versus Manserum filium Aaron et omnes alios calumpriantes. Et ad hoc obligavit omnia bona sua mobilia et inmobilia. Et hoc recognovit pro se et heredibus suis. Et hoc starrum et vendicionem fecit per licenciam domini Regis per breve suum patens quod irrotulatur in rotulis etc. ad scaccarium judeoum. Acta.... ....apostolorum Philippi et Jacobi anno regis Edwardi nono.

(876)

Lond'. Manserus filius Aaron judeus recognovit per starrum suum quod vendidit unum debitum .xx. librarum sub nominibus Saeri de Hay filii Guydonis . . . . . . judeo. Et concedit quod totum debitum est predicti Abrahe et quod . . . Egidii de Garderoba de dicto debita sit bona . . . . nec heredes nec assignati sui aliquid calumpriare seu exigere . . . . finem. Et eciam juravit lege sua quod . . . . quod nullum starrum fecit de dicto . . . Acta die dominica proxima ante festum apostolorum Philippi et Jacobi . . .

(877)

Warr'. Aaron filius Vyves judeus recognovit per starrum . . . . de una obligacione .c. quarteriorum frumenti . . . . tempore et loco reperiatur quod . . . sanctorum anno regis Edwardi . . . .

MEMBRANE 5

Essonia de quindena Pasche anno regni regis Edwardi filii regis Henrici nono. nono

(878)

Devon'. Willelmus de Compton', attornatus Humfridi Kael, versus Johannem filium Bernardi de placito acquietacionis debiti per Gilbertum le Warener.

(879)

Glouc'. Willelmus de Hertford', attornatus Rogeri Barbaustre <executoris>[77] testamenti Johannis le <Ware,>[78] versus Alexandrum de Aunho de placito acquietacionis debiti per Johannem de Merdon'.

[77] coexecutoris *37*. [78] Warre *37*.

Ricardus de Acre, alter [attornatus][79] dicti Rogeri, versus eundem Alexandrum de eodem per Johannem de Merdon'.

(880)

Essex'. Willelmus de Twynstede, attornatus Stephani le Keu de Wythermondeford', versus Mosseum de Clare judeum de placito debiti per Rogerum de Oxon'.

Essonia de tribus septimanis

(881)

Kanc'. Johannes Malemeyn versus Rogerum de Tylmanston', [i]<Loram uxorem ejus et Nicholaum Bret>[i] et alios in brevi de placito acquietancie debiti per Johannem de Clare. In octabis sancte Trinitatis. Affidavit.

MEMBRANE 5 DORSE

Attornati, Prece Parcium de termino Pasche anno regni regis Edwardi filii regis Henrici Nono. Nono. Nono. Nono

(882)

Norff'. Simon de Greynvill' et Isabella uxor ejus ponunt loco suo Willelmum de Kimingham versus Henricum le Chat de placito debiti Judaismi.

Idem Simon ponit loco suo Willelmum de Kimingham versus Willelmum de Carleton' de placito debiti.

(883)

Norff'. Reginaldus rector ecclesie de Massingham, Willelmus Stage, David de la Grene, Robertus de Swathing' de Houghthon', Hugo de la Mare de Massingham, Odo filius Willelmi de Harpele, Robertus Quyntin de eadem et Simon Nosce ponunt loco suo Johannem de Harpele vel Willelmum filium Ivonis versus Regem et Johannem filium Willelmi de Harpele de placito debiti.

(884)

Norff'. Willelmus Roscelyn ponit loco suo Ricardum filium Margarie de Audely vel Robertum de Beccl' versus Reginam consortem Regis de placito debiti.

(885)

Essex'. Abbas de Strateford' ponit loco suo Ricardum de Wyttham versus magistrum Eliam filium magistri Mossei judeum de placito debiti.

(886)

Suff'. Herveus de Hegesete ponit loco suo Stephanum filium Benedicti de Sancto Eadmundo versus Ricardum de Cokefeld, custodem heredis Johannis de Norton', de placito debiti.

(887)

Bokingham. Agnes que fuit uxor Johannes le Sauvage ponit loco suo Barnabam de Hertwelle vel Radulfum Sampson vel Isak' de Suwerk' judeum versus Aliciam de Luton' et Willelmum filium ejus attornatos Mossei filii Isak' judei de placito compoti.

(888)

Norff'. Thomas de Eylesham et Levota uxor ejus ponunt loco suo Robertum de Sancto . . . . versus Avegotam filiam Chere judeam de placito debiti.

(889)

Suff, Sussex'. Concessum est Joeli Payn et Nigello Payn per justiciarios et . . .[Isak de Su]werk' judeus prosequatur loco eorum versus tenentes terrarum que fuerunt Gilberti de Baseville de placito debiti.

(890)

Norff'. Priorissa de Carrow ponit loco suo Robertum de Middelton' versus Reginam consortem Regis etc. de placito debiti.

(891)

Leyc'. Rogerus de Somerville ponit loco suo Radulfum de Shoynton' versus Aaron filium Vyves judeum de placito debiti.

(892)

Norff'. Abbas de Crek' ponit loco suo Willelmum de Burnham Thorp versus [i]<Regem et>[i] Johannem filium Willelmi de Harpele de placito debiti.

(893)

Buk', Bed'. Johannes Druel ponit loco suo Johannem de Tevleby [i]<vel Robertum de Sancto Georgio>[i] versus Willelmum de Middelton', clericum de scaccario etc., de placito debiti.

(894)

Leyc'. Frater Johannes magister de Burton' sancti Lazari ponit loco suo Robertum de Babbegrave versus Johannem Fleg de placito debiti.

(895)

Norff'. Adam Boneyt ponit loco suo Johannem de Harpele vel Henricum de Sutham versus Johannem filium Willelmi et alios in brevi de placito debiti.

(896)

Kanc'. Rogerus de Tylemanston' ponit loco suo Johannem de Besil' versus Johannem Malemeyns de placito aquietancie debiti

Nicholaus le Bret ponit loco suo eundem Johannem versus eundem Johannem Malemeyns de eodem.

[79] *Supplied from 37.*

(897)

Cantebr'. Johannes Hamelyn ponit loco suo Johannem de Kyrkeby versus Josceum filium Sauloti de placito debiti.

(898)

North'. Johannes filius Eustachii de North' ponit loco suo Bartholomeum de North' ad prosequendum ad extrahendum quandam cartam sub nominibus ipsius Johannes et Sampsonis filii Sampsonis.

(899)

Linc'. Prior de Bolington' ponit loco Robertum filium Amandi de Impiton' vel Rogerum de Ormesby versus Johannem de Bathon' de placito debiti. Et amovet Adam Prodhomme quem prius etc.

(900)

Warr'. Johannes de Clynton' filius Thome de Clynton' senioris ponit loco suo Jacobum de Clynton' vel Robertum de Charnel' versus Regem de placito debiti.

(901)

Ebor'. Willelmus de Ros ponit loco suo Robertum de Coleville versus Regem et Johannem de Bathon' de placito debiti.

(902)

Warr'. Willelmus Hamelyn ponit loco suo Johannem de Blye vel Thomam Peverel versus Johannem de Hercy de placito acquietancie debiti.

(903)

Hereford'. Johannes Manyword ponit loco suo Sampsonem filium Isak' judeum versus Isak' de Caumpeden' et Floriam uxorem ejus de placito injuste detencionis.

MEMBRANE 6

(904)

Warr'. Preceptum fuit vicecomiti quod distringeret Johannem le Engleys de Upton' pro .xx. solidis quos Regi debet de debitis Salomonis filii Jacobi de Alecestr' judei dampnati; et quod distringeret eundem Johannem pro .ij. marcis de debitis Aaron filii Deulecres judei Warr' dampnati; et denarios haberet vel corpus etc.

Predictus Johannes venit et dicit quod satisfecit predictis judeis de debitis predictis tempore quo habuerunt liberam administracionem de bonis et catallis suis et inde protulit starra predictorum judeorum. Et petit quod veritas inde inquiratur. Et preceptum est vicecomiti quod venire faciat coram etc. sex probos et legales homines de Alecestre et sex legales judeos de villa Norht' de hiis qui solebant manere apud Warr' a die sancte Trinitatis in .xv. dies ad recognoscendum etc. Ad quem diem inquisicio non venit et datus est dies a die sancti Michaelis in .xv. dies. Et preceptum est vicecomiti quod juratores dicte inquisicionis distringantur per terras etc., et quod habeat corpora eorum coram etc. Ad quem diem inquisicio venit et predictus Johannes venit et protulit predicta duo starra, unum in hec verba 'Aaron filius Deulecr' judeus recognovit per starrum suum se recepisse de Johanne le Engleys de Upton .xx. solidos die sancti Michaelis anno regis Edwardi tercio de quodam debito duarum marcarum sub nominibus predictorum Johannes et Aaron. Et quod recognovit etc..' et aliud starrum in hec verba 'Salomon filius Jacobi judeus recognovit per starrum suum quod Johannes le Engleys de Upton' et heredes sui quieti sunt de ipso judeo et heredibus suis de omnibus debitis, demandis et calumpniis a creacione seculi usque ad festum sancti Edwardi anno regis Edwardi tercio. Et quod recognovit etc.' Et inquisicio inde capta fuit per sacramentum Willelmi Eude de Bumpton', Roberti El' de eadem et aliorum christanorum de comitatu Warr', Samuelis de Staunff', Samuelis filii Jude et aliorum judeorum. Qui dicunt super sacramentum suum quod starrum quod dictus Johannis protulit coram etc. de acquietancia .xx. solidorum quod Aaron filius Deulecres ei fecit de quodam debito .ij. marcarum est factum ipsius Aaron et manu sua signatum tempore quo habuit liberam administracionem. Et quod starrum quod idem Johannes protulit de acquietancia predictorum .xx. solidorum de quodam debito .xx. solidorum de debitis Salomonis [i]<filii Jacobi>[i] est starrum ipsius Salomonis etc. tempore debito etc. Ideo consideratum est quod[80] predictus Johannes de .xx. solidis in quibus tenebatur dicto Salomone sit quietus et quod carta inde eidem liberetur quiete dampnata; et quod de .xx. solidis quos solvit dicto Aaron in parte solucionis .ij. marcarum sit quietus et quod solvat Regi dimidiam marcam que ad huc restat solvendum. Et datus est ei dies ad dictam dimidiam marcam solvendum in crastino sancti Nicholai. Et quod, soluta dimidia marca, carta predicti debiti .ij. marcarum eidem Johanni liberetur quiete dampnanda.

(905)

Warr'. Cum Thomas de Bromwyz filius Rogeri de Bromwyz districtus fuisset pro .xx. libris ad opus Regis reddendum de debitis Mossei filii Leonis judei Warr' dampnati, idem Thomas venit coram etc. et tulit breve Regis de magno sigillo in hec verba: 'Edwardus etc. justiciariis etc. salutem. Ex querela Thome de Brumwych' accepimus quod, cum ipse Mossekino judeo nostro Warr' satisfecerit de .xiij. marcis in quibus eidem judeo [tenebatur][81] per quoddam scriptum suum quod in archa cyrographariorum adhuc residet, sicut sufficienter docere paratus est, vos, pro eo quod bona et catalla dicti judei pro transgressionibus quas fecit et pro quibus suspensus fuit capi fecimus in manum nostram, pecuniam predictam racione scripti illius ab eo exigitis nobis iterato solvendum minus juste in dampnum ipsius non modicum et

[80] *Followed in MS. by* de. [81] *MS. omits.*

gravamen; nos igitur super premissis cerciorari volentes vobis mandamus quod per inspeccionem rotulorum scaccarii predicti vel per sacramentum proborum et legalium hominum tam christianorum quam judeorum, per quos rei veritas melius sciri poterit si necesse fuerit, diligenter inquiratis si prefato judeo antequem bona et catalla sua ad manum nostram devenerunt de prefata pecunia in toto vel in parte per prefatum Thomam satisfactum fuerit an non. Et si sic, tunc quo anno et quando et in quorum presencia et per quem et qualiter et quo modo. Et inquisicionem illam inde distincte et aperte factam nobis sub sigillo scaccarii predicti et sigillis eorum per quos facta fuerit sine dilacione mittatis et hoc breve. Teste me ipso apud Westm' .xv. die Maii anno regni nostri nono.' Et quia predictus Thomas non protulit starrum vel talliam ab acquietancia dicti debiti per hoc breve preceptum est vicecomiti quod venire faciat coram etc. a die sancte Trinitatis in .xv. dies .xij. tam milites etc. de visneto de Bromwyz et vicecomiti Norht' quod venire faciat ad eundem diem sex legales judeos de villo Norht' de hiis qui solebant manere apud Warr', per quos etc., ad recognoscendum etc. Ad quem diem inquisicio non venit. Et datus est dies a die sancti Michaelis in tres septimanas. Ad quem diem predictus Thomas venit et inquisicio venit per Robertum le Wronge, Rogerum de Blyth' et alios christianos et Samuelem de Staunff', Samuelem filium Jude et alios judeos. Qui dicunt super sacramentum suum quod predictus Thomas satisfecit predicto Mosseo de .xiij. marcis, videlicet per .ij. equos precii .ix. marcarum et .iiij. marcas in denariis tempore quo idem Mosseus habuit liberam administracionem bonorum suorum etc. Et missus est processus loquele predicte una cum inquisicione et breve supradicto domino Regi sub sigillo scaccarii etc.[82]

MEMBRANE 6 DORSE

Adhuc Memoranda de termino Pasche anno regis Edwardi ix°

(906)

Ebor'. Memorandum quod Samuel filius Aaron de Ebor' et Antera filia Aaron de Ebor' judei venerunt coram etc. in pleno scaccario et reddiderunt Ade Verdonel civi <Lond'>[83] totum jus, clamium et calumpniam que habuerunt vel aliquo modo habere potuerunt occasione cujusdam mesuagii siti in vico de <Brancegate>[84] in parochia sancti Petri [Parvi][85] de Ebor', quod quidem mesuagium idem Samuel habuit ex vendicione predicte Antere, et eadem Antera ex dono predicti Aaron, patris eorundem Samuelis et Antere, pro multiplicibus arreragiis in quibus predictus Samuel tenebatur predicto Ade de redditu ejusdem [mesuagii,][86] et pro quatuor marcis quas idem Adam prefato Samueli solvit pre manibus, ita quod idem Samuel et Antera seu eorundem heredes jus, clamium seu calumpniam nullo modo decetero poterunt exigere vel vendicare inperpetuum.

[82] *At the bottom of the membrane is written* Pascha anno .ix.
[83] Ebor' *37*. [84] Brettegate *37*. [85] *Supplied from 37*.
[86] *MS. reads* Mossei; mesuagii *37*.

(907)

Summa catallorum Isak' filii Bonamy de Oxon' judei mortui in archa Lond' existencium .cxvj. solidi .viij. denarii, videlicet unum debitum decem librarum sub nominibus Petri de Denhull' de comitatu Kanc' et predicti Isak', reddendo ad Mediam Quadragesimam anno regni regis Edwardi tercio; et unum decem librarum sub nominibus Petri et Isak', reddendo ad quindenam sancti Martini in Hyeme anno regis Edwardi secundo, Acta .ij. die Augusti anno regis Edwardi primo; et unum octo librarum sub nominibus eorundem Petri et Isak, reddendo ad festum sanctum Petri ad Vincula anno regis Henrici .Lvij. Acta.xvij. die Octobris anno .Lvj.^{to}, que quidem debita Drua que fuit uxor predicti Isak appurat ad quatuor marcas. Et unum .xij. solidorum sub nominibus Willelmi filii Gilberti de <Faukeham>[87] [et Isak',][88] reddendo ad festum sancti Hillarii anno regis Henrici .xl.°, Acta .xxj. die Julii anno .xxxix.°, quod appuratur per dimidiam marcam per eandem Druam. Et unum unius marce sub nominibus Godefridi Prat et predicti Isak, reddendo ad Pentecosten anno regis Henrici .xl., Acta .xxv. die Februarii anno eodem, quod appuratur ad .x. solidos. Et unum quinque marcarum sub nominibus Baldewyni de Weyford' de comitatu Devon' et predicti Isak, reddendo ad Purificacionem beate Marie anno regis Henrici .xlij.°, Acta .xij. die Octobris anno .xlij.°. Et unum .xl. solidorum sub nominibus Roberti de Berchamsted' et predicti Isak, reddendo ad quindenam sancti Michaelis anno regis Henrici .xlj.°, Acta .xj. die Julii anno eodem.

Unde tercia pars Regis est .xxxviij. solidi .ij. denarii obulus, per quod Rex capit se ad tria debita, videlicet ad unum debitum .xij. solidorum sub nominibus Willelmi filii Gilberti de Faukeham et predicti Isak', et unum unius marce sub nominibus Godefridi Prat et predicti Isak', et unum .xl. solidorum sub nominibus Roberti de Berchamsted' et predicti Isak'. Et super hoc predicta Drua concessit quod, si alique carte invente fuerunt in archa cyrographariorum infra regnum etc. sub nominibus quorumcumque christianorum et predicti Isak', eedem carte sint Regis. Ideo preceptum est cyrographariis christianis et judeis Lond' etc. quod habeant coram etc. predictas cartas ad quas Rex se cepit pro tercia parte catallorum predicti Isak' a die sancte Trinitatis in .xv. dies. Et interim preceptum est eisdem quod predicte Drue de residuo catallorum que ei liberantur ut supradictum est liberam habere permittant administracionem.

(908)[89]

Oxon'. Concessum est Jacobo le Ballede de <Henle>[90] quod de centum solidis quos debet Regi de debito

[87] Faucham *37*. [88] *MS. omits.*
[89] *This entry is marked for deletion in 66, but not in 37.*
[90] Henleye *37*.

Cressei de Ebor' judei forisfacti, idem Jacobus solvat quinquaginta solidos ad quindenam sancti Michaelis anno regis Edwardi nono, et quinquaginta solidos ad quindenam Pasche proximo sequentem.[91]

(909)[92]

Norff'. Preceptum fuit vicecomiti quod distringeret Willelmum de <Halveryate>[93] tenentem <partem>[94] terrarum et tenementorum que fuerunt Bertrami de Werdun per terras etc. ad <reddendum>[95] sibi ad opus Regis .xviij. libras occasione terrarum etc. de debito Senioris le Eveske judei; et denarios haberet coram etc. vel corpus etc.

Predictus Willelmus venit et recognovit se esse tenenetem[96] terrarum et tenementorum que fuerunt predicti Bertrami et de dicto debito vocat ad warantum Robertum de Molton' qui ipsum inde acquietare debet ut dicit. Et preceptum est vicecomiti quod ipsum venire faciat coram etc. in octabis sancte Trinitatis etc. ad acquietandum etc., sicut rationabiliter etc.[97]

Ad quem diem predictus Robertus venit et optulit se primo, secundo, tercio et quarto die versus predictum Willelmum, et ipse non venit. Et predictus Robertus petit judicium de defalta ipsius Willelmi et qui non recedere debeat a curia. Et [e]<consideratum est>[e] quia predictus Willelmus versus eum nec aliquis pro eo prosequitur, ideo consideratum est quod predictus Robertus eat inde quietus; et dictus Willelmus, quia non est prosecutus versus ipsum de dicto debito, remaneat oneratus et nichilominus pro se et plegiis suis de prosequendo, quia non est prosecutus, in misericordia;[98] et quod distringatur pro toto predicto debito.

(910)

Warr'. Vyves le Romanzur judeus, qui tulit breve regis de placito debiti super priorem de Kenilworth et alios in brevi, petit licenciam recedendi de brevi suo, et habet. Et dictus prior et alii in brevi inde sine die.

(911)

Oxon', Berk'. Frater Alanus de Shesecote monachus et procurator abbatis de la Bruere, qui tulit breve regis super Salomonem Tapay, Josceum filium Syggh' et terciam uxorem ejus, Benedictum de Kauz et Meyr de Brug' judeos de placito transgressionis, quia non est prosecutus ideo in misericordia.

Et predicti judei non venerunt. Et vicecomes mandavit quod Salomon Tappay et alii judei non fuerunt inventi in balliva sua post recepcionem brevis; set quod Samuel de Staunff' et Manserus de la Venele manuceperunt Benedictum de Kauz judeum, quem non habuerunt. Ideo in misericordia. Judicium quod distringat per terras etc. et quod habeat corpus ejus coram etc. a die sancti Michaelis in .xv. dies, et quod attachiet corpora predictorum judeorum et ea habeat coram etc. ad eundem diem ad respondendum Regi de quibusdam privilegiis et aliis catallis, que ceperunt de dicto fratre Alano in villa Oxon' contra pacem etc.

(912)

Rotel'. Bernardus de Brus miles de comitatu Rotel' venit coram etc. et recognovit per scriptum etc. se debere Cresseo filio Cressei et Leoni fratri ejus judeis Lond' .iiij. saccos et dimidium lane vel pro quolibet sacco .x. marcas, reddendo inde medietatem ad festum nativitatis beati Johannis Baptiste anno regis Edwardi nono, et aliam medietatem ad festum sancti Michaelis proximo sequens. Et, nisi fecerit, concedit quod de terris et catallis suis ad quorumcumque manus devenerunt fiant.[99]

MEMBRANE 7

Adhuc Memoranda de termino Pasche anno regis Edwardi nono

(913)

Ebor'. Preceptum fuit vicecomiti, sicut continetur in termino sancti Michaelis ultimo preterito, [i]<quod>[i] inquireret si Isac le Eveske de Denec' judeus fuisset attornatus Milonis filii Milonis judei dampnati ad recipiendum et ad acquietandum Walterum le Grant de sex marcis in quibus tenebatur predicto Miloni tempore quo idem judeus habuit liberam administracionem bonorum suorum. Et vicecomes mandavit quod capta fuit inquisicio per sacramentum Johannis le Blund, Petri de Oxenholm' et aliorum christianorum, Mossei filii Bonamy, Davyd filii magistri et aliorum judeorum, sicut continetur inter inquisiciones hujus termini retornatas. Qui dicunt super sacramentum suum quod predictus Isac fuit attornatus predicti Milonis, habens plenam potestatem recipiendi et acquietandi unum debitum sex marcarum, unde fecit eidem Waltero starrum suum pro predicto Milone quod ipsum Walterum inde deberet acquietare. Ideo consideratum est quod carta predicti debiti liberetur predicto Waltero quiete dampnata, et quod predictus Isac quietus sit de predictis sex marcis.

(914)[100]

Lond'. Johannes de sancto Dionisio, custos domus conversorum, tulit breve regis de magno sigillo in hec verba: 'Edwardus etc. justiciariis etc. salutem. Ex parte conversorum domus nostre Lond' nobis est ostensum quod, cum medietas bonorum et catallorum judeorum

[91] *37 adds here* per plegium.
[92] *There is also a cancelled version of this entry on m. 11. See below, no. 1011.*
[93] Halvergate *37*.
[94] *37 omits.*
[95] respondendum *37*.
[96] *37 adds* cujusdam partis.
[97] *The version in 37 ends here.*
[98] *The word* misericordia *is repeated in the margin.*
[99] *At the bottom of this membrane in a later hand are written the words* 9 E.I *upside down.*
[100] *Previously printed by Rigg in* Select Pleas, *p. 114.*

conversorum seu convertendorum ad fidem catholicam ad conversos domus nostre predicte racione concessionis nostre eis inde facte pertineat, alia medietate illis qui se a tempore concessionis nostre predicte converterunt reservata, ac Belassez et Hittecote judee Oxon' nuper ad fidem catholicam se converterunt, per quod conversi domus nostre predicte medietatem bonorum et catallorum ipsorum juxta formam concessionis nostre predicte pecierunt a vobis sibi liberari, vos, ut accepimus, pro eo quod dicte judee parum ante tempus hujus concessionis nostre se ad fidem catholicam converterunt, predictam medietatem conversis dicte domus liberare contradicitis. Nos autem ad necessitatem dictorum conversorum pium respectum habentes et graciam eis facere volentes, vobis mandamus quod bona et catalla predictarum judearum seu valorem eorumdem, si alicui alii de precepto nostro prius assignata non fuerunt, dilecto clerico nostro Johanni de Sancto Dyonisio custodi domus predicte vel ejus attornato plenarie liberare faciatis et unam medietatem inde ad sustentacionem conversorum dicte domus retineat et aliam medietatem eisdem Belasset et Hittecot' faciatis assignari juxta formam concessionis nostre supradicte. Teste me ipso apud Wodestoke .xxvij. die Aprilis anno regis nunc nono.' Per hoc breve liberantur eidem Johanne bona et catalla subscripta, videlicet de bonis et catallis predictarum conversarum unus Liber Presciani constr' precii .xij. denariorum, unum Grecismus precii sex denariorum, una Logica Vetus precii .x. denariorum, unum Doctrinale Magnum precii .xvj. solidorum, quidam Liber Institutionum precii .iiij. solidorum, quidam Codex precii .xvj. soldiorum, quoddam Inforciatum precii .xvj. solidorum, Liber Nature precii .viij. solidorum, quidam Grecismus precii .xij. denariorum, et .x. solidi in denariis pro pannis qui fuerunt predictarum conversarum venditis etc.

(915)

Ebor'. Memorandum quod Alanus de Walkyngham solvit in pleno scaccario .x. libras in quibus Andreas de Gramar' tenebatur Josceo le Joefne judeo Ebor', que quidem debita atterminantur ad .cvj. solidos .iij. denarios per annum, et predicte .x. libre sunt de annis preteritis, que liberantur Aaron filio Vyves in recompensacionem debitorum Gilberti Pecche etc.[101]

(916)

Suff'. Loquela inter Johannem de Bayfeld' clericum querentem et Johannem de Clare de placito transgressionis et debiti patet inter placita de termino sancte Trinitatis anno regis Edwardi .viij. Et preceptum est vicecomiti quod non omittat propter libertatem sancte Etheldrede quin eam etc. et venire faciat tot et tales etc. de visneto de Hollesl' coram etc. in octabis sancte Trinitatis ad faciendum inquisicionem, nisi H. Haut' vel R. de Ludham prius etc.

(917)

Not'. Radulfus Hutte a quo exiguntur ad opus Regis .lx. solidi de debito in quo tenebatur Samueli de Not' judeo converso venit coram etc., et protulit starrum predicti judei de acquietancia dicti debiti et de hoc ponit se super cyrographarios et alios christianos et judeos. Et preceptum est vicecomiti quod venire faciat coram etc. in octabis sancti Johannis ad recognoscendum etc.

(918)

Essex'. Per breve regis de magno sigillo patens in hec verba: 'Edwardus etc. omnibus ad quos presentes littere pervenerunt salutem. Sciatis quod de gracia nostra speciali dedimus licenciam Mansero filio Abrahe et Abrahi filio Isac judeis nostris Lond' vendendi dilecto clerico nostro Egidio de Audenarde quoddam debitum .xxiiij. librarum in quo Saerus filius Godini Hay de Waltham per cartas suas predictis judeis tenetur. Dedimus eciam licenciam eidem Egidio debitum illud a prefatis judeis emendi, prout sibi magis viderit expedire, nisi debitum illud nobis fuerit forisfactum vel alio modo jus habeamus in eodem. In cujus rei testimonium has litteras nostras fieri fecimus patentes. Teste me ipso apud Wyndes' .xx. die Februarii anno regis nostri nono.'[102]

(919)

Hertff'. Johannes filius Johannis de Brokeshevede de Staundon' et Willelmus de Hemelhamsted' de comitatu Hertf' venerunt coram etc. et recognoverunt per scriptum etc. se debere Aaron filio Vyves centum quarteria frumenti vel pro quolibet quarterio .v. solidos, reddendo ad Pentecosten anno regis Edwardi .ix. Et, nisi fecerint, concedunt quod de terris et catallis suis fiant etc.

(920)

Lond'. Aaron filio Vyves judeus ad instanciam Regine consortis Regis ponit in respectum demandam quam facit versus Willelmum de Lyndes', tenentem quandam partem terrarum que fuerunt Roberti de Hereford', qui vocavit Ricardum de Brus ad warantum, de quodam debito .c. librarum usque in octabas sancti Michaelis proximo futuras.

(921)

Linc'. Hawysia de Benyngworth' pro pluribus defaltis in misericordia.[103]

Preceptum fuit vicecomiti quod distringeret Hawisiam de Benyngworth', tenentem quandam partem terrarum que fuerunt Gilberti de Benygworth', per terras etc. ad respondendum Regi una cum Johanne de Bathon', tenente quandam partem terrarum que fuerunt predicti Gilberti, de .ccclx. libris in quibus dictus Gilbertus Regi tenebatur de debitis judaismi. Predicta Hawisia per attornatum suum venit et per auxilium curie vocat ad warantum de porcione ipsam contingente de debito predicto

101 *The name* Pecche *is repeated in the margin.*

102 *This entry appears to be unfinished.*

103 *The word* misericordia *is repeated in the margin.*

occasione terrarum etc. Rogerum de Mortuo Mari et Luciam de Chauncy, heredes predicti Gilberti, qui ipsam inde acquietare debent, ut dicit. Et preceptum est vicecomiti quod venire faciat coram etc. a die sancte Trinitatis in .xv. dies predictos Rogerum et Luciam ad acquietandum etc. sicut racionabiliter etc.

(922)

Bed', [Buk'.][104] Alexander le Botiler de [Eydon'][105] de comitatu Bed' et Nicholaus Baynel filius domini Willelmi Baynel de comitatu Buk' venerunt coram etc. Et recognoverunt per scriptum suum se debere Vyves filio Aaron judeo centum quarteria frumenti vel pro quolibet quarterio .v. solidos, reddendo ad quindenam sancti Michaelis anno regni regis Edwardi .ix. Et, nisi fecerint, concedunt quod de terris et catallis suis [et heredum suorum et tenencium terrarum suarum, ad quorumcumque manus devenerint, fiant etc.][106]

(923)

Linc'. Abbas de Revesby pro pluribus defaltis in misericordia.[107]

Preceptum fuit vicecomiti quod distringeret abbatem de Revesby, tenentem quandam partem terrarum que fuerunt Gilberti de Benyngworth', per terras etc. ad respondendum Regi una cum Johanne de Bathon', tenente quandam partem predictarum terrarum, de porcione etc. .ccclx. librarum de debitis Judaismi etc.

Predictus abbas per attornatum suum venit et recognovit se esse tenentem partis predictarum terrarum et per auxilium curie vocavit ad warantum Rogerum de Mortuo Mari et Luciam de Chauncy, heredes predicti Gilberti, qui ipsum inde acquietare debent, ut dicit. Et preceptum est vicecomiti quod ipsos venire faciat coram etc. a die sancte Trinitatis in .xv. dies ad acquietandum etc., sicut racionabiliter etc.

(924)

Linc'. Prior de Ormesby pro pluribus defaltis in misericordia.[108]

Prior de Ormesby, tenens quandam partem terrarum que fuerunt Gilberti de Benygworth', districtus per terras etc. ad respondendum Regi una cum Johanne de Bathon', tenente quandam partem predictarum terrarum, de porcione etc. .ccclx. librarum de debitis Judaismi occasione predictarum terrarum etc. venit coram etc. et recognovit se esse tenentem cujusdam partis predictarum terrarum, set dicit quod inde feoffatus fuit antequam dictus Gilbertus se obligavit in Judaismo et petit quod inquiratur. Ideo preceptum est vicecomiti quod venire faciat coram etc. a die sancte Trinitatis in .xv. dies .xij. tam milites etc. de visneto de Fresken', per quos etc., ad recognoscendum etc. quibus die et anno etc.

104 *37 omits.*
105 Eyden' *37*.
106 fiant in quorumcumque manus devenerint etc. *37*.
107 *The word* misericordia *is repeated in the margin*.
108 *The word* misericordia *is repeated in the margin.*

(925)

[Linc.] Willelmus de Ros pro pluribus defaltis in misericordia.

Idem Willelmus, tenens quandam partem terrarum que fuerunt Gilberti de Benygworth', attachiatus ad respondendum Regi una cum Johanne de Bath', tenente quandam partem terrarum que fuerunt predicti Gilberti, de porcione ipsum contingente de quodam debito .ccclx. librarum de debitis Judaismi venit coram etc. et sine licencia recessit. Ideo distringatur etc.

(926)

[Not'.] Memorandum quod Gervasius de Clyfton' vicecomes Not' debet de residuo compoti sui de quo oneratur .clxxvj. libras .xviij. solidos .v. denarios obulum. Et habet diem ad computandum a die sancti Michaelis in .xv. dies.

(927)

. . . . , ... s de Clynton' de Willelmus Baggod manuceperunt Willelmum de Stafford' ad habendum corpus ejus coram etc. die lune ante Ascensionem Domini.

MEMBRANE 7 DORSE

Adhuc memoranda

(928)

Norff'. Willelmus de Ormesby, a quo exiguntur ad opus Regis .xxx. libre in quibus idem Willelmus tenebatur Josceo filio Benedicti per cartam suam, tulit breve regis de magno sigillo in hec verba: 'Edwardus etc. justiciariis etc. salutem. Monstravit nobis Willelmus de Ormesby quod, cum dudum satisfecerit Josceo filio Benedicti quondam judeo nostro Norwic', qui pro transgressione monete nostre suspensus fuit, de quodam debito .xxx. librarum in quo idem Willelmus per cartam suam dicto judeo aliquo tempore tenebatur, per quod idem judeus tempore quo de bonis et catallis suis ante mortem suam liberam habuit administracionem et potestatem per starrum suum predictum Willelmum de toto debito supradicto plenius acquietavit, vos nichilominus prefatum debitum a dicto Willelmo ad opus nostrum exigi et ipsum ea occasione distringi faciatis minus juste ad dampnum suum non modicum et gravamen. Et quia ei injuriari nolumus in hac parte, vobis mandamus quod, vocato coram vobis prefato Willelmo et inspecto starro predicto et plenius examinato, si vobis legitime constare possit ita esse, tunc cartam predictam ab archa cyrographariorum extrahi et eidem Willelmo liberari ac prefatum Willelmum de debito predicto quietum esse faciatis, prout de jure et secundum legem et consuetudinem judaismi nostri fuerit faciendum. Teste me ipso apud Walsyngham .vj. die Januarii anno regni nostri .ix.º.' Per hoc breve emanavit breve vicecomiti Norff' quod venire faciat coram etc. apud Norwic' die mercurii in septimana Pasche anno regis Edwardi nono .xij.

probos et legales homines de villa Norwyc', tam christianos quam judeos, per quos etc. ad certificandum etc. de confeccione et acquietacione dicti starri. Ad quem diem inquisicio venit per Simonem le Palmer, Hubertum de Morle et alios christianos, Isac filium Deulecres, Isac le Chapeleyn et alios judeos juratos, qui dicunt super sacramentum suum quod predictus Willelmus de Ormesby per starrum quod protulit coram etc. quietus est de omnibus debitis in quibus tenebatur Josceo filio Bendyt a creacione seculi usque ad festum Omnium Sanctorum anno regis Edwardi sexto. Et dicunt quod dictum starrum fecit tempore quo habuit liberam administracionem bonorum suorum, videlicet ad festum Nativitatis Beate Marie anno regis Edwardi sexto. Ideo consideratum est quod predictus Willelmus de predicto debito .xxx. librarum sit quietus et quod carta dicti debiti eidem Willelmo liberetur quiete dampnata.

(929)

Cant'. Josceus filius Sauloti Motun judeus solvit in recepta regis dimidiam marcam de fine pro catallis predicti Sauloti habendis et habet inde talliam.

(930)

Linc'. Isac de Provyns judeus Linc' ex parte Regis calumpniatus coram etc. de platis conflatis ex argento contra statutum etc., que fuerunt de catallis judeorum dampnatorum et aliorum catallorum, ut dicebatur, fecit finem pro secta regis relaxanda per .x. solidos solvendum ad scaccarium sancti Michaelis proximo futurum, salva querela quorumcumque versus eum loqui volencium. Et preceptum est vicecomiti quod ad corpus ejus etc. ea occasione manum non apponat etc.

(931)

<*Glouc'.*>[109] Johannes de <Langele,>[110] tenens terrarum que fuerunt <Roberti>[111] de Bulers, venit coram etc., et recognovit quod <satisfaciet>[112] Aaron filio Vyves judeo ad quindenam sancti Michaelis anno regis Edwardi nono de quodam debito .x. marcarum de catallo et .c. marcarum de lucro, nisi tunc acquietacionem inde ostendere poterit. Et, nisi fecerit, concedit quod de terris et catallis suis fiant. Ad quem diem dictus Johannes non venit. Ideo preceptum est vicecomiti quod de terris et catallis suis fieri faciat dictum debitum ad opus ipsius Aaron.

(932)[113]

Buk'. Rogerus de <Bachesworth'>[114] venit coram etc., et recognovit se debere Aaron filio Vyves judeo .lx. quarteria frumenti, reddendo in crastino Animarum proximo futuro vel pro quolibet quarterio dimidiam marcam ad eleccionem ipsius judei. Et, nisi fecerit, concedit [pro se et heredibus suis][115] quod de terris et catallis suis [ad quorumcumque manus devenerint][116] fiant.

[109] Warr' *37*. [110] Langelegh' *37*. [111] Johannis *37*.
[112] satisfecit *37*. [113] *Cf. No. 989*. [114] Bacheworth' *37*.
[115] *Supplied from 37*. [116] *Supplied from 37*.

(933)

Lond'. Aaron filius Vyves judeus solvit in recepta regis .xx. solidos de fine et habet talliam etc.

(934)

Warr'. Thomas de Arderne <venit coram etc. et>[117] recognovit se debere Aaron filio Vyves .cc. libras, reddendo inde in octabis sancti Johannis Baptiste anno regis Edwardi .ix.º .c. libras, et ad quindenam sancti Michaelis proximo sequentem .c. libras. Et, nisi fecerit, concedit quod de terris et catallis suis fiant.

(935)

Leyc'. Thomas de Linc' solvit in recepta regis .xx. solidos de debitis patris sui de debitis judaismi et habet inde talliam.

(936)

Warr. Johannes Perceval de Somery <venit coram etc. et>[118] recognovit se debere Aaron filio Vyves .xx. libras et unum palefridum precii .v. marcarum, reddendo dictum palefridum vel quinque marcas ad festum Pentecosten anno regis Edwardi .ix.º , et ad quindenam sancti Michaelis proximo sequentem .xx. libras. Et, nisi fecerit, concedit quod de terris et catallis suis fiant.

(937)

Kanc'. Willelmus le Joefne miles et Ricardus filius ejus <de comitatu Kanc' venerunt coram etc. et>[119] recognoverunt se debere per scriptum suum [i]<Aaron filio Vyves>[i] .viij. marcas .v. solidos .iiij. denarios, reddendo ad quindenam Omnium Sanctorum <anno regis Edwardi .ix.º>[120] Et, nisi fecerint, concedunt quod de terris et catallis suis fiant etc. Et per istam recognicionem predictus Willelmus debet esse quietus de quadam recognicione .x. librarum quam eidem Aaron fecit in termino sancti Michaelis anno regis Edwardi .viij.º, incipiente .ix., <sicut patet per starrum dicti Aaron quod idem Willelmus penes se habet.>[121] Et istam recognicionem predicti Willelmus et Ricardus fecerunt predicto Aaron pro quodam debito .iiij. librarum in quo predictus Willelmus Salomoni de Staunf' judeo Cantuar' dampnato per cartam suam tenebatur, quod quidem debitum idem Aaron recepit in recompensacionem <debiti Gilberti Pecche.>[122]

(938)

Wilt'. Cum Vyves filius Batemanni de Brugewat' judeus indictatus fuisset in villa Wylton' pro quibusdam platis et quodam feretro de ecclesia conventuali Wilton' asportato, nec super hiis per aliquem vel per aliquos fuit inculpatus seu calumpniatus nisi per sectam regis, idem judeus venit coram etc. et fecit finem per quinque solidos ad scaccarium sancti Michaelis proximo futurum solvendum pro secta regis relaxanda. Et preceptum est vicecomiti quod ad corpus ejus etc. manum non apponat etc.

[117] *37 omits.* [118] *37 omits.* [119] *37 omits.*
[120] *37 omits.* [121] *37 omits.* [122] *37 omits.*

(939)

Derb', Not'. Preceptum fuit vicecomiti quod distringeret Urianum de sancto Petro, tenentem terrarum que fuerunt Willelmi de Meysham junioris, per terras etc. ad reddendum Regi .xxxv. libras de debitis Benedicti de Wynton' judei dampnati occasione terrarum etc., et denarios haberet etc. vel corpus etc.

Predictus Urianus venit et dicit quod non tenetur de dicto debito respondere, eo quod non tenet aliquas terras vel tenementa que fuerunt Willelmi filii Willelmi de Meysham, et de hoc ponit se super patriam. Et Aaron filius Vyves, cui istud debitum assignatur in recompensacionem etc., dicit pro rege quod predictus Urianus tenet terras et tenementa que fuerunt predicti Willelmi et quod per feoffamentum predicti Willelmi ea tenet et per predictum Willelmum feoffatus fuit de terris et tenementis illis, ita quod de terris et tenementis illis nullam securitatem habuit nisi per factum. Et hoc petit similiter quod inquiratur. Et predictus Urianus dicit quod predictus Willelmus nunquam feoffavit eum de dictis terris seu tenementis nec quicquam juris in eis habuit. Et hoc petit similiter quod inquiratur. Et preceptum est vicecomiti quod venire faciat coram etc. a die sancte Trinitatis in .xv. dies sex probos et legales homines de visneto de Eyton' et sex legales judeos de villa Not', per quos etc., ad recognoscendum etc. Ad quem diem inquisicio non venit et datus est dies dicto Uriano a die sancti Michaelis in tres septimanas. Ad quem diem inquisicio venit per Galfridum de Skyftyngton', Robertum de Accorn' milites et alios christianos, Isac Colemyn, Pictavinum filium Isac et alios judeos, sicut patet inter brevia de termino sancti Michaelis proximo sequentis retornata. Qui dicunt super sacramentum suum quod dictus Urianus non tenet aliquas terras vel tenementa que umquam fuerunt Willelmi de Meysham junioris nec idem Willelmus umquam habuit seisinam de terris seu tenementis que idem Urianus modo tenet de terris et tenementis que fuerunt Willelmi de Meysham senioris, patris predicti Willelmi; et quod idem Willelmus junior nunquam habuit seisinam aliquarum terrarum in comitatu predicto. Et ideo consideratum est quod predictus Urianus de predictis .xxxv. libris in quibus Willelmus de Meysham junior tenebatur predicto Benedicto sit quietus et carta dicti debiti in hec verba: 'Willelmus de Meysham filius Willelmi de Meysham militis de comitatu Derb' debet Benedicto filio Abrahe de Wynton' judeo .xxxv. libras, reddendo ad quindenam sancti Michaelis anno regis Edwardi primo. Acta .xiij. die Julii anno eodem' eidem Uriano in pleno scaccario liberatur quiete dampnata.

(940)

Warr', Leyc'. Preceptum fuit vicecomiti quod non omitteret propter libertatem de Pathelawe quin eam etc. et distringeret Nicholaum le Webbe per terras etc. ad reddendum Regi .xv. marcas que devenerunt ad manus ejus de bonis et catallis que fuerunt Bonamy de Beaudesert judei dampnati; et quod distringeret eodem modo Jacobum de Clopt . . . pro .lxviij. solidis, qui[123] ad manus ejus devenerunt de bonis et catallis que fuerunt predicti Bonamy; et quod distringeret Willelmum Purcel, Nicholaum le Webbe et Rogerum le Clerc pro .xxv. marcis que ad manus eorum devenerunt de bonis etc. que fuerunt predicti Bonamy; et quod distringeret eodem modo Luciam Purcelote pro .xj. marcis que ad manus ejus devenerunt de bonis et catallis predicti Bonamy; et quod distringeret eodem modo Radulfum le Barber et Cristianam uxorem ejus pro .xix. libris .xvj. solidis .viij. denariis que ad manus eorum devenerunt de bonis et catallis predicti judei; et quod distringeret eodem modo Julianam la Dystere pro sex marcis que ad manus ejus devenerunt de bonis et catallis que fuerunt predicti judei; et denarios haberet coram etc. a die Pasche in tres septimanas nunc vel corpora etc. Et predicti Nicholaus, Jacobus et alii veniunt et defendunt etc. Et dicunt quod de denariis, bonis seu catallis predicti Bonamy nichil habuerunt nec aliquid de catallis suis receperunt nec aliquid ei debuerunt et petunt quod inquiratur etc. Et preceptum est vicecomiti quod venire faciat coram etc. in crastino sancti Johannis Baptiste .xij. etc. de visneto de Henle, per quos etc., ad recognoscendum etc. Ad quem diem inquisicio non venit nec vicecomes breve retornavit. Ideo datus est dies dictis Nicholao et aliis a die sancti Michaelis in tres septimanas. Et preceptum est vicecomiti, sicut alias etc. Postea a die Pasche in tres septimanas anno regis Edwardi .x.° inquisicio venit per Johannem de Heref', Robertum Lyun et alios christianos, Samuelem de Staunff', Vyves le Romaunzur et alios judeos, sicut patet inter brevia ibidem retornata. Qui dicunt super sacramentum suum quod Willelmus Purcel, Nicholaus le Webbe et Rogerus le Clerc conjuncti de .xxv. marcis, Lucia Purcelot de .xj. marcis, Radulfus le Barber et Cristiana uxor ejus de .xix. libris .xvj. solidis .viij. denariis, Juliana le Dyster de .vj. marcis nichil receperunt nec aliquid de catallis que fuerunt Bonamy de Beaudesert salvo suo receperunt. Ideo consideratum est quod predicti Nicholaus, Jacobus, Willelmus, Rogerus, Lucia, Radulfus, Cristiana et Juliana de denariis ab ipsis superius petitis recedant quieti et quod Rex ab eis ea occasione nichil capiat etc.

MEMBRANE 8

<Memoranda>[124] *Pasche anno regis Edwardi Nono*

(941)

Suth'. Preceptum fuit vicecomiti quod non omitteret propter libertatem Suth' quin eam etc., et venire faceret coram etc. a die Pasche in tres septimanas nunc Robertum le Mercer de Suth' et Feliciam uxorem ejus ad respondendum Regi de tribus ciphis argenti cum pedibus argenti deauratis precii quatuor et decem

[123] *Followed in MS. by* devenerunt.

[124] *This word is interlined above* Placita de tribus septimanis *which is marked for deletion.*

solidorum, quatuor ciphis de mazor' cum pedibus argenteis precii .xl. solidorum, tribus zonis de serico argent' barratis precii quatuor librarum et decem solidorum et aliis minutis jocalibus et catallis ad valenciam decem librarum, que bona et catalla devenerunt ad manus predicti Roberti et Felicie uxoris ejus de bonis et catallis que fuerunt Salomonis filii Salomonis de Suth' judei dampnati etc.

Predictus Robertus pro se et Felicia uxore sua venit et defendit etc., et dicit quod predicti quatuor ciphi argent', quatuor ciphi de mazar', tres zone seu aliqua alia bona vel jocalia precii supradicti ad manus ejus seu predicte Felicie uxoris sue non devenerunt ex tradicione predicti Salomonis nec ex tradicione alicujus pro eo. Et de hoc pro se et uxore ponit se super patriam. Et preceptum est vicecomiti quod venire faciat coram etc. in octabis sancte Trinitatis sex probos et legales homines de villa Suth', <sex probos et legales homines>[125] de civitate Wynton', et qui nulla affinitate etc., ad recognoscendum etc.[126]

Postea in termino sancti Hillarii anno regis Edwardi decimo venit inquisicio, sicut patet inter brevia ibi retornata, per Robertum Bonet, Hugonem de Hereff', Rogerum Alred, Stephanum de la Prise, Andream de Portesmue et Johannem Dyset christianos, Cokerel filium Licoricie, Abraham filium Cokerel, Lumbardum le Petyt, Swettmanum filium Licoricie, Abraham filium Cressei et Beycoc filium Bonamy judeos. Qui dicunt super sacramentum suum quod predicti Robertus et Felicia uxor ejus de supradictis ciphis, mazeris, zonis seu aliis catallis vel jocalibus que fuerunt dicti Salomonis nichil receperunt. Ideo consideratum est quod predicti Robertus et Felicia inde sint quieti etc., et quod Rex nichil ab eis capiat.

(942)

Suth'. Preceptum fuit vicecomiti quod venire faceret coram etc. Ricardum le Engleys, Johannem Wodhorn et Johannem Page juniorem ad respondendum Regi de viginti libris que devenerunt ad manus predictorum Ricardi, Johannis et Johannis de denariis que fuerunt Salomonis filii Salomonis de Suth' judei dampnati per manus <Douce>[127] uxoris predicti Salomonis ad inquisicionem inde procurandum ad deliberacionem predicti Salomonis.

Predicti Ricardus, Johannes et Johannes veniunt et defendunt vim etc., et dicunt quod de denariis seu catallis dicti <Salle>[128] ex tradicione predicte <Duce>[129] uxoris sue seu alicujus alterius per eam <non>[130] devenerunt nec aliquid de bonis suis habuerunt. Et de hoc ponit se super patriam. Et preceptum est vicecomiti quod venire faciat coram etc. in octabis sancte Trinitatis etc. [131]

[125] et sex legales judeos *37*.

[126] *The remainder of this entry is a later addition to 66 and is omitted from 37*.

[127] Duce *37*. [128] Salamonis *37*. [129] Douce *37*.

[130] nulla *37*.

[131] *The remainder of this entry is a later addition to 66 and omitted from 37*.

Postea in termino sancti Hillarii anno regis Edwardi .x.º inquisicio venit, sicut patet inter brevia ibidem retornata, per Robertum Bonet, Hugonem de Hereff' et alios christianos, Cokerel filium Licoricie, Abraham filium Cokerel judeos et alios judeos. Qui dicunt super sacramentum suum quod predicti Ricardus, Johannes et Johannes de denariis, bonis seu catallis que fuerunt dicti Salomonis nichil receperunt nec habuerunt. Ideo consideratum est quod predicti Ricardus, Johannes et Johannes inde sint quieti et quod Rex nichil capiat etc.

(943)

Suth'. Preceptum fuit vicecomiti quod venire faceret coram etc. Ricardum Seld ad respondendum Regi de duobis firmaculis auri, una zona de serico argento barrata precii quinque marcarum que devenerunt ad manus predicti Ricardi de catallis que fuerunt Salomonis filii Salle de Suth' judei dampnati etc.

Predictus Ricardus venit et defendit vim etc., et dicit quod predictus Salomon ab eo emit unam pipam vini pro triginta solidis multo tempore elapso antequam predictus Salomon captus fuisset pro tonsura monete pro qua suspensus fuit, et pro predicta pipa ei tradidit in vadium unum fermaculum auri et unam zonam de serico argento barratam, que vadia detulit coram Bartholomeo de <Sulleie>[132] et sociis suis justiciariis ad bona judeorum dampnatorum inquirendum deputatis, et coram eis predicta vadia ei, ut supradictum est, invadiata esse legittime probavit, qui sibi dicta vadia pro predicto precio concesserunt, et ea pro predicto precio aquietare recusarunt. Et quod aliter predicta firmaculum et <zona>[133] ad manus ejus non devenerunt nec aliqua alia catalla de catallis predicti judei. Et de hoc ponit se super patriam. Et preceptum est vicecomiti quod venire faciat coram etc. in octabis sancte Trinitatis etc.[134]

Postea in termino sancti Hillarii anno regis Edwardi .x.º venit inquisicio, sicut patet inter brevia ibidem retornata, per Robertum Bonet, Hugonem de Hereff' et alios christianos, Cokerel filium Licoricie, Abraham filium Cokerel et alios judeos. Qui dicunt super sacramentum suum quod predictus Ricardus non habuit sive recepit de catallis dicti Salomonis nisi unum fermaculum et unam zonam ut vadia pro predicta pipa vini, ut supradictum est, que quidem vadia predicti justiciarii pro predictis .xxx. solidis ei concesserunt, ut superius dictum est. Ideo consideratum est quod predictus Ricardus de predictis firmaculo et zona sit quietus etc. et quod rex nihil capiat etc.

(944)

North'. Preceptum fuit vicecomiti quod per sacramentum proborum et legalium hominum de comitatu suo diligenter inquireret quibus die et anno magister hospitalis sancti Johannis North' feofatus fuit de terris et tenementis que tenet in villa de Tyffeud que fuerunt Alani de

[132] Suthleye *37*. [133] zonam *37*.

[134] *The remainder of this entry is a later addition to 66 and is omitted from 37*.

Tyffeud, qui se dicit prius feofatum fuisse de predictis terris et tenementis quam predictus Alanus se obligavit Benedicto filio Isac per cartam suam .xl. solidorum. Et vicecomes retornavit inquisicionem coram se captam per sacramentum Roberti filii Stephani de Tyffeud, Philippi filii Roberti de eadem et aliorum, sicut patet inter inquisiciones hujus termini retornatas. Qui dicunt super sacramentum suum quod magister dicti hospitalis feofatus fuit de decem et novem acris et dimidia ad festum Natalis Domini anno regis Henrici .xl.°, et eisdem die et anno de sex acris bosci et quatuor solidatis redditus assise. Dicunt eciam quod idem magister feofatus fuit in eadem villa ad festum sancti Johannis Baptiste anno regis Henrici .xlij.° de decem et octo acris terre arabilis et decem denariis annui redditus. Dicunt eciam quod idem magister feoffatus fuit in eadem villa die Pasche anno regis Edwardi tercio de uno mesuagio et uno columbario, octodecim acris terre dimidia et una roda terre, tribus solidis et sex denariis annui redditus, una libra piperis et quinque acris bosci.

(945)[135]

Suth'. Cristiana Dykevin, attachiata ad respondendum Regi de quibusdam robis, tapetis, pannis et aliis bonis et catallis ad valenciam .x. librarum que devenerunt ad manus ipsius Cristiane de bonis et catallis que fuerunt Cote que fuit uxor Michaelis le Eveske judee dampnate, per attornatum suum venit et dicit quod de bonis et catallis predicte Cote nichil recepit nisi tantummodo .xx. denarios et duo tapeta ut vadia pro .v. solidatis cervisie quam Michaeli quondam viro predicte Kote accomodavit dum vixerit et habuit liberam administracionem bonorum suorum, quos quidem .xx. denarios et tapeta predicta ad communem clamacionem de bonis et catallis judeorum dampnatorum factam detulit coram Bartholomeo de Sul', Willelmo de Brayboef et sociis suis justiciariis ad bona judeorum dampnatorum recipiendum deputatis, et dictos denarios et tapeta eisdem liberavit, ita quod nichil penes se remansit. Et de hoc ponit se super patriam. Ideo preceptum est vicecomiti quod venire faciat coram etc. In octabis sancte Trinitatis sex probos et legales homines et sex legales judeos de civitate Wynt', per quos etc., ad recognoscendum etc. Ad quem diem inquisicio non venit. Et datus est dies a die sancti Michaelis in tres septimanas. Ad quem diem inquisicio venit per Willelmum Strut, Hugonem le Noreys et alios christianos, Cokerel filium Licoricie, Abraham filium Cokerel et alios judeos. Qui dicunt super sacramentum suum quod predicta Christiana non recepit de bonis seu catallis predicte Kote nisi .xx. denarios et duo tapeta que liberavit Willelmo de Brayboef et sociis suis justiciariis etc., et quod nichil penes ipsam Christianam remansit. Ideo consideratum est quod ipsa Christiana inde sit quieta etc. Et rex nichil inde capiat etc.

(946)

Somers'. Preceptum fuit vicecomiti quod venire faceret coram etc. Willemum le <Long'>[136] Keu, Thomam <Tuprest,>[137] <Hismond'>[138] servientem, Johannem Fabrum, et Petrum <Coky>[139] ad respondendum Regi de novem libris que devenerunt ad manus ipsorum de bonis et catallis que fuerunt Jacobi de Shaston' judei dampnati, et quod venire faceret Michaelem le Seler ad respondendum Regi de .lij. solidis, qui devenerunt ad manus ipsius Michaelis [de catallis ipsius judei].[140]

Et <ipsi>[141] veniunt et defendunt vim etc., et dicunt quod de predictis denariis nec aliquibus aliis bonis seu catallis que fuerunt predicti Jacobi ex tradicione Florie de Shaston judee seu alicujus alterius nichil receperunt. Et de hoc ponunt se super patriam. Et preceptum est vicecomiti quod venire faciat coram etc. in crastino sancti Johannis Baptiste sex probos et legales homines de villa de Shaston' et sex legales judeos de villa Wilton', et qui nulla etc., ad recognoscendum etc.[142]

Postea a die sancti Michaelis in tres septimanas inquisicio venit per Johannem Seled, Stephanum le Bray et alios christianos, Cresseum de Bristoll', Cokerel filium Licoricie et alios judeos, sicut patet inter brevia ibidem retornata. Qui dicunt super sacramentum suum quod predicti Willelmus, Thomas, Osmund et alii nichil receperunt de bonis seu catallis que fuerunt predicti Jacobi ex tradicione predicte Florie. Ideo consideratum est quod inde sint quieti etc. et quod rex nichil capiat etc.

(947)

North'. Preceptum fuit vicecomiti quod venire faceret coram etc. Adam le Porsere ad respondendum Regi de uno cipho de mazaro precii .xl. solidorum, Willelmum <de Bockebrock'>[143] ad respondendum Regi de .xl. solidis argenti, Ricardum de la Hulle ad respondendum Regi de quinque marcis argenti et Osbertum de <Crowstorpe>[144] ad respondendum Regi de septem marcis, videlicet duabus marcis in denariis et in ciphis argenti et de mazaro pannis et aliis minutis jocalibus ad valenciam quinque marcarum, que bona et catalla devenerunt ad manus predictorum Ade, Willelmi, Ricardi et Osberti de catallis que fuerunt Sampsonis filii Sampsonis judei North' dampnati ex tradicione <Beleassez>[145] que fuit uxor predicti Sampsonis die dominica in Media Quadragesima anno regis Edwardi sexto salvo custodiendum, ut predicta Beleassez dicit.

Predicti Adam, Willelmus, Ricardus et Osbertus veniunt et defendunt vim etc., et dicunt quod de bonis et catallis predicti Sampsonis ad manus eorum ex tradicione predicte Beleassez nichil devenit, et de hoc

[135] *This entry appears to be a late addition to the roll and in the same hand as the additions to entries 941–3.*

[136] Lung *37*. [137] Touprest *37*. [138] Hismound' *37*.

[139] Goky *37*. [140] *Supplied from 37*.

[141] predicti Willelmus, Thomas, Ismund, Johannes, Petrus et Michael *37*.

[142] *The remainder of this entry is a later addition to 66 and is omitted from 37*.

[143] Bockebroke *37*. [144] Crowesthrop *37*.

[145] Belasez *66 (and subsequently)*.

ponit se super patriam. Et preceptum est vicecomiti quod venire faciat coram etc. in octabis sancte Trinitatis sex probos et legales homines de villa North' et sex legales judeos de eadem villa, et qui nulla etc., ad recognoscendum etc.[146]

Postea a die sancti Michaelis in .xv. dies venit inquisicio per christianos et judeos. Qui dicunt super sacramentum suum quod predicti Willelmus et Ricardus de bonis seu catallis dicti Sampsonis nichil receperunt, et quod dictus Osbertus de Crowethorp' non recepit de bonis seu catallis dicti Sampsonis nisi .j. marcam, quam liberavit ad communem clamacionem de catallis judeorum Hugoni de Kandal' ad hoc deputato. Ideo consideratum est quod predicti Willelmus, Ricardus et Osbertus de bonis et catallis superius ab eo petitis sint quieti. Et predicta Belassez pro falso clamore committitur prisone.

(948)

Norff'. Aaron filius Vyves judeus venit coram etc. et recognovit se recepisse .xij. marcas de Willelmo de Rothynghe quos ei debuit per recognicionem factam ad scaccarium judeorum.

MEMBRANE 8 DORSE

(949)

Kanc'. Johannes filius Ricardi de <Schardstede,>[147] a quo exiguntur .xl. solidi ad opus Regis de debitis Salomonis de Stamford' judei dampnati, dicit quod quietus est de dicto debito et inde habet starrum dicti judei de aquietancia de quo posuit se [i]<in>[i] inquisicionem, ut patet in termino sancti Hillarii proximo preteriti, quod starrum protulit coram etc. in hec verba: 'Salomon de Stanford' judeus recognoscit per starrum suum quod Johannes filius Ricardi de Scharstede et heredes sui quieti sunt de ipso judeo et heredibus suis de omnibus debitis, demandis et calumpniis factis sub nominibus ipsorum Johannis et Salomonis a creacione seculi usque ad festum Omnium Sanctorum anno regni regis Edwardi filii regis Henrici sexto. Et, si inveniatur carta, tallia vel obligacio in archa cyrographariorum vel extra sub nominibus predictorum Johannis et Salomonis, concedit quod quieta sint et nichil valeant. Et quod recognovit hoc idem sigillavit.' Et inquisicio inde venit a die Pasche in tres septimanas nunc per Thomam <Chiche,>[148] Johannem <Huberd>[149] cyrographarios christianos, Willelmum Calvesfot, Willelmum le Fevere et alios christianos, Aaron de Wynton', Haginum le Eveske cyrographarios judeos, Leonem filium Abrahe, Sampsonem de Sidingburn' et alios judeos, sicut patet inter brevia hujus termina retornata, qui dicunt super sacramentum suum quod predictum starrum est factum predicti Salomonis et littera ebrayca manu sua propria signatum. Et quod dictum starrum fecit tempore quo habuit liberam administracionem bonorum suorum. Et quod de predicto debito dictus Johannes eidem Salomoni satisfecit in autumpno anno regis Edwardi sexto ante communem capcionem judeorum pro tonsura monete pro qua dampnati fuerunt. Ideo consideratum est quod predictus Johannes de predicto debito .xl. solidorum quietus sit. Et carta predicti debiti eidem <Johanni>[150] liberetur quiete dampnata. Et preceptum est vicecomiti quod predicto Johanni de predicto debito de cetero pacem habere permittat, et si quid etc.

(950)

Norht'. Inquisicio ad inquirendum de confeccione cujusdam starri de acquietancia decem librarum quod Mosseus filius Leonis judeus dampnatus fecit Johanni de Clynton' de Napton' de dicto debito, quod starrum Hawysia que fuit uxor dicti Johannis protulit coram etc. in hec verba: 'Mosseus filius Leonis recognoscit per starrum suum quod Johannes de Clynton' de Napton' et heredes sui quieti sunt de ipso et heredibus suis de omnibus debitis, demandis et calumpniis a creacione seculi usque in crastinum sancti Michaelis anno regni regis Edwardi filii regis Henrici tercio. Et quod recognovit hoc idem sigillavit.' venit ad hunc diem per Philippum le Noricesone cyrographarium Warr', Walterum de Estthorp' et Petrum de Porta christianos, Vyves le <Rumanzur,>[151] Salomonem de Stanff' et alios judeos, sicut patet inter brevia hujus termini retornata, qui dicunt super sacramentum suum quod predictum starrum est factum predicti Mossei et littera ebrayca manu sua propria signatum, et quod dictum starrum fecit tempore quo habuit liberam administracionem bonorum suorum die in starro confecto. Et quod per predictum starrum predictus Johannes de dicto debito decem librarum quietus est. Ideo consideratum est quod predictus Johannes de dicto debito decem librarum quietus sit. Et carta predicti debiti eidem liberetur quiete dampnata. Et preceptum est vicecomiti quod predicto Johanni et tenentibus terrarum suarum de predicto debito decetero pacem habere permittat. Et si quid etc.

(951)

Kanc'. Inquisicio ad inquirendum de confeccione cujusdam starri de aquietancia .xx. solidorum, quod starrum Johannes de Roda protulit coram etc., et quod starrum Josceus filius Cressei ei fecit de aquietancia dicti debiti in hec verba: 'Josceus filius Cressei judeus recognoscit per starrum suum quod Johannes filius Wyberti de Rod' et heredes sui quieti sunt de ipso judeo et heredibus suis de omnibus debitis calumpniis, querelis et plegiagiis a creacione seculi usque ad festum sancti Michaelis anno regni regis Edwardi filii regis Henrici sexto. Et si inveniatur carta, tallia vel aliquod aliud instrumentum infra archa cyrographariorum vel extra sub nominibus predictorum Johannis et Joscei facta ante dictum terminum predictus

[146] *The remainder of this entry is a later addition to 66 and is omitted from 37.*
[147] Sharstede *37*. [148] Chycche *37*. [149] Hubert *37*.

[150] *This word is repeated in MS.* [151] Romansour *37*.

judeus recognoscit quod quieta sunt et nichil valeant', et inquisicio inde venit per Thomam Chicche et Johannem Hubert cyrographarios christianos, Willelmum Kalvesheved, Willelmum le Fevre et alios christianos, Aaron de Linc', Haginum le Eveske cyrographarios judeos, Leonem filium Abrahe et alios judeos, sicut patet inter brevia hujus termini retornata. Qui dicunt super sacramentum suum quod predictus Josceus dictum starrum fecit de acquietancia dicti debiti .xx. solidorum prefato Johanni tempore quo habuit liberam administracionem bonorum suorum, et littera ebrayca manu sua propria signavit. Et quod dictus Johannes prefato Josceo de dictis .xx. solidis satisfecit in autumpno anno regis Edwardi sexto. Et ideo consideratum est quod predictus Johannes de dicto debito .xx. solidorum sit quietus, et carta inde liberetur quiete dampnata.

(952)

Kanc'. Inquisicio <facta>[152] de confeccione cujusdam starri de aquietancia tercie partis quinque marcarum sub nominibus Johannis filii Thome de Strode et Salomonis de Stanff' judei dampnati, quod quidem starrum predictus Salomon eidem Johanni fecit de aquietancia dicti debiti ipsum contingente in hec verba: 'Salomon de Staunf' judeus recognoscit per starrum suum quod Johannes filius Thome de Strode et heredes sui quieti sunt de ipso judeo et heredibus suis de omnibus debitis, calumpniis et querelis factis sub nominibus Thome patris predicti Johannis et dicti Salomonis a creacione seculi usque ad finem. Et quod recognovit hoc idem sigillavit.' Et inquiscio venit [ad hunc diem][153] per Thomam Chicche, Johannem Hubert cyrographarios christianos, Willelmum Calvesfot, Willelmum le Fevere et alios christianos, Aaron de Wynton', Hagynum le Eveske cyrographarios judeos, Leonem filium Abrahe, Sampsonem de Sydingburn et alios judeos, sicut patet inter brevia hujus termini retornata. Qui dicunt super sacramentum suum quod predictum starrum est factum predicti Salomonis et littera hebrayca est manu sua propria signatum. Et quod dictum starrum fecit eo tempore quo habuit liberam administracionem bonorum suorum. Et quod per predictum starrum predictus Johannes quietus est de porcione dicti debiti ipsum contingente. Ideo consideratum est quod dictus Johannes de tercia parte dicti debiti quinque marcarum quietus sit. Et preceptum est vicecomiti quod predicto Johanni pacem etc.

(953)

Kanc'. Preceptum fuit vicecomiti quod distringeret Nigellum de Crowthorn' filium Walteri et tenentes terrarum suarum ad reddendum sibi ad opus Regis unam marcam de debito Joscei filii Salle judei dampnati; et denarios haberet coram etc. ad hunc diem. Et Nicholaus filius et heres predicti Nigelli venit coram etc. et protulit starrum predicti judei in hec verba: 'Josceus filius Salle judeus recognoscit per starrum suum quod Nigellus de Crouthorn' filius Walteri et Nicholaus filius ejus et heredes sui quieti sunt de ipso judeo, heredibus suis et assignatis de omnibus debitis, demandis, calumpniis et plegiagiis a creacione seculi usque ad Pentecosten anno regis Edwardi filii regis Henrici quarto. Et si inveniatur carta, tallia vel aliquod aliud instrumentum factum sub nominibus predictorum Nigelli, Nicholai, et Joscei ante predictum terminum in archa cyrographariorum vel extra idem judeus concedit quod quieta sint et nichil valeant etc.' Et Nicholaus filius et heres predicti Nigelli dicit quod dictum starrum est factum ipsius judei et illud fecit patri suo et sibi de aquietancia dicti debiti tempore quo habuit liberam administracionem bonorum suorum. Et petit quod inquiratur. Et inquisicio <venit per>[154] Thomam Chicche, Johannem Hubert cyrographarios christianos, Willelmum Calvesfot, Willelmum le Fevere et alios christianos, Aaron de Wynton', Haginum le Eveske cyrographarios judeos, sicut patet inter brevia hujus termini retornata. Qui dicunt super sacramentum suum quod predictum starrum est factum predicti Joscei et littera ebrayca manu sua propria signatum. Et quod dictum starrum fecit tempore quo habuit liberam administracionem bonorum suorum. Et quod per predictum starrum predicti Nicholaus et Nigellus de dicto debito unius marce quieti sunt. Ideo consideratum est quod predicti Nigellus et Nicholaus de predicto debito unius marce sunt quieti. Et carta predicti debiti predictis Nigello et Nicholao liberetur quiete dampnata. Et preceptum est vicecomiti quod ipsum Nicholaum de dicto debito pacem etc.

(954)

Warr'. Inquisicio ad inquirendum de confeccione cujusdam starri de aquietancia quatuor marcarum quod starrum Willelmus Woleward protulit coram etc. et quod starrum <asserit>[155] Aaron filium Deulecress judeum <fecisse>[156] in hec verba: 'Aaron filius Deulecress judeus Warr' recognoscit per starrum suum quod Willelmus Woleward' et heredes sui quieti sunt de ipso et heredibus suis de una carta .iiij. marcarum sub nominibus predictorum Willelmi et Aaron a creacione seculi usque ad festum Omnium Sanctorum anno regis Edwardi secundo. Et quod recognovit hoc idem sigillavit.' Et inquisicio venit ad hunc diem per Philippum le Noricesene cyrographarium Warr', Walterum de Estthorp', Petrum de Porta christianos, Vyves le <Rumanzur,>[157] Salomonem de Staunff' et alios, sicut patet inter brevia hujus termini retornata. Qui dicunt super sacramentum suum quod predictum starrum est factum predicti Aaron et littera ebrayca manu sua propria signatum. Et quod dictum starrum fecit tempore quo habuit liberam administracionem bonorum suorum. Et quod per predictum starrum predictus Willelmus de dicto debito .iiij. marcarum sit

152 ad inquirendum *37*. 153 *Supplied from 37*.

154 presens fuit, videlicet *37*. 155 *37 omits*.
156 ei fecit de aquietancia dicti debiti *37*.
157 Romaunsour *37*.

quietus. Ideo consideratum est quod predictus Willelmus de predicto debito .iiij. marcarum quietus sit. Et carta predicti debiti eidem liberetur quiete dampnata. Et preceptum est vicecomiti quod pacem etc.

(955)

Warr'. Preceptum fuit vicecomiti quod distringeret Humfridum de Hastyng' per terras et catalla sua ad reddendum sibi ad opus Regis .x. libras de debito [in quo tenebatur][158] Isac filio Joscei judeo Warr' dampnato.

Predictus Humfridus venit et dicit quod satisfecit predicto judeo tempore quo habuit liberam administracionem bonorum suorum de duabus marcis et inde habet starrum predicti judei de aquietancia quod protulit coram etc. in hec verba: 'Isac filius Joscei judeus recognoscit per starrum suum se recepisse de Humfrido de Hasting' duas marcas die lune proxima post festum beate Marie in Martio anno regis Edwardi sexto de quodam debito decem librarum sub nominibus predictorum Humfridi et Isac infra archam cyrographariorum Warr'. Et quod recognovit etc.' Et petit quod inquiratur. Et inquisicio presens fuit per Philippum le Noricesone cyrographarium Warr', Walterum de <Estchep',>[159] Petrum de Porta christianos, Vyves le <Rumanzur,>[160] Salomonem de <Stansted'>[161] et alios judeos, sicut patet inter brevia hujus termini retornata. Qui dicunt super sacramentum suum quod predictum starrum est factum predicti judei et littera sua signatum et quod predictum starrum fecit tempore quo habuit liberam administracionem bonorum suorum. Ideo consideratum est quod predicte .ij. marce eidem Humfrido in predicto debito x librarum allocentur.

Idem Humfridus venit coram etc. et dicit quod per districcionem quam Gilbertus de Kyrkeby ei fecit per breve regis pro predicto debito levare fecit de bonis et catallis predicti Humfridi .c. solidos et eos predicto judeo solvit et inde protulit starrum predicti judei in hec verba: 'Isac filius Joscei judeus recognovit per starrum suum se recepisse de Humfrido de Hastyng' .c. solidos per manus Gilberti de Kyrkeby vicecomitis Norht' de quodam debito .x. librarum in quo idem Humfridus eidem judeo tenebatur per cyrographum quod est infra archa cyrographariorum Warr' et predictus judeus tulit breve regis predicto vicecomiti ad levandum de catallis predicti Humfridi predictos .c. solidos et predictos .c. solidos recepit predictus judeus; et quod recognovit hoc sigillavit.', et dictus Gilbertus presens recognovit se per breve regis predictos .c. solidos levasse et eidem judeo liberasse, sicut continetur in starro predicto. Ideo consideratum est quod predicti .c. solidi in predicto debito .x. librarum predicto Humfrido allocentur.

Et Aaron filius Vyves, qui presens fuit coram etc., recognovit se recepisse de predicto Humfrido quinque marcas et dimidiam que aretro fuerunt de predicto debito .x. librarum, cui istud debitum assignatum fuit in recompensacionem debiti Gilberti Pecche. Et sic predictus Humfridus de predictus .x. libris quietus est.

158 *Supplied from 37.*
159 Estthorp' *37.*
160 Romaunsour *37.*
161 Staunford *37. The version of this entry in 37 ends at this point.*

(956)

Johannes de Hercy, Johannes de la Porte, Willelmus Ingeram de comitatu Warr' manuceperunt Willelmum de Duddel' ad satisfaciendum regi de .j. marca in festo sancti Dunstani.

(957)

Cantebr'. Willelmus de Royng' vicecomes protulit coram etc. .xx. solidos de exitibus terrarum Willelmi le Moygne et soluti sunt clericis pro summonicionibus scribendis.

(958)

Norht'. Preceptum fuit vicecomiti quod venire faceret coram etc. Milicenciam de Lungevyle ad respondendum Belasset que fuit uxor Sampsonis filii Sampsonis, que sequitur pro rege et pro se, de quinque marcis quas ei et Jordano Knyt viro suo tradidit salvo custodiendum, ut dicit, et hoc offert etc.

Et predicta Milicencia venit et petit judicium si debeat respondere de dictis denariis quos ab ea et Jordano viro suo exigit cum esset .... Jordani viri sui dum vixerat. Et consideratum est quod ei inde non respondet set [eat inde sine] die. Postea ..... fuit ... principalis executrix testamenti dicti Jordani viri sui et bona ejusdem ad manus eius devenerunt ..... predicta Belasset ... inde ...

Et predicta Milicencia dicit quod plures sunt executores dicti testamenti sine quibus respondere non potest. Postea predicta Belasset retraxit se ...... let dicit se nullam habere accionem versus predictos executores etc.

MEMBRANE 9

Adhuc Memoranda de termino Pasche anno regni regis Edwardi Nono

(959)

Ebor'. Concessum est Deudoni Crespyn judeo Ebor' quod de sex marcis et dimidia quas debet Regi de diversis amerciamentis solvat per annum .x. solidos, videlicet ad scaccarium sancti Michaelis .v. solidos et ad scaccarium Pasche .v. solidos, incipiente primo termino in termino sancti Michaelis anno regis Edwardi nono; et sic de anno in annum ad eosdem terminos donec etc. per plegium Isac filii Urselli de Denecastr', Jurnini filii Deudon' et Elie Crespyn, quorum unusquisque tenetur in solidum.

(960)

Lond'. Memorandum quod de .xx. solidis qui venerunt de exitibus Willelmi le Moygne liberantur Rogero de Flete, servienti de scaccario etc., quinque solidi ad diversa brevia pro rege deferendum per diversos comitatus Anglie et residuum, videlicet .xv. solidi, clericis pro scriptura summonicionum et pergameno.

(961)

Hereff'. Walterus de Hampton', manucaptus veniendi ad juratam inter Johannem filium Walteri de Thornebur', tenentem quandam partem terrarum que fuerunt Willelmi Deveroy, et Aaron filii Vyves judeum, non venit. Ideo in misericordia.[162] Et Rogerus de Hampton' et Johannes Snel, quia non habuerunt predictum Walterum quem manuceperunt, in misericordia.[163] Thomas de Wyke manucaptus veniendi pro eadem causa, quia non venit, in misericordia.[164] Walterus le Palmere et Thomas le Talyur, quia non habuerunt predictum Thomam quem manuceperunt, in misericordia.[165]

(962)

Hereff'. Preceptum fuit vicecomiti quod distringeret Johannem Juniorem de Lugwardyn per terras et catalla sua ad reddendum sibi ad opus Regis .viij. solidos quos Regi debet occasione terrarum etc. que fuerunt Roberti de Weston' de debitis Urselli filii Isac. Et vicecomes mandavit quod Johannes Cole et Thomas le Wyte manuceperunt predictum Johannem, quem non habuerunt. Ideo in misericordia.[166] Et quod distringeret eodem modo Thomam de Hagelewe, tenentem quandam partem predictarum terrarum, pro .viij. solidis. Et vicecomes mandavit quod Ricardus filius Edrich' et Thomas de la Heche manuceperunt predictum Thomam, quem non habuerunt. Ideo in misericordia.[167] Et quod distringeret Walterum de la Hulle pro .viij. solidis. Et vicecomes mandavit quod Ricardus filius Gilberti de Haume et Matheus de Checkeleye manuceperunt predictum Walterum. Et quod distringeret eodem modo Philippum de Stapelton pro .x. solidis. Et vicecomes mandavit quod Ricardus de Wlveshegh' et Willelmus Pope manuceperunt predictum Philippum. Et quod distringeret eodem modo Rogerum de Pyrebrok', custodem <heredis>[168] et cujusdam partis terrarum que fuerunt Roberti de Weston', pro .cx. solidis. Et vicecomes mandavit quod Hugo de Molendino et Johannes le Joefne manuceperunt predictum Rogerum. Et quod distringeret eodem modo Rogerum filium Ricardi de Hereff', tenenetem terrarum predictarum, pro .xl. solidis etc. Et vicecomes mandavit quod predictus Rogerus nichil habet per quod possit distringi. Et quod distringeret eodem modo Robertum de Meysy, tenentem terrarum etc., pro sex solidis. Et vicecomes mandavit quod Walterus Sywaunt et Rogerus de la Pole manuceperunt predictum Robertum. Quos non habuerunt. Ideo in misericordia.[169] Judicium quod distringat per terras etc., et quod de exitibus etc., a die sancti Johannes Baptiste in .xv. dies etc.

(963)

Wygorn'. Prior de Parva Malvern' pro pluribus defaltis in misericordia.[170]

Idem prior attachiatus ad respondendum Regi de .lvj. solidis .vj. denariis de debitis Aaron filii Isac judei per quandam talliam inter ipsum priorem et prefatum judeum confectam etc., venit et totum defendit etc., et dicit quod aliquo tempore quidam prior predecessor ejus mutuo recepit de dicto Aaron .xiiij. marcas super quedam vadia ei pro eisdem denariis inpignorata ad valenciam .xx. marcarum et amplius, que tradita fuerunt Hugoni le Clerc in equali manu custodiendum donec predicto judeo de predictis .xiiij. marcis esset satisfactum. Et postea predictus prior in presencia Egidii de Berkel' vicecomitis Hereff', coronatorum ejusdem comitatus, cyrographariorum arche cyrographariorum Hereff' et aliorum proborum et legalium hominum de Hereff' computavit cum predicto Aaron de predictis .xiiij. marcis et ei inde satisfecit et vadia sua pro predictis denariis impignorata dicto priori liberata fuerunt, infra quam summam .xiiij. marcarum predicta tallia contenta fuit et pro ea infra summam predictam per predictum compotum inter eos habitum satisfecit, ita quod nichil per eam debuit. Et convencio fuit coram prefatis vicecomite, coronatoribus, cyrographariis et aliis probis hominibus quod, si dicta tallia vel aliqua alia de dicto debito inter eos facta inveniri contingeret, pro nichilo haberetur. Et de hoc ponit se super patriam.

Et dictus Aaron per attornatum suum dicit pro Rege quod dicta tallia infra summam .xiiij. marcarum non erat contenta set per quandam aliam convencionem postea inter eos factam de quodam alio debito facta fuit et hoc petit quod inquiratur. Et preceptum est vicecomiti quod venire faciat coram etc. a die sancti Michaelis in .xv. dies cyrographarios Hereff' et sex probos et legales homines et sex legales judeos Hereff' ad recognoscendum etc.

(964)

Wygorn'. Preceptum fuit vicecomiti sicut alias quod distringeret Johannem de Fraxino per terras etc. ad reddendum sibi ad opus Regis .vj. marcas de debitis Jacobi filii Salomonis judei; et denarios haberet coram etc. Et vicecomes mandavit quod retornavit breve inde sibi directum ballivis libertatis Wygorn', qui sibi respondent quod dictus Johannes non habet catalla nisi terram friscam per quam ipsum non distrinxit. Ideo ipse Thomas de Newenham vicecomes [i]<in misericordia.>[i][171] Et preceptum est ei, sicut pluries, in quindena sancti Johannis etc.

(965)

Oxon'. Berk'. Preceptum fuit vicecomiti quod de terris et catallis Johannis Hereward' et Johannis Alisaundre fieri

[162] *The word* misericordia *is repeated in the margin.*
[163] *The word* misericordia *is repeated in the margin.*
[164] *The word* misericordia *is repeated in the margin.*
[165] *The word* misericordia *is repeated in the margin.*
[166] *The word* misericordia *is repeated in the margin.*
[167] *The word* misericordia *is repeated in the margin.*
[168] *MS. reads* Reg'.
[169] *The word* misericordia *is repeated in the margin.*

[170] *The word* misericordia *is repeated in the margin.*
[171] *The word* misericordia *is repeated in the margin.*

faceret ad opus Joscei de Walyngff' judei .xl. solidos et eos haberet coram etc. Et vicecomes mandavit quod returnavit breve inde sibi directum ballivis libertatis de Redyng' qui nichil inde sibi respondent. Judicium quod non omittat propter libertatem etc. quin eam etc. a die sancte Trinitatis in .xv. dies etc.

(966)

Oxon'. Berk'. Preceptum fuit vicecomiti quod non omitteret propter libertatem de Walyngford' quin eam etc. et venire faceret magistrum Petrum de Benham ad respondendum Regi de diversis cartis que deposite erant in archa cyrographariorum Walyngf' et per ipsum extracte et elongate dum fuit cyrographarius arche predicte una cum Roberto Malet, qui se posuit inde in inquisicionem. Et inquisicio venit et predictus Robertus venit et magister Petrus non venit et datus est dies dicto Roberto propter absenciam dicti Petri a die sancte Trinitatis in .xv. dies etc. Et preceptum est vicecomiti, sicut alias, quod non omittat etc. et venire faciat predictum Petrum etc., et quod venire faciat predictam inquisicionem. Et quia vicecomes a die Pasche in tres septimanas nunc non fecit venire predictum Petrum nec aliquam mencionem de eo fecit, ideo ipse vicecomes, videlicet [blank], in misericordia.[172]

(967)

Linc'. Preceptum fuit vicecomiti quod distringeret tenentes terrarum et tenementorum que fuerunt Thome de Somercote per terras etc. ad reddendum sibi ad opus Regis .x. libras de debitis Sauloti Motun judei etc., et denarios haberet coram etc. Et vicecomes mandavit quod magister Willelmus de Somercote est tenens terrarum que fuerunt predicti Thome et quod manucaptus est veniendi ad diem in brevi contentum per Gilbertum le Lung de Somercote et Walterum fratrem ejus de eadem, qui ipsum non habuerunt. Ideo in misericordia.[173] Judicium quod distringat per terras etc., ita quod nec ipse etc., et quod de exitibus etc., et quod habeat corpus ejus coram etc.

(968)

Bed'. Buk'. Preceptum fuit vicecomiti, sicut pluries, quod distringeret Alinam et Johannam filias Jacobi Wake, Willelmum Pydifis, Johannem de Bowel', Walterum Gleve et Johannem de Stevenach', tenentes terrarum que fuerunt Jacobi Wake, per terras etc. ad reddendum sibi ad opus Regis .iiij. marcas quas Regi debent occasione predictarum terrarum etc. de debitis Isac de Suthwerk' judei; et denarios haberet coram etc. Et vicecomes mandavit quod predicti Alina, Johana, Walterus Gleve et Johannes non habent terras etc. per que possunt distringi. Et quod Willelmus le Graunt de Aston' et Lucas de eadem manuceperunt predictum Willelmum Pidifys, et quod Willelmus le Graunt de Wardon' et Lucas de eadem manuceperunt Johannem de Stevenach'; quos non habuerunt. Ideo in misericordia.[174] Et preceptum est ei, sicut pluries, a die sancte Trinitatis in .xv. dies etc.

(969)

Kanc'. Preceptum fuit vicecomiti quod de bonis et catallis Alani de Morton fieri faceret ad opus Roberti de Ludham .xiij. marcas quas recepit etc. Et vicecomes mandavit quod senescallus libertatis archiepiscopi Cant', cui istud breve returnatum fuit, sibi respondit quod predictus Alanus nulla habet bona de quibus aliqui denarii fieri possunt citra autumpnum. Ideo, sicut alias, a die sancte Trinitatis in .xv. dies.

(970)

Essex'. Jacobus de Marny, attachiatus veniendi etc. pro quadam inquisicione inter Galfridum de Waldegrave et Josceum filium Isac de Norht' judeum, non venit. Ideo ipse Jacobus in misericordia. Et Gilbertus Clericus, Stephanus Clericus, Johannes Dobbe et Ricardus Dobbe, plegii dicti Jacobi de veniendo, quia non habuerunt dictum Jacobum, in misericordia. Thomas le Clerc de eadem inquisicione non venit. Ideo in misericordia. Et Johannes Cistelote, Johannes Hervy, Walterus le Carpenter et Willelmus le Bercher, quia non habuerunt predictum Thomam, in misericordia. Hugo atte Berne de eadem inquisicione non venit. Ideo in misericordia. Et Rogerus Babbe, Walterus Babbe, Rogerus filius Reginaldi et Walterus de Bed' manuceperunt predictum Hugonem, quem non habuerunt. Ideo in misericordia. Rogerus Wolwich' de eadem inquisicione non venit. Ideo in misericordia. Et Robertus le Herd, Henricus frater ejus, Ranulfus Dune et Rogerus Dune, quia non habuerunt predictum Rogerum, in misericordia.[175]

(971)

Lond'. Manserus filius Aaron judeus, unus de inquisicione inter Henricum de Well' et Cresseum filium Gente, quia recessit sine licencia in contemptu curie, in misericordia.[176]

Cok' filius Hagini unus juratorum dicte inquisicionis, quia non venit, in misericordia.

MEMBRANE 9 DORSE

Adhuc memoranda

(972)

Wyltes'. Preceptum fuit vicecomiti quod non omitteret propter libertatem prioris Wynton' de Elestubbe quin eam etc., et distringeret Rogerum de Radenham per terras etc., et quod haberet corpus ejus coram etc. ad respondendum Regi de duabus cartis .ix.^{xx} marcarum

172 *The word* misericordia *is repeated in the margin.*

173 *The word* misericordia *is repeated in the margin.*

174 *The word* misericordia *is repeated in the margin.*

175 *The word* misericordie *is written twice in the margin opposite this entry.*

176 *The word* misericordia *is repeated in the margin.*

sub nominibus Alexandri de Authno et Salomonis de Merleberge judei et aliis diversis cartis sub nominibus diversorum christianorum et judeorum quas recepit de cyrographariis arche cyrographariorum Merleberg' tempore quod fuit constabularius castri Merleberg' et quas liberasse debuit justiciariis etc., et nondum liberavit etc. [i]<Et ipse non venit.>[i] Et vicecomes mandavit quod Reginaldus de Molendino, Johannes de Rotelaund', Willelmus filius ejus, Adam in la Felde, Willelmus Russel, Adam Maneye, Thomas le Thresschere et Gilbertus le Puleter manuceperunt predictum Rogerum, quem non habuerunt. Ideo in misericordia.[177] Et sunt exitus terrarum predicti Rogeri .v. solidi, de quibus vicecomes respondit. Et preceptum est vicecomiti, sicut alias, a die sancti Johannes Baptiste in .xv. dies etc.

(973)

Glouc'. Preceptum fuit vicecomiti quod attachiaret Thomam de Evesham, cyrographarium arche cyrographariorum Glouc', ita quod haberet corpus ejus coram etc. ad respondendum Regi una cum Thoma Chu, Roberto le Cornewaleys et Henrico de Penedoc, executoribus testamenti Johannis Cornubiensis quondam cyrographarii arche predicte, de diversis cartis que ab archa predicta extracte fuerunt et quas liberasse debuerunt justiciariis etc., et nondum liberaverunt. Et predictus Thomas non venit. Et vicecomes mandavit quod retornavit breve inde sibi directum ballivis libertatis Glouc', qui sibi responderunt quod predictus Thomas non habet terras nec tenementa per que possit distringi seu attachiari. Et preceptum est vicecomiti quod non omittat propter libertatem etc. quin eam etc. propter eorum insufficientem responsionem; et attachiet etc., ita quod habeat corpus ejus coram etc. a die sancti Johannis in .xv. dies etc. ad respondendum etc. una cum predictis executoribus, qui habent eundem diem etc.

(974)

Wyltes'. Prior de Bradenestoke pro pluribus defaltis in misericordia.[178]

Preceptum fuit vicecomiti quod distringeret priorem de Bradenestoke, tenentem terrarum que fuerunt Thome de Wynterburne et Rogeri le Joefne, per terras etc. ad reddendum sibi ad opus Regis .lx. solidos de debitis Lumbardi de Wyndes' judei.

Predictus prior per attornatum suum venit et dicit quod non tenet terras Rogeri le Joefne et petit quod veniat de dicto debito responsurus. Et preceptum est vicecomiti quod ipsum Rogerum venire faciat coram etc. a die sancti Johannis Baptiste in .xv. dies ad respondendum etc. una cum predicto priore etc.

(975)

Kanc'. Preceptum fuit vicecomiti quod venire faceret coram etc. Willelmum de Brokehulle ad respondendum Regi de uno cipho argenti precii quatuor librarum et de aliis bonis et catallis ad valenciam .ix. librarum que devenerunt ad manus dicti Willelmi de bonis et catallis Mossei de Doggestrete judei; et denarios haberet coram etc. Et vicecomes mandavit quod senescallus libertatis archiepiscopi Cant', cui istud breve fuit retornatum, sibi respondit quod Simon de Brokhull' et Johannes le Bedel de Aldyngton' manuceperunt predictum Willelmum, quem non habuerunt. Ideo in misericordia.[179] Judicium quod distringat per terras etc. et quod de exitibus etc. et quod habeat corpus ejus coram etc. a die sancte Trinitatis in .xv. dies ad respondendum etc. et ad audiendum etc.

(976)

Wygorn'. Preceptum fuit vicecomiti quod distringeret Robertum filium Roberti de Grafton' per terras etc. ad reddendum sibi ad opus Regis .iiij. marcas quas Regi debet de debito Sampsonis filii Isac judei, et denarios haberet coram etc. Et vicecomes mandavit quod Willelmus Payn, Walterus Payn de Huntingdrop, Willelmus de Oddingelegh' et Adam de eadem manuceperunt predictum Robertum, quem non habuerunt. Ideo in misericordia.[180] Et preceptum est ei, sicut pluries, a die sancte Trinitatis in .xv. dies. Et vicecomes sit etc. Et quia vicecomes non habuit predictos denarios sicut ei preceptum fuit, ideo ipse vicecomes, videlicet Thomas de Nywenham, in misericordia.

(977)

Linc'. Preceptum fuit vicecomiti quod distringeret Hugonem de Paunton', Hugonem Merle de Swynthorpe, Radulfum de Butayte, Andream de Hocheham, Robertum de Timberlond', Walterum Brid de Bekeryng', Henricum West de Ludeford', Simonem Mustel de Tyrington', Ranulphum Mustel de eadem, Johannem de la Grave de Bekering', Robertum West de Lassington', Johannem North de Houton', Galfridum de Radn', Johannem Rocelyn de Wolyngham et Robertum filium Johannis de eadem, juratores inquisicionis inter priorem de Bolyngton' et Johannem de Bathon', tenentem quandam partem terrarum que fuerunt Gilberti de Benygworth,' per terras etc., et quod haberet corpora eorum coram etc. a die Pasche in unum mensem nunc ad recognoscendum etc. Et ipsi non venerunt. Et vicecomes mandavit quod Ricardus prepositus de Paunton', Rogerus prepositus de eadem, Rogerus West de eadem et Willemus West de eadem manuceperunt Hugonem de Paunton; et quod Ricardus Carettarius de Snelleslond', Radulfus frater ejus de eadem, Nicholaus Piscator de eadem et Henricus frater ejus de eadem manuceperunt Hugonem de Merl'; et quod Teling' de Hogoteby, Henricus frater ejus de eadem, Gilbertus le Tannur de eadem et Alanus Gos de eadem manuceperunt Randulfum Botegate; et quod Willelmus le Mourier de

[177] *The word* misericordia *is repeated in the margin.*

[178] *The word* misericordia *is repeated in the margin.*

[179] *The word* misericordia *is repeated in the margin.*

[180] *The word* misericordia *is repeated in the margin.*

Bleseby, Johannes filius ejus de eadem, Robertus Hode de eadem et Alanus frater ejus de eadem manuceperunt Robertum de Timberlond'; et quod Johannes filius Simonis, Henricus frater ejus, Willelmus frater ejus et Thomas frater ejus manuceperunt Walterum Wryde; et quod Hugo Skut de Tyryngton', Alanus de Langwath' de eadem, Willelmus le Messer de eadem, et Henricus frater ejus de eadem manuceperunt Simonem Mussel de Tyrington', et quod Robertus filius Simonis de Bekering', Willelmus frater ejus de eadem, Rogerus le Serjaunt de eadem et Willelmus filius Willelmi de eadem manuceperunt Johannem de la Grave de Bekering'; et quod Henricus frater Roberti West de Lassington', Henricus de Bathon' et Radulfus frater ejus de eadem manuceperunt Robertum West de Lassington'; et quod Ricardus filius Johannis de Houton', Radulfus frater ejus de eadem, Galfridus frater ejus de eadem manuceperunt Johannem North de Houton'; et quod Gilbertus Biscop de Houton', Galfridus Biscob de eadem, Robertus West de eadem et Henricus filius Radulfi de eadem manuceperunt Galfridum de Raund'; et quod Johannes subballivus de Wranghowe, Thomas West de Burgo, Robertus Germeyn de Houton et Thomas serviens ejus manuceperunt Johannem Rocelyn'; et quod Willelmus de Westhawe, Robertus frater ejus de eadem, Robertus Tyle de eadem et Ricardus frater ejus de eadem manuceperunt Robertum filium Johannis de Wolyngham; quos non habuerunt. Ideo in misericordia.[181] Judicium, sicut pluries, quod distringat etc. a die sancte Trinitatis in .xv. dies etc. ad recognoscendum etc.

(978)

Linc'. Preceptum fuit vicecomiti, sicut pluries, quod salvo custodiet in manu regis terras etc. per que distrinxit Henricum de Lacy comitem Linc' et Helewysam de Neyvile, tenentes quandam partem terrarum que fuerunt Gilberti de Benyngworth', et quod haberet corpora eorum coram etc. ad respondendum etc. Et vicecomes mandavit quod Simon de Graffam capitalis ballivus de Northtreyingo sibi respondit quod non fuit ausus facere aliquam districcionem super predictum Henricum. Et ideo de ipso nichil actum est. Et quod Willelmus prepositus de Magna Straton', Willelmus North' de eadem, Ricardus Gamb' de eadem et Henricus le Pinder de eadem manuceperunt predictam Helewysiam, quam non habuerunt. Ideo in misericordia. Judicium, sicut pluries, a die sancte Trinitatis in .xv. dies ad respondendum etc. et ad audiendum etc. Et quia vicecomes nichil respondit de exitibus terrarum dicte Helewysie. Ideo ipse vicecomes, videlicet [blank], in misericordia.[182]

(979)

Linc'. Preceptum fuit vicecomiti quod salvo custodiret terras etc. per que distrinxit Lambertum filium Hugonis de Bussey, Johannem Abraham, Ricardum de Molton', Ricardum de Oteby, Robertum de Oteby et Robertum Dun, tenentes quandam partem terrarum que fuerunt Gilberti de Benyngworth', et quod haberet corpora eorum coram etc. ad hunc diem. Et vicecomes mandavit quod Ricardus prepositus de Hogham, Adam filius Simonis de eadem, Willelmus filius Hugonis de eadem et Walterus le Paumer de eadem manuceperunt predictum Lambertum; et quod Robertus ballivus de Wranghou, Eudo le Skynnere de Marbirthorp', Adam de Grimwelby et Johannes serviens ejus manuceperunt Robertum Doun; quos non habuerunt. Ideo in misericordia.[183] Et quod Johannes Abr' et Ricardus de Oteby mortui sunt. Et quod plures sunt in balliva sua qui vocantur Ricardus de Molton' et quia non specificatur in brevi cujus filius fuerit, ideo de ipso nichil actum est. Et quia vicecomes retornavit quod plures sunt in balliva sua qui vocantur hoc nomine Ricardus de Molton' et nullum eorum fecit venire nec distrinxit sicut ei preceptum fuit, ideo ipse vicecomes, scilicet [blank], in misericordia.[184] Et vicecomes mandavit quod Robertus de Oteby nichil habet in balliva sua per quod potest distringi. Et preceptum est ei, sicut pluries, a die sancte Trinitatis in .xv. dies ad respondendum etc. Et quia predictus vicecomes nichil respondit de exitibus terrarum predicti Lamberti et aliorum supradictorum, ideo ipse vicecomes, videlicet [blank], in misericordia.[185]

(980)

Suth'. Preceptum fuit vicecomiti quod distringeret Willelmum de Merse per terras etc. ad reddendum sibi ad opus Regis .xx. solidos quos Regi debent de debitis Hagini de Byrkehamsted'; et denarios haberet coram etc. ad hunc diem. Et vicecomes retornavit breve inde sibi directum ballivis libertatis de Andevere, qui nichil inde fecerunt. Judicium quod non omittat etc. quin eam etc. et denarios habeat coram etc. a die sancti Johannis in .xv. dies Regi solvendum.

MEMBRANE 10

Adhuc Memoranda de termino Pasche anno regis Edwardi nono

(981)

Wyltes'. Inquisicio ad inquirendum de confeccione cujusdam starri de acquietancia cujusdam debiti .xxij. librarum, quod starrum Mosseus filius Salomonis de Merleberge judeus dampnatus fecit Roberto Burdun tempore quo habuit liberam administracionem bonorum suorum, quod starrum Robertus de Romeseye coexecutor testamenti predicti Roberti Burdun protulit coram etc. in hec verba: 'Mosseus filius Salomonis recognoscit per starrum suum quod acquietavit Robertum Burdun et

[181] *The word* misericordia *is repeated in the margin.*
[182] *The word* misericordia *is repeated in the margin.*
[183] *The word* misericordia *is repeated in the margin.*
[184] *The word* misericordia *is repeated in the margin.*
[185] *The word* misericordia *is repeated in the margin.*

heredes suos de predicto judeo et heredibus suis de quodam debito viginti duarum librarum sub nominibus predictorum Roberti et Mossei a creacione seculi usque ad finem anno regni regis Edwardi quinto. Et si veniat aliquis homo et calumprietur aliquid super predictum Robertum occasione predicti debiti super predictum judeum et heredes suos est acquietare predictum Robertum et heredes suos warantizare et defendere contra omnes homines et hoc sigillavit.' venit per Johannem le Teynturer, Galfridum Buchard cyrographarios christianos, Robertum Prat, Thomam de Mommeham et alios christianos, Salamonem filium Salamonis, Josceum filium Symonis et alios judeos, sicut patet inter brevia hujus termini returnata. Qui dicunt super sacramentum suum quod predictum starrum est factum predicti Mossei et illud fecit tempore quo habuit liberam administracionem bonorum suorum et littera sua ebrayca manu propria signatum et quod starrum illud fecit anno regis Edwardi quinto. Ideo consideratum est quod predictus Robertus et executores sui de predicto debito .xxij. librarum quieti sint et carta predicti debiti eis liberetur quiete dampnata. Et preceptum est vicecomiti quod ei pacem etc. Et si quid etc.

(982)

Linc'. Benedictus de Linc' judeus dat Regi quatuor bissancia pro quodam debito .xx. librarum levando nomine Regis sub nominibus Hugonis de Coleworth' et predicti Benedicti, ita tamen quod scribatur vicecomiti pro Rege et predicto judeo.

(983)

Wyltes'. Inquisicio ad inquirendum de confeccione cujusdam starri de acquietancia duorum debitorum, videlicet de uno debito .xl. solidorum et alio quinque marcarum, quod starrum Jacobus de Wodeberg' protulit coram etc., et quod starrum Mosseus filius Salomonis ei fecit de acquietancia dicti debiti in hec verba: 'Mosseus filius Salomonis de Merleberge recognoscit per starrum suum quod perdonavit et acquietavit Jacobo de Wodeberge unum debitum .v. marcarum et aliud debitum .iij. marcarum quod ipse Jacobus et heredes sui quieti sunt de ipso judeo et heredibus suis de omnibus demandis et calumpniis a creacione seculi usque ad festum sancti Michaelis anno regni regis Edwardi quarto et, si contingat quod aliquis homo veniat calumpniari versus predictum Jacobum, super ipsum judeum est defendere predictum Jacobum et hoc sigillavit.' venit per Johannem le Teynturer, Galfridum Buchard cyrographarios christianos, Robertum Prat, Thomam de Mommeham et alios christianos, Salomonem filium Salomonis, Josceum filium Salomonis et alios judeos, sicut patet inter brevia hujus termini returnata. Qui dicunt super sacramentum suum quod predictus Mosseus fecit predictum starrum tempore quo idem Mosseus habuit liberam administracionem bonorum suorum et illud manu sua propria littera ebrayca signavit et illud starrum fecit anno regis Edwardi quarto de acquietancia dicti debiti. Ideo consideratum est quod predictus Jacobus de predictis duobus debitis .viij. marcarum sit quietus et quod carte dictorum debitorum et liberentur quiete dampnata. Et preceptum est vicecomiti quod ipsum decetero pacem habere permittat etc.

(984)

Kanc'. Preceptum fuit vicecomiti quod distringeret Hugonem filium David de Bleddyng' ad reddendum sibi ad opus Regis .xxxiij. solidos quos Regi debet de debitis Isac filii Benedicti judei dampnati. Predictus Hugo venit et dicit quod satisfecit predicto Isac de predicto debito tempore quo predictus Isac habuit liberam administracionem de bonis suis et inde starrum de acquietancia dicti debiti ei fecit, quod protulit coram etc. in hec verba: 'Isac filius Benedicti recognoscit per starrum suum quod Hugo filius David de Bleddyng', heredes et assignati sui quieti sunt de ipso judeo et heredibus suis de omnibus debitis, demandis et calumpniis a creacione seculi usque ad Pascham anno regni regis Edwardi sexto. Et si inveniatur carta, tallia vel aliquod aliud instrumentum infra archa cyrographariorum vel extra sub nominibus predictorum Hugonis et Isac a principio seculi usque ad Pascham predictum, sciant universi quod inde quietus est et hoc sigillavit.' et petit quod inquiratur. Et inquisicio presens fuit per Thomam Chicche, Johannem Hubert, cyrographarios Cant' christianos, Willelmum Calvesfot, Willelmum le Fevre et alios christianos, Aaron de Wynton', Haginum le Eveske cyrographarios judeos, Leonem filium Abrahe, Sampsonem de Sydingburn' et alios judeos, sicut patet inter brevia hujus termini retornata. Qui dicunt super sacramentum suum quod predictus Isac predictum starrum fecit eidem Hugoni tempore quo idem Isac habuit liberam administracionem bonorum suorum, videlicet ad Pascham anno regis Edwardi sexto, ut supradictum est, et manu propria signatum, et quod dictum starrum ei fecit de acquietancia dicti debiti. Ideo consideratum est quod predictus Hugo de predicto debito .xxxiij. solidorum quietus sit et quod carta dicti debiti ei liberetur quiete dampnanda. Et preceptum est vicecomiti quod ipsum pacem etc.

(985)

Wyltes'. Preceptum fuit vicecomiti quod distringeret Willelmum filium Willelmi [Quintini][186] de <Bubbeclyve>[187] et tenenetes terrarum suarum ad reddendum sibi ad opus Regis .l. solidos quos Regi debent occasione etc. de debito Salomonis filii Joscei de Marleberge judei fugitivi. Walterus de Barevile, tenens terrarum predicti Willelmi, venit et protulit coram etc. starrum predicti Salomonis de acquietancia dicti debiti quod predictus Salomon prefato Willelmi inde fecit ut dicit in hec verba: 'Salomon filius Joscei recognoscit per starrum suum quod acquietavit et quietumclavit [Willelmo filio][188] Willelmi Quintin de Bubbeclyve

[186] *Supplied from 37.* [187] Bubeclive *37.*
[188] Willelmum filium *37.*

omnia debita, calumpnias et demandas quas idem Willelmus, heredes et tenentes terrarum suarum umquam ei [debuerunt;][189] quieti sunt de ipso judeo, heredibus et assignatis suis de omnibus querelis et demandis a creacione seculi usque ad festum sancti Michaelis anno regnis regis Edwardi sexto. Et si contingat quod aliquis judeus vel judea veniat et calumpnietur versus predictum Willelmum aut tenentes terrarum suarum occasione alicujus debiti quod umquam sibi <debuit>[190] infra archam cyrographariorum super ipsum judeum est acquietare et defendere predictum Willelmum et tenentes terrarum suarum. Et hoc sigillavit ad instanciam Rogeri de Evesham clerici domini regis.' Inquisitum fuit de confeccione dicti starri per sacramentum Johannis le Teynturer, Galfridum Buchard cyrographariorum christianorum, Roberti Prat, Thome de Mommeham et aliorum christianorum, Salomonis filii Salomonis, Joscei filii Salomonis et aliorum judeorum, sicut patet inter brevia hujus termini returnata. Qui dicunt <super sacramentum suum>[191] quod predictus Salomon predictum starrum ei fecit tempore quo idem Salomon habuit liberam administracionem bonorum suorum <et illud starrum manu sua propria littera ebrayca signavit>[192] et illud starrum ei fecit anno regni regis Edwardi sexto, ut supradictum est, de aquietancia dicti debiti. Ideo consideratum est quod predictus Willelmus Quintyn de predicto debito .l. solidorum sit quietus et predicta carta eidem Willelmo liberetur quiete dampnata. Et quod decetero pacem etc.

(986)

Norff', Suff'. [Abbas de Langel' pro pluribus defaltis in misericordia.][193]

Preceptum fuit vicecomiti quod distringeret Emmam relictam Rogeri filii Johannis de <Korpesty>[194] et abbatem de Langhel', tenentes terrarum que fuerunt predicte Emme, ad reddendum sibi ad opus Regis .xij. marcas de debito Manseri filii Urselli <judei dampnati, et denarios haberet coram etc.>[195]

Predictus abbas venit et dicit quod [non tenetur de dicto debito sive parte ejusdem debiti respondere quia][196] non tenet aliquas terras vel tenementa que fuerunt predicte Emme; et <de hoc ponit se super patriam.>[197] Et preceptum est vicecomiti quod venire faciat coram etc. a die sancte Trinitatis in .xv. dies .xij. tam milites etc. de visneto de Corpesty, et qui nulla affinitate etc., ad recognoscendum etc., nisi H. Hauteyn interim etc.

(987)

Warr'. Inquisicio ad inquirendum de confeccione cujusdam starri de acquietancia decem marcarum quod Mosseus filius Leonis judeus dampnatus fecit Willelmo de Nafford' de dicto debito, quod starrum predictus Willelmus protulit coram etc. in hec verba: 'Mosseus filius Leonis judeus recognovit per starrum suum quod Willelmus de Nafford' et heredes sui quieti sunt de ipso judeo et heredibus suis de omnibus demandis et calumpniis a creacione seculi usque ad festum sancti Andree anno regis Edwardi sexto.' Et inquisicio venit ad hunc diem per Philippum le Noricesone cyrographarium Warr', Walterum de Estthorp', Petrum de Porta christianos, Vyves le Rumanzur, Salomonem de Staunff' et alios judeos, sicut patet inter brevia hujus termini retornata. Qui dicunt super sacramentum suum quod predictus Mosseus prefatum starrum predicto Willelmo non fecit nec littera sua signavit. Et quia convictum est per inquisicionem etc. quod predictum starrum non est factum dicti Mossei, ideo consideratum est quod predictus Willelmus satisfaciat Regi de predictis .x. marcis. Et committitur prisone pro falso starro quod protulit etc.

(988)

Norff'. Cum quoddam debitum decem marcarum exigeretur de Andrea le Waleys filio Willelmi le Waleys de Sweynesthorp' de comitatu Norff' de debitis Salomonis filii Jornini judei Norwyc' ad fidem christianam conversi in quo eidem judeo per cartam suam tenebatur, predictus Andreas venit et dicit quod nulla habet catalla mobilia unde aliquem denarium Regi de dicto debito solvere possit, et petit quod terre et tenementa sua extendantur ut Regi satisfacere possit secundum extentam inde factam; et concessum est ei quod terre et tenementa sua extendantur. Et preceptum est vicecomiti quod per sacramentum etc. in pleno comitatu etc. extendi faciat omnes terras etc. predicti Andree, videlicet quantum valent per annum in omnibus exitibus salvo etc., et extentam etc. scire faciat justiciariis etc. a die Pasche in unum mensem nunc. Et vicecomes mandavit quod extendi fecit etc. omnes terras etc. per sacramentum Willelmi de Sweynesthorp', Georgium de Merkesal' et aliorum juratorum, sicut patet inter inquisiciones hujus termini returnatas. Qui dicunt super sacramentum suum quod predictus Andreas habet unum mesuagium et valet per annum .iij. solidos, .lx. acras et unam rodam terre arabilis et valent per annum .l. solidos .ij. denarios obulum, precium acre .x. denarii, tres acras prati et valent per annum tres solidos, .xxviij. solidos .viij. denarios obulum quadrantem annui redditus, unam summam annui redditus et valet .ij. solidos, .xj. opera precii .xj. denariorum, duas precarias cum carucis et valent .iiij. denarios, tres capones et unam gallinam precii .v. denariorum obuli salvis serviciis dominorum feodi. *Summa* .iiij. libre, .viij. solidi .vj. denarii obulus quadrans. Et concessum est predicto Andree quod solvat ad scaccarium sancti Michaelis anno regis Edwardi nono .xx. solidos et ad scaccarium Pasche proximo sequens .xx. solidos et sic de anno etc. annum ad predictos terminos quousque etc. Et preceptum est vicecomiti quod ipsum pro predicto debito non distringat.

189 *MS. reads* debuit; tenebantur *37*. 190 tenebatur *37*.
191 *37 omits.* 192 *37 omits.* 193 *Supplied from 37.*
194 Corpesty *37*. 195 *37 omits.* 196 *Supplied from 37.*
197 hoc petit quod inquiratur *37*.

(989)[198]

B[u]k. Rogerus de B[a]chew[orth] ... recognovit se [debere Aa]ron filio Vyves judeo .lx. quarteria frumenti, reddendum in crastino Animarum proximo futuro, vel pro quolibet dimidiam marcam ad electionem ipsius judei. Et, nisi fecerit, concedit pro se et heredibus suis quod de terris et catallis suis fiant.

(990)

Ebor'. Josceus filius Benedicti [venit][199] coram etc., et recognovit quoddam debitum .x. librarum sub nominibus Roberti de Stanleye et ipsius Joscei esse quietum. Et quia idem Josceus amisit partem cyrographi sui, preceptum est cyrographariis [christianis et judeis arche cyrographariorum][200] Ebor' quod cartam predicti debiti a prefata archa extrahant et eandem predicto Roberto liberari faciant quiete dampnatam.

(991)

[*Ebor', Linc', Norff'*.][201] Ricardus Folyot miles de comitatu Ebor', Edmundus Folyot et Ricardus Folyot filii ejusdem Ricardi venerunt coram etc. et recognoverunt se debere Benedicto de Linc' judeo .ccclxiij. quarteria frumenti, reddendo [i]<inde>[i] ad quindenam sancti Michaelis anno regis Edwardi nono sexies viginti quarteria et unum frumenti vel .xxiiij. libras, et ad Pascham proximo sequens sexies viginti quarteria et unum vel .xxiiij. libras, et ad quindenam sancti Michaelis proximo sequentem, scilicet anno regis Edwardi decimo, sexiesviginti et unum quarteria vel .xxiiij. libras, ad eleccionem predictorum Ricardi, Edmundi et Ricardi, precium cujuslibet quarterii .iiij. solidi. Et, nisi fecerunt, concedunt quod de terris et catallis suis <fiant.>[202] Et per istam recognicionem predictus Benedictus recognovit pro se et heredibus suis, uxore et omnibus filiis suis quod predicti Edmundus, Ricardus et Ricardus et heredes Willelmi Folyot quondam filii predicti Ricardi Folyot militis quieti sunt de ipso Benedicto, heredibus, uxore et omnibus filiis suis de omnibus debitis, calumpniis et omnimodis exaccionibus in quibus predicti Ricardus, <Willelmus, Edmundus et Ricardus>[203] filii predicti Ricardi umquam tenebantur predicto Benedicto, heredibus, uxori sue vel cuicunque filiorum suorum quoquo modo vel ex quacunque causa a creacione seculi usque ad festum Invencionis sancte Crucis anno regis Edwardi nono. Et quod predictus Benedictus tenetur reddere omnia scripta obligatoria, cartas et omnia alia instrumenta per que predicti Ricardus, Willelmus, Edmundus et Ricardus in aliquo debito tenebantur eisdem Benedicto, heredibus, uxori sue et omnibus filiis suis [conjunctim et divisim][204] a temporibus elapsis usque ad predictum festum. Et si carta, scriptum obligatorium, vel aliquod aliud instrumentum remanserit penes predictum Benedictum, uxorem vel heredes suos sub nominibus predictorum Ricardi, Willelmi, Edmundi et Ricardi et Benedicti, uxoris sue vel heredum suorum quod nichil valeant [et omnino cassentur].[205]

(992)

Cantebr'. Johannes Ernald' de Trumpeton' venit coram etc. et recognovit se teneri pro se et heredibus suis Mansero filio Aaron judeo .xxiiij. quarteria frumenti vel pro qulibet quarterio dimidiam marcam reddendo ad festum Omnium Sanctorum anno regis Edwardi nono. Et, nisi fecerit, concedit quod de terris et catallis suis, ad quorumcumque manus devenerunt, fiant.[206]

(993)

Willelmus Paynel et Willelmus de [blank] venerunt coram etc. et recognoverunt pro se et heredibus suis teneri Aaron filio Vyves judeo in viginti saccis lane, reddendo a die sancti Michaelis in .xv. dies anno regis Edwardi nono, vel pro quolibet sacco .x. marcas. Et, nisi fecerit, concedit quod de terris et catallis suis fiant.

MEMBRANE 10 DORSE

(994)

Linc'. Lond'. Cum Willelmus de Appelterfeld' habuisset quedam debita ex vendicione Hagini filii magistri Mossei judei sub nominibus Johannis de Nevyl de Cotes et ipsius Hagini, videlicet unum trescentarum librarum sub nominibus predictorum Johannis et Hagini, reddendo ad festum sancti Martini anno regni regis Henrici .lv.^{to}, Acta die jovis proxima post conversionem sancti Pauli anno regni regis Henrici .liiij.^{to}, et unum ducentarum et sex librarum sub nominibus eorundem Johannis et Hagini, reddendum medietatem ad Nativitatem beati Johannis Baptiste anno regis Henrici .liiij.^{to}, et aliam medietatem ad festum sancti Martini proximo sequens, Acta die veneris proximo post festum sancti Hillarii anno predicto; et unum .l. marcarum sub nominibus predictorum Johannis et Hagini, reddendo ad Nativitatem beati Johannis Baptiste anno regis Henrici .lv., Acta in vigilia sancti Marci Evangeliste anno predicto; unde carte de predictis debitis posite fuerunt in quadam pixide sigillata sigillo predicti Willelmi et inbillate ad opus ipsius Willelmi in custodia justiciarorum in thesauro regis ad transmittendum ad archam cyrographariorum vel alibi ubi dictus Willelmus voluerit, ita quod dictus Willelmus posset semper inde habere administracionem, idem Willelmus venit coram etc. et recognovit quod Andreas de Nevyle, frater et heres predicti Johannis, satisfecit eidem Willelmo pro predictis debitis et ipsum Andream

[198] *This entry is marked for cancellation with the words* vacat quia in rotulo precedenti. *See above, no. 932.*

[199] *MS. omits.*

[200] *Supplied from 37.*

[201] *Supplied from 37; the margin of 66 is damaged at this point.*

[202] leventur *37*.

[203] Foliot, Willelmus filius ejusdem Ricardi defunctus, Edmundus Foliot et Ricardus Foliot *37*.

[204] *Supplied from 37.*

[205] *Supplied from 37. It continues* Et quod *but ends there.*

[206] *37 adds* et leventur.

et omnes tenentes terrarum que fuerunt predicti Johannis de eisdem debitis inperpetuum quietavit. Ideo predicte carte in presencia ipsius Willelmo predicto Andrea in pleno scaccario liberantur quiete dampnate.

(995)

Lanc'. Robertus de Holond miles venit coram etc. et recognovit se teneri Nicholao de la <Hose>[207] in ducentis marcis, reddendo inde centum marcas ad festum sancti Michaelis anno regnis regis Edwardi nono et ad Pascham proximo sequens quadraginta marcas et ad festum Nativitatis beati Johannis Baptiste subsequens sexaginta marcas. Et, nisi fecerit, concedit pro se et heredibus suis et pro tenentibus terrarum suarum, ad quoruncumque manus devenerunt, quod de terris et catallis suis fiant. Et <ad hanc solucionem faciendum>[208] invenit manucaptores subscriptos qui una cum eo constituerunt se principales debitores, et unusquisque eorum in solidum, videlicet Robertum <Grely,>[209] Johannem Deuyas, William le <Botilyer>[210] milites et Gilbertum filium Gilberti de Suthworthe de comitatu Lanc' sub hac forma, scilicet quod, si predictus Robertus de Holond' predictas soluciones terminis predictis non fecerit vel si aliquem terminum preterierit, iidem Robertus Grely, Johannes et alii manucaptores prenominati concedunt pro se et heredes suis et tenentibus terrarum suarum quod predicta pecunia tam de terris et catallis suis propriis quam de terris et catallis predicti Roberti de Holond' ad opus predicti Nicholai fiat et levetur. Et predictus Robertus de Holond' recognovit et concessit quod ipse et heredes sui tenentur acquietare predictos Robertum Grely et alios manucaptores suos prenominatos versus predictum Nicholaum de predictis .cc. marcis et de omnibus dampnis <et expensis>[211] que <vel quas>[212] <predicti Robertus Grely et alii manucaptores prenominati>[213] pro defectu <soluccionis>[214] <predicte pecunie incurrent.>[215] Et, nisi fecerit, quod de terris et catallis suis fiat. Et pro ista recognicione predictus Nicholaus recognovit et concessit quod Thurstanus de Hoyland, Robertus Greley, Herbertus Greley et Robertus de Hoyland sint quieti de quadam recognicione ducentarum marcarum quas recognoverunt coram justiciariis domini regis de Banco se debere predicto Nicholao; et eciam idem Nicholaus concessit et recognovit quod per illam recognicionem ibidem factam nichil decetero exigere poterit seu vendicare de predicto Thurstano et aliis manucaptoribus suis. Et quod illa recognicio pro nullo computetur nec aliquid valeat. [Postea venit idem Robertus et solvit predicto Nicholao centum marcas de termino sancti Michaelis anno regni regis Edwardi nono incipiente decimo.][216]

[207] Huse militi *37*.
[208] super hac recognicione et solucione facienda *37*.
[209] de Grelley *37* (and so elsewhere in this entry).
[210] Botyler *37*. [211] *37 omits*. [212] *37 omits*.
[213] eis quoquomodo accidere poterint *37*.
[214] acquietancie *37*. [215] predicti debiti *37*.
[216] *Supplied from 37*.

(996)

Buk'. Barnabas de Hertwelle, filius domini Willelmi de Hertwell, venit coram etc. et recognovit per scriptum suum obligatorium se debere magistro Elia filio magistri Mossei judeo Lond' .xl. quarteria frumenti vel pro quolibet quarterio dimidiam marcam reddendo ad octabas sancti Michaelis anno regis Edwardi .ix.º. Et, nisi fecerit, concedit quod de terris et catallis suis, ad quorumcumque manus devenerunt, fiant.

(997)

Buk'. Barnabas de Hertwelle, filius domini Willelmi de Hertwelle, venit coram etc. et recognovit per scriptum suum se debere magistro Elia filio magistri Mossei .xx. marcas reddendo ad octabas sancti Michaelis anno regis Edwardi nono. Et, nisi fecerit, concedit quod de terris et catallis suis, ad quorumcumque manus devenerint, fiant.

(998)

Surr'. Radulfus Wauclyn de Kyngeston' de comitatu Surr' venit coram etc. et recognovit per scriptum suum obligatorium se debere Cresseo filio Gente judeo viginti quarteria frumenti vel pro quolibet quarterio dimidiam marcam, reddendo eidem judeo in crastino apostolorum Philippi et Jacobi anno regis Edwardi decimo. Et, nisi fecerit, concedit quod de terris et catallis suis fiant etc.

(999)

Wyltes', Suth'. Johannes de Havering' quondam vicecomes Suth' pro pluribus defaltis in misericordia.

Idem Johannes attachiatus ad respondendum de .c. libris .xij. solidis .x. denariis quos levare fecit de bladis, redditibus, finibus, perquisitis curie et cicera proveniencia de gardinis Thome de Chelewarton' ad opus Benedicti de Wynton' judei dampnati per brevia regis eidem Johanni inde directa, quos quidem denarios et bona ad valenciam summe predicte per se [i]<et ballivos suos>[i] dum exstitit vicecomes Suth' per ipsum apud Chelewarton' missos levavit et ad voluntatem suam [abduxit][217] et adhuc penes se dicta catalla detinet, nullam restitucionem seu allocacionem dicto Thome seu alicui alii pro eo inde facit set dicta bona duci fecit ad manerium suum de Grafton', ut dicitur.

Predictus Johannes venit et defendit etc. et dicit quod nunquam per ipsum vel aliquos ballivos suos dum exstitit vicecomes comitatus predicti per breve regis seu sine brevi aliquid de bonis seu catallis predicti Thome, ut in redditibus, finibus terrarum, perquisitis curie, bladis, cicera vel aliis exitibus aliquid levari fecit nec [abduxit][218] et hoc petit quod inquiratur etc. Et dicit quod adeo cito quod aliquod breve sibi venit, dictus Thomas munitus fuit per prefatum judeum et per composicionem inter eos factam quedam bona sua eidem judeo liberavit, ipso et omnibus suis quid et quantum penitus ingnorantibus, quia sine aliqua districcione in absencia sua et ministrorum suorum. Et hoc petit similiter quod inquiratur etc. Et

[217] *MS. reads* adduxit. [218] *MS. reads* adduxit.

preceptum est vicecomiti quod venire faciat coram etc. a die sancte Trinitatis in .xv. dies et .vj. milites et sex alios probos et legales homines de visneto de Chelewarton', et qui nulla affinitate etc., ad recognoscendum etc.

(1000)[219]

Warr'. Cum dominus Rex assignasset magistro Elie filio magistri Mossei judeo [de thesauro suo][220] in recompensacionem quorundam debitorum in quibus abbas de Straff' eidem judeo tenebatur, unum debitum .lx. librarum sub nominibus Henrici de Benygton' et Cressei filii [i]<ejusdem>[i] magistri, prout patet inter memoranda de termino sancti Hillarii anno regis Edwardi quinto, ac cum idem magister Elias exigeret predictum debitum .lx. librarum de Elia de Wonecot', tenente terras que fuerunt predicti Henrici, idem Elias de Wonecot' venit coram etc. et recognovit se esse tenentem terrarum que fuerunt predicti Henrici, videlicet duarum parcium terrarum illarum, quia dicit quod Alicia de Benygton' tenet terciam partem terrarum illarum in dotem, et bene recognovit predictum debitum esse totaliter debitum et clarum excepto tantummodo .xiiij. marcis quas dicit inde solutas fuisse predicto Cresseo in vita sua, et inde protulit starrum predicti Cressei de illis .xiiij. marcis sic eidem Cresseo solutis; et idem magister Elias, habita inde inspeccione, bene recognoscit dictum starrum esse factum dicti Cressei et concedit quod ille .xiiij. marce allocentur eidem Elie de Wonec' in predicto debito .lx. librarum. Et idem Elias de Wonec' concedit quod idem magister Elias teneat medietatem predictarum terrarum secundum statutum etc. quousque predictum debitum .lx. librarum ei solvatur, salvis predictis .xiiij. marcis prius solutis predicto Cresseo. Et postea predictus magister Elias concessit, tradidit et dimisit predicto Elie de Wonec' predictam medietatem terrarum tenendam pro sex marcis sibi singulis annis solvendis ad duos terminos, videlicet unam medietatem a die sancti Michaelis in tres septimanas et aliam medietatem a die Pasche in tres septimanas. Et quamcito predicta dos sibi acciderit, extunc solvet idem Elias de Wonec' singulis annis predicto magistro Elie .ix. marcas ad terminos predictos quousque predictum debitum plenarie persolvatur, salvis predictis .xiiij. marcis inde prius predicto Cresseo solutis. Et idem Elias de Wonec' concedit quod, si in aliquo predictorum terminorum defecerit vel cessaverit, [i]<quod>[i] vicecomes Warr' et Leyc' totum predictum debitum de omnibus terris suis predictis ad opus predicti judei fieri faciat et levari, ita tamen quod eidem Elia de Wonec' allocetur quicquid inde solutum fuerit. Et per predictas recogniciones et concessiones et predicte pecunie solucionem in forma predicta faciendam idem magister Elias recognovit quod ipse et heredes sui tenentur warantizare, defendere et acquietare predictum Eliam et Aliciam uxorem ejus, heredes et assignatos suos de toto predicto debito .lx. librarum contra quoscumque calumpniantes.

[219] *There is another version of this entry on m. 11d of this roll (no. 1015). Significant variants from that version are recorded in the footnotes to this enrolment with the siglum B.*

[220] *Supplied from B.*

MEMBRANE 11

Memoranda de termino Pasche anno regni regis Edwardi nono. De quindena

(1001)

Sutht'. Preceptum fuit vicecomiti quod venire faceret coram etc. ad hunc diem Radulfum le Orfevre ad respondendum Regi de .xxv. solidis, Willelmum Mot ad respondendum Regi de decem solidis, Willelmum Cornealond' de decem solidis, Johannem Moraunt aurifabrum ad respondendum Regi de auro ponderis decem denariorum et quatuor petris preciosis sculptis precii quinque solidorum, Henricum Henwe de Twyford' ad respondendum Regi de una vacca et duobus vitulis precii unius marce, et Petrum Ascelyn de Andevere ad respondendum Regi de pellibus lanatis precii quinque marcarum de bonis et catallis Abrahe filii Benedicti. Et ipsi non venerunt. Et vicecomes mandavit quod returnavit breve inde sibi directum ballivis libertatum Wynton', Sutht', episcopatus Wynt', Andevere et Basingstok, qui nichil inde <responderunt.>[221] Judicium quod non omittat propter libertates etc. quin eas etc. et venire faciat coram etc. in octabis sancte Trinitatis [predictos Radulphum, Willelmum, Willelmum, Johannem, Henricum et Petrum][222] ad respondendum <etc.>[223]

(1002)

Sutht'. Preceptum fuit vicecomiti quod venire faceret coram etc. ad hunc diem Mabiliam que fuit uxor Emeryci de Cancellis ad respondendum Regi de bonis et catallis ad valenciam .xx. librarum que devenerunt ad manus dicte Mabilie de bonis et catallis que fuerunt Samuelis de Arundel judei, qui Regi in diversis debitis tenetur. Et ipsa non venit. Et vicecomes mandavit quod <Reginaldus>[224] prepositus, Galfridus de Bradeford, Radulfus de Fraxino et Johannes le Crek' manuceperunt predictam Mabiliam, quam non habuerunt. Ideo in misericordia.[225] Judicium quod distringat per terras etc., ita quod nec ipsa etc., et quod de exitibus etc., et quod habeat corpus ejus coram etc. in octabis sancte Trinitatis ad respondendum etc. et ad audiendum etc.

(1003)

Sutht'. Preceptum fuit vicecomiti quod venire faceret coram etc. ad hunc diem Walterum <Dalerun>[226] et Thomam le Paumer, ballivos Wynton' in anno regis

[221] fecerunt *37*. [222] *Supplied from 37.*

[223] regi de denariis, bonis et catallis supradictis que devenerunt ad manus ipsorum de denariis, bonis et catallis que fuerunt Abrahe filii Benedicti de Wynton' judei *37*.

[224] Rogerus *37*.

[225] *The word* misericordia *is repeated in the margin.*

[226] Dalroun *37*.

Edwardi tercio, et Johannem [de][227] Gys, clericum eorum eodem anno, ad respondendum Regi de .xj. libris de claris debitis Judaismi, et aliis transgressionibus. Et ipsi non venerunt. Et vicecomes mandavit quod returnavit breve inde sibi directum ballivis libertatis Wynton', qui nichil inde fecerunt. Judicium quod non omittat propter libertatem etc. quin eam etc. et venire faciat coram etc. in octabis sancte Trinitatis etc.

(1004)

Sutht'. Preceptum fuit vicecomiti quod venire faceret ad hunc diem Wyot' le Mouner et Orengam uxorem ejus ad respondendum Regi de diversis bonis et catallis ad valenciam .xl. marcarum que devenerunt ad manus ipsorum Wyoti et Orenge ex tradicione Jacobi <Mawe judei>[228] de bonis et catallis Abrahe filii Benedicti judei [de Wynton',][229] qui Regi in diversis debitis tenetur. Et ipsi non venerunt. Et vicecomes mandavit quod returnavit breve inde sibi directum ballivis libertatis [e]<predicte>[e] Wynton', qui nichil unde fecerunt. Judicium quod non omittat propter libertatem etc. quin eam etc. et venire faciat coram etc. in octabis sancte Trinitatis [predictos Wyot et Orengam ad respondendum Regi de predictis bonis][230] etc.

(1005)

Northt'. Preceptum fuit vicecomiti quod distringeret Margeriam [i]<que fuit uxor Willelmi>[i] de Pelevyle, Walterum filium ejus [i]<et>[i] Robertum de <Shrapetoft,>[231] executores testamenti predicti Willelmi, per terras etc. et quod haberet corpora eorum coram etc. ad hunc diem ad respondendum Regi de diversis bonis et catallis que devenerunt ad manus predictorum Willelmi et Margerie de bonis Isac de Lond' judei dampnati. Et ipsi non venerunt. Et vicecomes mandavit quod Willelmus Makeman et Ricardus le Westreys manuceperunt predictam Margeriam, quam non habuerunt. Ideo in misericordia.[232] Et quod predictus Walterus non fuit inventus in balliva sua post recepcionem hujus brevis, nec aliquid habet in ea per quod possit distringi. Et quod predictus Robertus de <Shrapetoft>[233] non habet terras nec tenementa in balliva sua per que possit distringi nec potuit manucaptores invenire veniendi ad diem [hic quia pauper est.][234] Ideo, sicut pluries, in octabis sancte Trinitatis etc.

(1006)

Hereff'. Abraham le Prestre judeus, qui tulit breve regis de placito debiti super Johannem Lovekyn, Julianam uxorem ejus et alios in brevi, non est prosecutus versus eos. Ideo ipse Abraham, pro se et plegiis suis de prosequendo, in misericordia.[235]

[227] *Supplied from 37.* [228] Manne *37.*
[229] *Supplied from 37.* [230] *Supplied from 37.*
[231] Strapetoft *37.*
[232] *The word* misericordia *is repeated in the margin.*
[233] Strapetoft *37.* [234] *Supplied from 37.*
[235] *The word* misericordia *is repeated in the margin.*

(1007)

Hereff'. Preceptum fuit vicecomiti quod de bonis et catallis Willelmi Deveroys, Rogeri <Springehose,>[236] Rogeri Tyrel, Johannes de Baskervyle, Gilberti de Bosco et Walteri Tyrel' fieri faceret ad opus Johannis de Pycheford' .xij. marcas que ei aretro sunt de <.cc. et .xl. marcis>[237] quas predicto Johanni debent per recognicionem suam inde factam coram etc. et denarios haberet coram etc. ad hunc diem. Et vicecomes mandavit quod Rogerus Springhose, Johannes de Baskervyle et Walterus Tyrel nichil habent in balliva sua; et quod Rogerus Tyrel mortuus est; et quod Gilbertus de Bosco est de libertate Leomenstr' et pro ipso returnavit breve ballivis libertatis predicte, qui nichil inde fecerunt. Judicium quod non omittat propter libertatem etc. quin eam etc. Et vicecomes mandavit quod de bonis et catallis Willelmi Deveroys fecit quinque marcas quas secum deferet a die Pasche in unum mensem <etc.>[238]

(1008)

Kanc'. Preceptum fuit vicecomiti quod venire faceret coram etc. ad hunc diem Gilbertum le Peyntur et Matildam uxorem ejus ad respondendum Regi de .xl. solidis quos receperunt de bonis et catallis que fuerunt Sampsonis de Sydingburne judei ex tradicione dicti Sampsonis, cujus debita capta sunt in manus Regis pro diversis debitis in quibus Regi tenetur, et adhuc dicta catalla penes dictos Gilbertum et Matildam remanent, ut dicitur.

Predicti Gilbertus et Matilda veniunt et defendunt vim etc. et dicunt quod predictos .xl. solidos ex tradicione dicti Sampsonis non receperunt nec aliquid aliud de bonis seu catallis dicti Sampsonis penes se habent nec habuerunt et de hoc ponunt se super patriam. Ideo preceptum est vicecomiti quod venire faciat coram etc. in octabis sancte Trinitatis .xij. probos etc. de Sydingburn' et visneto ejusdem ville, et qui nulla affinitate etc., ad recognoscendum etc.[239]

Ad quem diem inquisicio venit per Benedictum Aurifabrum, Rogerum de Wormedale, Adam Taylur, Willelmum Brut, Rogerum de Bundestrete, Jordanum Belejambe, Johannem filium Petronille, Hugonem Bolle, Johannem de Lond', Alanum le Taverner, Hamonem Dru et Stephanum le Taverner, qui jurati dicunt super sacramentum suum quod predicti Gilbertus et Matilda predictos .xl. solidos seu aliqua alia bona vel catalla ex tradicione predicti Sampsonis non receperunt nec aliquid [e]<inde habent>[e] ei debent. Ideo consideratum est quod predicti Gilbertus et Matilda inde sint quieti et dictus Sampson committatur prisone donec de dicta transgressione Regi satisfecerit et nichilominus in misericordia.[240]

[236] Springehuese *37.*
[237] .xx. marcis per annum de quodam debito .ccxl. marcarum *37.*
[238] Ad parliamentum predicto Johanni solvendas *37.*
[239] *The remainder of this entry is a later addition to 66 and is omitted from 37.*
[240] *The word* misericordia *is repeated in the margin.*

(1009)

Bristoll'. Petrus de la Mare constabularius Bristoll' solvit in recepta regis de catallis Hake de Dorkyng' judei .xxx. solidos et habet inde talliam.

(1010)

Kanc'. Preceptum fuit vicecomiti quod venire faceret coram etc. ad hunc diem Willelmum de Renham drapparium de Maydenston' ad respondendum Regi de .xl. solidis quos recepit ex tradicione Sampsonis de Sydingburn' judei custodiendum, cujus debita capta sunt in manum Regis pro [diversis][241] debitis in quibus Regi tenetur. Et ipse non venit. Et vicecomes mandavit quod returnavit breve inde sibi directum senescallo libertatis archiepiscopatus Cant', qui sibi respondit quod breve sibi adeo tarde venit quod exequi non potuit. Ideo, sicut alias, in octabis sancte Trinitatis.

(1011)[242]

Norff'. Preceptum fuit vicecomiti quod distringeret Willelmum de Halvergate, tenentem terrarum et tenementorum que fuerunt Bertrami de Verdun, per terras et catalla sua ad reddendum sibi ad opus Regis .xviij. libras quas Regi debet occasione terrarum etc. de debito Senioris le Eveske judei; et denarios haberet coram etc. ad hunc diem vel corpus etc. ad ostendendum etc.

Predictus Willelmus venit et recognovit se esse tenentem cujusdam partis terrarum et tenementorum que fuerunt predicti Bertrami et de porcione dicti debiti ipsum inde contingente vocat ad warantum Robertum de Molton' quod ipsum inde acquietare debet, ut dicit. Et preceptum est vicecomiti quod venire faciat coram etc. in octabis sancte Trinitatis predictum Robertum ad acquietandum prefatum Willelmum de porcione ipsum contingente de predicto debito, sicut racionabiliter etc.

(1012)

Surr', Sussex'. Preceptum fuit vicecomiti quod venire faceret coram etc. ad hunc diem Radulfum de la Forde ad respondendum Regi de diversis bonis et catallis ad valenciam .c. solidorum que deverunt ad manus ejus ex tradicione Mossei de Doggestrate judei, cujus debita capta sunt in manum regis pro [diversis][243] debitis in quibus Regi tenetur; et quod venire faceret ad hunc diem Lambertum Conent ad respondendum Regi de quatuor libris de debito dicti Mossei, ut supra. Et ipsi non venerunt. Et vicecomes mandavit quod predictus Radulfus nichil habet nec fuit inventus post recepcionem brevis sibi inde directi. Et quod Willelmus de Sneylham, Rogerus <Bullok',>[244] Willelmus <filius>[245] Hughe, Johannes Warde et Hamo Berte manuceperunt predictum Lambertum, quem non habuerunt. Ideo in misericordia.[246] Judicium quod distringat per terras etc., ita quod nec ipsi etc., et quod de exitibus etc., et quod habeat corpora eorum coram etc. in octabis sancte Trinitatis ad respondendum et ad audiendum etc.

(1013)

Sussex'. Radulfus de Stopham miles venit coram etc. et recognovit se teneri Mansero filio Aaron judeo per scriptum suum obligatorium in ducentis quarteriis frumenti, reddendo die Omnium Sanctorum anno regis Edwardi nono, vel pro quolibet quarterio dimidiam marcam argenti, quam partem idem judeus eligere maluerit. Et, nisi fecerit, concedit pro se et heredibus suis quod de terris et catallis suis fiant, ad quorumcumque manus devenerunt.

MEMBRANE 11 DORSE

Adhuc Memoranda de quindena Pasche

(1014)

Surr'. Sussex'. Preceptum fuit vicecomiti quod venire faceret coram etc. ad hunc diem Willelmum [i]<de>[i] <Wykes>[247] filium et heredem Johanne de Wyke, Johannem de <Wykeford,>[248] Robertum de Wyvelehol', Ricardum de <Wyke,>[249] Walterum de <Wyke,>[250] Johannem de <Polyngfaud,>[251] Willelmum de Hoston', Thomam de Kepeston', priorem de Eringeham et Nigellum <Payn,>[252] tenentes quandam partem terrarum et tenementorum que fuerunt Gilberti de Basevyle, ad respondendum Regi una cum <Joel' Payn,>[253] qui habuit hunc diem, de quater viginti libris, in quibus predictus Gilbertus tenebatur Aaron Crespyn judeo dampnato. <Joel>[254] Payn et Nigellus Payn venerunt et alii supradicti non venerunt. Et vicecomes mandavit quod Johannes Pepyn de Wyk' et Henricus de Uppehell' de eadem manuceperunt Willelmum filium et heredem Johanne de Wyk'; et quod Laurencius de <Cokel'>[255] de Werplesdon' et Willelmus de la Grave de eadem manuceperunt Johannem de Wykeford'; et quod Johannes le Bude et Gilbertus <Bicchewot>[256] manuceperunt Robertum de Wyvelehole; et quod Gilbertus de <Pennestand>[257] et Radulfus Orday manuceperunt Ricardum de <Wyk';>[258] et quod Willelmus Leveron de <Billing>[259] et Willelmus Ruffus de eadem manuceperunt Walterum de <Wyk';>[260] et quod Adam de Cruce de <Billingherst>[261] et Willelmus <Simond>[262] de eadem manuceperunt Johannem de <Pollingfaud;>[263] et quod Bartholomeus de <Pullebergh'>[264] et Willelmus Pyghou de eadem manuceperunt Willelmum de Hogthon'; et quod Adam Attefanne de Novo Ponte et Thomas Gylemyn de eadem manuceperunt Thomam de Kepeston'; et quod

[241] *Supplied from 37.*
[242] *This entry is marked for deletion with the words* vacat quia alibi inter memoranda hujus termini. *See above no. 909.*
[243] *Supplied from 37.* [244] Bollok' *37.* [245] *37 omits.*
[246] *The word* misericordia *is repeated in the margin.*

[247] Wyke *37.* [248] Wykesforde *37.* [249] Wykes *37.*
[250] Wykes *37.* [251] Polingefald *37.* [252] Payen *37.*
[253] Juello Paen *37.* [254] Juellus *37.* [255] Cokelye *37.*
[256] Bythewot *37.* [257] Pennefaud *37.* [258] Wikes *37.*
[259] Bylingeherst *37.* [260] Wykes *37.*
[261] Bylingeherst *37.* [262] Symod' *37.*
[263] Polingefaud *37.* [264] Pulebergh' *37.*

Willelmus le Messer de <Herinngeham>[265] et Johannes Atteherst de eadem manuceperunt priorem de <Hermyngheham;>[266] quos non habuerunt. Ideo in misericordia. Judicium quod distringat per terras etc., ita quod nec ipsi etc., et quod de exitibus etc., et quod habeat corpora eorum etc. in octabis sancte Trinitatis ad respondendum etc. et ad audiendum etc.

(1015)

[This is a second version of an enrolment on m. 10d (no. 1000). Significant variants are noted in the footnotes to that entry.]

(1016)

Bed'. Buk'. Preceptum fuit vicecomiti quod de bonis et catallis Walteri de Gayton' fieri faceret ad opus Regis viginti libras de quibus aquietasse debuit Hugonem de Coleworth' versus Regem de debito Benedicti de Linc' judei, et quod denarios illos haberet coram etc. ad hunc diem. Et vicecomes mandavit quod retornavit breve sibi inde directum ballivis libertatis Leyc', qui nichil inde responderunt. Judicium quod non omittat propter libertatem predictam quin eam etc. <et de bonis et catallis predicti Walteri fieri faceret denarios supradictos et eos habeat coram etc.>[267] in octabis sancte Trinitatis Regi solvendum.

(1017)

Wyltes'. Preceptum fuit vicecomiti quod non omitteret propter libertatem de Selkel' quin eam etc., et distringeret Johannem Brun et Robertum Harevest, tenentes quandam partem terrarum que fuerunt Johannis filii Nicholai Wace, per terras etc. ad <reddendum>[268] sibi ad opus regis decem libras quas Regi debent occasione terrarum etc. de debito Isac de Suthwerk' judei. Et vicecomes mandavit quod breve adeo tarde venit [post decessum vicecomitis, predecessoris sui][269] quod exequi non potuit. Ideo, sicut alias, in octabis sancte Trinitatis.

(1018)

<*Linc'.*>[270] Ricardus Guydicionis, civis [i]<et mercator>[i] <Lucan',>[271] venit coram etc. et recognovit pro se et sociis suis se recepisse de domina A. Regina consorte Regis nunc per manus fratris Johannis grangiarii hospitalis <sancte Katerine>[272] extra Linc' centum libras in partem solicionis debiti in quo eadem Regina eis tenebatur. Et quia predictus frater Johannes servat terminos suos de debito in quo tenetur predicte Regine, preceptum est vicecomiti quod <ipsum fratrem de predictis .c. libris pacem habere permittat etc.>[273]

[265] Heringeham *37*. [266] Heringeham *37*.
[267] *37 omits.* [268] respondendum *37*.
[269] *Supplied from 37*.
[270] Kanc' *37*. *In 66* Kanc' *is written above* Linc' *but has been deleted.*
[271] Lanc' *37*. [272] Sancti Sepulcri *37*.
[273] dictus frater et domus sua de dicto debito centum librarum pacem habeant *37*.

(1019)

Leyc'. Rogerus de Somervyle [de comitatu Leyc'][274] venit coram etc. et recognovit per scriptum obligatorium etc. se debere Aaron filio Vyves [judeo Lond'][275] octo libras, reddendo a die sancti Michaelis in .xv. dies anno regis Edwardi .ix.°. Et, nisi fecerit, concedit quod de terris et catallis suis [heredum et tenencium terrarum suarum, ad quorumque manus devenerunt][276] fiant. Istam recognicionem dictus Rogerus fecit pro .vij. libris in quibus Gerardus de Hamelton' per cartam suam .x. librarum tenebatur Elie filio Manseri judeo Staunff', quod quidem debitum idem Aaron recepit de thesauro in recompensacionem debitorum Gilberti Peche etc.

(1020)

Wygorn'. Walterus de Bello Campo miles venit coram etc. et recognovit per scrpitum suum etc. se debere eidem <Aaron>[277] .c. et .l. quarteria frumenti, vel pro quolibet quarterio dimidiam marcam, reddendo inde medietatem ad festum sancti Petri ad Vincula anno regis Edwardi nono et aliam medietatem ad quindenam sancti Michaelis proximo sequentem. Et, nisi fecerit, quod de terris et catallis suis [heredum et tenencium terrarum suarum,][278] ad quoruncumque manus devenerint, fiant.

(1021)

Norht'. Willelmus Hanret filius domini Ricardi Hanret de comitatu Norht' venit coram etc. et recognovit se debere magistro Elie filio magistri Mossei [judeo Lond'][279] .lx. quarteria frumenti, reddendo a die sancti Michaelis in .xv. dies anno regis Edwardi nono, vel pro quolibet quarterio dimidiam marcam. Et, nisi fecerit, concedit quod de terris et catallis suis fiant.

(1022)

Cant', Norff'. Johannes Canon solvit Aaron filio Vyves .iiij. marcas quas idem Aaron recepit in recompensacionem etc. Et Baldewinus de Maners manucepit solvere eidem Aaron pro predicto Johanne .ij. marcas a die sancti Michaelis in tres septimanas. Et, nisi fecerit, concedit quod de terris et catallis suis fiant etc.

(1023)

Kanc'. Preceptum fuit vicecomiti quod distringeret Ricardum Eustach' de Peccham et tenentes terrarum suarum per terras etc. ad reddendum sibi ad opus Regis .iiij. libras de debitis Aaron filii Benedicti de Cant' judei defuncti. Et Willelmus atte Wode, tenens terrarum que fuerunt predicti [i]<Ricardi>[i] Eustach', venit coram etc. et protulit starrum dicti judei de acquietancia predicti debiti in hec verba: 'Aaron filius Benedicti judeus Cant' recognovit per starrum suum quod Ricardus Eustach' et heredes sui et assignati quieti sunt de ipso judeo,

[274] *Supplied from 37*. [275] *Supplied from 37*.
[276] *Supplied from 37*.
[277] Aaron filio Vives judeo Lond' *37*.
[278] *Supplied from 37*. [279] *Supplied from 37*.

heredibus et assignatis suis de omnibus debitis, querelis, calumpniis et plegiagiis a creacione seculi usque ad festum sancti Martini anno regis Edwardi primo. Et si inveniatur carta vel tallia infra archa cyrographariorum vel extra facta ante predictum terminum, idem judeus recognovit quod quiete sint et nichil valeant etc.' Et inquisicio presens fuit per Thomam Chicche, Johannem Hubert cyrographarios christianos, Willelmum Kalvesfot, Willelmus le Fode et alios christianos, Aaron de Wynton', Haginum le Eveske cyrographarios judeos, Leonem filium Abrahe et alios judeos, sicut patet inter brevia hujus termini retornata. Qui dicunt super sacramentum suum quod predictum starrum est factum predicti Aaron et littera sua ebrayca signatum, et quod dictum starrum fecit tempore quo habuit liberam administracionem bonorum suorum. Ideo consideratum est quod predictus Ricardus et tenentes terrarum suarum de predicto debito .iiij. librarum sint quieti et quod carta inde liberetur Willelmo atte Wode tenenti predictarum terrarum quiete dampnata. Et preceptum est vicecomiti quod predictos tenentes pacem habere permittat etc. Et si quid etc.

(1024)

Cant'. Galfridus de Suthorp' venit coram etc. et recognovit se debere Aaron filio Vyves .xxij. libras, reddendo inde ad quindenam sancti Johannis Baptiste anno regis Edwardi nono .x. libras, et ad quindenam sancti Michaelis proximo sequentem .xij. libras. Et, nisi fecerit, concedit quod de terris et catallis suis fiant.

(1025)

Leyc'. Willelmus <Mordak'>[280] et Willelmus de Boyvyle venerunt coram etc. et recognoverunt se debere Aaron filio Vyves .xxxvij. marcas et dimidiam, reddendo inde a die Pasche in unum mensem anno regis Edwardi .ix.º .l. solidos, et in crastino sancte Trinitatis .l. solidos et ad quindenam Nativitatis beati Johannis Baptiste proximo sequentem .x. marcas et ad Natale Domini proximo sequens .x. marcas, et ad quindenam Pasche proximo sequentem .x. marcas. Et, nisi fecerint, concedunt quod de terris et catallis eorum fiant. Postea, videlicet in quindena nativitatis beati Johannis Baptiste, Willelmus de Boyvile solvit inde <in pleno scaccario>[281] .x. marcas.

(1026)

Rotel'. Memorandum quod Willelmus de Boyvile vicecomes Rotel' habet diem ad solvendum .l. solidos .ij. denarios in octabis sancte Trinitatis de quibus oneratur pro manucapcione Theobaldi de Nevyle.

(1027)

Rotel'. Cum Reginaldus Turnehare de Seyton' districtus fuisset pro quodam debito .iiij. librarum sub nominibus ipsius Reginaldi et Samuelis filii Saulin judei, predictus Reginaldus venit et solvit per manus Willelmi de Boyvyle vicecomitis predictas .iiij. libras in recepta regis per .ij. tallias eandem summam continentes, prout patet in pipa. Et predicta carta in hec verba: 'Sciant etc. quod Reginaldus Turnehare de Seyton' de comitatu Rotel' debet Samueli filio Saulini judeo Staunff' .iiij. libras, reddendo ad festum sancti Michaelis anno regis Edwardi primo. Acta die veneris proxima post festum sancte Trinitatis anno regis Edwardi primo.' liberatur predicto Reginaldo in pleno scaccario quiete dampnata.

(1028)

Kanc'. Memorandum quod Willelmus de Oxenhale, filius Godefridi de Oxenhale, venit coram etc. et solvit Aaron filio Vyves in recompensacionem debiti Gilberti Pecche per preceptum justiciariorum .vj. libras et .iiij. solidos de uno debito .x. librarum in quo idem Willelmus tenebatur Avegaye relicte Salle judee dampnate et residuum solverat eidem judee, scilicet .lxxvj. solidos, tempore quo ipsa habuit liberam administracionem etc. Et predicta carta in hec verba: 'Willelmus de Oxenhale filius Godefridi debet Avegaye relicte Salle .x. libras, reddendo in quindena Omnium Sanctorum anno regis Henrici .lvij.º. Acta .xviij. die Aprilis anno .lvj.[to]' predicto Willelmo in pleno scaccario liberatur quiete dampnata.

ROLL 37

MEMBRANE 1

Adhuc de termino Pasche anno [regis Edwardi] nono

(1029)

Suth'. Nicholaus Horsenemayn pro pluribus defaltis in misericordia.

Idem Nicholaus attachiatus ad respondendum Regi de .xx. saccis lane, qui devenerunt ad manus predicti Nicholai de bonis et catallis que fuerunt Kote que fuit uxor Michaelis le Eveske judee dampnate ad valenciam .cc. marcarum, ut dicitur.

Predictus Nicholaus venit et defendit etc. et dicit quod numquam alisquos saccos lane seu aliqua bona vel catalla de catallis predicte Kote recepit seu custodiam habuit. Et petit quod inquiratur etc. Et preceptum est vicecomiti quod venire faciat coram etc. [i]<a>[i] die sancte Trinitatis in .xv. dies sex probos et legales homines et sex legales judeos de civitate Wynton' per quos etc., et qui nulla affinitate etc. ad recognoscendum etc.

Ad quem diem inquisicio non venit, et datus est dies dicto Nicholao a die sancte Michaelis in tres septimanas. Ad quem diem inquisicio venit per Willelmum Strut, Hugonem le Noreys et alios christianos, Cokerel filium Licoricie, Abraham filium Cokerel et alios judeos, sicut patet inter brevia de termino sancti Michaelis anno regis Edwardi nono retornata. Qui dicunt super sacramentum suum quod predictus Nicholaus de bonis seu catallis que

[280] Mordack *37*. [281] *37 omits.*

fuerunt predicte Kote nichil recepit nec aliquam societatem in lanis vel aliis bonis cum predicta Kote habuit nec aliquid ei debuit. Ideo consideratum est quod predictus Nicholaus de predictis .xx. saccis lane sit quietus et quod Rex nichil inde capiat. Et Douce soror dicte Cote, ad cujus sectam predictus Nicholaus attachiatus fuit, committitur prisone etc.

(1030)

Suth'. Johanna Thurmound, Willelmus Thurmound et Alicia uxor ejus pro pluribus defaltis in misericordia.

Iidem Johanna, Willlelmus et Alicia attachiati ad respondendum Regi de quibusdam jocalibus auri et argenti et aliis bonis et catallis ad valenciam .l. marcarum, que devenerunt ad manus predictorum Johanne, Willelmi et Alicie salvo custodiendum de bonis et catallis que fuerunt Kote que fuit uxor Michaelis le Eveske [judee][282] dampnate; et eciam predicti Willelmus et Alicia atachiati ad respondendum Regi de uno forcerio cum jocalibus, auro et argento precii .x. librarum quod devenit ad manus ipsorum Willelmi et Alicie ex tradicione Duce que fuit uxor Salomonis filii Salomonis judei Suth' dampnati de bonis et catallis que fuerunt predicti Salomonis.

Predictus Willelmus venit et Johanna et Alicia per attornatos suos veniunt et defendunt etc., et dicunt quod de bonis, jocalibus seu catallis predicte Kote nichil receperunt nec habent. Et predicti Willelmus et Alicia dicunt quod de bonis, jocalibus seu catallis Salomonis filii Salomonis judei dampnati ex tradicione dicte Duce nichil receperunt nisi duos anulos auri parvi valoris quos protulerunt coram etc. et quos dicunt se recepisse de dictis Salomone et Duce pro conductione duorum equorum ad opus ipsorum multo tempore elapso antequam dictus Salomon captus esset pro retonsura monete etc., et quos anulos ad communem clamacionem de catallis judeorum dampnatorum apud Wynton' factam Bartholomeo de Sully, Willelmo Brayboef et sociis suis justiciariis ad catalla judeorum dampnatorum recipiendum deputatis ostenderunt, qui dictos anulos pro conductione dictorum equorum legittime coram eis probata concesserunt. Et de hoc ponunt se super patriam. Et preceptum est vicecomiti quod venire faciat coram etc. a die sancte Trinitatis in .xv. dies sex probos et legales homines et sex legales judeos de civitate Wynton' per quos etc., et qui nulla affinitate etc., ad recognoscendum etc.

Ad quem diem inquisicio non venit. Et datus est dies a die sancti Michaelis in tres septimanas. Ad quem diem inquisicio venit per Willelmum Strut, Hugonem le Noreys et alios christianos, Cokerel filium Licoricie, Abraham filium Cokerel et alios judeos, sicut patet inter brevia termini sancti Michaelis proximo [i]<sequentis>[i] retornata. Qui dicunt super sacramentum suum quod predicti Johanna, Willelmus et Alicia nichil receperunt de bonis et catallis predictorum judeorum nec aliquid inde habent nisi dictos duos anulos precii .iiij. solidorum pro conduccione dictorum .ij. equorum, ut predictum, qui anuli concessi sunt eisdem Willelmo et Alicie pro conductione dictorum equorum. Et ideo consideratum est quod predicti Johanna, Willelmus et Alicia de bonis et catallis ab ipsis petitis sint quieti et quod Rex nichil capiat ab eis. Et predicta Duca committitur prisone etc.

(1031)

Suth'. Thomas le Cornwaleys tabernarius et Johanna uxor ejus pro pluribus defaltis in misericordia.[283]

Idem Thomas et Johanna attachiati ad respondendum Regi de .xxx. marcis que devenerunt ad manus eorum de catallis que fuerunt Kote que fuit uxor Michaelis le Eveske [judee][284] dampnate. Predicti Thomas et Johanna veniunt et defendunt etc. et dicunt quod nullos denarios nec catalla que fuerunt predicte Kote receperunt nec habent. Et de hoc ponit se super patriam. Et preceptum est vicecomiti ut supra. Ad quem diem inquisicio non venit et datus est dies a die sancti Michaelis in tres septimanas. Ad quem diem inquisicio venit per Willelmum Strut, Hugonem le Noreys et alios christianos, Cokerel filium Licoricie, Abraham filium Cokerel et alios judeos, sicut patet inter brevia ibidem retornata. Qui dicunt super sacramentum suum quod predicti Thomas et Johanna de predictis catallis nichil receperunt nec aliquid predicte judee debuerunt. Ideo consideratum est quod inde recedant quieti et quod Rex nichil capiat etc.

(1032)

Suth'. Walterus Pofray et Christiana uxor ejus pro pluribus defaltis in misericordia.[285]

Iidem Walterus et Christiana attachiati ad respondendum Regi de quibusdam robis, pannis, utensilibus et aliis bonis et catallis ad valenciam .x. librarum que devenerunt ad manus eorum de bonis et catallis que fuerunt Kote que fuit uxor Michaelis le Eveske judee dampnate.

Predicti Walterus et Christinana veniunt et recognoscunt se recepisse per manus dicte Kote unum trussellum pannorum, videlicet duo mantella de scarleto penulata, unam supertunicam de Worsted', duo tapeta lanea et unum tapetum de Reyns, unam robam veterem de bluete et .xv. solidos in denariis, que omnia supradicta liberaverunt Willelmo de Brayboef et aliis sociis suis justiciariis apud Wynton' ad catalla judeorum dampnatorum ad communem clamacionem factam etc. Et de hoc ponunt se super recordum rotulorum dicti Willelmi de Brayboef. Et quod plura bona seu catalla de catallis predicte Kote non receperunt ponunt se super patriam. Et preceptum est vicecomiti, ut supra, et mandatum est Willelmo de Brayboef quod scire faciat justiciariis etc. recordum rotulorum suorum de dictis particulis sub sigillo suo a die sancte Trinitatis in .xv. dies etc.

282 *MS. reads* judei.

283 *The word* misericordia *is repeated in the margin.*

284 *MS. reads* judei.

285 *The word* misericordia *is repeated in the margin.*

Ad quem diem inquisicio non venit et datus est dies a die sancti Michaelis in tres septimanas. Ad quem diem inquisicio venit per Willelmum Strut et alios christianos, Cokerel filium Licoricie et alios judeos, sicut patet inter brevia hujus termini retornata. Qui dicunt super sacramentum suum quod predicti Walterus et Christiana nichil receperunt de catallis predicte Kote nisi predictum trussellum in quo fuerunt duo mantella de scarleto et alios pannos superius nominatos; et Willelmus Brayboef, cui mandatum fuit quod justiciariis certificaret de dictis pannis, mandavit quod per breve regis sibi directum scrutari fecit rotulos suos de receptis catallorum que fuerunt Cote de Wynton' judee dampnate et invenit quod Walterus Pyrfrayt ei liberavit de catallis ipsius Kote tria tapeta precii octo solidorum, unam tunicam de burneto, unam supertunicam de perseto precii .v. solidorum, unam supertunicam de Bynel' et unam de Worthested' lyniatam de syndone precii .j. marce, .ij. mantella et unam supertunicam de scarleto furrata de minuto varo precii .lx. solidorum et .xv. solidos in denariis quos liberavit Johanni le Faukoner ad catalla judeorum dampnatorum deputato. Et juratores dicunt quod predicti Walterus et Johanna nichil aliud receperunt custodiendum de catallis ipius Kote. Ideo consideratum est quod inde sint quieti et quod Rex ab eis nichil capiat.

(1033)

Suth'. Egidius le Flemeng' burgensis Suth' pro pluribus defaltis in misericordia.[286]

Idem Egidius attachiatus ad respondendum Regi de duabus marcis quas debet Regi de debitis Salomonis filii Salamonis judei Suth' damnati per talliam inde inter eos factam, ut dicitur.

Predictus Egidius venit et defendit etc. et dicit quod predicti Salamoni nichil debuit nec per talliam nec sine tallia. Et de hoc ponit se super patriam. Et preceptum est vicecomiti quod venire faciat coram etc. a die sancte Trinitatis in .xv. dies .vj. probos et legales homines de villa Suth' et sex de visneto ejusdem ville et sex legales judeos de civitate Wynton' per quos etc., et qui nulla etc., ad recognoscendum etc. Quia tam etc.

(1034)

Norff'. Preceptum fuit vicecomiti quod venire faceret coram etc. cyrographarios christianos et judeos arche cyrographariorum Norwyc', sex probos et legales homines de civitate Norwyc', et qui nulla etc. attingerent Walterum de Lenn', Willelmum Gore et Ricardum filium Roberti de Farnham ad recognoscendum etc. si predictus Walterus solverit Josceo filio Benedicti de Lond' judeo dampnato centum solidos in quibus eidem judeo per cartam suam tenebatur tempore quo idem judeus habuit liberam administracionem bonorum suorum et unde dictus judeus starrum suum de aquietancia dicto Waltero fecit quod protulit coram etc. de aquietancia dicit debiti, ut dicit; et si dictus judeus dictum starrum sigillavit tempore quo illud fecisse potuit etc. et si Willelmus Gore de Herdingham satisfecerit Salamoni filio Jornini judeo Norwic' dampnato de .xl. solidis in quibus eidem judeo per cartam suam tenebatur tempore quo etc. et starrum de aquietancia dicti debiti eidem Willelmo fecit etc. quod protulit coram etc. et si predictus Ricardus satisfecerit Isak' filio Benedicti de Lond' judeo dampnato de .xxx. libris in quibus eidem Isak' per cartam suam tenebatur in domo Simonis le Paumer unius cyrographariorum arche cyrographariorum Norwyc' antequam dictus Isak' captus fuisset pro transgressione monete etc. et unde starrum aquietancie ei fecit quod protulit coram etc. Et Simon le Paumer, Johannes Gamen, Ricardus le Botman christiani, Isak filius Deulecres, Isak le Chapeleyn, Josceus filius Isak de Norwyco, Jacobus de Colec', Jacobus de Novo Mercato, Olekinus filius Elie, Isak de Colec', Benedictus le gendre Vyves judei venerunt. Et quia non venerunt nisi tantummodo tres christiani datus est partibus dies et christianis et judeis qui venerunt in octabis sancte Trinitatis. Et vicecomes mandavit quod Ricardus de Mickeberton', Willelmus de Senges, Rogerus de Senges et Andreas de Kentishale manuceperunt Willelmum de Yrsted; et quod Galfridus Moddok', Willelmus Hodio, Reginaldus le Grey, Richerus Swan, Andreas le Cheweyt manuceperunt Ricardum de Heylesham; et quod Willelmus de Redenh', Robertus de Stamene lindraper, Galfridus de Wymondham et Rogerus le Teler de eadem manuceperunt Johannem Fyn, quos non haberunt. Ideo in misericordia. Et mandavit quod Willelmus Deleton de Cranesford, Willelmus de Valoynes de Redham, Johannes Codit de Farnham, Johannes filius magistri Rogeri de Glenham, Johannes le Hanebere de Northglemham et Rogerus Fausebr ... de Scrafford' sex de visneto de Farnham de comitatu Suff' attachiati, unusquisque per alterum, prout vicecomes mandavit pro eadem inquisicione. Et quia vicecomes insufficienter pro eis de manucaptoribus respondet, ideo ipse vicecomes, scilicet Willelmus de [Re]dham, in misericordia. Judicium quod distringat per terras etc. et quod habeat corpora eorum coram etc. in octabis sancte Trinitatis etc. ad recognoscendum etc., nisi H. [Haut]eyn vel [R.] de Ludham prius etc. Interim inquisicio capta fuit apud Norwyc' coram H. Hauteyn per sacramentum Willelmi de Hyrsted ... ham et alios christianos, Isak filium Deulecres, Isak le Chapeleyn et alios judeos. Qui dicunt quod Willelmus Gare de Hardyngham satisfecit [Salamoni] filio Jornini de Norwyc' judeo de .xl. solidis in quibus ei per cartam suam tenebatur tempore quo habuit liberam administracionem bonorum suorum. Ideo [consideratum] est quod predictus Willelmus de predicto debito .xl. solidorum sit quietus et carta predicti debiti eidem liberetur quiete dampnata. Et die veneris in septimana Pentecostes [coram] predicto H. Hautein apud Norwyc' predictus Walterus de Len protulit duo starra de acquietancia, unum de acquietancia trium cartarum, videlicet une .c. solidorum, alterius quinque marcarum,

286 *The word* misericordia *is repeated in the margin.*

et tercie .c. solidorum. Inquisita veritate super confeccione dicti starri per sacramentum predictorum juratorum, sicut patet inter brevia [hujus] termini returnata. Qui dicunt super sacramentum suum quod predictum starrum non est factum ipsius Isak filii Benedicti de Lon' nec manu sua ebrayca signatum. Ideo ipse Walterus in misericordia, pro qua finem fecit per dimidiam marcam per plegium Henrici de Norwyco clerici. Idem Walterus protulit aliud starrum de quietancia omnium debitorum in quibus eidem Isak per cartas suas umquam tenebatur. Predicti juratores dicunt quod predictum starrum est bonum et littera ebrayca manu predicti Isak signatum et quod per predictum starrum quietus esse debet de .l. solidis in debito .c. solidorum superius petito sub nominibus dicti Walteri, Willelmi et dicti Isak. Ideo consideratum est quod predictus Walterus de .l. solidis in dicto debito .c. solidorum contentis pro parte sua sit quietus et dictus Willelmus pro parte sua ... preceptum est vicecomiti quod predicto Waltero de predicto debito .c. solidorum pacem habere permittat. Et si quid etc.

MEMBRANE 1 DORSE

(1035)

Norff'. Simon de Grenvyle, a quo exiguntur ad opus Regis .lvj. libre de debito Joscei filii Benedicti de Tykehulle et Abrahe filii Deulecres judeorum dampnatorum, fecit venire Willelmum de Kerelton' quondam vicecomitem Norff' et petit quod ipsum acquietet de .v. marcis quas per breve regis de bonis et catallis suis levari fecit ad opus ipsius Abrahe et nullam inde fecit allocacionem ad dampnum suum etc.

Predictus Willelmus venit et protulit coram etc. quandam talliam continentem centum solidos contra predictum Abraham scriptum. Et quia non constat justiciariis si predictus Simon solvit predicto judeo prefatos .c. solidos quia non peciit allocacionem nisi de .v. marcis per breve suum requisitus qualiter solucionem dicte tallie eidem judeo factam verificare voluerit petit quod inquiratur per patriam. Ideo preceptum est vicecomiti quod venire faciat coram etc. a die sancte Trinitatis in .xv. dies sex probos et legales homines etc. de visneto [blank] sex legales judeos de Norwyc' per quos etc., et qui nulla affinitate etc., ad recognoscendum etc.

(1036)

Suth'. Inquisicio ad inquirendum de confeccione cujusdam starri quod Petrus Self de Petresfeld', a quo exiguntur ad opus Regis .ix. libre de debitis Benedicti filii Abrahe de Wynton' judei dampnati, protulit coram etc. de acquietacione dicti debiti, ut dicit, in hec verba: 'Benedictus filius Abrahe recognoscit per starrum suum quod Johannes Self de Petresfeld' et heredes sui quieti sunt de ipso Benedicto et heredibus suis de quodam debito .ix. librarum sub nominibus predicti Johannis et Lumbardi fratris predicti Benedicti, que liberata fuit eidem Benedicto de thesauro regis.' Et inquisicio inde venit per Adam Poveray cyrographarium christianum, Ricardum de Werewell', Henricum Ospreng et alios christianos, Kokerell filium Licoricie, Abraham filium Cokerell' et alios judeos, sicut patet inter brevia hujus termini returnata. Qui dicunt super sacramentum suum quod predictus Johannes satisfecit predicto judeo de predictis .ix. libris in domo dicti Ade unius cyrographariorum arche cyrographariorum Wynton' et quod pro predictis .ix. libris de dicto debito quietus esse debet, set dicunt quod dictum starrum non est littera ebrayca manu dicti Benedicti signatum. Ideo consideratum est quod predictus Johannes de predicto debito .ix. librarum sit quietus et carta dicti debiti eidem Johanni liberatur quiete dampnata, set quod pro predicti falso starro quod protulit coram etc. sit in misericordia,[287] et committitur prisone donec satisfecerit Regi de predicta transgressione. Et postea finem fecit pro predicta transgressione per unam marcam.[288]

(1037)[289]

Hereff'. Preceptum fuit vicecomiti quod venire faceret coram etc. cyrographarios arche cyrographariorum Hereff' et sex probos et legales homines de viseneto de Galmeshull' Gamayg', recognitores inquisicionis in quam Willelmus Rygge, Rogerus le Fevre et Nicholaus le Mercer se posuerunt. Et ipsi non venerunt. Et vicecomes mandavit quod Willelmus Bydel et Willelmus de Lungeford' manuceperunt Willelmum Mayl; et quod Willelmus Ingod et Johannes filius la Lavenderie manuceperunt Ricardum le Usser; et quod Philippus Snygge et Johannes Bullok' manuceperunt Adam Germayn; et quod Adam filius Mauricii et Johannes filius Alexandri manuceperunt Ricardum Bot'; et quod Willelmus de Cabbel' et Ricardus de la Were manuceperunt Willelmum Aytrop de la Were; et quod Robertus filius Rogeri de Crendenhille et Robertus Faber de eadem manuceperunt Willelmum le Jevene de Stretton'; et quod Henricus Patric et Rogerus Owen manuceperunt Willelmum clericum de Stretton'; et quod Johannes de Buford' et Nicholaus Norwy manuceperunt Ricardum de Crasselond'; et quod Johannes Prude et Walterus de Fonte manuceperunt Radulphum Litelberi; et quod Willelmus filius Nicholai et Andreas de Standich' manuceperunt Walterum le Waleys; et quod Benedictus le Eveske et Mosseus de Glouc' manuceperunt Manserum filium Joscei, quem non habuerunt. Ideo in misericordia.[290] Et predicti Willelmus, Ricardus et alii manucapti, quia non venerunt, in misericordia.[291]

(1038)

Wygorn'. Preceptum fuit vicecomiti quod distringeret Johannem filium Roberti de Cradecote ad reddendum

287 *The word* misericordia *is repeated in the margin.*

288 *The words* .j. marca *are written in the margin.*

289 *In the margin just above this entry are the words* Incip' alius rotulus.

290 *The word* misericordia *is repeated in the margin.*

291 *The word* misericordia *is repeated in the margin.*

Regi .iiij. marcas de debito Mossei filii Bonefey, et denarios haberet etc. Et ipse non venit. Et vicecomes mandavit quod Gilbertus le Hopere, Robertus Schyne, Philippus de Bradecote et Gilbertus le Wodeward manuceperunt predictum Johannem, quem non habuerunt. Ideo in misericordia.[292] Judicium, sicut alias, a die sancte Trinitatis in .xv. dies etc.

(1039)

Warr', Leyc'. Preceptum fuit vicecomiti quod venire faceret coram etc, sex probos et legales et legales homines de visneto de Alcestre, recognitores inquisicionis in quam Johannes le Engleys de Upton' se posuit. Et ipsi non venerunt. Et vicecomes mandavit quod Rogerus de la Pole de Bovyngton' et Henricus Edward de eadem manuceperunt Willelmum Cede de Bonitton'; et quod Johannes Molendinarius de Bonitton' et Willelmus Silivrelok' de eadem manuceperunt Robertum Elis de Bonitton'; et quod Willelmus le Baxtere de Grafton' et Johannes de Poddenhou manuceperunt Alanum de Fonte de Grafton'; et quod Johannes le Rowere de Alcestre et Robertus le Rowere de eadem manuceperunt Johannem Roumay de Alcestre; et quod Johannes Freman de Alcestre et Henricus le Mareschal de eadem manuceperunt Willelmum de Freines de Alcestre; et quod Willelmus Basley de Haseloure et Willelmus Edwayne de eadem manuceperunt Willelmum Elias de Haseloure; quos non habuerunt. Ideo in misericordia.[293] Judicium quod distringat per terras etc., et quod de exitibus etc., et quod habeat corpora eorum coram etc. in octabis sancte Trinitatis etc. ad recognoscendum etc. et ad audiendum etc. Et Vyves le Romanzur, Samuel de Staunff', Samuel filius Jude, Cresseus filius Sarre, Saulot le Petyt et Bonamy filius Deudonis recognitores dicte inquisicionis, qui presentes fuerunt, habent eundem diem. Et dictus Johannes habet eundem diem.

(1040)

Rotel'. Preceptum fuit vicecomiti quod distringeret Robertum de Nevyle de Tykynton' ad reddendum sibi ad opus Regis .viij. libras de debitis Manseri filii Elie judei dampnati. Et vicecomes mandavit quod Ricardus de Caldecote de Stoke, Walterus ad Portam de eadem, Willelmus Sampson de eadem, Robertus Pulint' de eadem, Robertus Gerrard de eadem et Simon Faber de eadem manuceperunt predictum Robertum, quem non habuerunt. Ideo in misericordia.[294] Judicium, sicut alias, in octabis sancte Trinitatis etc.

(1041)

Norff'. Preceptum fuit vicecomiti quod venire faceret coram etc. Willelmum de Carleton' ad acquietandum Simonem de Greynvyle et Isabellam uxorem ejus de .v. marcis quas ab eis recepit ad opus Abrahe filii Deulecres judei. Et ipse non venit. Et vicecomes mandavit quod Johannes le Bretun de Carleton', Robertus Dune de eadem, Simon Dune de eadem et Stephanus Blunte de eadem manuceperunt predictum Willelmum, quem non habuerunt. Ideo in misericordia.[295] Judicium quod distringat per terras etc., et quod habeat corpus ejus coram etc. a die sancte Trinitatis in .xv. dies etc.

(1042)

Warr', Leyc'. Preceptum fuit vicecomiti quod venire faceret coram etc. cyrographarios christianos Warr' et sex probos et legales homines de eadem villa, recognitores inquisicionis in quam Hawysia que fuit uxor Johannis de Clynton' de Napton', Thomas de Cherlecote et Willelmus de Nafford' se posuerunt. Et ipsi non venerunt. Et vicecomes mandavit quod Petrus de Cave de Warr' et Coleman de eadem manuceperunt Rogerum Helewys; et quod Willelmus le Blake de Warr' et Nicholaus le Rowr de eadem manuceperunt Ricardum Miche; et quod Thomas le Fosse de Warr' et Robertus Piscator de eadem manuceperunt Johannem de Cumpton'; et quod Ricardus le Tippere de Warr' et Johannes Piscator de eadem manuceperunt Thomam Colet; et quod Willelmus Lyun de Warr' et Robertus Edward de eadem manuceperunt Johannem le Hosyer; et quod Willelmus de Stretford et Henricus de Henle de Warr' manuceperunt Ricardum Eve; et quod Johannes de Coleshille et Ricardus Mercator de Warr' manuceperunt Hugonem atte Schite; et quod Ricardus le Scherman et Robertus le Mareschal manuceperunt Coleman Mercatorem; et quod Adam Cokul de Warr' et Ricardus Miche de eadem manuceperunt Adam Bercarium, quos non habuerunt. Ideo in misericordia.[296] Judicium quod distringat per terras etc., et quod habeat corpora eorum coram etc. in octabis sancte Trinitatis etc.

(1043)

Warr', Leyc'. Preceptum fuit vicecomiti quod distringeret Johannem filium Thome de Clinton' seniorem ad reddendum Regi .xij. libras .xiij. solidos .iiij. denarios de debitis Mossei de Warr' judei dampnati, et denarios haberet etc. vel corpus etc. Et vicecomes mandavit quod Alexander Ive de Coleshill', Ricardus Davy de eadem, Simon Fox de eadem et Simon de Godelisdon' de eadem manuceperunt predictum Johannem, quem non habuerunt. Ideo in misericordia.[297] Judicium, sicut alias, a die sancti Johannis Baptiste in .xv. dies etc.

(1044)

Warr', Leyc'. Preceptum fuit vicecomiti quod venire faceret coram etc. sex probos et legales homines de Alecestre, sex de visneto ejusdem ville, recognitores inquisicionis in quam Willelmus de Stoke de Alecestre et Willelmus Brun de eadem se posuerunt. Et ipsi non

[292] *The word* misericordia *is repeated in the margin.*
[293] *The word* misericordia *is repeated in the margin.*
[294] *The word* misericordia *is repeated in the margin.*
[295] *The word* misericordia *is repeated in the margin.*
[296] *The word* misericordia *is repeated in the margin.*
[297] *The word* misericordia *is repeated in the margin.*

venerunt. Et vicecomes mandavit quod Alanus le Chaluner de Alec' et Willelmus le Flecchere de eadem manuceperunt Adam de Ponte de Alecr'; et quod Stephanus de Curia de Alec' et Johannes le Rowr de eadem manuceperunt Johannem Romay de Alc'; et quod Willelmus le Porter de Alec' et Stephanus frater ejus manuceperunt Johannem le Tanur de Alc'; et quod Rannulphus de Cotton' de Alc' et Johannes Brice de eadem manuceperunt Adam de Kent; et quod Johannes de Podenho de Grafton' et Thomas filius Osberti de eadem manuceperunt Alanum de Fonte de Grafton'; et quod Willelmus le Waleys de Grafton' et Walterus Faber de eadem manuceperunt Willelmum atte Nasse de Grafton; quos non habuerunt. Ideo in misericordia.[298] Judicium quod distringat per terras etc., et quod de exitibus etc., et quod habeat corpora eorum coram etc. a die sancte Trinitatis in .xv. dies ad recognoscendum etc. et ad audiendum etc.

(1045)

Somers', Dors'. Preceptum fuit vicecomiti quod venire faceret coram etc. ad hunc diem priorem de Monte Acuto, fratrem Willelmum ballivum de Tyntehull', Philippum Bastard et Henricum fratrem ejus, executores testamenti Willelmi Bastard, et Walterum de Bradeford' ad respondendum Regi de diversis bonis et catallis que devenerunt ad manus ipsorum de catallis que fuerunt Isak de Ivelcestre judei dampnati. Et ipsi non venerunt. Et vicecomes mandavit quod Willelmus Hobard de Tyntehill' et Galfridus Wyn de eadem manuceperunt predictum priorem; et quod Galfridus le Heyward de Tyntehill' et Osbertus le Foel de eadem manuceperunt Willelmum ballivum de Tyntehill'; et quod Osbertus Molendinarius de Northoure et Willelmus Bastard de eadem manuceperunt Philippum Bastard; et quod Walterus le Heyward de Nortoure et Ricardus de Ponte de eadem manuceperunt Henricum Bastard, quos non habuerunt. Ideo in misericordia.[299] Judicium quod distringat per terras etc., et quod de exitibus etc., et quod habeat corpora eorum coram etc. a die sancte Trinitatis in .xv. dies ad recognoscendum etc. et ad audiendum etc.

(1046)

Norht'. Preceptum fuit vicecomiti quod venire faceret coram etc. cyrographarios arche cyrographariorum Norht' et sex probos et legales homines et sex legales judeos de eadem villa, recognitores inquisicionis in quam Johannes Gylemyn de Burton se ponit. Et ipsi non venerunt. Et vicecomes mandavit quod Johannes Muleton' et Eustachius le Vyneter manuceperunt Johannem Eustach'; et quod Radulphus de Hampton' et Hugo le Palmer manuceperunt Willelmum de Buckebrok'; et quod Danyel le Ferrur et Johannes Godseye mauncceperunt Ricardum super Montem; et quod Simon Wygor et Willelmus de Tynewell' manuceperunt Adam le Fermerye; et quod Philippus le Regrater et Rogerus le Rus manuceperunt Johannem ad Portam; et quod Hugo de Thorp et Philippus Davy manuceperunt Robertum de Sybeford'; et quod Walterus de Forho et Walterus de Dulton' manuceperunt Adam de Waltham; quos non habuerunt. Ideo in misericordia.[300] Judicium quod distringat per terras etc., et quod de exitibus etc., et quod habeat corpora eorum coram etc. a die sancte Trinitatis in .xv. dies ad recognoscendum etc. et ad audiendum etc.

(1047)

Norht'. Preceptum fuit vicecomiti quod venire faceret coram etc. sex legales judeos de hiis qui solebant manere apud Warr', recognitores inquisicionis in quam Thomas de [Ch]erlecote se posuit. Et ipsi non venerunt. Et vicecomes mandavit quod Sampson le Frere et Mosseus filius Avegaye manuceperunt Samuelem de Staunff' et quod Mosseus filius Avegaye et Sampson le Frere manuceperunt Samuelem filium Jude, et quod Abraham le Chaplein et Mosseus filius Avegaye manuceperunt Cresseum filium Sarre, et quod Mosseus filius Avegaye et Abraham le Chapelayn manuceperunt Saulot le Peyt, et quod Mosseus Avegaye et Isak filius Benedicti manuceperunt Bonamy filium Deudonis, quos non habuerunt. Ideo in misericordia. Judicium quod distringat per terras etc. et quod habeat corpora eorum etc. in octabis sancte Trinitatis etc. ad recognoscendum etc.

(1048)

Norht'. Preceptum fuit vicecomiti quod venire faceret coram etc. cyrographarios christianos et judeos arche cyrographariorum Norht' et sex probos et legales homines et sex legales judeos, recognitores inquisicionis in quam Hugo filius Hugonis de Shytelond' se posuit. Et ipsi non venerunt. Et vicecomes mandavit quod Radulphus de Hampton' et Hugo le Paumer manuceperunt Willelmum de Buckebrok'; et quod Danyel le Ferrur et Johannes Godhegh' manuceperunt Ricardum super Montem; et quod Simon Wyger et Willelmus de Tynewell' manuceperunt Adam de la Fermereay; et quod Philippus le Regrater et Ricardus le Rus manuceperunt Johannem ad Portam; et quod Hugo de Thropp et Philippus Davy manuceperunt Robertum de Sibbeford; et quod Walterus de Forho et Walterus de Duston' manuceperunt Adam de Waltham; et quod Sampson le Frere et Mosseus filius Avegaye manuceperunt Samuelem de Stanff'; et quod Abr' le Chapeleyn et Mosseus filius Avegaye manuceperunt Cresseum filium Sarre; et quod Mosseus filius Avegaye et Sampson le Frere manuceperunt Samuelem filium Jude; et quod Abraham le Chapeleyn et Mosseus filius Avegaye manuceperunt Saulotum le Petyt; et quod Mosseus filius Avegaye et Isak filius Benedicti manuceperunt Bonamy filium Deudonis; quos non habuerunt. Ideo in misericordia.[301] Judicium quod distringat per terras etc., et quod

[298] *The word* misericordia *is repeated in the margin.*
[299] *The word* misericordia *is repeated in the margin.*
[300] *The word* misericordia *is repeated in the margin.*
[301] *The word* misericordia *is repeated in the margin.*

habeat corpora eorum coram etc. a die sancti Johannis Baptiste in .xv. dies ad recognoscendum etc. et ad audiendum etc.

(1049)

Norht'. Preceptum fuit vicecomiti quod venire faceret coram etc. cyrographarios christianos et judeos Norht' et sex probos et legales homines et sex legales judeos de eadem villa, [recognitores] inquisicionis in quam Simon de Harewedon' se posuit. Et ipsi non venerunt. Et vicecomes mandavit quod Radulphus de Hampton' et Hugo le Paumer manuceperunt Willelmum de Buckebrok'; et quod Daniel le Ferrur et Johannes Godeshegh' manuceperunt Ricardum super Montem; et quod Simon Wyger et Willelmus de Tynewell' manuceperunt Adam de la Fermereye; et quod Philippus le Regrater et Ricardus le Rus manuceperunt Johannem ad Portam; et quod Hugo de Throp et Philippus Davy manuceperunt Robertum de Sybbeford; et quod Walterus de Forho et Walterus de Duston' [manuceperunt] Adam de Waltham; et quod Sampson le Frere et Mosseus filius Avegaye manuceperunt Samuelem de Staunff'; et quod Mosseus filius Avegaye et S[ampson] le Frere manuceperunt Samuelem filium Jude; et quod Abraham le Chapeleyn et Mosseus filius Avegaye manuceperunt Cresseum filium Sarre; et quod Abraham le [Chapeleyn] et Mosseus filius Avegaye manuceperunt Saulot le Petyt; et quod Mosseus filius Avegaye et Isak filius Benedicti manuceperunt B[onamy filium Deudonis]; quos non habuerunt. Ideo in misericordia.[302] Judicium quod distringat per terras etc., et quod habeat corpora eorum coram etc. a die sancti Johannis Baptiste in [.xv. dies ad recognoscendum] etc. et ad audiendum etc.

(1050)

Sutht'. Preceptum fuit vicecomiti quod venire faceret coram etc. tenentes terrarum que fuerunt Willelmi Tyrel de Wordy et Wymundi de .... de S... ad respondendum Regi de diversis bonis et catallis que devenerunt ad manus predictorum Willelmi et Wymundi de bonis et catallis Salle de Sutht' et Cote judeorum dampnatorum. Et ipsi non venerunt. Et vicecomes mandavit quod Robertus Tyrel et Hugo de Berstrete manuceperunt Johannem de Pade, tenentem terras que fuerunt predicti Willelmi; et quod Willelmus Baldewyne et Willelmus le Flemyng' manuceperunt Egidium le Flemyng, tenentem terras que fuerunt predicti Wymundi; quos non habuerunt. Ideo in misericordia. Judicium quod distringat per terras etc. a die sancti Michaelis in tres septimanas ad respondendum etc. et ad audiendum etc.

(1051)

Sutht'. Preceptum fuit vicecomiti quod venire faceret coram etc. Nicholaum filium Ade Thuremund ad aquietandum Simonem de Wynt' de .xx. libris que ab eos exig[untur de] debitis Benedicti filii Abrahe judei dampnati. Et ipse non venit. Et vicecomes mandavit quod dictus Nicholaus clericus est et non habet laycum feodum. Ideo [preceptum est episcopo] Wynt' quod ipsum distringat per bona sua ecclesiastica, ita quod habeat corpus ejus coram etc. a die sancti Johannis Baptiste in .xv. dies etc.

(1052)

[Norff', S]uff'. Preceptum fuit vicecomiti, sicut alias, quod non omitteret propter libertates Norwyc', sancti Edmundi, Gernem', sancte Etheldrede de Mitford' quin eas etc. et distringeret Willelmum filium Johannis Rodland de Corpston' et alios in brevi. Et vicecomes mandavit quod Willelmus Thebaud, Willelmus filius Stephani Textoris de Norwyc', Johannes Rodland de Creston et Thomas filius Eve de eadem manuceperunt Willelmum filium Johannis Rodland; et quod Willelmus de Kyrkeby de Norwyco, Walterus le Mercer de eadem, Stephanus de Mundham de eadem et Gerardus le Especer de eadem manuceperunt Bartholomeum le Especer, tenentes terras Ade le Especer, quos non habuerunt. Ideo in misericordia. Judicium, sicut pluries, quod non omittat etc. et ipsos distringat etc. et denarios habeat etc. a die sancti Johannis in .xv. dies. Et quod ... filius Rogeri, Johanna que fuit uxor Willelmi Herbert, Robertus filius Willelmi Rose, Adam filius Galfridi de Aldeberg' et alii in brevi non habent unde possint distringi. Ideo, sicut pluries, ad diem supradictum etc.

MEMBRANE 2

(1053)

Norff, Suff'. Preceptum fuit vicecomiti, sicut alias, quod distringeret Ricardum filium Albini de Seccheford' et tenentes terrarum suarum et alios in brevi pro denariis in brevi ab ipsis petitis de diversis debitis judeorum dampnatorum. Et vicecomes mandavit quod Johannes Lytel de Jakesle, Robertus del Gap, Nicholaus le Grone de eadem et Johannes Borman de eadem manuceperunt Adam B..., quem non habuerunt. Ideo in misericordia.[303] Et quod Ricardus filius Albini clericus est. Et quod alii in brevi nichil habent unde aliqui denarii levari possint. Et preceptum est ei, sicut pluries, a die sancti Johannis Baptiste in .xv. dies etc.

(1054)

Norff'. Preceptum est vicecomiti, sicut alias, quod de terris et catallis Roberti Thurkyl de Magna Gernem' et aliorum in brevi et tenencium terrarum suarum fieri faceret denarios ab ipsis in brevi petitis de debitis diversorum judeorum dampnatorum. Et vicecomes mandavit quod dicti debitores non habent unde dicti denarii levari possint. Et preceptum est ei, sicut pluries, a die sancti Johannis Baptiste in .xv. dies etc.

[302] *The word* misericordia *is repeated in the margin.*

[303] *The word* misericordia *is repeated in the margin.*

(1055)

Warr', Leyc'. Preceptum fuit vicecomiti, sicut pluries, quod distringeret Henricum Skyrewyt, Adam Ledet de Badesle et alios in brevi pro denariis ab ipsis in brevi petitis, et denarios haberet coram etc. Et vicecomes mandavit quod Henricus, Adam et alii in brevi nichil habent unde denarii levari possint. Et preceptum est ei, sicut pluries, a die sancti Michaelis in tres septimanas.

(1056)

Linc'. Preceptum fuit vicecomiti [i]<sicut alias>[i] quod non omitteret propter libertatem civitatis Linc' vel Bullingbrok' quin eas etc. et distringeret Hugonem filium Nicholai Munde de Linc' et tenentes terrarum suarum suarum pro .iiij. marcis de debitis Urselli filii Sampsonis Levy, et Henricum le Coylter de Kyrkeby pro .xvj. libris de debitis Abrahe filii Isak; et denarios haberet etc. Et vicecomes mandavit quod predictus Hugo nichil habet unde dicti denarii levari possint. Et preceptum est ei, sicut alias, a die sancti Johannis in tres septimanas. Et quod Alanus Buche de Kyrkeby, Alanus de Sancto Botulpho de eadem, Willelmus frater ejus de eadem, et Robertus West de eadem manuceperunt predictum Henricum quod satisfaciat Regi ad hunc diem etc., quem non habuerunt. Ideo in misericordia.[304]

(1057)

Sutht'. Preceptum fuit vicecomit, sicut pluries, quod non omitteret propter libertates Wynton', episcopatus Wynton', Andevre et Basyngstok quin eas etc. et distringeret Thomam le Messager de Andevre, Thomam Ketyl de Rumesy, et alios in brevi et tenentes terrarum suarum ad reddendum sibi ad opus Regis denarios in brevi contentos. Et vicecomes mandavit quod Mattheus Lucas, Willelmus de Anne de Lokerle, Lucas le Bercher et Petrus Cole manuceperunt Willelmum le Heyward, tenentem terrarum Serlonis de Lokerle, quem non habuerunt. Ideo in misericordia.[305] Et quod Thomas le Messager de Andevre et alii in brevi non sunt inventi in balliva sua. Et preceptum est ei, sicut pluries, a die sancti Michaelis in .xv. dies etc.

(1058)

Kanc'. Preceptum fuit vicecomit, sicut pluries, quod distringeret Thomam filium Guydonis de Herbaldun', Willelmum filium Johannis de Herndenn' et alios in brevi et tenentes terrarum suarum ad reddendum sibi ad opus Regis denarios in brevi petitos. Et vicecomes mandavit quod predictus Thomas et alii in brevi nichil habent unde denarii levari possint nisi Robertus Germeyn, Ricardus Bruily, Willelmus filius Ricardi de la Dune, Rogerus Talebot, Willemus Godefray et Hamo de Beracres, qui satisfecerunt Aaron filio Vives. Et preceptum est ei, sicut pluries, a die sancti Michaelis in tres septimanas.

[304] *The word* misericordia *is repeated in the margin.*

[305] *The word* misericordia *is repeated in the margin.*

(1059)

Not', Derb'. Preceptum fuit vicecomit, sicut pluries, quod distringeret Adam Malerbe de Shelford, Johannem Gernet de Bischopcropil' et alios in brevi et tenentes terrarum suarum ad reddendum sibi ad opus Regis denarios in brevi petitos. Et vicecomes mandavit quod predictus Adam et alii nichil habent unde denarii levari possint. Et preceptum est ei, sicut pluries, a die sancti Michaelis in tres septimanas etc.

(1060)

Sutht'. Preceptum fuit vicecomiti quod non omitteret propter libertates Wynton' et prioratus Wynt' quin eas etc. et venire faceret coram etc. Walterum de Valle civem Wynt' cum quadam tallia etc., Simonem de Wynton' et alios in brevi et preter eos etc., recognitores inquisicionis in quam Hugo de Fulflode se posuit versus Benedictum filium Abr'. Et ipsi non venerunt. Et vicecomes mandavit quod Stephanus Goldcnap, Willelmus le Barbur, Johannes de Wycumbe et Ricardus le Seler manuceperunt Walterum de Val; et quod Galfridus Gerland, Robertus le Veleter, Radulphus Bischop et Johannes Cocus manuceperunt Gilbertum Cole, quos non habuerunt. Ideo in misericordia.[306] Et ipsi Gilbertus et Walterus, quia non venerunt, in misericordia. Et Simon de Wynton' et Nicholaus de la Berton', Johannes Cras, Johannes Tyting, Ricardus de Wherwelle et alii christiani in brevi, Cokerel filius Licoricie, Abraham filius ejus et alii judei in brevi, qui venerunt, habent diem in octabis sancti Johannis Baptiste ad recognoscendum etc. Et predictus Hugo habet eundem diem etc.

(1061)

Wylt'. Preceptum fuit vicecomiti quod non omitteret propter libertates de Alwaldburi, Wrth', Chipenham, Kynwarston, episcopi Sar', Glouc' vel Walyngf' quin eas etc. et de terris et catallis Roysie filie Roberti de Elyng' de Estgrimsted, Cristiane Rowe [et aliorum in] brevi et tenencium terrarum suarum fieri faceret ad opus Regis denarios in brevi ab ipsis petitos, et denarios haberet coram etc. a die Pasche in unum mensem. Et vicecomes mandavit quod predicta Roysia tulit breve regis de respectu habendo usque hunc diem; et quod Christiana Rowe non habet nisi blada in terra crescencia, ad que emenda nullum invenit emptorem. Et quod cepit in manum regis de averiis Walteri Lillebon', tenentis terrarum que fuerunt Willelmi filii Willelmi Lillebon', ad valenciam .vij. marcarum, ad que emendum nullum invenit emptorem. Et quod custos vallis scolarium Novi Sarum tulit sibi breve de districcione super ipsum facta sibi relaxanda et quod cepit in manum regis averia abbatisse de Wylton', tenentis partem terrarum Galfridi de Wyneleff' etc., et nullum invenit emptorem. Et quod Willelmus de Weil' nichil habet in balliva sua unde possit distringi. Et quod Willelmus de Well', Willelmus Quintyn, Johannes filius Nicholai de Wace de

[306] *The word* misericordia *is repeated in the margin.*

Wyntreburn Basset nichil habent unde denarii levari possint nisi blada in terra crescencia etc. Et preceptum est ei, sicut pluries, quod non omittat etc. et predicta averia et blada vendi faciat etc. et denarios habeat etc. a die sancti Michaelis in unum mensem Regi solvendum etc.

MEMBRANE 2 DORSE

[This is blank except for contemporary notes *terminus Pasche anno regis Edward non ad scaccarium Judeorum*; *Pascha .ix.*^{o} i; and *Ex' n. est dom. R. .xij.*]

MEMBRANE 3

Essonia ad Scaccarium Judeorum de quindena Pasche anno regni regis Edwardi nono

(1062)

Wiltes'. Feynkyn de Crickelade judeus versus Philippum le But, Thomam le Mercer et alios in brevi de placito debiti per Sampsonem filium Ysak'.

MEMBRANE 3 DORSE

(1063)

Blyssota judea de Norht' ponit loco suo Saulot maritum suum versus Adam de la Fermerie et Matildam uxorem ejus de placito debiti et transgressionis.

(1064)

Belassez que fuit uxor Leonis filii Presciose ponit loco suo Meir filium Sampsonis versus Gilbertum le Ceintor et alios in brevi de placito debiti.

(1065)

Miliscenta de Longevile ponit loco suo Rogerum servientem de scaccario versus Belasez [i]<que fuit>[i] uxor Sampsonis Norht' de placito debiti.

(1066)

Willelmus de Harpeley ponit loco suo Johannem de Harpeleye versus Johannem filium Willelmi de Harpeleye et alios in brevi contentos de placito debiti.

(1067)

Linc'. Salomon de Lond' judeus ponit loco suo Isac de Suwerk' versus Adam Hake de Linc' de placito transgressionis.

MEMBRANE 4

Memoranda de termino Pasche anno regis Edwardi nono

(1068)

Rogerus de Somervyle de comitatu Lincoln' venit coram etc. et recognovit se debere Aaron filio Vyves judeo septem libras, reddendo ad quindenam sancti Michaelis proximo futuram. Et, nisi fecerit, concedit pro se et heredibus suis quod de terris et catallis suis fiant.

(1069)

Surr'. Johannes Camoeys filius Radulphi de Camoys venit coram etc. et recognovit se debere Cok Hagin judeo .cc. libras reddendo ad quindenam sancti Michaelis anno regis Edward .ix.^{o} ·.l. libras et ad quindenam Pasche proximo sequentem .l. libras. Et, nisi fecerit, concedit quod de terris et catallis suis ad quorumcumque manus devenerint.

(1070)

Ebor'. Frater Henricus abbas de Kirkestalle venit coram etc. et recognovit se debere Cok' Hagin judeo mille marcas, reddendo .cc. marcas ad quindenam nativitatis Sancti Johannis Baptiste anno regis Edwardi nono, et sic de anno in annum quousque etc. Et, nisi fecerit, concedit etc.

MEMBRANE 4 DORSE

Adhuc Memoranda

(1071)

Suht'. Preceptum fuit vicecomiti quod non omitteret propter libertates prioratus Winton' vel Andevre et venire faceret coram etc. sex milites et sex probos et legales homines de visneto de Chelewarton' et Anne et preter eos Matheum Novel, Robertum de Popham et alios in brevi, recognitores inquisicionis in quam Johannes de Haveringe se posuit, sicut patet inter memoranda termini Pasche proximo preteriti. Et plures de dicta inquisione non venerunt. Et vicecomes mandavit quod Johannes de la Mare, Robertus de la [blank], Willelmus Gillemin et Willelmus de Chartres manuceperunt Philippum Gret; et quod Henricus Bug' de Oterburn, Rogerus le Dunt de eadem, Ricardus Cocus de Draiton' et Johannes le Gaunt manuceperunt Simonem de Winton'; et quod Robertus le Hare, Robertus le Pouk', Ranulphus le Gothurde et Johannes le Gray manuceperunt Oliverum de Punchardun; et quod Thomas Kingman, Yvo Maneyt, Rogerus Litle et Henricus Dunstighelle manuceperunt Rogerum Launceleve; et quod Johannes le Bietere et Johannes de Maundevile, Willelmus Whitside et Ricardus Cornubiensis manuceperunt Ricardum de Poites'; et quod Robertus Launcelevee, Johannes Attehuld, Ysac Clute et Willelmus Puerich manuceperunt Johannem de Grinstede; et quod Rogerus Trays, Henricus le Bec, Petrus Bec et Thomas Comin manuceperunt Ricardum de Burghunte; et quod Willelmus Curpse, Willelmus Aynolf, Johannes de Val et Willelmus Scut manuceperunt Robertum Duredent; et quod Radulphus Berethorn, Radulphus Heringe, Henricus Rubayl, et Petrus Suur manuceperunt Henricum Thuremunde; et quod Johannes Sim', Willelmus le Turner, Gilbertus le Bacheler et Ricardus le Claperwine manuceperunt Gilbertum de Botes; et quod Hugo Colewys, Walterus le Taylur, Johannes Man et Willelmus Godegrom manuceperunt Willelmum de Putton'; et quod Thomas le Mouner, Johannes de Northleye, Willelmus de Benetleye et Hugo Piscator manuceperunt Ricardum le Queynte; et quod Radulphus Bissop, Robertus Molendinarius, Willelmus Wysdom et Robertus Faber manuceperunt Johannem de Marisco; et quod Radulphus le Herl, Willelmus Seolf, Johannes Reymund et Johannes Somer manuceperunt Matheum Nowel; et quod Henricus le Paumer, Simon Caretarius, Johannes Wodewardon' et Ricardus Heyward manuceperunt Robertum de Popham; et quod Thomas Trot, Adam de Corboyl, Johannes de Putelinch et Radulphus Pit manuceperunt Rogerum de Kaleston'; et quod Johannes Joye, Rogerus Dikere, Ricardus Gos, et Henricus le Dikere manuceperunt Walterum de Maeys; et [i]<quod>[i] Johannes le Frie, Robertus Bastard, Johannes Hep et Thomas filius ejus manuceperunt Thomam Gateling; et quod Robertus le Ryde, Willelmus Rolf et Johannes Duk manuceperunt Robertum filium Alani; et quod Rogerus Pistor, Radulphus le Taillur, Ricardus le Freke, et Galfridus Sifrith manuceperunt Alexandrum le Ryche; et quod Johannes le Dumbe, Robertus le Stur, Thomas Fot et Robertus Roland manuceperunt Johannem de Wenmeledon', quos non habuerunt. Ideo in misericordia.[307] Judicium quod distringat per terras etc., ita quod nec ipsi etc., et quod de exitibus etc., et quod habeat corpora eorum coram etc. a die sancti Michaelis in .iij. septimanas, nisi H. Hauteyn interim ad partes illas venerit, ad recognoscendum etc. et ad audiendum etc. Et Robertus de Aundeli, Henricus Morterel, Johannes de Wyn', Robertus Launceleve, Henricus de Foxkote, Edmundus le Cornwaleys, Johannes Leyr, Lucas Kyng', Johannes Seled', quidam recognitores dicte inquisicionis, qui presentes fuerunt, habent eundem diem. Et Johannes de Havering', qui presens fuit, habet eundem diem.

(1072)

Kanc'. Preceptum fuit vicecomiti quod distringeret Johannem filium Simonis Talebot de Harnhell' per terras etc. et quod haberet corpus ejus coram etc. ad respondendum Regi de .iij marcis de debitis Mossei filii Aaron judei Cant' dampnati. Et ipse non venit. Et vicecomes mandavit quod retornavit breve sibi inde directum senescallo libertatis archiepiscopatus Cant', qui nichil inde fecit. Judicium quod non omittat etc. et distringat predictum Johannem per terras etc., ita quod nec ipse etc., et quod de exitibus etc. et quod habeat corpus ejus coram etc. a die sancti Michaelis in unum mensem ad respondendum etc. et ad audiendum etc.

(1073)

Surr' Sussex'. Preceptum fuit vicecomiti quod distringeret Thomam de Rulte per terras etc., et quod haberet corpus ejus coram etc. ad respondendum Regi de .x. et ix. quarteriis frumenti vel eorum precio que Regi debet de debitis Mossei filii Aaron judei dampnati. Et ipse non venit. Et vicecomes mandavit quod Robertus le Deveneys de Northflete et Johannes Rabel de Gynesford' manuceperunt predictum Thomam, quem non habuerunt. Ideo in misericordia.[308] Et interim predictus Thomas venit et dictum debitum dedicere non potuit quin teneatur. Et preceptum est vicecomiti quod valorem dicti frumenti de terris et catallis dicti Thome levari faciat et valorem inde habeat coram etc. a die sancti Michaelis in .iij. septimanas Regi solvendum.

MEMBRANE 7

Starra de termino Pasche anno regni regis Edwardi nono

(1074)

Hereford'. Manser filius Aaron judeus recognovit per starrum suum quod Johannes de Gatisden' et heredes sui quieti sunt de ipso judeo et heredibus et assignatis de quodam debito sexaginta quarteriorum frumenti in quibus ei tenebatur per scriptum suum obligatorium.

(1075)

Hereford'. Sampson filius Isak recognovit per starrum suum pro se et Ursello fratre ejus [i]<tanquam>[i] attornato ejusdem Urselli quod perdonavit Roberto de Lammartin [i]<et>[i] magistro Willelmo de Breaus episcopo Landafennsi et magistro Willelmo de Radenovere, heredibus, successoribus et eorum assignatis totum jus, demandam, calumpniam, obligacionem et potestatem quam habuerunt vel habere potuerunt versus predictos Willelmum episcopum, Robertum et magistrum Willelmum occasione terrarum, boscorum, <pratarum>[309] et reddituum cum pertinenciis quas prefatus Robertus tenet in manu sua die confeccionis hujus starri, unde predicta terra cum pertinenciis Willelmus de Radenovere predictus emit de Roberto de Weston' infra villa de Arkeston' ante coronacionem regis Edwardi, ita quod nec heredes nec assignati aliquid possint exigere, calumpniari versus predictos Willelmum episcopum, Robertum et Willelmum vel eorum heredes seu successores vel eorum assignatos pretextu predictarum terrarum, boscorum, pratorum et reddituum cum pertinenciis que predictus Robertus [e]<modo>[e] tenuit die confeccionis hujus starri que fuerunt empte ante predictam coronacionem. Acta a die Pasche in unum mensem anno regni regis Edwardi nono.

[307] *The word* misericordia *is repeated in the margin.*

[308] *The word* misericordia *is repeated in the margin.*

[309] *MS.* pratis.

MEMBRANE 8

Recogniciones de termino Pasche anno regis Pasche anno regis Edwardi nono

(1076)

Wygorn'. Walterus de Bello Campo recognovit per starrum suum se debere Aaron filio Vives judeo .c. et .l. quarteria frumenti vel dimidiam marcam etc., reddendo medietatem ad festum sancti Petri ad Vincula anno nono et aliam medietatem ad quindenam sancti Michaelis proximo sequentem. Et nisi etc.

(1077)

Cant'. Baldewynus de Mansereys manucepit pro Johanne Canun solvere eidem Aaron duas marcas a die sancti Michaelis in tres septimanas. Et nisi etc.

TRINITY TERM, 9 EDWARD I [1281]

Exchequer of Jews, Plea Roll No. 38 [E 9/38]

Membrane 12 of this roll was transferred here from Roll 37, of which it had been membrane 5, in 1975, since it was clear both from its heading and from internal evidence that it belonged to a roll for this term rather than to a roll of the preceding Easter term. It is not, however, certain that it belongs to this Roll rather than to a duplicate Roll for the same term. The other membranes are also probably not in their original order. What are now membranes 6 and 7 were probably originally the first two membranes of the roll and membrane 4 must have followed them.

MEMBRANE 1

Memoranda de termino sancte Trinitatis anno regni regis Edwardi Nono

(1078)

Devon'. Preceptum fuit vicecomiti quod venire faceret coram etc. Rogerum de Mueles et Benedictam que fuit uxor Baldewyni de Wayford', tenentes quasdam partes terrarum que fuerunt predicti Baldewini, ad respondendum Regi una cum Jacobo de Mohun, qui habuit hunc diem, de diversis debitis que ab eodem Jacobo exiguntur per summonicionem scaccarii judeorum de debitis Judaismi. Et ipsi non venerunt. Et vicecomes mandavit quod Wymundus de Combe et Ricardus Glas manuceperunt Rogerum de Mueles; et quod Johannes de Holewele et Johannes de Backeton' manuceperunt Benedictam de Wayford', quos non habuerunt. Ideo in misericordia.[1] Judicium quod distringantur per terras etc., ita quod nec ipsi etc., et quod de exitibus etc., et quod habeat corpora eorum coram etc. a die sancti Michaelis in unum mensem ad respondendum etc. et ad audiendum etc. Et dictus Jacobus per attornatum suum habet eundem diem.

(1079)

Oxon'. Preceptum fuit vicecomiti, sicut pluries, quod de terris et catallis Edmundi filii Johannis de Glouc' fieri faceret ad opus Ade de Stratton' decem libras et eas haberet coram etc. Et vicecomes mandavit quod predictus Edmundus terras suas vendidit Roberto Malet ante recepcionem istius brevis, et tamen tres acras terre ordeo et siligine seminatas et quoddam pratum non falcatum pro predicto debito cepit in manum regis. Et preceptum est ei quod de predictis blado, prato et aliis catallis dicti Edmundi fieri faciat dictas decem libras et eas habeat coram etc. a die sancti Michaelis in .xv. dies eidem Ade solvendas.

(1080)

Oxon'. Bark'. Preceptum fuit vicecomiti quod distringeret Johannem de Shotesbroke et alios tenentes terrarum que fuerunt Simonis de Ordeston' ad reddendum sibi ad opus Regis .xxiiij. marcas et dimidiam de debito Henne et Belie filiarum Joscei de Marleberg' judei; et denarios illos haberet coram etc. vel corpora predictorum tenencium ad ostendendum etc. Et vicecomes mandavit quod retornavit breve sibi inde directum ballivis libertatis de Schrivenham, qui nichil inde fecerunt. Judicium quod non omittat etc. et distringat predictos tenentes pro denariis predictis et eos habeat coram etc. a die sancti Michaelis in .xv. dies Regi solvendum.

(1081)

Glouc'. Preceptum fuit vicecomiti quod non omittat propter libertatem Glouc' etc. et attachiaret Thomam de Evesham cyrographarium arche cyrographariorum Glouc', ita quod haberet corpus ejus coram etc. ad respondendum Regi una cum Thoma de Cheu, Roberto le Cornwaleys et Henrico de Penedot, executoribus testamenti Johannis le Cornewaleys quondam cyrographarii arche predicte, qui habuerunt hunc diem, de diversis cartis que ab archa predicta per preceptum regis extracte fuerunt et quas justiciariis etc. liberasse debuerunt et nondum liberaverunt ad dampnum regis etc.

Predictus Thomas venit et deffendit vim etc. et bene recognovit quod per preceptum regis ab archa predicta extraxerunt quasdam cartas que tradite fuerunt Johanni le Cornewaleys socio suo cyrographario Lond' deferendum justiciariis etc. ibidem liberandas.[2]

(1082)

Norff'. Suff'. Preceptum fuit vicecomiti quod de terris etc. Johannis de Geddinges et Roberti filii sui fieri faceret ad opus Aaron filii Vives judei Lond' .xxxv. libras quas iidem Robertus et Johannes recognoverunt etc., et denarios illos haberet coram etc. Et vicecomes mandavit quod retornavit breve sibi inde directum ballivis libertatis sancti Edmundi, qui sibi responderunt quod predicti Johannes et Robertus nichil habent in balliva sua nisi bladum in terra quod apreciatur ad .xiiij. solidos. Et quia testificatum est quod satis habent unde dictum debitum fieri facere potuissent, si voluissent, preceptum est vicecomiti quod non omittat etc. et de bonis et catallis dictorum Johannis et Roberti fieri faciat et denarios illos

[1] *The word* misericordia *is repeated in the margin.*

[2] *This entry is unfinished.*

habeat coram etc. a die sancti Michaelis in .xv. dies dicto judeo solvendum etc.

(1083)

Norff'. Suff'. Preceptum fuit vicecomiti quod de terris et catallis Johannis de Hadeshawe fieri faceret ad opus Johannis de Bayfelt .lx. [et] .vij. marcas et dimidiam quas idem Johannes versus eundem Johannem de Hadeshawe per consideracionem curie coram etc. recuperavit etc., et denarios illos haberet coram etc. Et vicecomes mandavit quod predictus Johannes de Hadeshawe ob timorem istius brevis abscondit bona sua mobilia, ita quod nichil inde inveniri poterit nisi bladum in terra crescens de quo nullum denarium citra autumpnum levare potest. Et preceptum est ei, sicut alias, quod de blado et aliis catallis dicti Johannis dictas .lxvij. marcas et dimidiam fieri faciat et eas habeat coram etc. in quindena sancti Michaelis eidem Johanni solvendum.

(1084)

Linc'. Preceptum fuit vicecomiti quod venire faceret coram etc. cyrographarios christianos et judeos arche cyrographariorum civitatis Linc' et .vj. legales homines et .vj. legales judeos de eadem civitate et visneto de Gunwardeby, juratores inquisicionis in qua magister Johannes le Graunt se posuit. Et ipsi non venerunt. Et vicecomes mandavit quod Robertus de Greygham de Linc' et Thomas de Bulyngbrok' manuceperunt Osbertum filium Egidii, unum cyrographariorum christianorum; et quod Jacobus Brond de Linc' et Walterus Brond de eadem manuceperunt Jacobum de Ponte, alium cyrographarium; et quod Simon de Bridelingeton' de Linc' et Alanus de Leyc' de eadem manuceperunt Ivonem le Cordewaner de Linc'; et quod Rogerus Bat de Linc' et Alanus de Ebor' manuceperunt Willelmum de la Neueland cordwaner; et quod Brunrobyn le Gaunter de Linc' et Nicholaus Cokewald de eadem manuceperunt Rogerum de Filingheye de Linc'; et quod Robertus Cokewald de Linc' et Radulfus le Fevere de eadem manuceperunt Willelmum le petit pier de Linc'; et quod Willelmus filius Albr' de Linc' et Adam de Norfolch' de eadem manuceperunt Alanum le Taillier de Wykeford' de Linc'; et quod Johannes de Bello Fago de Linc' et Nigellus Pally de eadem manuceperunt Johannem le Peleter de Wykeford' de Linc', quos non habuerunt. Ideo in misericordia. Et quod Isac filius Samuelis et Elias filius Diey manuceperunt Salmonem filium Cresse; et quod Samuel filius Manseri et Jacobus filius Samuelis manuceperunt Jacobum filium Isac; et quod Abraham de Not' et Manser Lacop manuceperunt Isac filium Samuelis; et quod Elias de Huntyndon' et Jacobus de Ebor' manuceperunt Samuelem filium Manseri; et quod Isac filius Manseri et Manserus filius Elie manuceperunt Abraham filium Abr'; et quod Samuel filius Mosse et Diey filius Diei manuceperunt Sam' filium Jacobi; et quod Abraham Levi et Bonamy filius Jacobi manuceperunt Eliam filium Samuelis; et quod Jacobus filius Abrahe et Benedictus filius Abrahe manuceperunt Die filium Abrahe, quos non habuerunt. Ideo in misericordia. Judicium quod distringat per terras etc., ita quod nec ipsi etc., et quod de exitibus etc., et quod habeat corpora eorum etc. a die sancti Michaelis in unum mensem ad recognoscendum etc. et ad audiendum etc. Et predictus magister Johannis, qui presens fuit per attornatum suum, habet eundem diem etc.

MEMBRANE 1 DORSE

(1085)[3]

Hereford'. Preceptum fuit vicecomiti quod distringeret Henricum Bret per terras etc. ad [reddendum][4] sibi ad opus Regis .v. marcas; et denarios illos haberet coram etc. in octabis sancte Trinitatis nunc. Et vicecomes mandavit quod breve sibi inde directum adeo tarde venit quod exequi non potuit. Ideo preceptum est ei, sicut alias, a die sancti Michaelis in tres septimanas.

(1086)[5]

Suthp'. Preceptum fuit vicecomiti quod distringeret Robertum de <Harnhell'>[6] et Johannam uxorem ejus, tenentes terras que fuerunt Nicholai de Cundy, per terras etc. ad reddendum sibi ad opus Regis .xxxvj. solidos .viij. denarios de debitis Mossei filii magistri Aaron judei Wynton' dampnati et denarios illos haberet coram etc. vel corpora predictorum Roberti et Johanne ad ostendendum etc. Et predictus Robertus pro se et Johanna uxore sua venit et vocat ad warentum Willelmum le Dun per auxilium curie quod ipsos inde aquietare debet. Et preceptum est vicecomiti quod venire faciat coram etc. a die sancti Michaelis in tres septimanas predictum Willelmum ad acquietandum predictos Robertum et Johannam de predicto debito etc.

(1087)[7]

Sutht'. Preceptum fuit vicecomiti quod venire faceret coram etc. Simonem de Wynton', Johannem de Windeshor' et alios in brevi, recognitores inquisicionis in qua Hugo de Fulflod et Benedictus filius Abrahe se posuerunt dum idem Benedictus vixerat, sicut patet inter placita termini [blank][8] anno regni regis Edwardi sexto. Et ipsi non venerunt. Et vicecomes mandavit quod retornavit breve sibi inde directum ballivis libertatum prioratus Wynton', Basingestok', civitatis Wynton', qui nichil inde fecerunt. Judicium quod non omittat propter libertates predictas quin eas etc., et venire faciat coram etc. a

[3] *This entry is also to be found on m. 12d, where it is marked for omission.*

[4] *MS. reads* respondendum.

[5] *This entry is also to be found on m. 12d, where it is marked for omission.*

[6] Harnhull' *m. 12d.*

[7] *This entry is also to be found on m. 12d, where it is marked for omission.*

[8] *There is only a blank in the version on m. 12d as well, but the name of a specific term is required by the sense.*

die sancti Michaelis in unum mensem predictos Simonem, Johannem et alios ad recognoscendum etc., et quod venire faciat .xij. legales judeos de civitate Wynton' etc.

(1088)[9]

Linc'. Preceptum fuit vicecomiti quod venire faceret coram etc. sex liberos et legales homines et sex legales judeos de civitate Linc', recognitores inquisicionis in qua Rogerus de Somerville, tenens terras que fuerunt Gerardi de Hamelton', se posuit, sicut patet inter memoranda termini Pasche proximo preteriti. Et recognitores non venerunt. Et vicecomes mandavit quod Willelmus <Unwyne>[10] de Linc' et Alanus de Ebor' de eadem manuceperunt Simonem <Onewyne;>[11] et quod Radulfus le Taillur ad Arthus de Linc' et Brunrobin le Gaunter de eadem manuceperunt Rogerum de Heydore de Linc'; et quod Rogerus Mille de Linc' et Gilbertus Giselin de eadem manuceperunt Ricardum le <Pero>[12] de Linc'; et quod Johannes filius prepositi de Linc' et Rogerus de Gresthrop' de eadem manuceperant Adam Page de Linc'; et quod Robertus de Cestrefeud de Linc' et Robertus Brungaunter de eadem manuceperunt Willelmum le Petit seler de Linc'; et quod Willelmus Scot frater Roberti Scot tronur de Linc' et Nicholaus de London' de eadem manuceperunt Rogerum de Filingeye de Linc'; quos non habuerunt. Ideo in misericordia.[13] Et quod Salomon filius Isac et Jacobus filius Samuelis manuceperunt Isac filium Samuelis; et quod Samuel filius Isac et Isac filius Salomonis manuceperunt Jacobum filium Abrahe; et quod Diei filius Abrahe et Elias filius Jacobi manuceperunt Samuelem filium Manseri et quod Isac gener Samuelis et Salomon filius Jacobi manuceperunt Manserum filium Salomonis; et quod Manserus filius Isac et Abraham filius Abrahe manuceperunt Abraham de Staumford'; et quod Vyves filius Elie et Elias filius Deudoneye manuceperunt Eliam filium Abrahe, quos non habuerunt. Ideo in misericordia.[14] Judicium quod distringat per terras etc., ita quod nec ipsi etc., et quod de exitibus etc., et quod habeat corpora eorum coram etc. a die sancti Michaelis in quindecim dies ad recognoscendum etc. Et predictus Rogerus, qui presens fuit per attornatum suum, habet eundem diem.

(1089)[15]

Wygorn'. Preceptum fuit vicecomiti quod distringeret tenentes terras et tenementa que fuerunt Willelmi de Bleys per terras etc. ad reddendum sibi ad opus Regis centum solidos de debitis Sampsons filii Isac. Et vicecomes mandavit quod Willelmus de <Blois>[16] non habet terras neque tenementa in comitatu Wygorn'. Et quia testificatum est quod habuit terras in comitatu Heref', preceptum est vicecomiti [Heref'][17] quod distringat tenentes terras dicti Willelmi pro centum solidis supradictis et eos habeat coram etc. a die sancti Michaelis in .xv. dies Regi solvendum.

(1090)[18]

Wygorn'. Preceptum fuit vicecomiti, sicut pluries, quod distringeret Robertum filium Roberti de Grafton' per terras etc. ad reddendum sibi ad opus Regis .iiij. marcas de debitis Sampsonis filii Isac judei. Et vicecomes mandavit quod Godefridus Silat, Johannes de Peredoc, Hugo de Hodeshovere et Willelmus <Hiceret>[19] manuceperunt predictum Robertum ad satisfaciendum Regi de denariis in brevi contentis, quem non habuerunt. Ideo in misericordia.[20] Et mandavit quod citra autumpnum nichil de predicto Roberto levari posset. Et preceptum est ei quod de blado et aliis catallis predicti Roberti in autumpno predictas .iiij. marcas levare faciat et eos habeat coram etc. a die sancti Michaelis in .xv. dies Regi solvendum. Et quia vicecomes respondit de manucapcione dicit Roberti cum ei preceptum fuit quod de denariis supradictis tantummodo responderet, ideo ipse vicecomes, scilicet Thomas de Neywenham, in misericordia.[21]

(1091)

Salop'. Preceptum fuit vicecomiti, sicut pluries, quod de terris et catallis.[22]

(1092)[23]

Buk'. Hugo de Brock' miles recognovit se debere Aaron filio Vives et magistro Elie filio magistri Moyssei .xx. saccos lane vel valorem dicte lane, reddendo medietatem ad octabas Purificacionis beate Marie anno regis Edwardi .x., et aliam medietatem ad octabas sancti Johannis Baptiste proximo sequentes etc.

(1093)

Suth'. Philippus de Wauton' recognovit se debere eidem Aaron .vi.^{xx} quarteria frumenti vel dimidiam marcam etc., reddendo ad festum Omnium Sanctorum anno regis Edwardi nono. Et nisi etc.

9 *This entry is also to be found on m. 12d, where it is marked for omission.*

10 Onwyne *m. 12d.* 11 Onwyne *m. 12d.*

12 Percy *m. 12d.*

13 *The word* misericordia *is repeated in the margin in the version on m. 12d only.*

14 *The word* misericordia *is repeated in the margin in the version on on m. 12d only.*

15 *This entry is also to be found on m. 12d but it is not marked for omission in either place.*

16 Bleys *m. 12d.*

17 *Supplied from the version on m. 12d.*

18 *This entry is also to be found on m. 12d but it is not marked for omission in either place.*

19 Hutret *m. 12d.*

20 *The word* misericordia *is repeated in the margin of m. 12d only.*

21 *The word* misericordia *is repeated in the margin of m. 12d only.*

22 *This entry is left unfinished.*

23 *Cf. no. 1184*

(1094)

Warr'. Petrus Mounfort miles, filius Petri de Mounfort, recognovit se debere eidem Aaron .xviij. libras reddendum ad festum sancti Michaelis anno regis Edwardi nono. Et nisi etc.

(1095)

Buk'. Walterus de Gayton' recognovit per scriptum suum se debere eidem .c. quarteria frumenti vel dimidiam marcam etc., reddendo ad quindenam sancti Michaelis anno regis Edwardi nono.
Dictum debitum quietum est etc.

(1096)

Kanc'. Johannes Malemeyn miles recognovit se debere eidem .xxx. quarteria frumenti vel dimidiam marcam etc., reddendo ad festum sancti Petri ad vincula anno regis Edward nono. Et nisi etc.

(1097)

Norff'. Jacobus filius Gilberti de Dileketshale miles recognovit per scriptum suum se debere eidem .cc. quarteria frumenti vel dimidiam marcam etc. reddendo a die Pasche in unum mensem anno regis Edwardi nono. Et nisi etc.

MEMBRANE 2

Adhuc memoranda de termino sancte Trinitatis anno regni regis Edwardi nono

(1098)

Suht'. Preceptum fuit vicecomiti quod venire faceret coram etc. sex probos et legales homines et sex legales judeos de civitate Winton' ad recognoscendum si Walterus de Wyk' solvit Benedicto de Winton' judeo .xx. marcas dum habuit liberam administracionem bonorum suoram. Et jurata non venit. Et vicecomes mandavit quod retornavit breve sibi inde directum ballivis libertatis Wynton' pro christianis, qui nichil inde fecerunt. Judicium quod non omittat etc. Et vicecomes mandavit quod Pictavinus filius Urselli et Ursellus filius Bonamy manuceperunt Kokerellum filium Licoricie; et quod Mille filius Jacobi et Jacobus filius Bonamy manuceperunt Abraham filium Kokerel; et quod Vives filius Milonis et Jacobus filius Abrahe manuceperunt Josceum filium Troyt; et quod Elias filius Lumbardi et Lumbardus filius Jacobi manuceperunt Abraham filium Cressei; et quod Manserus filius Cokerel et Kokerel filius Jacobi manuceperunt Beycoc filium Bonamy; et quod Mulle filius Vives et Lumbardus filius Abrahe manuceperunt Josceum de Caleys, quos non habuerunt. Ideo in misericordia. Judicium quod distringat per terras etc., et quod habeat corpora eorum coram etc. a die sancti Michaelis in tres septimanas ad recognoscendum etc. Et predictus Walterus, qui presens fuit per attornatum suum, habet eundem diem.

(1099)

Oxon'. Bark'. Preceptum fuit vicecomiti, sicut alias, quod venire faceret .xij. probos et legales homines de villa de Walingford' et sex probos et legales homines visneti ejusdem ville, juratores cujusdam inquisicionis in qua Robertus Malet se posuit, ut patet inter memoranda termini sancti Hillarii proximo preteriti. Et sex de visneto de Walingford' non venerunt. Et vicecomes mandavit quod Robertus Lovete de Chalgrave et Robertus de Buriende manuceperunt Willelmum de Barantin; et quod Willelmus filius Willelmi et Ricardus Germayn manuceperunt Thomam deu Park; et quod Theobaldus Aubin et Willelmus Modi manuceperunt Willelmum Quatrmeyns; et quod Alexander de Lacheford' et Galfridus de Leukenore manuceperunt Petrum filium Elmery; et quod Walterus le Pur et Ricardus le Tylie manuceperunt Ricardum Morin; et quod Willelmus Faber et Hugo Carettarius manuceperunt Hugonem Frelond', quos non habuerunt. Ideo in misericordia. Judicium quod distringantur per terras etc., ita quod nec ipsi etc., et quod de exitibus etc., et quod habeat corpora eorum coram etc. a die sancti Michaelis in unum mensem ad recognoscendum etc. una cum Eustachio Clemente, Bartholomeo de Shirebourne, Petro Hentelove de Walingford', Gregorio de Waltham de eadem, Thoma Chaumpeneys de eadem, Petro Osbern de eadem, Willelmo de la Wyke de eadem, Radulfo Honeye de eadem, Johanne Bernard de eadem, Rogero Malvey de eadem, Roberto de Brihtwalton' de eadem et Reginaldo de Aula de eadem, qui venerunt et habent eundem diem. Et predictus Robertus Malet, qui presens fuit, habet eundem diem. Et preceptum est vicecomiti, sicut alias, quod non omittat propter libertatem Walingeford' quin eam etc., et venire faceret magistrum Petrum de Benham ad respondendum Regi una cum predicto Roberto [de][24] diversis cartis, que deposite erant in archa cyrographariorum Walingford' tempore domini Ricardi regis Alemannie in custodia dictorum Petri et Roberti, ut dicitur. Et vicecomes nichil de predicto Petro respondit, sed breve quantum ad dictum Petrum vacuum retornavit. Ideo ipse vicecomes in misericordia.[25] Et preceptum est ei, sicut pluries, quod non omittat etc. et predictum Petrum venire faciat ad diem supradictum.

(1100)

Wygorn'. Preceptum fuit vicecomiti quod venire faciat coram etc. Willelmum de Kemesing', Simonem Alayn, Willelmum de Chiltenham, et Agnetem de Okle, tenenetes quasdam partes terrarum que fuerunt Ricardi de Wyz, ad respondendum Regi de .vj. libris et .x. solidis de debitis Manseri filii Joscei judei. Et ipsi non venerunt. Et vicecomes mandavit quod Willelmus de Kemesinge et Willelmus de Chiltenham nichil habent in comitatu Wygorn' nisi quandam parvam porcionem terre, que

24 *MS. omits.*
25 *The word* misericordia *is repeated in the margin.*

jacet inculta. Et quia predictus vicecomes predictam terram in manum regis non cepit, ideo ipse vicecomes in misericordia. Et preceptum est ei, sicut alias, quod eos venire faciat coram etc. a die sancti Michaelis in quindecim dies etc. Et mandavit quod Thomas Grene et Robertus Renaud' manuceperunt Simonem Alayn; et quod Johannes le Rawe de Aclye et Henricus Attegate de eadem manuceperunt Agnetem de Ocle, quos non habuerunt. Ideo in misericordia. Judicium quod distringat per terras etc., et quod habeat corpora eorum etc. ad diem supradictum ad respondendum etc. et ad audiendum etc.

(1101)

Warr'. Preceptum fuit vicecomiti quod venire faceret coram etc. .xij. tam milites quam alios etc. de visneto de Braundwyz ad recognoscendum etc. si Thomas de Braundwych' satisfecit Mosseo de Warr' dum vixerat et habuit liberam administracionem bonorum suorum in parte vel in toto de .xiij. marcis in quibus eidem judeo tenebatur per cartam suam. Et jurata dicte inquisicionis non venit. Et vicecomes mandavit quod Adam Lovekoc de Bromwyz et Alanus Smalberde de eadem manuceperunt Henricum de Castello; et quod Rogerus Drake de Bromwiche et Adam de Mere manuceperunt Thomam le Wrenge; et quod Simon de Bardimoz et Jacobus frater ejus manuceperunt Reginaldum de Blythe; et quod Rogerum Faber de Scustoke et Willelmus atte Hulle manuceperunt Willelmum de Edrichele; et quod Robertus Abel de Bromwihc et Anselmus de Watele manuceperunt Ricardum filium Henrici; et quod Willelmus super la Hull de Merxton' et Ricardus de Coleshulle manuceperunt Thomam le Fraunceys; et quod Hugo de la Haye et Rogerus Somerlove manuceperunt Henricum Orin; et quod Ricardus de Rokeby et Thomas Crowe manuceperunt Robertum de Rokeby; et quod Robertus Jordan et Ricardus frater ejus manuceperunt Willelmum Leyr de Erdinton; et quod Willelmus Tamon et Jordanus Faber manuceperunt Galfridum de Mumeworth'; et quod Robertus le Carpenter et Willelmum Long Axs manuceperunt Nicholaum de la Hethe; et quod Robertus Wombestrong et Johannes Smalbret manuceperunt Rogerum de Sidinhale; et quod Radulfus de Bosco et Simon filius Petri manuceperunt Rogerum atte Londesende; et quod Walterus Brag et Osbertus filius Lone manuceperunt Rogerum Ramage, quos non habuerunt. Ideo in misericordia. Judicium quod distringat per terras etc,. ita quod nec ipsi etc., et quod de exitibus etc., et quod habeat corpora eorum coram etc. a die sancti Michaelis in tres septimanas ad recognoscendum etc., et preter eos etc.

(1102)

Leyc'. Preceptum fuit vicecomiti quod, si Willelmus Murdac sibi invenerit securitatem quod solvet Aaron filio Vives sex libras ad quindenam sancti Martini anno regnis regis Edwardi nono et sex libras ad quindenam Pasche proximo sequentem, tunc predictum Willelmum pro predicto debito non distringeret. Et vicecomes mandavit quod Robertus Wade de Stokfaston, Ricardus Wade de eadem, Simon in le Wro de eadem, Johannes Wrayn de eadem, Robertus le Hunte de eadem, Willelmus Wade de eadem, et Ricardus le Bercher de eadem manuceperunt quod predictus Willelmus satisfaciet predicto Aaron de denariis supradictis ad terminos supradictos.

(1103)

Northt'. Preceptum fuit vicecomiti quod distringeret Osbertum de Crauthorp per terras etc., et quod haberet corpus ejus coram etc. ad respondendum Regi de diversis bonis et catallis, ut in auro, argento, pannis et aliis minutis jocalibus, ad valenciam .xxx. librarum que devenerunt ad manus predicti Osberti de catallis que fuerunt Isac de Celario judei forisfacti. Et ipse non venit. Et vicecomes mandavit quod ballivi Northt', quibus istud breve returnatum fuit, sibi responderunt quod predictus Osbertus districtus est per duas domos de quibus nulli exitus proveniebant et quod dictus [Osbertus][26] non fuit inventus post recepcionem brevis. Ideo, sicut alias, a die sancti Michaelis in xv dies etc.

(1104)

Kanc'. Preceptum fuit vicecomiti quod de terris et catallis Alani de Morton' fieri faceret ad opus Roberti de Ludham .xiij. marcas quas idem Alanus etc. Et vicecomes mandavit quod returnavit breve sibi inde directum senescallo libertatis archiepiscopatus Cantuar', qui nichil inde fecit. Judicium quod non omittat etc., et de terris et catallis predicti Alani prefatas .xiij. marcas fieri faciat et eas habeat coram etc. a die sancti Michaelis in .xv. dies eidem Roberto solvendas etc.

(1105)

Kanc'. Preceptum fuit vicecomiti quod attachiaret Thomam Chiche, ita quod haberet corpus ejus coram etc. ad respondendum Regi [de][27] eo quod sine licencia et contra fidem suam recessit a curia in contemptum Regis cum attachiatus esset pro diversis debitis Regi reddendis. Et vicecomes mandavit quod returnavit breve sibi inde directum ballivis libertatis Cantuar', qui nichil inde fecerunt. Judicium quod non omittat etc. et attachiari faciat predictum Thomam, ita quod habeat corpus ejus coram etc. a die sancti Michaelis in .xv. dies ad respondendum Regi de debitis ab eo petititis [et][28] contemptu predicto etc.

[26] *MS. reads* Robertus. [27] *MS. omits.* [28] *MS. reads* in.

MEMBRANE 2 DORSE

Adhuc memoranda de termino sancte Trinitatis

(1106)[29]

Willelmus de <Brokhulle>[30] pro pluribus defaltis in misericordia.

[Kanc'.][31] Preceptum fuit vicecomiti quod [non omitteret propter libertatem archiepiscopatus Cantuar' quin eam etc. et][32] distringeret Willelmum de Brokhulle per terras etc., et quod haberet corpus ejus coram etc. [ad hunc diem][33] ad respondendum Regi de uno cypho de mazero cum pede argenti precii .vj. marcarum et aliis bonis et catallis ad valenciam .xiij. librarum que devenerunt ad manus predicti Willelmi de bonis et catallis que fuerunt Mossei de Doggestrete judei pro transgressione monete Regi forisfactis.

Et predictus Willelmus venit et deffendit vim etc., et dicit quod de catallis predicti Mossei <nichil recepit nec penes se aliquid de catallis suis habuit seu habet;>[34] et de hoc ponit se super patriam. Et patria presens fuit per Rogerum <Hurre,>[35] Rogerum de Leyc' et alios christianos, Samuelem le Fraunceys, Josceum <filium Mulle>[36] et alios judeos, sicut patet inter brevia hujus termini returnata [in brevi tangenti Dyonisiam que fuit uxor Stephani le Taylur de Cantuar'.][37] Qui jurati <concordare>[38] non potuerunt. Et datus est eis dies a die sancti Michaelis in tres septimanas ad veredictum <inde dicendum,>[39] nisi Rogerus de Northwode interim ad partes <Kanc'>[40] venerit.

(1107)

Kanc'. Preceptum fuit vicecomiti quod venire faceret coram etc. Johannem filium Simonis Talebot de Harnhulle ad respondendum Regi de .iij. marcis quas Regi debet de debito Mossei filii Aaron judei Cantuar' dampnati. Et ipse non venit. Et vicecomes mandavit quod Thomas Baudi et Robertus frater ejus manuceperunt predictum Johannem, quem non habuerunt. Ideo in misericordia. Judicium quod distringat per terras etc., et quod habeat corpus ejus coram etc. a die sancti Johannis Baptiste in .xv. dies ad respondendum Regi de predicto debito etc.

(1108)

Bed', Buk'. Preceptum fuit vicecomiti quod distringeret Robertum de Cave, Rogerum filium Johannis de Hampslep et alios in brevi per terras etc., et quod haberet corpora eorum coram etc. ad respondendum Regi de .lv. marcis de debitis Sampsonis filii Sampsonis. Et ipsi non venerunt. Et vicecomes mandavit quod Johannes le Notte de Schirington', Willelmus Cosin de eadem manuceperunt Rogerum filium Johannis, quem non habuerunt. Ideo in misericordia.[41] Et idem Rogerus, quia non venit, in misericordia.[42] Et sunt exitus terrarum dicti Rogeri .xviij. denarii.[43] Et quod Willelmus filius Hugonis de Emberton' et Johannes filius Galfridi de eadem manuceperunt Willelmum de Scakeleston', quem non habuerunt. Ideo in misericordia.[44] Et idem Willelmus, quia non venit, in misericordia.[45] Et sunt exitus terrarum dicti Willelmi .xij. denarii.[46] Et quod Thomas Mayn de Harrmed' et Johannes Mayn de eadem, quia non habuerunt Ricardum Gerveys quem manuceperunt, ideo in misericordia.[47] Idem Ricardus, quia non venit, in misericordia.[48] Et sunt exitus terrarum dicti Ricardi .xij. denarii.[49] Et quod Johannes Brid de Chechelye et Willelmus Brid de eadem manuceperunt Rogerum Goulde, quem non habuerunt. Ideo in misericordia.[50] Idem Rogerus, quia non venit, ideo in misericordia.[51] Et sunt exitus terrarum dicti Rogeri .vj. denarii.[52] Et quod Walterus Fraunceys de Sirington' et Simon le Suur de eadem, quia non habuerunt Henricum le Bret quem manuceperunt, ideo in misericordia.[53] Idem Henricus, quia non venit, in misericordia.[54] Et sunt exitus terrarum dicti Henrici .vj. denarii.[55] Et quod Simon le Petit de Schirington' et Willelmus Dyrmal de eadem manuceperunt Willelmum filium Ade, quem non habuerunt, ideo in misericordia.[56] Et idem Willelmus, quia non venit, in misericordia.[57] Et sunt exitus terrarum dicti Willelmi .vj. d. Robertus de Cave, quia non venit, in misericordia.[58] Ranulphus le Fevre pro eodem in misericordia.[59] Et Simon filius Simonis Gerveys pro eodem in misericordia.[60]

(1109)

Not', Derb'. Preceptum fuit vicecomiti quod venire faceret coram etc. sex probos et legales homines de

[29] *This entry is repeated on m. 12 (no. 1235). Significant variants are noted in the footnotes.*

[30] Brochulle *m. 12.* [31] *Supplied from m. 12.*

[32] *Supplied from m. 12.* [33] *Supplied from m. 12.*

[34] ad manus ejus, ut in denariis, cyphis seu aliis catallis, nichil devenit *m. 12.*

[35] Burre *m. 12.* [36] Molekin *m. 12.*

[37] *Supplied from m. 12.* [38] unanimes esse *m. 12.*

[39] super premissis recognoscendum *m. 12.*

[40] illas *m. 12.*

[41] *The word* misericordia *is repeated in the margin.*

[42] *The word* misericordia *is repeated in the margin.*

[43] *The words* .xviij. denarii *are repeated in the margin.*

[44] *The word* misericordia *is repeated in the margin.*

[45] *The word* misericordia *is repeated in the margin.*

[46] *The words* .xij. denarii *are repeated in the margin.*

[47] *The word* misericordia *is repeated in the margin.*

[48] *The word* misericordia *is repeated in the margin.*

[49] *The words* .xij. denarii *are repeated in the margin.*

[50] *The word* misericordia *is repeated in the margin.*

[51] *The word* misericordia *is repeated in the margin.*

[52] *The words* .vj. denarii *are repeated in the margin.*

[53] *The word* misericordia *is repeated in the margin.*

[54] *The word* misericordia *is repeated in the margin.*

[55] *The words* .vj. denarii *are repeated in the margin.*

[56] *The word* misericordia *is repeated in the margin.*

[57] *The word* misericordia *is repeated in the margin.*

[58] *The word* misericordia *is repeated in the margin.*

[59] *The word* misericordia *is repeated in the margin.*

[60] *The word* misericordia *is repeated in the margin.*

visneto de Eyton', et sex legales judeos de villa Notingham, recognitores inquisicionis in qua Urianus de sancto Petro se posuit, ut patet inter memoranda termini Pasche proximo preteriti. Et ipsi non venerunt. Et vicecomes mandavit quod Rogerus Faber de Mackelye et Willelmus le Lung de eadem manuceperunt Johannem Wace de Mackelye; et quod Robertus Chef de Foston et Simon Massecreu de eadem manuceperunt Johannem filium Simonis de Foston; et quod Willelmus Wyldegos de Foston' et Nicholaus de Kortecunte de eadem manuceperunt Robertum de Cryton; et quod Thomas Molendinarius de Kenlond' et Willelmus frater Nicholai de eadem manuceperunt Oliverum de Kenlond'; et quod Henricus Arnald' de Holmton' et Willelmus de Chebbeseye manuceperunt Oliverum le Foune de Holmton; et quod Rogerus Faber de Makkelye et Willelmus atte Tounesende junior de eadem manuceperunt Henricum Rowe de Matworth', quos non habuerunt. Ideo in misericordia.[61] Et quod Hugo filius Bateman et Isac Colemin manuceperunt Pictavinum filium Isac; et quod Pictavinus filius Isac et Ursellus filius Bateman manuceperunt Isac Colemin; et quod Isac Colemin et Pictavinus filius Isac manuceperunt Haginum filium Bateman, quos non habuerunt. Ideo in misericordia.[62] Judicium quod distringat per terras etc., ita quod nec ipsi etc., et quod de exitibus etc., et quod habeat corpora eorum coram etc. a die sancti Michaelis in tres septimanas ad recognoscendum etc., et preter eos etc. Et predictus Urianus non venit. Ideo in misericordia.[63]

(1110)

Not'. Preceptum fuit vicecomiti quod venire faceret coram etc. cyrographarios christianos et judeos arche cyrographariorum Not' et sex probos et legales homines et sex legales judeos de eadem villa, recognitores inquisicionis in qua Radulfus Hunt' se posuit, sicut patet inter memoranda termini Pasche proximo preteriti. Et jurata non venit. Et vicecomes mandavit quod Adam le Paumer et Sewal Brian cyrographarii christiani, uterque manucaptor alterum, non venerunt. Ideo in misericordia. Et quod Willelmus Jordan et Robertus Gos manuceperunt Ricardum Becok; et quod Robertus Gos et Ricardus Becok manuceperunt Willelmum Jordan; et quod Ricardus Becok et Willelmus Jordan manuceperunt Robertum Gos; et quod Robertus Dast et Rogerus de Landeford' manuceperunt Mattheum de Sutton'; et quod Mattheus de Sutton' et Rogerus de Landeford' manuceperunt Robertum Dafs; et quod Matheus de Sutton' et Robertus Dast manuceperunt Rogerum de Landeford, quos non habuerunt. Ideo in misericordia.[64] Et quod Pictavinus filius Isac et Isac Coleman manuceperunt Bateman de Wynton'; et quod Bateman de Wynton' et Isac Colemun manuceperunt Pictavinum filium Isaac; et quod Bateman de Winton' et Pictavinus filius Isac manuceperunt Isac Colemun; et quod Haginus filius Batemanni et Abraham filius Joscei de Staunf' manuceperunt Isac de Provinz; et quod Isac de Provinz et Abraham filius Joscei de Staunf' manuceperunt Haginum filium Bateman; et quod Haginus filius Bateman et Isac de Provinis manuceperunt Abraham filium Joscey de Staunf', quos non habuerunt. Ideo in misericordia.[65] Judicium quod distringat per terras etc., ita quod nec ipsi etc., et quod de exitibus etc., et quod habeat corpora eorum coram etc. a die sancti Michaelis in unum mensem ad recognoscendum etc. Et predictus Radulfus, quia non venit, distringatur pro predicto debito.

(1111)

Not'. Preceptum fuit vicecomiti quod venire faceret coram etc. Willelmum Dalby personam de Humberton', Johannem filium Stephani de Brokton, Johannem servientem domine de Bretton' et Ricardum Henfray, tenentes quasdam partes terrarum que fuerunt Johannis de Suthleye, ad respondendum Regi una cum Gervasio de Clifton', tenenti quandam partem terrarum que fuerunt predicti Johannis, de septem marcis que de dicto Gervasio ad opus Regis exiguntur de duobus debitis Samuelis filii Mossei de Pavyly et Deulecresse filii Bonefey judeorum forisfactorum. Et ipsi non venerunt. Et vicecomes mandavit quod Stephanus filius Hugonis de Bretton' et Robertus de Wydmerpole de eadem manuceperunt Willelmum de Dabley; et quod Adam super montem de Bretton' et Nicholaus clericus de eadem manuceperunt Johannem filium Stephani de Bretton'; et quod Adam Lorz et Ricardus Fisch' manuceperunt Johannem servientem domine de Bretton'; et quod Robertus de Brademere de Bretton' et Ranulphus filius Radulfi de eadem manuceperunt Ricardum Henefray, quos non habuerunt. Ideo in misericordia.[66] Judicium quod distringat per terras etc., ita quod nec ipsi etc., et quod de exitibus etc., et quod habeat corpora eorum coram etc. a die sancti Michaelis in tres septimanas ad respondendum etc. et audiendum etc. Et predictus Gervasius, qui presens fuit per attornatum suum, habet eundem diem.

MEMBRANE 3

Adhuc Memoranda de termino sancte Trinitatis anno regni regis Edwardi Nono

(1112)

Suth'. Preceptum fuit vicecomiti quod non omitteret propter libertatem Wynton' etc., et venire faceret coram etc. Willelmum Cote et Dyonisiam uxorem ejus ad respondendum Regi de .xx. solidis etc., et una zona de serico argento barrata precii unius marce, que catalla

61 *The word* misericordia *is repeated in the margin.*
62 *The word* misericordia *is repeated in the margin.*
63 *The word* misericordia *is repeated in the margin.*
64 *The word* misericordia *is repeated in the margin.*
65 *The word* misericordia *is repeated in the margin.*
66 *The word* misericordia *is repeated in the margin.*

devenerunt ad manus predictorum Willelmi et Dionisie de bonis et catallis que fuerunt Salamonis filii Belecote judei dampnati, quos quidem denarios receperunt de Petro Neweman de Andevre, et predicta Dyonisia uxor predicti Willelmi predictam zonam recepit de Belecote judea dampnata, ut dicitur.

Predictus Willelmus pro se et Dyonisia uxore sua venit et deffendit vim etc., et dicit quod de predictis Salomone seu Belecote matre sua judeis dampnatis de predictis denariis, zona vel aliis bonis seu catallis nichil receperunt et de hoc ponunt se super patriam. Et preceptum est vicecomiti quod venire faciat coram etc. a die sancti Michaelis in tres septimanas sex probos et legales homines de civitate Wynton' et sex legales judeos de eadem civitate, per quos etc., et qui nulla affinitate etc., ad recognoscendum super premissis veritatem.

(1113)

Sutht'. Preceptum fuit vicecomiti quod non omitteret propter libertatem Wynton' etc., et venire faceret coram etc. Adam Gappe et Julianam uxorem ejus ad respondendum Regi de .ccxvj. coclеariis argenti precii .x. librarum et .xvj. solidorum, sex ciphis argenti precii sexaginta solidorum et uno firmaculo aureo precii .xl. solidorum et [auro][67] ponderis duodecim marcarum, que bona et catalla devenerunt ad manus predictorum Ade et Juliane de bonis et catallis que fuerunt Belecote et Salomonis filii sui judeorum dampnatorum.

Predictus Adam pro se et Juliana uxore sua venit et deffendit vim etc. et recognovit quod ante communem capcionem judeorum pro transgressione monete habuit in custodia sua duo forceria clausa clavibus dicte Belecote, set nichil sciebat quid interius erat, et duos ciphos argenti et unum ciphum de mazero, que bona in capcione judeorum pro transgressione predicta Walterus del Wal tunc major Wynton' venit ad domum dicti Ade et exigebat si aliquid habebat de catallis judeorum custodiendum, tunc ei predicta duo forceria et tres ciphos ei ostendit, que forceria et ciphos dictus Walterus sigillo suo signavit et sub sigillo suo dicta bona Willelmo Braybuef et sociis suis justiciariis ad bona dampnatorum judeorum recipienda deputatis ad communem clammacionem inde factam quod nullus bona judeorum concelaret sub periculo etc. liberavit et hoc ponit super rotulos et recordum predicti Willelmi de Braybuef. Et mandatum est dicto Willelmo quod dictum recordum scire faciat justiciariis etc. a die sancti Michaelis in tres septimanas sub sigillo suo etc. Et dictus Adam dicit quod nulla bona de bonis dictorum judeorum recepit et de hoc ponit se super patriam. Et preceptum est vicecomiti quod venire faciat coram etc. a die sancti Michaelis in tres septimanas sex probos et legales homines de civitate Wynton' et sex legales judeos de eadem civitate, per quos etc., et qui nulla affinitate etc., ad recognoscendum super premissis veritatem etc.

(1114)

Sutht'. Preceptum fuit vicecomiti quod non omitteret propter libertatem Wynton' etc., et venire faceret Simonem le Mostarder et Matildam uxorem ejus ad respondendum Regi de quodam forcerio, una mappa et uno tapeto precii .x. solidorum, que catalla devenerunt ad manus predictorum Simonis et Matilde de catallis que fuerunt Salomonis filii Belecote judei dampnati.

Predictus Simon pro se et Matilda uxore ejus venit et deffendit vim etc. et dicit quod de predicto Salomone de predictis forcerio, mappa, tapeto vel aliis bonis seu catallis nichil receperunt et de hoc ponunt se super patriam. Et preceptum fuit vicecomiti quod venire faciat coram etc. a die sancti Michaelis in tres septimanas sex probos et legales homines de civitate Wynton' et sex legales judeos de eadem civitate, per quos etc., et qui nulla affinitate etc., ad recognoscendum super premissis veritatem etc.

(1115)

Sutht'. Preceptum fuit vicecomiti quod non omitteret propter libertatem ville Sutht' quin etc. et venire faceret Walterum le Horder burgensem Sutht' ad respondendum Regi de tribus firmaculis auri precii .iiij. marcarum, duobus ciphis argenteis cum pedibus [precii][68] .c. solidorum, duabus zonis de serico argento barratis precii .xxiiij. solidorum et aliis bonis et catallis ad valenciam .xxij. solidorum et .viij. denariorum, que bona et catalla devenerunt ad manus predicti Walteri de catallis que fuerunt Deudoneye de Winton' judei dampnati, ut dicitur.

Predictus Walterus venit et deffendit vim etc., et dicit quod de predictis firmaculis, ciphis, zonis, bonis seu catallis predicti Deudonis nichil habuit seu recepit et de hoc ponit se super patriam. Et preceptum est vicecomiti quod venire faciat coram etc. a die sancti Michaelis in tres septimanas sex probos et legales homines de villa Sutht' et sex legales judeos de civitate Wynton' per quos etc., et qui nulla etc., ad recognoscendum super premissis veritatem etc., quia predictus Walterus etc.

(1116)

London'. Reginaldus de Suff' civis London' venit coram etc. et recognovit se debere Aaron filio Vyves judeo centum quarteria frumenti, reddendo eidem judeo a die sancti Hillarii in quindecim dies anno regnis regis Edwardi decimo vel dimidia marca pro quolibet quarterio. Et nisi fecerit, concedit quod de terris et catallis suis, ad quorumcumque manus devenerint, fiant etc.

(1117)

Oxon'. Jacobus le Ballede de Henle venit coram etc. et recognovit se debere Mansero filio Isac de Warr' judeo sex quarteria frumenti, reddendo inde medietatem a die sancti Michaelis in .xv. dies, et aliam medietatem in octabis sancti Andree apostoli proximo sequenti. Et, si non solverit frumentum predictum terminis predictis,

[67] *MS. reads* aurum.

[68] *MS. omits.*

concedit quod de terris et catallis suis et heredum suorum fiat. Et pro ista recognicione prefatus Manserus remisit et quietum clamavit pro se et heredibus suis predicto Jacobo et heredibus suis omnimoda debitum, accionem et calumpniam quas habuit vel habere potuit quocumque modo versus eundem Jacobum a creacione seculi usque ad octabas sancti Johannis Baptiste anno regni regis Edwardi nono.

(1118)

Northt'. Johannes de Wahelle miles de comitatu Northt' venit coram etc. et recognovit se debere domine Regine consorti Regis etc. .xx. marcas pro Jacobo filio Pictavini de Bed' judeo per quas idem Jacobus finem fecit pro quibusdam platis que fuerunt Cressey de Hanerberg' quas penes se detinuit; ita videlicet quod, si predictus Jacobus predictas .xx. marcas non solverit ad terminos subscriptos, scilicet quinque marcas ad quindenam sancti Michaelis anno regni regis Edwardi nono et .v. marcas ad quindenam sancti Hyllarii proximo sequentem, et decem marcas ad quindenam Pasche proximo sequentem, tunc idem Johannes concedit pro se et heredibus suis quod predicte .xx. marce de terris et catallis suis fiant etc.

(1119)

Ebor'. Breve directum justiciariis[69]

(1120)

Essex'. Gilbertus Peche venit coram etc. et recognovit se debere Aaron filio Vyves judeo .x. marcas, reddendo eidem in octabis sancti Martini. Et, nisi fecerit, concedit quod de terris et catallis suis fiant etc.

(1121)[70]

Lond'. Adam de Fulham venit coram etc. et recognovit se recepisse de Aaron filio Vyves .xx. marcas ad opus magistri Radulfi cementarii, ita quod idem Radulfus levabit et construet quemdam domum ipsius Aaron in vico de Cattestrete in parochia sancti Laurencii in Judaismo London' citra Natale domini anno regni regis Edwardi decimo juxta convenciones habitas in quodam scripto [inter][71] ipsum Radulfum et Aaron, cui quidem scripto sigillum ipsius Ade et Radulfi est appensum. Et, nisi contruccio predicte domus se perfecerit per predictum magistrum Radulfum citra terminum supradictum, idem Adam concedit quod predicti .xx. marce de terris et catallis suis una cum dampnis que idem Aaron sustinuerit occasione predicte construccionis non consummate fiant et leventur.

(1122)

Isac filius Aaron judeus manucaptus per Aaron filium Isac et Pictavinum filium Aaron. Vyves le Petit manucaptus per Mosseum filium Jacobi et Benedictum filium Jacobi. Vyves filius Molle per Aaron filium Hake et Staunf'. Antera que fuit uxor Vyves le Long manucaptus per Jacobum le Clerk et Meyr nepotem L.[72]

MEMBRANE 3 DORSE

Adhuc de termino sancto Trinitatis anno regni regis Edwardi Nono

(1123)

Ebor'. Per breve domini regis directum justiciariis etc. in hec verba: 'Edwardus dei gracia rex Anglie, dominus Hybernie et dux Aquitanie justiciariis suis ad custodiam judeorum assignatis salutem. Cum nuper dederimus licenciam Henne filie Leonis judee de Ebor' et Elye filio ejus vendendi Henrico de Brylaunde quandam domum cum pertinenciis in Ebor', et idem Henricus domum suam adhuc non emerit, ut accepimus, vobis mandamus quod, si vobis constare possit ita esse, tunc predictos Hennam et Elyam domum suam predictam cum pertinenciis Roberto de Conteclive vendere et ipsum Robertum domum illam ab ipsis emere permittatis, nisi domus illa sit eschaeta nostra vel alio modo jus habeamus in eadem. Teste me ipso apud Westm' .x. die Junii anno regis nostri nono.' capta est inquisicio si predicti Elyas et Henna vendiderunt predictam domum, ut supradictum est, predicto Henrico de Brylaund' vel non, per Gamalielem de Oxon' et alios judeos, prout patet etc. Qui dicunt super sacramentum suum quod predicti Elyas et Henna nunquam vendiderunt predictam domum prefato Henrico nec instrumenta alicujus vendicionis ipsius domus erant confecta. Tamen verba convencionalia inita fuerunt inter eos, de quibus nulla sortiebatur vendicio, eo quod condiciones super forma illius vendicionis neuter ipsorum tenebat. Et quia compertum est per predictam inquisicionem quod predictus Elyas et Henna nullam vendicionem fecerunt predicto Henrico de predicta domo, consideratum est quod juxta formam brevis supradicti vendicionem predicte domus faciant Roberto de Conteclyve, si sibi viderint expedire.

(1124)

Surr'. Preceptum fuit vicecomiti quod venire faceret coram etc. a die sancte Trinitatis nunc[73] Henricum de Donelegh', Johannem servientem ejus, Alanum Paynot, Ricardum le Fruter, Willelmum de Bernewell', Robertum de le Stake et Johannem Russel ad respondendum Regi ex eo quod, cum Jorninus filius Abrahe, serviens Turris Lond', Aaron filius Elye et Mossevin de Doggestret' judei Lond' ducebant corpus Joscy de Geldeford' judei interfecti per vicum pupplicum de Suwerk', predictos judeos insultaverunt, verberaverunt et male tractaverunt et quoddam tabardum pro teolonio ab eis ceperunt et carettam, in qua corpus predicti judei

[69] *This entry is unfinished.*

[70] *This and the following entry are written on an additional sheet attached to the bottom of the membrane.*

[71] *MS.* in.

[72] *This name has been left unfinished*

[73] *Sic.*

[i]<defuncti>[i] ferebatur, evertebant et conculcabant contra pacem regis etc.

Et predicti Johannes serviens Henrici de Donelegh', Alanus Paynot, Ricardus le Fruter et Willelmus de Bernewelle veniunt et deffendunt vim etc., et dicunt quod predictos Jorninum, Aaron seu Mosseum judeos ducentes corpus predicti defuncti non insultaverunt nec aliquid mali eis fecerunt nec carettam in qua corpus dicti defuncti ferebatur evertebant, ut supradictum est. Et de hoc ponunt se super patriam. De tabardo dicunt quod ballivus domini regis de Suthwerk' illud pro teolonio domini regis cepit et illud adhuc penes se detinet de quo nullam deliberacionem facere possunt. Et hoc petunt quod inquiratur. Et preceptum est vicecomiti quod venire faciat coram etc. in octabis sancti Johannis Baptiste sex probos et legales homines de Suthwerk', per quos etc., et qui nulla affinitate etc., et constabulario Turris quod venire faciat ad eundem diem sex legales judeos de civitate Lond', ut supra, ad recognoscendum super premissis veritatem.

Ad quem diem inquisicio venit per Martinum Coleman, Johannem le Pestur et alios christianos, Mosseum de Doggestrete, Elyam de Cornhell' et alios judeos, sicut patet inter brevia hujus termini retornata. Qui dicunt super sacramentum suum quod Johannes serviens Henrici de Doneleye, Alanus Paynot, Johannes de Ponte cordewanarius per preceptum Henrici de Doneleye ballivi Sutwerk' cum multis aliis ignotis predictam carettam, in qua corpus predicti judei ferebatur, pro tollonio arestabant, evertebant et conculcabant et predictos judeos verberaverunt et male tractaverunt et quoddam tabardum ab eis pro dicto tollonio ceperunt, quod adhuc remanet in custodia Thome le Serjaunt ballivi consortis dicti Henrici, contra pacem regis, cum dicti judei nullum tollonium per totum regnum Anglie dare debeant. Ideo consideratum est quod predicti Johannes, Alanus et Johannes attachientur et in prisona custodiantur donec Regi et predictis judeis de predicta transgressione satisfecerint.

Et predictus Henricus de Donelegh', Robertus de la Stake et Johannes Russel non venerunt. Et vicecomes mandavit quod retornavit breve sibi inde directum ballivo libertatis archiepiscopi Cantuar' pro Henrico de Donelye, qui nichil inde responderunt. Judicium quod non omittat etc. et venire faciat coram etc. in octabis supradictis predictum Henricum ad respondendum Regi de placito predicto. Et mandavit quod Robertus de la Stake et Johannes Russel nichil habent in balliva sua et quod manent in civitate Lond'. Et preceptum est vicecomitibus quod venire faciat coram etc. ad eundem diem etc. Ad quem diem predictus Henricus attachiatus venit et deffendit vim etc. et recognovit quod caretta ferens corpus predicti defuncti arestata fuit per suos [blank] et socium suum conballivum Suthwerk' per comitem Warenn' pro duobus solidis quos habere debent et habere consueverunt de costuma de carettis corpora judeorum [i]<defunctorum>[i] portantibus, pro qua custuma ceperunt de dictis judeis dictum tabardum et vadium pro custuma predicta. Requisitus si quid habeat de Rege per quod recipere potest custumam de judeis dicit quod ballivi predecessores sui hoc fecerunt. Et quia nullum warentum habet de Rege per quod possit recipere custumam de judeis, cum omnes judei per totum regnum Anglie per cartam Regis quieti sint de omnimodis custumis, ideo dictus Henricus pro predicta transgressione committitur prisone donec Regi et predictis judeis inde satisfecerit.

(1125)

Essex'. Preceptum fuit vicecomiti quod levari faceret ad opus Regis de tenentibus terrarum que fuerunt Henrici de la Rokele de Wendenlaut et Johannis filii Johannis de Essigdon' .c. solidos et dimidium quarterium frumenti, quos Regi debent occasione predictarum terrarum quas tenent que fuerunt predictorum Johannis et Henrici de debitis Samuelis filii Ysac judei.

Johannes Passemer, tenens quandam partem terrarum que fuerunt predicti Henrici, venit et dicit quod non tenetur de dicto debito seu aliqua porcione ejusdem debiti respondere ex eo quod non tenet aliquas terras seu tenementa que predictus Henricus in Judaismo invadiare possit, quia ea tenuit secundum legem et consuetudinem regni[74] Anglie post mortem Duce uxoris sue et hoc petit quod inquiratur. Et preceptum est vicecomiti quod venire [faciat][75] coram etc. ad hunc diem .xij. probos et legales homines de visneto de Wandenlout per quos etc., et qui nulla affinitate etc., ad recognoscendum super premissis veritatem. Et inquisicio venit a die sancte Trinitatis in .xv. dies nunc per Radulfum Ernis et magistrum Gilbertum et alios, sicut patet inter brevia hujus termini retornata. Qui jurati dicunt super sacramentum suum quod predictus Henricus tenuit terras et tenementa que nunc Johannes Passemer tenet ad terminum vite sue secundum legem et consuetudinem regni Anglie post mortem predicte Duce uxoris sue, quas terras seu tenementa invadiare seu alienare non potuit nisi tantummodo dum vixerat, et post mortem dicti Henrici dicte terre et tenementa hereditarie descenderunt Roberto de la Rokele ut proximo heredi matris sue et ea tenuit ut proximus heres et postea idem Robertus.[76]

(1126)

Bed'. Preceptum fuit vicecomiti quod per sacramentum proborum et legalium hominum tam christianorum quam judeorum de balliva sua, per quos etc., diligenter inquireret que bona et catalla Josceus de Geldeford' judeus nuper interfectus habuit die quo interfectus fuit, ut in auro, argento, jocalibus, domibus, terris, redditibus et omnibus rebus aliis mobilibus et immobilibus extra archam cyrographariorum existentibus et ad quorum manus bona et catalla illa post mortem dicti Joscey devenerunt. Et vicecomes mandavit quod inquisicionem illam coram se inde cepit per sacramentum Walteri de

[74] *Followed in MS. by* Angli. [75] *MS. omits.*
[76] *This entry is unfinished.*

Runhey, Roberti le Mareschale et aliorum christianorum, Milonis de Luton' et Isaac le Eveske de Northt' et aliorum judeorum, sicud patet inter inquisiciones hujus termini retornatas. Qui dicunt quod dictus judeus non habet domos, terras nec tenementa die quo interfectus fuit, sed habuit bona mobilia ut in auro, argento, vadiis, jocalibus, cunis, vasis eneis et pannis ad valenciam .ij. marcarum, que omnia sunt in custodia Formose que fuit uxor dicti Joscey.

Summa .ij. marce, unde tercia pars Regis est .viij. solidi .xj. denarii.

Et predicta Formosa, que finem fecit cum Rege pro predictis catallis habendis, habet terminos solvendi predictos .viij. solidos et .xj. denarios ad terminos subscriptos, videlicet.[77]

(1127)[78]

Kanc. Preceptum fuit vicecomiti, sicud pluries, quod distringeret Jacobum Hunfrey de Romenhale per terras etc. ad reddendum sibi ad opus Regis .xv. libras quas Regi debet de debitis Salomonis de Staunford' judei Cantuar' dampnati, et denarios illos haberet coram etc.

Predictus Jacobus venit et recognovit se adhuc teneri in .x. libris de dicto debito .xv. librarum. Et habet terminos ad dictas .x. libras solvendas Aaron filio Vives judeo, cui istud debitum assignatum in recompensacionem debitorum in quibus Gilbertus Peche ei tenebatur, videlicet .c. solidos ad quindenam sancti Michaelis anno regni regis Edwardi nono, et .c. solidos ad quindenam Natalis Domini proximo sequentem super fidem suam ad dictos terminos observandum. Et de residuo dicti debiti .xv. librarum, videlicet de .c. solidis, dicit quod satisfecit predicto Salomoni antequam captus fuit pro tonsura monete pro qua suspensus fuit, dum idem judeus liberam habuit administracionem bonorum suorum, et inde habet starrum dicti judei de acquietancia dictorum .c. solidorum et hoc petit quod inquiratur. Et preceptum est vicecomiti quod venire faciat coram etc. a die sancti Michaelis in .xv. dies cyrographarios christianos et judeos arche cyrographariorum civitatis Cantuar', sex probos et legales homines et sex legales judeos de eadem civitate, per quos etc., et qui nulla etc., ad recognoscendum super premissis veritatem.

(1128)[79]

Omnibus Christi fidelibus presentem cartam visuris vel audituris Henna relicta Aaron quondam judei Ebor' et Elyas filius ejus salutem in domino. Noveritis nos dedisse, concessisse et hac presenti carta nostra confirmasse Roberto de Conesclyve civi Ebor' et Avice uxori ejus totam illam terram cum omnibus pertinenciis suis et cum omnibus domibus superedificatis sine aliquo retenemento que jacet in villa Ebor' in quodam videlicet vico qui vocatur Coningestrete, scilicet inter terram ecclesie beati Petri Ebor' quam Nicholaus Doggeheved quondam tenuit que vocatur Suwynlending' et extendit se a regia strata de Coningstrete usque ad aquam de Owse omnino ita integraliter, prout Leo judeus dictus episcopus vel Samuel filius ejus cum omnibus edificiis et aliis omnibus pertinenciis unquam habuerunt tempore eorum, habendum et tenendum de nobis et heredibus nostris predictis Roberto et Avicie et heredibus eorum vel assignatis quibuscumque libere, quiete, bene et in pace, hereditarie in feodo inperpetuum, reddendo inde annuatim nobis et heredibus nostris unam rosam ad festum Nativitatis sancti Johannis Baptiste, et faciendo capitalibus dominis feodi servicia inde debita et consueta pro omni servicio, exaccione et demanda. Et nos, predicti Henna et Elyas, et heredes nostri warantizabimus, acquietabimus et defendemus predictis Roberto et Avicie et eorum heredibus vel assignatis quibuscumque totam predictam terram cum omnibus domibus superedificatis et omnibus aliis pertinenciis suis, ut predictum est, contra omnes gentes christianos et judeos per predicta servicia in perpetuum. In cujus rei testimonium presentem cartam sigillorum nostrorum apposicione roboramus. Hiis testibus Johanne de Lydegraynes tunc vicecomiti Ebor', domino Hugone de Viene, Emgrameo de Estrus, Johanne Sampson de Ebor', Johanne le Especer, Johanne filio ejus, Stephano Wyles, Nicholao de Seleby, Roggero Basy, Johanne de Cantebr', Waltero Takel, Joricio le Flemming, Copino le Flemming, Thoma del Wak, Thoma Tabernario, Aaron judeo domini Edmundi, Bonamy judeo Ebor', Benedicto Crespin judeo et aliis.

MEMBRANE 4

Adhuc placita de quindena sancte Trinitatis anno regni regis Edwardi Nono

(1129)

Oxon'. Philippus Walensis fecit venire Belyam que fuit uxor Lumbardi de Oxon' judei et exigit ab ea quandam Summam Galfridi precii .xiiij. solidorum, quam predictis Lumbardo et Belye inpignoravit pro .xij. denariis dum idem Lumbarus vixerat, et post mortem dicti Lumbardi sepe fuit ad domum dicte Belye et optulit ei dictos .xij. denarios pro predicta Summa pro tanta pecunia impignorata. Et predicta Belya recognovit sepius ei penes se predictam Summam habere et quod eam dicto Philippo habere faceret et hucusque dictam Summam ei injuste detinet ad dampnum suum .x. solidorum, et hoc offert se etc.

Predicta Belya sine brevi venit et deffendit vim etc., et dicit quod post mortem dicti Lumbardi quondam viri sui dictam Summam ad manus suas non devenit nec aliquam recognicionem ei inde fecit post mortem dicti Lumbardi. Et hoc petit quod inquiratur. Et quod predictam

[77] *This entry is unfinished.*

[78] *Above the first line of this entry and opposite the marginal heading is another erased line.*

[79] *This entry is written on an additional sheet attached to the bottom of the membrane.*

Summam penes se habuit post mortem dicti Lumbardi, dictus Philippus petit similiter quod inquiratur. Et preceptum est vicecomiti quod per sacramentum proborum et legalium hominum tam christianorum quam judeorum, nisi Adam de Winton' clericus prius ad partes illas venerit, diligenter inquirat etc. et inquisicionem illam etc. scire faciat justiciariis etc. a die sancti Michaelis in .xv. dies etc.

(1130)

Linc'. [i]<Ricardus>[i] rector ecclesie de Algarkerke pro pluribus defaltis in misericordia.[80] Idem Ricardus attachiatus ad respondendum Regi de porcione ipsum contingente occasione quarumdam parcium terrarum quas tenet que fuerunt magistri Thome de Cappelade de quodam debito .xlvj. librarum in quibus idem magister Thomas Regi tenebatur de debito Abrahe filii Muryele venit et de porcione dicti debiti ipsum inde contingente occasione predictarum terrarum etc. vocat ad warantum Edmundum de Cappelade quod ipsum inde acquietare debet. Et predictus Edmundus, qui presens fuit, venit et dictum Ricardum de porcione sua warantizat. Ideo consideratum est quod predictus Ricardus eat inde quietus et dictus Edmundus de porcione sua oneratus. Et preceptum est vicecomiti quod predicto Ricardo de predicto debito pacem habere permittat.

(1131)

Linc'. Edmundus de Cappelade optulit se quarto die versus Hawysiam Chaumpeneys de Sutterton', Thomam filium Alani Fabri de eadem, Isoldam Chaumpeneys de eadem, Johannem filium Alexandri de Cappelade, et Sarram filiam Roberti le Blunt, tenentes quasdam partes terrarum que fuerunt magistri Thome de Cappelade, de placito acquietacionis debiti. Et ipsi non venerunt. Et preceptum [fuit][81] vicecomiti quod ipsos [distringeret][82] per terras etc. et quod haberet corpora eorum coram etc. Et vicecomes mandavit quod breve sibi inde directum adeo tarde venit quod exequi non potuit. Ideo, sicut alias, in tribus septimanis sancti Michaelis etc.

(1132)

Linc'. Jorninus filius Abrahe judeus optulit se quarto die versus Walterum le Marescal, Simonem le Botoner, Thomam Fabrum, tenentes terras que fuerunt Willelmi le Mareschal de Stowe, de placito debiti. Et ipsi non venerunt. Et preceptum fuit vicecomiti quod ipsos distringeret per terras etc. et quod haberet corpora eorum coram etc. Et vicecomes mandavit quod Johannes Wyner de [blank], Johannes Kok de eadem, Willelmus persone de eadem et Henricus le Mazon manuceperunt predictum Walterum. Et sunt exitus terrarum predicti Walteri .xl. solidi.[83] Et quod Wilellmus Faber de Stowe, Rogerus Bernard de eadem, Robertus Kokes de eadem et Willelmus Monde de eadem manuceperunt predictum Simonem; et sunt exitus terrarum predicti Simonis .x. solidi.[84] Et quod Thomas filius Roberti de Stretton', Henricus filius Martini de eadem, Jordanus filius Radulfi de eadem et Robertus filius Juette de eadem manuceperunt predictum Thomam, quem non habuerunt. Ideo in misericordia.[85] Et sunt exitus terrarum predicti Thome .x. solidi.[86] Judicium quod distringat per terras etc., ita quod nec ipsi etc., et quod de exitibus etc., et habeat corpora eorum coram etc. a die sancti Michaelis in .xv. [dies][87] ad respondendum etc., et ad audiendum etc.

(1133)

Devon'. Petrus de Grenham per attornatum suum optulit se quarto die versus Warinum de Sechevile, quondam vicecomitem Devon', de placito injuste ejeccionis manerii sui de Weborneford'. Et ipse non venit. Et preceptum fuit vicecomiti quod non omitteret propter libertatem de Witeringe quin eam etc. et distringeret predictum Warinum per terras etc. et haberet corpus ejus coram etc. ad hunc diem. Et vicecomes mandavit quod Osmundus le Someter et Galfridus Bozoun manuceperunt predictum Warinum, quem non habuerunt. Ideo in misericordia.[88] Judicium, sicud alias, quod non omitteret propter libertatem predictam etc., et distringat predictum Warinum per terras etc., ita quod nec ipse etc., et quod de exitibus etc., et quod habeat corpus ejus coram etc. a die sancti Michaelis in tres septimanas ad respondendum predicto Petro de predicto placito; et ad audiendum etc. Et sunt exitus terrarum predicti Warini .v. solidi.[89] Et preceptum est vicecomiti quod dictos .v. solidos habeat ad eundem diem etc.

(1134)

Surr', Sussex'. Magister Elyas filius magistri Mossey judeus per attornatum suum optulit se quarto die versus Robertum Agelun de placito debiti. Et ipse non venit. Et preceptum fuit vicecomiti quod ipsum distringeret per terras etc. et quod haberet corpus ejus coram etc. ad hunc diem. Et vicecomes mandavit quod Willelmus prepositus de Adinton', Willelmus le Fox juvenis, Radulfus Lok de eadem, Alexander Rossel de eadem, Galfridus Sovereyn de eadem et Johannes Gengel de eadem manuceperunt predictum Robertum, quem non habuerunt. Ideo in misericordia.[90] Judicium, sicud alias, quod distringat per terras etc., ita quod nec ipse etc., et quod de exitibus etc., et quod habeat corpus ejus coram etc. a die sancti Michaelis in tres septimanas ad respondendum predicto judeo de placito predicto; et ad audiendum etc. Et nulli sunt exitus terrarum predicti Roberti, prout significavit.

[80] *The word* misericordia *is repeated in the margin.*
[81] *MS. reads* est.
[82] *MS. reads* distringat.
[83] *The words* exitus .xl. solidi *are repeated in the margin.*
[84] *The words* exitus .x. solidi *are repeated in the margin.*
[85] *The word* misericordia *is repeated in the margin.*
[86] *The words* exitus .x. solidi *are repeated in the margin.*
[87] *MS. omits.*
[88] *The word* misericordia *is repeated in the margin.*
[89] *The words* exitus .v. solidi *are repeated in the margin.*
[90] *The word* misericordia *is repeated in the margin.*

(1135)

Lond'. Mosseus de Doggestrete et Bona uxor ejus attachiati ad respondendum Matildi la Megre de placito injuste detencionis vadiorum; et unde queritur quod, cum eis et Belaset [blank] invadiasset septem ulnas de burnetto precii ulne .iij. solidorum pro sex solidis die martis proxima post festum sancti Benedicti anno regni regis Edwardi nono sub hac condicione, videlicet quod quacumque die infra quindenam post invadiacionem predictam predictis judeis de dictis sex solidis satisfaceret, dictum vadium ei libaretur pro predictis sex solidis, infra quam quindenam predicta Matillis venit ad domum dictorum judeorum et optulit eis predictos sex solidos et predicta Belasez tres solidos inde recepit pro tribus solidis quos eidem Matillidi super predictum vadium accomodaverat. Et predicti Mosseus et Bona alios tres solidos recipere recusabant, exigentes ab ea .x. solidos de catallo et lucro pro predictis .iij. solidis contra statutum regis, et vadium suum reddere contradicebant nisi pro eo dictos .x. solidos reddere volebat et ad huc dictum vadium ei injuste detinent ad dampnum suum .xl. librarum et contra statuta regis et hoc offert verificare.

Predicti Mosseus et Bona venerunt et deffendunt vim etc. et negant precise et dicunt quod de dicta Matillide nichil receperunt nec aliquid de bonis suis penes se habent ex tradicione dicte Matillidis set predicta Belasez eis quoddam pannum burneti pro octo solidis et novem denariis invadiavit et pro predictis .viij. solidis et .ix. denariis pro quibus dictus pannus invadiatus fuit prompti fuerunt dictum pannum eidem Matildi reddere. Et quod pro tanta peccunie summa dictus pannus invadiatus fuit, petunt quod justiciarii inquirant de dicta Belasez, que presens fuit coram etc. Dicit quod una vice dicta Matildis peciit quod accomodaret ei .v. solidos super pannum predictum que tunc dictam pecuniam non habuit et peciit a Bona uxore dicti Mossey ut medietatem dictorum .v. solidorum secum eidem Matildi super vadium predictum accomodaret, que Bona tunc eidem Matildi super vadium predictum accomodavit .ij. solidos et .vj. denarios et ipsa Belasez .ij. solidos et .vj. denarios. Et alia vice super idem vadium eedem Bona et Belasez accomodaverunt eidem Matildii .xij. denarios, ita quod in universo ab eis habuit .vj. solidos de quibus .iij. solidi fuerunt predicte Bone et .iij. solidi dicte Belasez pro quibus dictum pannum ambabus invadiavit. Et dicta Belasez dicit quod dicebat predictis Mosseo et Bone quod eidem Matildi pannum supradictum pro .iij. solidis quos eidem Matilidi accomodaverant deliberarent quia ipsi Belasez de tribus solidis satisfecit et ipsi dictum pannum reddere contradicebant nisi eis dicta Matillis pro dicto panno .x. solidos reddere volebat. Et quia convictum est per veredictum dicte Belasez, super quam dicti Mosseus et Bona uxor sua se posuerunt, quod dicta Matilda super pannum predictum debuit eis .viij. solidos et .ix. denarios, quod non accomodavit ab eis nisi .iij. solidos pro quibus exigebant .x. solidos nomine usure contra statuta regis, predicti Mosseus et Bona committuntur prisone Turris Lond' salvo custodiendum, donec Regi de dicta transgressione satisfecerint. Et dictus pannus eidem Matilidi pro tribus solidis, ut supradictum est, mutuatis liberatur.

(1136)

Kanc'. Walterus de Chitelcroft venit coram etc. et recognovit se debere Aaron filio Vyves judeo .cc. quarteria frumenti vel dimidiam marcam pro quolibet quarterio reddendo eidem judeo a die sancti Michaelis in quindecim dies. Et, nisi fecerit, concedit quod de terris et catallis suis fiant, ad quorumcumque manus devenerunt.

(1137)

Oxon'. Manserus de Brackele judeus, qui tulit breve regis de placito debiti super Petrum de Wymburn', non est prosecutus versus eum. Ideo ipse Manserus, pro se et plegiis suis de prosequendo, in misericordia.[91] Et preceptum fuit vicecomiti quod non omitteret propter libertatem ville Oxon' quin eam etc. et venire faceret coram etc. predictum [Petrum.][92] Et vicecomes mandavit quod Johannes Spryng et Walterus de Keneby de Oxon' manuceperunt predictum Petrum, quem non habuerunt. Ideo in misericordia.[93]

(1138)

Oxon'. Mosseus filius Jacobi judeus, qui tulit breve regis de placito arreragiorum redditus assise super Robertum de Driffelt et Aliciam uxorem ejus, non est prosecutus versus eos. Ideo ipse Mosseus et plegii sui de prosequendo, videlicet Cok' Hagyn et Sampson filius Isac de Wygorn' judei, in misericordia.[94] Et preceptum fuit vicecomiti quod venire faceret coram etc. predictos Robertum et Aliciam. Et vicecomes mandavit quod Hugo le Hore et Philippus le Serjant de Oxon' manuceperunt predictos Robertum et Aliciam, quos non habuerunt. Ideo in misericordia etc.[95] Postea dictus Mosseus petit licenciam recedendi de brevi suo et habet. Et misericordia dicti Mossei et manucaptorum suorum condonatur per justiciarios etc.

(1139)

Bed'. Simon Pertesoyl pro pluribus defaltis in misericordia.

Belya de Bed' venire fecit Simonem de Pertesoyl tenentem terras etc. que fuerunt Rogeri Pertesoyl patris sui et exigit ab eo .lvj. marcas, quas ei debet occasione predictarum etc., per duo cyrographa, unum .xx. marcarum et aliud .xxxvj. marcarum sub nominibus predictorum Rogeri et Belye, unde altere partes depredate fuerunt tempore turbacionis regni Anglie per inimicos regis et asportate in insulam Eliensem, ut dicitur.

Predictus Simon venit et petit diem premeditandi et habet a die sancti Michaelis in unum mensem.

91 *The word* misericordia *is repeated in the margin.*
92 *MS. reads* Philippum.
93 *The word* misericordia *is repeated in the margin.*
94 *The word* misericordia *is repeated in the margin.*
95 *The word* misericordia *is repeated in the margin.*

(1140)

Buk'. Robertus filius Nigelli venit coram etc. et recognovit se debere Aaron filio Vyves judeo centum quarteria frumenti vel dimidiam marcam pro quolibet quarterio reddendo eidem judeo in crastino Animarum anno regni regis Edwardi nono. Et, nisi fecerit, concedit pro se et heredibus suis quod de terris et catallis suis fiant etc.

MEMBRANE 4 DORSE

Adhuc Memoranda

(1141)

Bed, Buk'. Warinus de Dene pro pluribus defaltis in misericordia.

Benedictus de Bedeford' judeus per Sampsonem de Wygorn' attornatum suum venire fecit eundem Warinum de Dene et exigit ab eo .xl. solidos quos ei debet, sicut continetur in quodam scripto obligatorio inter eos inde confecto et sigillo dicti Warini signato, quos .xl. solidos hucusque eidem injuste detinet ad dampnum suum .xx. solidorum, quod scriptum protulit coram etc.

Predictus Warinus venit et defendit vim etc. et dicit quod nichil dicto Benedicto debet per dictum scriptum nec in aliquo debito ei tenetur et quod maliciose dictum scriptum nomine suo fecit et illud quodam sigillo sibi ignoto signari ex eo quod nunquam aliquid inde scivit nec sigillum suum dicto scripto est appositum nec aliquod aliud sigillum pro eo. Et hoc petit quod inquiratur. Et predictus Benedictus per attornatum suum dicit quod dictum scriptum de dicto debito ei fecit et illud sigillo suo signavit et petit similiter quod inquiratur. Et preceptum est vicecomiti quod venire faciat coram etc. a die sancti Michaelis in unum mensem sex probos et legales homines de visneto de Dene et sex legales judeos de villa Bedef', per quos etc., et qui nulla affinitate etc., ad recognoscendum super premissis veritatem etc.

(1142)

Hereford'. Abraham le Prestre per essoniatorem suum optulit se quarto die versus Johannem Lovekyn, Julianam uxorem ejus, Johannem fratrem dicti Johannis, Johannem Laur', Aliciam uxorem ejus et Walterum le Chapeleyn de placito debiti. Et ipsi non venerunt. Et preceptum fuit vicecomiti quod non omitteret propter libertatem Hereford' quin eam etc. et ipsos venire faceret coram etc. hic. Et vicecomes mandavit quod Johannes Lovekin, Juliana uxor ejus, Johannes frater dicti Johannis Lovekin, Johannes Laur' et Alicia uxor ejus nichil habent per quod possint distringi. De ipsis, sicut alias, quod non omittat etc. et quod distringat predictum Walterum per terras etc., ita quod nec ipse etc., et quod de exitibus etc. et quod habeat corpus ejus coram etc. a die sancti Michaelis in unum mensem ad respondendum etc. et ad audiendum etc.

(1143)

Hereford'. Mosseus filius Abrahe judeus de Hereford' optulit se quarto die versus Robertum le Parchiminer, Ricardum le Teynturer de placito detencionis catallorum. Et ipsi non venerunt. Et preceptum fuit vicecomiti quod ipsos venire faceret coram etc. hic. Et viecomes mandavit quod ballivi libertatis Heref', quibus istud breve retornatum fuit, sibi responderunt quod Petrus Irinmangour et Willelmus le Parchiminur manuceperunt Robertum le Parchiminur, quem non habuerunt. Ideo in misericordia. Judicium quod distringat per terras etc., et quod habeat corpus ejus coram etc. a die sancti Michaelis in unum mensem ad respondendum etc. Et quod multi sunt in civitate Hereford' qui vocantur hoc nomine, Ricardus le Teynturer, et nullum eorum attachiaverunt veniendi hic ad hunc diem. Ideo ipsi ballivi in misericordia, videlicet Johannes le Gaunter et Willelmus Godknave. Et preceptum est vicecomiti, sicut alias, quod predictum Ricardum venire faciat coram etc. ad diem supradictum ad respondendum predicto Mosseo de predicto placito etc.

(1144)

London'. Memorandum quod Meyr nepos Belasez venit coram etc. et recognovit se debere magistro et fratribus Domus Conversorum London' novem marcas sterlingorum percipendas de debitis ipsius Meyr quamcito per brevia domini regis possunt levari de debitis suis. Et idem magister et fratres per istam recognicionem concedunt quod, receptis predictis novem marcis de debitis ipsius Meyr ut predictum est, idem Meir liberam administracionem habeat de residuo debitorum suorum et insuper quietum clamarunt et perdonarunt predicto Meyr omnem forisfactionem debitorum suorum quam nuper calumpniarunt sibi adjudicari ex concessione Regis etc. occasione cujusdam concelamenti de quo convictus erat etc.

MEMBRANE 5

Adhuc Memoranda de termino sancte Trinitatis

(1145)

Kanc'. Robertus de Hardres miles venit coram etc. et recognovit se debere Aaron filio Vyves judeo centum libras reddendas ad quindenam sancti Michaelis anno regni regis Edwardi nono. Et, nisi fecerit, concedit quod de terris et catallis suis et heredum et tenencium terrarum suarum etc.

Idem Robertus venit coram etc. et recognovit se debere prefato Aaron ducentas marcas, reddendo inde quinque marcas anno regni regis Edwardi nono, et .v. marcas ad .xv. Pasche anno regni regis Edwardi .x.º. Et sic de anno in annum decem marcas ad predictos terminos quousque dictas ducentas marcas plene persolvent. Et, nisi fecerit, concedit pro se, et heredibus et tenentibus terrarum suarum in quorumcumque manus devenerint fiant etc.[96]

[96] *The word* Samps' *is written at the end of the line after a large blank space.*

(1146)

Lond'. Memorandum quod cum Hamo Hauteyn peteret versus Deudonem le Orfevre et Willelmum le Herevy, executores testamenti Hervey le Ferun, quasdam cartas et scripta que ad ipsum pertinent racione tenementi sui quod habet in cyvitate Lond', idem Deudone et Willelmus venerunt in pleno scaccario et differebant duo scrinia sigillo Gregorii de Rokesle tunc majoris Lond' consignata, quorum unum scrinium fractum erat antequam deferebatur in scaccario et per eundem Gregorium sigillo suo [reconsignatum,][97] que quidem scrinia in pleno scaccario aperiebantur et in uno eorundem scriniorum fracto et postea consignato inventa sunt scripta subscripta, videlicet unum in quo continetur quod Alanus abbas et conventus sancti Stephani Cadamensis tradiderunt et consesserunt et carta capituli sui confirmarunt Ricardo Aurifabro filio Henrici totum mesuagium [i]<apud>[i] Lond' quod Brand' clericus de eis tenuit in parochia sancti Petri apud Wodestrete, habendum sibi et heredibus suis inperpetuum; et unum in quo continetur quod Walterus filius Johannis quietum clamavit et carta sua confirmavit Gervasio Alutario quicquid juris habuit in quadam selda sua in parochia sancti Petri Lond', habendum sibi et heredibus suis inperpetuum; et una carta in qua continetur quod Gervasius Alutarius civis et aldirmannus Lond' dedit, concessit et carta sua confirmavit magistro Johanni Rosamund totam terram suam cum omnibus super edificatis quam habuit retro seldas suas in foro in parochia sancti Petri de Wodestrete, habenda sibi et heredibus suis inperpetuum; et unum scriptum in quo continetur quod Jordanus filius Walteri Burlyman alutarius Lond' vendidit et quietumclamavit Herveo le Ferun et heredibus suis totam terram suam cum domibus superedificatis quam habuit in parochia sancti Petri de Wodestr' in Lond', habendum sibi et heredibus suis inperpetuum; et unum scriptum in quo continetur quod Cristina relicta quondam Walteri Burlyman alutarii Lond' in viduitate sua vendidit et quietum clamavit Herveo le Ferun et heredibus suis totam terram suam cum domibus superedificatis quod habuit in eadem, habendum et tenendum sibi et heredibus suis inperpetuum. Que quidem carta et scripta liberata fuerunt dicto Hamoni in pleno scaccario eo quod tangebant predictum tenementum suum. Et una carta de novo confecta que fuit in eodem scrinio in qua continetur quod magister Johannes Rosamund dedit, concessit et carta sua confirmavit Herveo le Ferun et Sabine uxori sue totum capitale managium suum cum pertinenciis in Wodestrete in parochia sancti Petri, quod managium predictum cum pertinenciis fuit Ricardi patris sui et Rosamunde matris sue, habendum et tenendum dictis Herveo et Sabine et heredibus de dicta Sabina exeuntibus in perpetuum, reddendum inde annuatim dominis feodi debita servicia; et una carta in qua continetur quod Johanna Rosamund dedit, concessit et carta sua confirmavit Radulfo filio Hervey Lond' viginti quinque solidos annui redditus percipiendum de terris et domibus superedificatis quod Stephanus Cyssor de ipsa tenuit extra Crepilgate in parochia sancti Egidii; item dedit, concessit et carta sua confirmavit Radulfo filio Hervey decem solidos annui et quieti redditus ad quatuor anni terminos principales pro equali porcione percipiendos de toto tenemento quod tenet Herveus le Ferrun in parochia de Fanechirch, habendum et tenendum sibi et heredibus suis libere, quiete etc. Et, si contingat quod dictus Radulfus [infra][98] religionem vel sine herede de se obierit, vult et concedit quod predictus redditus Johanni et Godefrido fratribus predicti Radulfi sine alicujus contradiccione vel impedimento revertant. Et inter eos pro equali porcione dividantur.

Et in eodem scrinio inventa est una pixis in qua est testamentum Matilde Flael cum una carta quam idem Matilda fecit Johanni filio Hervey de feofamento cujusdam domus in cyvitate Lond' apud Stanigecherche versus Alegate.[99]

Et in alio scrinio [i]<integro et consignato>[i] inventa est una carta quod Willelmus filius Benedicti vendidit Gervasio Barn' unam seldam in Wodestrate.

Et una carta quod Johannes Rosamund dedit, concessit et hac presenti carta sua confirmavit Herveo le Ferun et Sabine uxori sue et Godefrido filio eorundem totum capitale mesuagium suum cum pertinenciis suis in Wodestrate in parochia sancti Petri inter dictam ecclesiam versus austrum et managium Edmundi filii Roberti de Basinges versus aquilonem cum illa placia terre quam emit de Gervasio Barn versus occidentem et viam regiam de Wodestrate versus orientem, quod managium predictum fuit Ricardi patris sui et Rosamunde matris sue, habendum et tenendum dicto Herveo et dicte Sabine uxori sue quoad vixerint et dicto Godefrido filio eorundem Hervei et Sabine in feodo, jure et hereditarie, libere, quiete, bene et in pace inperpetuum, reddendo inde annuatim sibi et heredibus suis sive assignatis suis unam rosam ad festum sancti Johannis Baptiste et dominis feodi[100] servicium debitum et consuetum pro omni servicio, consuetudine et demanda. Et predictus Johannes et heredes sui assignati sui predictum mesuagium cum pertinenciis suis dicto Herveo et dicte Sabine quo ad vixerint et dicto Godefrido filio dictorum Hervei et Sabine, ut predictum est, per predicta servicia [warentizabunt, defendent et acquietabunt][101] contra omnes homines christianos et judeos inperpetuum. Et ut hec sua donacio et presentis carte sue confirmacio rata et stabilis et inconcussa permaneat huic presenti scripto sigillum suum inpressione roboravit. Hiis testibus domino Radulfo Hardel, tunc majore London', Thoma filio Thome, Mattheo [Bokerel][102] tunc vicecomitibus London', Ricardo de Ewelle tunc aldermanno ejusdem garde, Ada de Benetleye, Alano de Benetleye, Petro de

97 *MS. reads* recongnacum.

98 *MS. reads* extra.

99 *There is a finger in the margin pointing to this paragraph.*

100 *Folowed in MS. by* debitum.

101 *MS. reads* warantizabit, defendet et acquietabit.

102 *MS. reads* Pokerel *but the initial letter has been altered.*

Standon', Roberto de Wynton', Willelmo de Farindon', Nicholao Hardel, Deodato Aurifabro, Galfrido de Sancto Albano, Nicholao le Convers, Waltero le Mareschal, Ricardo de Kirkested, Johanne le Ferun, Rogero de Caunterbir', Johanne de la Cornere, Rogero de Bristehulle, Elya de Cicestr', Johanne le Barbour, Godefrido le Hurdlere, Roberto Skeleman, Willelmo filio Henrici, Elya le Bedel, magistro Godefrido de sancto Dunstano. Et multis aliis.

Que quidem carte similiter liberantur dicto Hamone eo quod tangebant predictum tenementum suum; et omnia alia scripta et carte in eisdem scrineis inventa retradita fuerunt predictis Deudon' et Willelmo sigillo capitali de scaccario judeorum consignata.

MEMBRANE 5 DORSE

[blank]

MEMBRANE 6

Essonia de octabis sancte Trinitatis ad scaccarium judeorum anno regni regis Edwardi Nono, Nono, Nono

(1147)

Cantebr'. Johannes Portehors versus Josceum filium Sauloti judeum de placito debiti per Thomam de Newynham.

Johannes Lewyn versus eundem Josceum de eodem placito per Willelmum de Kyngeston'.

Henricus de Berton' versus eundem Josceum de eodem placito per Andream de Fluete.

(1148)

Leyc'. Frater Johannes de Herdeling', magister domus sancti Lazari de Borton', versus Johannem Fleg' de placito debiti, unde jurata, per Johannem le Careter.

(1149)

Hereford'. Sarra de Hereford' versus Lucam de Bergeveny et alios in brevi de placito debiti per Thomam le Messager.

(1150)

Essex'. Ricardus de Wytham, attornatus abbatis de Stratford', versus magistrum Eliam judeum de placito debiti per Rogerum de Kyngton'.

(1151)

Cantebr'. Rogerus Mauniaunt de Karleton' versus Josceum filium Sauloti judeum de placito debiti per Johannem de Norht'.

(1152)

Sutht'. Robertus de Harhulle versus Kokerel filium Likorice judeum de placito debiti per Robertum de Staunford'.

Johanna uxor dicti Roberti versus eundem judeum de eodem.

Robertus filius Rogeri, quem prior Sancte Fidis vocavit ad warantum versus Alienoram Reginam Anglie consortem Regis, de placito debiti per Johannem le Norman.

(1153)

Salop, Heref'. Johannes filius Aeri.[103]

MEMBRANE 6 DORSE

(1154)

Kanc'. Floria que fuit uxor Mossei le Graunt ponit loco suo Mosseum le Petyt de fine faciendo pro catallis viri sui habendis.

MEMBRANE 7

Placita ad scaccarium judeorum de termino sancte Trinitatis anno regni regis Edwardi Nono

(1155)

Lond'. Johannes de Axebrigg' optulit se quarto die versus Walterum de Oxon' alutarium Lond' de placito transgressionis. Et ipse non venit post diem amoris. Ideo consideratum est quod dictus Walterus distringatur per terras etc., ita quod nec ipse etc., et quod de exitibus etc., et quod habeant corpus ejus coram etc. in octabis sancti Johannis Baptiste ad respondendum et ad audiendum etc.

(1156)

Essex'. Saerus Hay per attornatum suum optulit se quarto die versus Hardewynum Spyht de placito quod ei reddat decem marcas quas ei tradidit in deposito custodiendas ad ipsum inde de Judaismo acquietandum. Et ipse non venit. Et preceptum fuit vicecomiti quod ipsum venire faceret coram etc. ad hunc diem. Et vicecomes mandavit quod retornavit breve sibi inde directum ballivis libertatis de Waltham, qui nichil inde fecerunt. Judicium quod non omittat propter libertatem predictam etc., et venire faciat coram etc. a die sancti Johannis Baptiste in .xv. dies predictum Hardewynum ad respondendum predicto Saero de predicto placito etc.

(1157)

Meyr filius Gamalielis judeus optulit se quarto die versus Laurencium Hardel, tenentem terras que fuerunt Jollani de Cokham, de placito debiti. Et ipse non venit. Et preceptum fuit vicecomiti quod ipsum distringeret per terras etc., ita quod nec ipse etc., et quod de exitibus etc. et quod haberet corpus ejus coram etc. ad hunc diem. Et vicecomes mandavit quod Ricardus filius Willelmi de Terling', Willelmus filius Roberti de eadem, Radulfus

[103] *This entry is unfinished.*

Mouner de eadem et Nicholaus le Hurd' de eadem manuceperunt predictum Laurencium, quem non habuerunt. Ideo in misericordia.[104] Et quia vicecomes nichil respondit de exitibus terrarum predicti Laurencii, ideo ipse vicecomes, videlicet [blank], in misericordia.[105] Et preceptum est vicecomitibus Lond', in quorum balliva manet, sicut alias, quod predictum Laurencium distringant per terras etc., et quod nec ipse etc., et quod de exitibus etc., et quod habeant corpus ejus coram etc. a die sancti Johannis Baptiste in .xv. dies ad respondendum predicto judeo de predicto placito etc. et ad audiendum etc.

(1158)

Heref'. Sarra vidua judea per essoniatorem suum optulit se quarto die versus Lucam de Bergeveny, Dyonisiam uxorem ejus, Robertum de Wyteshale et Agnetem uxorem ejus de placito detencionis catallorum.

Predictus Lucas per attornatum suum pro se et uxore sua venit et datus est eis dies a die sancti Michaelis in .xv. dies.

Et predicti Robertus et Agnes non venerunt. Et preceptum fuit vicecomiti, sicud alias, quod non omitteret propter libertatem Hereford' et ipsos distringeret per terras etc. et quod haberet corpora eorum coram etc. ad hunc diem. Et vicecomes mandavit quod Johannes Hotthe et Thomas de Ideshale manuceperunt predictos Robertum et Agnetem, quos non habuerunt. Ideo in misericordia.[106] Judicium, sicut pluries, quod non omitteret propter libertatem etc. et distringat per terras etc., ita quod nec ipsi etc., et quod de exitibus etc., et quod habeat corpora eorum coram etc. a die sancti Michaelis in .xv. dies ad respondendum etc. et ad audiendum etc.

(1159)

Hereford'. Walterus Balun, qui tulit breve compoti super Aaron le Blunt judeum Hereford', non est prosecutus versus eum. Ideo ipse Walterus in misericordia.[107] Et ipse Aaron inde sine die.

(1160)

Surr', Sussex'. Walterus de Wouborn' optulit se quarto die versus Rogerum le Meyne, Laurencium le Bakere de Blechesworthe <de placito>[108] debiti et injuste detencionis catallorum. Et ipsi non venerunt. Et preceptum fuit, sicut alias, quod ipsos venire faceret. Et vicecomes mandavit quod Johannes le Mestre de Blechchingele et Ricardus le Lepere de eadem manuceperunt Laurencium le Bakere, quem non habuerunt. Ideo in misericordia.[109] Judicium quod distringat per terras etc., ita quod nec ipsi etc., et quod de exitibus etc., et quod habeat corpora eorum coram etc. a die sancti Johannis Baptiste[110] ad respondendum etc. et ad audiendum etc.

(1161)

Essex', Hertford'. Johannes de Caunvile, qui tulit breve regis de placito debiti super Walterum de Stivekele, Willelmum de Bradefeld, Erardum le Parker, Galfridum Corpul, Johannem Besse, Ricardum de Sucherche militem et Rogerum de Cogeshale, non est prosecutus versus eos. Ideo ipse Johannes in misericordia.[111] Et predicti Walterus et alii prenominati non venerunt. Et preceptum fuit vicecomiti quod ipsos venire faceret coram etc. Et vicecomes mandavit quod Walterus de Stivekele non est de balliva sua, Johannes de Esse mortuus est, Galfridus Corpil et Ricardus Sucherch' et Rogerus de Cogeshale nichil habent in balliva sua per quod possint distringi. Et quod Petrus Bonde et Willelmus Mariot manuceperunt Willelmum de Bradefeud; et quod Edmundus de Bradefeud et Willelmus Gunild manuceperunt Everardum Parkere, quos non habuerunt. Ideo in misericordia.[112]

(1162)

Essex'. Robertus de Ludham optulit se quarto die versus Willelmum ⁱ<de>ⁱ Appelford et Johannem de Appelford de placito transgressionis. Et ipsi non venerunt. Et preceptum fuit vicecomiti quod ipsos venire faceret coram etc. ad hunc diem. Et vicecomes mandavit quod breve sibi inde directum adeo tarde venit quod exequi non potuit. Ideo, sicut alias, a die sancti Michaelis in .xv. dies.

(1163)

Wiltes'. Preceptum fuit vicecomiti quod venire faceret coram etc. ad hunc diem Johannem de Pateneye, filium et heredem Nicholai de Pateneye, ad respondendum Salomoni filio Simonis judeo de placito debiti. Et ipse non venit. Et vicecomes mandavit quod Willelmus Acreman et Adam de Oxon' manuceperunt predictum Johannem, quem non habuerunt. Ideo in misericordia. Judicium quod distringat etc.

(1164)

Wiltes'. Daunzele que fuit uxor Jacobi de Shafton' judei optulit se quarto die versus Radulfum du Boys de placito transgressionis. Et ipse non venit. Et preceptum fuit vicecomiti quod ipsum attachiaret, ita quod haberet corpus ejus coram etc. ad hunc diem. Et vicecomes mandavit quod dictus Radulfus nichil habet in balliva sua per quod possit distringi nec corpus ejus fuit inventum post recepcionem hujus brevis. Ideo, sicut alias, a die sancti Michaelis in .xv. dies.

(1165)

Lond'. Manserus filius Aaron per attornatum suum optulit se quarto die versus Deutetum Gillame, tenentem

[104] *The word* misercordia *is repeated in the margin.*
[105] *The word* vicecomes in misericordia *are in the margin.*
[106] *The word* misericordia *is repeated in the margin.*
[107] *The word* misericordia *is repeated in the margin.*
[108] *These words are repeated in MS.*
[109] *The word* misericordia *is repeated in the margin.*
[110] *Sic.*
[111] *The word* misericordia *is repeated in the margin.*
[112] *The word* misericordia *is repeated in the margin.*

quandam partem terrarum que fuerunt Ade de Novo Mercato, de placito debiti. Et ipse non venit. Et preceptum fuit vicecomitibus quod ipsum distringerent per terras etc., ita quod haberent corpus ejus coram etc. Et vicecomes mandavit quod predictus Deutettus districtus est per terras et catalla sua, set nulli exitus inde proveniebant post recepcionem brevis; et quod corpus ejus non fuit inventum in balliva sua post recepcionem brevis. Ideo, sicut alias, a die sancti Johannis Baptiste in .xv. dies.

(1166)

Northt'. Adam de la Fermerie et Matilda uxor ejus optulerunt se quarto die versus Saulotum le Petit et Bissam uxorem ejus judeos de placito transgressionis, unde inquisicio. Et predicti Saulottus et Blissa uxor ejus venerunt. Et inquisicio perfecte non venit. Ideo datus est dies partibus a die sancti Michaelis in .xv. dies. Et preceptum fuit vicecomiti quod dictam inquisicionem venire faceret. Et vicecomes mandavit quod Elias Tinctor et Thomas Albas manuceperunt Willelmum Trul; et quod Johannes de Catesby et Walterus filius Gregorii manuceperunt Johannem de Wenlinby', quos non habuerunt. Ideo in misericordia. Judicium quod distringat per terras etc., ita quod nec ipsi etc., et quod de exitibus etc., et quod habeat corpora <eorum coram>[113] etc. a die sancti Michaelis in .xv. dies ad recognoscendum etc. una cum Willelmo de Beuver, Willelmo Durvassal, Johanne de Catesby, Simone de Upton' christianis, Samuele de Staunford', Samuele filio Judas, Cresseo filio Sarre, Bonamico filio Deudonis, Josceo filio Salmonis judeis, qui habent eundem diem. Et mandavit quod Samson de Stanford' et Saulotus le Petit manuceperunt Isac filium Isac judeum, quem non habuerunt. Ideo in misericordia. Judicium quod distringat per terras etc., ut supra.

(1167)

Norff'. Johannes de Bayfeld, clericus de scaccario etc., optulit se quarto die versus Reginaldum de Bintre, Radulfum filium ejus, et Henricum de Suanton' capellanum, executores testamenti magistri Thome de Byntre, de placito debiti. Et ipsi non venerunt. Et preceptum fuit vicecomiti, sicut alias, quod ipsos venire faceret coram etc. Et vicecomes mandavit quod Robertus de Bintre, Johannes Faber de eadem, Willelmus de Byntre de eadem et Johannes Martin de eadem manuceperunt predictum Reginaldum, quem non habuerunt. Ideo in misericordia. Judicium quod distringat per terras etc., ita quod nec ipse etc., et quod de exitibus etc., et quod habeat corpus ejus coram etc. in octabis sancti Michaelis ad respondendum et ad audiendum etc. Et quod Radulfus filius predicti Reginaldi et Henricus capellanus de Suanton' nichil habent in balliva sua per quod possint distringi. De ipsis, sicut alias, ad eundem diem. Et preceptum fuit eidem vicecomiti quod attachiari faceret Johannem de Fraxino, ballivum de Eyneford', ita quod haberet corpus ejus coram etc. ad respondendum Regi ex eo quod contempsit exequi breve regis sibi inde directum, sicut vicecomes significavit. Et vicecomes mandavit quod Willelmus de Plomestede, Petrus de Cotton', Rogerus Maulyon' et Johannes Rivet de Rudham manuceperunt predictum Johannem, quem non habuerunt. Ideo in misericordia.[114] Et preceptum est ei, sicut alias, quod ipsum attachiet, ita quod habeat corpus ejus coram etc. ad diem supradictum.

(1168)

Norff'. Willelmus de Havergate, tenens quandam partem terrarum que fuerunt Bertrami de Verdun, qui tulit breve regis de placito porcionis ipsum contingentis de .xviij. libris in quibus dictus Bertramus tenebatur Seniori le Eveske judeo super Robertum de Molton', tenentem quandam partem predictarum terrarum, ad ipsum inde acquietandum, non est prosecutus versus eum. Ideo predictus Robertus, qui presens fuit, inde sine die et predictus Willelmus de porcione sua inde remaneat oneratus.

(1169)

Sutht'. Magister Radulfus Salsarius optulit se quarto die versus Simonem de Wynton' et Beatricem uxorem ejus de placito acquietacionis .viij. solidorum redditus assise. Et ipsi non venerunt. Et preceptum fuit vicecomiti, sicut alias, quod ipsos distringeret per terras etc., ita quod haberet corpora eorum coram etc. Et vicecomes mandavit quod Rogerus le Dent de Otrebourne, Henricus le Burgeys de eadem, Johannes le Gaunt de Drayton', Robertus Baroun de Folflod, Ricardus le Cok de Drayton' et Thomas de Otrebourne manuceperunt predictos Simonem et Beatriciam, quos non habuerunt. Ideo in misericordia.[115] Judicium quod salvo custodiat etc. et quod habeat corpora eorum coram etc. a die sancti Johannis Baptiste in .xv. dies ad respondendum et ad audiendum etc. Et nulli sunt exitus, prout vicecomes mandavit.

MEMBRANE 7 DORSE

Adhuc Placita de Quindena

(1170)

Wilec'. Salamon filius Simonis judeus, qui tulit breve regis de placito debiti super Johannem de Pateney, filium et heredem Nicholai de Patenay, non est prosecutus versus eum. Ideo ipse Salamon, pro se et plegiis suis de prosequendo, in misericordia.[116]

(1171)

Sutht'. Abraham filius Benedicti de Winton' judeus optulit se quarto die versus Edmundum de Sutton' de placito transgressionis. Et ipse non venit. Et preceptum fuit vicecomiti quod ipsum distringeret per terras etc., ita

[113] *These words are repeated in MS.*

[114] *The word* misericordia *is repeated in the margin.*

[115] *The word* misericordia *is repeated in the margin.*

[116] *The word* misericordia *is repeated in the margin.*

quod nec ipse etc., et quod de exitibus etc., et quod haberet corpus ejus coram etc. ad hunc diem. Et vicecomes mandavit quod Willelmus Aylwyne, Willelmus Weswode, Robertus Berkarius, Robertus le Careter, Johannes le Pottere et Henricus le Niue manuceperunt predictum Edmundum, quem non habuerunt. Ideo in misericordia. Judicium, sicut alias, quod distringat per terras, ita quod habeat corpus ejus coram etc., a die sancti Michaelis in .xv. dies ad respondendum predicto judeo de predicto placito, et ad audiendum etc.

(1172)

Norff'. Johannes de Bayfeld, clericus de scaccario etc., optulit se quarto die versus Johannem de Clare, rectorem ecclesie de Holesle, de placito debiti, unde jurata. Et jurata non venit. Et preceptum fuit vicecomiti quod eam venire faceret. Et vicecomes mandavit quod Johannes de la Ho de Asfeud et Robertus Haliday de eadem manuceperunt magistrum Johannem de Asfeud; et quod Johannes magister de Asfeud et Robertus Haliday de eadem manuceperunt Johannem del Ho; et quod Johannes magister de Asfeud et Johannes del Ho manuceperunt Robertum Haliday; et quod Walterus Hingered de Debeham et Willelmus Spurneshut de eadem manuceperunt Wilelmum filium Nicholai de Framesden'; et quod Willelmus filius Nicholai de Framesden' et Willelmus Spurneshut de eadem manuceperunt Walterum Hyngered de Debeham; et quod Willelmus filius Nicholai de Framesdon et Walterus Hingered de Debeham manuceperunt Willelmum Sporneshot de Debeam; et quod Johannes Dispensarius de Debeham et Hervicus Faber de eadem manuceperunt Lambertum mercatorem de Debeham; et quod Lambertus mercator de Debeam et Hervicus Faber de eadem manuceperunt Johannem Dispensarium de eadem; et quod Lambertus mercator de Debeham et Johannes Dispensarius de eadem manuceperunt Hervicum Fabrum de eadem; et quod Josceus clericus de Debeham et Willelmus del Fon de Wyneston' manuceperunt Robertum Cage de Debeham; et Willelmus del Fon de Wyneston' manucepit Josceum clericum de Debeham; et quod Robertus Cage de eadem et Josceus clericus de eadem manuceperunt Willelmum de Fou de Wyveleston; et quod Johannes Underwode de Peche et Robertus Rauf de eadem manuceperunt Thomam Estred de Pethehawe; et quod Thomas Estreld de eadem et Robertus Rauf de eadem manuceperunt Johannem Underwode de eadem; et quod Thomas Estreld de Pecchwe et Johannes Underwode de eadem manuceperunt Robertum Rauf de eadem; et quod Johannes Underwode de Pecchawe et Robertus Rauf de eadem manuceperunt Johannem Haude de eadem, quos non habuerunt. Ideo in misericordia.[117] Et quia vicecomes male respondit de manucaptione predictorum juratorum, ideo ipse vicecomes, videlicet Willelmus de Redham, in misericordia.[118] Judicium quod distringat per terras etc., ita quod nec ipsi etc., et quod de exitibus etc., et quod habeat corpora eorum coram etc. in octabis sancti Michaelis ad recognoscendum etc.

(1173)

Essex'. Johannes de Caunvile venire fecit Sawalrum de Brunfeud, Hervicum Folkel, Reginaldum Lucas, Willelmum le Parkere, Adam Martin, Willelmum Andr', et Gervasium de Heldholte et exigit ab eis .xj. libras quas ei debent ut fidejussores Johannis Fylol et dicti debiti principales debitores secundum tenorem cujusdam scripti obligatorii quod idem Johannes protulit coram etc., in quo sigilla eorum dependent, ut predictus Johannes dicit, et in quo continetur quod unusquisque eorum tenetur in solidum et quos denarios ei hucusque injuste detinent ad dampnum suum .x. librarum et hoc offert etc.

Predictus Sawalrus venit et deffendit vim etc. et dicit quod nunquam fuit plegius dicti Johannes Fylol nec aliquid pro eo manucepit nec sigillum suum predicto scripto obligatorio quod idem Johannes protulit coram etc. apposuit. Et quod odio per emulos suos in absencia sua nomen ejus in dicto scripto appositum fuit et nomine suo signatum, ipso penitus ignorante. Et hoc petit quod inquiratur. Et predicti Hervicus, Reginaldus, Willelmus, Adam, Willelmus [i]<et>[i] Gervasius eandem responsionem in omnibus faciunt et petunt quod inquiratur. Et quod pro predicto Johanne Fylol manuceperunt et sigilla sua in dicto scripto apposuerunt, sicut predictum est, predictus Johannes petit quod inquiratur. Et preceptum est vicecomiti quod venire faciat coram etc. a die sancti Michaelis in tres septimanas .xij. de visneto, per quos etc.

(1174)

Kanc'. Stephanus Chiche, tenens quandam partem terrarum que fuerunt Guydonis de Brussele, a quo Mosseus le Petit judeus Cantuar' exigebat octo libras occasione terrarum quas tenet que fuerunt predicti Guydonis per quandam cartam octo librarum, unde pars ubi cera dependet est in archa cyrographariorum Cantuar' ut dicit, venire fecit Aldinum de Corbaeyl, executorem testamenti Walteri Carbonel, quem idem Stephanus vocavit ad warantum de acquietacione dicti debiti octo librarum quod ipsum inde acquietare debuit per quandam cartam feofamenti dictarum terrarum quam ei inde fecit et quod dictum Stephanum acquietare debuit, sicut continetur in dicta carta inter eos inde confecta, idem Walterus recognovit coram etc., sicut patet inter placita termini sancte Trinitatis anno regni regis Edwardi octavo inter eos habita, et petit quod dictus Alanus, ad cujus manus bona et catalla dicti Walteri defuncti devenerunt, quod dictum Stephanum acquietet versus dictum Mosseum le Petit de dictis octo libris, de quibus ipsum acquietare debet per recognicionem dicti Walteri coram etc. factam dum vixerat.

Predictus Alanus venit et non potuit dedicere quin predictum Stephanum de predicto debito octo librarum, ut executor testamenti dicti Walteri, versus dictum judeum acquietare debet. Et petit diem [i]<ad>[i] solvendum

[117] *The word* misericordia *is repeated in the margin.*

[118] *The words* vicecomes in misericordia *are in the margin.*

centum solidos a die sancti Michaelis in .xv. dies anno regni regis Edwardi nono predicto Stephano, quos centum solidos recognovit se habere penes se de catallis predicti Walteri, et idem dies per justiciarios concessum est ei. Et preter hoc petit quod Johannes de Covenham, alius executor testamenti predicti socius suus, veniat ad diem predictum secum responsurus de .lx. solidis qui aretro sunt de predictis octo libris. Et preceptum est vicecomitibus Lond' quod venire faciant dictum Johannem de Covenham ad diem predictum.

MEMBRANE 8

Memoranda de Termino sancte Trinitatis Anno regni regis Edwardi Nono

(1175)

Lond'. Henna que fuit uxor Aaron de Ebor' solvit in recepta regis de fine .vj. solidos .viij. denarios et inde habet talliam.

(1176)

Lond'. Reginaldus de Suff' civis Lond' recognovit per scriptum suum se debere Aaron filio Vives judeo centum quarteria frumenti boni et mundi mensurati secundum mensuram ripe regine Lond' vel dimidiam marcam pro quolibet quarterio, quam partem judeus maluerat, solvendi eidem judeo vel suo attornato ad Purificacionem beate Marie anno regni regis Edwardi filii regis Henrici decimo. Et, nisi fecerit, concedit quod de terris et catallis suis et heredum suorum in quorumcumque manus devenerint fiant etc.

(1177)

Kanc'. Preceptum fuit vicecomiti quod venire faceret coram etc. ad hunc diem Dyonisiam que fuit uxor Stephani le Taylur de Cantuar' ad respondendum Regi de .xj. marcis argenti et uno cypho argenti precii .vj. marcarum, que bona et catalla devenerunt ad manus dicte Dyonisie ex tradicione Mossey filii Abrahe judei, cujus debita sunt in manu Regis pro diversis debitis in quibus Regi tenetur.

Predicta Dyonisia venit et deffendit vim etc. et dicit quod de predicto Mosseo de predictis .xj. marcis, cipho argenti precii .vj. marcarum, ut superius dictum est, nichil recepit seu custodiam habuit et de hoc ponit se super patriam. Et preceptum est vicecomiti quod venire faciat coram etc. a die sancti Johannis Baptiste in .xv. dies sex probos et legales homines de civitate Cantuar' et sex legales judeos, per quos etc., ad recognoscendum super premissis veritatem etc.

(1178)

Norht'. Preceptum fuit vicecomiti quod venire faceret coram etc. Adam le Porsere ad respondendum Regi de uno cypho de mazero precii quadraginta solidorum qui devenit ad manus dicti Ade de catallis que fuerunt Samsonis filii Samsonis judei dampnati ut dicitur.

Predictus Adam venit, defendit vim etc. et dicit quod Belasez que fuit uxor dicti Samsonis ei impignoravit quendam cyphum de mazero pro tribus solidis ante communem capcionem judeorum pro retonsura monete, quem ad communem clamacionem catallorum judeorum dampnatorum factam quod nullus ea concelaret protulit coram vicecomite Norhtht', majore dicte ville et Hugone de Kandale ad bona judeorum Northt' recipienda deputato, coram quibus predictum cyphum sibi per prefatam judeam pro tribus solidis impignoratum legittime probavit, quod sibi dictum cyphum sub sigillo vicecomitis et majoris et [blank] sibi retradiderunt, sub quibus sigillis dictum cyphum protulit coram etc.[119]

(1179)

Norht'. Preceptum fuit vicecomiti quod venire faceret coram etc. Rogerum de Cowe ad respondendum Regi de diversis bonis et catallis ad valenciam .vij. marcarum que devenerunt ad manus dicti Rogeri salvo custodiendum de catallis que fuerunt Sampsonis filii Sampsonis judei dampnati, ut dicitur.

Predictus Rogerus venit et deffendit vim etc. et dicit quod de catallis dicti Sampsonis ad manus ejus non devenerunt nisi unum firmaculum aureum precii .x. solidorum et unus cyphus argenteus precii dimidie marce, que firmaculum et chiphum judeus ei optulit in exennium per judeos Northt' ut esset amicus eorum in tempore capcionis judeorum, cum tunc erat ballivus predicte ville predicte. Et dicit quod dicta bona recipere recusavit; et cum dictus judeus dicta bona reportare noluerit ea majori dicte ville, constabulario castri et aliis probis hominibus Northt' monstravit et sub sigillis dictorum majoris et constabularii ea custodivit usque ad communem clamacionem de bonis judeorum dampnatorum quod nullus ea concelaret, ad quam clamacionem prefati ciphus et firmaculum per manum unius servientum vicecomitis liberata fuerunt Hugoni de Kendale ad dicta bona recipenda deputato. Et quod nulla alia bona seu catalla dicti Sampsonis recepit nec penes se retinuit petit quod inquiratur.[120]

(1180)

Surr', Sussex'. Preceptum fuit vicecomiti quod venire faceret coram etc. ad hunc diem Willelmum le Fischere et Ricardum de Hamme, tenentes quasdam partes terrarum que fuerunt Gilberti de Bassevile, ad respondendum Regi de porcionibus ipsos contingentibus occasione terrarum quas tenent que fuerunt predicti Gilberti de quodam debito .iiij. librarum in quibus dictus Gilbertus Aaron Crespin judeo dampnato per cartam suam tenebatur.

Predicti Willelmus et Ricardus veniunt et deffendunt vim etc. et dicunt quod de aliqua porcione dicti debiti non tenetur respondere eo quod de terris et tenementis[121] que

119 *This entry is unfinished.*
120 *This entry is unfinished.*
121 *Followed in MS. by* que tenementa.

fuerunt predicti Gilberti feofati fuerunt ante quam predictus Gilbertus per cartam suam predicto Aaron in dicto debito se obligavit. Et preceptum est vicecomiti quod per sacramentum proborum et legalium hominum etc., per quos etc., et qui nulla affinitate etc. diligenter inquirat quibus die et anno feofati fuerunt; et inquisicionem illam scire faceret justiciariis etc. a die sancti Johannes Baptiste in .xv. dies sub sigillo etc.

(1181)

[Surr'],Sussex'. Preceptum fuit vicecomiti quod distringeret Walterum de Wykes, tenenetem quandam partem terrarum que fuerunt predicti Gilberti de Bassevile, ad respondendum Regi de porcione ipsum contingente de dicto debito .iiij. librarum sub nominibus dicti Gilberti et Aaron Crespyn judei dampnati. Et ipse non venit. Et vicecomes mandavit quod Willelmus atte Span' de Byllinghurst, Willelmus Leveron de eadem, Nicholaus Rinchwine de eadem et Galfridus de la Broke de eadem manuceperunt predictum Walterum, quem non habuerunt. Ideo in misericordia.[122] Et Nicholaus le Gras vicecomes, quia non respondit de exitibus terrarum dicti Walteri, ideo in misericordia.[123]

Ladareyne de Valoignes, una tenens terrarum que fuerunt predicti Gilberti, attachiata ad respondendum regi de porcione dicti debiti ipsam contingente occasione predictarum terrarum etc. non venit. Et vicecomes mandavit quod Willelmus de Schire et Willelmus Harefot manuceperunt predictam Ladarenam, quam non habuerunt. [i]<Ideo>[i] in misericordia.[124] Johannes de Tyweleby attachiatus pro eodem non venit. Et vicecomes mandavit quod [blank] atte Stile de Bebitone et Willelmus prepositus de eadem manuceperunt predictum Johannem, quem non habuerunt. Ideo in misericordia.[125]

Thomas de la Chaumbre attachiatus pro eodem non venit. Et vicecomes mandavit quod Ricardus de Uppehelle de Werplesdon' et Robertus de Bethewell' de eadem manuceperunt predictum Thomam, quem non habuerunt. Ideo in misericordia.[126] Judicium quod distringat per terras etc., et quod habeat corpora eorum coram etc. a die sancti Johannes Baptiste in .xv. dies ad respondendum etc.

Robertus de Wyveleshole unus tenens, qui habuit hunc diem,[127] vocat ad warrantum ad [acquietandum][128] ipsum de porcione dicti debiti ipsum contingente occasione terrarum quas inde tenet Nigellum Pain, qui presens fuit et ipsum warrantizat. Ideo consideratum est quod dictus Robertus inde eat sine die et dictus Nigellus pro eo de porcione dicti debiti ipsum Robertum contingente remaneat oneratus.

[122] *The word* misericordia *is repeated in the margin.*
[123] *The words* vicecomes in misericordia *are written in the margin.*
[124] *The word* misericordia *is repeated in the margin.*
[125] *The word* misericordia *is repeated in the margin.*
[126] *The word* misericordia *is repeated in the margin.*
[127] *Followed in MS. by* et.
[128] *MS. omits.*

Johannes filius Johannis de Polingfaud, prior de Heringham, Ricardus de Wykes, Juellus Pain et Nigellus Payn venerunt et recognoverunt se esse tenentes quarundam parcium terrarum que fuerunt predicti Gilberti. Et Ricardus de Wykes et Juellus Payn vocant ad warrantum Willelmum de Wykes, filium et heredem Johanis de Wykes, ad ipsos de porcionibus dicti debiti ipsos inde contingentibus acquietandum, qui profectus est ad Terram Sanctam per recognicionem dictorum Ricardi et Juelli. Et quia vocant ad warrantum dictum Willelmum in partibus transmarinis existentem ad prorogandum debita regis, dictum est eis quod de porcionibus ipsos contingentibus Regi respondeant et habeant recuperare suum versus predictum Willelmum in redditu suo a partibus predictis. Et preceptum fuit vicecomiti quod in propria persona sua extendi faciat omnes terras et tenementa que predicti Walterus, Johannes, prior, Willelmus, Ricardus, Robertus, Juellus, Nigellus, Ladarena, Thomas, Johannes, Willelmus, Ricardus tenent de terris et tenementis que fuerunt predicti Gilberti; quid et quantum etc.; et si plures tenentes invenerit extendi faciat, ut supra; et extentam illam scire faciat justiciariis etc. a die sancti Johannis Baptiste in .xv. dies; et venire faciat ad eundem diem omnes quos predictarum terrarum invenerit tenentes ad respondendum Regi de predicto debito. Et preceptum est vicecomiti Sutht' quod venire faciat ad eundem diem priorem de Suthwyk, tenentem .x. libratas redditus qui fuerunt predicti Gilberti, ad respondendum Regi una cum predictis tenentibus de predicto debito.

(1182)

Sussex, Dors'. Radulfus de Stopenham miles de comitatu Sussex' et Johannes de la Tyle filius Ricardi de la Tyle de comitatu Dors' venerunt coram etc., et recognoverunt per scriptum suum se debere, obligari et teneri, quilibet ipsorum in solidum, Mansero filio Aaron judeo Lond' in centum et quinquaginta quarteria frumenti reddendum eidem judeo a die sancti Martini anno regni regis Edwardi nono terminante in quindecim dies vel pro quolibet quarterio dimidiam marcam [i]<secundum quod idem judeus maluerit eligere.>[i] Et, nisi fecerint, concedunt quod de terris et catallis suis leventur etc. ad quoruncumque manus devenerint.

MEMBRANE 8 DORSE

(1183)

Pro Willelmo de Valance.Willelmus de Valance tulit breve regis de magno sigillo in hec verba. 'Edwardus dei gracia etc. justiciariis suis ad custodiam judeorum assignatis salutem. Cum celebris memorie dominus H. rex Anglie pater noster per litteras suas patentes [quas][129] inspeximus concesserit pro se et heredibus suis dilecto avunculo et fideli nostro Willelmo de Valance quod ipse et heredes sui quieti essent inperpetuum de omnimodis

[129] *MS. reads* quos.

debitis in quibus ipsi qui maneria de Cherdelegh' et Policote in comitatu Buk', maneria de Posseby et Lecchesbirn in comitatu Norff' et manerium de Roydon' in comitatu Suff' tenuerunt tenebantur quibuscumque judeis, que quidem debita ad opus ipsius patris nostri vel quorumcumque judeorum exigi possent, ante quam dicta maneria ad manus predicti Willelmi de dono dicti patris nostri devenerunt, vobis mandamus quod eundem Willelmum contra quietanciam predictam non gravetis nec in aliquo vexetis. Et districciones si quas eidem fieri feceritis contra formam quitancie predicte sine dilacione relaxari faciatis eidem. Teste me ipso apud Westm' .xxviij. die Maii anno regni nostri nono.'

(1184)[130]

Buk'. Hugo de Brok miles venit coram etc. et recognovit se debere magistro Elye filio magistro Mossey judeo et Aaron filio Vives .xx. saccos lane bene mercatorios vel valorem dicte lane ad terminos subscriptos, reddendo eisdem judeis inde medietatem ad octabas Purificacionis beate Marie anno regni regis Edwardi decimo, et aliam medietatem ad octabas sancti Johannis Baptiste proximo sequentes. Et, nisi fecerit, concedit quod de terris et catallis suis fiant etc.

(1185)

Surr'. Johannes de Wauton' miles de comitatu Surr' venit coram etc. et recognovit per scriptum suum obligatorium se debere Aaron filio Vives judeo Lond' sexies viginti quarteria frumenti vel pro quolibet quarterio dimidiam marcam, reddendo ad festum Omnium Sanctorum anno regni regis Edwardi filii regis Henrici nono. Et, nisi fecerit, concedit quod de terris et catallis suis fiant etc.

(1186)

Kanc'. Preceptum fuit vicecomiti quod non omittat propter libertatem de Middelton' etc. et distringeret Matildam que fuit uxor Reginaldi de Sidingburn' per terras etc., et quod haberet corpus ejus coram etc. hic ad respondendum Regi de diversis bonis et catallis ad valenciam .xiiij. marcarum que deverunt ad manus dicte Matilde de catallis que fuerunt Salle Poleyn judei dampnati. Et ipsa non venit. Et vicecomes mandavit quod predicta Matilda non habet terras nec tenementa neque catalla per que possit distringi. Et preceptum est vicecomiti, sicud pluries, quod non omittat etc., et attachiet predictam [Matildam,][131] ita quod habeat corpus ejus coram etc. in octabis sancti Michaelis ad respondendum etc. et ad audiendum etc.

(1187)

Warr'. Preceptum fuit vicecomiti quod distringeret Willelmum Ende de Benton', Robertum Elys de eadem et alios juratores inquisionis ad inquirendum de duobus starris que Johannes le Engleys de Upton' protulit coram etc. de acquietacione duorum debitorum, ut dicit. Et ipsi non venerunt. Et vicecomes mandavit quod Willelmus le Hunte de Bunton', Ricardus le Careter de eadem, Willelmus ad Fontem de eadem, et Johannes prepositus de eadem manuceperunt Willelmum Ende; et quod Simon filius Johannes de Buniton', Johannes le Loverd' de eadem, Henricus Edward de eadem et Adam de Boveton' de eadem manuceperunt Robertum Elys; et quod Nicholaus le Clerk' de Grafton', Willelmus Swift de eadem, Johannes Podithowe de eadem et Thomas Osby de eadem manuceperunt Alanum de Fonte; et quod Stephanus de la Court de Alincestre, Adam de Kent de eadem, Johannes le Welwrite de eadem, et Johannes Burgeys de eadem manuceperunt Johannem Romay; et quod Willelmus Ray de Grafton', Willelmus filius Johannes de eadem et Rogerus de la Marche de eadem manuceperunt Willelmum de Fraxino; et quod Willelmus de Hampton' de Hesilovere, Nicholaus ad crucem de eadem, Walterus Edwyne de eadem et Johannes Edwyne de eadem manuceperunt Willelmum Elys, quos non habuerunt. Ideo in misericordia.[132] Et mandavit quod nulli sunt exitus terrarum predictorum juratorum post recepcionem brevis. Judicium, sicud alias, quod distringat per terras etc., ita quod nec ipsi etc., et quod de exitibus etc., et quod habeat corpora eorum coram etc. a die sancti Michaelis in .xv. dies ad recognoscendum etc.

(1188)

Northt'. Samuel de Staunford', Samuel filius Judas, Cresseus filius Sarre et Bonamy filius Deudonis judei Northt' pro pluribus defaltis in misericordia. Vives le Romaunsor, qui habuit hunc diem veniendi pro predicta inquisicione, non venit. Ideo in misericordia.[133] Predicti Samuel, Samuel, Cresseus et Bonamy, juratores dicte inquisicionis, attachiati venerunt. Et Saulottus le Petit unus juratorum, qui habuit hunc diem, venit. Et christiani, ut patet superius, non venerunt. Et datus est eis dies a die sancti Michaelis in .xv. dies ut supra etc.

(1189)

Oxon'. Preceptum fuit vicecomiti quod distringeret Willelmum [i]<filium>[i] Roberti de Wykenholt, Ricardum Jacob de Newber' et Robertum Godeman de eadem per terras etc. ad reddendum sibi ad opus Regis .iiij. marcas quas Regi debent de debito Abrahe filii Hagini de Berkhamstede judei dampnati; ita quod denarios haberet coram etc. Et vicecomes mandavit quod retornavit breve sibi inde derectum ballivis honoris Walingford', qui nichil inde fecerunt. Judicium quod non omittat etc. a die sancti Michaelis in .xv. dies etc.

(1190)

Oxon'. Josceus filius Jacobi de Alemannia judeus, qui tulit breve regis de placito debiti super Roggerum de Budene monacum, coquinarium abbacie de Abindon',

130 *Cf. no. 1092.*

131 *MS. omits.*

132 *The word* misericordia *is repeated in the margin.*

133 *The word* misericordia *is repeated in the margin.*

non est prosecutus versus [eum.][134] Ideo ipse Josceus in misericordia.

(1191)

Preceptum fuit vicecomiti quod de bonis et catallis Johannis Brond fieri faceret ad opus Isaac Leveske judei .xxxv. marcas, quas ei debet per recognicionem coram etc. inde factam, et denarios illos haberet coram etc. ad hunc diem. Et vicecomes mandavit quod retornavit breve sibi inde directum ballivis libertatis quatuor hundredorum et dimidii de Ciltre, qui nichil inde responderunt. Judicium quod non omittat etc. a die sancti Michaelis in .xv dies.

(1192)

Sutht'. Preceptum fuit vicecomiti quod venire faceret coram etc. sex probos et legales homines de civitate Winton', .vj. de villa Sutht', .vj. de visneto ejusdem ville et .vj. legales judeos de civitate Wynton' ad recognoscendum veritatem super quibusdam bonis et [catallis] salvo custodiendum traditis Roberto le Mercer, Felicie uxori ejus, Ricardo Selde, Ricardo Lengleys, Johanni Page le Jufne et [Christiane] Dykevin de catallis judeorum dampnatorum ut dicitur. Et inquisicio non venit. Et vicecomes mandavit quod retornavit breve sibi inde directum ballivis libertatum Wynton', episcopatus Wyton' et Sutht' pro christianis, qui nichil inde fecerunt. Judicium quod non omittat propter libertates predictas etc. et venire faciat coram etc. a die sancti Michaelis in .xv. dies .vj. de Wynton', .vj. de visneto, .vj. de villa Sutht' ad recognoscendum etc. Et pro judeis vicecomes mandavit quod Salomon filius Jacobi et Dyey filius Mulle manuceperant Kokellum filium Liquoricie et quod Bonami filius Joscey et Copinus filius Isac et Abraham filius Cressaunt manuceperunt Abraham filium Cokerel; et quod Pictavinus filius Jacobi et Haginus filius Pictavini manuceperunt Josceum generum Kokerel; et quod . . . filius Dyey et Mulle filius Joscey manuceperunt Beycoc filium Bonamy; et quod Pictavinus filius Hagini et Jacobus filius Copin manuceperunt Josceum de Kaleys, quos non habuerunt. Ideo in misericordia. Judicium quod distringat per terras etc., ita quod nec [ipsi] etc., et quod de exitibus etc., et quod habeat corpora eorum coram etc. ad diem supradictum ad recognoscendum etc.

(1193)

Sutht'. Preceptum fuit vicecomiti quod venire faceret coram etc. Petrum Asselin de Andevre ad respondendum Regi de pellibus lan[atis] precii .v. marcarum; et Alexandrum de Mennevile de Colebrokstreet ad respondendum Regi de sexaginta solidis; et Henricum de Cok ... et Johannam uxorem ejus ad respondendum Regi de quodam forcerio cum jocalibus ad valenciam .c. solidorum. Et ipsi non venerunt. Et vicecomes mandavit quod Walterus Postrome, Robertus Hod, Roggerus Pistor et Roggerus le Parcheminur manuceperunt Petrum Asselin, quem non habuerunt. Ideo in misericordia. Judicium quod distringat per terras etc., ita quod nec ipse etc., et quod de exitibus etc., et quod habeat corpus ejus coram etc. in octabis sancti Michaelis ad respondendum etc. et ad audiendum etc. Et vicecomes mandavit quod retornavit breve sibi inde directum ballivis libertatis Wynton' pro predictis Alexandro et Henrico, qui nichil inde [responderunt.][135] Judicium quod non omittat etc. in octabis sancti Michaelis etc.

(1194)

Northt'. Preceptum fuit vicecomiti quod venire faceret coram etc. Benedictum le Chapeleyn judeum, quem cepit et arestavit cum omnibus ...onibus per quas ipsum fecit ad standum recto omnibus super hiis secundum legem et consuetudinem regni. Et vicecomes mandavit quod predictus Benedictus judeus captus est et inprisonatus pro una supertunica de viridi furrata de cuniculis, una supertunica de burello, una furrura agnina, que furata fuerunt in domo Willelmi de Thorp' clerici, ut idem Willelmus dicit. Et idem [Benedictus][136] nichil [habet][137] in bonis unde sumptibus suis propriis cariari possit; et quod judei comunitatis Northt' [noluerunt] sumptus invenire ad ipsum cariandum. Et quod, si ipsum apud Westm' habere voluerint ad custum domini regis, fieri fiant inde habere allocacionem. Et judei Northt', qui presentes fuerunt coram etc., petunt quod ipsum Benedictum cariari possint custibus suis propriis periculo eorum. Et concessum est eis per manucapcionem Sampsonis de Staunford' et Bonamy filii Deudonis, Saulotti filii S..., Cressey filii Sarre, Sampsonis filii Sarre, Aaron filii Sampsonis, Sampsonis filii Judas, Isac filii Benedicti, Joscey filii Sa..., Sampsonis de Bed', Isac le Eveske judei Lond' et Salomonis filii Isac, quorum unusquisque manucepit predictum Benedictum, corpus pro corpore, quod salvo ipsum duceret una cum attachiamento ipsum tangente. Et preceptum est vicecomiti quod predictum Benedictum eisdem manucaptoribus deliberet et attachiamentum dictum judeum tangens sub sigillo suo ad hunc . . . diem ad dictum judeum cum attachiamento producend' coram etc. a die sancti Johannis Baptiste in .xv. dies etc.

(1195)

Norff'. Inquisicio capta coram H. Hauteyn apud Norwyc' in crastino sancte Trinitatis proximo preterito super quodam starro quod Walterus de Lenne protulit et per quod clamat habere quietanciam de centum solidis qui ab eodem Waltero exigebantur ad opus Regis de debito Isak' filii Benedicti per Simonem le Paumer et alios etc., et Isak' filium Josce et alios judeos etc. Qui dicunt super sacramentum suum quod unum starrum sub nominibus predictorum Walteri et Isak' in quo continetur quod predictus Walterus quietus est de una carta centum

[134] *MS. reads* eus.

[135] *MS.* respondit. [136] *MS. reads* Willelmus.
[137] *MS. omits.*

solidorum et alia carta centum solidorum et tercia carta centum solidorum sub nominibus predictorum Walteri et Isak' falsum est et non consignatur manu predicti Isak'; tamen aliud starrum in quo continetur quod predictus Walterus quietus est de omnibus debitis et demandis per quascumque cartas a principio seculi usque ad diem Cinerum anno regni regis Edwardi nunc sexto verum est et consignatum manu judei. Ideo datus est eis dies ad audiendum judicium suum a die sancti Johannis Baptiste in .xv. dies. Ad quem diem predictus.[138]

MEMBRANE 9

Starra de termino sancte Trinitatis anno regni regis Edwardi Nono

(1196)

Wiltes'. Isac de Suwerk' recognovit per starrum suum quod aquietavit et quietum clamavit Johanni Brunyg et Roberto Hernyst de Marleberg' et eorum heredibus et assignatis totum jus, demandam et calumpniam que habuit vel habere potuit versus eos occasione terrarum, redditum, pratorum que modo tenent die confeccionis istius starri que fuerunt aliquo tempore Johanni Wasce debitori meo et Mabilie uxori ejusdem, unde iste predicte terre obligate fuerunt sibi racione dicti debiti, ita quod nec ego nec heredes mei aliquid possint exigere seu calumpniari versus predictos Johannem et Robertum vel heredes seu eorum assignatos occasione terrarum, redditum, et prati predictarum que predictus Johannes Brunyng et Robertus tenent que quondam fuerunt Johanni Wasce et Mabilie predictis debitore meo, ut predictum est, a creacione seculi usque ad finem. Et si quis homo vel femina, judeus vel judea aliquid calumpniatur super predictas terras, redditus vel prata que predicti Johannes et Robertus tenent occasione alicujus debiti in quo prefatus Wasce aliquando michi tenebatur, volo et concedo quod ipsum teneor aquietare et omnino defendere. Acta in crastino Apostolorum Petri et Pauli anno regni regis Edwardi nono.

(1197)

Kanc'. Drua que fuit uxor Isac filii Bonamy judea de Oxon' recognovit per testimonium Meyr filii Benedicti et Sampsonis filii Isac quod Petrus de Denholl' de comitatu Kanc' et Willelmus de Botaylles, heredes sui, antecessores et eorum assignati quieti sint de ipsa judea, heredibus et assignatis [i]<suis>[i] et de Isac filio Bonaymy domino suo et de omnibus aliis debitis, cyrographiis, demandis, calumpniis et plegiagiis que predictus Petrus et Willelmus de Botayles eidem judeo unquam tenebantur vel predicto Isac domino suo judeo a creacione seculi usque sancti Johannis Baptiste in quindecim dies anno regni regis Edwardi nunc nono. Et si inveniatur carta, cyrographum, tallia vel aliquod aliud instrumentum vel indossamentum carte pro Isac filio Bonamy judeo predicto, faciens mencionem de ipso Isac vel nomine predictorum Willelmi et Petri vel nomine Manseri filii Aaron vel nomine alicujus alii judei, quod quietum sit et nichil valeat.

(1198)

Essex'. Aaron filius Vives judeus recognovit per starrum suum quod Ricardus de Tany et heredes et assignati sui de omnibus debitis, demandis et clamiis et plegiagiis et obligacionibus que unquam ei debuit vel per que idem Ricardus extitit obligatus dicto Aaron sub quibuscumque cartis sub nominibus eorundem [i]<Ricardi et Aar'>[i] a principio seculi usque a die sancti Johannis Baptiste in .xv. dies anno regni regis Edwardi nono quietus est. Et si contigerit in aliqua archa cyrographariorum domini regis aut extra sub nominibus eorundem Ricardi et Aaron invenire cartam, cyrographum, talliam vel aliud quodcumque instrumentum confectum ante predictum festum Nativitatis sancti Johannis Baptiste concedit quod quitati sint et pro nullo habeantur. Et similiter concedit quod predictus Ricardus et heredes sui quieti sint de se et heredibus suis de omnimodis recognicionibus recognitis in rotulis domini regis de scaccario judeorum ante predictum festum sancti Johannis Baptiste.

Cresseus filius Cresse concedit predictam quietanciam pro se et heredibus suis a principio seculi usque ad predictum festum nativitatis sancti Johannis Baptiste, videlicet de debitis, obligacionibus et talliis.

(1199)

Wiltes'. Elias filius magistri Mossei, Aaron filius Vives et Vives filius Aaron recognoverunt per starrum suum quod Willelmus Paynel, filius Willelmi Paynel, miles de comitatu Wiltes', antecessores et heredes sui quieti sunt de eis et heredibus eorundem et de omnibus pueris eorundem de omnibus debitis, calumpniis, demandis, plegiagiis, obligacionibus, irrotulacionibus et recognicionibus factis coram justiciariis etc. que unquam fuerunt facta sub nominibus dictorum Willelmi et judeorum prenominatorum ante festum sancti Johannis Baptiste anno regni regis Edwardi filii regis Henrici nono usque ad finem seculi. Et si carta, tallia, obligacio vel aliud instrumentum, irrotulacio seu recognicio facta coram justiciariis etc. sub nominibus dictorum Willelmi et judeorum prenominatorum ante diem predictum inveniatur, recognoscunt iidem judei esse quieta et nullius valoris.

(1200)

Northt', Lond'. Isaac le Eveske judeus Lond' tanquam attornatus Florie que fuit uxor David de North' judei recognovit per starrum suum quod ipse recepit de Walkelino le Macegref de Northt' centum solidos de decem libris in quibus Walkelinus condempnatus fuit coram justiciariis domini regis ad custodiam judeorum assignatis ad opus domini Regis per inquisicionem christianorum et judeorum de catallis predicti David, de

[138] *This entry is unfinished. But see no. 1034.*

quibus decem libre [concesse][139] et [assignate][140] fuerunt Florie que fuit uxor predicti David per assignacionem et concessionem predictorum justiciariorum et residui centum solidi sunt domini Regis. Et quod recognovit hoc sigillavid tanquam attornatus predicte Florie et per preceptum ipsius Florie.

(1201)

Lond'. Isaac le Eveske, Meyr filius Jacobi et Mosseus filius Jacobi judei testantur pro Belasez que fuit uxor Leonis filii Preciose et recognoverunt per starrum suum quod Johannes filius Petri civis Lond' et heredes et assignati sui quieti sunt de ipso Belasez et heredibus et assignatis suis de quodam debito .xl. solidorum sub nominibus Willelmi de Dunstaple feliparii de Colemanestrate et predicti Leonis filii Preciose quondam viri ipsius Belasez, quod quidem debitum fuit predicte Belasez per finem quem fecit cum domino Rege pro debitis predicti Leonis habendis post mortem ipsius Leonis, unde predictus Johannes et heredes et assignati sui quieti sunt de predicta Belasez et heredibus suis a creacione seculi usque ad finem. Acta die in octabis sancti Johannis Baptiste anno regni regis Edwardi nono.

Et Jorninus filius Abraham recognovit per starrum suum et concessit totam quietanciam predictam pro et heredibus et assignatis suis predicto Johanni et heredibus et assignatis suis inperpetuum.

(1202)

Kanc'. Manserus filius Aaron judeus recognovit per starrum suum quod Petrus de Deneherst et Willelmus de Botayles et heredes et assignati sui quieti sunt de ipso judeo et heredibus et antecessoribus suis de omnibus debitis, demandis et calumpniis que ipsum contingunt de porcione sua ipsum de debitis illis contingente. Et si inveniatur carta, tallia vel aliquod aliud instrumentum sub nominibus predictorum Petri et Willelmi et predicti Manseri, idem Manserus recognovit quod tota porcio sua ipsum inde contingens quieta sit pro ipso Mansero et heredibus suis predictis Petro et Willelmo et heredibus eorum.

(1203)

Warr'. Aaron filius Vyves judeus recognovit per starrum suum quod recepit de Ricardo de Ammundevill' .xij. libras .x. solidos per manus Rogeri de Pevlisdon' in termino sancti Michaelis anno regni regis Edwardi nono de debito in quo tenebatur predicto Aaron et eciam recepit .xx. solidos pro una roba in qua tenebatur predicto Aaron. Et quod recognovit, hoc idem sigillavit.

139 *MS. reads* concessi.
140 *MS. reads* assignati.

MEMBRANE 9 DORSE

(1204)

Leyc'. Aaron filius Vives judeus Lond' recognovit per starrum suum quod recepit de Willelmo de Boyville vicecomite Rotelandie decem marcas ad quindenam sancti Johannis Baptiste anno regni regis Edwardi filii regis Henrici nono, quos quidem denarios idem Willelmus recognovit se debere eidem Aaron pro quodam debito in quo Willelmus de Mordak tenebatur Dyei de Hulmo judeo dampnato, quod quidam debitum assignatum fuit eidem Aaron in recompensacionem quorundam debitorum in quibus Gilbertus Peche tenebatur eidem Aaron.

(1205)

Ebor'. Magister Elias filius magistri Mossei judeus recognovit per starrum suum quod recepit quinque marcas de Johanne de Eyville de termino trium septimanarum post festum sancti Johannis Baptiste anno regni regis Edwardi filii regis Henrici octavo de quodam debito viginti librarum in quo ei tenetur, sicut continetur in rotulis justiciariorum etc., videlicet pro quodam debito sub nominibus Elie le Blund et predicti Johannis de Eyville, unde tercia pars predicti debiti est predicti magistri Elie.

(1206)

Roteland'. Bernardus de Brus miles de comitatu Roteland' venit coram etc. et recognovit se debere Cresseo filio Cressei judeo Lond' in .xl. quarteriis frumenti vel pro quolibet quarterio dimidiam marcam, reddendo medietatem ad quindenam sancti Johannis Baptiste anno regis Edwardi nono, et aliam medietatem ad quindenam sancti Michaelis proximo sequentem. Et, nisi fecerit, concedit quod de terris et catallis etc.

(1207)

Lancastr'. Aaron filius Vyves judeus recognovit per starrum suum quod Henricus de Lathum et Johannes de sancto Edmundo et eorum heredes quieti sunt de ipso judeo et ipsius heredibus de quadam obligacione de centum et sexaginta quarteriis frumenti de termino satisfaccionis predicte obligacionis, medietas cujus satisfaccionis [i]<fuit>[i] in termino Pentecostes anno regni regis Edwardi nono, aliam vero medietatem in festo sancti Michaelis proximo sequenti, a creacione seculi usque in finem. Et quod recognovit, hoc idem sigillavit.

MEMBRANE 10

Adhuc Memoranda de termino sancte Trinitatis anno regni regis Edwardi nono

(1208)

Somerset'. Willelmus de Favelore attachiatus ad respondendum domine Regine consorti Regis etc. de placito transgressionis et injuste detencionis debiti etc. Et unde queritur quod, cum breve domini regis nuper directum fuisset vicecomiti Somers' et Dors' ad levandum de terris et catallis Walteri de Furneus trescentas marcas ad opus prefate Regine, in quibus idem Walterus tenebatur Hagino filio magistri Mossei judeo, cujus quidem debita Rex eidem Regine donavit, idem Willelmus, dum subvicecomes fuit <vicecomitis>[141] predicti, sciens hujusmodi preceptum domino suo emanasse, terciam partem manerii de Heynton' Sancti Georgii in comitatu Somers' de predicto Waltero emit et seysinam inde per feoffamentum ejusdem Walteri cepit et pro empcione ejusdem manerii et feoffamento solvit Hagino filio magistri Mossei judeo .xl. et unam libras per voluntatem predicti Walteri, quasi satisfaciendo eidem Hagino pro omnibus debitis in quibus idem Walterus tenebatur eidem Hagino, pro eo quod idem Willelmus asserebat se habuisse breve domini regis in quo continebatur quod predictus Haginus finem fecit cum domino Rege pro catallis suis habendis et quod idem Walterus distringeretur pro debito predicto ad inpetracionem predicti Hagini, per quos quidem denarios quos prefato Waltero solvit pro tercia parte manerii sui predicti distrinxisse et eosdem denarios prefate Regine in partem solucionis debiti supradicti solvisse potuit, idem Willelmus in decepcionem et subtraccionem debiti prefate Regine per collusionem inter ipsum et prefatum [i]<Haginum>[i] habitam predictos denarios eidem Hagino solvit ad dampnum suum centum marcarum etc.

Et predictus Willelmus venit et defendit omnem transgressionem et quicquid etc., et dicit quod legaliter et antequam quod breve directum fuit vicecomiti Somers' domino suo ad levandum de terris et catallis dicti Walteri debitum supradictum idem Willelmus terciam partem dicti manerii de predicto Waltero emit et seysinam inde habuit et .xl. et unam libras prefato Waltero solvit pro predicta empcione.

Et Walterus de Forneaus, qui presens fuit, venit et precise dedicit quod nunquam sibi aliquos denarios solvit pro tercia parte predicti maneri, set si quos solvit prefato Hagino solvit nec sibi vel alii et inde protulit quoddam scriptum sigillo predicti Willelmi consignatum in quo continetur quod idem Willelmus solvit Hagino filio magistri Mossei judeo pro predicto Waltero et pro feoffamento predicti manerii habendo .xl. et unam libras.

Et predictus Willelmus bene recognovit predictum scriptum set dicit quod eosdem denarios solvit predicto Hagino tempore quo idem Haginus liberam habuit administracionem bonorum suorum et antequam Rex debita ipsius Hagini prefate Regine donavit terciam partem dicti manerii de predicto Waltero emit et seysinam inde habuit et predictas .xl. et unam libras eidem Hagino solvit per voluntatem ipsius Walteri.

Et prefata Regina per Walterum de Kanc' attornatum suum petit judicium desicut primo recognovit predictas .xl. et unam libras solvisse predicto Waltero de Forneaus et postea per scriptum suum quod liquide testabatur non potuit dedicere quin predictos denarios prefato Hagino solvit et sic sibi ipsi contrariatur.

Et quia constat per rotulos de scaccario etc. et recordum justiciarorum etc. quod breve regis directum fuit vicecomiti Somers' ad levandum de terris et catallis predicti Walteri predictum debitum per duos annos antequem emit terciam partem predicti manerii et seysinam inde habuit et predictas .xl. et unam libras solvit prefato Hagino, quas solvisse debuit prefate Regine et eas subtraxit in dampnum ipsius Regine, consideratum est quod predicta domina Regina habeat suum recuperare versus prefatum Willelmum de predictis .xl. et una libris. Et predictus Willelmus pro injusta detencione in misericordia.[142]

(1209)

Willelmus de Favelore attachiatus ad respondendum Waltero de Furneaus de placito transgressionis. Et unde idem Walterus queritur quod predictus Willelmus hostia domorum et grangiorum suorum nuper clausit et consignavit et blada sua ad voluntatem suam triturari fecit et alias districciones diversaque gravamina eidem intulit, asserendo Haginum filium magistri Mossei judeum finem fecisse cum domino Rege pro catallis suis habendis et breve domini regis ad impetracionem predicti Hagini habuisse ad levandum debita in quibus predictus Walterus prefato Hagino tenebatur ad opus ipsius Hagini, cum nullum breve seu preceptum super hoc habuit, quarum quidem districcionum pretextu et diversorum gravaminum que ei inferrebat sibi vendi fecit terciam partem manerii sui de Henton' Sancti Georgii ad satisfaciendum predicto Hagino de predictis debitis per collusionem maliciosam inter predictos Willelmum et Haginum habitam et provisam ad dampnum predicti Walteri ducentarum librarum et exheredacionem suam manifestam. Et inde producit sectam etc.

Et predictus Willelmus venit et defendit vim et injuriam et quicquid etc. Et bene dicit quod predictum Walterum distrinxit per bona et catalla sua pro diversis debitis que idem Walterus debuit consorti Regis etc. per quoddam breve domini regis domino suo vicecomiti Somers' directum. Set quod nunquam asseruit predictum Haginum finem fecisse cum domino rege pro catallis suis habendis nec breve domini regis super hoc habuisse ad levandum aliqua debita ad opus predicti Hagini nec quod pretextu aliquarum districcionum que ei <eadem>[143] causa intulisse debuerat sibi vendi fecit terciam partem predicti manerii ad satisfaciendum predicto Hagino de debitis suis set bene gratis ipsius Walteri et certis condiccionibus pro voluntate ipsius Walteri predictam terciam partem manerii de predicto Waltero emit bene et legaliter pro .xlj. libris sterlingorum quas ei solvit ponit se super patriam.

Et predictus Walterus venit et dicit quod nunquam

[141] *Corrected in MS. from* comitatus.

[142] *The word* misericordia *in the margin has been deleted with the explanation* condonatur per W. de Kanc' *written above.*

[143] *This word is repeated in MS.*

terciam partem predicti manerii ei vendidit per voluntatem suam set per diversas districciones quas ei fecit et quod asserciones predictas et districciones ei fecit in forma predicta ponit se super patriam. Et predictus Willelmus similiter. Ideo preceptum est vicecomiti quod venire faciat coram etc. duodecim milites gladiis cinctos [i]<de comitatu suo,>[i] .xij. probos et legales homines de visneto de Heinton' ad recognoscendum etc. a die sancti Michaelis in .xv. dies. Ad quem diem vicecomes non retornavit breve. Ideo, sicut alias, in octabis sancti Hillarii. Ad quem diem vicecomes retornavit nomina recognitorum, qui non venerunt. Ideo preceptum est vicecomiti quod ipsos distringat etc. per terras etc., et quod de exitibus etc., et quod habeat corpora eorum coram etc. in crastino Cinerum ad recognoscendum etc. et eundem diem [habet][144] dictus Willelmus, qui presens fuit. Ad quem diem inquisicio non venit. Ideo, sicut alias, in octabis sancte Trinitatis. Ad quem diem dictus Willelmus venit et inquisicio venit per [blank] et alios etc. juratos. Qui dicunt super sacramentum suum quod dictus Willelmus blada dicti Walteri triturari fecit pro debito domine Regine ad opus ipsius Regine levandum et quod nunquam asserit breve domini regis habuisse ad levandum debita dicti Hagini ad opus ipsius Hagini nec ipsum Walterum pro debito ipsius Hagini ad opus ipsius Hagini distrixit set ad opus domine Regine, nec eciam idem Walterus coactus seu invite vendidit terciam partem manerii [Henton'][145] Sancti Georgii dicto Willelmo nec sibi vendi fecit, [set][146] bene gratis et spontanea voluntate sine coaccione, districcione, minis seu molestia eandem terciam partem dicto Willelmo vendidit pro .xlj. libris quas ei solvit. Ideo consideratum est quod dictus Willelmus habeat et teneat dictam terciam partem dicti manerii [Henton'][147] Sancti Georgii in forma qua prius tenuit ex vendicione dicti Walteri, et dictus Walterus pro falso clamore in misericordia.

(1210)

Cantebr'. Gilbertus Pecche miles venit coram etc. et recognovit se debere Aaron filio Vyves judeo ducentas libras, reddendo eidem judeo ad festum sancti Michaelis anno regni regis Edwardi nunc filii regis Henrici decimo. Et, nisi fecerit, concedit quod de terris et catallis suis, ad quorumcumque manus devenerunt, fiant etc.

(1211)

Gloucestr'. Johannes de Clyfford miles venit coram etc. et recognovit se debere Aaron filio Vyves judeo .xx. solidos, reddendo eidem judeo ad festum sancti Michaelis anno regni regis Edwardi nunc nono. Et, nisi fecerit, concedit quod de terris et catallis suis, ad quorumcumque manus devenerunt, fiant etc.

(1212)

Surr', Suss'. Johannes de Middilton' venit coram etc. et recognovit se debere Aaron filio Vyves judeo centum quarteria frumenti vel dimidiam marcam pro quolibet quarterio et .xviij. marcas sterlingorum, reddendo eidem judeo [e]<a die Pasche in .xv dies>[e] apud Hokeday anno regni regis Edwardi .x.°. Et, nisi fecerit, concedit quod de terris et catallis suis fiant etc. ad quorumcumque manus devenerunt etc.

(1213)

Leyc'. Benedictus de Rolleston' miles venit coram etc. et recognovit se debere Abrahe Grugan et Jornino filio Abrahe judeis in tribus saccis lane precii cujuslibet sacci novem marcas, [i]<reddendo a die sancti Michaelis in unum mensem.>[i] Et, nisi fecerit, concedit quod de terris et catallis suis fiant etc. ad quorumcumque manus devenerunt.

(1214)

Norff'. Cum Willelmus Gare de Hardyngham districtus fuisset pro .xl. solidis in quibus ipse et Gilbertus Overbek' et Johannes Hony tenebantur Salomoni filio Jornini judeo Norwycensi nuper ad fidem catholicam [converso,][148] predictus Willelmus venit et protulit quoddam starrum [ejusdem judei][149] confectum de aquietancia porcionis sue ipsum contingentis de predicto debito, et dicit quod predictus judeus tempore quo habuit administracionem catallorum suorum fecit ei predictum starrum. Et petit quod inquiratur per patriam tam per christianos quam judeos. Ideo preceptum est vicecomiti Norff' quod venire faciat coram justiciariis etc. in octabis sancti Johannes Baptiste, nisi H. Hauteyn et R. de Ludham prius etc. Et interim venerunt predicti H. et R. Et predicta inquisicio venit coram eis apud Norwic' tam per cyrographarios christianos quam judeos et per alios probos et legales homines de visneto de Norvic'. Qui dicunt super sacramentum suum quod predictus judeus tempore quo habuit administracionem catallorum suorum fieri fecit predictum starrum per quendam alium judeum in presencia ipsius Salominis et per preceptum suum, eo quod idem Salomon fere laicus fuit de lege judayca et non litteratus. Ideo datus est ei dies de audiendo judicio coram etc. apud Westm' a die sancti Michaelis in unum mensem. Ad quem diem predictus Willelmus venit et instanter petit judicium suum etc. Et quia attinctum est per inquisicionem predictam quod predictum starrum factum fuit tempore debito et per preceptum et voluntatem ipsius judei, consideratum est quod predictus Willelmus quietus sit de porcione sua ipsum contingente de predicto debito, salvo domino regi recuperare suo versus predictos Gilbertum et Johannem etc.

[144] *MS. omits.* [145] *MS. omits.* [146] *MS. reads* se.
[147] *MS. omits.*

[148] *MS. reads* conversi. [149] *MS. reads* eidem judeo.

MEMBRANE 11

Adhuc Memoranda de termino sancte Trinitatis anno regni regis Edwardi nono

(1215)

Warewyk', Glouc'. Petrus de Mounford et Radulfus de Welington' [venerunt][150] coram etc. et recognoverunt se debere Aaron filio Vives judeo Lond' centum quarteria frumenti vel pro quolibet quarterio dimidiam marcam, reddendo a die sancti Michaelis in .xv. dies anno regni regis Edwardi nono. Et, nisi [fecerint, concedunt][151] quod de terris et catallis suis fiant.

(1216)

Norf'. Preceptum fuit vicecomiti quod haberet corpus Cok filii Salomonis le Convers coram etc. a die sancte Trinitatis nunc in .xv. dies ad satisfaciendum Regi de .v. marcis de fine suo pro transgressione monete regis de qua rettatus fuit. Et predictus vicecomes per quendam de suis corpus predicti Cok' protulit coram etc. Et quia nichil habuit in bonis unde Regi de predictis .v. marcis satisfacere possit, magister Elyas, Haginus filius Deulecres', Aaron filius Vives pro se et communitate judeorum Anglie manuceperunt satisfacere Regi de predictis .v. marcis pro prefato judeo per quendam communem collecionem inter eos faciendam. Et quod predictus Cok pro predicta transgressione ei imposita abjuraret regnum per triennium, qui statim coram etc. juravit quod transmearet ad partes transmarinas ad proximum passagium infra quindenam; ita quod in regnum Anglie non rediret nisi haberet inde warentum de domino Rege super forisfacturam inde provisam.

(1217)

Lond'. Hake de Dorkinge attachiatus per constabularium castri Bristoll' cum quadam plata falsa conflata, <quam Petronille Nerewyt uxor cujusdam monetarii de Bristoll' pro quadraginta solidis inpignorata in redempcione dicte Petronille,>[152] ut constabularius mandavit. Et, quia predictus Hake nullos manucaptores invenire potuit quod se fideliter versus quoscumque gereret, pro predicta transgressione et aliis transgressionibus ei impositis abjuravit regnum Anglie per tres annos a festo sancti Michaelis proximo sequenti; ita quod infra predictum terminum non redibit sine licencia domini regis sub forisfactura inde provisa. Et mandatum est constabulario de Dovoria quod ipsum transmeare permittat.

(1218)

Elias de Hauvile miles venit coram etc. et recognovit se recepisse de Aaron filio Vives judeo .xl. marcas de quindena sancti Johannis Baptiste nunc in partem solucionis centum marcarum in quibus Aaron eidem Elye per recognicionem inde factam in cancellaria domini regis tenetur.

[150] *MS. reads* venit. [151] *MS. reads* fecerit, concedit.
[152] *Sic in MS.*

(1219)

Rotelaund'. Preceptum fuit vicecomiti quod distringeret Galfridum filium Thome de Emplingham per terras etc. ad reddendum sibi ad opus Regis unam marcam quam Regi debet de debitis Manseri filii David judei dampnati; et denarios illos haberet coram etc. vel corpus predicti Galfridi ad ostendendum etc.

Predictus Galfridus venit et dicit quod satisfecit Reyne matri predicti Manseri judei per preceptum ejusdem de dicta marca et vocat predictam Reynam quod ipsum inde acquietare debet. Et preceptum est vicecomiti [i]<Linc'>[i] quod predictam Reynam venire faciat coram etc. a die sancti Michaelis in unum mensem, nisi interim H. Hauteyn ad partes illas venerit, ad acquietandum predictum Galfridum de predicta marca, sicut racionabiliter etc.

(1220)

Norff'. Willelmus filius Hugonis de Wygenhale protulit breve regis de magno sigillo in hec verba: 'Edwardus dei gracia etc. justiciariis suis ad custodiam judeorum assignatis salutem. Cum Willelmus filius Hugonis de Wygenhale teneretur in quibusdam debitis Ysaac de la Selerie judeo Norwyci, qui pro transgressione monete suspensus fuit, ut dicitur, et cujus debita capi fecimus in manum nostram, ac idem Willelmus debita illa salvo tenemento suo nobis solvere non possit nisi racionabiles terminos solucionis eorundem ei concederemus, ut dicit, nos statui ipsius Willelmi conpacientes in hac parte vobis mandamus quod, facta extenta omnium terrarum et tenementorum ipsius Willelmi, racionabiles terminos ad quos debita illa, salvo contenemento suo, nobis solvere possit juxta extentam illam assignari faciatis eidem. Teste me ipso apud Sanctum Edmundum .vij. die Februarii anno regni nostri nono.' Per hoc breve preceptum est vicecomiti quod extendi faciat omnes terras et tenementa predicti Willelmi, et extentam illam scire faciat justiciariis etc. Et vicecomes mandavit quod per inquisicionem inde coram eo factam per sacramentum Laurencii de Maneris, Galfridi de Upgate et aliorum, sicut patet inter brevia hujus termini retornata, terre ejusdem Willelmi, videlicet .xxiiij. acre terre, extunduntur per annum ad .xij. solidos. Et concessum est predicto Willelmo per breve regis predictum quod reddat regi per annum per extentam.

(1221)

Hunt'. Concessum est Roberto filio Roberti de Watervile quod de duabus marcis in quibus tenebatur Josceo filio magistri de Stanf' judeo pro tonsura monete suspenso solvat per annum unam marcam, videlicet ad scaccarium sancti Michaelis dimidiam marcam et ad scaccarium Pasche dimidiam marcam, et sic de anno in annum ad eosdem terminos donec predicte due marce regi persolvantur, incipiendo ad scaccarium sancti Michaelis anno regni regis Edwardi .ix.º.

(1222)

Norff'. Adam de Creting' miles venit coram etc. et recognovit se debere Aaron filio Vives judeo viginti marcas, reddendo eidem judeo a die sancti Michaelis in unum mensem anno regni regis Edwardi nono. Et, nisi fecerit, concedit quod de terris et catallis suis et heredum suorum fiant.

(1223)

Lond'. Cresseus filius Florie, Mosseus filius Jacob, Isaac de Warr', et Jorninus filius Abrahe judei Lond' ceperunt per ballium Abraham filium Benedicti de Winton' judeum in prisona apud Turrim Lond' existentem pro morte cujusdam hominis in civitate Winton' interfecti, de qua morte indicatus fuit coram coronatoribus civitatis predicte et quod indictamentum predicti coronatores protulerunt coram justiciariis itinerantibus ibidem et, quia predictus Abraham coram dictis justiciariis cum essent ibi in itinere non venit, utlagaria ibidem super eum in pleno comitatu ter fuit [promulgata,][153] pro qua in prisona se posuit, de habendo corpus suum coram etc. a die sancti Michaelis in .xv. dies ad standum recto de predicto indictamento et ad faciendum quod de jure fuerit faciendum.

(1224)

Ebor'. Preceptum fuit vicecomiti quod per sacramentum proborum et legalium hominum tam christianorum quam judeorum.[154]

(1225)

Lond'. Per breve domini regis quod Jacobus filius Joscei protulit coram etc. in hec verba 'Edwardus dei gracia etc. omnibus ad quos presentes littere pervenerint salutem. Sciatis quod dedimus licenciam Jacobo filio Joscei judeo London' vendendi Gregorio de Rokesley medietatem unius mesuagii cum pertinenciis in London' quod est inter terram magistri Elie filii magistri Mossei judei London' versus aquilonem et terram Sleme que fuit uxor magistri Isak' de Oxon' judei versus austrum, cujus capud occidentale abutat super regium vicum qui vocatur Collecherche Lane et capud orientale super terram fratrum de Penitencia Jhesu Christi ibidem. Dedimus eciam licenciam eidem Gregorio medietatem mesuagii predicti a prefato judeo emendi, prout sibi magis viderit expedire, nisi medietas illa sit eschaeta nostra vel alio modo jus habeamus in eodem. In cuius rei testimonium has litteras nostras fieri fecimus patentes. Teste me ipso apud Westm' .xviij. die Maii anno regni nostri nono.' idem Jacobus vendidit predicto Gregorio medietatem predicti mesuagii pro .xx. marcis quas ei solvit pre manibus.

[153] *MS. reads* provulgata.

[154] *This entry is unfinished.*

MEMBRANE 11 DORSE

[Blank except for a cover sewn to the bottom with the heading *Rotuli de termino sancte Trinitatis anno regni regis Edwardi nono*]

MEMBRANE 12

Adhuc Memoranda de termino sancti Johannis Baptiste anno regni regis Edwardi Nono

(1226)

Linc'. Preceptum fuit vicecomiti quod distringeret Thomam de Schirlond' per terras etc. et quod haberet corpus ejus coram etc. ad respondendum Regi de .xx. quarteriis frumenti que regi debet de debitis Samuelis filii Manseri judei forisfacti. Et ipse non venit. Et vicecomes mandavit quod Walterus atte Larde de Wrangeby, Nigellus Ardegrey de eadem, Simon atte Lard de eadem, Walterus clericus de eadem manuceperunt predictum Thomam, quem non habuerunt. Ideo in misericordia.[155] Judicium, sicut alias, quod distringat per terras etc., ita quod nec ipse etc., et quod de exitibus etc., et quod habeat corpus ejus coram etc. a die sancti Michaelis in tres septimanas ad respondendum etc. et ad audiendum etc.

(1227)

Essex', Hertf'. Preceptum fuit vicecomiti quod distringeret Thomam de Flaundene et tenentes terrarum suarum ad reddendum sibi ad opus Regis .x. marcas de debitis Hagini de Berkhamsted', et denarios illos haberet coram etc. Et vicecomes mandavit quod retornavit breve sibi inde directum ballivis libertatis de Berkhampsted', qui nichil inde fecerunt. Judicium quod non omittat etc. et distringat predictos Thomam et tenentes terrarum suarum ad reddendum sibi ad opus Regis dictas .x. marcas et eas habeat coram etc. a die sancti Michaelis in unum mensem Regi solvendas.

(1228)

Essex, Hertf'. Preceptum fuit vicecomiti quod de bonis et catallis Edmundi de Foleham fieri faceret .x. marcas ad opus Henrici le Blunt de .xl. marcis quas idem Edmundus recognovit coram etc. Et vicecomes mandavit quod predictus Edmundus nulla habet mobilia nisi blada in terra crescencia ad quod emendum nullum invenit emptorem. Et preceptum est vicecomiti quod de bladis et aliis catallis dicti Edmundi fieri faciat dictas .x. marcas et eas habeat coram etc. a die sancti Michaelis in .xv. dies predicto Henrico solvendas.

(1229)

Warr'. Preceptum fuit vicecomiti quod venire faceret coram etc. Philippum le Norizun cyrographarium arche cyrographariorum Warr' et alios in brevi, recognitores

[155] *The word* misericordia *is repeated in the margin.*

inquisicionis in qua Johannes de la Porte de Warr' se posuit, ut patet inter memoranda termini sancti Illarii proximo preteriti. Et ipsi non venerunt. Et vicecomes mandavit quod Willelmus de Doddeuuell' de Warr' et Johannes le Careter manuceperunt Philippum le Norizun; et quod Rogerus de Alecestr' de Warr' et Robertus de Caumpeden' manuceperunt Robertum Torold'; et quod Vincencius le Barkere de Warr' et Robertus Begus de eadem manuceperunt Willelmum le Carpenter; et quod Johannes de Cumpton' et Willelmus juxta aquam manuceperunt Galfridum de Radeford'; et quod Johannes Molendinarius de Warr' et Henricus de Claverdon' manuceperunt Petrum de Porta; et quod Ricardus Banel de Warr' et Walterus Vale de eadem manuceperunt Walterum de Thorp; et quod Walterus Ban de Warr' et Thomas Molendinarius de eadem manuceperunt Thomam de Saltreford; et quod Thomas Colet de Longo Ponte et Robertus le Rede de eadem manuceperunt Robertum de Lalleford'; et quod Ricardus Mich' de Warr' et Walterus Plane de eadem manuceperunt Thomam Lovecok'; et quod Alanus Marescallus de Warr' et Henricus Hevet de eadem manuceperunt Willelmum de Pouterel; et quod Galfridus de Etindon' et Ricardus Mercator de Warr' manuceperunt Robertum Russel; et quod Ricardus de Herdewyk' et Simon Phelp de eodem manuceperunt Eustachium Brunyng, quos non habuerunt. Ideo in misericordia. Judicium quod distringat per terras etc., ita quod nec ipsi etc., et quod de exitibus etc., et quod habeat corpora eorum coram etc. a die sancti Michaelis in unum mensem ad recognoscendum etc. et ad audiendum etc. Vives le Romaunsur, Samuel de Staunford', Samuel filius Jude, Cresse filius Sarre, Saulot le Petit et Bonamy filius Deudone, recognitores dicte inquisicionis qui presentes fuerunt, habent eundem diem. Et Johannes de la Porte qui presens fuit habet eundem diem.

(1230)

Warr'. Preceptum fuit vicecomiti quod venire faceret coram etc. Amabiliam Comin de Nywebaud ad respondendum Regi de .x. libris argenti que devenerunt ad manus predicte Amabilie de bonis et catallis que fuerunt Mossei filii Leonis judei dampnati. Et predicta Amabilia venit. Per licenciam justiciariorum ipsa et Chera que fuit uxor dicti Mossei, ad cujus sectam predicta Mabilia venit, concordate sunt sub hac forma, videlicet quod predicta Amablia dat predicte Chere dimidiam marcam pro secta sua relaxanda et pro omnimodis exaccionibus et calumpniis quas dicta Chera versus dictam Amabiliam habuit occasione cujusdam scripti obligatorii de .x. libris quod dicta Chera de predicta Amabilia habuit; ita quod de cetero occasione dicti scripti nil ab ea exigere potuit etc.

(1231)

Ebor'. Preceptum fuit vicecomiti quod distringeret Simonem de Resebi et tenentes terrarum suarum etc. ad reddendum sibi ad opus Regis centum solidos de debitis Sampsonis filii Josce; et denarios illos haberet coram etc. Et vicecomes mandavit quod retornavit breve sibi inde directum ballivis libertatum de Hold' et Beverl', qui nichil inde fecerunt. Judicium quod non omittat etc. et distringat predictos Simonem et tenentes terrarum suarum ad reddendum sibi dictos denarios; et eos habeat coram etc. a die sancti Michaelis in .xv. dies Regi solvendos etc.

(1232)

Suthp'. Preceptum fuit vicecomiti quod venire faceret coram etc. priorem de Suthewik', tenentem .x. libratas redditus assise qui fuerunt Gilberti de Basevill', ad respondendum Regi de .iiij. libris quos Regi debet occasione dictorum reddituum quos tenet etc. Et ipse non venit. Et vicecomes mandavit quod Willelmus Baseli, Ricardus Faber de Axeye, Nicholaus de eadem et Willelmus de Ede manuceperunt predictum priorem, quem non habuerunt. Ideo in misericordia. Judicium quod distringat per terras etc., ita quod nec ipsi etc., et quod de exitibus etc., et quod habeat corpus ejus coram etc. a die sancti Michaelis in unum mensem ad respondendum et ad audiendum etc.

(1233)

Suthp'. Preceptum fuit vicecomiti quod venire faceret coram etc. tenentes terrarum que fuerunt Willelmi Lillebon ad respondendum Regi una cum Waltero Lillebon, qui habuit hunc diem, de .vij. marcis de debito Salmonis de Beverlee judei dampnati. Et ipsi non venerunt. Et vicecomes mandavit quod retornavit breve sibi inde directum ballivis libertatis Sutht', qui nichil inde fecerunt. Judicium quod non omittat etc. et venire faciat coram etc. a die sancti Michaelis in unum mensem predictos tenentes ad respondendum Regi una cum predicto Waltero de predicto debito.

(1234)

Somers', Dors'. Preceptum fuit vicecomiti quod venire faceret coram etc. Ricardum de Emmelberg' et priorem sancti Jacobi Bristoll', tenentes quasdam partes terrarum que fuerunt Johannis de Brutasch', ad respondendum domine Regine matri Regis una cum Rogero de Dykel', tenenti quandam partem terrarum predictarum, qui habuit hunc diem, de quater .xx. librarum que ab eo exiguntur de debitis Abrahe filii Ysac de Karlion, que debita Manserus filius Aaron habuit de thesauro Regis et liberavit eidem domine Regine pro auro suo. Et ipsi non venerunt. Et vicecomes mandavit quod Ricardus Wylwy de Badwelle et Nicholaus le Yrisse de eadem manuceperunt predictum Ricardum, quem non habuerunt. Ideo in misericordia. Judicium quod distringat per terras etc., ita quod nec ipse etc., et quod habeat corpus ejus coram etc. a die sancti Michaelis in .xv. dies ad respondendum et audiendum etc. Et mandavit quod prior sancti Jacobi nihil habet in balliva sua. Et quia testatum est quod magister hospitalis de Rededive tenens est de terris predictis, preceptum est vicecomiti quod ipsum venire faciat ad diem supradictum de predicto debito responsurum; et Rogerus de Dykele habet eundem diem.

(1235)

[This is a second version of no. 1106 and significant variants are noted in the footnotes to that entry]

(1236)

Dors'. Preceptum fuit vicecomiti quod venire faceret coram etc. .vj. probos et legales homines de visneto de Wike et Horton', recognitores inquisiciones in qua Walterus de Wyke se posuit. Et ipsi non venerunt. Et vicecomes mandavit quod Nicholaus de Burton' et Thomas de eadem manuceperunt Robertum de Burton'; et quod Thomas le Mouner de Gillingham et Robertus Diwele de eadem manuceperunt Ricardum Cressebin; et quod Rogerus de Gillingham et Ricardus Heym de eadem manuceperunt Nicholaum de Karentham; et quod Willelmus de Dilinton' et Robertus Berkarius de eadem manuceperunt Johannem de Wiltes'; et quod Ricardus Calabrey et Johannes Calabrey de Gossych' manuceperunt Johannem de Gussich', quos non habuerunt. Ideo in misericordia. Judicium quod distringat per terras etc., ita quod nec ipsi etc., et quod de exitibus etc., et quod habeat corpora eorum coram etc. a die sancti Michaelis in tres septimanas ad recognoscendum etc. et ad audiendum etc. Et dictus Walterus de Wyke, qui per attornatum suum presens fuit, habet eundem diem.

MEMBRANE 12 DORSE

Adhuc memoranda de termino sancte Trinitatis

(1237-1240)

These entries are marked for omission by the words *vacat quia alibi* in the margin, and they are to be found on m. 1d (nos. 1085-8). Significant variants are noted in the footnotes to those entries.

(1241-2)

These entries are also duplicated on m. 1d (nos. 1089-90) but are not marked for omission. Significant variants are noted in the footnotes to those entries.

(1243)

Salopia. Preceptum fuit vicecomiti sicut pluries quod de terris et catallis Willelmi Devros, Rogeri Springehose, Rogeri Tirel, Johannis de Baskervile, Gilberti de Bosco et Walteri Tyrel fieri faceret ad opus Johannes de Picheford .xxv. marcas, que ei aretro sunt de .xx. marcis per annum de quodam debito .cc. et .xl. marcarum. Et vicecomes mandavit quod Willelmus Devros, Walterus Tyrel, Johannes de Bas' et Gilbertus de Bosco nichil habent in balliva sua et quod Rogerus Tyrel mortuus est. Et quod de bonis et catallis Rogeri Springehose nichil citra autumpnum levari possit, quia nichil habet nisi blada in terra. Et preceptum est vicecomiti quod de bladis et aliis catallis dicti Rogeri in autumpno fieri faciat predictas .xxv. marcas, et eas habeat coram etc. a die sancti Michaelis in tres septimanas eidem Johanni solvendas etc.

(1244)

Heref'. Preceptum fuit vicecomiti quod non omitteret propter libertatem de Lemenistre quin eam etc. et de terris et catallis Willelmi Devros, Rogeri Springehose, Rogeri Tyrel, Johannis de Baskereville, Gilberti de Bosco et Walteri Tyrel fieri faceret ad opus Johannes de Picheford .xvij. marcas que ei aretro sunt de .xx. marcis per annum de quodam debito .cc. et .xl. marcarum. Et vicecomes mandavit quod levare fecit de catallis Willelmi Devros .iiij. marcas quas solvit dicto Johanni de Picheford' in pleno scaccario. Et sic dictus vicecomes inde quietus est. Et mandavit quod ad presens de catallis dicti Willelmi et aliorum supradictorum plus levare non potuit citra autumpnum quia vix habent unde vivunt. Ideo preceptum est ei, sicut alias, quod non omittat etc. et de terris et catallis predictorum Willelmi et aliorum supradictorum fieri faciat .xiij. marcas et eas habeat coram etc. a die sancti Michaelis in tres septimanas eidem Johanni solvendas.

(1245)

Northt'. Preceptum fuit vicecomiti quod distringeret Willelmum de Buckebrok', Adam de la Fermerie et alios juratores inquisicionis in qua Johannes Gilemin de Burton' et Hugo filius Hugonis de Schitelond', Johannes filius Hugonis le Jofne de Hampslap et Simon de Horvadon' se posuerunt. Et dicti juratores non venerunt. Et vicecomes mandavit quod ballivi libertatis ville Northt', quibus istud breve retornatum fuit, sibi respondent quod Osbertus de Tyringham et Walterus de Bavintre manuceperunt Willelmum de Buckebrok'; et quod Johannes Caudron et Walterus de Boseyate manuceperunt Ricardum super montem; et quod Simon Wyger et Willelmus le Poleter manuceperunt Adam de Watham; et quod Willelmus filius Marsille et Ricardus de Pudinton' manuceperunt Willelmum Medicum; et quod Johannes le Mengeter et Simon de Rowell manuceprunt Rogerum de Alkemundeber'; et quod Walterus de Weydon' et Simon Baret manuceperunt Robertum de Sileford, quos non habuerunt. Ideo in misericordia. Judicium, sicut alias, quod distringat per terras etc., ita quod nec ipsi etc., et quod de exitibus etc., et quod habeat corpora eorum coram etc. a die sancti Michaelis in unum mensem ad recognoscendum etc. et ad audiendum etc. Et Vives le Romaunzor, Samuel de Staunford', Samuel filius Jude, Cresseus filius Sarre, Saulot le Petit et Bonamy filius Deudone, juratores predicte inquisiciones qui presentes fuerunt, habent eundem diem. Et predicti Johannes Gilemin, Hugo filius Hugonis, Johannes filius Johannis et Simon de Harwedon', qui presentes fuerunt, habent eundem diem. Johannes Eustach' et Robertus de Kyleby, juratores dicte inquisicionis, qui habuerunt hunc diem, non venerunt. Ideo in misericordia. Judicium quod distringat ut supra etc.

INDEX I

Marginal headings of counties etc.

Note: Many individual English counties were regularly paired during the period of these rolls with another county for administrative purposes under a single sheriff. The marginal headings sometimes reflect this administrative reality by giving the names of both counties even in entries which clearly refer only to people or places in just one of them. Other headings give only the name of a single county even though it is one of these paired counties. Most clearly relate to individuals and places within that county, but others seem to refer to people and places not in that county but in its twin. This index has therefore adopted the expedient of bringing together all the references to such headings under the names of both twinned counties. The references are to the individual numbered entries.

INDEX II

Jewish names, references to Jewish groups and references to places of Jewish settlement

Note: The names of individual Jews on the rolls have been arranged in this index by the alphabetical order of their first name. The arrangement within each heading is to give first those individuals identified as the sons or daughters of other named individuals, followed by those identified as some other relative and then the remainder of the names following the alphabetical order of the next significant element in the second name (ignoring 'de', 'le' and 'of'). As far as possible, entries relating to particular individuals known by more than one name have been brought together under a single name, but it is probable that the index still contains separate entries for some individuals who were referred to by more than one name.

The following abbreviations are used: br.= brother of; da.= daughter of; m.=mother of; s.= son of; s.-i.-l.= son in law of; sis.=sister of; w.=wife of; wid.=widow of. The numbers refer to the individual entries. There are also headings for the other significant elements in Jewish names, whether bynames, surnames or place names, under which will be found cross-references to the individual entries containing these elements. A third element in this index is a place name one bringing together references to chirograph chests located at places possessing Jewish communities, references to one or more Jewish jurors from named towns, references to Jewish communities of specific towns and other evidence suggesting Jewish residence there.

INDEX III

Non-Jewish Names and Places

Note: This is an index to the non-Jewish persons and to the places mentioned in these rolls. Every reasonable effort has been made to identify the places and the main entry for them is under the modern version of the place name, with cross-references from the forms found on the rolls. For the personal names, the index is arranged by surname or byname and as far as possible under the modern version of the occupational name or place name concerned, again with cross-refeences to the versions found on the rolls.

The following abbreviations are used in this index: b.=bailiff (and bs.=bailiffs) ; br.=brother; da.=daughter; EJ=Exchequer of the Jews; exec.=executor (of); jr.=junior; kt.=knight; m.-i.-l=mother in law; s.=son (of); s.-i.-l.=son in law; sh.=sheriff of; sr.=senior; w.=wife (of); wid.=widow (of). The numbers refer to the individual entries.

INDEX IV

Analytical Table of Contents

Note: This analytical table follows in general outline that developed for the previous volume. It is intended to provide a general guide to the contents of the volume and to assist in tracking related entries throughout the volume. Its arrangement is as follows:

(A) LITIGATION

The main entries relating to individual cases are in **bold.**

1. about title to real property

2. about possession of movable property (detinue)

(a) brought by Jewish plaintiffs

(b) brought by Christian plaintiffs

3